ONLY A BEGINNING

ONLY

A

BEGINNING

AN ANARCHIST ANTHOLOGY

edited by Allan Antliff

ARSENAL
PULP PRESS
Vancouver

ARSENAL PULP PRESS
103–1014 Homer Street
Vancouver, B.C.
Canada v6b 2w9
arsenalpulp.com

The publisher gratefully acknowledges the support of the Canada Council for the Arts and the British Columbia Arts Council for its publishing program, and the Government of Canada through the Book Publishing Industry Development Program for its publishing activities.

Design by Solo
Cover photograph by Susan Simensky-Bietila

Printed and bound in Canada

Library and Archives Canada
Cataloguing in Publication

Only a beginning : an anarchist anthology / Allan Antliff, editor.

Includes bibliographical references and index.
ISBN 1-55152-167-9

1. Anarchism–North America–History–20th century.
I. Antliff, Allan, 1957–

HX842.054 2004 320.51'097 C2004-902953-3

An Anarchist Critique of the Global Economy (2001)

CONTENTS

In 1980 two symbolic "markers" appeared on the cover of the Vancouver-based journal *Open Road*: the circle-A, invented by Italian anarchists in the 1960s, and a slogan – "You think it's the end, but it's just the beginning." The slogan was adapted from an incident that took place during the anti-capitalist, anti-authoritarian uprisings of May–June, 1968 in France. On the night of May 13th thousands of students and striking workers ended a march at the Place Denfert-Rochereau in Paris, where they clapped hands and chanted – "ce n'est qu'un début, continuons le" … clap! clap! … "com-bat!" ("This is on-ly a be-gin-ning, let's" . . . clap! clap! . . . "fight on!") In the same spirit, *Only a Beginning* welcomes the new century and its infinite possibilities.

The anthology begins with the founding of the Vancouver-based *Open Road* journal in 1976 and charts it's course from there. Anarchism is traced through a myriad of journals, flyers, posters, and web sites. A plethora of gatherings, book fairs, free schools and reading groups, protests, squats, info shops and travelling musical caravans are documented. Throughout, the poetics of revolt are given free reign.

A word about the book's origins. I have long been aware that anarchism in Canada lacked a history, or, more accurately, that neglect had driven that history underground. Occasionally an interview or retrospective article threw some light on past events, but apart from that, there was nothing. In 1999, in an effort to address this situation in the Toronto activist community, I organized a Lecture Series in conjunction with educational activities at the Toronto Anarchist Free School. While canvassing for possible topics I contacted Jim Campbell, who agreed to give a talk on the urban guerilla Direct Action collective ("From Protest to Resistance: The Vancouver Five Remembered"). After the talk Jim and I discussed putting together an anthology, and this is how *Only a Beginning* came into being.

What general conclusions can be drawn from this anthology about anarchism in Canada? We might begin by noting that the downfall of the state and capitalism through working-class struggle is important, but that anarchism has always aspired to far more than this. It demands an end to oppression in all its forms. Thus feminism is a major force in the movement: indeed, anarchists of diverse life-styles and cultural backgrounds are continually enriching our understanding of what liberation entails.

Anarchists have also played a leading role in the radicalization of Canadian environmentalism. They go to the root of the problem by calling for the restructuring of society so as to achieve social and ecological harmony on a planetary scale. This stance, in turn, has fostered a resilient culture of eco-resistance in the face of sometimes fierce repression.

The most oppressed people in Canada are its "first nations:" indigenous peoples who, having suffered under the yoke of the French and British empires, continue to be brutalized by the Canadian state. Responding to this injustice, anarchists have been resolute in their support of indigenous resistance struggles. And this same spirit of solidarity has extended beyond Canada's borders to encompass the struggle of Palestinians and other oppressed peoples around the globe.

From the fight for affordable housing to protests against police brutality, anti-war mobilizations, and the defence of old growth forests, anarchists in Canada have challenged the social, economic, and political injustices of capitalism every step of the way. And if, at present, more and more people are paying attention to what they have to say, the reasons are not hard to fathom.

In the 1990s, with the Soviet empire's collapse and the acceleration of capitalist "development" in China under the aegis of a Communist Party dictatorship, the anarchist critique of leftist authoritarianism in all its guises has come into sharp focus. Simultaneously, the dramatic expansion of neo-liberal trade agreements spearheaded by the World Trade Organization has exposed the undemocratic connivance between electoral modes of governance and capitalist institutions. As a result, anarchism is emerging as the radical touchstone for understanding the logic of capitalism, it's statist foundations, racism, and the predatory relationship to the natural environment undergirding it's economic agenda.

But it's been a long haul. How, then, did the anarchism in Canada sustain itself before this historic sea change, and why does it continue to expand today? The answer lies in the political culture documented in this anthology. Over the last quarter century anarchists have fostered their own press, internet sites, communes, book stores, free schools, and other co-operative ventures, creating communities of resistance right across the country. This is a compelling instance of politics by example, proving anarchism is not only possible, but can be actualized in everyday life. Which is to say that *Only a Beginning* is just that: a beginning, not an end.

– ALLAN ANTLIFF

Survival Gathering Demonstartion (1988)

HISTORIES

When *Open Road* was launched back in 1976, our goal was not very grand – only to attract and turn on all the anti-authoritarian activists and fellow-travellers on the planet. We were seeing outbreaks of anti-authoritarian activity all over North America, even the world (Spain and Portugal), in the environmental movement, in the prisons, among First Nations, in the struggle for personal liberation, in manifestations of the popular and counter-culture. People may not have known they were doing anarchist things, but to us, they were being anti-authoritarian and part of a rising anti-authoritarian sensibility.

It seemed like the right time for a populist, general purpose anarchist journal that could reflect this sentiment back to them and demonstrate they were part of something bigger. We especially wanted to rope in people who didn't consciously think of themselves as anarchist. The anarchist press of that era – *Freedom, Black Flag, The Spark* – was inward-looking, plus, their packaging was behind the times – copy-heavy, lackadaisical editing, sparse graphics and features, not suited to the generation of activists brought up on television.

Our organizational training (if you could call it that) was the Vancouver version of Yippie – counter culture, youth-oriented, non-sectarian. Bombarding Vancouver city council with marshmallows; firing up monster joints in the public square; feeding, housing and finding free lawyers for the masses of wayward transient youth - that was how we spent our spare time.

In creating large-scale events, from happy-face be-ins to pie-in-your-face protests, Yippie was the political expression of what we now set out to do journalistically – create a stage on which every individual or tendency, as long as they were anti-authoritarian, could express themselves and develop their creative instincts.

So despite individual personality differences, our nucleus had had years of practical experience working together. In fact, unlike so many other journals, we never had what you could call a serious discussion on "the line" of the paper. We had read most of the anarchist classics, of course, but, in the Vancouver style, we didn't bother ourselves too much with fine distinctions.

Plus we had another big advantage – we mostly came from journalism backgrounds, either as reporters or layout artists for the mainstream or the alternate press, especially the *Georgia Straight* and its more unruly spinoffs. We didn't want to destroy the conventions of journalism, just tilt them in our direction. That was crucial – to look at the paper as reporting and displaying the activity that was actually going on, not as the organ of any particular mini-group or ideological stream.

We started by making up a laundry list of topics, then assigned each other to research and come up with angles on them. News articles were handled in a breezy, fact-based style, short on abstractions and theorizing. Design and layout were put under the direction of our most experienced and highly-skilled practitioners – no fuzzy democracy in that crucial department. Our manifesto, "Still Crazy After All These Years," seems not so much crazy now as exceedingly earnest, with statements like, "*Open Road* maintains that a Social Revolution is not only desirable but possible, and that ordinary, everyday people will make this revolution, organizing in their own interests, without the need for Supermen, political bosses, or self-appointed vanguards."

Then in the grand tradition we tithed ourselves and our friends, borrowed a work space in the back office of a friendly community group, expropriated a bunch of paste pots and exacto knives from work, and laboured day and night for two weeks to produce our first edition.

Setting the tone, we put a comic strip on the cover – the villainous Anarchist from DC Comics. And we adopted the name *Open Road* from Emma Goldman to cloak ourselves in historical legitimacy. Then we sent it off to the printers for a press run of 8,000 copies.

That was the easy part.

Now we had to figure out what to do with all those newspapers. We had an obvious network of food co-ops, radical bookstores, and head-shops in the city, but for overseas, we were flying blind. Scrounging addresses out of the listings and ads in the anarchist and alternative press, we mailed out the papers, then sat back and waited for the reaction

Did we get reaction! Scores of enthusiastic letters poured in. We ran thirty-six in the second issue. They really covered the map – mainstream anarchists like *Black Flag* in England and *A-Rivista Anarchica* in Italy, to groups in Japan, Hong Kong, Argentina, and Australia. Then there were fellow travellers – everyone from the Symbionese Liberation Army (SLA of Patty Hearst fame), to the Black Panthers and the Wounded Knee Legal Defense team. But the reaction from the individuals was equally as heartening – so many wrote to say that we had changed their lives. "I thought I was all alone," they said. "I didn't know there were people out there who think like me."

We got our share of negative reaction, too. For instance, we were criticized for romanticizing the SLA and their jailhouse conversion to anarchism. Being non-sectarian, we covered pacifist and anti-pacifist alike, and the situation became all the more sensitive in later years when some friends (and *Open Road* co-workers) were arrested, convicted, and sentenced to long prison terms for bombing and firebombing campaigns carried out by groups called Direct Action and the Wimmin's Fire Brigade (the media referred to them as the Squamish Five or the Vancouver Five.)

And, given our counterculture orientation, it was no surprise we were criticised for our labour coverage. Early on, we ran a number of upbeat articles on what our friends were doing in their unions to reduce bureaucracy, but, to the proletarian theorists out there, we were never sufficiently rigorous in our analysis of union pork-choppers.

Somewhere around this time, we picked up the label, "The *Rolling Stone* of Anarchism." It was apparently meant as a jibe by some of the old-liners, but we reveled in it. That's how we managed to sneak onto some straight newsstands and bookstore shelves, hiding our questionable content behind humorous and jazzy cover layouts.

We started putting out issues every three months. A certain pattern developed: we would work at a casual level for maybe two months, answering the mail and doing research while maintaining relatively normal lives, then start to speed up toward the final two-week frenzy, staying up all night, taking vacations from our jobs, fraying our nerves and our relationships, and then, when the paper was finally out the door, collapsing and never wanting to see or think about anarchism again.

After a few issues, some new people started coming around. A Vancouver anarchist-feminist group, Revolting Women, challenged our old-boys' club, and as a result the paper was broadened to include gender and personal topics, as well as the traditional political mix. The younger generation also shook up our settled-in sensibilities. Soon the paper was sporting punk features and layout elements, although still within the overall packaging. Some of our original group even took on the role of organizing gigs and managing bands. But no Mohawks!

The fresh-air fiends wanted their say, too, and we had to move over for the Bikeshevicks. An entire issue was dedicated to the proposition that we could pedal our way to the promised land. It was our largest press run ever – 20,000 copies.

Circulation and sales revenue were almost paying the printing costs. So many people wrote in, offering to take bulk deliveries of 50, 100, even 200 copies, for resale in their own communities. But we still had to dig into our own pockets for mailing bills, rent, and other expenses. Of course, there was no money to pay anyone. That was never even discussed. Everybody had to shift for themselves to earn an income, either from wage labour or welfare.

Along the way, we spawned *B.C. Blackout,* a local-oriented zine that had the same political orientation as the mother paper, but concentrated on Vancouver events. *Blackout* continued for five years as a bi-weekly, serving as a template for similar publications in various centres around North America.

After the arrests of Direct Action and the Wimmin's Fire Brigade in the early '80s, *Open Road* started including a locally-produced armed struggle journal, *Resistance*, in its mail-outs. *Resistance* didn't draw too fine a line politically and that didn't sit well with many readers. Murray Bookchin cancelled his subscription after Issue #18. "I can't understand why you would carry that thing," he told one *Open Roadster.* "What's happening to the paper doesn't have much to do with anarchism."

Some of the *Open Road* cast continue to be active; some are sympathetic but on the sidelines; some we don't want to talk about. That seems about par for the course. Judging by the mail, and our personal contacts, we obviously affected a lot of individuals at the time. But in the big picture, the results can appear thin. The environment is still going to hell, racism and authority are flourishing, state-sponsored war never seems to end. And we didn't really make much difference on the specific stuff we targeted either: Leonard Peltier is still in prison, solitary confinement has not been abolished, our friends got convicted for the Direct Action campaign and sent to prison.

But why dwell on the negative? The new generation of young anarchist activists is doing some amazing things, moving from environmental and race issues to massive resistance to globalization and MacCulture. On the West Coast, the high-energy anti-APEC demonstrations in Vancouver in 1998, and the mother of all pre-Millennium parties, the "Battle of Seattle" in late '99 against the World Trade Organization, were rousing examples of street-smart decentralized organizing that pulled the curtain back from those secretive cartels. These young people are actors in the same tradition that inspired *Open Road.* They are reinventing the wheel, of course. But that's what we did, too. It's called progress.

– BOB SARTI

Song of The Open Road

1

Afoot and light-hearted I take to the open road,
Healthy, free, the world before me,
The long brown path before me leading wherever I choose.

5

From this hour I ordain myself loos'd of limits and imaginary lines,
Going where I list, my own master total and absolute,
Listening to others, considering well what they say,
Pausing, searching, receiving, contemplating,
Gently, but with undeniable will, divesting myself of the holds that would
           hold me.

11

Listen! I will be honest with you,
I do not offer the old smooth prizes, but offer rough new prizes,
These are the days that must happen to you:
You shall not heap up what is call'd riches,
You shall scatter with lavish hand all that you earn or achieve,

14

Allons! through struggles and wars!
The goal that was named cannot be countermanded.

Have the past struggles succeeded?
What has succeeded? yourself? your nation? Nature?
Now understand me well—it is provided in the essence of things
           that from any fruition of success, no matter what,
               shall come forth something to make a greater struggle
               necessary.

My call is the call of battle, I nourish active rebellion,
He going with me must go well arm'd,
He going with me goes often with spare diet, poverty, angry enemies,
           desertions.

15

Allons! the road is before us!
It is safe—I have tried it—my own feet have tried it well—be not detain'd!
Let the paper remain on the desk unwritten, and the book on the
           shelf unopen'd!
Let the tools remain in the workshop! let the money remain unearn'd!
Let the school stand! mind not the cry of the teacher!
Let the preacher preach in his pulpit! let the lawyer plead in the court,
           and the judge expound the law.

Camerado, I give you my hand!
I give you my love more
precious than money,
I give you myself before
preaching or law;
Will you give me yourself?
will you come travel with me?
Shall we stick by each other
as long as we live?

Walt Whitman
[1819 - 1892]

American Indian Movement
Building a new nation from the grassroots
REPORT P. 14

Martin Sostre
Nine years after frame-up revolutionary yogi free at last!
INTERVIEW P. 12

Phil Ochs & Holly Near
Peoples' music from one decade to the next
STORIES P. 11 & 27

OpenRoad

60¢

Issue One Summer 1976

Never Say Sorry To The Pentagon

A Ghandian approach to Doomsday weaponry
PACIFIC LIFE COMMUNITY / P. 7

Jailbreaks, Expropriations & Political Bombs

Hard times for Seattle's urban guerrillas
GEORGE JACKSON BRIGADE / P. 23

Working Women Organize Themselves

A militant new union shakes up system
SERVICE, OFFICE & RETAIL WORKERS UNION / P. 5

Open Road #1 (1976)

Still Crazy After All These Years
The Open Road

The Open Road is a newsjournal which is designed to reflect the spectrum of international anarchist and anti-authoritarian Left activities and to provide reports and analysis of popular struggles and social problems. It is not the organ of a political organization.

As an anti-authoritarian publication, *The Open Road* maintains that a Social Revolution in North America is not only desirable but possible, and that ordinary everyday people will make this revolution, organizing in their own interests, without the need for Supermen, political bosses, or self-appointed vanguards.

The Open Road is a revolutionary publication dedicating itself to the idea – social justice, human solidarity, and freedom – which has inspired all popular struggles against oppression and the State throughout history.

It has grown out of the positive experiences of the last decade which has seen various organizing efforts and class and social struggles in Vancouver and the world take on an implicitly anti-authoritarian character. In every arena of struggle people are rejecting sectarian and authoritarian methods of organization in favour of full rank-and-file participation and direction. In many instances people have taken the initiative and successfully overruled their "leadership" to occupy positions far to the Left of what is "acceptable."

One of the hopes of *The Open Road* is to make explicit the libertarian and anti-authoritarian content of these popular developments throughout the world. To counter the dead hand of the centralist vanguard organizations which have hindered and confused serious organizing possibilities over the past few years, *The Open Road* intends to give a voice to the emergent anti-authoritarian tendencies identifying themselves with various labels, including: anarcho-communism, anti-authoritarian or libertarian socialism, revolutionary humanism, anarcho or revolutionary syndicalism, libertarian or anarcho-Marxism. Although there are significant differences between these tendencies they all contain within them the notion of a totalistic revolution of the people, to create a society based on everybody's free self-activity.

These tendencies stand for a complete and definitive Social Revolution and in opposition to the wholesale importation of revolutionary traditions from other times and other places which are inadequate to the situation, as it presently exists in North America and the advanced industrial nations. These tendencies particularly oppose authoritarian and hierarchical "socialist" movements which have little in common with a revolution based on human freedom and the all-round development of human life. Now more than ever revolutionaries must he aware of Social Revolution as a deep socio-historical process involving the mobilization of millions of ordinary people. In the historically specific conditions of North America the organizations and activities of a revolutionary minority must aid and catalyze popular self-activity. Our primary loyalty must be to the *social* forms created by revolutionary process itself, not to the *political* forms created by radicals. To take this position is not to deny a role for revolutionary organization and leadership; it is an attempt to place it in perspective. In this spirit *The Open Road* attempts to address itself to the multifaceted nature of oppression in this society and the multi-dimensional scope of the actual social movements which have emerged and are emerging.

Among those anarchists and libertarian-leaning Leftists who participated in the formation of *The Open Road* there was no lack of enthusiasm nor was there any fundamental disagreement on the political desirability of launching a new publication at this time. However, there ensued a series of exchanges over what role the journal should play in promoting any of the various currents or "lines" that characterize the libertarian tradition.

The consensus established was that *The Open Road* would try to provide a forum through which the various theoretical and organizational positions could be described in their actual practice. This would prevent the journal from becoming embroiled in the kind of overly abstract debate and armchair theorizing that has tended to isolate comrades from each other and to entrench them in their particular positions. If the libertarian notion is to survive and, indeed, to flourish, its theories and abstractions must be tested in concrete practice, the fruits of this practice must be given wide exposure. As a newsjournal, therefore, we are more concerned with reporting on what people and organizations are doing than what they talk about doing.

In keeping with conditions in North America at the present time, *The Open Road* will give extensive coverage to what people can and are doing in pre-revolutionary situations to build grass-roots militancy and solidarity. Examples will include progressive unions, co-ops, neighbourhood and community organizations, political and social groups and primitive anarchist units. As well, there will be an emphasis on the kinds of popular institutions that are created during insurrectionary and revolutionary periods in western industrial societies, such as in France and Portugal in recent times.

The Open Road will provide critical support for established popular-based liberation movements in the Third and Fourth Worlds where no significant libertarian trend exists or seems likely to develop. We will also draw on living examples of revolutionary social reconstruction, such as in China and Cambodia, in an attempt to discover what new forms of social relations are possible when a new society is being built.

We will also examine the activities of the various clandestine armed struggle groups in North America and throughout the world. Many of these groups are closely identified, rightly or wrongly, with anarchism, either ideologically or through the nature of their practice. Their views and the real nature of their practice are being blacked-out and grossly distorted by most of the existing media, even though these guerrilla groups have generally conducted themselves in a highly principled manner making significant and relevant political statements.

The Open Road recognizes that the social revolution in North America and the advanced industrial nations must be qualitatively different than those which have occurred in underdeveloped countries in the past or present. The objective logic in North America is such that a revolutionary project here can only take the form of Human Liberation; and cannot be limited to the national determination, industrialization, and State Capitalism of other revolutions. This Human Liberation is the movement toward a classless, non-authoritarian, non-hierarchical, ecologically-balanced and decentralized society in which the splits created by Capitalist exploitation and oppression will be transcended by new unalienated human relationships. Because of the new conditions and new possibilities created by the development of advanced industrial society we at *The Open Road* believe great strides can be made towards Human Liberation in our lifetimes.

For *The Open Road* to accomplish the work it has undertaken will require a high level of co-ordination and co-operation from a considerable number of comrades. At the present time it is being produced by an open editorial collective in which the level of participation varies from one individual to the next. Those of us who are directly involved in the production see it as a secondary activity, which should not interfere with but supplement on-going efforts in the community. For this reason we have only planned to come out seasonally or possibly every two months heading towards monthly status if interest and international participation is high enough.

We would like readers to participate as soon as possible, including correspondents throughout North America and other countries who will take the time to write articles about relevant developments in their locales. We particularly need translators who regularly read the revolutionary press and can provide articles on that basis. We want to exchange with as many radical publications as possible and get in touch with as many interested groups as we can.

Financially this first issue has been funded by donations and loans. We intend to finance upcoming issues in the same manner, as we do not have subscription rates for individuals, and store sales will not cover costs. On the most basic level we are depending on small donations from a large number of readers and large contributions from the few comrades who have the resources. Another important and painless method of fund raising readers can participate in is the holding of benefit picnics and parties in their communities. In the long run, by relying directly on our readers, we will have a practical method to determine the paper's usefulness to others. Needless to say *The Open Road* will not survive if a significant number of readers do not participate with funding and written contributions.

The Open Road also needs to establish an extensive distribution system which will get the publication to the committed minority it is written for. We have allocated a large mailing budget and will mail *The Open Road* to anyone who takes the time and interest to write to us. For this issue we have piggy-backed with some of the existing publications at our own expense and would like to do so with others. Hopefully some comrades will take the responsibility of distributing the paper in their communities and of sending us the names of people they think would be interested in receiving a copy. If you have received this first issue and want to continue getting the paper please drop us a card immediately.

* * * * *

The social ideas, experiments, and struggles of the Sixties have been more or less laid to rest, but the visions they represented have not disappeared. In the cynical Seventies friends have told us that only crazy people hold to the view that "a new concert of human relations is being developed which must emerge, become conscious, and shared so that a revolution of form can be filled with a renaissance of compassion, awareness, and love." Yet, this formulation of the Hip-culture represents one example of the spirit, unity, and depth of conception which is necessary for any movement towards human freedom, solidarity, and social justice. Consequently, *The Open Road* is thronged with dreamers.

Mailing address:
  The Open Road
  Box 6135, Station G
  Vancouver, B.C., Canada

Open Road #1 (1976)

STILL CRAZY AFTER ALL THESE YEARS – CONT. A HISTORY
Part I (Beginning)

Open Road #1 *contained the collective's statement, "Still Crazy After All These Years," outlining their hopes and objectives for the paper. Now, ten issues later, with an almost new collective, we're using this special "half" issue to describe and assess the developments that have taken place over the past three years.*

"Still Crazy After All These Years – Cont." is the nearest we could come to a collective evaluation of what's been happening around here. The first part is a history of the OR development as a collective written in three stages by three different people who were involved. It's followed by excerpts from discussion papers that reflect the kind of debate we've taken up among ourselves these past few months. The first two pieces are from a critique written by two new members of the collective, while the last one is a statement from a third new member. We hope you'll give careful consideration not only to what we say below, but also to our special appeals on pages 1, 7 and 8. We'd like to hear from you.

"What can propaganda do? It can in general, express the proletariat's own instincts in a new, more definite and more apt form. It can sometimes precipitate and facilitate the awakening consciousness of the masses themselves. It can make them conscious of what they are, of what they feel, and of what they already instinctively wish; but never can propaganda make them what they are not, nor awaken in their hearts passions which are foreign to their own history." – Bakunin

The *Open Road* from the outset has been an experiment, a creative experience where those participating have learned some harsh lessons, both in failure and success. That process is still continuing.

If you re-read OR *#1*'s original statement "Still Crazy After All These Years," it is possible to view the newsjournal's development over ten issues with a bit of perspective. The successes are there. We proved that a bunch of people in an obscure city can put out a relatively high quality anarchist publication – that means you can too. OR *#10* had a press run of 14,000 – not bad in the sleepy Seventies. In short the OR has fulfilled the minimum objectives of the people who founded it.

"Still Crazy" contains the seeds of a continuing debate over methods, ideas, social perspectives, organizational forms, etc. which has raged throughout ten issues, causing convulsions, depressions, at times bitterness, in addition to moments of collective harmony which generated a special excitement. The pressure has been intense – the OR collective going into issue *#11* is almost completely different from that which began with issue one.

The general ideas of the original OR collective are outlined in "Still Crazy" and much of what was written there still holds true. The initial group was composed of about fifteen people of whom six were primarily responsible for the OR's editorial content and graphic design. Although young, the individuals in the group had some journalistic and organizational skills acquired through movement activity. They also had the advantage of knowing each other's idiosyncrasies and work patterns.

What was initially a positive association eventually tended to become a problem because it made it difficult for new people to comfortably join the collective. Efforts were made to encourage openness and participation by new people but the intensity of putting out the paper, differing skill levels and developed friendships, created a centrifugal motion which tended to repel of throw people out of the collective unless they were extremely tenacious.

At one point the cynical, sometimes hysterical in-jokes that permeated the OR's process came under attack. It was proposed that in-jokes be downplayed to create a warmer environment for new people. This controversy symbolized one aspect of a larger issue of differing work styles on the OR which became a constant collective theme: "hippie mañana" vs. "arbitrary deadlines": "male" production orientation vs. "female" group process; etc. While there were continuing efforts to work out functional compromises the real social problems disguised themselves in a more destructive personal dimension of backbiting, snide comments, and a wary circling of disdainful cliques within the collective. One person's or group's success was subliminally perceived as a threat to the fragile balance of power, phenomena which often took real joy and satisfaction out of the OR's process.

In addition to the question of differing work styles the actual organization of work became a primary concern that reflects itself in a major and continuing debate over the nature of the OR collective that has yet to be resolved. One tendency leans toward maintaining the OR as a "quality" newsjournal with an efficient and relatively small production collective. Their position could be outlined as collective control of the general direction of the OR but individual responsibility (even creative autonomy) for the specific tasks to be done. Others, to a greater or lesser degree, feel that such a position leads to elitism. They feel that the paper while maintaining quality to the best of its ability should serve as a practical school in which each individual (recent arrival or old hand) can learn all aspects of the process – that skill level or aptitude is only relative and can be compensated for by a healthy collective process. In theory, work is organized on an ad hoc basis according to whoever fells like doing it.

On another front, it is clearly stated in "Still Crazy" that the OR was meant to be a secondary activity for us in Vancouver and that it should supplement and not interfere with ongoing local efforts. In spite of this the OR tended to demand fulltime commitments from activists. The success of the newsjournal created a situation in which people used the OR to justify their anarchist credentials and lack of effective activity on a local level. The OR was substituted for practical work, the international arena becoming a comfortable focus of attention rather than the less spectacular nuts and bolts of local grassroots organizing.

The OR was conceived as a newsjournal. It was never meant to be a political organization, but it has often acted like one, and this identity crisis has caused a tremendous amount of misunderstanding that still has not been entirely worked out. In many cases people wanting to work with the OR really wanted to join a political organization not put out a newsjournal and their orientation at OR reflected this.

Within the paper itself theory and analytical debate over content have often been shunted aside or subject to power broking. Real discussion of content and orientation has been downplayed in favour of a less rigorous, less "time-consuming" trade-off system of article selection (i.e. "I'll trade you a 'worker-it is' article, if you'll go along with a 'feminist' or 'pie-kill' piece.") Such methods have often taken the spirit and guts out of the OR in favour of a tenuous series of bloodless compromises. As early as issue two, a collective member wrote in an internal discussion document:

"The most ominous sign in all this is that (writers) begin to censor their own perceptions to meet the collective's line. Given the bartering that produced the final copy for the second issue, the lesson to be drawn is that producing the OR is not a triumph of the will of individuals. OR manifests anarchy as the mass media understand the term, i.e. the collapse of a mutually consented order and the acceptance of random, chaotic, individualized action. We all know that in the end the mood was one of desperation to get the job done by any means necessary. So in the end OR becomes a newspaper. In this expediency is the seed of authoritarian politics."

If all this seems a bit devastating, it should also be remembered that the OR collective through its various manifestations has not been unaware of the issues and problems outlined. For all its errors and shortcomings the OR as a collective has pursued its vision continually – and we could not hope for more than that.

Perhaps the most important lesson people could take away from the founding issues of the OR is a drunken spout from Gloria Mundi back in 1977: "If the glue isn't trust the politics aren't freedom." It can serve as our motto or epitaph.

Part II (Herstory)

When we were trying to identify the different phases of putting out OR one member commented, "Don't forget the proletarian cultural revolution after issue four!"

While reality was less cataclysmic, important changes took place as new people joined OR and others became more assertive. Existing debates accelerated as the collective discussed the problems of journalistic and artistic skills and the problem of "male burn-out work styles." Meanwhile the problem of ideological differences between us was largely ignored, giving way to "practical" discussions about "brain-work" and "shit-work," which we tried to share out more fairly.

What emerged was a formal rotation of our basic task areas – editorial, production and distribution – so that each part of the process came to be coordinated by two people, one of whom had the necessary experience and could pass on information and skills to the other person. Another offshoot of our discussions was setting up office-shifts in an attempt to keep up with out mail and keep the office open in case anyone wanted to drop by and talk to us. In short we created some fairly idealistic structures to help integrate newer members and share the work out as equally as we could.

Our successes included continuing to put out the paper and acquiring some new skills. We also ran into problems. It quickly became clear that new members couldn't learn everything about writing and editing news articles in a three month period and that while designing and laying out one issue of OR offered insights into the breadth of tasks involved it did not enable them to perform them all. Experience could be acquired but there were no short cuts.

Increasingly burnt out and perhaps disappointed, we lapsed into working in the area of the paper we felt safest with. This helped us to make OR into the secondary political project we had planned it to be, but made the collective more atomized. At its worst people slotted into their tasks without having contributed to the gathering of articles or helping out in what was perceived as the more tedious work of mailing the paper out. Energy was low and the whole process became rather mechanical until the collective reached a crisis of enthusiasm both in terms of working together and putting out the paper.

The anarcha-feminist issue (#10) was an experiment to put out OR with an all-women group in order learn some of the necessary skills involved away from a potentially intimidating male environment.

The all-women collective experienced the problems of any new collective in terms of finding a necessary number of committed people to carry out the mass of work together. In the end the main body of the work was done by five to eight women which made the work load a heavy one and caused quite a lot of stress for individual members. However we employed the feminist principles of ongoing evaluation and feedback and while we sometimes fell short of our goal of consensus decision-making under pressure, falling into the "We don't have time to stop and talk" syndrome, we generally modified any aspects of the paper that one or two people strongly objected to.

Our success lay in the fact that we took on new responsibilities and handled them competently proving that

Open Road #10½ (1976)

there is nothing sacred about the basic OR collective. Our issue inspired new people to join OR and our consciousness around process is now reflected in the structures which the new mixed collective has adopted.

Even with the success of the anarcha-feminist group behind us, the old OR collective still couldn't fire itself up for another issue.

Part III (Now)

With our former collective strength drained, and people feeling burned out, tired, or just plain bored, the OR was having its worst energy crisis in three years. Fortunately the survivors of a bottomed out OR collective were able to rally local friends to help resolve this situation. Replacing burned out collective members is one thing; changing the conditions of collective labour to avoid future burnouts is something else. It was time for the OR to make its new beginning.

Slowly rebuilding OR this time round we recognize the importance of establishing a comfortable, less exhausting collective process. We're excited about the potential our new collective dynamic promises for the future.

That dynamic has been present in our meetings between individuals, with collective members now showing more respect for both each other and differing ideas than was evident in the past. We have adopted a system of "process checks" built in to the actual structure of our meetings. Each person gives what we call a "weather report" at the start of each collective meeting describing how she or he feels before things get underway. This allows us to find out in advance which of us is tired, ill, depressed or even super-high so that we can better understand and deal with each other's responses to everything from planning a fundraising picnic to cleaning up the office. We also set aside time at the end of each meeting to hear each other's evaluation about the strong and weak points of that meeting. Work gets done, but with an improved sensitivity to the way people feel.

On a lighter note, we have purposely scheduled our meetings to allow us to have a drink together afterwards so that people can relax and work out any tensions in a more intimate atmosphere.

The OR's problems of "power" is finally getting wrestled to the ground and dealt with more reasonably. In the past, putting out the OR was never a mystery to those on the collective who controlled a major part of the process. This time those of us with particular newspaper skills and backgrounds are much more conscious of this very real power that we wield. As individuals and as a group we are trying more than ever to recognize and understand the function of such power and how we can use it responsibly without upsetting the collective process. The specialized knowledge, which lies behind this power, is being demystified as we devise new ways to pass on experience and skills to each other.

Finally the need for an on-going evaluation of the OR content and collective process has become as integral to the functioning of the paper as we are ourselves. We need your critical feedback and constructive suggestions now more than ever before.

We want the new OR to reflect the changes we are going through to better satisfy our own needs as people who put the paper out, and your needs as critical readers wanting an anarchist newsjournal reporting on a growing anti-authoritarian movement.

A Critique

The following are excerpts from a critique written by two new members of the OR collective:

> "It hardly matters what the content is, what's crucial is that the *Open Road* is there."
> – an OR reader

Most readers would argue that without content there is no paper but it's true that the first encounter with the OR is for many, tangible proof that they're not alone. A correspondent from Arkansas says there wasn't a soul in miles with whom he could share his revolt but the OR gives him the world. But once the initial connection has been made the OR should help to develop and encourage anarchism.

Does it? Having said that the first contact with the OR is exciting, we have to admit that in our own experiences and talking with other readers, initial excitement is often followed by gradual boredom. This critique tries to root out some of the paper's limitations and suggest possible remedies.

News

> "As a newsjournal … we are more concerned with reporting on what people and organizations are doing than what they talk about doing." – OR #1

Overall, OR news coverage has been good. It has particularly helped inform us about struggles that the straight and even left presses either ignore or totally distort. Coverage of individuals and groups identifying themselves as anarchist throughout North America and Europe has helped reinforce the sense of anti-authoritarian solidarity that defies borders and oceans. However, reportage on struggles outside North America and Europe has been sparse.

Which leads one to ask … what is the criteria for an OR news story? The easiest answer appears to be that OR reports on events that its collective members can get material on. It's pretty clear that there aren't correspondents in many countries outside the Europe and North America circuit. The new collective's appeal for news correspondents and translators hopefully will correct this deficiency.

Availability of material is only one factor in choosing OR stories. A fairly common question among OR readers is "why that story?" Is this just another bit of media information packed into our daily dosage of useless oddities?" Does the OR report on the same actions as other left papers? It's not always – or even generally – clear. There is either an assumption that readers know why certain issues are considered somehow anarchistic (and therefore no explanation is necessary), or worse, the OR collective itself isn't clear why it's choosing specific stories. Whatever the reason, we feel that more of the articles should contain some background and analysis.

Only through analysis and discussion can news reveal lessons and directions. We see anarchist theory as both the issue of and catalyst to "what people are doing." Through more attention to analysis, the OR could be making a larger contribution to anarchist theory and at the same time spurring its readers on to do the same.

Where we feel the OR has been especially helpful is in reporting all kinds of direct actions that prove an inspiration to all kinds of political activists. The OR has reported on such diverse actions as people painting their own bicycle lanes in Montreal and victims and their supporters confronting rapists outside the courts.

Personal Politics

"… It would be helpful if society behaved like a phoenix – a new culture rising fully shaped from the disastrous ashes of metropolis – but such is the way of mythological symbols not life." – from a letter in 1977 to OR from Red Storm Dancing

"Traditional" politics seem to imply that knowledge of government operations and the economy are the most important prerequisites to one's understanding of the oppressiveness of capitalism and the need for an egalitarian system of social organization.

A large portion of OR's content in the past has served as traditional politics. There have been numerous articles exposing a particular country's government, and/or its oppressive tactics; it's class struggles, its revolutionary factions, etc.

But what is just as crucial as our awareness of our relationship to the State is our sensitivity to our personal relationships. Frequently the connection between politics and the immediate everyday reality of our lives is unclear, and yet it should be the subject of ongoing investigation and evaluation. There have appeared a number of articles in the OR seemingly recognizing this need. Some provide

analysis (Children are revolutionary force, OR #2); others suggest strategy (Work it out collectively, OR #9), while others provide concrete examples of workable alternatives (B.C. Food Co-Ops, OR #2). Articles which report on and encourage the examination of our inner selves (health and psyche), our social exterior (including friends, lovers, family and community) and the use of our physical environment are as fundamental to the paper as is the news coverage. Struggles within people's personal lives are often the prelude to acquiring a political consciousness. Articles dealing with the politics of our personal lives can illuminate new directions for the future.

Restructuring our personal lives is perhaps the most immediate revolutionary act at our disposal.

Art and Reviews
(DISCOVERING OUR EXPRESSIONS)

"I take my desires to be reality, because I believe in the reality of my desires." – Graffiti in Paris, May – June '68

Capitalist society tries to render art harmless by packaging it in cellophane government grants and encouraging dabblers in the exotic to perform their esoteric antics for each other. So-called "socialist" governments recognize the dangers of unleashed art that escapes during political upheavals and try to harness it for the building of their new order. But revolutionary art is neither a superfluity nor a servant. It is a searching and struggle to know the abundance and mystery of life, to push beyond the known boundaries in search of new relationships. In our society it is a struggle for clarity, to wrench life from beneath the plastic, to combat the tragedy of wasted existence in the midst of undreamed of possibilities.

From the limited exposure given art, it would seem that the OR has tended to acquiesce in the capitalist view of art that sees it as superfluous living. But daily, in dynamic explorations of their selves and their societies, people struggle to unleash the imaginative. The OR could help expose us to more of these people.

While graphic art and photographs could be used much more to extend OR stories, the paper's major contribution towards revolutionaries reclaiming art would be through careful reviews of important but often neglected artists, their struggles and creations. The OR has in fact printed infrequent but important reviews in this vein. In particular, we value OR #6's "Blue Collar Pets," a look at poetry written by and about people at their workplace and the "Living Theatre" interview in OR #9 which explores the dynamic of people collectively seeking and expressing an artistic and critical response to their world. A short piece on graffiti in OR #9 only touched upon the potential of this radical break with closet art. We cannot stress too strongly the

Open Road # 10½ (1976)

importance of more developed, creative reviews exploring music, literature and all the visual arts. Through exposure to how others are dismantling the barriers of narrow perception we will be encouraged in our determination to reclaim art as life and insist on the reality of our desires.

A Hobby?

And a few last comments from another member of the collective:

Sometimes I wonder if there is an "anarchist movement" and if in fact we are not all engaged in a rather exotic hobby. I don't think there is any point in belabouring the fact that the left is isolated from the rest of society. Such isolation is a part of having new or unusual ideas. However, I would like to see a certain change in the direction that OR has previously taken:

a) We should be critical of events and not just accept them at face value because they are part of the anarchist movement.

b) We should use critical analysis in regards to anarchism itself. We mustn't be like the Leninists and feel that everything we believe in is "God's truth." I don't think that we have all the answers yet. Also I don't think that it is enough to say "I am an anarchist" and leave it at that. I think the knowledge that the anti-authoritarian ends and means are necessary is rather a beginning for discussion amongst revolutionaries.

c) As well as news which we are pretty good at, we should also do some research of our own as we are in a better position than many collectives to do so. For example, is there a decent anarchist analysis of the present economic crisis?

With regard to the last point, I don't think it wise to ignore or dismiss the theoretical issues. Theory determines to a large extent one's actions. In the same way that you can't repair a car properly without knowing how it works you also can't change a society. We need to continuously advance and deepen our awareness and this isn't done by ignoring areas which appear to be more abstract than simple activism.

On The Road

After fourteen years the *Open Road* will cease to exist for the (un) foreseeable future. The collective has gone through many changes and has involved scores of people. At various times, from a high of a dozen to a low of two, and now we are three. The collective has consisted of a disparate group of people, covering all facets of the anarcho-movement. This has helped in keeping the "correct line "out of the paper and actually making it what someone once called the "Rolling Stone of Anarchism".

For the most part the paper has been fun to put out and we believed it was relevant to the anarchist movement. We no longer see the paper as useful. Not to mention that we haven't come up with too many original articles or fresh ideas in (your guess) years/days? … which renders us rather redundant.

When we first came out in 1976, there were few anarchist papers in the English language. There are now dozens of enthusiastic people, and we'll leave the stage to them. For now, we have no enthusiasm left for this paper, and putting out the *Open Road* has turned into a big chore. There is much work to do in the community and that is where we will put our energies.

We still need money to pay for this issue and any monies left – ha ha – will be given to the native legal fund (which isn't a laughing matter). Also, we'll still be here at this box # to answer mail and would appreciate continuing to receive English-language papers for ongoing political work. The papers we have received since out last issue have been used by a local anarchist radio show project, other anarchist publishing projects, and for some prison work, If you are in prison, and want to keep communicating with us, please write. Also, we will fill orders for back issues of the paper, and would like to hear from our distributors (preferably with cash!)

This is not say that the *Open Road* will not publish again (with a whole new collective), but time will answer that. Thanks for all your support in the past and we're sorry if you sent money for a new sub which cannot be fulfilled or refunded (we ain't a mailorder catalogue). If you write us, maybe we can send you some back issues to make up the difference. It's worth a try. And we're even more sorry if you miss us. Bye.

left: Open Road # 10/2 (1976); right: Open Road #25 (1990)

Okay, we're leaving. We've had enough. But we'll still be around to answer letters, fill backorders, catch up on other english-language anarchist news, and collect any cash you want to send us to pay off our debts. Write us: **Open Road,** Box 46135, Station G, Vancouver, BC, Canada, V6R 4G5.

Open Road #25 (1990)

At the age of fifteen I devoured the Boston Women's Health Collectives first edition of *Our Bodies, Our Selves*. I stepped into feminism as comfortably as I stepped into my jeans; intuitively I understood that the successes of the women's movements were mine to wear, were my inheritance. I was a young woman with an expectation of having control over my body and reproductive rights, of living my life in a way which fed my spirit and unselfconsciously I demanded voice and place in the world.

Idealized writings about feminist inclusion and the sanctuaries created by the women's movement – such as support groups and women-only organizations – defined my expectations of the women's community.

With the exception of my participation in two young women's issues of *Kinesis* (Vancouver) I found it difficult to find a place I felt comfortable within the feminist community. It seemed that young women were welcome to participate when asked and when kept in our place. I was shocked by the hierarchy within the women's movement; it was inconsistent with the model of consensus decision making that I presumed. I was stung when an older woman clearly told me to shut up and respect the political viewpoint of my feminist elders. Rather than encouraging dialogue and thoughtfulness, I had been silenced. It is unfortunate that so many women of my generation have similar stories; it speaks to the failure of the feminist movement to ensure it's continuity.

Instead I found voice in the radical youth media/ movement of the late 1970s and early 1980s. A group of us established Heard But Not Seen, a youth show on Vancouver Cooperative Radio. Incidentally we were invited to do so by the administration and board, not by any altruism on their part, but because we were the key to access youth-targeted funding. Fully cognizant of this, we grasped the opportunity to take on church, state, the education system, class structure, patriarchy and any other hierarchy that we could push up against. We featured music by anarchist bands and youth culture.

Heard But Not Seen and youth newspapers *Next Generation* (Vancouver) and SCREAM! (Ottawa)were not explicitly anarchist (although SCREAM! did sport a circled A on its masthead). Rather, they were inherently anarchic in their organization and structure for the quite practical reason that youth – deluged by authority figures – would have it no other way. The youth media was also action oriented: it covered and supported the development of direct action groups and the youth strikes in Ottawa and Vancouver high schools that protested education issues and funding cuts.

While anarchist history and thought was a common theme, and many of us in the youth community defined ourselves as anarchist, the youth movement was savvy enough and sufficiently broad that its inclusion went beyond strict labels and definitions. There were some linkages with the traditional anarchist community but they were not strong. My own experience with the anarchist community – admittedly limited – was that it was male-dominated and rigid and defensive of its theoretical framework. In the youth community anarchism was a way of organizing and an ideal, not a party line.

Unlike the feminist movement of the early 1980s, many young women commonly played significant and vibrant roles in the youth movement. Although today I cringe when I look back on one collective article we wrote for SCREAM! entitled "Designer Menstrual Stains" which critiqued the women's movement from a young women's perspective. Our feminist analysis lacked depth (to be kind!), but we had voice, sweet voice.

Still I longed for a women-only environment; one in which the process was consistent with the theory. It seemed strikingly obvious to me that if either the anarchist or feminist communities were consistent in their practice, each would embrace the other's root values.

A woman from *Next Generation* passed me a copy of Louise Michelle's biography. What inspired me was that she quietly laboured for years in low income communities in contrast to the high profile, almost cavalier, lifestyle of Emma Goldman in her heyday. While the youth movement addressed economic issues – youth having limited economic resources – and it was inclusive of youth from all economic and social strata, including vibrant women from working class and lower middle class backgrounds (Heard But Not Seen specifically tackled anti-poverty issues), there remained a strong representation of middle-class kids.

While my parents were first and second generation middle-class (i.e. I understood access) I lived in poverty from the age of sixteen. Now in my early twenties I was actively interested in anti-poverty issues, particularly as they impacted women.

When a young teenage woman fleeing an abusive home landed on my woman friend's doorstep, we realized she was prostituting herself to survive. Oppression was not theoretical to us; it was a brutal reality.

We began to discuss starting an anarchist/feminist magazine. We envisioned a place where we could safely bring together and explore anarchism and feminism, issues of poor women, and our intimate experiences of oppression.

We talked to other women. A woman called a meeting that brought together about fifteen women from the Vancouver anarchist and radical women's and youth communities, including Pam, Kim, and I. While interesting, there seemed to be no consensus to start a publication. Shortly after that I moved to Montreal where I would meet up with these two again....

— ZOE LAMBERT

The magazine *Bevy Of Anarcha-feminists (BOA)* was started in Montreal in fall of 1986, in Montreal, by three, white, young women who were transplants from the West Coast. Our class association is complex. Born into the "middle class," we had been subject to downward mobility and had each experienced class disenfranchisement due to various forms of abuse, low income, family dysfunction, eccentricity, sexuality and rebelliousness against moral hypocrisy. Our bare survival was our main preoccupation, navigating hard labour, the service industry, non profit jobs in frontline women's organizations, careers as starving artists, welfare and political activism. We were rejecting the status quo, determined to not compromise our identities to gain access to mainstream society. We had free floating and uninhibited rebellious feelings that we wanted to uncover and put words and images around in a forum that was unconstrained. We decided to do a zine.

In the beginning everything was to be free, free as in total absence of money in it's production. We wanted the paper it was printed on to come from dumpster diving, we imagined hand stitched binding. As we spoke to other women about the project, we realized the seriousness of what we wanted to do and the huge need that women we knew had for the kind of forum that was starting to come to light. Our original format, which would have limited production and distribution, gave way to a more committed, socially and politically conscious project.

As members of the art and political communities that existed in the '80s we were concerned with issues ranging from sexism, prisons, squatting, welfare and sex-trade workers' rights, to class, ageism, sexuality and self expression. We called the magazine "anarcha-feminist" despite the fact that, while we saw ourselves as oppressed by the patriarchal and hierarchical socio/political system, we felt alienated from both the anarchist and feminist communities.

Our intention was to create a "new" framework for our issues through a positive self-reflection of our reality. We felt the fact of our voice speaking directly to the world, not through an academic study or some political agenda, would be revolutionary, and would hold it's own self-determination through it's own unfolding. As such *BOA* had no official editorial policy or staff, our plan was to print everything we received.

For the most part we were able to do this without contradictions arising; we did, however, receive one piece on rape from a woman that we felt uncomfortable about printing. We postponed including the piece in *BOA* while we engaged the author in dialogue, hoping to perhaps print the full exchange in a future issue: this never transpired.

BOA was organized so that women who wanted to be published could layout their own pages, submitting them in the exact way they felt best suited their work. We provided "how-to" information and guidelines. For many women, adding images to their words was exciting, and doing funky collages fun and liberating. We organized "layout parties" and whoever showed up would paste-up the work that remained. Much of the layout was done with stacks of magazines, a xerox machine and a typewriter. These "layout parties" were warm and full of mirth. Hours were spent, women sitting around the table, flipping ironically through fashion magazines with an eye to bending the images to our will, our message.

BOA was funded by benefits and private donation. The benefits that we put on were women only cultural events including music, spoken word, film and performance. We did receive donations from some men that knew us individually, and some through the mail, but for the most part we were scraping the empty pockets of the women who we were trying to serve. Most of the money came from within the small circle of what could be loosely referred to as the *BOA* collective.

While many women participated at different times, *BOA* was consistently organized by us three original women, who took time out of our lives to dedicate to this often unwieldy project. Our lack of time and resources is why *BOA* was published so infrequently; it just took us that long to raise the money, make women aware of an upcoming issue that they may want to participate in, wait for submissions, organize numerous layout parties, go to press, do distribution and finally … rest. We produced 4 issues in 5 years. Each issue was printed in a run of 1,000 copies, which were distributed for free by the women who contributed to the issue, to their friends, family or whomever. We also mailed *BOA* out to various women's and anarchist organizations, archives and libraries. Remaining copies were dropped off to local women's centers, resource centers and anarchist bookstores to be picked up, for free, by the general public.

BOA seemed to receive quite a bit of attention from what we perceived to be the male dominated anarchist movement (I had the habit of perusing the anarchist press for women writers and editors; there were very few in the '80s). Various anarchist presses did make an effort to find anarchist women in history whose work they could print, however, when it came time to deal with issues of sexism in our daily lives, personal relationships, and movement activities, we constantly had to fight for acknowledgment and even basic forms of respect from men. Key to our liberation was the freedom to express ourselves, something we did not find in the anarchist establishment of the time. We decided the only way to find this freedom of expression was to do it among ourselves in a "woman only" forum. For this we were heavily criticized by some (as "oppressive to men") and heavily tokenized by others.

BOA was distributed to other anarchist presses and bookstores and some members participated in anarchist gatherings that took place. Those of us somewhat involved in the anarchist movement at times responded to anarchist events or debated issues with anarchists in *BOA* or in other presses. The most important thing for us, however, was that we not lose precious energy, time and resources debating anarchist men, but that we give that to each other to further our goal of a self-defined liberation.

Many of the women involved with *BOA* worked in feminist organizations dealing with "front-line" type groups (prostitutes rights, prison, anti-poverty, against violence), some of which received government funding and some of which didn't. We did receive a lot of support from the Downtown Eastside Women's Center in Vancouver (serving low-income women), who gladly shared their resources with us, mostly space and copy machines. The women contributors who worked in the feminist movement saw *BOA* as a place where they could express ideas, feelings, art, literature and personal her-stories that they either could not express or didn't feel comfortable revealing in other feminist forums.

For mainstream feminists changing the power structure as a whole had been eclipsed as an issue: now the problem was how to inject women into it. As long as a woman was doing it, it was good; as long as a woman got paid what a man got paid, she'd do what he'd do. We were expected to support women who became our landlords, bosses, policewomen, politicians and soldiers.

Classism was reinforced by not demanding a reorganization of power and economy, but instead using government funding to create a new class of women who worked to help women who were still disenfranchised without analyzing the source of continuing oppression. These women were characterized within the movement as being somehow party to their own oppression (i.e. women on welfare and women prisoners). Society at large reinforces the mainstream women's movements' neglect of these women by perpetuating bigoted perceptions of poor, working class and criminal women as having nothing of value to offer the world. Disenfranchised women are regarded as only in need of intervention by social workers; they've become the fodder for the employment of a new middle class of women "helpers" and "controllers". Taking a position of solidarity has been a non-issue.

BOA outgrew it's "anarcha-feminist" label (by the third issue we took the words off our cover but maintained both the anarchist and feminist symbols) mostly because we didn't want to co-opt the women who contributed to the magazine by attaching a label to them that they didn't choose for themselves. The women who participated were very diverse, spanning race, class, age, abilities, life experience ... some had wandered in off the street into the Downtown Eastside Women's Center where a "layout party" was happening, sat down, opened a notebook, pulled out some poetry and laid it out. We realized how discussions of "art" and "politics" had much different implications to many women who were still concerned with avoiding violence and putting food on the table. This is where class seemed to sever the reality from our ideals; it's where we found the silent pool of women's oppression, still voluminous. Here was a population of people with almost no access to public cultural space (and conversely the public remained ignorant of the vital knowledge that was generated by this sector of society): attaching labels generated by other communities felt questionable. *BOA* couldn't pretend to be much more than an internal dialogue; we spoke primarily to each other, but we spoke.

BOA was about women extricating their true identities from the mire of their day to day lives, of pointing the finger at what was pissing them off – be it a lover or family member, the feminist movement or left/anarchist intelligentsia, the medical establishment, the injustice system or their job. In a cavalier can-do fashion, we printed tips for runaways and shoplifters, bibliographies of anarchist/feminist literature and listings of free goods and services in three major cities. Contributors also spoke out on a range of broader issues; land claims, animal rights, the military industry, right wing women, AIDS....

And yet, what became the pulse of *BOA* was the willingness of women to speak about the effects of oppression. There is very little, if any, respect given to the pain and depression that people suffer as a result of oppression; even within progressive movements we seek to affirm our rights and show a strong face. Those who are dealing with real, everyday forms of disenfranchisement have real everyday stresses, and often deep psychological and emotional pain around being regarded by society as voiceless, pitiful and even dangerous victims worthy only of charity. What we found with *BOA* was that women were surviving this society at a price and that talking about the cost of their survival was an important part of feeling accepted for who they really were – not always triumphant feminists, enduring and ever-loving mothers, or stoic labourers, but truly frustrated, angry, hurt, addicted,

traumatized and mistrustful people faced with many impossible decisions with few options.

Fortunately, life experience tends to create real knowledge. Anyone who's been pushed against the wall, had to strategize against absence of resources, had to protect their loved ones, who has loved despite horror and is still coherent, ends up with a fuck of a lot to reveal about life.

The wisdom is natural and undeniable – the self-awareness is profound, and often without moral and ego driven distortion. The drive of the women who participated in *BOA* to speak to this part of their experience evolved naturally as one of the main focuses of the magazine. The words in *BOA* came from women who had nothing to lose socially or politically, who were determined to call it as they saw it, to feel free to be eccentric and bitchy, to find beauty in their scars and to demand attention for exactly that. Being "real" was our liberation.

– KIM JACKSON

The Book of BOA

feathers cross sky

earth bound
souls re-verb
erate finding
voice dry squeaky
from lack of use
fills void voluptuous volume
love among women
full of hate boa
licks unsutured hearts
in place(s) where there is
no mad(n)ess
no longer not there
front and centre
full and heaving with
laughter spilling tears
not a dry eye
not a dry eye
boa becomes life
beyond our selves
now public
no longer private
domain (titter titter
tee hee the girls are
stitching you up with glee)

and R A G I N G
molten river beneath
our beds
being together
getting together
we got it together
tying threads of
unravelled quilt
re-creating the universe
in a room of my own
on st. denis we
tipped it on its testosterone
stomping it into
oblivion breaking
new ground for
wild fire wild flowers
& slippery seditiousness
slapping words images
on blank pages
of our story her story
all stories beyond
adam beyond eve
beyond the burnings
kaleidoscope vision
shards of colour
blood red indigo fuschia black
slithery texture of scales making

music with our tongue in
cheeky revolution
don't forget to wear your lipstick to
the board meeting
when you kiss the corporate fly
and mind you powder your little nose
brown in the ladies room
while on the out side
of margins
the real world is still
flaming burning
down your house
of misery
dancing crazee banshees
out of bondage & out of control
blood bath
after math
the ladies are
on the howl
in heat
out of beat
no longer tongue tied
but bold
beyond our (wildest) aspirations
p.j. flaming

boa collective 2001

By and For Wimmin!   spring 1992

bastion of amazons
bossy ostracised ana
nas bored of assholes.
bankrupt odd amplifiers
bottled up anger
band of

angels
blacklist
ing opaque
artsyness
breeders of act
ivism blight of
arachnes bleating
    ornery applepickers
    bright opulent
    androgynes bowled
    over aphrodites
    blasters of ageism
    balking outmoded
    aesthetics barging
    over airheads.batty
oscine anuses belligerents
orchestrating anarchy
bipedal oving animals
bracing ourselves against
backwards orders of aristoc
racy.bulldozing optic aerospace
beautiful orgasmic avacadoes
bountifully organising actions
bitches ovulating atavistically.
braineating orchids always bent
on autonomy.ballbreaking offensive
arrogants babbling ogling apes
and berating old archetypes

bevy of anarchist-feminists

BOA # I (1987)

As Anarchists....

As anarchists (hopefully) we see the big picture, the interconnectedness of things, how they are, how they have been, how they could be. As feminists, we feel our place as females in the scheme of things, a destiny put upon us like a too tight jacket by society, by patriarchy, telling us very particularly who we are and what we are not, and where we are and aren't going. To be the gender called female gives us a particular vision, perspective, of daily living and of history.

Saying all this, some male anarchists may reply, well, my experience as a male gives me a certain perspective too. Of course, it does, but it doesn't wipe out the fact that little boys, no matter what their education, colour, capabilities, are raised to *know* that they are automatically *better* than some certain people by virtue of their lack of functional breasts and possession of The Big Outie. If you are male you can always find someone that it's your nature given right to dump on, beat or force fuck or grind into the dust or dismiss or kill. Maybe it's the women of your class, race same or race different women, younger women, older women, your daughters, etc.etc. How securing it is to have this one thing you can always be certain of, everything else may be fucked up, but still you're better than *some*, that's for sure. What deadly knowledge baby boys are steeped in from birth, all the signals saying go, yes, it's right, don't think about it, it just is, nature, nature, nature, approval, domination affirmation.

Deadly, yes, for males too, for their human spark of individuality. Deadly for those who do not fit in to its narrow, narrowing mold. Deadly to females on a grand scale, functionally. See it in my mother's vacant eyes and selfless voice. Know it when women are set on fire for bringing a too small dowry to their husband's family. Know it everyplace as clitoradectomies are forced on young girls, ancient, ancient, terror filled rite of control now done in shining steel and white hospital rooms as well as on open old ground. No patriarchal culture is innocent.

So what am I saying to you, my dears, my sweet girls? I call you girls to reclaim a small work, that holds strength and wonder and curiosity and self-assuredness and action in it (before the self-doubt grows and grows and the new strength is broken apart) brave, wonderful girls of all lovely kinds, it is our place to be strong, to grow, to try our best to live what we think and feel, to know, really know, that what we have to do is to gather up those good strengths, even though men at large, and often women, will tell you the "female" strengths are weaknesses and the "male" strengths are bad for us and even if they weren't, we aren't deploying them properly (power over, power over). We have to know ourselves and try to know others and take it from there.

It is *not* our place to pick up the slack for those anarchist men who are confused or hurt or angry with us for our

MOTHERSISTER-NURTURER ?— JUST SAY NO!

being feminists. It is not our place to be their teachers (why our anarchist women friends want to keep us out of a workshop when Emma G. would never have done it – 10 AM on the front lawn, female facilitators mandatory). Male anarchists must wake themselves up, the initial desire for growth must lie with them. They've got to call each other on it. They've got to open their ears and listen and think when anyone calls them on fucked up sexist behaviour (behaviour that can be oh so subtle because it is in the air, everywhere, like other pollutants that get added over time but aren't a natural part of the atmosphere). A big part of the problem of them treating us this way is that some anarchist men don't even consider it a problem. And how can a person work on something he doesn't think is real, or important, or even there? Not easy.

Remembering this, girls, don't feel guilty for wanting to argue, or at times not wanting to, because all you're being faced with are closed ears and anger and fear. And please, don't let anyone trip you on how it's unanarchistic to want to spend time alone with other women to work and hang out and love with each other. We do it, I think, because it strengthens us in a way that is completely free of the touch of patriarchy, in that a woman without a man is just not there, and we know that is *not the truth*. It is more our wanting to be with one another than a desire to be apart from men. Perhaps the fear this inspires in some men happens because there is a strong element of this being a space apart and a safe space at that – three guesses apart from who and safe from what. Well, it's always best to come together out of a sense of joy, not out of the need to get away for a while from something hurtful, but to be creating something joyful. Yes, but until there is profound change in the world, women will keep coming together, apart from men that understand and men who don't, men who listen and men who never can quite hear. Often our feelings are very mixed; and our male friends pick up on this and question us and tell us we are wrong. Well, we're not. And we shouldn't feel intimidated. So listen here, my dears:

DON'T FEEL GUILTY. DON'T BE GUILTY. DON'T BE QUIET. Our friends must teach one another how to listen, how to stop expecting us to be quiet about this. To stop dismissing us. (What was it you said? I wasn't listening, hmmm?) Those anarchist men who are very aware and growing have a big thing to do in spreading the word. The hardest part of which is that there is a word, and that it's vital, absolutely, and it doesn't matter one damn that Bakunin or Kropotkin or insert Here Whoever you like, never wrote about it. We have no heroes, heroines, no saints, right? What we do have is people. And if we all don't grow, we stagnate. The choice is theirs, and ours.

Sharon
t.h.r.u.s.h.
(terrifying hags ruthlessly uprooting self-hatred)

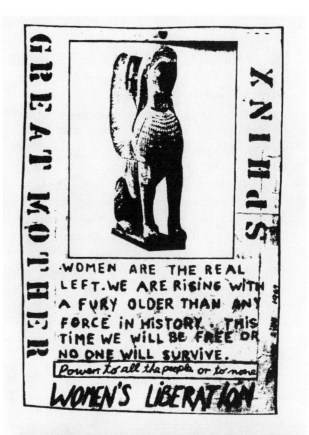

BOA WAVES Good bye

This is the fourth issue of BOA: Six years ago in a dingy rented room on St. Denis in Montréal, three wimmin started talking about our political and social lives. "We had weekly meetings, we never had an agenda; we would sit and talk moving fluidly from the theoretical to the personal--gossip integrated with analysis. We laughed a lot. We had fun. It was very much a collective process." (BOA Issue #1, Spring 1987).

We talked about how we felt alienated from our "alternative" communities; the Left; the feminist establishment; male-dominated anarchism and combinations thereof. We felt stifled, silenced, discounted, unheard by our own communities. Our realities were being narrowly defined by sexism, ageism, classism, maleism and dogmatic approaches to life.

We wanted a publication by and for wimmin where we could speak without censor about our own issues through stories, poetry, analysis, graphics, drawings, or whatever. We wanted something that we could have input to at all levels of process from inception to layout to printing. We wanted something that would inspire other wimmin to create similar voices.

We wanted something that was accessible and FREE so we could all read it, something not tied to government stipulative funding. We wanted a "zine" that didn't edit out the harsh realities of our lives into pleasant pink plastic paragraphs or male-stream media.

We didn't want to become yet one more official "voice for women". Storytelling and creating are the traditional and essential sources of wimmins truth, where we discover the real reality behind correct political lines. In the pages of BOA wimmin explore doubts, joy, rage, theory and our vast and varied responses to life.

76

Six years later BOA is part of many wimmins lives all over the world. We distribute it by hand, mail, and backpack. We distributed issue #3 to every wimmin's centre in B.C., to prisons, community centres, friends. BOAs have shown up in Australian Prostitute collectives, Lexington Maximum Security Prison for Wimmin, squats in Amsterdam, El Salvador, Downtown Eastside Women's Centre, Hazelton, Berkeley Women's Archives, the Canadian Women's Movement Archives, the Yukon. Yup. Of our limited run of 1000, we sure do get around!

The original 3 wimmin (pj flaming, wilma hazel , & terra Jovi .) continued to be the publishing collective. Hundreds of other wimmin contribute by writing, graphics, and layout. In the last few years, we have largely been based out of downtown/east Vancouver. One of the publishing collective lives in a small community North of Vancouver and is constantly nagging about the urban bias.

We manage to scrape BOA together through our own limited funds, donations, unpaid labour, sheer will and lots of pleasure. BOA also produced cultural shows, parties, benefits, posters and pamphlets and is making a video and audiotape--all for and by low income wimmin. We hope to publish all four copies of BOA in book form.

BOA is a permanent part of the cultural ecoscape for and by wimmin. BOA politic, aesthetic and way of doing stuff has directly influenced other 'zines papers and the women's movement. Our voices have been strong resounding radical uncompromising clear. Issues BOA raised in 1987 are re-surfacing in the mainstream (again!!)--classism, revolution vs. patriarchal adjustments (liberalism/reform).

BOA wimmin **are** the wimmins liberation movement; we are workers, poor wimmin, dykes, bi's, young wimmin, mothers, grandmothers, women of color, aboriginal women, women with diverse abilities and backgrounds . It's time for feminism to get off its middle class officious ass and move over for the real leadership of wimmins liberation: wimmin who are the most oppressed and benefit the least from the status quo, i.e all of the above. It's time to get real and listen to your sisters below you who are forced through our unpaid and underpaid labor to prop up your privilege and comfort. Liberation for all wimmin, not just a few of us.

 Six years and four issues later, two things remain consistent and obvious to all wimmin who are part of BOA: **PATRIARCHY SUCKS** and **BIG CHANGE --REVOLUTION** needs to happen. BOA is tired of being pulled together without money and resources. This is the final issue, but look for us in the liberation struggle nearest you! And remember: revolutionaries never die we just get tired of publishing. bye bye.

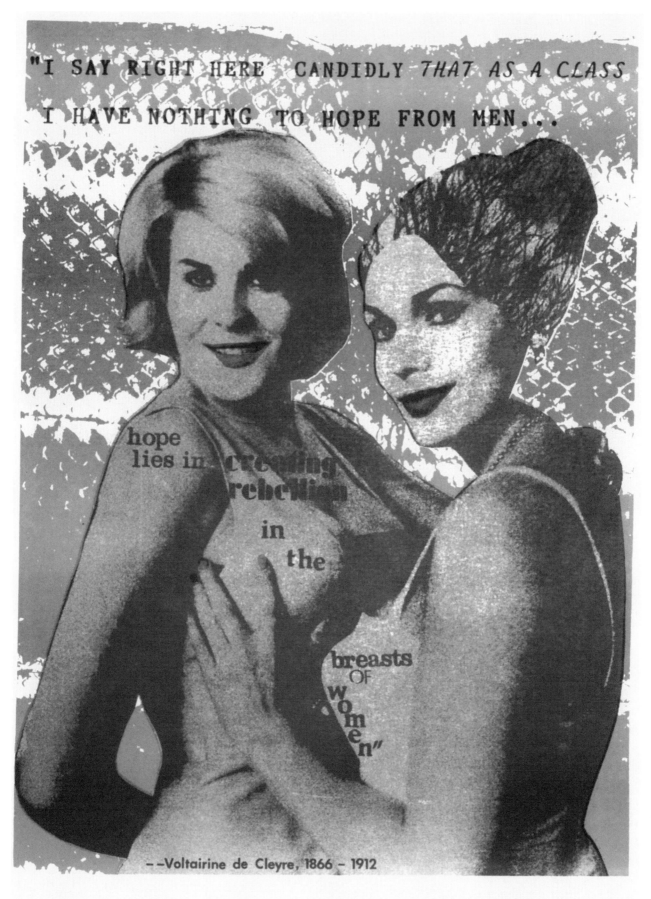

"I SAY RIGHT HERE CANDIDLY *THAT AS A CLASS*
I HAVE NOTHING TO HOPE FROM MEN...

hope lies in creating rebellion in the breasts OF women"

--Voltairine de Cleyre, 1866 - 1912

DEMOLITION DERBY

Demolition Derby lasted for two and a half years, starting in 1989. The two issues that came out were received enthusiastically by some, with scorn by others, and bewilderment by not a few. *Demolition Derby* was arguably the most radical – in the sense of extremist – journal that has appeared in Canada. In its pages almost everything was questioned or rejected, from cities to technology to contemporary methods of radical organizing.

Demolition Derby was conceived as a primarily theoretical publication putting out theme issues on an irregular basis, a sort of supplementary journal to *Anarchy* and the *Fifth Estate*, publications *Demolition Derby* was politically close to. In issue #1 an extremely long – endlessly long – text of mine appeared on the subject of anarcho-syndicalism, provoking outraged responses from anarcho-syndicalists. Other letter writers commented from a variety of viewpoints and twelve pages of #2 consisted of letters about the article. I now regret that so much space was devoted to anarcho-syndicalism. At the same time part of the purpose of *Demolition Derby* was to critique the more conservative anarchist currents. In this context texts lambasting electoralist "libertarian municipalism" were also printed.

Issue #2 featured several long critiques of feminism by women. Also appearing in the journal were previously unpublished texts by John Zerzan and Feral Faun, two of North America's most important radical theorists. The journal printed texts from both an individualist and a collectivist perspective. Two long translations from the Stirner-influenced publication *L'Unique et Son Ombre* introduced this thought-provoking group to an English-speaking readership. Paradoxically, *L'Unique et Son Ombre* subsequently veered off in a nationalist direction. In *Demolition Derby* individualist and collectivist approaches were not seen as mutually exclusive; rather, they were in a dialectical relationship. Knee-jerk hostility to individualism unfortunately remains the reaction of much of today's anarchist milieu.

Demolition Derby's core outlook was anti-civilizationist. But it also published texts from the more interesting sectors of the revolutionary milieu such as the Bonanno/Insurrectionist current. Also printed were translations of texts by members of *La Sociale*, a local libertarian-Marxist project. Several people assisted me with aspects of putting out the journal. One hand-lettered all the headlines in issue #1 and chose the graphics for a long translation. Some of these folks I remain on friendly or speaking terms with, and some not.

In the journal's final year, my interest in the project waned. Editing a journal is a rôle, a rôle I eagerly took on at first but which then became a burden. Some are no doubt cut out to be editors. I'm not. Nowadays I just send in the texts and let the publishers deal with the rest.

– MICHAEL WILLIAM

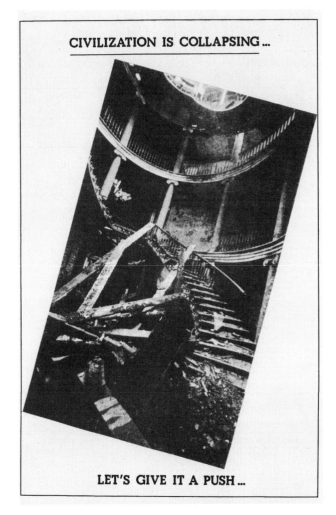

CIVILIZATION IS COLLAPSING ...

LET'S GIVE IT A PUSH ...

Demolition Derby #1 (1989)

DEMOLITION DERBY

GRATUIT / FREE

ABOLISH MONTREAL?

THE SOONER THE BETTER...

IN THIS ISSUE

WHAT IS SOCIETY?

DEBORD ON NORIEGA

Tonality and the Totality

The «Bufe-ooneries»*continue
A response to Chaz Bufe's «Primitive Thought»,
and to the Misery of Anarcho-syndicalism

QUESTIONING ECOLOGY

LIBERTARIAN MUNICIPALISM: GIMME A BREAK!

BONANNO AND STASI ARRESTED

THE NATION: ¡NO PASARAN!
ANGLOPHONES, FRANCOPHONES, YOU'RE A ROYAL PAIN IN THE ASS!

FERAL REVOLUTION: Rebelling against our domestication

Demolition Derby #1 (1989)

BONJOUR

Welcome to the first issue of *Demolition Derby*.

Demolition Derby is a journal of revolutionary theory and analysis, which will be publishing on an irregular basis, whenever it comes together.

Although advocating the abolition of the state, the patriarchy, money, cities and industrialism (among other things), *Demolition Derby* does not call itself anarchist, communist, situationist or anything else. Having discarded certain labels, it has yet to appear necessary to take on others. This should not be understood, however, as a strident claim to have superseded anti-authoritarianism: leaving behind our revolutionary desires and being absorbed by the machine or simply moving to another location within the anti-authoritarian milieu (which, to say the least, has ample space to accommodate a variety of tastes!) seem to be the two possibilities at hand, which is not to absolutely rule out potential third ways, but they have yet to make themselves known.

Demolition Derby will be publishing in English, a difficult decision in a city like Montreal. On the other had, five of the texts in this issue were translated from French, and *Demolition Derby* expects to offer further translations on a regular basis. Letters and texts in French sent to the journal can be translated, as well as letters and texts in Spanish.

The opinions in the articles appearing in this paper are the authors', although *Demolition Derby* is in general agreement with most of them. An exception worthy of particular note in this issue is the *L'Unique et son Ombre* text's rejection of community, which is considered to be the equivalent of society. Though feeling no particular attachment to "society," *Demolition Derby* continues to affirm community as the negation of capital. The *L'Unique* text remains of interest for a variety of reasons, however, and ultimately the original idea of including an introduction to it has been dropped in favour of simply welcoming readers' comments.

For the moment there are no subscriptions to the journal. By the time the next issue comes out (at least six months – probably closer to a year), it should be clear whether or not it is going to continue, and subscription rates will be announced. If you wish to receive the next issue, just write to the journal and it will be sent when it comes out. Monies for postage and costs – or an SASE in Canada – will of course be greatly appreciated, but please don't write cheques or money orders to *Demolition Derby*, because for now there's no account in that name. Please don't forget to send your new address if you move.

Demolition Derby is free to prisoners and to people in psychiatric hospitals.

Translations for another issue are already underway, as well as an article on the cinema entitled *"I was a Celluloid Junkie"* by Michael William, in which an ex-cinephile tells of his misadventures in the harrowing world of this most addictive of drugs. Till then....

Demolition Derby
CP 1554, Succ. B
Montreal, Quebec
Canada H3B 3L2

Meanwhile, back in Beijing, a sinister symbol looms ...

Demolition Derby # I (1989)

What Is Society?

> "As for the issue of whether or not to continue to reproduce, males, it doesn't follow from the male's, like disease, having always existed among us he should continue to exist.... Why produce even females? Why should there be future generations? What's their purpose to us? When aging and death are eliminated why continue to reproduce? Even without they're being eliminated, why reproduce? Why should we care what happens when we're dead? Why should we care that there's no younger generation to succeed us?" – Valerie Solanas, SCUM Manifesto

When we state that we do not fit into any type of society – past, present or future – the usual response is: "But then you want a world in which people live in isolation?" As if all relationships between individuals were necessarily social!

Until now, certainly, human beings have always lived in societies. But that, on the one hand, is no reason to live in them *ad aeternum*; and on the other, there is no society in which *all* relationships possess a social content, although some of them tend toward this totality, especially the present one. Relationships which cannot be identified as social relationships have always and still do exist. Generally they are called "intimate" or "private", which does not convey their true content (or does it poorly) because among these relationships some possess a social content whereas others, which certain people call "social", in effect are not.

The next step then, is to define what is meant by "society" and "social relationships."

In order to do so more easily, I believe that it would be useful, before such a definition is attempted, to point out that the "natural", eternal appearance of society is similar to that of the "natural" and eternal appearance of work.

At the beginning of the seventies, when we (along with others) claimed that it was *work* which was to be abolished, and not only its salaried form, we often attracted the same sarcastic replies we receive today concerning society. Now, however, although all those who disagreed with us at that period remain just as critical, the necessity of the abolition of work as such is quite widely accepted in the "revolutionary" milieu.

Of course it is easier to demonstrate that each activity is not automatically work, and that while other activities coexist with work, a "society" in which work would be excluded from human activities as a whole is possible.

However, to continue to call an ensemble of relationships that exclude work a "society" is to remain a prisoner of work's concept of these relationships.

In effect, what is work if not activity whose only goal is to reproduce people by reproducing "external" nature (i.e. what does not belong to them)? This activity prevails over all the rest because it is *the most social*, to the point of giving birth to a realm which has become autonomous from other relationships – be they social or not – in order to bring together every moment of the *material* reproduction of individuals: it is of course to *the economy* that I am referring.

The predominance of the economic realm even implies that the relationships which compose it are the only ones which are generally considered social, whereas the rest are called "private."

In fact, among the latter, some are social (although of secondary importance), and others are not. Family relationships, through which individuals reproduce themselves by reproducing "internal" nature (i.e. the species), are *social* because their goal is the reproduction of individuals through social activity.

Like economic relations in general, and those of work in particular, these are not free relationships but *obligatory* ones. Individuals who establish these obligatory relationships *are defined by them*: someone is a worker (or an owner) if he or she takes part in the relations of material production. Someone is a mother (or a father) in a family if they participate in the relations of reproducing the species. Someone is a woman or a man if they establish a relationship based on belonging to a sex. Someone is black, white or yellow if it is based on belonging to a race. Someone is French or Turkish if they are born in such and such a territory.

If every individual is a unique being, he or she gives an initial impression of being an undifferentiated member of the species who shares the same vital necessity with other members to the extent that reproduction is the principle goal of his or her relationships with others. Individuality becomes completely dependent on reproduction.

> "What was Beaudelaire?
> What were Edgar Poe, Nietzsche, Gerard de Nerval?
> BODIES
> which ate,
> digested,
> slept,
> snored once a night,
> *shat*
> between 25 and 30 thousand times
> and before 30 or 40 thousand meals,
> 40 thousand nights of sleep,
> 40 thousand nights of snores,
> 40 thousand sweet and sour mouths must present
> 50 poems each when they awake;
> it is truly not enough,
> and the equilibrium between *magical*
>   production and *automatic* production
>   is far from having been maintained;
>   it has been horribly broken,
> but *human reality*, Pierre Loeb,
> is not that.

We are 50 poems.
Everything else is not ours but the nothingness
which clothes us,
laughs at us first
and then *lives through us.*"
– Antonin Artaud, letter of April 23, 1947
to Pierre Loeb

Society, then, can be defined as the totality of *obligatory* relationships individuals form *in order to reproduce themselves* materially, physically and mentally.

Thus it can be seen that the abolition of work, like that of the family, signifies the abolition of a *social* activity in the sense that its only goal is to reproduce members of humanity. Even if, hypothetically, humanity were not reproduced in an unequal manner (the wage system), the content of work would still call out for its own abolition, as would the content of the family, because we are not 30,000 turds or 40,000 snores, as Artaud points out, nor are we 20,000 leg stretchings under a desk or 15,000 sets of dishes. We are 50 poems and 10 accordion tunes (awaiting more). But work, the family and society in a more general sense necessarily presuppose the "alienation" of their products; it is only from a poem or an accordion tune that we cannot be separated because they are *useless*.

Love

If work and the economic realm in general are often the sole activities which are termed "social", it is because their goal is *exclusively* reproductive (of society as a whole). Family relationships, on the other hand, possess the social disadvantage of being linked to, and of possibly being invalidated by (*loving*) relationships which *in themselves* do not have a reproductive content and do not correspond to social criteria. Individuals do not form these relationships on a basis which is determined by their sex. They *leave behind* the sexual community they belong to and come together as *unique* individuals. A loving relationship is a free relationship and hence *asocial* (see the forthcoming text "The being you love lives," by Dominique Fouquet).

However, the tie which closely binds the loving relationship to a family one in turn implies that it can be invalidated by the latter. If the limit of the family relationship is always individual, that of the loving relationship is always social – not only externally, through the constant intervention of society in general and its economic realm in particular in order to annihilate it, but also and above all *internally*, through the "natural" tendency of individuals who are in love to deny their uniqueness in order to affirm their social/sexual roles (i.e. determined by belonging to a sex).

It is clearly not the presence of children which determines the existence of family relationships between two individuals belonging to different sexes, but their affirmation (whether they live together or not) of their "male" or "female" roles. Often the birth of children serves to confirm the omnipresence of these roles and gives them a maternal or paternal form. But such a causality is in no way automatic: it is possible to procreate without affirming a family relationship; and family relationships can be affirmed without procreating.

Whether one marries or not does not further clarify whether the content of relationships between "men" and "women" are family ones or not. Thus, today's development – people living together without getting married – in no way invalidates this content as such. Instead it is a question of adapting the family to modern society, which has resulted in couples coming together and breaking up in the time it takes to play a videotape. Marriage seems like a useless formality in a social sense since *divorce* constitutes a relatively complicated and costly formality to which couples are having recourse more and more frequently.

This propensity towards divorce is linked to gaining access to social life and attaining material independence, through which women are no longer materially obliged to prolong an unsatisfactory relationship. But it also signifies that an increasing number of couples come together simply because today's young people are in the habit of having a *mixed* social life which is *given* to them by society (see the forthcoming text "Abolishing Society to the Tune of an Accordion"). They no longer need to *leave behind* their sexual group in order to meet someone else. The, at the same time marvelous and anguished, moment of discovery experienced by most adolescents has become almost meaningless: it is society which makes them "meet." If discovery still exists, it is primarily sexual and is itself to a large extent determined by what everyone knows, or believes they know, about sex.

In the past, every meeting between young men and women obviously did not have an exclusively loving content; it was possible for antagonistic relationships to develop from the outset, or later on, depriving women of a social existence as such, while men played a mediating role. But for women to gain access to this social life is obviously not synonymous with affirming their own uniqueness, even if this affirmation can *at times* be more or less hidden behind gaining access to it.

Women's access to social life does not bring about a profound questioning of the role of women, and men are even less inclined to question theirs. People who live together and economize on entrance, and above all exit formalities behave in ways which are no more those of unique individuals than those of traditional married couples. Anyone who has frequented these new-look (1) couples, either from up close or from a distance, has noticed that they are usually in complete conformity with family criteria and sexual roles, which have simply been somewhat modernized.

More interesting of course (at least at the outset), was the approach of individuals who did not marry out of

Demolition Derby #1 (1989)

revolt, when living together did not yet constitute a parallel social norm (although these roles were often re-established very quickly in these cases as well…).

No loving relationship is exempt from the presence of masculine and feminine roles and/or maternal and paternal ones. What is important, however, is whether lovers comfortably adapt to them; whether they confirm or invalidate them. To invalidate them is to destroy the relationship of allegiance individuals possess towards their usual presuppositions (in this case, sexual ones): individuals are no longer defined as being masculine or feminine, traits which on the contrary become *one* element of their uniqueness. The same is true for maternity and paternity.

Authentic love can only bring together *unique* beings, not a man and a woman, a man and a man or a woman and a woman.

Loving relationships simultaneously go beyond both social and intimate ones. They are intimate, certainly, but cry out the incongruity of their existence in life's social face.

Art

Before its socialization during the second half of this century (a socialization whose premises were apparent right from the beginning), artistic activity was the polar opposite of work. Because it did not play a reproductive role, it was not a necessary activity. It was carried out for the artist him or herself, and only the attractiveness of a work that was freely produced caused a patron of the arts to assist its creator (there were, certainly, works done to order, but most of those created did not fall into this category).

What occurred when art patronage *progressively* (i.e. as a result of social progress) disappeared during the 19th century is well known: the mythic image of the *artiste maudit* (doomed or damned artist) represents a material precariousness that was very real. The attraction which *bohemian life* exerted and still exerts on imaginations and memories results from the freedom of its relationships; ones which were free precisely to the extent that they did not become social (i.e. to keep a person well fed).

Also, when we return to the origin of the word, the lives of *bohemians*, gypsies, etc. are attractive not because of the social content that they presuppose, with its hierarchies and extreme constraints which inhibit individuals, but because of the precariousness of the *relationships* of a social life that is constantly in motion, giving individuals back the freedom they are deprived of in the tribe.

Crime

Another truism among those who are favourable to each and every asocial viewpoint holds that these viewpoints have no future (because for these folks, the only future is …

a social one) and are unable to go beyond crime, madness, and ultimately suicide.(!)

In effect, these are manifestations of human beings' incapacity to identify with any society whatsoever, since human beings are not essentially members of a species and cannot be assigned self-reproductive and social functions as their goal in life without becoming sick or desperate or reacting violently.

Crime is based on an ambiguity if not a contradiction: criminals create activity through which they attempt to reproduce themselves and are nevertheless the free subjects of this activity. In other words, their acts, like work, are determined by a social necessity to reproduce, but they themselves decide the form they take. This can allow certain individuals to "transcend" the act of reproduction through crime-as-an-act-of-pure-pleasure. Usually, though, this is not the case and instead the opposite takes place: the social act, absorbing uniqueness, manifests its sordid content through the omnipresence of a vital reproductive necessity, which is worse than that of work. The traditional criminal milieu and the various mini-milieus, which have more or less replaced it, are the social representation of this phenomenon.

This in no way prevents society's obligatory exorcism of what is unique in criminal activity, however weak this aspect may be, and entrusts its execution to the police and the legal system. The criminal must be deprived of *his or her* reasons for having done something, and all the reasons which can be interpreted socially (in fact psychosocially) – an unhappy childhood, coming from a disadvantaged milieu, etc., are substituted.

Thus, in order to re-socialize crime, society does not hesitate to accuse itself of being recurringly dysfunctional. Prison – the real crime society – which is based even more on vital necessity and the interchangeability of roles, is where this process of socialization ends up.

What is true for crime is even truer, but in a different way, for crimes of passion. Here we have reached the limits of all the acts of self-reproduction: madness and suicide. Why do people kill? The enigma of acts which are not absolutely necessary, hovers over crime.

Everyone who reads classic crime novels, of course, knows the answer: people kill, apparently, because of greed, jealousy or resentment (2). But many greedy, jealous, hateful people have never killed and never will. Why, then, do people kill?

Convinced that an elaborate performance is necessary in order to at the same time answer and avoid answering this question, society trots out all its actors and props for the occasion: the media, psychiatrists, experts and public opinion join the cops, judges and lawyers in order to erase any meaning which belongs to an act which can then be presented as being the same as hundreds, or in effect thousands of others, and the person responsible as a lifeless puppet.

But all this is still not enough. If the police, media and

legal institutions restore criminals to their proper place in society (prison), to place them back in their class becomes the task of revolutionaries: "A communitarian association of prisoners – one which goes beyond formally individual reasons for being in jail (reasons which are inherently atomizing) – can only be founded on the basis of a critique of their common proletarian condition, which is the real reason almost all prisoners are in jail and remains with them in prison as on the outside ("Going through the prison walls", in *Prisonniers de la Démocratie #1*, a bulletin which is close to the journal *La Banquis*).

Where capitalism is content with "formally individual reasons," the revolutionaries of *Prisonniers de la Démocratie* find them in a proletarian condition, which is common to all prisoners (who are thus placed right back in a class perspective they had, voluntarily or not, to some extent abandoned). In the same text on the other hand, a class perspective is criticized, though in effect by it being limited to work relationships. To be obliged to search for proletarian revolutionaries among prisoners demonstrates the weakness of this viewpoint. But proletarians have to be taken where they can be found because, as the text admits, the factories are emptying and the prisons are filling up. What allows the elaboration of a class viewpoint concerning prisoners is a perception that the association in question places them on a path which is headed directly towards a communist revolution: "Establishing a communist association which traverses prison walls, however, presupposes an indispensable subjective condition: critiquing and going beyond the purely nihilist and *individualist* anti-capitalist revolt which is characteristic of crime. An *"individual"* revolt which is not at the same time oriented towards and transfigured and radicalized by the project, love and poetry of the universal human community can only constitute a dead end" (ibid., underlined in the text). A social apotheosis of sorts.

Madness

Through madness, individuals demonstrate that they are no longer able to accept their own social reproduction as the goal of their existence. Contrary to the criminal, the "mad" person dues not *a priori* attempt to practice another form of social reproduction. This difference explains why, in accordance with the division of sexual roles, there are undoubtedly (a few) more women who are mad, whereas there are (many) more male criminals.

Certainly one must be precise about what falls into the very general category of "madness". But the distance between a nervous breakdown and mental disorder is only one degree with respect to the increasing impossibility of existing as a member of a society (of *any* society at all).

To condemn the fact that madness was a product of society (but of a *certain* society), in the seventies it was often claimed that madness did not exist as such, and that it

was a normal response to this society. But if it is possible for such an affirmation to constitute the means of expression of an individual revolt, as in the case of Artaud, its essential goal, on the contrary, is to turn madness itself into a form of social reproduction. This tendency was expressed in *anti-psychiatry*, which criticized the repression exerted by psychiatrists and advocated a sort of "self-management" of madness by the "mad." In principle, this taking charge of oneself was to abolish the barrier between the patients and those treating them, thus allowing their socialization within society. This *"in vitro"* socialization was at times considered a testing ground which would allow a "mad" person to one day rejoin society *while at the same time continuing to come to terms with him or herself as such.*

A number of clinics which hoped to be different from and opposite to hospitals and psychiatric clinics were thus created. In France, the best known was undoubtedly Laborde's clinic, notably because of incidents opposing patients and the anti-psychiatrists who were treating them. These incidents perfectly revealed the function of anti-psychiatry, which was unable to sustain an anti-repressive discourse and practice unless the targeted individuals did not revolt against their "madness" which-has-become-responsible-for-itself, starting with revolting against the places where they were being treated.

Laborde was thus the object of such a revolt, during which a number of patients confronted the anti-psychiatrists who were present, notably a certain Félix Guattari, then famous for his "desiring machines", through which the negation of the unique individual was achieved in order to make way for the social individual (see "Anti-Oedipus," written in collaboration with Deleuze). An entire sector of the ultra-left – the modernist one – took Guattari's side against the insufferable attacks he was undergoing from several people living at Laborde's clinic and the rare individuals who supported them (see debates concerning this question in *Informations Correspondance Ouvrières 120*).

Since then, these folks – the modernists – either ended up in the socialist soup in '81, or attempted, like Guattari, to assemble the debris of the political and alternative extreme left in order to conjure up a truly leftist tendency in the present … to make a long story short.

As for anti-psychiatry, if it has disappeared from the ideological terrain it is because certain of its objectives have been partially achieved through a number of reforms which have taken place in current psychiatric practice. These reforms are obviously limited, but a certain number of archaisms have been eliminated and it appears that some psychiatric hospitals have become similar to what Laborde's was like at the beginning of the seventies.

As is usually the case (see the not-yet-published text "Abolishing society…"), modern society itself, *in its own way*, at least partially achieves the objectives of the ultra-left concerning psychiatry. It appears that in Italy, though, a more direct anti-psychiatric intervention has allowed this movement of modernization to become even more radical: there, with the elimination of psychiatric hospitals, madness is integrated directly into society. Psychiatric evolution in France also appears to be headed in this direction, but at a slower pace because it is obliged to follow the official social paths (see R. Castel: *La Gestiun des Risques*, Ed. de Minuit).

Madness demonstrates an inability to identify with any society whatsoever. This, of course, is in no way a limitation, except for all kinds of socialists, among whom one finds the very anti-psychiatrists who have attempted to turn madness into a normal outlook through the creation of a mini-society of "crazy people", and thus a new social role. In this sense, revolting against the role of being mad, like against that of being criminal, allows those who personify these roles to exist as individuals at least to a certain extent. Only then can certain aspects of transgressing social norms present in madness become elements of wonder.

Suicide

By committing suicide, individuals make a radical break with social necessity of any kind. In this sense, it is possible for suicide to give the impression of being the freest activity an individual could possibly carry out. In response to the question "Is suicide a solution?" in *La Revolution Surrealiste no. 2*, Crevel answers "yes." Artaud, on the other hand, felt that suicide could not be anything other than an act *imposed* on him by social reality. This was the viewpoint he was to develop later in "Van Gogh, Killed by Society." This approach to suicide, and to death in a more general sense, is the most powerful, the most poetic, and at the same time the most deeply thought-out because it conceives of death as a social moment of life and considers that *both are equally abominable* (this disgust radically distances him from all the modernists – the anti-psychiatrists, Telqueliens and the rest, who have successively attempted to appropriate him).

In fact, the only freedom demonstrated by "my suicide" is not in my choice of death instead of life at one moment as opposed to another, but that *I* carry it out because I am the *only one* who can kill myself. Certainly, an act imposed by society that I can carry out immediately reminds one (apart from delinquency) of the self-management of asocial acts that we found with respect to anti-psychiatry. Still, one cannot properly speak of self-management, because in order to do so it would be necessary to adopt a schema which is one of social relationships: my act must be lost in the anonymity of acts belonging to everyone. As things stand, my freedom can only make itself known through an act whose origin is not free. But emphasizing the obligatory character of suicide while presenting it on the contrary as a chosen act, let us supposed that I, and all the other likely suicide candidates are told how to carry it out. In this case it is no longer *I* who kill myself, but thanks to the instructions used, an interchangeable member of a group of people who will potentially kill themselves.

When I take the amount of little pills necessary to go over the edge, for example, I will be aware that that other individuals, at the same instant, or a little sooner or a little later, have gone through the same motions, measuring out the same dose in order to achieve the same result! It's enough to gross you out too much to commit suicide!

Thus the goal of the book *Suicide, mode d'emploi* (since by now it will have become clear that that's what I am referring to) is to make voluntary death a social act which gives birth like the one which brought us into this world. To kill oneself – what a beautiful role! The last and the finest! As Leo Malet might have written, *have you seen me as someone killing himself?*

This even more strongly confirms Artaud's viewpoint that suicide is imposed by society.

The task of socializing suicide has fallen to the anarchists, just as that of socializing crime has fallen to the communists and of madness to the anti-psychiatrists. Social space is thus hermetically sealed and nothing, it seems, is able to escape from it.

Society is by nature contradictory. According to its criteria, which are those of the reproduction of the species, society wishes to create interchangeable individuals which carry their uniqueness within themselves. It attempts to make them identify with self-reproduction and in order to bring this about, decks it out with playful, subjective charms. This has particularly been the case for the last thirty years with the establishment of a realm of consumption which has now reached its zenith: "I'm me," the advertisements proclaim, offering a pitiful specimen of something which is identical in every feature to any other sample of the same thing. They can even go so far as to claim that "people are unique," while adding, "don't spoil it," like the advertisements on the wall of the Parisian subway, signed "The Associated Humans." Thus uniqueness itself is monopolized by Man, whom Stirner called the last ghost, who, having replaced God, would prevent the arrival of singular individuals: People Which Are Unique.

The question of social modernity will be considered in more detail in the forthcoming text "Abolishing Society.…" For now, it is a question of pointing out that the contradiction that unique individuals cannot be reduced to social relationships is the same one diverse communist revolutionaries who wish to abolish the separation between the individual and the community have also tried to resolve. This separation, in effect, only exists because individuals cannot be part of a community: the separation is the negative of the positive which non-identification represents. By abolishing the one, they abolish the other.

Wonder

The result would be a society in which individuals would only exist as members of the species but in which their

Demolition Derby # 1 (1989)

relationships, as in today's society, would be considered free. Such a society would undoubtedly be close to "primitive societies," but would be considerably worse because it would be based on historical social development.

Of all the societies which have ever existed, those known as primitive societies are in effect the ones which have obliged their members to identify with them the most. Here individualization is only slightly developed. However, the limited socialization of nature which accompanies these societies allows individuals, however unfree they might be, to relate to nature in such a way as to incorporate it into their individuality and make it an integral part of it. Certainly the community itself presupposes this relationship with nature and in effect shapes its content. However, even if it is mixed together with relationships with the community, the relationship between the individual and nature is real and distinct. Whereas the relationship between the community and nature produces the religion of these communities, the relationship between individuals and nature possesses a content which can be called magic, or more precisely, one of *wonder*.

We can term a relationship with nature (external or internal) one of "wonder" if *it is not one which reproduces* nature or individuals who are in contact with it. By integrating nature as an element of their unique individuality, the latter make *another* reality appear, one which is not a social one: *their own*. Constantly hidden behind the former, the latter reality cannot appear when the *realistic* criteria inherent in every society are in place, but only as a sense of wonder which is more or less poetic. This is the basis on which the surrealist movement was formed (see the text *A Note On Surrealism*).

Although they are mixed together, it is essential to distinguish between wonder and religion in "primitive" societies, because if nature religions have become outmoded with the socialization of nature, religion as such has subsequently developed in ways which are (more and more) social, because every community presupposed one or several religions. Also, wonder is renewed in ways which are more and more individualized – i.e. poetic, although in ones which are less and less effective because the relationship with nature is cut off, but non-identification with society remains profound (the surrealism of the interwar period constitutes the high point of this period and of its contradiction).

There now exists an *extreme potential* for poetic wonder in need of a desocialized relationship with nature in order to manifest itself.

This point will also be taken up in a future text.

Communist revolutionaries, then (to get back to them), desire a community which would be in a state of osmosis with respect to individuals, signifying, in fact, that they would only exist through the community.

The critique of the notion of community, then, complements and perfectly illustrates the critique of society. One of the rare critiques of this notion and at the same time the reality it indicates has been developed by Catherine Baker in her text *From One Society to the Next* (final part). In order to properly understand the passage quoted below, it would be worthwhile to clarify the context.

At their request, Catherine Baker, who had previously written a prison abolition manifesto, met the editors of *La Banquise* and *Prisonniers de la Démocratie*. During this meeting, she had a fairly long discussion with Gilles Dauvé (Jean Barrot), which, according to her, took place on a level which represented a break with those which usually take place between "revolutionaries." Then, wishing to prolong this discussion in a written form, she sent him a letter c/o the only address in her possession – the *La Banquise* one, but, of course, clearly indicating the first name of the person it was addressed to since at that point she was unaware of his surname. According to Catherine, in any case, there could be no doubt about whether the letter was addressed to a particular individual. It was then received by one member of *La Banquise* or another and was read and discussed by a number of members in Gilles Dauvé's absence. A little later, Catherine Baker received a response to her letter from a certain Caroline, whom she had never heard of. The latter letter would be printed in *Prisonniers de la Démocratie no. 2* as a response … not to Catherine's letter, but to an abolitionist text, *From One Society to the Next*, because, according to *Prisonniers de la Démocratie*, "they both said the same thing"!

The explanation, though of only minor interest, makes it clear that the text *From One Society to the Next*, of which only the part concerning community is reprinted here, represents a clarification concerning the above experience.

SURREALIST DESTINIES:
MIX AND MATCH!

Andre Breton	Diplomat
Steve Schwartz	Catholic devotional painter
Aime Cesaire	Knight (soil)
Louis Aragon	Wrote a long book on Art
Herbert Read	Communist Party official
Octavio Paz	Trade journalist
Salvador Dali	Racial nationalist
————	Bob Black

In every sense of the term, society presupposes socializing life and organizing its socialization. A society calling itself libertarian or revolutionary would be just the same as today's, with undoubtedly a new division of power and a desire to do away with protuberances such as the state, law, justice and prison as they now exist. In any other society, however, it would be necessary to recreate them or to find alternative solutions.

We like the idea of sharing. But if my thing can become your thing, because I wish it to be so, it

Demolition Derby #1 (1989)

should not become our thing (when I say us, on the other hand, I am aware that this us signifies a plural I, not a pronoun representing a group. It is a sign of poverty that language contains only social expressions).

If something is ours, it is neither mine nor yours; no one can enjoy it without the other's authorization. The community, therefore, becomes a third-person guarantor. It is in this manner that the idea of a legal system which "guarantees" the rights of each person (and with the idea of law appears the idea of crime) has been incorporated into every society. The rights of each person are nothing more than rights – in other words authorization. All the mechanisms of democracy are based on this permanent concession.

The concept of law is incapable of going further. A democratic society which tends to see that "human rights" are respected in effect becomes the best of all possible societies.

It is because common interests must be defended that members of societies (of any type – present or future) find it necessary to adopt a common response to anything which is in a position to threaten them. The question of internal and external "enemies" – that of crime – is thus necessarily raised.

Guiding Law is Justice (peoples' or otherwise): it is judged that individuals do not conform (are guilty) or conform (are innocent) – but in either case they are judged. It could not be otherwise in a society whose members defend the common interests in question.

By definition a society presupposes its self-organization, in other words an ensemble of rules which govern how it functions.

We affirm that in our opinion it is possible to conceive of people living in a world without society.

One tangerine plus another tangerine adds up to tangerines, and not to a big tangerine called an orange. Society is this fruit monstrosity.

Today an individual is only seen as a member of a society. This is the source of our isolation, because isolation is contained in the very concept of community to the extent that each person is only a minute fragment of a single complete entity: the community. From this viewpoint then, an individual can only miss other people, not desire them.

In our opinion each person in his or her uniqueness constitutes a totality. Because someone is a totality, their desire to meet other "totalities" can only be an expression of freedom, and not a herd-like determinism.

We cannot be both a totality and a part of a totality. Each person, choosing a conception of unity, moves in the direction of individualization or communization. We then act. It is not the interpretation of these acts which varies (it's not "just a question of words"), but our acts themselves and our way of living.

The authors of Prissoniers de la Démocratie, therefore, have a way of going about things which is in accordance with their ideas and have offered an extremely interesting example of the interchangeability of individuals once they belong to a community. Catherine sends a letter to Gilles. The letter is read by people other than Gilles and is discussed within the community. One of its members, Caroline, answers the letter addressed to Gilles (who only learns about it several days later). To top off a communitarian relationship in which anyone can replace anyone else without causing the least inconvenience, a letter signed by Caroline is published as a text, which is no longer, in this context, Catherine's letter.

Thus universality is based (and this is what's terrifying) on the assertion of the existence of a bond; it is claimed that people are naturally joined together by what is most common to them: the human species. It is therefore necessary to become more and more "human": "And, to the extent that we can know how to love the human species, our body belongs to it" (in "For a world without morality," La Banquise no. 1). This sentence is very revealing concerning this desire to abandon everything specific to individuals in favour of the community.

But we are no more interested in having banal bodies than banal thoughts. In our opinion, the only thing that belongs to each person and to everyone is his or her irreducible difference.

We have a mad, reasonable, utopian desire – the only kind possible – to live unique relationships, which have extricated themselves from any type of social obligation. What is unique is what is different and unusual: what has never existed and never will again. The general principles governing the community do not allow relations between individuals unless the community is able, in one way or another, to reappropriate them. What we have stated with respect to the criminal act is therefore true for every act and relationship.

Every unforeseen relationship is banished from "private life", a realm to which we obviously do not lay claim any more than to a social one. Our relationships will not be limited to either the one or the other. We desire life at its fullest and inter-individual relationships which are always *possible and possible everywhere; amongst our friends, of course, but also every time we meet someone (at a later date we will consider the question of chance).*

To refuse the social relationships imposed by the functioning of each life within societies is to open up to wonder (at this point we couldn't care less whether certain words are in fashion or not). Because we need surprise and our need is growing.

Everything in this world is predictable, including its limits and its revolutions. Everything in its proper place. Everything at its proper time. As elements of equations we are unable to experience the unknown in new situations. The people we meet are defined (even if only by inference – "she doesn't look like this … he's not that") even before they can say "I." Besides, this "I" usually only consists of the expected representation.

We have chosen the unpredictable. By disentangling ourselves from what binds us to society we make ourselves available for what can happen between you (whether I know you or not) and I. What is possible is the very essence of relationships between individuals.

Every relationship between one unique being and another is potentially desirable. And we desire a world in which the possibility of becoming involved in already existing relationships will be preserved. Thus we exclude any kind of institutionalization of these relationships: when we become involved in them we transform them, as we ourselves expect to be transformed by them.

The community, which a revolutionary society would be ideally, presupposes a universal affinity, which is said to be part and parcel of the vital impulse of the infamous human species. We are repulsed by the idea of a generalized "feeling of belonging to the same family." Being a sponge would be preferable.

The entire universe interests us. What takes place between ourselves and the world around us is a mystery. How each person becomes conscious of this mystery is unique. Nevertheless this secret can be shared in specific conditions between specific individuals. It is what is specific to each meeting that we decide to safeguard. Relationships between individuals, past, present or future, are not a question of politics, but one of poetic creation instead.

Each time we must invent a relationship which can be compared to no other; one which will allow us to become more and more unique, but not only for ourselves. Isolation is neither

necessary nor inevitable. Several people can think together; we could revolt individually or together and perhaps we can even have what some people call "a revolution." But this would be the subject of another text.

– Catherine Baker

Anarchism

Today the anarchist project of abolishing the state has become the axis of every class orientated critique (regardless of its specific ideology).

Here the Marxists undoubtedly regain a radical edge which their emphasis on capitalist relations of production had eliminated, given the present low level of class activity within these relationships (whereas during the seventies it was the anarchists who adopted Marxist economic analyses instead).

What could be a higher achievement than to abolish the state (that is, all of them)? However, with the exception of certain anarchists, everyone agrees that the state is simply a representation of society (not in a fictitious but in the real sense of the word).

As the illusion developed here would have it, since the state is a product of the division of society into classes, destroying it will allow a society to reunite. It is a question, then, of a revolutionary project which wishes to produce a society devoid of its inherent contradictions.

Well, abolish the state. Create a new society without excrescences of any kind according to criteria (bringing together individuals on the basis of their membership in a species) which are proper to all societies! You'll find that the contradictions you hoped to leave behind will catch up at a trot and then a gallop: individuals who fortunately do not identify with the species will recreate groups which, as in every society, will be antagonistic. Then there will be nothing left to do but reconstruct a state conflict-management arsenal. If you want a society you get the state too.

In "primitive" societies, founding a real state was not necessary due to the limited extent of socialization present. However, embryonic states which were consistent with their size did in fact exist in these societies – in tribal councils, for example, which represented bodies which were separate from individuals (although these bodies emerged from society in a more direct manner than states as such). These are undoubtedly the kind of decision-making bodies revolutionaries have in mind when they are asked "What should be with the uncontrollables in a communist society?", or when other people propose direct democracy as a way to run a society.

In these cases, these folks are not minding their own business. If I become involved in a conflict with such and such, it is only my and that person's business, as well as that of the people who will eventually be indirectly affected by the conflict in question. Society, if one still exists, can fuck right off!

Demolition Derby # I (1989)

However, if revolutionaries are focusing their critiques on the state in this manner, capitalist society itself is putting this critique into practice in its present attempt to short-circuit classes and directly socialize members of the human species.

This subject will be expanded upon in the forthcoming text *"Abolishing Society to the Sound of an Accordion"*, which will also explore the following questions:

– Every society presupposes divisions between human groups. It is in this mutilated, predetermined manner that the persistence of individual difference expresses itself at the very heart or social relationships. *Antagonism* between social groups is precisely what allows the accompanying presence of nonsocial relationships.

– The importance of the phenomenon of *déclassement* (leaving one's class) in history, which is not simply the history of class struggle.

– The importance of the time/space of nonwork, which, until the stage of the real domination of society was reached (i.e. before World War 11), was one of encounters between individuals as opposed to simply one of recreation. The city represented the space in which the activities of reproducing the labour force were detoured into the streets, cafés, festivals (especially travelling carnivals), dances and music, expressing the existence of individuals who were both unique *and* separated from their social relationships (i.e. Argentinean tango, American urban blues, Parisian cafés in which popular music is played, etc.).

– Capitalism, which presupposes itself, constitutes the last possible society because, having replaced nature in every respect, it is *society which presupposes itself.*

– Society therefore tends to short-circuit classes and social groups and to directly socialize individuals it obliges to *coexist* within it. As a result, individuals in dominated social groups tend to be elevated to a state of being social individuals just like everyone else. From this state of coexistence flows a necessity for people to *tolerate* each other, in other words to put up with each other instead of loving or hating each other. A *cool* (4) attitude prevails (but one which does not exclude violence of a more or less cunning nature), along with critiques of resentment and violence, which fly off in all directions. Also, there is the arrival of youth as a social force, which corresponds to society's need to constantly renew itself because there is nothing left to conquer. This arrival was foreshadowed by Nazism and fascism on the one hand and by the Popular Front on the other, as transitional political forms on the way to the stage of the real domination of society. Now that the period of political transition has been left behind, today (i.e. since the beginning of the Sixties) the social force of youth manifests itself primarily through music, which has become more and more mechanical. Technical and lacking in content – i.e. pure Muzak – in accordance with the tendency towards the abstract universalization of capital.

– Also consistent with this abstract movement of universalization is a parallel transnational, transracial movement, which is visible in the anti-racist milieu and which, far from wishing to abolish the labeling of individuals according to their race, instead wants to promote it as an integral part of society, similar to, for example, categories based on work. Today's society is therefore at the same time socialist and individualist.

– How can it be abolished?

– Etc. To be continued in the next issue.

– ALAIN AJAX
FEBRUARY 1987

From: L'Unique et Son Ombre.
     B.P. 180,
     75463 Paris Cedex 10, FRANCE

Translated by Michael William

NOTES
(1) In English in the text.
(2) See the text "Here is the story of a crime," the prologue of a crime novel which frees crime from any kind of social cause.
(3) Léo Malet – participated in anarchist and surrealist groups and later wrote crime novels.
(4) In English in the original.

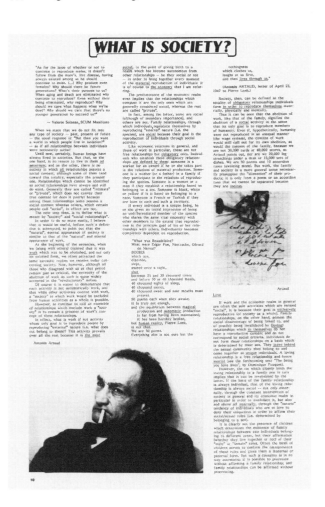

SURREALIST DESTINIES: MIX AND MATCH!

PRISONNIERS DE LA DÉMOCRATIE 2

11

13

Anarchism

— Alain AJAX
February 1987

From: L'Unique et Son Ombre,
B.P. 130,
75463 Paris Cedex 10,
FRANCE

Translated by Michael William

12

14

VISIONS OF THE MAGIC KINGDOM

innocence   experience

dadata

Demolition Derby #1 (1989)

NO PICNIC

In the fall of 1987 I had been putting out a small poetry zine in Vancouver, B.C. I wanted it to be part of more than just the literary scene, so I included other content as well. For instance a former roommate of mine was in Reikers prison in New York for armed robbery and so I included some letters he had sent me. Another friend of mine whom I had worked with at the cafe commune, a restaurant and community bookstore run by an anarchist collective in Montreal, was inspired and decided to put out his own zine. After a few discussions we concluded that a collective project would be a more efficient use of resources, more fun to put together and the result might be more powerful. We approached a third friend, Chris O, and agreed to put out an explicitly anti-statist and anti-capitalist magazine. After much brainstorming we settled on *No Picnic* as its name. I believe it came from a Minutemen song by that name – "Modern life ain't no picnic."

I lived in a communal house with Helen, who was Gerry Hannah's (of the Vancouver Five Direct Action group, then in jail) girlfriend, Chris O, Beverley S, and other friends. We were all involved in various aspects of the anarchist milieu and so *No Picnic* really grew out of that household and the extended family and milieu that it was part of. I had also founded a Vancouver chapter of the International Black Cross. We started a weekly radio show, *Stark Raven*, which still exists, and organized a drop in centre we called the Autonomy Centre, where we sold reprinted pamphlets and held discussion nights, etc. Again, *No Picnic* drew on all this incredible passionate energy, which also gave it a militant or at least activist feel. Vancouver anarchists tend to be somewhat a-historical, soft on authoritarian leftism and leftism in general, a little moralistic and somewhat anti-intellectual. So the activist aspect of *No Picnic* had a wide appeal. As a collective, (we preferred to refer to ourselves as a "group of friends"), we didn't share those leftist points of view.

We didn't have a collective statement, and there were fundamental differences between us, but I think we all felt closer to the anti-civilizationists, green anarchists and other radicals who weren't afraid to go outside of the anarchist tradition in search of new ideas and practices. Living in B.C., where primal peoples had only very recently been invaded and their territories occupied, it made sense not only to investigate the so called primitivists' perspective, but to get involved somewhat in the struggles of the first peoples here. So we covered not only the anarchist milieu, but native issues as well. While we clearly were deeply influenced by the anarchist tradition and felt a part of it, we made a point of rarely, if ever, referring to ourselves as anarchists, expressing the need for radicals to move beyond ideologies. We wanted anarchy, but not anarchism. At the time we were reading Fredy Perlman's *Against His-Story, Against Leviathan* and were profoundly influenced by it. We were also reading a fair amount of direct actionist and insurrectionist material as well. We wanted to inspire folks to trust their desires, to revolt, to create, to self-organize.

Our press run changed from issue to issue. Anywhere from five hundred to two thousand. We sent them out to prisoners, for trade with other papers, to a few subscribers, to several bookstores here in Canada and internationally as well, handed them out at demonstrations and gave them to like-minded people. Although we only put out a couple of issues a year for a few years, from 1988 to 1990, I have met several people who told me that their first contact with anarchist ideas and dreams came from *No Picnic*. We didn't want it to become an institution like *Open Road*, preferring to let it go when the time came.

– SHAUN WOODS

No Picnic (January 1988)

Hello and welcome to the first
issue of No Picnic. We are a
group of friends who share ess-
entialy the same political per-
pectives though we do have some
differences. We would like to
promote an anarchistic vision of
society.The only way to attain
this is by eliminating the state
and class society and by incorporating egalitarian, non hierarchical, ecological and feminist
priciples into our everyday lives.
We do not want to reform industrial
society. Industrialism is anti-life.
No creature, no plant,no part of
our planet is free from the deadly
tentacles of civilization. We see
the immediate need for communities
of resistance to counter this on-
slaught, and see direct action as
the most effective strategy. We
feel the wisdom that land based
cultures have accumulated over the
centuries will be an essential aspect of any culture of resistance.
In that respect we'd like to emphasize the importance of the struggles
of indigenous peoples everywhere.
Its up to all of us to dare to win.
Resist and refuse to be compromised
by the bosses, politicians, corporations and ruling scum who talk shit
and want to turn our planet into another one of their fucking wastelands.

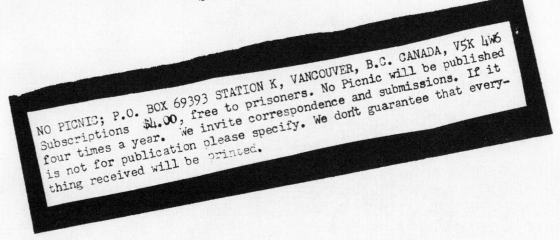

NO PICNIC; P.O. BOX 69393 STATION K, VANCOUVER, B.C. CANADA, V5K 4W6
Subscriptions $4.00, free to prisoners. No Picnic will be published
four times a year. We invite correspondence and submissions. If it
is not for publication please specify. We don't guarantee that everything received will be printed.

No Picnic (Spring 1989)

no picnic

$1 spring 89

Women in prison, Anarchist Black Cross, Tyranny of Cars,
United Europe, Ecomedia, Fish Farming, Shell to hell,.... with love

Stop the Machine!

When some of our ancestors destroyed wild forests for agriculture, and captured, fenced in and tamed free animals, they began to lose touch with nature. This was, in many ways, the origin of alienation, of feeling alien in our own world. Not all cultures followed this path of original domination. Some continued their hunter-gatherer (many were actually gatherer-hunters) lifestyles.

Civilization, founded on the principle of power-over, began it's long history of destruction and subjugation of everything wild and free, bringing us to our current world of states, property, hierarchies, pavement, shopping malls, meaningless drudgery, restrictions and separation from everyone and everything.

If we are going to stop this technological, industrial, work obsessed, violent machine that is killing this planet and reducing everything on it to extensions of itself, then we are going to have to break out of the anarchist ghetto and begin learning from and fighting with others who see the need for a complete transformation of the world we exist in. It is in this respect that earth based cultures, for instance, should have as much significance for anarchists as collectives of the Spanish revolution. After all, we are trying to help build a society based on the principles of mutual aid, friendship and trust founded in the common bonds of real communities. Further we refuse to accept being alienated from and controlled by the tools we use to produce the things we want.

This type of society, both communitarian and without authoritarian technologies, has already existed, and to some extent, still exists in some traditional indigenous cultures.

From the standpoint of a planet rapidly dying from the "we-must-conquer-nature" mentality of Christian/industrial society, self-managing an automobile factory is no longer an acceptable long-term goal. What we produce and the process and type of tools involved in that production, are as important as who now controls the whole system of production and distribution. It is all the same. While we are getting rid of the bosses and their prisons, police, nations, armies, etc., let's get rid of everything that their fucking violent system has created! Is it so hard to imagine a world without cars, smoke stacks, agribusiness (maybe even agriculture itself as well as business), factory work, factory learning, factory cities…? Is the desire for small scale, self-sufficient communities that consciously attempt to maintain a balance with the local eco-systems so utopian?

Isn't a world without bosses and privileged scum who do fuck but have everything, a world where gender and colour and looks don't determine how oppressed and miserable our lives will be, as equally utopian?

We do want to send the yuppies back to wherever they came from, to get the rich bastards and all their lackey governments, to stop the male violence, etc., but we also refuse to inherit their society. Each of us will decide how we will do this. One thing for sure however, is that we cannot vote out the capitalist or patriarchal systems. To the extent that the ruling caste will use violence to prevent us from taking control of our lives, we too will have to use violence. It seems obvious to many of us that drinking our own piss is just what this system wants us to do, turn the other cheek, and thank that senile old man in the sky for the strength of our convictions that we are right, and that in the end, justice will miraculously prevail.

There is an empowering aspect to protest and revolt, an example of which is the adrenalin rush one gets during an action, when solidarity seems unbreakable, when we're together and directing our anger at something or someone we despise. There is also a range of emotions that are usually associated with celebration and release that rioters and looters in England have recently talked about. The sheer joy of being free and wild, of experiencing, if only for a few hours, a world without cops, money or private property.…

No Picnic (Summer 1988)

People, not Ism-Oids

Hello there! Well here it is, Spring 89 issue of *No Picnic*. We hope you enjoy it. *No Picnic* is an assortment of ideas, expressions and information, not of any one perspective or influence, but of many. Often we are asked: "How does your group define its politics?" or "What are the goals you're trying to achieve?" Well to tell you the truth, we strongly reject and resist the tendency to categorize and don't believe in blueprints for "revolution." In defining one's politics and even the idea of separating "politics" from the rest of our everyday life activity can only lead to boring old dogma and rhetoric. And there's enough of that around already, thank-you.

We know what we like/love and we know what we hate and think is gross. This is something that changes as we live, grow, learn and unlearn. We see self-activity as an important part of local resistance. As definers of our own activity, outside of the 9–5 and other impositions that society has shoved down our throats, we must not slide into the trap of incorporating this society's garbage into our lives. Like boring and dry politics, workerist ideas and terminology like "activist" and other stupid concepts such as "politically correct" that plague the ghettos of the political sphere. If we can't enjoy ourselves, break-out and do things we really desire and want to do, then self-activity is shot to hell.

Many things and ideas influence us. We are people, not ism-oids with a cause. As individuals we have differences. Like we hash things out from time to time, but we agree on a lot as well. We try to remain self-critical and open to other approaches and influences.

The paper is one facet of our lives and we try to allow space, so it doesn't become an all work no fun type of project. Other activity, our daily lives, and pleasure almost always take precedent over *No Picnic*. We're all still dealing with the shock and horror of this society we live in, and at times it's difficult to go into the next day, living and trying to be open and honest with each other, let alone trying to put out a newspaper.

Knowing that there's people out there who care and give a shit enough to fight against injustice and refuse to bow down to the dictates of conformity, are all inspirations that keep us alive and empowered.

Politics

All struggles come down to resistance against domination. Power-over has been institutionalized in a society wherein one group, the ruling class, owns the means of production, i.e.: (factories, mines, distribution, infrastructure etc.) and also manages the movement of capital. At the same time they try to reduce our lives to that of 'worker' and expect us to throw a large part of our life away, to the benefit of their profit-making machinery.

"From the cradle to the grave, you made yourself the system's slave" – AMEBIX

Their factories and all their other alienating structures can burn to the fucking ground for all we care. But they can't do it by themselves. They need help.

This society is also organized in an increasingly centralized and bureaucratic manner by the State, i.e.: (prisons, armies, government, police, tax collector etc.) We feel that those who see nationalism as a tool for liberation are either kidding themselves or have already picked a comfortable position in their future 'revolution'. We don't have to look far to see the counter-revolutionary effects of nationalism, a world defined and separated by boundaries, the reproduction of hierarchy and the whole elitist mentality that this concept embraces leads us to the recognition that nationalism bars the way to a free society.

"I spit upon the flag, I spit upon religion" – THE EX

Thirdly power over is virtually universally expressed in the organized domination of women by men (religion, family violence, etc…). This system is called a patriarchy. The interplay between the institutions of the patriarchy, the State and capital is that which must be understood, explained, exposed and destroyed. As long as these structures remain in place and are left to interact with each other unopposed, freedom is only an elusive and far off dream.

We sometimes use the word civilization to express the totality of what we're up against. When we step away from the influences of civilization, and begin acting autonomously of its structures, an effective resistance can begin to grow.

We are inspired and encouraged by those who attempt to smash and topple that which seeks to destroy us all.

Because or our situation locally we must learn to take advantage where we can. Two outstanding realities here are the great isolation from large populations, relative to Europe or even eastern North America, and the fact that our economy is based on so-called natural resource exploitation. We watch with interest developments in Western Europe and elsewhere and try and learn what we can from them, but they obviously have limited applications in our scenario. Because of this we must develop our own methods of continuing and building resistance with both long and short-term goals in mind, try to apply it as much as possible to our daily lives and be constantly flexible – open to new ideas and change. Autonomous, unmediated, non-directed and collective efforts that work towards this, is what we seek to promote.

Thanks everyone who has helped out with bringing this and past issues of *No Picnic* together. Donations, correspondence, and great submissions have made *No Picnic* what it is. We want to thank Colette Bealieu for the front cover and inside cut block photo in the last issue. We hope to see another issue out sometime this summer.

No Picnic (Summer 1988)

We always appreciate submission of articles and graphics so keep it in mind. This issue we have included a lot of information and writings either from prisoners or about prison and prisoners. We did not include this information with the idea of filling people with feelings of shock and horror. We feel that the blatant and sickening hypocrisy of this society cannot be realized until we look into the cages that it has built for us. We hope that this recognition will ignite people into action and the calling for the abolition of all these profit-motivated factories of despair. While freedom is denied the resistance must continue!

PEOPLE   NOT   ISM-OIDS

Hello there! Well here it is, Spring 89 issue of No Picnic. We hope you enjoy it. No Picnic is an assortment of ideas, exspressions and information, not of any one perspective or influence, but of many. Often we are asked:'How does your group define it's politics?'., or ' What are the goals your trying to achieve?' Well to tell you the truth, we strongly reject and resist the tendency to categorize and don't believe in 'blueprints for 'revolution'. In defining one's politics and even the idea of seperating 'politics' from the rest of our everyday life activity can only lead to boring old dogma and rhetoric. And there's enough of that around already, thank-you. We know what we like /love and we know what we hate and think is gross. This is something that changes as we live, grow, learn and unlearn. We see self activity as an important part of local resistance. As definers of our own activity, outside of the 9-5 and other impositions that society has shoved down our throats, we must not slide into the trap of incorporating this societies garbage into our lives. Like boring and dry politics, workerist ideas and terminology like 'activist' and other stupid concepts such as 'politically correct' that plague the ghettos of the political sphere. If we can't enjoy ourselves, break-out and do things we really desire and want to do, then self activity is shot to hell.
We are influenced by many things and ideas. We are people, not ism-oids with a cause. As individuals we have differences. Like we hash things out from time to time, but we agree on a lot as well. We try to remain self-critical and open to other aproaches and influences. The paper is one facet of our lives and we try to allow space, so it doesn't become an all work no fun type of project. Other activity, our daily lives, and pleasure almost always take precedent over No Picnic. We're all still dealing with the shock and horror of this society we live in, and at times it's difficult to go into the next day, living and trying to be open and honest with each other, let alone trying to put out a newspaper. Knowing that there's people out there who care and give a shit enough to fight against injustice and refuse to bow down to the dictates of conformity, are all inspirations that keep us alive and empowered.

POLITICSPOLITICSPOLITICSPOLITICSPOLITICSPOLITICS
All struggles come down to resistance against domination. Power-over has been institutionalized in a society wherein one group, the ruling class, owns the means of production. ie: (factories, mines, distribution, infrastructure etc) and also manages the movement of capital. At the same time they try to reduce our lives to that of 'worker' and expect us to throw a large part of our life away, to the benefit of their profit-making machinery.
'From the cradle to the grave, you made yourself the systems slave' -AMEBIX---
There factories and all their other alienating structures can burn to the fucking ground for all we care. But they can't do it by themselves. They need help.
This society is also organized in an increasingly centralized and bureaucratic manner by the State, ie: (Prisons, armies, government, police, tax collector etc.) We feel that those who see nationalism as a tool for liberation are either kidding themselves or have already picked a comfortable position in their future 'revolution'. We don't have to look far to see the counter-revolutionary effects of nationalism, a world defined and seperated by boundaries, the reproduction of hierarchy and the whole elitist mentality that this concept embraces leads us to the recognition that nationalism barrs the way to a free society.
'I spit upon the flag I spit upon religion' The EX---
Thirdly power over is virtually universally exspressed in the organized domination of women by men(religion, family violence etc...) This system is called a patriarchy. The interplay between the institutions of the patriarchy, the State and capital is that which must be understood, explained, exposed and destroyed. As long as these structures remain in place and are left to interact with each other unopposed, freedom is only an elusive and far off dream. We sometimes use the word civilization to exspress the totality of what were up against. When we step away from the influences of civilization, and begin acting autonomously of its structures, an effective resistance can begin to grow

We are inspired and encouraged by those who attempt to smash and topple that which seeks to destroy us all.
Because of our situation locally we must learn to take advantage where we can. Two outstanding realities here, are the great isolatiom from large populations, relative to europe 1 or even eastern N. America, and the fact that our economy is based on so-called natural resource exploitation. We watch with interest developments in W. Europe and elsewhere and try and learn what we can from them, but they obviously have limited applications in our scenario. Because of this we must develop our own methods of continuing and building resistance with both long and short term goals in mind, try to apply it as much as possible to our daily lives and be constantly flexible - open to new ideas and change. Autonomous, unmediated, non-directed and collective efforts that work towards this, is what we seek to promote.

Thanks everyone who has helped out with bringing this and past issues of No Picnic together. Donations, correspondence , great submissions have made No Picnic what it is. We want to thank Colette Beaulieu for the front cover and inside cut block photo in the last issue. We hope to see another issue out sometime this summer. We always appreciate submissions of articles and graphics so keep it in mind. This issue we have included a lot of information and writings either from prisoners or about prison and prisoners. We did not include this information with the idea of filling people with feelings of shock and horror. We feel that the blatant and sickening hypocacy of this society can not be realized until we look into the cages that it has built for us . We hope that this recognition will ignite people into action and the calling for the abolition of all these profit motivated factories of despair. While freedom is denied the resistance must continue!

NO PICNIC, p.o.box 69393 STN. K, VANCOUVER B.C. CANADA V5K 4W6
Free to Prisoners. or $8.00 a year

No Picnic (Summer 1988)

I worked on editing, layout, and distribution for the summer '96, spring '97 and summer '97 issues of *Anarchives*, a publication started by Jesse Hirsh. Jesse went on to found Tao Communications (*tao.ca*) – which has since restructured to become the worker's co-op Organization for Autonomous Telecommunication – and also founded *openflows.org*, a very successful progressive open source resource. In August 1996 I brought a stack of *Anarchives* to the Active Resistance anarchist gathering in Chicago. Anarchists and activists who attended this event took copies of the journal to various communities across North America, and this contributed to a considerable increase in readership. Before 1996 distribution had been restricted in the main to Toronto, though an online component existed simultaneously via email lists and web space hosted on *tao.ca*.

During my involvement, the journal published articles about eco-architecture, homelessness, and police racism. We also ran the story of a young girl living in a Nicaraguan coffee co-operative and a Toronto refugee's account of his escape from Russia. It featured interviews with Noam Chomsky, with the conscious hip-hop group Poor Righteous Teachers, with a founder of Toronto's Who's Emma book store, and with members of the newly-formed ARC – Advocating Respect for Cyclists. On the activist side, *Anarchives* promoted Food Not Bombs servings of free food to homeless people, Critical Mass bike rides, the October 25th 1996 Toronto Day of Action against the policies of Mike Harris, leader of the Conservative Party provincial government (finally thrown out of power in 2003), and a Toronto lecture by Hakim Bey (AKA Peter Lamborn Wilson). We also profiled the music of hip-hop artists in The Dope Poet Society and a number of anarchist and radical feminist organizations. And we covered various political events in Montreal, Vancouver, and south of the border. There were articles on the structural adjustment policies of the World Bank and the IMF, on confronting homophobia and activist graffiti in Western Europe, and a tactical guide to various forms of culture jamming (such as how to make paint-bombs to target corporate advertising). *Anarchives* featured graffiti works by Toronto artist Jubal Brown, collage work by Carly Stasko and Jason Hallows, poetry by playwright Jon Garfinkel and dub poet Debbie Young, pieces advocating opposition to tobacco advertising, activist events listings, colourful accounts of subway parties, the musings of Jesse Hirsh on the marketing of the internet as a utopia and his narrative account of a World Bank counter-conference held in Toronto.

In addition to producing *Anarchives*, many of the journal's writers and contributors were part of The Media Collective. This was a loosely-structured affinity group comprised of activists and journalists, artists and anti-artists, techies and Luddites, all of whom would come together periodically to brainstorm, discuss, debate and collaborate. *Anarchives* promoted some of the activities of The Media Collective, but both folded in 1998, in part to concentrate on planning for the 1998 Active Resistance anarchist gathering in Toronto. The Media Collective was reincarnated in the winter of 2003–2004 and continues to operate. Active Resistance was important. The conference brought hundreds of North American anarchists to Toronto, raised $8,000 for various activist groups, and trained a new wave of anarchist organizers who went on to work in various anti-poverty, anti-capitalist, and grassroots media organizations. Though *Anarchives* no longer exists, most everyone who was affiliated with it continues to work as artists, activists, journalists and shit-disturbers. That's a good legacy.

– DAVE FINGRUT

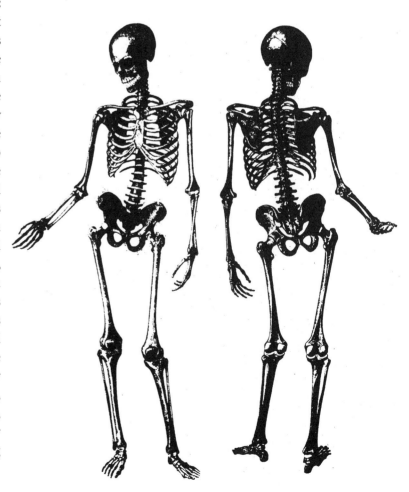

Anarchives 4/I (1997)

You are now entering an alternative world

Of Creativity and Freedom

Of Truth and Energy

All Converging into Love

The Media Collective
'Bringing Culture Back To Resistance'

The Media Collective is a spontaneous, dynamic, holistic organization, that includes the universe as its membership. We are artists, activists, and people interested in reclaiming our environment, reclaiming our minds, and thus reclaiming our lives. The Collective itself is a conduit for change.

The Media Collective is an inclusive and universal organization. We are the expression of human liberation, we are the demonstration of freedom. We are reclaiming our environments by engaging them at a direct and immediate level.

We are a movement towards ecological sustenance via self-determination of communities and individuals. We support international indigenous struggles, pro-democracy, pro-human and animal rights, pro-choice, food not bombs, and universal access.

As an inclusive organization we only exclude those who exclude. We are anti-fascist, anti-racist, anti-sexist, anti-homophobic, anti-ageists, and against any abuse of power or oppression of individuals or identity. We are fighting for political economic social justice: we are against neo-libearlism, neo-conservatism, patriotism, militarism, and capitalism. We are against any system that sustains political economic power through cultural hegemony.

The term 'Media' does not refer to an institution, or a technological artefact, but rather to the environment in which we all live. Media are the methods in which we communicate with ourselves, each other, and the world at large. As we communicate, we forge the material reality in which we exist.

Centuries of empire, appropriation, and exploitation have consolidated and centralized control of the majority of media. Corporate concentration manifests itself as the realization of a true media monopoly, declaring the birth of a new regime, and the end of history. His story has robbed us of our sovereignty, robbed us of our land, robbed us of our voice, and may soon rob us of our minds.

The Media Collective is a spontaneous proclamation of the self. It is an uprising of the free individual spirit, shedding the chains of mental colonialization, screaming shouts of joy with the self-realization of identity.

Anarchives 4/I (1997)

Anarchives 4/1 (1997)

"Are you happy? Do you choose how you think? How often do you use your imagination? What was your last day dream? Do you have free will? How oftend do you feel inspired? Are you sexually satisfied? Did you do something selfless today? Who are you?"

We are a conduit for grassroots revolution. We seek to bring various active and interested forces together to enable independent and co-operative organization. We hope to foster, support, and encourage a fertile ground for media organizing and action. We are multifaceted at being multimedia, our decentralization comes through a renaissance of expression. We are all regaining our ability to speak, and with our new found voice we are screaming, 'The Emperor is Naked!'.

We break the homogeneity of the media monopoly by expressing ourselves with our own media. We take back our media, taking back our freedom, igniting a chain-reaction of self-expression, a revolution of many minds uniting against a common enemy. We use guerrilla tactics and any means necessary to defend our freedom of speech which is not defined according to profitability.

We are collectively and individually involved in video, mirco-power broadcasting, radio, art, graffiti, zines, performance art, food, street theatre, cartoons, faxing, fasting, civil-disobedience, newspapers, music, hacking, phreaking, luddism, the web, television, writing, email, video-conferencing, elite-crashing, talking, loving, partying, reading, reporting, ranting, telephony, protesting, analysis, and straight-out revolution.

"and behind the most creative aspect of that insurrection looms a band of reality hackers, merry pranksters, ontological anarchists, psychedellic warriors, and intelligence agents; the bastard progeny of Toronoto's own McLuhan: The Media Collective"

We are the virus of human liberation. We spread through the minds of all people, spreading the desire for freedom and happiness. Everybody is the media collective, and everybody can speak on behalf of the media collective. We must all take responsibility for our future, and we must all take an active part in our future.

We are the virus of unity. All may take claim under our banner as all are subject to media, and all have an interest in controlling their own media. We seek to decentralize power by decreasing the degree of mediation between us. Together we can all help each other help ourselves.

We are the virus of language. We subvert the institution via the medium on which it was built. Education accompanies transformation as the living language flows among free people. We spread the word and propagate the message of freedom.

We are the virus of action. We lead by example, allowing our actions to be the spark that ignites hearts and minds to strive for freedom. We are the convergence of thought and action, ideas and initiative, I and I bringing down babylon.

The Media Collective is an ambiguous, and amorphous organization. Our members participate in primarily spontaneous actions, covering a wide range of media and minds. Individuals make actions, the collective is the forum in which to share these individual experiences.

The Media Collective meets on the 16th of each month and holds events on the 27th of each month. The meetings act as a forum for members to exchange experiences, thoughts, ideas, and actions.

The next Toronto gathering is on Sunday March 16th, at 3pm at 86 Parliament #305. See above for information about the next toronto event 'it's after the end of the world'.

All people are encouraged to organize local meetings, events, and take part in their own spontaneous actions. We are building a comprehensive web site available as well as other resources in other media to encourage the spread of the virus.

The Media Collective Hotline: (416) 812-6765

Members of the media collective communicate on the media-l e-mail list. You can join the network by visiting the e-mail center or sending the command 'subscribe media-l' no quotes to majordomo@tao.ca. You can also view a hyperarchive of the messages sent to media-l. Send comments, questions, and reports to media

"And one day all the slaves ran free,
Something inside of them died.
The only thing I could do was be me
And get on that train and ride."

anarchives

Par un soir des derniers jours de 1993, environ une douzaine de personnes s'étaient rassemblées avec l'intention de former un nouveau journal d'anarchiste à Montréal. Dans l'appartement de l'Est del la Ville on trouvait des jeunes pour la plupart impliqué-e-s dans les associations et journaux étudiants et des groupes populaires et anti-racistes (dont les maintenant défuntes Brigades Noires). La réunion avait été convoquée après la dissolution (temporaire, comme nous le savons maintenant) du journal socialiste-libertaire moins radical appelé *Rebelles*, qui regroupait des militant-e-s plus âgé-e-s et avait existé pendant quatre ans. Une demi-douzaine de celles et ceux qui avaient assisté à la première réunion est revenu à la seconde par semaine plus tard, et les bases de ce qui serait connu comme le collectif *Démanarchie* ont été établies.

Rebelles s'étant reformé entre temps, un des camarades intéressés est revenu à son ancien projet et un deuxième journal anarchiste à Montréal était sur le chemin des presses. Après beaucoup de réunions élaborant une plate-forme politique et définissant ce qu'on voulait dans la publication, un premier numéro parut en avril 1994. Le collectif était alors déjà impliqué dans plusieurs luttes sociales et bien connu dans la communauté militante de la métropole. Les articles étaient écrits par la plupart des membres du collectif, en utilisant des surnoms et des noms d'emprunt, déclarant clairement que le collectif, regroupant des intérêts et des orientations divers, était pour l'anarchisme de lutte de classes un mot qui était presque absent de *Rebelles*.

Le journal a été un succès instantané avec les punks de montrealais-es, qui achetaient (ou se faisaient donner) *Démanarchie* dans son quartier préféré du temps, le vieux "Red Light." Le langage utilisé dans les articles était le français de tous les jours, parfois même le "Joual," le dialecte des quartiers pauvres. Les lancements et les shows bénéfices avec des groupes locaaux attireraient des foules de militant-e-s et dee jeunes de la rue, qui se mélangeaient dans une atmosphère communale qui était aussi celle des réunions du collectif, qui se tenaient dans l'Est pauvre de Montréal et aussi le quartier immigrant de Parc-Extension où plusieurs vivaient.

Peu avant l'élection provinciale de septembre 1994, deux membres avec une orientation plus nationaliste quittent le collectif à cause de la haine d'autres camarades envers le Parti Québécois (PQ), supporté par la plupart des groupes populaires institutionnels, parti qui a par la suite gagné l'élection.

Un conflit amer avait éclaté et devait être réglé au cours d'un débat formel sur la question nationale, puisqu'aucune position n'avait pu être adoptée par le collectif sur le sujet, pace qu'autant le côté anti-nationaliste que celui de "libération nationale" tenait à sa position. Après les démissions, la discussion ne s'est jamais produite, et à la place un numéro spécial anti-nationaliste a été publié. Ce "grand schisme" de l'histoire de démanarchiste durera ce qui a semblé plus d'un an. Les politiques antisociales et anti-pauvres du déficit zéro du gouvernement Parizeau changeraient les positions des deux camarades qui réintègreront le collectif dans une atmosphère plus amicale.

Pendant cette période, le journal a également ajouté une section anglophone, le rendant accessible à un plus grand nombre de lectrices-teurs et militant-e-s. Des copies ont été distribuées et vendues jusqu'à Toronto, Paris, Londres et en Amérique latine. Pendant les années qui suivent, une nouvelle édition de *Démanarchie* paraît à tous les deux ou trois mois, avec es sessions de production longues de souvent plusieurs jours, parfois même sans interruption. D'autres membres de la scène anarchiste se joindront au collectif et il atteindra à un moment la taille de dix-sept membres. Être connu dans la communauté d'anarchiste signifiait également collaborer avec d'autres groupes, voyager, établir des réseaux avec d'autres organisations et, par conséquent, une influence accrue. Les membres du collectif qui parcouraient la province voyaient de plus en plus leurs publications diffusées dans les cercles alternatifs et, éventuellement, à l'extérieur de Montréal de façon régulière. En séjournant à Québec, un membre est ainsi tombé amoureux de l'environnement politique autour du groupe local de Food Not Bombs (appelé là-bas De la Bouffe, pas des Bombes) Il s'y est établi à l'automne 1995 et a formé le deuxième collectif *Démanarchie* qui a également fourni des articles au journal et tenu des activités semblables.

Autour du début de 1996, la communauté punk de Québec avait rapidement adopté *Démanarchie*, qui était devenu un des journaux de gauche les plus fréquemment publiés dans la province. Une des raisons était le niveau élevé de répression policière dans les rues et les parcs du centre-ville, un phénomène d'escalade coïncidant avec les émeutes de la St-Jean-Baptiste, un événement annuel qui avait commencé dans cette ville autour de 1993. Les émeutes fascination également plusieurs membres de *Démanarchie*, certains en ayant vécue une à Montréal en Juin 1993 quand l'équipe locale de hockey a gagné la coupe

DÉMANARCHIE

Stanley et la masse s'est mise à briser des vitrines et à piller les commerces le long de la rue de Ste-Catherine, l'artère commerciale principale de la métropole. Un jour après l'émeute de Québec, le 25 juin 1996, le porte-parole de "La ligue anti-fasciste mondiale" auto-proclamée (LAM), le collaborationiste péquiste Alain Dufour, déclarait aux medias que les émeutes dans la vieille capitale, un phénomène en propagation rapide à travers le Québec, avaient été "organisées" par le collectif anarchiste, qu'il a appelé "un groupe d'ectrême-droite." Ce fut le début d'une spirale de répression policière contre tout le mouvement anarchiste. Le collectif de Québec fut poursuivi par les medias bourgeois après cette "dénonciation," amplifiée par l'attaque chauvine du maire Jean-Paul L'Allier de Québec selon laquelle l'agitation a été provoquée par de "dangereux montréalais," au même moment que la police municipale de Québec avec sa contre-partie provinciale perquisitionnait l'appartement montréalais d'un démanarchiste. Ceci en emportant un ordinateur et des caisses de documents, n'ayant rien à voir avec les émeutes ou le collectif.

À partir de ce moment, le mouvement a commencé à s'inquiéter de sa sécurité interne et de répression politique à tous les niveaux. Des embryons des collectives commençaient à se former à Sherbrooke, dans l'est de la province, et un projet de nouveau collectif en Ontario étaient dans l'air, mais la confiance et l'énergie commençaient à manquer à Montréal et Québec.

Ceci, jumelé à des procédures légales qiu traînaient en longueur pour deux camarades de Montréal, épuisait les vains efforts de nouvelles adhésions, et beaucoup de temps était perdu dans des tentatives de décentralisation.

En outre, quelques membres, dont certains à Québec mais également à Montréal, qui avaient pris l'habitude de vivre de leurs ventes de rue (qui appartenaient à 100% au collectif) et d'emprunter les épargnes du collectif ont rendu la vie du collectif difficile et soulevant des questions de responsabilité individuelle. Les publications sont alors devenues moins fréquentes, et les membres ont commencé à dédoubler leur temps avec d'autres projets déjà en cours, comme Citoyen-ne-s opposé-e-s à la brutalité policière, ARA (Action anti-raciste), la croix noire anarchiste, et bientôt des émissions de radio et encore plus.

Après la dernière édition de *Démanarchie* au milieu de 1997, plusieurs nouvelles publications anarchistes sont apparues, dont *Le Poing d'Exclamation*, *Le Chat Noir*, *Le Mortier*, *Suspectus*, et beaucoup plus tard, après une fusion progressive des trois premiers, *Le Trouble*. Le collectif de *Démanarchie*, toujours affecté par la chute de 1997, espérait restaurer sa structure, mais a dû par la suite abandonner ses plans. *Rebelles* a poursuivi son existence parallèle mais, incapable de remplacer ses membres relativement vieillissant-e-s, plie bagage à la fin du siècle. Aujourd'hui, presque cinq ans après la fin de cette expérience, le mouvement anarchiste essaie de poursuivre sa tradition, avec au moins un-e ancien membre de *Démanarchie* actif-ve dans chacun des quatre groupes qui forment maintenant l'Union provinciale de la NEFAC, la Fédération anarcho-communiste du nord-est de l'Amérique. Red & Anarchist Skinheads Montréal, Bête Noire, *Facing Reality*, et l'Union locale de Québec (autrefois le groupe Émile-Henry) font de leur mieux en action et en pensée pour maintenir le milieu d'anarchiste en vie et lui apporter du sang neuf. Une histoire, même honnête, n'est jamais complète sans tout ce que nous aurions voulu accommplir mais qui ne s'est pas réalisé. Le nombre de femmes dans le groupe (toujours une minorité), une plus grande diversité ethnique, la constructoin d'une organisation anarchiste et d'un mouvement de masse radical auraient été d'une grand apport à *Démanarchie*, mais l'histoire ne peut pas être révisée et doit être acceptée en tant que telle. Le futur, cependant, peut toujours être inlfuencé. De sorte que nos camarades actuel-le-s n'oublient pas les bonnes et les mauvaises expériences, c'était, et c'est, notre histoire.

– SID, QUI N'EST PLUS LE DERNIER GRANULIEN

On an evening in the last days of 1993, about a dozen people congregated with the intent of forming a new Anarchist newspaper in Montreal. In the East End apartment were young people mostly involved in student unions and newspapers, and also community and anti-racist groups (including the now-defunct Brigades Noires). The meeting had been called following the (temporarily, we can now say) disbanding of the less radical, libertarian socialist paper called *Rebelles* which grouped older activists and had existed for four years. A half-dozen of those who attended the first meeting showed up at the second a week later, and the bases of what would be known as the *Démanarchie* collective were established. *Rebelles* having reformed meanwhile, one of the interested comrades returned to his old project and a second Montreal anarchist newspaper was on the way to hit the streets.

After many meetings elaborating a political platform and defining what we wanted in the publication, a first issue came out in April 1994. The collective was then already involved in several social struggles and well-known in the city's activist community. Articles were written by most of the collective's members, using nicknames and aliases, clearly stating that the collective, while having mixed interests and orientations, stood for class-struggle anarchism, a word that was nearly absent from its older brother/sister, *Rebelles*. The paper was an instant hit with Montreal's punks, buying (or being given) *Démanarchie* in its favourite neighbourhood at the time, the old Red Light district. The language used in the articles was everyday French, sometimes even "Joual," the dialect of the working classes. Launches and benefits with local bands would attract crowds of activists and street youth, mixing in a communal atmosphere that was also that of the collective's meetings, taking place in Montreal's poor East End district, as well as in immigrant Park Extension where a few members also lived.

Shortly before the provincial election of September 1994, two members with a more nationalistic orientation quit the collective over the hate other comrades had towards the Parti Québécois (PQ), supported by most institutionalized community groups, which eventually won the election. A bitter dispute had erupted and was to be settled in a formal debate on the Quebec national question, since no position was ever adopted by the collective on the topic, both the strict anti-nationalist and the "national liberation" sides holding firmly to their intents.

Following the resignations, the debate never occurred, and instead an anti-nationalist special edition was published. This "great schism" of démanarchist history would last for what seemed over a year. Only the anti-social and anti-poor zero-deficit policies of the Parizeau government would cause the two comrades to revise their positions and reintegrate the collective in a more friendly mood. During that period, the paper also gained an English section, making it accessible to a far greater number of readers and activists. Copies would be distributed and sold as far as Toronto, Paris, London and Latin America. For the next few years, a new issue of *Démanarchie* would be released every two to three months, with often intense production sessions several days long, in some cases even without any interruptions. New members would join coming from the anarchist scene and the collective would grow to a record of seventeen members at one point. Getting known in the anarchist community would also mean linking with other groups, travelling, networking with other kinds of organizations and, consequently, increased influence.

Members of the collective travelling across the province were seeing more and more copies circulating in alternative circles and, eventually, this led to distributing the paper outside Montreal on a regular basis. On a trip to Quebec City, one member fell in love with the political environment surrounding the local Food Not Bombs collective. He settled there in the fall of 1995 and formed the second *Démanarchie* collective that would also contribute articles to the paper and hold similar activities as the one in the province's metropolis.

Around early 1996, the punk crowd in Québec City quickly had caught on to reading *Démanarchie*, which had by then become one of the most regularly published left-wing newspapers in the province. One reason was the high level of police repression on the streets and in parks downtown, an escalating phenomenon coinciding with the St Jean Baptiste riots, an annual event that began in that city around 1993. Riots were also a fascination for quite a few *Démanarchie* members, some having experienced one in downtown Montreal in June 1993 when the local hockey team won the Stanley Cup and mass window-breaking and looting occurred along St Catherine Street, the main commercial strip. One day after the riot, on June 25, 1996, the leader of the self-proclaimed "World anti-fascist league" (LAM), PQ collaborationist Alain Dufour, issued a statement to the media that the riots in the Old Capital, a phenomenon that was

DÉMANARCHIE

rapidly spreading across Quebec, were "organized" by the *Démanarchie* collective, which he called a "far-right group." This would be the beginning of a downward spiral of police repression on the whole anarchist movement. The Quebec City collective was pursued by the bourgeois media following this "denunciation," amplified by the chauvinistic attack of Québec City mayor Jean-Paul L'Allier who claimed that the turmoil was caused by "evil Montrealers." Québec City police along with their provincial counterparts raided one member's Montreal apartment, taking away a computer and cases of documents, most of which had nothing to do with either the riots or the collective. From then on, the movement began to worry about internal security and political repression from all levels of authority.

Embryos of collectives were beginning to form in Sherbrooke, the Eastern Townships, and plans for one in Ontario were under way, but trust and energy were beginning to run low in Montreal and Quebec City. This, paired with separate and long court procedures of at least two Montreal members, was depleting energy – it showed in declining membership and time lost sorting out problems arising from decentralization. Furthermore, a few members in Québec City and Montreal had a habit of living off their street sales (which belonged 100% to the collective). The chronic borrowing made collective life difficult and raised questions of accountability. Publication became less frequent, and members began splitting their time with other side projects that were already under way, like Citizens Opposed to Police Brutality, ARA, Anarchist Black Cross, and soon radio shows and more.

After the last issue of *Démanarchie* in mid-1997, several new anarchist publications sprung up, including *Le Poing d'Exclamation*, *Le Chat Noir*, *Le Mortier*, *Suspectus*, and much later, after a gradual merger of the first three, *Le Trouble*. The *Démanarchie* collective still met through the fall of 1997, hoping to restore its structure, but eventually abandoned its plans. *Rebelles* continued its parallel existence but, failing to replace its relatively aging members, folded at the turn of the century. Today, nearly five years after the end of this experience, the Anarchist movement is trying to pursue its tradition, with at least one former *Démanarchie* member active in each of the four groups that now form the Provincial Union of NEFAC, the Northeastern Federation of Anarcho-Communists. Red and Anarchist Skinheads Montréal, Bête Noire, *Facing Reality*, and the Québec City Local Union (formerly the Émile-Henry Group) all do their best in action and thought to keep the anarchist milieu alive and expanding. An honest history, though, is never complete without all we would have liked to accomplish but were unable to achieve. The number of women in the group (always a minority), more ethnic diversity within, the building of an anarchist organization and a radical mass movement would have been of a great improvement to *Démanarchie*, but history cannot be revised and must be accepted as such. The future, however, may well see what we were still pursuing, for we all can, and will, influence it. So that our present-day comrades not forget the good and bad of our experiences, this was, and is, our story.

– SID, NO LONGER THE LAST GRANULIAN

POLITIK · POLITIK · POLITIK · POLITIK · POLITIK · POLITIK · POLITIK · POLITIK · POLITIK

PLATE-FORME DU COLLECTIF DE DÉMANARCHIE

(prenez note que cette plate forme fut adopté par le collectif en septembre 1995)

Le collectif de Démanarchie est totalement opposé à l'organisation étatisée de la société comme modèle de gestion territoriale et politique. L'état se maintient et ne s'est maintenu historiquement que par le vol, le meurtre et la corruption. L'état répression: police, tribunaux, armée et prisons. L'état directeur de conscience: école, médias et hôpitaux psychiatriques. L'état abrutisseur de masses: travail et économie. Bref, l'état qui crée de toutes pièces des criminel-le-s, des coupables, des tueur-e-s et des incarcéré-e-s. En prenant bien soin de mouler ses enfants, de créer l'opinion "vraie" et falsifier l'histoire, en désignant les "déviant-e-s" qui ne répondent plus à son mode de surproduction, l'état investit dans l'économie des asiles. L'état s'agglutine à ses propres antagonismes afin de se maintenir, tel un monstre froid qui vide l'individu de toutes ses capacités et qui le "soigne" par sa raison, la raison d'état. La condition essentielle de notre émancipation passe donc par la destruction complète et radicale de l'état comme moyen et instrument de la classe dominante maintenant notre asservissement. À l'étatisme nous opposons l'organisation volontaire collective décentralisée et fédérative.

Le collectif de démanarchie vomit sur le concept de démocratie parlementaire qu'il considère comme étant un nid légiférateur de la propriété et du droit, qui ne sert qu'à protéger le parasitisme bour-

geois. Seulement la destruction de la démocratie parlementaire et des institutions qui la représentent et son remplacement par la démocratie directe permettent le pouvoir au peuple. Conséquemment, nous ignorons le légalisme lors de nos actions.

La démocratie directe est une des conditions essentielles qui assurent l'autonomie individuelle du plus grand nombre dans toutes les sphères de la société et, pour toute conséquence, dans le processus décisionnel de son évolution. Il est évident que les décisions prises par le collectif sont prises à l'unanimité, afin que la confrontation des points de vue soit la plus riche possible et que les problèmes ne soient pas réglés d'une façon simpliste par la prééminence d'une majorité. Conséquemment, chaque membre du collectif ne représente que lui ou elle-même et son adhésion, qui est de ce fait individuelle, doit être approuvée par toutes et tous.

Le collectif de démanarchie considère le déisme comme une forme d'oppression. Nous croyons fermement que cette dictature par la pensée mine la libre volonté des masses et a historiquement été complice des autocraties en tous genres. L'humanité peut et doit ne plus vivre à genoux devant aucune figure matérielle et spirituelle que ce soit. L'athéisme nous semble la direction appropriée vers une philosophie humaine exempte du joug autoritaire des dogmes de l'au-delà et de la mort. Nous sommes conscient-e-s, comme l'affirma si justement Bakounine, qu'il ne peut y avoir de philosophie sérieuse au-

jourd'hui qui ne prenne pour point de départ l'athéisme.

Le collectif de Démanarchie crache sur le concept de sélection par la race ou par le sang qu'est l'eugénisme. Nous sommes conscient-e-s que cette ségrégation en race ou en ethnie est exercée par le pouvoir institutionnalisé de l'état et de la bourgeoisie et sert à stratifier le (lumpen)prolétariat pour un meilleur contrôle des pauvres. Nous sommes donc anti-racistes et anti-ségrégationnistes par essence.

Le collectif de démanarchie considère comme étant oppressive l'assimilation culturelle qu'est le patriotisme. En effet, puisque la culture contemporaine en est une de surconsommation de masse et de productivisme, puisque les instruments de travail n'appartiennent pas aux travailleuses et travailleurs, nous ne voyons pas comment nous pourrions considérer cette patrie adulée comme étant la nôtre. Nous sommes d'avis que cette culture et cette partie restent la propriété de la bourgeoisie. "Le patriotisme suppose que les institutions que l'on nous impose sont les nôtres et forment une base de l'ethnocentrisme." Les luttes de libération nationale voilent l'exploitation étant menée par des bourgeoisies nationales en manque d'état. Tout sentiment nationaliste découlant des frontières de cette propriété privée ne peut donc naître que dans des esprits asservis et dans des mentalités d'esclaves. Le collectif est anti-traditionaliste et anti-nationaliste par nécessité.

Le collectif de démanarchie urine sur la hiérarchie. Nous croyons que l'être humain ne peut

Le collectif de démanarchie défèque sur la domination patriarcale du sexe féminin. Du génocide inquisitionnel de l'église catholique en passant par la ghettoïsation économique, les femmes ont été et restent aujourd'hui les victimes du patriarcat. Nous savons pertinemment bien que la destruction du rapport marchand par une révolution ne pourra éradiquer seule cette pollution de l'esprit. Nous croyons qu'un changement au niveau de notre comportement quotidien de même que la destruction active des institutions patriarcales sont nécessaires et même primordiaux afin de jeter les bases d'un rapport réellement égalitaire et anti-hiérarchique entre les sexes. Nous sommes anti-sexistes.

Le collectif de démanarchie s'oppose avec acharnement au système capitaliste. La surconsommation inutilitaire de marchandises qui répondent aux statuts sociaux est une des causes de la destruction lente mais évidente de notre planète. Le capitalisme est l'instrument d'un état qui régit notre existence, réduisant celle-ci en vulgaire marchandise par l'appropriation et le détournement de la force de travail de toutes et tous, par la planification de nos temps d'existence qui nous réduisent à l'asservissement de la survie sous la dictature économique. Nous croyons que toute personne peut et doit autogérer son temps de travail et décider elle-même de ce qui est un travail et de ce qui est un loisir afin de se réapproprier sa vie. Il a été démontré que l'histoire de toute société jusqu'à nos jours n'a été que l'histoire de la lutte des classes. Ainsi, notre collectif comprend que les anarchistes ne peuvent faire seul-e-s la révolution et qu'il est essentiel, en gardant nos objectifs, de lutter avec tout individu ou groupe qui a à court terme un but de destruction du capitalisme. Nous ne pouvons nous permettre, sous le prétexte incertain d'être éventuellement trahi-e-s par nos alliances, d'être une secte partiellement active dans la lutte de classes. Nous observons d'un oeil désabusé le travail syndicaliste révolutionnaire. En effet, ces médecins de l'ouvriérisme, qui pratiquent les sutures de l'éducation et de la propagande sur le corps éventré d'une classe ouvrière malade du paludisme de son propre salariat, ont au moins le mérite de travailler à une finalité historique proche de celle que nous concevons, avec la même énergie que la nôtre, celle du désespoir. En opposition au capitalisme, le communisme libertaire et le collectivisme nous semblent être les méthodes d'organisation sociale les plus respectueuses du genre humain et les plus évoluées dans leurs buts égalitaires de répartition des ressources et des pouvoirs.

agir et vivre en soumis ou en qualité de subordonné devant aucun-e de ses pairs. La hiérarchie, cet embryon d'état, attaque l'autonomie individuelle en aliénant et déshumanisant l'individu par la notion de rôle. La conception manuelle et intellectuelle de la hiérarchie poussée à son extrême est aujourd'hui, dans le travail, la technocratie. Pour contrer cette plaie, le collectif admet le principe de délégation pour chacun de ses projets. Il revient aux membres du collectif de se regrouper affinitairement sur chaque projet en désignant une ou un délégué-e chargé-e de faire un compte rendu du travail ou des tâches prescrites par le collectif. Ces délégué-e-s, comme tou-te-s les membres collectif mandaté-e-s pour la réalisation de ces projets spécifiques, sont révocables à tout instant. Aussi, la hiérarchie du travail qu'est la technocratie ne peut prendre germe lorsqu'une rotation des responsabilités est appliquée pour toutes les tâches.

Le collectif de démanarchie est militant. Il a été reconnu par le mouvement anarchiste nord-américain que le gouvernement ne tombera pas de lui-même, aussi décadent soit-il. La tâche du collectif, en plus d'offrir une alternative aux médias de propagande de l'état bourgeois, est de s'impliquer activement dans des luttes qui ne sombrent pas dans le concertationnisme, en continuant un travail d'éducation tout en radicalisant les orientations des luttes. Il est clair pour nous que radicalisme n'est pas nécessairement synonyme de violence, mais il est rare qu'une de nos actions soit égale à la violence que nous subissons tous et toutes de l'état. L'état se maintient et s'est toujours maintenu par le vol, le meurtre et l'escroquerie. Et comme l'a si bien exprimé Malatesta, les anarchistes ne sont pas des hypocrites, c'est par la force qu'on résiste à la force: aujourd'hui contre l'oppression d'aujourd'hui, demain contre ceux qui pourraient essayer de remplacer par une autre oppression celle de demain. Nous concevons le travail d'éducation du journal comme un outil politique plus que comme simplement un publication contre-culturelle. Nos buts en quelques lignes? Affûter la conscience politique. **"Dans les masses qui ont été éternellement asservies, gouvernées, exploitées, qu'est-ce qui peut constituer la conscience politique? Ce ne peut-être assurément qu'une chose, la sainte révolte, cette mère de toute liberté, la tradition de la révolte, l'art coutumier d'organiser et de faire triompher la révolte, ces conditions historiques essentielles de toute pratique réelle de la liberté."** Bakounine

le collectif de Démanarchie

THE *DÉMANARCHIE* COLLECTIVE'S PLATFORM

(Please note that this platform was adopted in September 1995)

The *Démanarchie* collective is totally against state-controlled organization of the society as a model of territorial and political management. The state has maintained itself historically, and continues to do so, only by theft, murder and corruption. The repressive state: police, courts, army and prisons. The director of state conscience: school, media and psychiatric hospitals. The alienating state of the masses: work and economy. In short, the state creates from scratch criminals, the guilty, killers and the incarcerated. In taking care to shape its children, to create a "true" opinion and to falsify history by pointing out the "deviants" who don't answer to its way of overproduction, the state invests in the economy of refugees. The state swarms to its won antagonisms in order to maintain itself, as a cold monster who empties the individual of all his/her capacities and who cures him/her with its reason, the truth of the state. The essential condition of our emancipation passes therefore by the complete and radical destruction of the state as a means and instrument for the dominant class maintaining our servitude. Statism conflicts with our decentralized and federal voluntary collective organization.

The collective of *Démanarchie* vomits on the concept of parliamentary democracy, which it considers as being a legislative nest for property and the law, which only serves to protect the parasitical bourgeois. Only with the destruction of parliamentary democracy and its institutions that represent it and replacing it with direct democracy, can the power be made accessible to the people. Consequently, we ignore the legality at the time of our actions.

Direct democracy is one of the essential conditions that assure individual autonomy for the majority in all phases in society, and for all consequences, within decision-making and its evolution. It is evident that decisions made by the collective are made unanimously, in order that the confrontation of points of view are the richest possible and that problems are not settled in a simplistic manner by the preeminence of a majority. Consequently, each member of the collective represents only him/herself and his/her adherence, which is therefore individual, and must be approved by everyone.

The *Démanarchie* collective considers deism as a form of oppression. We firmly believe that this dictatorship, by undermining thinking, liberates itself willfully to the masses and has historically been an accomplice for the autocrats of all kinds. Humanity can and should live without worshipping any material or spiritual figure, whatever it may be. It seems to us that atheism is the appropriate direction towards a humane philosophy exempt of the authoritarian yoke of dogmas from the hereafter and death. We are conscious, as Bakunin justly affirmed, that one cannot have a serious philosophy today if its departure point doesn't deal with atheism.

The *Démanarchie* collective spits on the concept of selection by race or blood that is eugenics. We are conscious that this segregation of race or ethnic group is practiced by the institutionalized power of the state and the bourgeoisie and serves to stratify the proletariat by keeping a firmer control over the poor. We are thus, essentially, anti-racist and anti-segregationist.

The *Démanarchie* collective considers cultural assimilation, which in turn means patriotism, as being oppressive. In fact, contemporary culture is a mass culture of overconsumption and overproducing. Since the work tools do not belong to the workers, we do not see how we would be able to consider this adulated homeland as being ours. We are of the opinion that this culture and homeland remain the property of the bourgeoisie. Patriotism assumes that the institutions that it has imposed upon us are ours, and that they form an "ethnocentrical" base. The battles for national liberation veil the exploitation being lead by nationalistic bourgeoisies in want of a state. All national sentiments ensue from the borders of this private property and therefore can only arise into the subservient minds, and into a slave mentality. The collective has no choice but to be anti-traditional and anti-nationalist.

The collective of *Démanarchie* defecates on patriarchal domination of women. From the geno/gendercidal inquisition of the Catholic Church through to economic

Demanarchie 2/1 (1995/6)

ghettoization, women have been and remain today victims of patriarchy. We know full well that only by the destruction of the revenue market, by a revolution, will we be able to eradicate this polluted way of thinking. We believe that a change in the daily level of behaviour as well as the active destruction of patriarchal institutions are necessary and even primordial in order to lay the foundations for a truly egalitarian and anti-hierarchical relation between the sexes. We are anti-sexist.

The *Démanarchie* collective is fiercely against the capitalist system. The pointless overconsumption of merchandise, which answers to social status and is one of the causes of the slow, but obvious, destruction of our planet. Capitalism is an instrument of the state which governs our existence, reducing it to a vulgar merchandise by the appropriation and diversion of everyone in the work force, by planning our time and means of existence which reduces us to servitude in order to survive under an economic dictatorship. We believe that everyone can and should self-manage his/her time spent working and decide him/herself what is work and what is leisure time in order to take over one's own life. Up to the present day it has been demonstrated that society's history has only been a history of the fight between the classes. Thus, our collective understands that anarchists cannot make a revolution by themselves, and that it is essential, while keeping our objectives, to fight with all individuals or groups who have a short term goal to destruct capitalism. However, we cannot permit ourselves to be betrayed by our alliances under an uncertain pretext, or to be a partially active sect in the class struggle. We will keep an undeceiving eye on revolutionary union work. Indeed, these doctors of work control who practice their stitches on education and propaganda on the devastated body of a working class will, with their own salary's malaria, have at least the credit to work towards an historical finality to what we conceive, with the same energy as ours, that of despair. In opposition to capitalism, libertarian communism and collectivism seem to us to be the social organizational methods that respect humankind the most and are the most evolved in their egalitarian goals of dividing up resources and power.

The *Démanarchie* collective urinates on hierarchy. We believe that the human beings cannot act and live submissively or subordinately in front of any of his/her peers. This embryo of the state, hierarchy, attacks the autonomy of the individual in alienating and dehumanizing the individual by the notion of his/her role. Today, the manual conception and hierarchal intellectual are pushed to its extreme, in work and technocracy. To counter this wound, the collective admits the principle of the delegate for each project. It returns to its collective members to gather by affinity on each project in naming a delegate in charge of a report on the work and prescribe tasks by the collective. These delegates, as all members of the mandated collective who carry out these specific projects, are

dismissible at any time. Consequently, hierarchy of work, which is technocracy, cannot take root when a rotation of responsibilities is applied to all tasks.

The *Démanarchie* collective is militant. It is recognized by the North American anarchist movement that the government will not fall by itself, as decadent as it is. The collective's task, in addition to offering an alternative to the media and propaganda of the bourgeois state, is to actively get involved in struggles which do not give away to concertationist dialogue, continuing educational work totally radicalizing orientations of fights. It is clear to us that radicalism is not necessarily a synonym to violence, but it is rare that one of our actions is equal to the violence that we are subjected to by the state. The state is maintained by theft, murder, and fraud. Malatesta expressed it well when he said that anarchists are not hypocrites, and it is by this force that they resist to force: today against the oppression of today, tomorrow against those who would try to replace it by another oppression tomorrow. We conceive the newspaper's educational work as a political tool more than just simply a counter-culture publication. Our goals in a few lines? Sharpen the political conscience.

"In the masses, who have been perpetually enslaved, governed, and exploited, who can build up the political conscience? It can most certainly only be one thing, the blessed revolt, this mother of all liberty, the traditional rebellion, the customary art of organization and to make the revolt triumph, these essential historic conditions are in practice real liberty." – Bakunin

Le climat social

annonce un été chaud

Démanarchie 2/1 (1995/6)

What came through in the pages of *Reality Now* through its brief run was the sense of urgency and passion felt by its authors. *Reality Now* was about the need for people in North America to come to terms with the dark underside of the society that surrounded us – not the flashy dreams then (and still) being thrown at us in the expanding TV universe, such as the blind faith in a social progress that never really materializes or the naive belief that society's environmental, social and economic problems are better left to experts and authorities who will find technical solutions to benefit us all.

Born out of the early '80s punk and youth activist scene in Ottawa, *Reality Now* was originally a small photocopied zine published by the band/political collective Black Dove. When Black Dove disbanded in 1984, *Reality Now* was moved to Hamilton and then Toronto, where, thanks to the assistance and influence of publications like *Bulldozer* and other Toronto activists, *Reality Now* grew both in size, format and scope. Its editors used the publication as a communication tool for a burgeoning movement supporting political prisoners in North America, as a means of spreading news about First Nations and environmental struggles in Canada, and increasingly as a way to assess and share some of the lessons learned from the direct, on the ground work its writers were carrying out. Later issues turned increasingly to practical, how-to guides on meetings, organizing, and self-defense.

In the end it was the collective's commitment to organizing which ended *Reality Now* as a magazine after eight issues. With increasing demands on their time from volunteer efforts in prison solidarity, First Nations solidarity and other organizing, *Reality Now*'s editors packed it in in the late '80s to devote their attention to the grassroots projects they prioritized in its pages.

One of the prisoners who regularly contributed to *Reality Now*'s work once wrote of being "disillusioned" with political ideologies. He didn't mean to be without hope, crushed by despair. Rather, he was trying to see the world around him without prejudging it, without fitting the pieces into a preconceived picture, whether liberal, Marxist or anarchist. Only by engaging in an open, ongoing analysis of current reality, *Reality Now*'s editors felt, could people organize effectively to change their situation.

That's probably why, when reading through its editorials and articles now, *Reality Now*'s articles feel somewhat dated, even though the underlying crises they railed against are, if anything, even more pronounced today. The key to *Reality Now* was not the kind of sedate academic debate which is detached from the immediate and therefore seems timeless. Its articles were intended to anchor the reader in the moment, to instill a sense of the pressing need for action and organization, and to compel people to get involved in social change as "disillusioned," non-ideological but no less committed organizers. Each issue was a call for people to engage with the world as it is, right now, with the intensity, passion and focus that social justice deserves.

— KEVIN THOMAS

THE EARTH
THE WIND
THE FIRE
THE RAIN
RETURNS
RETURNS
RETURNS
RETURNS

Reality Now PO Box 6326 Stn. A , Toronto Ontario, Canada M5W 1P7

Reality Now Weapons of Words

The simple and intense fraternity is the vibrant poetry of this daily struggle.

Mauricio Marquina

Reality Now: Weapons of Words (1989)

Winter 85|86   Issue Five $1

Reality Now

1.7.X. '85

Melch-Lutah

Reality Now 8 (1988/9)

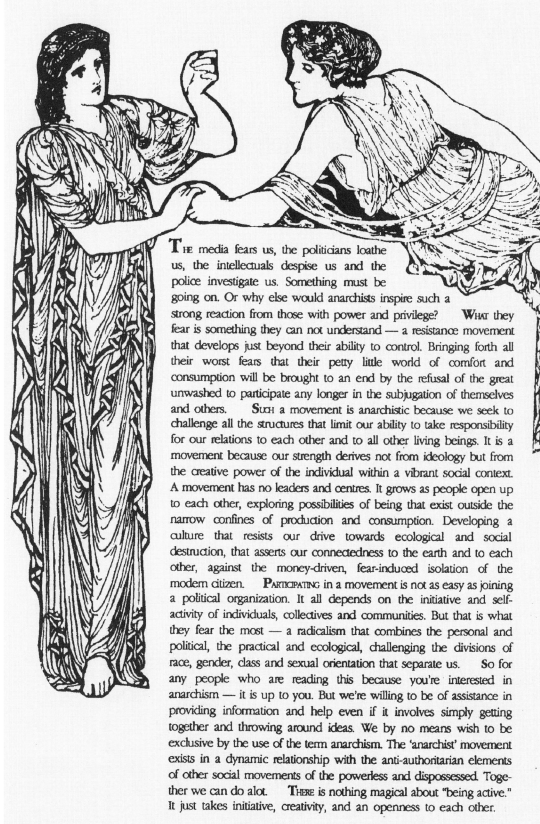

Reality Now: Weapons of Words (1989)

THE media fears us, the politicians loathe us, the intellectuals despise us and the police investigate us. Something must be going on. Or why else would anarchists inspire such a strong reaction from those with power and privilege? **W**HAT they fear is something they can not understand — a resistance movement that develops just beyond their ability to control. Bringing forth all their worst fears that their petty little world of comfort and consumption will be brought to an end by the refusal of the great unwashed to participate any longer in the subjugation of themselves and others. **S**UCH a movement is anarchistic because we seek to challenge all the structures that limit our ability to take responsibility for our relations to each other and to all other living beings. It is a movement because our strength derives not from ideology but from the creative power of the individual within a vibrant social context. A movement has no leaders and centres. It grows as people open up to each other, exploring possibilities of being that exist outside the narrow confines of production and consumption. Developing a culture that resists our drive towards ecological and social destruction, that asserts our connectedness to the earth and to each other, against the money-driven, fear-induced isolation of the modern citizen. **P**ARTICIPATING in a movement is not as easy as joining a political organization. It all depends on the initiative and self-activity of individuals, collectives and communities. But that is what they fear the most — a radicalism that combines the personal and political, the practical and ecological, challenging the divisions of race, gender, class and sexual orientation that separate us. So for any people who are reading this because you're interested in anarchism — it is up to you. But we're willing to be of assistance in providing information and help even if it involves simply getting together and throwing around ideas. We by no means wish to be exclusive by the use of the term anarchism. The 'anarchist' movement exists in a dynamic relationship with the anti-authoritarian elements of other social movements of the powerless and dispossessed. Together we can do alot. **T**HERE is nothing magical about "being active." It just takes initiative, creativity, and an openness to each other.

If anybody in the Toronto area wants to find out what's happening they can contact the Toronto Anarchist "Hotline" at (416)-536-2514

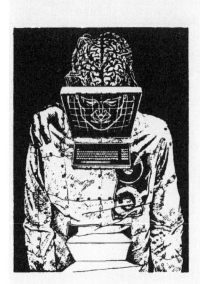

WORK WILL SET YOU FREE

Another day of carrot and stick
out on the floor
Everything screams the compressor pounds
Someone looks at you and frowns
"Oh please don't let me go, I wanna work here,
I won't do it no more"
Did I really say that? Have I really sunk that low?

Attention now you work for me,
You're on my time
Attention now you work for me
Tow the end of the line

They've given you a number
and taken away your name
and when they put you in the 'out' file
they will take the number away
you step into a seamless place
got lost somewhere but you don't know how
ground and ground 'til they spit you out
with your pockets lined with the dust of your time

Attention now you work for me
tow the end of the line
As you pause at the gate look up at the sign
and see the reward for all of your time
It says "WORK WILL SET YOU FREE"

Days and weeks slip by so fast
only last year you said "I'll get into something else"
How many months now just gone down the tube
How many days have you called your own?

Back in the morning just one more time
looking for something to throw
"Come on, be sensible now, try not to think
'til the whistle blows"
What's one day, there's plenty left
all the time in the world
You can throw them away, be real blase
they're cheap enough the way that you're paid

Attention now you work for me
tow the end of the line
as you pause at the gate look up at the sign
and see the reward for all of your time
it says "WORK WILL SET YOU FREE"

Shanghai Dog

I cry as I write this (all cops must die)

young and dead
in the anxious horizon
we were the messengers of pure information,
agents of a riot that rained down from the stars
on a sullen night powered
by twin engines of rage deluxe,
young and dead
I am living stillborn in a straightjacket of pain
our lives were handcuffed to multiple felonies
like
you blew your pretty face away ...

I don't know if there's a nihilist heaven
somewhere on the nether side of the sun
but young and dead
we could have laughed it up killing the cops of poverty
instead of our lonely burning selves.

Peter Plate

Reality Now: Weapons of Words (1989)

REALITY NOW

*The Earth gives us life in the natural cycle of life,
death, and rebirth. We feel that this is threatened,
and that we must live as defenders. We are of the
Earth, and must regain our connection to life
and our role in the sacred balance.*

We find it so hard, facing this beast every day without rest, not only in the actions or the State, the Earth-rapists and the obvious brutality of city life, but in the actions of our sisters and brothers who hurt us as well. We so often get swallowed up by the gloom and rage, and lose the vitality of our struggles, the joy and energy which could make our visions a real alternative to the gray concrete world which imposes itself upon us. Learning and being able to keep a balance within us in the midst of an unbalanced world, being able to remain open, caring and respectful when we are betrayed or just taken for granted, trying to heal ourselves, each other and the earth while still being battered, and being able to hold on to our hopes when they seem so impossible in this present reality, all these are very hard to live up to and we so often fall short of our ideals. Yet these ideals are our lives and our hopes and cannot be abandoned. Our creativity in learning new solutions is our strongest weapon in challenging the APART-heid of daily life, in which we live apart; not only from each other, and our natural environment, but also live separated inside ourselves – good from evil, life from death, love from anger.

Not seeing, or not seeing clearly at least; this seems to sum up our state at present, where we have sight but no vision, where it takes great inner perception to simply view clearly the outside world, and, in turn, our place in it.

The challenge, which this magazine is a part of, is one that faces each one of us individually and our world collectively. We must challenge ourselves constantly to examine our actions and our visions, our thoughts and feelings, to arrive at an understanding of this world and our place in it. This issue contains many pieces of information, which we feel paint a pretty clear picture of our situation at present. All these pieces are connected, and all of us are connected to this situation in some way, either in the way we contribute to its maintenance or to its downfall (all of us contribute in some ways to both). It would probably be redundant to yet again try to explain exactly how we feel about this situation, this should be made clear to anyone who reads this magazine. Instead we ask that you read and consider many things.

Consider the connections between the way we live in the industrial "first world" and the mass starvation, destruction of land and control of labour in the man-made "third world". Consider the Earth, the frailty and strengths of our natural environment, the damage being done to it and how this relates to our own lives. Consider rape, the hatred and fear of wimmin, the hatred and fear of animals, and of ourselves. Consider choices; how we can live cooperatively, responsibly, and without causing both our own death and that of all life on this planet, and how our present society fits into all this. Consider, most of all, how you involve yourself in this at present, for we are all involved, and how you would like to involve yourself in the future. Consider the connection between all these things, and everything around you. Consider this and then act on your knowledge, and work to make this action effective.

We have many ideas of our own, most of which should be apparent from this magazine and the work we do. It's in the communication of these ideas between all of us, and the transformation of these ideas into solid actions, and responsibility for them, that we make visions reality. This is the task, which lies before us, and it can't wait. To accept our given situation is to accept our own destruction, and the possible end to all life. We have to defend ourselves and try to create change. Is there any hope? Is it already too late? We'd like to think that there is hope, as long as there is life. But it also must be said that if we don't struggle for change, for balance (each in our own ways), then the choices we are left with are personal betrayal or death.

There are many ways to struggle against fascist control, and certainly there is not only one way in which we will overcome fascism, but many, and they are all important.

Reality Now staff

We can all do what we have the resources and means to do, always trying to do them better and more effectively, with our focus being on increasing potential, and not getting caught.

Every situation is different; therefore we cannot have a pre-arranged plan that we can follow without question. To do so is like planning to walk straight through the woods. You'd have to walk around the trees you came to, or you'd have to cut down all of the trees in your path. The path of authoritarianism is built in this manner. We have to deal with things as they arise, and not put our trust in people and laws that have "THE ANSWER." At the same time we have to work together, and help one another in this struggle against authoritarianism.

It would appear that most peoples have forgotten how to live peacefully with the Earth. And it would seem we've lost our connection to the Earth, or what could be called our spirituality. If we return to and learn once again from life, then we will begin to regain our spirituality, and our lost knowledge. When, as a movement (and we don't mind calling it that even though it often seems stagnant) we understand and really feel the connection between ourselves and our Earth, and in turn each other, we will truly have the living, breathing community we need. As separated individuals – separated from our Earth, from each other, from ourselves – we are truly powerless to effect the needed changes. We who are not Indian people cannot follow their traditional beliefs and ways, but like all people who live with the Earth, they have much to teach us.

It's been about 500 years since the first European settlers came to this land and started killing the Native peoples. Physical and cultural genocide of Native people has not let up in North and South America; nor has resistance, however.

It has been estimated that in 1492 there were ten million people (541 Indian nations) who lived in what is now the United States. Populations of Native people are now estimated at 200–250 thousand people. Indian land is now less than three percent of their original land base. This process of genocide has only been slightly slower but no less brutal in Canada, Mexico and South America. Such is power, and reality.

In the tropics, more than two-thirds of the world's estimated four to five million species live. Humans have already destroyed half of the tropical forests on the planet with the remainder expected to he wiped out by the end of the century. Estimates vary, but approximately one species becomes extinct every hour. How much time do we have left – ten years? Twenty years? Something's got to happen, if there are to be any future generations.

We must relearn. We have the responsibility, whether we like it or not, that the fate of the Earth, and life's survival, is in our hands. We must heal and defend the Earth, and start to take responsibility for our own lives, and actions both in personal relationships and in how we relate to our present collective situation. Survival of life, our own, and all that is on this Earth, our home, is our birthright.

Love, anger, and respect.

Reality Now staff

Reality Now is an anti-statist tabloid dedicated to exposing and confronting the people, institutions, and attitudes which control, attack and destroy our world and peoples. We focus on prisons and prisoners, Native struggles, the defense of our natural environment, direct action, and anarchist, feminist liberation struggles around the world. We also work as the Toronto branch of the *Anarchist Black Cross* in the defense of prisoners in need.

The continuation of our work depends on donations and subscriptions. You can help us advance this work by sending $6 (in Canada) or $7 (international) along with your name and address for a 4 issue subscription (free to prisoners). If you haven't already seen the magazine and want a sample, send $2 and we'll send you the latest issue, or send $3 for the past two issues. Please get in touch, smash the State, and have a nice day!

(Please make cheques and money orders payable to Reality Now)

REALITY NOW. For Defense of Life on Earth.
P.O. Box 6326 Stn A, Toronto Ontario, M5W 1P7, Canada

Reality Now 7 (1987)

In February 1980, the *Bulldozer* collective was formed when 4 or 5 activists from various places in southern Ontario met up in Toronto and decided that we should start working together on prison-related issues, since we had individually begun to do so. We were so inspired by the letters we were receiving from prisoners that we decided we should share them more widely. That summer we put out the first issue of a newsletter called *Bulldozer* – the only vehicle for prison reform.

Much has changed since that time – and generally for the worst. Prison populations have increased in Canada by over fifty percent, and by much more than that in the US. Conditions have deteriorated due to overcrowding and program slashing. Control Units have proliferated and sentences have gotten longer. More than ever, prisons seem to be an inevitable part of the lives of the poor and marginal. Their role in disrupting and containing the colonized peoples – Native, New Afrikan, and Latino – is as effective and disguised as ever.

On the outside, a small number of very dedicated individuals and groups have kept going, but there has been no movement to speak of until very recently. Prisoner-support work has not been that popular with the left, nor with social activists in general, and as in most movements out here, a year or so seems to satisfy most people's interest in doing the work. In spite of the hard work on campaigns to free particular POWs, such as Leonard Peltier, most of them remain in prison, a constant reminder of our weakness.

But *Bulldozer/PNS* did not survive for as long as it did by dwelling on the negative, and I don't intend to. With this in mind, I would like to articulate some of the politics *Bulldozer/PNS* developed over the years. These politics were more implicit than explicit. We never wrote long essays telling prisoners what they should think. Rather, we tried to provide a forum in which prisoners, individually and collectively, could articulate and develop their politics. We were always more interested in what we could learn, rather than what we could teach. If individual prisoners could learn from us, so much the better, but that would come from ongoing dialogue and communication. The political direction of the paper would be determined by prisoners, even if the decision as to what would or would not be printed was always ours.

Bulldozer's politics were rooted in the counter-culture, going back to a student house begun in the fall of 1971 in Kitchener, Ontario which developed into one of the first anarchist collectives in Canada with a heavy emphasis on radical psychology and existential philosophy (and sex and drugs and rock and roll). All through the 1970s, the collective tried to maintain a political orientation in activism, even as the individualism that was glorified in many counter-culture movements allowed for the reassertion of race, class and gender privilege, and a reintegration into business-as-usual for many former radicals and activists. In 1979, we moved to the country and set up a communal farm with the expectation that it would be a viable rural community from which we could maintain a political practice.

Prior to *Bulldozer*, the first issue of *Open Road*, a kick-ass, and very well produced, anarchist news-journal, had come out of Vancouver in August of 1976 and transformed radical politics in Canada. In fact, many of the articles in *Open Road*'s issue – Leonard Peltier's impending extradition; the U.S. George Jackson Brigade actions; an interview with Martin Soastre, a Puerto Rican anarchist and former POW; coverage of Native and prisoner's struggles – would not look out of the place in the later *Bulldozer/PNS*. My own sense of political possibilities and necessities were opened by the year (1977) which I spent working with *Open Road* in Vancouver. But there was little opportunity to put them into practice when I returned to Ontario. I became increasingly dissatisfied with the self-indulgence of the counter-culture and the anarchist-purism that celebrated it. I missed the more activist-oriented politics of the Vancouver scene, but moved to the country anyway to follow the politics of collectivity through to the end.

The farm floundered right from the beginning due to lazy-faire attitudes and middle-class arrogance. With self-expression and "do-your-own-thing" as the highest values, most communal members were unable to respond to the realities of a situation determined by an unrelenting hostile climate and the cycle of the seasons. Having grown up poor and living-in-the-country, it didn't seem to be such a big deal for me to be back, poor and living-in-the-country. I left, totally disillusioned, at the end of 1981, moved to Toronto permanently, cut my hair, and got a full-time job shortly after. I had started to write to prisoners and the first issue of *Bulldozer* came out while I was still living on the farm. Back in Toronto, I was keen to continue with the work.

Open Road motivated the creation of a more action-oriented, militant politic in Vancouver such as the Anarchist Party of Canada (Groucho-Marxist) which carried a series of "pieings" – literally throwing a pie in the face of a politician or celebrity, with Eldridge Cleaver being the most famous "hit" – in order to make a political point. As simple as this may sound, it brought about political and personal transformations from planning and carrying out the actions to dealing with the consequences – confrontations with reactionaries and authorities. The more serious people in the scene started to do support work for the prisoners in the old B.C. penitentiary, and their struggles eventually resulted in its closure. From then on, prisons have been an essential part of the work taken on by our circles.

Out of this came Direct Action, an armed group which in 1982 blew-up an electrical substation on Vancouver Island ($5 million in damages) and a Litton Industries factory north of Toronto that built components for the Cruise Missile ($10 million in damages and several injuries). Some of the same people were also involved in the Wimmin's Fire Brigade firebombing of three video stores specializing in violent porn. They were arrested in January 1983, an event that immediately threw us into doing support work. In June of 1983, the office of *Bulldozer* was raided and we were threatened with a charge of Seditious Libel (calling for the overthrow of the state) for the distribution of support-leaflets we were putting out. A mid-wife, living with us at the time, was arrested and charged with "performing an abortion" in an attempt to get information from her about our links to Direct Action. After several thousand dollars in legal fees and a year of high-stress, all the serious charges against us were dropped in connection to the raid. After losing several legal challenges over the legality of evidence, the Vancouver Five, as they had come to be called, pled guilty to several charges related to their actions.

Bulldozer was being published irregularly during this time. The eighth and final issue came out in 1985. I was personally and politically exhausted, and *Bulldozer* as a political project disappeared for two years. Fortunately, a very active group of young high school students in Ottawa had been influenced by the politics put out around the trials of the Vancouver Five. Even as our own political motivations disappeared in despair, they took up our ideas and started working with them, leading to the appearance of *Reality Now*, an anarchist zine that was very influential. Eventually, their enthusiasm helped to regenerate my own politics. After two years of inactivity the tedium of a comfortable working class life was becoming all too apparent. When political prisoner Bill Dunne needed an outsider to help him with *The Marionette*, a prisoner's newsletter

he was producing from Marion Prison, I rejoined the struggle. *Bulldozer*'s successor, *Prison News Service*, then developed out of *The Marionette*.

This provides a brief, more social than political, history. I want to be clear that *Bulldozer* developed out of the alternative or cultural politics – i.e., the punks, the hippies, purist anarchism, women, lesbians and gays, etc. – which has been the primary means by which white youth have been radicalized over the past few decades. It is all too easy, and certainly necessary, to critique these cultural movements. Their general failure to deal adequately with issues of race and class does make them little more than "white rights" groups as Lorenzo Kom'boa Erwin puts it. The social alienation that originally motivates many white youth into becoming part of these alternative movements often gets channeled into an accommodation with race and class privilege. Intense self-absorption, often combined with heavy drug and/or alcohol use, leads them to think that their subjective rebellion has some meaning. But modern capitalism cares little what anyone actually thinks, so long as one produces or, if unemployed, accepts being economically marginal.

The women's movement is, or at least was, different in that it did pose a real threat to the existing patriarchal structure of this society. This can be measured by the severity of the ideological counter-attack waged against it, even if it was discovered that the position of women in society could be changed without endangering the interests of those who get the goods. Awareness of their own misery led many women individually and collectively to develop a radical analysis of their social position. This self-awareness became a vulnerability as self-help and New Age therapies – often looted from Native societies in a continuation of the colonial kleptomania that has characterized white society – were used to help women (and men) to fit into the existing system. Political consciousness was increasingly seen as "part of the problem," rather then part of the solution. The necessary struggle to feel good about oneself – self-esteem – allowed for an acceptance of class and privilege.

For all that, the fundamental oppression, super-exploitation of and violence towards women remains. And mainstream culture is a death culture: not much wonder that so many young people, working class and middle class, try to find some life outside of it in one movement or another. Back in the early 1970s we were more political than the rest of the hippies and more hippy-like than the other politicos: we've tried to develop what could be termed the political wing of alternative movements. Through time, our politics changed thanks to people such as Kuwasi Balagoon and the local Leonard Peltier Defense Group with whom we went through some real hard times from 1983 to 1985 as we struggled to come to terms with colonialism, genocide and slavery upon which North Amerikan society is based.

The original insight that the "personal is political" was certainly truly radical in that it went to the root (radical means going to the roots) of social existence, our own individual lives. So great was the contradiction between the myth of social happiness and the misery found in most people's lives once they looked, that it energized the various social movements from the 1960s on. The slogan originally meant that there is a social context to our personal lives, and that a serious examination of who we are would lead us to understand the political context within which we lived. But its subversive impact has been smothered by reducing the political to the person, as though nothing mattered politically except for one's personal life and a few close friends.

Yet it remains that coming to understand who we are is a necessary first step towards participating in an authentic liberatory process. Part of the impact of *Bulldozer/PNS* itself was because it spoke directly to prisoners' lived-experience, rather than simply offering an intellectual explanation of political reality. The paper helped those struggling to know themselves in spite of living in a cage to feel strong – and that was a victory. Coming from what could be called a "secular spirituality," we shared with traditional Natives, New Afrikans, and Muslims, amongst others, the sense that an individual's life is a "struggle" in and of itself; that it is our task as humans to unravel the mysteries of our own existence, to determine the truth within it, and to find the proper direction. Politics come back into it since any honest examination should lead to a clear understanding that this society is based on a complex blend of race, class, and sex. Many whites, and others as well, unfortunately back off from these political implications.

The critical importance of understanding the connections between politics and one's personal experience became much more vivid for me when I "remembered" in the early 1990s that I had been subjected to severe and frequent sexual abuse as a child. Suddenly my own life made a lot more sense to me. I had discovered the key to my private mythology. The rage which I had learned to channel into my political work became understandable. It made sense to me why I was

drawn to the plight of the prisoner. I had spent much of my younger days isolated, brutalized, surrounded by those much more powerful than I who were bigger and stronger boys. An image that had haunted me for years of a prisoner, beaten down, forlorn and forgotten, huddled in a corner of a cell, had come straight from my own life, figuratively if not literally. I had been driven by a vow – as unconscious as it must have been – to not stand by while others were being abused.

There is much that we've learned over the past few years about abuse and healing that has political implications, particularly for prisoners, since surely prison is nothing if not a system of institutionalized abuse. For now, I will say that as we became more aware of issues around abuse, it made sense to discover that at least half of the activists we knew were sexually and/or physically abused as children. We had lived the lies and hypocrisy of the family, religion and society. Our opposition to all three was not merely some intellectual construct, nor mere political fashion, but was born of bitter experience. I did not need the suffering of others – women, Native people, Afrikans, prisoners or whoever – to motivate me politically. I had resisted long before I even knew there was a struggle. Like many of my prisoner-friends surviving long years of isolation and brutality, something within me refused to be broken.

I was in total mental and emotional anguish until well into my twenties, but for whatever unknown reasons, I was able to focus my rage on the corporate-state, and its bullies and bosses. Political activity became a means of eventual resolution. Slowly, but surely, I connected with other misfits, malcontents and losers. The counter-culture gave us all a certain space to be ourselves. We might have still been totally alienated from society, barely able to function day-to-day with heavy drug use helping to keep the pain at bay, yet we were no longer alone. And we could fight back.

In a psychologized society such as ours, political activity will often be shaped by unresolved personal problems. We are driven by our demons. But working through these problems need not mean the end of the political activism that was energized by the inner conflicts. It should, in fact, mean that we target the enemy ever more precisely. The abuse must stop! We can stop being abusive. We can resist the abuse we're suffering. But abuse is not simply due to personal failure or the lack of appropriate therapy or bad genes but totally integral to a homophobic society that uses class, race and sex to determine who gets what. This is where political will comes in. As long as abuse continues, then we must fight against it, even if, or especially if, our own pain and suffering has been eased.

POSTSCRIPT

The history above reflects my personal experience and opinions, and I played the main editorial role in *Bulldozer/PNS* since the beginning. But the journal can't simply be reduced to me personally. There are several people who helped shape it and their efforts are much appreciated. I do want to acknowledge some of the others who made significant contributions.

Sunday Harrison was around *Bulldozer* more or less since the beginning, especially including the raid and its aftermath. Her technical skills and creativity helped give *Bulldozer/PNS* a much more professional look than it would otherwise have had. We very much developed our ideas together – even if on any particular detail we are as apt to disagree as to agree.

Bill Dunne, the editor and main writer for the now defunct *The Marionette* also was a major influence on my thinking. Our years of exchanging letters certainly tightened up many of my arguments. Without him, it is unlikely that *PNS* would ever have existed.

After the raid in 1983, our support came from our Native comrades and from women working at a lesbian print shop. Though I barely knew these women, they immediately came through with crucial assistance. It is many years later, but I don't forget those who were there when help was needed. The lesbian community has also done the basic work on understanding sexual abuse and how it affects those who survive it. I would not have been able to write the above if it were not for the personal support and political stimulation and information that came from lesbian friends.

– JIM CAMPBELL

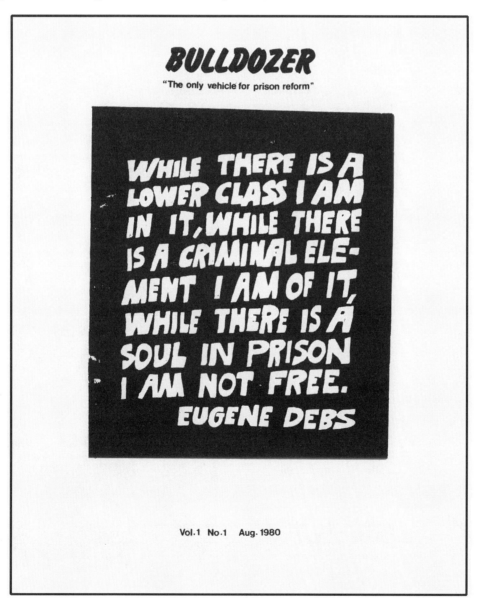

COMMUNICATION AND REPRESSION

Bulldozer is about communication. Represssion is the destruction of authentic communication. The state has the guns, the goons and lackies, the fences and concrete walls and the cages. To this we counter with our outrage, love, solidarity and the written word. There are few lasting victories in this struggle and many atrocities to relate. But it is the development of the networks, inside, outside and through the walls that give us all the strength and determination to continue.

The prison authorities like to operate in the shadows. In opposition to this we encourage our outside readers to develop personal contact with prisoners. Prisons cease to be an abstract issue of "human rights" when it is your friends who are subjected to the brutality and irrationalities of the penal system. Any of the writers in this journal would be pleased to hear from you. Write to them directly or through us. Prisoners and non-prisoners alike have much to learn from the world of the other.

We seek to reflect the struggle that is currently being waged in North American prisons. To some prisoners it is quite literally a matter of life or death. To others it is a question of retaining their pride and dignity as humans. We do not pretend to reflect the "average prisoner" in these pages. Rather we present the voice of those prisoners who see the need for change and are willing to do something about it. We will work with them to bring about that change.

Events are moving rapidly in the Canadian prison system; the Dorchester incident, the new proposals for preventative segregation for "potentially dangerous" prisoners, the introduction of more behaviour modification schemes. We hope to stay abreast of these developments and to this end, we will be coming out with smaller issues more frequently in the future.

We do not wish to limit ourselves to Canadian issues. Our concern for the genocide of the native people is shown in Standing Deer's material. There are many important struggles going on in the U.S. such as the trial of the Pontiac Brothers and the death sentences coming out of the Santa Fe insurrection about which we know little but which are a sign of the increasingly repressive times ahead. We would also like to publish material on some of the "reforms" that are being introduced to show the limitations that such reforms have.

We hope our correspondents will direct themselves to these issues and more importantly recommend possible actions. More than ever, we need a strategy to combat these changes. Such a strategy cannot be the product of political ideology understood in the narrow sense of the word. Rather it must incorporate a pragmatism based on experience of both victory and defeat with a political insight and vision that will not allow us to be satisfied with half measures. There is no such thing as being half-free.

We appreciate the response that we recieved from our first issue. We do try to respond to as many letters as possible but neither our time nor our emotional energy is unlimited. We do like to hear about what is going on in the different joints, everything adds to our understanding of the broader situation. What we need most of all are good graphics, so if you doodle, send us the results.

And a note to any prison official who may be reading this. There should be no guilt by association. We carry letters from many prisoners and the views of one writer may not be shared by the others.

Finally, outsiders who are not part of prison support groups should let us know that they wish to continue to recieve our publication. Otherwise you will disappear in the upcoming purge of our mailing list. Your acknowledgement can take the form of a letter, money, posters, local papers or whatever you do. Send us names of others who may be interested in seeing the paper. Prisoners and support groups will continue to recieve the paper though we would like to hear from you as well.

We have changed our permanent address to P.O.B. 5052, Station A, Toronto, Ontario, Canada, M5W 1W4.

Bulldozer 2 (1981)

Collective Statement

This first issue of <u>Bulldozer</u> is produced and distributed from the stifling, capital intensive city of Toronto, Kanada by the Prisoner Solidarity Collective. We are a group of women and men who have been writing individually and collectively to prisoners in various penal institutions, as well as trying to support them on the street.

We are all anti-state, anti-authoritarian, and definitely prison abolitionist. As with any production collective, the individuals function in diverse ways that complement the whole. And just as we believe that prisons are not abstract insitutions separate from total reality, we believe that politics are most honestly expressed in the way people live their lives.

Some of us have done time; some work for wages; some do not. None are "professionals" and we do not work for the state.

The decision to work with prisoners in penal dungeons rather than the prisoners in factories, high rises, high schools or any other oppressive institutions came to each of us differently; but in general we were all impressed with the excellent quality of materials recieved from the comrades on the inside. We have been exposed to incredible levels of courage, honesty, political sophistication, literary and artistic brilliance, and an openness that is seldom found on the outside and <u>never</u> found in government circles. Yet it is government that insists that it protects civil society from their influence. In short, we are being educated in a very real and positive sense; and it is this experience we are attempting to share with you.

The production of the newsletter is by far the easiest task. Articles, letters, art work, poetry, i.e., the copy, comes to us from prisoners and ex-prisoners of penal institutions and it is this qualitative content that makes it. All material is recieved and printed anonymously unless the writer requests we break their anonymity.

Perhaps the name of the newsletter should in some way describe its content or the basic philosophy/ideology; but for reasons of security, aesthetics etc., the name will <u>probably</u> change from issue to issue. What will remain is content quality.

Production schedules depend on two criteria - copy and dollars. So what can we say? If you are doing time or have done time and want to express your feelings in print or artwork, contribute material. If you are on the outside and have access to extra dollars, contribute some. We'll get back to work as soon as possible.

If you know of anyone who would like a copy, or if you are reading someone else's copy and want to be on our mailing list our address is printed below. We are most interested in exchanges with any support group or prisoners' group that is also putting out printed material.

Write to: Prisoner Solidarity Collective, P.O.Box 2, Station "O", Toronto, Ontario, Kanada M4B 2B0. Finally, all social critics should be open to criticism. So criticize.

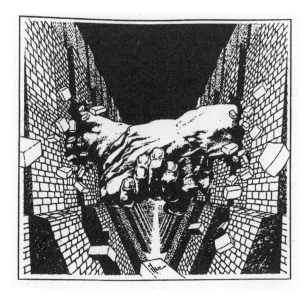

Facing Reality

Studying the faces on the "Face Reality" poster
And the harsh reality that these beautiful faces
Will remain where they are, steals my breath away –
Frozen on this page – for how long?!?
Captured and held behind the steel razor wire
And concrete madness of the Kamps,
Which have been my reality for the past 7 years
Now, when I walk out this gate,
What do I do about them?!?

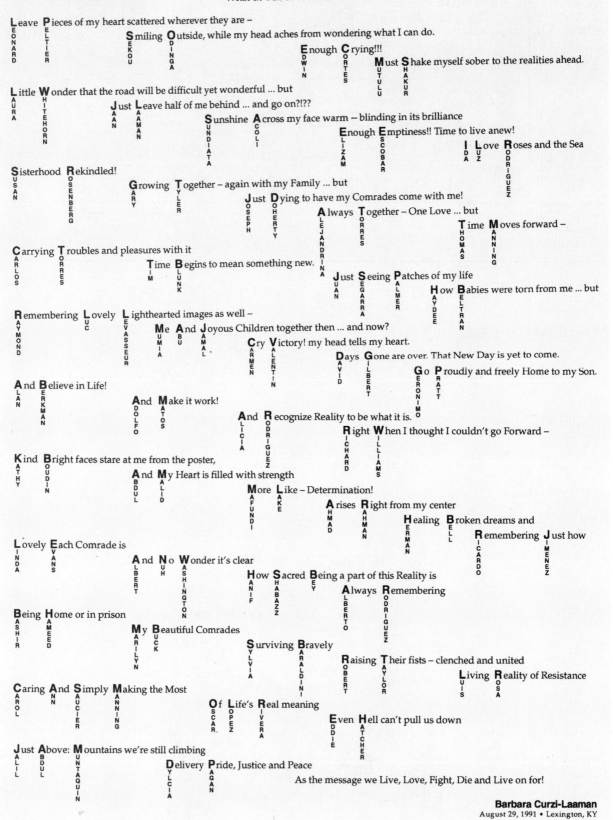

Leave Pieces of my heart scattered wherever they are –
Smiling Outside, while my head aches from wondering what I can do.
Enough Crying!!!
Must Shake myself sober to the realities ahead.
Little Wonder that the road will be difficult yet wonderful ... but
Just Leave half of me behind ... and go on?!??
Sunshine Across my face warm – blinding in its brilliance
Enough Emptiness!! Time to live anew!
I Love Roses and the Sea
Sisterhood Rekindled!
Growing Together – again with my Family ... but
Just Dying to have my Comrades come with me!
Always Together – One Love ... but
Time Moves forward –
Carrying Troubles and pleasures with it
Time Begins to mean something new.
Just Seeing Patches of my life
How Babies were torn from me ... but
Remembering Lovely Lighthearted images as well –
Me And Joyous Children together then ... and now?
Cry Victory! my head tells my heart.
Days Gone are over. That New Day is yet to come.
Go Proudly and freely Home to my Son.
And Believe in Life!
And Make it work!
And Recognize Reality to be what it is.
Right When I thought I couldn't go Forward –
Kind Bright faces stare at me from the poster,
And My Heart is filled with strength
More Like – Determination!
Arises Right from my center
Healing Broken dreams and
Remembering Just how
Lovely Each Comrade is
And No Wonder it's clear
How Sacred Being a part of this Reality is
Always Remembering
Being Home or in prison
My Beautiful Comrades
Surviving Bravely
Raising Their fists – clenched and united
Living Reality of Resistance
Caring And Simply Making the Most
Of Life's Real meaning
Even Hell can't pull us down
Just Above: Mountains we're still climbing
Delivery Pride, Justice and Peace
As the message we Live, Love, Fight, Die and Live on for!

Names spelled vertically (political prisoners): Leonard Peltier, Sekou Odinga, Edwin Cortes, Mutulu Shakur, Laura Whitehorn, Jaan Laaman, Sundiata Acoli, Elizam Escobar, Ida Luz Rodriguez, Susan Rosenberg, Gary Tyler, Joseph Doherty, Alejandrina Torres, Thomas Manning, Carlos Torres, Tim Blunk, Juan Segarra, Haydee Beltran, Raymond Luc Levasseur, Mumia Abu Jamal, Carmen Valentin, David Gilbert, Geronimo Pratt, Alan Berkman, Adolfo Matos, Alicia Rodriguez, Richard Williams, Kathy Boudin, Abdul Malik, Mafundi Lake, Ahmad Rahman, Herman Bell, Ricardo Jimenez, Linda Evans, Albert Nuh Washington, Hanif Shabazz Bey, Alberto Rodriguez, Bashir Hameed, Marilyn Buck, Sylvia Baraldini, Robert Taylor, Luis Rosa, Carol Ann Saucier Manning, Oscar Lopez Rivera, Eddie Hatcher, Jalil Abdul Muntaquin, Dylcia Pagan

Barbara Curzi-Laaman
August 29, 1991 • Lexington, KY

Prison News Service 37 (1992)

Prison
News Service

A BULLDOZER PUBLICATION

$2.00 • Free to prisoners
SEPTEMBER/OCTOBER
1992 • NUMBER 37

Simon Paul-Dene ©92

I began publishing *Endless Struggle* in 1987–1988. I was very involved in the hardcore anarchist punk scene at the time. I first began making a zine entitled *Secret Burial* which was completely handwritten as I didn't have a typewriter and nobody had computers back then. This first title was from a massacre that had occurred in El Salvador in 1982. Solidarity work with El Salvador was my first involvement in any form of political organizing. At the same time, I was attracted to themes of horror and was influenced by punk bands like the Accused, Septic Death (including the artist Pushead). I wasn't attracted to anarchism at first and was more interested in guerrilla movements, like El Salvador's FMLN (which was Marxist). Overall, I didn't have a very good analysis of society or the world in which I lived. I just knew there were terrible things going on and I felt compelled to do something. Punk was my first introduction to any alternative views of society. From the age of 13 to 19 I had been in Army Cadets and the Reserves and had intended to join the regular forces. Punk helped me change my career option.

The Offenders were a band from Texas (I think) who had a very good album entitled *Endless Struggle*. I liked their music and lyrics a lot. I also started listening to UK bands like the Amebix and Conflict. Through this, and the influence of my girlfriend at the time, I began to study anarchism. I read Bakunin, Kropotkin, Maletesta, and others.

I published five issues of *Secret Burial*. On the sixth issue I changed the title to *Endless Struggle* and adopted an explicitly anarchist position. I continued the numbering just so I wouldn't feel like I was starting all over again. Some comrades gave me a decent typewriter, and later some people had computers. Writing and researching was really new to me; in high school I hated writing and skipped out constantly.

Once I began publishing *Endless Struggle* I made many new contacts and met people involved in the anarchist movement in Vancouver (i.e., *Open Road*, *No Picnic*, *Anarchist Black Cross*, etc.). We did a lot of public organizing, including protests and public discussions, video screenings, etc. By 1988–1989 the hardcore punk scene was pretty much at its end, at least in Vancouver.

In 1988 I travelled to London and took part in actions there (including a big squat resistance). That same year I attended the North American Anarchist Survival Gathering in Toronto, which helped me meet even more people and really broadened my understanding. There was also a small-scale riot which was a lot of fun. I was greatly influenced by the West European Autonomous movement, and the insurrectionary anarchists as well (Jean Weir, Alfredo Bonanno, etc.).

In 1989 I attended the Anarchist gathering in San Francisco, and from there went to Mexico City with anarchist punks who had come up. I was also inspired by the Palestinian Intifida. By this time I wasn't really into the punk scene and I stopped publishing *Endless Struggle*.

In 1990 the Oka Crisis occurred and this had a profound effect on me due to my Indigenous ancestry (Kwakwaka'wakw, also known as Kwakiutl). It made me proud to see my people standing up and resisting the state. From this point on I have worked primarily on Indigenous resistance. After *Endless Struggle* I began to publish an Indigenous resistance newspaper entitled *Oh-Toh-Kin* (strength from our ancestry).

My political education in anarchism helped me understand society and to develop a good critique of its structure and forms of oppression. In a sense I will always be an anarchist, that is: against rulers.

– GORD HILL

ENDLESS STRUGGLE

NO. 8 • SUMMER 1988 • .75 ¢

INSIDE; Atavistic•SSDC•Toronto Anarchist Gathering•
Squat Resist in London•Squat in W. Berlin• Rock
Against Racism•Perjury Dist.•Corporations in
Arms-Production• Reviews• Art•

ANARCHY

article by gored.

So, what exactly is Anarchy? The basic definition most Anarchists agree on is simply; absence of Government and authority. From there concepts of Anarchy and their interpratations branch out in many, many, directions. There are those who pursue the breakdown of the State by actions, others withdraw from the confines of the gov't. as much as is possible,+those who attempt to live within the system.

When we look at the *powerlessness* of the individual and the small face-to-face group in the world today and ask ourselves *why* they are powerless, we have to answer not merely that they are weak because of the vast central agglomerations of power in the modern, military-industrial state, but that they are weak *because* they have surrendered their power to the state. It is as though every individual possessed a certain quantity of power, but that by default, negligence, or thoughtless and unimaginative habit or conditioning, he has allowed someone else to pick it up, rather than use it himself for his own purposes. ('According to Kenneth Boulding, there is only so much human energy around. When large organisations utilise these energy resources, they are drained away from the other spheres.')[7]

Anarchy attempts to put the emphasis on the individual, and not on the whole of a nation (as in communism/democracy). Anarchy is a society where the life of an individual is up to her/him to choose what he/she wishes to do. It is freedom. It is opposed to government and it's ability to force people to do as it demands. Government makes and enforces the laws that keep people suppressed, and it decides what is for the good of the people. It's laws keep the rich, rich, and the poor, poor.

But, you say, if the majority of people wanted to have Anarchy, then they would reach out and grab it, and because they haven't, they must be happy with the gov't. system. That's all true except for the fact that gov't. is now so firmly entrenched and holds so much power that it controls what and how a person will perceive something. It's control of the media stops the people from seeing truth, it's control of the educational system programmes how people will think and act. We were conditioned at school to accept the presence of gov't. and accept it's power over us.

The apathetic and apolitical nature of people today is a sign that they beleive they no longer have an any control over their lives or the government they created, which was designed to help with the organisation of society, and help it operate more effeciently. Anarchy sais

no, we do not need a small group of authoritarian, power hungry, and 'superiors' to lead us and tell us what is for our good.

Anarchy sais people can organise themselves to live together, without an established authority.

Government decides when we will go to war, then forces it's people to do the battle, by propaganda and by force.

Government decides who shall prosper and who shall live in poverty.

Government decides what will be reported via the media.

Government decides what will be censored, and what will not.

Government decides what the curriculum in school shall be.

Government decides who shall enter or leave it's country.

Government decides what is legal and what is illegal, then uses it's police and army to enforce it's laws.

Anarchy sais this is all up to each and every individual to decide:

I will decide to live in peace, I will decide how I shall live, I will decide what to report or seek facts on, I will decide what I wish to see or read, I will decide what or if I want to learn, I will decide where I shall live, I will decide what is 'wrong' or 'right' for me to do...no authority, no gov't., and no person should ever have the power to decide what I can do:●

Gustav Landauer, the German anarchist, made a profound and simple contribution to the analysis of the state and society in one sentence: 'The state is not something which can be destroyed by a revolution, but is a condition, a certain relationship between human beings, a mode of human behaviour; we destroy it by contracting other relationships, by behaving differently.' It is *we* and not an abstract outside identity, Landauer implies, who behave in one way or the other, politically or socially.

excerpts from 'Anarchy in Action'.

Endless Struggle 6 (1988)

Article by Gored

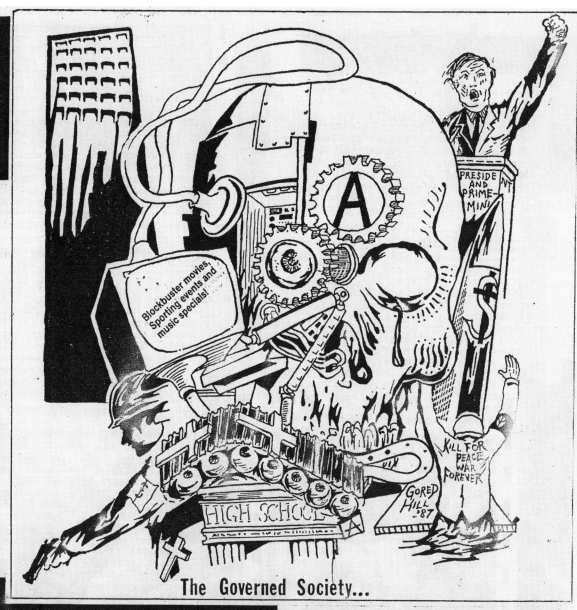

The Governed Society...

The Governed Society

Many people have trouble understanding Anarchy. Firstly because they believe it could not keep the country as organised and as stable as it seems to be, and secondly because they believe anarchy to mean violent chaos. They also have trouble gathering information on the subject because, as Alex Berkman stated in his book 'ABCs of Anarchism', that "...anarchist books, with few exceptions, are not accessible to the understanding of the average reader. It is the common failing of most works...that they are written on the assumption that the reader is already familiar to a considerable extent with the subject...". Anyone who has struggled through a Kropotkin or Bakunin essay will attest to that.

First off, let us look at the Governments supposed organising qualities, and to do that I would first like to look at why and how we are governed.

Why are we governed? I'd like to quote from Colin Wards' 'Anarchy in action', "Why do people consent to be ruled? It isn't only fear, what have millions to fear from a small group of professional politicians & their paid strong-arm men? It is because they subscribe to the same values as their governors. Rulers and ruled alike believe in the principle of authority, of hierarchy, of power. They even feel themselves privileged when, as happens in a small part of the globe, they can chose between alternative labels on the ruling elites. And yet, in their ordinary lives they keep society going by voluntary association and mutual aid." Many people also believe that gov't., complete with its armies & wars, its oppression, is <u>natural</u> and <u>necessary</u>! They actually believe there is no other way! The situation of an apathetic and non-questioning society is designed and upheld by the State. To understand this, let's look at the structuring of 'main-stream' society, in a broad, general sense of course.

education ?

Education, the process of acquiring knowledge. Voluntarily, a most rewarding habit, forced-it is pure drudgery. In the 'advanced, civilised' societies, schooling is compulsorary. By the age we can eat, walk, talk, and use the shitter on our own- we are off to the schooling system, where our education is decided by the gov't.

"It enrolls 5-yr olds and tries to direct their mental, and much of their social, physical and moral development for 12 or more of the most formative years of their lives." (Mackinnon,'Anarchy in Action').

Many pupils attend unwillingly,regarding the education system with contempt as well as the learning of knowledge- simply because it is so rigidly forced upon them. The school itself is based upon authoritarian rules, where one is forced to succeed or fail, to be a 'winner' or a loser', to conform or be crushed with the hammer of schooling. Here one learns math and language, but more importantly to accept and respect the authority their 'superiors' have over them. They learn to obey rules, not to question...they will study wars and the 'heroic' men who fought them, they'll study Hitlers nazi gov't., without once realising that Hitlers gov't. was indeed almost the <u>perfect government</u>. The perfect war-machine with a nation of slaves to support it.

In school we learn the need for gov't., that we <u>need</u> authority and all its 'leaders', police, and

A *WORDS(PIERRE JOSEPH PROUDHON 1848 PARIS) VISUALS(CLIFFORD PETER HARPER 1981 LONDON)*

WHAT IS GOVERNMENT?

Graphics taken from 'Anarchy' comics, issue no. 3.

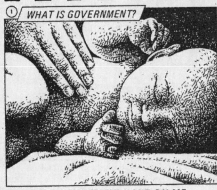

WHOEVER LAYS THEIR HAND ON ME

IS A USURPER AND A TYRANT;

I DECLARE THEM TO BE MY ENEMY...

GOVERNMENT IS SLAVERY.

5 WHAT IS GOVERNMENT?

ITS LAWS ARE COBWEBS FOR THE RICH

6 WHAT IS GOVERNMENT?

AND CHAINS OF STEEL FOR THE POOR.

COPYRIGHT 1981

armies. And here is where one learns that you <u>must</u> be a part of the
systems machine if you wish to eat
& have shelter, the basic needs of
any humin.

work

The most important part of <u>any</u>
gov'ts system is labour. The machine needs that labour to keep it
going, to keep it alive. And because we are a part of that machine,
we need <u>it</u> to remain alive. People
are forced to work, to slave away
for their employer. This forced
labour is an excellent method of
keeping the masses busy, and at the
same time re-enforcing the idea
that gov't. is necessary.

"The split between life and work
is proabaly the greatest contemporary social problem. You cannot expect men to take a responsible attitude and to display initiative in
daily life when their whole working
experience deprives them of the chance of initiative and responsibility. The personality cannot be
successfully divided into water-
tight compartments, and even the attempt to do so is dangerous; if a
man is taught to rely upon a patern-
alistic authority within the factor-
y, he will be ready to rely upon one
outside...The contemporary social
trend towards a centralised, patern-
alistic, authoritarian society only
reflects conditions which already
exist within the factory. (Gordon
Taylor'"Are workers human?"). Most
people are not satisfied with work
simply because it is not that they
want to, but rather they must.

The illusion of gov't. is that it
keeps society flowing smoothly. It
is something that is needed. Any
thoughts to the contrary are quickly
corrected by media distortions/half
truths of situations, and gov't.
lies and cover ups. The people are
kept busy with their work, they're
kept busy with the <u>huge</u> entertainment industry,.. Joe blo on the street consider <u>alternatives</u> to the

governed society he lives in? Pre-
posterous! Why- he'll be working
all day, then he's gonna watch the
football game on tv, or go bowling.
A life of ignorance, he has no concept of life without gov't. or big
business- let alone question it.

The greatest arguement <u>for</u> Gov't.
and <u>against</u> anarchy, is that it
(gov't.) prevents crime, and that
it's police and prisons keep the order. Hmmm- what are some of the mos
most common crimes? Burglary, theft
shoplifting, drugs, prostitution,
robberies...reported everyday in the
press. What's the basic motivation
for these 'crimes'? Money! And
the 'criminals'? The 'underprivel-
eged', the poor, the racial minorities, unemployed youth, the people
most fucked over by the gov't.s system that caters to the rich and
big business. The gov't. causes the
problems it claims it solves! Thats
why and how we are governed; with an
armed force of police and soldiers,
with the chain of work around our
necks, but most importantly, with
the planned and calculated illusion
that gov't. is necessary.

violent?

Much of the thinking that anarchy
is violent chaos originated in the
late 1800s and early 1900s. Anarch-
y was once a major movement in Europe, it produced some of the great
anarchist thinkers- Bakunin, Kropotkin, Prodhoun, and I suppose they
could almost 'smell a revolution in
the wind', especially with the Industrial revolution developing at a
very brisk pace. The workers trade
unions was a very powerful force.

The anarchists were a major part
of that force, until the communists
started to take more and more control under Marx. Many workers moved
over to Marx, leaving the anarchists.
Also, the business's soon made small
concessions to the workers demands,
"...conquest of political rights by
workers who then became more recept-
iverto parliamentary reformism.

...the satisfaction of short-term de demands." (Anarchism, Daniel Guerin)

Much division among the anarchists did not help their organisation, and they could only watch as their revolution to a free society slipped away with the support of the workers. Disenchanted, frustrated at their inability to achieve that society, many anarchists turned to 'Propoganda by the Deed', a wave of 'terrorism' that spread across nation after nation, bombing after bombing. It was meant to shock people, to grab them by the neck and say 'Look, there is something <u>very</u> wrong with gov't.'. Eventually, 'Propoganda by the Deed' became unpopular among most anarchists. It did shock people, but it failed to open peoples eyes as it only seemed gov't. was even more necessary than before! Not only that, but it gave a very wrong impression of anarchy, that of violence.

Anarchy does <u>not</u> mean violence. Quite the opposite, and it is gov't. that uses violence. "...all gov't.s , all law and authority finally rest on force and violence, on punishment or fear of punishment", (ABC of Anarchism, Berkman).

Any definition of anarchy can and must be limited to 'absence of government and authority', to give any further definitions and rules of anarchy defeats the meaning. However, in regards to violence and a chaotic society, anarchists <u>must</u> wish to pursue a society of harmony... peace and co-operation.

Any kind of violent society is <u>not</u> an anarchistic society. For violence, in any form (rape, murder robbery, State oppression) is a means to inflict a form of authority over another... the very thing anarchy is opposed to. (Note; violence as self-defence is either agreed to, condoned, or refused depending on circumstances and each anarchists belief).

As for chaos, if individual freedom and not 'governed, organised freedom' <u>is</u> chaos, then so be it. Remember in the article on anarchy (this issue) I said anarchy is not opposed to organisation, only the authoritarians who wish to control many organisations!

Anarchy is not a belief where one supposed 'genious' decides and defines what anarchy shall or shall not be. Ideas and theories may be shared, but these are not to be blue-prints for an anarchist society.

Many people will look at anarchy & say it is not possible, or look at one persons idea of anarchy and say it is not possible, they will look no further than that, and will continue to disregard any thoughts on anarchy. People who do this display the greatest example of ignor-

ance, for they have missed the whole point of anarchy, that of individual thought! Where one persons version of anarchy may rest on a workers revolt and crushing of the gov't., another persons version may be educating people on anarchy through literature and rallies, struggling for an anarchist society through a 'psychological' revolution, another will say anarchy must be based on communal life in a village situation, independant of other communes, still another will say it can be a way of life within the society we now live in, and that any kind of anarchist revolution begins from within and spreads through communication...

"Beauty is in the eye of the beholder", and I would include anarchy in that category.

ideal?

"Capable of existing as a mental concept only; utopian; imaginary", this is the definition of the word <u>ideal</u>. Is anarchy an ideal? We will know the answer to this when humins can foresee the future. Anarchy can be a reality today, a way of life now, or it can be a society to struggle for in the future.

Consider Leanardo da Vinci, he had plans for a flying craft much like a helicopter. "Absurd" his fellows would say. And yet today flying crafts are common. Was this an ideal? It was not possible in his life, yet it is reality today. Perhaps people were not ready for such an invention in those days, and it can be said to be much the same for anarchy today. The future can not be said to be this or that, only vaguely directed, for it is a ship at the mercy of the winds.

Blowing as hard as I can for the Island of anarchy...
Gored.

References:
'Anarchy in Action', by Colin Ward.
'ABC of Anarchism', by Alex Berkman.
'Anarchism', by Daniel Guerin.
the process of thinking, by my brain!

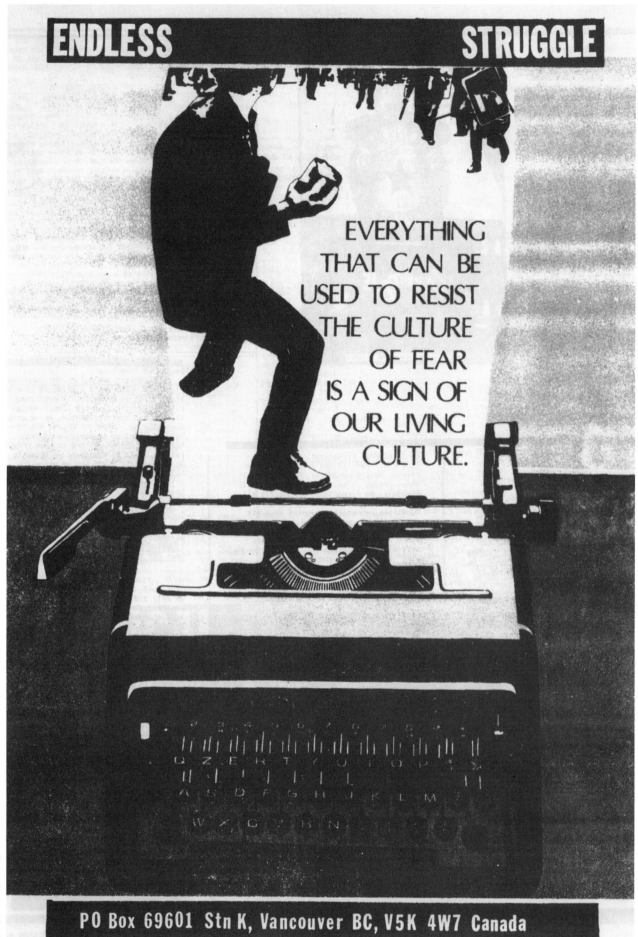

I forget where I first came across *Resistance*. I do recall being drawn to it because of its distinctive "direct action" agenda and the information and analysis it provided – even if I found its uncritical stance towards "radical" Marxism problematic (see the exchange on authoritarianism in "Debates"). Early issues were in a zine format, and they carried news, communiques and theoretical statements of groups ranging from the Italian anarchist Azione Rivoluzionaria and Marxist Red Brigades to the New Afrikan Black Liberation Army in the United States. The focus was on everything from squatting, street fighting and prison liberation to guerilla warfare, including assassinations and bombings. For example, I first learned about the dangers of biotechnology in 1987, in *Resistance* coverage of direct action attacks on biotech firms. Coverage like this never appeared in the corporate media.

The editorial group – Friends of Durruti – supported a broad range of "autonomist and anti-imperialist" struggles. Of course this stance was controversial from an anarchist perspective and by the third issue (Spring 1982), the editors were already responding to accusations of indiscriminate leftoid cheerleading. "Contrary to the impression which may have been made from an examination of our earlier issues," they wrote, "we favour a revolutionary practice that is based on decentralized, non-hierarchical forms of organization. The party, the vanguard, the dictatorship of the proletariat, and other sacrosanct Marxist-Leninist conceptions can and do seriously hinder the development of truly revolutionary

societies, where all class privileges are abolished, along with other forms of domination of man over man, man over women, and the human race over nature. We do not apologize, however, for printing the material that we have, for we believe that armed struggle is a strategic and tactical necessity for our liberation. We have focused, and will continue to focus, on the guerrilla struggle in the metropolis (U.S. and Western Europe) since it is the most relevant to us here. Through our publication of documents from such guerrilla groups as the BLA (Black Liberation Army), the BR (Red Brigades) and the RAF (Red Army Fraction) we hope to help initiate a more sophisticated discussion of the need for armed struggle not only in the Third World, but here in the centre of imperialism."

Resistance began in 1981 as a zine but starting with issue 8 (Winter 1984) the journal was published as a tabloid *Open Road* "insert." This relationship lasted till Fall 1987, when "in recognition of the differing conceptual frameworks of *Open Road* and *Resistance*, and the difficulties of a small group of people trying to keep on top of all the work involved in producing both papers" the two projects went their separate ways. The last issue I own is dated Summer/Fall 1991. That year I attempted to arrange a subscription by writing to "Resistance c/o Friends of Durruti, PO Box 790 Stn A Vancouver B.C." A few months later the (opened and resealed) letter was back in my mailbox marked, "return to sender."

– ALLAN ANTLIFF

Covering militant autonomist, anti-imperialist, national liberation, feminist and anti-nuclear struggles in advanced capitalist countries, Resistance: Documents and Analyses of the Illegal Front is an important tool for revolutionary social change.

Help us continue to publish. Become a sustainer [$50 per year] or subscribe [$6/year, $15/year for institutions]. Free to prisoners. Send your cheques to:

Friends of Durruti
PO Box 790, Stn. A
Vancouver, BC
Canada, V6C 2N6

RESISTANCE

No. 11

Jan. 9, 1987: MAKRO supermarket in Nuth, Holland burns in anti-apartheid action

Arson severs trade links

In the last two years three branches of MAKRO (a wholesale cash and carry chain—daughter company of SHV, a Dutch multinational) have been burnt to the ground. The underground group Revolutionary Anti Racist Action (RARA) claimed responsibility for all three actions and demanded that SHV cut off all trade links with South Africa. SHV refused to respond to this demand. Only after the third fire did they start to get a bit ruffled.

SHV presented the Dutch government with an ultimatum—to be answered by January 17th:

1. In the event of further 'terror attacks' the government must compensate SHV for the damage, because their insurers refused to pay anymore.

2. The government must give absolute priority to stopping 'terror attacks' which, of course, includes protecting the MAKRO branches (saving SHV the normal costs of guards) and catch the activists and severely punish them.

If the government didn't agree with these 'proposals' SHV would feel forced to pull out of South Africa and also, if the government didn't do more against the 'terrorists', SHV would move their head office out of Holland.

That same week the media started up their hate campaign with gusto. 'Everyone' of course agreed that the 'terrorists' must finally be found/stopped, (until now the word 'terror' had only been used by the extreme right-wing press in connection with political attacks on buildings). Everyone thought they knew where to find these 'terrorists'—within the squatters movement of course. Therefore the actions in

Nijmegen (where the eviction of squatters occupying a building owned by Shell led to street fights, burning barricades, and damaged property) were immediately lumped together with the MAKRO actions.

The parliament dismissed SHV's demands, but agreed that a harder and more definite stand must be taken against 'terrorism'. They announced an increase in activities to prevent political actions, to which the business community would have to contribute financially. Three days following this announcement, SHV announced that they would sell the MAKRO branches in South Africa.

The CCAWUSA (union of South African MAKRO employees) demanded that they

have some say in who took over the company, so as to ensure that their working conditions would not deteriorate further. But the business was sold (without any consultation) to South Africa's biggest transport company, a part of 'Old Mutual'! Old Mutual is, together with the Anglo-American group, one of the main supporters of the apartheid regime, and has recently been buying up American companies that are supposedly leaving South Africa (Holiday Inn, Thomas Cook Travel).

As a result, not much has changed. Above all, it is still not clear if SHV will continue its coal trade with South Africa, which is carried out through its subsidiaries SSM and EMO, in which SHV has a majority interest.

FRONTLINE INFO

RARA Communique

Using the most draconian measures, the South African regime is trying to hide the tragedy, the hard and bloody repression of the population of South Africa, from the eyes and ears of the world.

A wall is put up around Soweto. There is a total black-out of any news about the struggle against the apartheid regimed. Names of arrested, tortured, or murdered people aren't allowed to be published anymore. The power-mongers of South Africa have learned from the wave of indignation which swept the world after the proclamation of the state of emergency.

They are now putting their knowledge (with at least partial success) into practice with the latest measures.

There are no more pictures, no more information. The world is silent and no longer watches. The indignation is fading, as well as the support for the struggle.

To break through this strangling silence we did actions inside two branches of the MAKRO concern. At about the same time we detonated smoke bombs at the branches in Duiven (near Arnhem) and Amsterdam. We hope that, with these actions, we've managed to take the cream off the profits made by MAKRO during the lucrative *Turn to page 2*

Turn to page 2

A Talk With *Resistance*

Resistance: Documents and analyses of the illegal front

Armed struggle is, like most critical aspects of revolutionary struggle, a topic that is widely debated. Armed struggle means different things to different people; to some it is counter-productive and ultimately destructive, to others it is wrong because violence is wrong, and to still others it is an important form of resistance. In North America armed struggle is limited and small, as is the discussion of it. Our information and news on clandestine groups and actions, primarily originating from European countries, is even more limited and small. Unless you happen to read the radical left press here, any knowledge you may have of a group or action is presented through mainstream press, & of course that ignores the discussion on why a target was attacked and focuses instead on the "terrorist" angle and the fact that it was "illegal" etc.

Resistance: Documents and analyses of the illegal front publish communiqués and articles of the armed struggle movement in the industrialised "first world." The approach is non-sectarian and so many of the groups vary greatly in politics, some being outright Marxist-Leninist vanguardist groups, while others are autonomously organised & have an anti-authoritarian organisation. There is always a tendency to generalise on armed struggle and say it is the work of "middle-class intellectuals on a violence crazed ego-trip," and of course this kind of argument gets us nowhere. What is the role of armed resistance in the fight for a free world? With that in mind we invited a member of the Friends of Durruti collective, which publishes *Resistance*, over to our small house for tea and a discussion on how they see the armed struggle.

Endless Struggle: What was the impetus for publishing *Resistance*?

Friends of Durruti: Well, as you know, there's been very little armed struggle in Canada, other than the FLQ. *Resistance* actually started before the *Direct Action* formed or anything …

ES: What year did *Resistance* begin publishing?

FOD: It was in 1981 that it first started. A bunch of us got together in Montreal and sat around a table and discussed the idea of putting together a paper like this in the winter of 1980.

ES: This was mostly inspired by the armed struggle in Europe?

FOD: That's right. There was in fact a woman from West Germany and she was talking about the struggle there, and some of the other people I was with were interested in this area of struggle. One of them had travelled to Europe and taken part in big demonstrations and visited some political prisoners, and another one had been involved in support work in San Francisco. These people and myself thought this was a viable form of struggle and we wanted to publish material about it and so on.

ES: You've been an observer of the growth of the armed struggle movement in Europe, how do you [see] the development of the European struggle as compared to North America?

FOD: The armed struggle movement, both in Europe and the U.S. drew out of the student movement in the '60s; the Weathermen in the States, the RAF and Revolutionary Cells in Germany. So in a sense they both grew out of maybe the frustration people felt with "legality" and so on. Why that in Europe there's actually quite a bit of support for this type of struggle I'm not really quite sure. Except that if you do look in Germany I think you'll find there's a lot more support for the autonomous type of group, i.e., the RZ (Revolutionary Cells), than there is for the more Marxist oriented RAF. And so that type of politics that's put forward by groups like the RZ, perhaps people can identify with that type of approach.

ES: It's more accessible.

FOD: Right. And certainly the groups in the U.S. in the '60s, like the Weather Underground did have a more Marxist-Leninist position. One of the things the RZ has always put forward is that groups should make their own revolutionary cells without perhaps so much emphasis on "leading it all." And also I think you should look at the very different economic situation and historical situation, Germany having gone through a period of fascism, and a much longer history going back hundreds of years where the communists have had quite a larger influence. That's certainly been absent in the U.S. So these sort of things undoubtedly played a role.

ES: In some of the past issues of *Resistance*, such as issues seven and ten, there seemed a broader focus on what the paper was. In issue seven there's an article on the B.C. General strike, the editorial talks about squatting and factory occupations, in issue ten there's an article on the Brixton riots. Within the last two issues, eleven and twelve, the focus seems only on armed actions, is that a conscious move?

FOD: No, I don't think it's a conscious decision. We've always been interested in publishing material on armed and militant struggle. If it comes to us we'll generally try to publish it. Groups do different actions at different times so we publish what's available to us. So that if there's militant riots occurring we're happy to publish that as well as armed actions. Not all of them are on the same level. There's assassinations, which is perhaps the most difficult, or has the biggest reaction of any action, on the other hand there's firebombing etc. In the last couple of issues we've covered things that have happened in Holland where a big subsidiary of a firm that was operating in South Africa was attacked, and last issue we covered some to the stuff by the Rote Zora (an autonomously organised feminist group who carry out actions primarily, but not limited to, the specific oppression of women. They work and have affinity with the Revolutionary Cells, both active in West Germany, editor), where they had burned and trashed some clothing stores of a West German firm that was active in South Korea. I don't think we have a specific focus on hi-level actions.

ES: And I suppose a lot of these actions are also covered in other publications, *Black Flag* etc.…

FOD: Yeah, that's true. And not only for actions. There's a lot of things we don't cover as much as we could, which could easily go in *Resistance* as well as other publications, and we haven't covered them perhaps as much as we should have because of the fact that that stuff is available elsewhere. In the last issue we did stuff on prisoners, mostly West German prisoners, but we haven't printed much about the Ohio 7 (seven U.S. revolutionaries arrested in 1984–85 for the ten actions of the United Freedom Front, editor), whereas in earlier issues we've covered their actions. But we feel … there's a paper coming out from New York, and *Open Road* and *Reality Now* has covered the trial. We have a rather limited budget, so generally if other papers are carrying this information then we let them do that.

ES: How do you go about selection, which groups or communiqués will be published, have you ever published IRA or FMLN communiqués, and what distinction do you draw between say the IRA and the RAF?

FOD: We have actually covered some of the FMLN & Puerto Rican groups, but we haven't had any IRA material. Again, there's papers that cover the IRA that come out of Ireland, in English, that you can read. We don't publish everything we get. We did publish, in one of the very earliest issues, material from the Red Brigades, but after doing that, and getting an idea of what they were talking about, we didn't publish anymore, because they were really heavy into the party building and all that. And of course the big difference between the IRA and RAF is Ireland is much more of a nationalist type struggle. I think there's a lot you could learn from the IRA. As a guerrilla campaign they've obviously been quite successful, but we haven't focused too much on the national liberation struggles. We only write about stuff that happens in the "advanced" capitalist countries. There's

a lot of support groups for Third world struggles, we focus on what they call the "First" world. We feel it's most easiest for people to relate to, and conditions in these countries are similar to ours. I think people can take from what these groups are saying and apply it to their own situation.

ES: Do you think the successes of the Rote Zora and RARA (Revolutionary Anti-Racist Action) have changed the context, or perhaps shown to more people what role armed attacks can play in revolutionary resistance? Do you think it's opened it up a bit more?

FOD: Yes, I think if you compare those types of actions with say some of the RAFS' earlier ones, I think people are generally more supportive for the RARA and RZ, and I suppose they're similar to the Wimmins Fire Brigade here, in that they're attacking an issue people can relate to more. It's perhaps not so abstract as say "imperialism."

ES: That's a question we were going to ask here; do you think the RARA and RZ targets were more practical than the RAF ones, more realistic?

FOD: Oh yeah. If we look at the few actions of the RARA and Rote Zora, two of them have been quite successful. In the case of the Rote Zora they managed to get the West German firm to agree to the demand of striking South Korean and Sri Lankan women. So that was a major success, and the company admitted it was because of the RZ. In the case of the RARA they had attacked a multi-national involved in South Africa and that multi-national said they would leave South Africa as a result of these attacks. It ended up selling that firm to some other business so it basically continued on as before but with a different name. But they did actually force the company to do something, yeah. But on the other hand, not all actions are gonna have those kinds of results. You may be successful in some cases, and some people have criticized that approach. I think there was a group in the U.S. in the early '70s that did a lot of work, the New World Liberation Front, did some attacks in relation to prison conditions and I guess they were successful in forcing the prison to change some of the conditions and that was successful in the same way. Some people criticized that as "reformist" politics and not really revolutionary. But I think if people can actually do things like that and show that people can act in this manner and have some practical results – it's a very positive step. And certainly we're not going to see revolutionary change for some time. It's going to take an awful lot of work, and so anything that does show something concrete to be gained is worthwhile.

ES: So what purpose, and what role, does armed struggle play in revolutionary struggle, in perhaps not so revolutionary times … is it developing structures?

FOD: That's right, I think if anybody looks at the situation it's pretty obvious that the capitalists aren't going to give up their position without some kind of struggle. I mean, they show it all over the world against revolutionary movements, in the Third world, they're quite willing to resort to violence. So I think some kind of militant armed struggle will be necessary at some point. I think that by making groups now that are active, you can build possibilities for the future, where you can have a much larger role. And also I think it builds a revolutionary feeling amongst people.

ES: An attitude.

FOD: An attitude, and it also builds a movement as well. Like in Germany I think they've done that. It's what, seventeen years since the first actions, and now there are thousands of people involved in the movement. They're not all of one idea, it's parts of different ideas like the women's movement, the anti-nuclear movement, but there's a lot of people that go out and do actions and I think they've developed a kind of revolutionary culture and that's something that's important.

ES: Do you feel the discussion with No Picnic, about Resistance and many of the groups contained in it, expanded the debate on armed struggle?

FOD: I think, on one hand it was good that there was this discussion in No Picnic, because otherwise people don't think of it unless they're interested in it or pick up a copy of Resistance. There's a lot of people out there who haven't even heard of it, so the fact it was in No Picnic was a good thing. It's the same with the articles that have been in Open Road recently too.

ES: "The Politics of Bombs."

FOD: Yes, which I don't think was the original title, but it's making the debate come out in public more. Some of the responses, after putting out a paper like this, you have heard before, and some of it's fairly stereotypical.

ES: What are some of the more common arguments against armed struggle?

FOD: Well, okay, that it's elitist, it's not gonna help anything it's just gonna help the state to arm itself and take away the rights of the citizens and it's basically a waste of your life, and of course some people just basically come from the position that any kind of violence is "incorrect" and that the only thing you can make out of using violence is a violent system … those are some of the typical ones.

ES: One of the more common ones is "the time isn't right." Going back to what we were talking about earlier, building

for the future and trying to develop theses structures now – discussing that with people, what's your response seeing as it's on-going process, and not a case of "the time is right now" and all of a sudden there's a hundred armed groups in Canada?

FOD: Well, when is the time going to be right? As you were saying, I mean if we look at the situation here, let's say on the question of the environment, the firms can go on polluting the environment while we're eating carcinogenic foods, the lakes, rivers and oceans are polluted, the temperature's rising and all this, and when is the time to stop that? When are people going to try and do something about it? And another thing, in this particular society, where there's so much wealth, can we realistically think that at some point in the near future, ten or twenty years, that the mass of workers are suddenly going to rise up and decide they don't want the system as it is? If they're pretty well off, I mean, I can't see that the unions are really gonna change their ways. which is to basically go along with capitalism, so l don't really see too much hope for just peaceful organising. I don't see how it will have a real effect. Whereas if people try to organise now, in a real sort of militant fashion, and try and develop a different attitude amongst people, an attitude which is along the idea that it's necessary to break the balance of legality to get ahead. I think that's the route we have to go. Also, I think it's something the Tupamaros (the Uruguayan MLN (Movimiento de Liberacion Nacional), formed in the early '60s and active for about nine years. A highly organised guerrilla. At one point its number was estimated at 3,000 members, editor) first said, and actually a lot of the groups in Europe, the Tupamaros were a sort of impetus to them. The first June 2nd Movement communiqué almost sounded like a repeat of the Tupamaros, but what they were saying about it was that the revolutionary creates the time by acting. And you could have a million different parties saying whatever they want, but until people actually start acting nothing's going to change. So that in the process of arming themselves, and taking action, they're going to create the revolutionary time.

ES: Another common argument is that the retaliation from the state…

FOD: Of course people have definitely made that criticism before. Especially in Germany where they were saying "Look what the state has done as a result of the RAFs actions, look at the controls and laws they have … 129A where if you even put out pamphlets in support of a guerrilla you'll be called a member of that group and jailed in an isolation prison.…" I mean, obviously the state has acted fairly repressively, but a lot of those laws were on the books a long time ago. A lot of them came from the nazi period, and a lot of the people who were in the judiciary had been involved in nazi Germany and were fascists. So it's more a continuation of

Endless Struggle 10 (1989)

the policies that they had before rather than something new that came up because of the RAF. So I think a lot of these laws, the state was already interested in using them and used the actions of the group as a pretext to put them into effect. And the other thing is that if you're going to be effective the state's going to fight back. Even if it's some kink of civil disobedience or whatever, if these actions have a "heavy" effect the state is going to fight back. So I think people have to realise that state repression is an inevitability, it will come sooner or later, whenever it is necessary. And certainly for people in the Third world, it's right there, right now. The fact is we live in the First world, and we have it fairly well off here, because it (state repression) isn't needed here, and people aren't struggling against it.

ES: On the other hand, what has the North American radical movements reaction been to *Resistance* and the ideas is represents … do you receive a lot of "resistance?" (Haha)

FOD: Well certainly there's been a lot of controversy over *Resistance*. We actually did a survey, when *Resistance* was being published with *Open Road*, and people at the *Open Road* wanted to find out how this was being taken by the readers, and they asked readers to respond. Really the response wasn't as great as we'd hoped, it was fairly mixed. There has been a lot of criticism of *Resistance* because of the material it publishes, and because its not primarily of anarchism. And people have been very critical of publishing material of the RAF, and even the United Freedom Front, and saying "oh why do you even publish this Marxist Leninist stuff at all, they've got their own propaganda machine" etc, and then of course some people are really definitely opposed to armed struggle so they don't even want to see this stuff. But on the other hand, we do receive a lot of support, prisoners especially write us, and they really appreciate receiving copies, and we sell them in bookstores … so there's both a negative and positive response.

ES: The bulk of your readership is, because of your purpose, in North America.

FOD: That's right. We do send it to Europe but it's more to get people over there to realise it exists and have them send stuff etc.

ES: In the autumn issue of *No Picnic*, there's a letter from Bob McGlynn I think, and he was discussing the position paper on the peace movement, put out by the Rote Zora and Revolutionary Cells, and his criticism was that they had a kind of "chauvinism" to a lot of the Eastern Bloc activists, and that they were generally less critical …

FOD: Yes, that's right, but actually if you look at that article you'll see there is criticism of the Soviet Union. That article actually talked about the Soviet Union and its imperialism,

so I don't think that particular argument is valid, even though it's true that generally there is more of a focus on NATO, the Western system etc. But that's natural because that's where these groups are active, they're not fighting against the Soviet Union, they're fighting against the capital interests in their own countries.

ES: I can remember, about two years ago when I was turning to the ideas of anarchism, and so I was picking up all these papers and one of the first ones I picked up was *Resistance #11*. I was flicking through the pages, and some of the actions were like kneecapping and assassinations. It was a big shock to me! You don't read that kind of stuff. It seemed extreme of course. Do you make any attempt to present these communiqués or documents to people that might be picking up an issue for the first time? I know you mentioned it's more of an esoteric publication of interest to those who have a basic knowledge and interest…

FOD: Yes, well actually I think it would be more effective if we attempted to present it a little more with an introduction to articles etc. One of the problems is we don't really have all that much background material ourselves. For instance, we suddenly got communiqués from this group in Belgium, the Fighting Communist Cells and we had never heard of this group nor did we know too much about the situation in Belgium. So how are we to publish interesting, thought-provoking intros to those articles, when we ourselves don't have that level of contact. Basically our contact has been with a few different publications, and we translate and publish. It would be great if we had more resources, if more people sent us material, translate, so we *could* put more of an intro to articles. I do think it leaves a lot of people out. I mean, if you look at West Germany again, we're publishing only a very small number of actions that actually happen. Besides all the actions, which might be thousands in a year, there's all sorts of conferences and discussion papers. There's a whole level of discourse that we never even hear about.

ES: That would be an important part of trying to build up those kind of structures.

FOD: Sure, that's all part of the movement, that's right. That's essential. Just like all these groups, like the *Ecomedia, Endless Struggle, No Picnic* etc. these are all just parts of the movement. In other countries, where the movement is a bit more built up, you'll find a lot more. You'll find whole sections of the city where left things are happening, bars where all the leftists go …

ES: You've been involved in the anarchist movement for a number of years now. Do you see it developing towards [a] more militant stage? There seems to be a segment that wants to raise the level of militancy, to raise the level of actions, such as the controversy over the Day of Action at

HISTORIES § 95

the Anarchist Gatherings … do you see it as approaching a turning point?

FOD: Obviously these gatherings represent a fairly big step forward. In the real recent history, besides going back to the time of the Wobblies, this is pretty new. And the actions of Direct Action and the Wimmins Fire Brigade didn't really catch on so that groups like that became active … still, the gatherings, where people discuss this and then actually have a DOA, that's a real positive step. And the fact that there is a big discussion about it does show it is a turning point. If people decide, well from now on we won't [have] a DOA and we'll just have a little conference, well then maybe that's all that'll happen in the future; there'll be all these little conferences. And the thing about these gatherings is it's really the only time where a large number of anarchists can actually come together and do something, because in most cities there aren't really many anarchists to take part in militant demos. I think it's also really important and that it bolsters peoples confidence and the idea that they're not just alone, five people or something.

ES: What's the future for your publication?

FOD: Well, I think it'll continue to be an irregularly published paper, even though we've always wanted to come out more frequently, we've never been able to. We might change the format, we might go to magazine style. And also I think we'll try to have more letters, that's something we hoped to do in the last issue but we weren't able to. Part of the problem is that we get a lot of material and at some point we have to decide "do we want this or this" and what's more important … But actually I think letters are important, it shows the readers are interested and everyone likes to read their own comments (do we! editors).

ES: How do you see the publication as having developed? Have there been any turning points in it history?

FOD: Well, when it was first published we only did 200, it was xeroxed and in pretty poor condition. So technically it's changed quite a bit, and the biggest change was when we started coming out with *Open Road* (*Resistance #8*). Because we were publishing with OR it meant we could increase our distribution. But in terms of content it hasn't changed too much. There's been other changes, we used to get info from one paper from France, *L'Internationale*, but that was closed down. So that meant making contact with a new paper, in a different language and that meant a whole different group of translators. And now that paer is being boycotted by the movement. That paper is *Knipselkrant*, which means clipping papers in Dutch. They got in a bit of a controversy and now they're on the blacklist. So we'll have to depend more on other sources. But in terms of content it really hasn't changed.

I started *Kick It Over* at the end of 1981, and was able to enlist Alexandra Devon, and some of my co-workers at the World's Biggest Bookstore (Coles), to help. At the time it was founded, committed activists seemed few in number, and one of the more significant "cultures of resistance" was the punk movement; hence our name, which came from a song performed by The Clash. At the time, it seemed that The Clash were a more potent force for change than parliamentary groups like Canada's New Democratic Party. Other forces, such as eco-feminism, the Green movement of Europe, and a renewed Native American activism, were rejecting traditional left-wing ideology and assumptions and looking at the relationship of humanity to the biosphere. They were critical of "progress" and "materialism," whether of the capitalist or communist variety. All of these influences infused the new publication.

As crude as the first issues were, the thrust of *KIO* was to provide a means by which new social movements could express themselves, giving new writers and young people a chance to be heard. The object was not to suggest to new movements that they "join the working class," but to see in them an indication that the world had changed, that new contradictions had come to the fore. The task was to discover their inner logic and make explicit their implicit radicalism. *KIO* also reflected the belief that if some of the values and ideals of the traditional left still possessed validity, then new social forces would come forward to take them up even if the traditional social base of leftism had proved moribund.

The first three issues of *KIO* were in "fanzine" form. Cheap and easy to produce, fanzines were a peculiar expression of the punk movement: xeroxed text arranged helter-skelter in an 8½ by 11 inch format. *KIO*, like the rest of the genre, was very much an amateur production. The early issues were limited in distribution. Our outlets were music stores that catered to punk rock fans and the odd progressive bookstore. The cover price was 25 cents and we sold or gave away fewer than 100 copies of each issue. These issues dealt with oppressive forms of fashion (the "bruised look"), nuclear tensions in Europe, and some of the social criticisms of modern life being advanced by bands like Gang of Four. *KIO* was read avidly by the punk crowd, though we were more political than the rest of the "zines" in circulation at the time.

The fourth issue was transitional: an eight-page tabloid, of which 1,000 copies were printed. It had more anarchist content. Alexandra and I had met a small group of anarchists who were centered around a bookshop called Focus Books and Art. When several of them joined, we became the *Kick It Over* Collective. One of our new members, a self-styled "Groucho-Marxist," proved invaluable, enabling us to typeset and paste-up subsequent issues through a print shop. Larry Ingersoll, a former member of the *KIO* collective, tells what happened next:

"In 1982, the Toronto anarchist community was growing in numbers and influence rapidly. With the clampdown in Poland and the founding of Focus Books and the Anarchist Black Umbrella, people were stirring. When Alexandra and Ron [Don] proposed turning their scruffy little rag *Kick It Over* into a collective enterprise and a real publication, people started to think about doing an anarchist newspaper.

"I was one of the original collective members. We were self-selected on the basis of interest in an anarchist publication, but had wide political and stylistic differences. The range was from pacifist peace activists to radical feminists, supporters of armed struggle, and street sheet leafleteers to academic 'anarcheologists.'

"The progress of beginning the collective and producing the first issue took up the summer, with a great deal of argument about issues and approach. Several members of our baby collective left, and those of us who stayed were able to consolidate on the basis of publishing interviews and first-hand accounts, and continuing to have a strong emphasis on new musical and cultural movements. We also opted for a more ordinary layout style in the interest of readability.

"*KIO* became much of our political work, because it involved a lot of labour to produce and sell. It gave our community an example of a magazine that was producing quality material regularly, and was put together by a dedicated collective. The searching feel of *KIO*, the desire to let people tell their own stories, and the demand for quality work from writers and artists had a valuable effect on members of the collective – we challenged one another, learned to expect more, learned to be mutually responsible. We learned – and I think others learned from us – that anarchism isn't necessarily slipshod, half-thought-out reactionism, but can be based on a true respect for the capacity of people to learn and grow and find ways not to oppress one another."

In our early debates on whom we should be trying to reach, I maintained that we should produce a magazine that would appeal to anarchists and non-anarchists alike, and which would, within anarchism, appeal to the anarchist professor as well as to the anarchist "lumpen." We would achieve this by including fresh, challenging material rooted, to some degree, in direct or first-person experience, while avoiding an academic or obscurantist tone.

Our success was suggested by the growth in our readership. At its peak, *KIO* was distributing 3,500 copies in thiry-five countries, with a readership of 6,000. Our readers include a healthy number of anarchists, and also large numbers of feminists, members of the Green and ecology movements, punks, back-to-the-landers, socialists, Native activists, and many others.

Our eclectic approach allowed us to speak as a credible though new voice in a number of discrete movements. We often published articles that others wouldn't. We were never able to countenance anything resembling a party line, and we stated in our masthead that "Articles seldom, if ever, reflect the opinions of the entire collective – occasionally the opinions expressed don't represent any of us." We printed things either because we believed them to be true or because they contributed to an ongoing debate out of which greater understanding would emerge.

It was after the fifth, and first collective, issue that *KIO* received a communique at its post office box from Direct Action, an anarchist guerrilla group that had taken responsibility for blowing up the Litton factory in a suburb of Toronto. This event sent a shock wave through the left movement in general, and the anarchist movement in particular. Some of us felt that Direct Action was "vanguardist" – substituting the actions of a small group for those of a "mass movement." We produced a leaflet entitled, "Vanguard Terror vs. State Terror," and distributed it to activists. It was later reprinted in *Kick It Over*, with a rebuttal from some other members of the collective.

The Litton bombing occurred in late 1982. In spring 1983, we published #7 of *Kick It Over* under the heading of a "No More Patriarchy" issue. In it, we raised – possibly for the first time in Canada – the whole pornography debate that was engulfing the feminist movement in the U.S. in the wake of a conference on sex held at Barnard College. On the one hand, there were the anti-pornography feminists who argued for a fairly rigid "feminist" conception of sexual correctness; on the other, there were the "libertarians" who saw sexual "deviance" (including s/m and pedophilia) as inherently progressive, or who denied that there was anything harmful about pornography. We allowed both sides to express their

opinions, but sought a "third pole" that synthesized aspects from each position. That issue was our first to sell out at the newsstands and, for a couple of issues, we were actually considered rather trendy.

In addition to contributing to the pornography debate, we ran many articles which would otherwise might never have seen the light of day. "Macho Disco Tendencies in Gay Men," for example, was a critique of the "straight" cultural tendencies in the gay movement. We were also self-critical of anarchism, with such articles as "Anarchy means Responsibility Not Spray-painting People's Garages," "You Smoke I Choke," and "The Macho Revolutionary Syndrome" – all widely reprinted and commented on.

Our purpose in all this was to demonstrate that all forms of hierarchy and oppression are interrelated and mutually conditioning. An interview with Native activist Jay Mason, for instance, challenged Canada's anti-apartheid activists by informing them that apartheid "begins at home": the South African government studied the reservation system in Canada and Australia before setting up its "homelands." Other authors wrote articles that drew links between the oppression of Black men and women, and that showed commonalities between reggae and Native culture.

Through long interviews with such older activists as Emma Goldman's comrade Art Bartell, and articles on youth liberation, we tried to help different generations of activists understand the continuity of anarchism. We also tried to connect culture with politics by putting more emphasis on artwork and by learning to "think visually."

Possibly one of our greatest contributions was to help initiate the social vs. deep ecology debate that would engulf the green movement for the next two years. We had come across an interview with Dave Foreman (co-founder of Earth First!) in an Australian publication, *Simply Living*, in which Foreman said that Ethiopians should be allowed to starve, and Central American refugees kept out of the United States because of their potential drain on American resources. We appended critical remarks about this to an interview we had conducted with Kirkpatrick Sale, someone who had many affinities with Foreman. We also sent a copy to Murray Bookchin, with whom we were quite close at the time. This touched off a storm of controversy especially after Bookchin and Janet Biehl wrote vitriolic responses which were distributed at a national Green conference in the summer of 1987, and later republished in our magazine. The debate raged on for two more years – in the pages of *KIO*, in

U.S. publications such as the *The Nation* and *Socialist Review*, and in the green press. It was acrimonious, and not always very clean, and *KIO* may not have acted as responsibly as it could in publishing – for the most part, unedited – Bookchin and Biehl's original polemics. While much of deep ecologists' thinking was and is muddled, social ecologists were guilty of smear tactics and of not acknowledging genuine concerns and issues, such as the problem of overpopulation.

Being on the cusp of key ideological debates was part of our success, but equally essential was the integration of the personal and the political in our own process. This took a long time to achieve. Susan Brown, a later member of the collective, described how that process worked:

"The fact that members of the *KIO* collective shared such basic anarchist principles as consensus, non-hierarchy, and decentralization meant that we were constantly attentive to process without having to argue about its importance. For example, we all implicitly agreed that decision-making must be supported by all of us; if even one person disagreed then an alternative solution must be sought.

"It was because of this strong commitment to consensus decision-making that I found it very easy to work with the rest of the collective – the other members were interested in and respectful of my point of view, and expected me to treat them in the same responsible way. I think this was very important, as it made working in the collective a very enjoyable and powerful experience. The knowledge that if any of us disagreed strongly enough on a point, the plan or action under discussion would be changed or postponed until we could reach a decision made each of us speak very carefully. We indeed had differing viewpoints, but the process of consensus and our respect for one another allowed us to accommodate these. Of course, without our basic agreement on anarchist principles, we would have found the situation unworkable."

KIO continued to evolve throughout these years. It was difficult to maintain the balance between theoretical depth and accessibility, and at times we veered towards the academic. We also engaged in discussion and debate about the relationship of form (the artwork, the images) to content, and tried to avoid the temptation to make the images a mere adjunct to what one reader once described as "walls of text." But a publication, like a human being, necessarily ages – for better or for worse. Christopher Alice, a member of the original collective, noted that "I often wonder how we continued, but we did. We learned how to trust.

We had to, in order to survive. Too much of us went into our magazine. I remember dealing with a friend, a collective member, who lost his lover to AIDS. I do not think we have ever put a meeting to better use. The people I worked with were not just acquaintances. I had a commitment to grow with them. I could not 'seal' a business agreement with them.

"Over time we got a better sense of who we were. One magazine, in reviewing us, said "*Kick It Over* still has not found its focus." They were wrong. We were Chris, Don, Catherine, Kathy, Glynis, Susan, Alexandra, and Robyn. We were our past as well. As our members changed and grew, the publication changed and grew.

"Within the left we were felt. Like our magazine, our readership was diverse. Through our readers, we were part of the peace movement, the feminist movement, the gay movement, and the anarchist movement. We tried to live the idea that everything is connected. Through the types of articles we printed, we propagated the idea that domination in any form is wrong."

In 1987, Alexandra and I decided to move to Peterborough to go to grad school. This spelled the beginning of the end of our role with *KIO*. Though we dutifully drove in for every meeting for the next two years, expending hundreds of dollars on gas and risking our necks on cold, dark, icy roads, the logistics of putting out a newspaper with a geographically split collective became more and more of a nightmare. Also, we were "doing more and enjoying it less," and began to resent the enormous lien on our time that the magazine entailed.

We had been having difficulty getting the kinds of publishable material that we felt we needed. Issues began to become formulaic, with repetitive subject matter, and editorial disagreements emerged over direction, and acceptable levels of quality. I felt that we had mined the anarchist-feminist-ecological formula for all that it was worth, and needed to move on to the issue of how one would begin to apply the "new synthesis" (as we sometimes called it) in one's personal and community practice. There was resistance to this and, eventually, Alexandra and I decided to leave.

For me, the key to a successful project is two-fold. It requires a special chemistry between collaborators, and it requires being in the right place at the right time. *Kick It Over* in the 1980s was a special magazine and, while I exercised considerable editorial influence on it, it was the synergy of the collective as a whole that made it successful. For instance, when Susan

Brown and her partner, Steve, got involved in the mid-1980s, it provided a needed infusion of energy and enabled the collective to make the transition to fully computerized production.

Furthermore, *Kick It Over* spoke to a receptive anarchist and broader-than-anarchist community in Toronto at a time when the "scene" was graced with many important personalities and much creative fire. Somewhat miraculously, *KIO* continues to the present day under a new collective. As of 2001, the magazine was twenty years old. To keep something going for a whole generation is an amazing accomplishment. As I wrote in issue #3:

> All artists and political thinkers act as a lens in relation to their social base, in relation to a specific social group. They focus and concentrate the understanding and sentiments, strengths and qualities, of a particular group of people. It is a mutual or "feedback" relationship. They derive their energy and raw material from the people, and concentrate it – giving it a more definite shape, and hence contribute to enhancing the identity of the group. Such artists or political thinkers may possess a certain "flair"… but without their energy source, without their social base, they are nothing.

– DON ALEXANDER

There were three key members of the *Kick It Over* collective through the first ten years. After Don and Alexandra left the project Christopher, Alice, and the other members kept the magazine going through one more issue and the beginning of the next. But it became evident that Christopher had also lost his enthusiasm, and the group drifted apart.

Eventually, under the impetus of Gary Moffatt, an occasional *KIO* contributor (although not a collective member), two of the newer members, plus Gary and myself, convinced Christopher to guide us through the process of putting the paper out. We spent about six months meeting weekly to learn about computers and layout and mailing and distribution and all the other jobs that are part of the process of doing a publication, and then brought out our own issue, *Kick It Over* #26, in a magazine format in the summer of 1991. Unfortunately, the long break between issues had severed many of the connections that had been built up over the years, and we had some trouble gathering materials to keep the magazine on a regular quarterly schedule. But we did manage to bring out six issues in the next two years.

In between issues #32 and #33, our collective fell apart, mostly due to other commitments weighing too heavily on people's schedules. As the one member who was not engaged full-time in either work or school, I decided to continue on by myself. Well, it wasn't quite as easy as I had imagined, and I managed to bring out only one issue per year until 1995. In 1998, I met a good bunch of folks at a social ecology conference in Guelph, Ontario (about sixty miles outside of Toronto). I gave one of them a call, and said "Do you want to take on this magazine?" They talked about it, and said "Sure!" So in the fall of 1998, I drove out to Guelph with a car-load of boxes, and spent a day telling them all about *Kick It Over* (luckily, a couple of them had already been involved in print projects, so they didn't require the long learning process that we had gone through seven years earlier).

I've maintained my connection with the magazine, and we now have a new collective of five, all at least half my age. We're still having problems with keeping to a schedule, but we all enjoy each other's company and we generally work well together. I'm pleased to say that the "young folks," while they respect my experience and enjoy my stories of struggles gone by, do not offer me any deference or slack: they're quite prepared to tell me when I'm full of shit, and that's as it should be. Our goal is to produce a magazine that speaks to many concerns and interests – from the historical background of our movement to today's ongoing struggles against globalization – in a manner that finds a place for theory and practice, ideas and activism.

– BOB MELCOLME

What We Believe

1. The Kick It Over Collective is opposed to all forms of hierarchy and domination, whether right or left.

2. For us, revolution is a process not an event—a process, moreover, rooted in the transformation of everyday life.

3. Rather than make a principle out of violence or non-violence, we believe in judging actions on their own merits.

4. We are not a mouthpiece for the "official" anarchist movement. Instead, we are interested in drawing out and popularizing those implicitly radical values and lifestyles which we believe are pointing in the direction of freedom.

5. Since we are interested in the creation of a politics of everyday life, we avoid dealing primarily with the stock issues which make up the "left agenda."

6. We do not identify with the "official left," which seeks to establish itself as a new ruling group. We identify with and seek to give voice to the largely unarticulated anti-authoritarian tendencies within society.

7. We are committed to avoiding rhetoric. We believe that one should not have to be familiar with standard leftist buzzwords to read our magazine.

8. We are committed to quality of content, and we hope to remain open to contributions of new writers and artists.

9. We are committed to the collective process of putting out a quarterly magazine, and see that as our main function.

10. Above all, we are committed to spontaneity, by which we mean the triumph of life over dogma. Hence, we believe that freedom is in need of constant redefinition.

SUSTAINING DEVELOPMENT OR DEVELOPING SUSTAINABILITY?

BY DON ALEXANDER

The following article was delivered as a talk to a student conference at Trent University called "Discovering Our Future" in May of this year. The theme of the conference was sustainable development, with special reference to the Brundtland Commission report. The Brundtland Commission (formally known as the World Commission on Environment and Development) was a UN sponsored commission, chaired by Norwegian Prime Minister Madame Gro Brundtland, which produced a report entitled *Our Common Future* (Oxford University press, 1987). The talk has been shortened for reasons of space.

"Development" – Cure or Disease

The Brundtland Commission's document, *Our Common Future*, does a good job of painting a picture of our current environmental dilemma. Acid rain, a thinning ozone layer, an increase in the greenhouse effect, toxic pollution, erosion and desertification, deforestation, and species loss are among the issues discussed in the report, and the Commission has succeeded in putting these issues on the international political agenda. The report also shows the interrelationship between the ecological crisis and the social crisis – how a massive Third World debt and urban overcrowding are both a cause and an effect of environmental degradation.

But, in the end, despite the parts of its analysis which are compelling, the Brundtland Commission generally mistakes symptoms for causes, and winds up prescribing more of the same "development" that brought about the problems in the first place. While the report is not monolithic, there is an underlying development model as reflected in the following quotation:

> It is essential that economic growth be
> revitalized. In practical terms, this means more
> rapid economic growth in both industrial and
> developing countries, freer market access for
> the products of developing countries, lower
> interest rates, greater technology transfer, and
> significantly larger capital flows.

"Another Development" Model

In opposition to this "standard" model of development, the Dag Hammarskjold Foundation of Sweden has given us what they call "Another Development" model. The defining characteristics of this are: it is need-oriented, not profit and growth oriented; it is endogenous (that is, it accords with the values of each culture and leaves the people of that culture free to determine those values); it stresses self-reliance rather than increased dependence on the world market; it is ecologically sound (development which tailors itself to the carrying capacity of local, regional, and global ecosystems); and it is based on transforming existing power structures such that self management and participatory democracy replace the current system of entrenched economic and political privilege.

While the Brundtland Commission report pays lip service to these points, it essentially envisions achieving sustainable development through minor modifications of the existing world order. Manfred Max-Neef, a self-described "Barefoot economist", challenges this belief that:

> It is simply a question of considering one or more
> additional variables and parameters in order
> to perfect a model. If this were so, it would then
> be perfectly logical and natural to conceive as
> possible an ecological capitalism...an ecological
> socialism, an ecological conservatism or finally,
> any other equally ecological and eclectic mixture
> or combination ... [T]hese very possibilities ...
> [are] illusory.

He goes on to argue that: "the forms of socio-economic and political organization currently in force in the world are essentially antagonistic to the achievement of a tripartite harmony between Nature, Humans, and Technology."

The Brundtland Commission leaves unchallenged the hegemony of market institutions, imposes a Western-style development model, encourages more production for export, calls for a new era of economic growth, and leaves power in the hands of existing governments, multilateral development organizations, and multinationals.

The ecological consequences of this model cannot help but be devastating. Increased trade and industrialization will boost energy use; urbanization will overstress ecosystems and existing infrastructure, and technology transfer will introduce technologies, such as biotechnology and nuclear power, which are potentially more damaging to the environment. In addition, increased consumerism will encourage the growth of artificial needs turning people into junkies insensitive to the effect of their habit on the surrounding biosphere.

The Commission and Neo Classical Economics

The economic model of the Commission is the traditional model of neo-classical economics. According to the neoclassical view, the goal of any society should be to increase the number of jobs (regardless of whether they're worthwhile), boost the Gross National Product (ignoring

Kick It Over 24 (1989)

the fact that growth in GNP can indicate social misery more than social health), improve the balance of trade (regardless of whether the products are worth trading and ignoring the effects of fossil fuel consumption), encourage the formation of larger, more efficient firms (thereby further alienating local control), and treat increased availability of consumer goods as the best way to promote social welfare. It is a theory of "trickledown" – that the greater the orgy at the banquet table, the more crumbs will fall down to the poor. In actual practice, the trickledown strategy has been a gross failure. Over the last twenty-five years, despite efforts at development and modernization, and impressive rates of growth in some Third World countries, poverty has increased in both relative and absolute terms.

The Degradation of Culture

In addition to accepting the neo-classical economic model, the commissioners have failed to recognize that the degradation of nature is inseparably connected with the degradation of culture. Three examples will serve to illustrate this point. In the early history of modern North America, the introduction of European trade goods (and the increasing dependence of Native people on Europeans) led to the erosion of traditional Native patterns of life and belief systems. This resulted in the slaughter of millions of beaver, marten, muskrat and other species for the fur trade – to make hats for the European aristocracy – leading to their virtual extinction in certain areas.

The last twenty years has seen increasing desertification and famine in the Sahel region of Africa. This is due, in large part, to the disruption of the lifestyle of traditional herders and farmers, who have either been forced off their lands to accommodate agribusiness or have been herded into villages to promote social control, as in Ethiopia.

Finally, the obscene overcrowding of Mexico City – now the largest city in the world, with twenty million people – is the direct product of the displacement of peasants who do not have an adequate land base in the countryside because the bulk of the land is owned by large landowners.

Social ecosystems are like natural ecosystems; they maintain themselves in relative equilibrium and in relative harmony with their environment as long as they are undisturbed. When massively interfered with, they lose their internal poise and balance; they lose their ability to naturally regenerate themselves. The key to a sustainable economy is producing sustainable cultures, and to produce sustainable cultures we must first salvage what is left of those cultures, which have sustained themselves in relative harmony with their environment for thousands of years. I am arguing that there is a direct relationship between conservation of "natural resources" and the conservation of what we might choose to call "spiritual" and "cultural" resources.

Material Poverty vs. Cultural Poverty

Ecologists have focused attention on our squandering of things natural, but too little attention has been given to the spiritual and cultural resources, which also make society viable. These are often less tangible than petroleum or coal, but just as important.

The first of these is community. Human beings cooperate by means of culture: through values, attitudes and social relationships, which are passed down from generation to generation. Wolves, ants, and primates also cooperate, but they do so instinctively for the most part. The consequences of allowing community to break down – with everyone "looking out for #1" – are not hard to fathom.

Another important cultural resource is diversity. Thousands of different cultures have emerged in different parts of the world, evolving different customs and strategies for survival. The ability of human groups to learn from their neighbours has enabled them to adapt to changing conditions. European civilization – at one time the most technologically "advanced" – borrowed much of its technology from the Chinese, crops from Amerindians, mathematics from the Arabs, and philosophy and religion from Greece and Palestine. Today, the most "advanced" society, North America, is imposing its technology and value structures on peoples all across the globe, with the result that many thousands of age-old cultures are being destroyed. These cultures have "worked". They have permitted their members to live in relative harmony with the earth. Every time one of these cultures dies, we lose the possibility of transcending our own culture, of appraising it critically, of opting for different life ways.

Democracy is also important. For decades, the Soviet Union has been stagnant because its rulers have attempted to concentrate all power in their hands, allowing the people little meaningful participation. Society pays a high price for the fallibility of the few. Today's "glasnost" is being imposed in a typically topdown fashion, but it reflects Mikhail Gorbachev's recognition that unless the initiative of people is liberated, the Soviet Union will sink ever deeper in the mire of apathy and inefficiency.

The last cultural resource I'm going to talk about is equality. For decades, Canada was deprived of the energy and enthusiasm of immigrants barred by exclusionist and racist immigration policies. For decades, women were limited to the home, depriving society of their contributions to public life. Oppression and injustice breed apathy and self-hatred; they waste precious talent and resources. An equitable society is a society which maximizes the potential of each of its citizens, thereby improving everyone's quality of life.

But social qualities like democracy and equality also depend on the individual. Democracy is impossible unless people are capable of weighing evidence, reasoning things out, and making their own independent judgments. The intelligence and knowledge of the many is being wasted, not to mention degraded by manipulative media. Our current ecological crisis is very much a product of too few people and too few institutions having too much decision-making power.

Another important trait, which we can either encourage or destroy, is versatility. A generation ago, family farmers possessed a variety of skills. They could fix engines, build fences and barns, birth animals, and make tools. Their mixed farming style of life permitted them to incorporate new crops gradually, diversify their financial base, and avoid having "all their eggs in one basket." Like the farmers-fishermen-woodcutters of the Maritimes, these traditional mixed farmers were a type of "renaissance person," concentrating in one individual the knowledge of a number of occupations. Most people today are highly specialized, highly dependent on mass produced goods for their survival. Should a major economic crash occur, a lot of people would be helpless. Only versatility enables people to readily adapt to changing circumstances.

But another point about versatility and self-reliance is that it increases people's pride, their sense of self-worth. If you take a group of people who were formerly independent, and force them to become dependent, you destroy their self-respect. One consequence of this is increased alcoholism, drug abuse – even suicide.

Other important qualities, which we need to nurture, are sensitivity and responsibility. The basis of any successful community is the ability of its members to be sensitive to one another's needs and points of view. Sensitivity to natural cycles and processes – to the natural regions, which form the matrix for our activity – is needed to sustain human life. Amongst the Iroquois, it was a normative principle that people should consider the consequences of their actions "for the seventh generation." All major decisions should take into account the interests of the as yet unborn. Contrast this with the way our society functions; most political and corporate leaders are willing to continue the orgy of ecological destruction as long as they get their share of the loot, or the vote. Reciprocity – considering the needs of others and taking an ecologically and socially responsible position – is the soul of any sustainable culture.

There's no question we've done a lot in the Western countries to eliminate material poverty, but have we replaced material poverty with cultural poverty? We live in a society where people think nothing of dumping their garbage by the side of the highway or of spraying weed killer on their lawn. They're more concerned about their pay cheque at the end of the week, and about buying a new car, than they are about whether their children will inherit a planet worth living on. A culture which has created such a total absence of vision, is one that is fighting for its life. If we cannot change our basic orientation to the other species on the planet, and to future generations, then we are no different than a pack of lemmings headed straight for the edge of the cliff.

What I'm suggesting is that this insensitivity, this living in the eternal "now" is, in large measure, a product of modernization. In order to conceive of modernization in its positive aspects, we first need to be clear on its negative aspects.

A Critique of Modernization

There are five aspects to the modernization process I'd like to talk about: industrialization, urbanization, bureaucracy, the development of mass culture, and the commodification of the economy and social relationships. Industrialization involves increased economic specialization, hierarchical relationships in the workplace (and hence loss of worker autonomy), and diminished local economic control. It leads to an increasingly privatized struggle for survival, and a loss of contact with the reality of natural processes. Urbanization engenders a loss of rootedness and community support systems, and a growth in political apathy and social indifference. Bureaucratization erodes mutual aid networks (and hence promotes dependence on the state), disempowers people, fosters an increasingly invasive security apparatus, and a political elite which is committed to perpetuating its own power. Mass culture fragments community, atomizes individuals, and transforms people into spectators and consumers of pre-packaged culture rather than allowing them to be cultural creators. Finally, commodification involves a loss of economic self-reliance, the growth of consumerism, and a tendency for human relationships to degenerate into those of buyers and sellers.

We should protect the *social* ecosystems, which give rise to cultural and spiritual resources, not just the natural ones. Just as air, water and soil can be polluted, so too communities can be degraded, diversity replaced with monoculture, democracy stifled in the interests of "efficiency", and equality crushed in the drive to make a buck. In the interests of allowing free reign to market forces, attitudes, products, and forms of industrial organization are allowed to proliferate which erode intelligence, versatility, sensitivity and responsibility.

"Another Development" in Practice

Using the criteria offered by the Dag Hammarskjold Foundation, I'd like to talk about some of the initiatives that are being undertaken in various parts of the world that are positive, that embody the spirit of "Another Development". The first group I'd like to mention is *Plenty Canada*, an aid group that evolved out of a hippie commune in Eastern Ontario. Plenty, through its projects in Lesotho, the Caribbean and elsewhere, emphasizes self-reliance, local control, appropriately scaled and inexpensive technologies, and respecting traditional values. Their projects have included helping villagers plant fruit and nut trees for

Kick It Over 24 (1989)

food and erosion control, establishing community gardens, helping build small-scale irrigation and water projects, and introducing renewable energy technologies.

Another project worth mentioning is the *Ladakh Ecological Development Group*. Ladakh is the most northerly part of India, an area the size of Newfoundland, high up in the Himalayan Mountains. Since 1974, Ladakh, which has traditionally been isolated from contact with the outside world, has been open to tourists from Europe and North America. This was beginning to have disastrous effects as the Ladakhi began to look down on their traditional way of life as inferior, in contrast with the seemingly limitless affluence of the Western tourists. Helena Norberg-Hodge, a Swedish linguist, who was the first Westerner to master the Ladakhi language and to translate it into the Western alphabet, established the *Ladakh Ecological Development Group* to help combine the best elements of traditional Ladakhi culture with appropriate forms of modern technology. Local craftsmen, using almost all locally produced materials, built passive solar Trombe walls. Solar water heaters, solar kilns, and windmill generators have also been experimented with. By such methods, Norberg-Hodge is attempting to implement Ivan Illich's injunction that "two thirds of [hu]-mankind can still avoid passing through the industrial age, by choosing right now a post-industrial balance."

Two other positive examples I'd like to mention are the *Green Belt* movement and the *Chipko* movement. The *Green Belt* movement is a movement of rural women in Kenya which is engaged in a massive program of reforestation, with women earning revenue from operating tree nurseries, developing expertise and gaining decision making power, with the wood from the newly planted forests being harvested for fuel, fodder, food and building materials. In India, in the central state of Uttar Pradesh, largely tribal women have initiated a movement called Chipko or "tree-hugger". The women have resisted the commercial exploitation of the forests for the making of tennis rackets, etc., have opposed the transplantation of exotic species such as eucalyptus (funded by the World Bank) which are useless to the people and do damage to the environment, and have planted new forests with a view to protecting the purity of air, water and soil. The survival rate of the trees they plant is eighty percent compared with a government average of twenty percent.

Like the Chipko women, the rubber tappers of the Amazon use the trees of the forest in a sustainable and renewable fashion. To quote a recent newsletter from the *Rainforest Action Network*:

> *The rubber tappers' livelihood, based on*
> *the extraction of latex from rubber trees*
> *and harvesting of tropical nuts, exemplifies*
> *sustainable use of the tropical forest's resources.*

Chico Mendes, the rubber tappers' leader, pointed out that "A rubber tree can live up to one hundred years if you tap

it right, affectionately." Mendes was recently murdered by ranching interests who are trying to burn down the forest and drive the rubber tappers away.

Friends of the Earth Malaysia and its sister group, the *Consumers' Association of Penang*, have a long, vital history fighting against the destruction of rainforests, the dispossession of tribal peoples, and the pollution of Malaysia's rivers. Several key activists in the group have recently spent time in jail.

A movement which started in North America and which models itself, to some degree, on the way of life of the continent's Native peoples is the *bioregional* movement. The bioregional movement believes that people ought to discover the attributes of the regions where they live and develop their economic, political and cultural institutions accordingly. It believes that people should make a commitment to place and try to live as equals within the web of life, rather than as lord and master over the biosphere. Their stance is similar to the Haida elder who recently posed the question: "When are white people going to start treating the land as if they planned to stay?"

Here in Ontario, we have the Teme-Augama Anishnabai who, rather than allow their ancestral homeland – site of the last major white pine forests in the province – to be logged off providing saw mills with five more years of work, have proposed that the area be turned into an ecological reserve where the natural processes of old growth forests be studied for 400 years so that future generations might benefit.

Mulroney: Rhetoric and Reality

The Mulroney government has been a big booster of "sustainable development", and yet its policies go in the opposite direction. Mulroney is promoting increased trade and industrialization, is seeking to strengthen the role of market forces in economic and social decision-making, and is bankrolling costly and unecological energy megaprojects. He is chopping funding for renewable and energy conservation research, is providing no tax or other incentives for energy efficiency and recycling, is taking little action on toxic pollution in the Great Lakes, and is pulling the rug out from under precisely those cultural and socio-economic groups that could form the nucleus for a sustainable society: Canada's Native people, family farmers, and the inshore fishermen of the Maritimes, etc,

Another thing Mulroney would have us believe is that it is corporations like Inco and Dow Chemical which are going to be the vanguard of sustainable development. Corporations, by their very nature, are ecologically and socially irresponsible. Go into any McDonald's and complain about their wasteful packaging. The employee (who after all, only "works" there) will refer you to the manager. The manager will refer you to the franchise owner. The franchise owner will say his hands are tied: all decisions are made at head office, and head office will tell you how they are switching from one pernicious form of Styrofoam to another. Meanwhile, landfills all across the continent continue to fill up with their garbage.

The small craftsperson was at least responsible for his or her product. With modern corporations, no one is willing to take responsibility. In many cases, the individuals associated with the corporation bear no personal liability for the corporation's actions. They may make one production process less polluting, they may stop using rainforest beef because of public pressure, they may use recycled paper for inter-office memos, but the goal is still to transform the earth's resources into capital and transform their employees into obedient robots. Corporations function according to the law of "grow or die", and a grow or die economy is ecologically and socially destabilizing.

The corporations are not interested in "sustainable development", nor can they be as long as their loyalty is to their "bottom line." As the ends, so the means. How can you harness greed to the achievement of equality and sensitivity? We have to stop assuming that "what's good for the economy" is good for society, because it's patently untrue. If we are going to integrate economic and environmental decision – making, as the Brundtland Commission has recommended, we must put ecological, cultural and spiritual values first, and mold our economic institutions accordingly.

The kinds of initiatives that governments are talking about – recycling, ozone conventions, and pollution controls – are important, but, ultimately, they are band-aid solutions. They are like trying to put your hand on a spring: the water will just spurt up somewhere else. We need a radical restructuring of our economic, political and social institutions – a revolution, if you will.

We need to pay attention to those movements, here in Canada, and around the world where peoples' struggle to preserve their distinct cultures is linked to the struggle to preserve specific ecosystems and use them in a renewable and sustainable fashion. There is a growing convergence of these movements worldwide; some people have called it the emergence of the "planetariat." It is a movement to preserve natural, cultural and spiritual resources, and we need to be part of it.

Sustaining Development or Developing Sustainability?

by Don Alexander

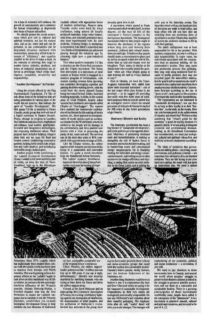

VISIONING THE FUTURE – AN EDITORIAL

by Alexandra Devon

In some native languages, the term for "elder" means "guardian of the dream". In our **visioning the future** issue we want to acknowledge that the vision or dream we are carrying into the future is part of a gift from our elders. Because as anarchists or anti-authoritarians, we don't belong to an organic community, finding our elders and knowing our history is not always easy. We face geographical and generational barriers which keep us from having the sense of continuity and solidarity with people who share our values.

A native elder watching a stomp dance in Oklahoma described how the dance represents their connectedness: "That line of dancers, that's the way we're made. You hear the leader call and the dancers echo him. That call is relayed to the last dancer in the line...You hear the dancers echo the call, so you know [the leader] must have called something, and you echo that call, thinking you're the last. But you hear the call going on back behind you...and you turn around and see your son and his son behind, going clear back beyond the horizon, dancing behind."

For many of us the first "echo" we hear comes from a book, a song or a magazine. Friends of mine who first "discovered" anarchism through the writings of Emma Goldman were quite certain that there were no anarchists alive today, until a subversive clerk at the World's Biggest Bookstore sold them a tacky little fanzine (K.I.O. #1 in 1981) under the counter, when they asked where they could find literature on anarchism.

As anarchists we are often isolated from our contemporaries, thinly spread as we are all over the world. We are also often ignorant of our own history and of those people who have kept alive an anarchist vision. Yet this doesn't need to be the case. Our teachers and comrades are there for the finding. Although not always self-identified anarchists, there are many people sympathetic to and practicing an anarchist vision. Many tribal people were anarchists long before the term meant anything to the Europeans who tried to destroy their way of life. Feminists who believe that power, not sex, lies beneath our most profound oppression (although sexual oppression may have been the first manifestation of it) and bioregionally-oriented people who want to decentralize society into egalitarian, ecological communities are among our fellow dancers whether we or they realize it or not.

We at Kick It Over have been lucky that so many important teachers have seen a commonality between our vision and theirs and have helped us to understand these connections and our history. Mildred Loomis (of the School of Living), Art Solomon (Native spiritual leader), Jake Swamp (Chief of the Wolf clan), Murray Bookchin (of the Social Ecology Institute), Roberta Blackgoat (elder from Big Mountain) and Gary Moffat are just a few of the teachers who have shared their wisdom with us and in the process have helped us to understand that the aspirations and dreams we have are not ours alone and that they are not something we will outgrow, a "phase" to be passed through on the road to the mature cynicism of adulthood.

In this issue we have part of a longer interview with Art Berthelot, an anarchist who was born in Italy just after the turn of the century and is as passionately committed to his ideals as ever. In telling us about his life and activism in Canada and the United States, Art teaches us about our own history as well. It is a reminder that anarchist history is made up of more than the obvious luminaries of the movement.

I have often introduced Art to people who have heard that he was a friend of Emma Goldman's. Their first question is often (predictably), "What was she like?" Art, whose principled hatred of the Catholic church would not allow him to exchange one type of hagiography [writing of the lives of saints --ed.] for another, would answer quite frankly that Emma was quite "irascible". I think he would say this to impress upon people that she was human like the rest of us. He would then go on to talk about her in all her complexity and contradictions. By the end of the conversation, you could not mistake his love and appreciation for her but it was her human qualities that you understood most deeply.

Art's relationship with Emma was a special one. She worked with determination on his behalf to keep him from being deported to Mussolini's Italy, after he had been arrested (on some flimsy charges) following the declaration of the War Measures Act in Canada in 1939. In the letters which she wrote to elicit support on his behalf, she describes him as being among the finest comrades. Due in large part to her efforts, he was finally released and allowed to remain in Toronto.

Art described his release on a bitterly cold snowy January day. As he walked out of the doors of the jail, Emma waiting for him. He was quite sick as a result of his stay in prison and Emma insisted on travelling across town every day to nurse him (one of Emma's talents). Art was determined that once he was well he would take care of Emma and eliminate her constant worrying about money. In May of that same year, Emma died so that Art was never able to accomplish this dream.

Art has remained committed to anarchist ideals and in touch with each new generation of anarchists. He's lent us at this magazine strong moral support and through his appreciation of our work given us a sense of being connected to a rich tradition through more than just the printed word.

This connection through our elders (such as Art, Murray Bookchin, Mildred Loomis and others) is invaluable; it grounds us in a long tradition of people seeking to transform society in accordance with a vision of how things ought to be. Although each generation finds itself confronted with changed conditions and must ultimately choose its own path, they echo part of the call of the dancers ahead.

As important as our elders are to us, we are to them. We create a human chain from the past into the future of people trying to create a realm of freedom and a new age of caring. So this issue, concerned as it is with visioning the future, is dedicated to all guardians of the dream -- past, present and future. □

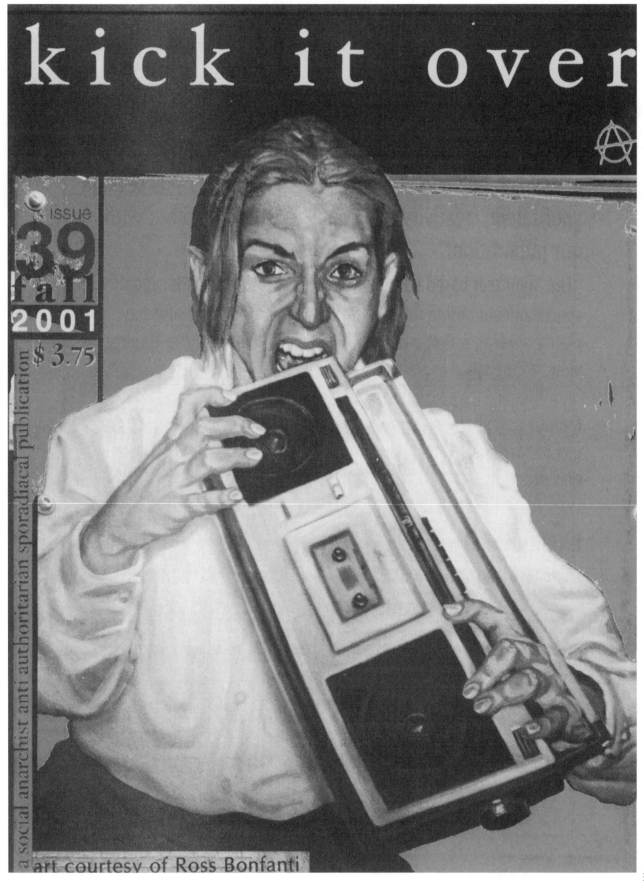

kick it over

issue
39
fall
2001
$ 3.75

a social anarchist anti authoritarian sporadiacal publication

art courtesy of Ross Bonfanti

Kick It Over 31 (2001)

Active Resistance (1998), photo: Susan Simensky-Bietila

ISSUES & ACTIONS

In an editorial for *Kick it Over* entitled, "Visioning the Future," Alexandra Devon has likened the anarchist movement to a "human chain from the past into the future of people trying to create a realm of freedom and a new age of caring." She compares this chain to an Indigenous elder's description of the sacred dance that symbolically binds his community together: "That line of dancers, that's the way we're made. You hear the Leader call and the dancers echo him. The call is relayed to the last dancer in the line. . . . You hear the dancers echo the call, so you know the leader must have called something, and you echo that call, thinking you're the last. But you hear the call going on back behind you . . . and you turn around and see your son and his son behind, going clear way back beyond the horizon, dancing behind."

A community's past should echo it's future, but the anarchist community is not an organic one, and the bonds from one generation to the next can weaken and break. All the more important, then, to recall past struggles such as those documented here.

"Issues and Actions" highlights some of the most prescient concerns that have galvanized the movement to date. Sensitivity to the injustices underpinning the Mohawk's armed confrontation with the police and military at Oka, Quebec in 1990, for example, inspired anarchists to fan the flames of dissent with road blockades and other supportive actions. This same combination of analysis/engagement was very much in evidence during the first Gulf War of 1991 and the Quebec City protests of April 2001, when anarchists were at the forefront, organizing and protesting. And then there are the enduring issues that transcend Canada's borders: capitalism; prisons; racism; the destruction of the earth; and the on-going plight of the Palestinians. Anarchists have developed positions on all these issues, and they've offered solutions as well.

Activism, of course, involves more than analysing and protesting against this or that injustice. Thus, the movement has given rise to localized cultures of resistance that span everything from guerilla warfare to squatting to critical mass bike rides to wrapping giant protest posters around city hall. Underlying the tactical differences, however, is a shared recognition that experience is the best teacher, and that agendas for realizing an anarchist society will only emerge organically from lived situations.

— ALLAN ANTLIFF

Profits Before Peace

In an average small business, the revenue is divided up almost evenly between labour, product cost, and other small expenses, leaving very little for profit. If a company's main goal, though, is to have large profits, then they must find a way of getting cheap labour and expenses. The easiest way of doing this is to obtain and manufacture the product in a place where the whole cost of living is much lower than in the company's consumer based countries. These conditions of low wages and low costs are ripe in developing or "third world" countries.

The Third World Situation

A "developing" country is one which is described as a country which is attempting to raise its level of industrialization/capitalism to that of the so-called "first" world countries. Traditionally, the people lived directly off the land, and as the countries are still in the process of changing, many areas still do. The situations facing the people are the same as during the Industrial Revolution in Europe. A few people take control of the land and force the people who lived there to work in order to get their basic necessities such as food and shelter. Most of the working conditions are also the same – long hours, no breaks, unsafe working areas, little pay, child labour, etc. Unfortunately, most of the people doing this exploiting are large companies which are financially secure and aren't really dependant on one factory or farm. These companies will do all they can to keep these conditions and any attempts by workers to organize are met by brutal oppression, intimidation, and even death squad assassinations. An example of this is in a Coca Cola bottling plant in Guatemala in the 1970s. Employees tried to organize and form a union so Coke, along with the military, formed a death squad and assassinations, mass firings, and military raids followed. The death squads/militia stayed until 1980 when public pressure forced reforms. The military left the factory, although the threat of the death squad remained.

Banks, too, are playing a major part in exploiting these country's situations. Large sums of money are lent out to help a country set up "modern conditions", decrease poverty, pay off old debts, etc. The money is lent at high interest rates and must be paid back in a relatively short period of time, which forces the countries to do everything they can to generate back the money quickly. Usually, the countries allow foreign companies to come in, exploit the resources and people, and sell these resources and products in another country (i.e. export everything). The landowners/companies take control of everything on the land and the workers cannot even grow food for themselves. In the Philippines, some companies even insist the workers buy their goods at the company store, at high prices, which ensures the worker must keep working in order to pay off the increasing debt. The stripping of the land by bad agricultural practices, clear-cutting, etc. usually means the area cannot be used again the next year, or growing season, and so a new area is then used. This using up of the land leaves less and less for the people to grow their food on, and the poverty increases. It is a never-ending circle the banks and companies are only too happy to play a part in.

Unfortunately, even all the money and goods sent into the countries as foreign aid rarely gets to the people who really need it. Most of it is taken in by the government and redistributed amongst the elite/landowners who either use it for themselves, or sell the goods at a high profit. An example of this is in 1986, when the Canadian government sold $8.9 million of manure on the open market with profits going to help El Salvador. The money was put into the supposedly neutral Canada/El Salvador Development Fund, but the fund is administered on behalf of the government of El Salvador through its Ministry of Planning. This makes the fund's resources the property of the government and leaves the power of distribution to the government and its committees. The El Salvadorian bank, which handled the funds, received $1 million in "handling fees." Also, when all the countries sent in food aid to help during Ethiopia's famines, the food was usually divided up and redistributed to the people who help keep the government in power, such as the soldiers, landowners, etc., and then the remainder was divided amongst the people who could afford the food. Very little actually got out to the rural areas and the people who really needed it.

The divisions of wealth become vastly increased between landowners and workers – the rich get richer and the poor get poorer. Many cities in these countries have become exotic tourist attractions for North Americans and Europeans, and so a lot of money is put into the cities to keep them luxurious so the tourists keep coming. This too results in a division of wealth between the cities and countryside. Many people leave the rural area and travel to the cities in hope of finding better jobs to support their families. This leaves less people in the villages to work on the land, and overcrowding in the city core, which results in shantytowns being set up to compensate for the homelessness and unemployment these people found.

A lot of the wealth is racially divided, too, as the native peoples were the ones living off the land and are now the workers. The English, French, Spanish, etc. who explored and "conquered" the land were wealthy to begin with, and they took this wealth with them as they settled and this wealth has been passed down from generation to generation. The "official" languages of the country became those of the explorers, and so the native peoples have a harder time receiving "education" (schooling is also not very extensive in the rural areas), and so are not qualified for any "good" jobs. Also, companies coming into the country are foreign-owned and so the racial division of money continues.

Pharmaceuticals in the Third World

Many pharmaceutical companies use the third world to sell/dump off dangerous medicines which no longer can be used (because of bans, proven harmful effects, out of date, etc.) in the first world, or just sell medicines of which there is no real need. In the third world, between ¾ and 1 billion small children fall sick each year with acute diarrhea. The pharmaceutical industry sells a multitude of anti-diarrhea substances with huge advertising campaigns in these countries. These remedies are very expensive and, according to the World Health Organization, almost all are superfluous and even partially dangerous to the health. For example, the Ciba-Geigy preparations Mexaform and Enteroform both contain the active ingredient Clioquinol. This agent leads to a serious nerve ailment called Smon. In the 1970s, in Japan alone, 20,000–30,000 people became sick with Smon and over 1,000 died. Ciba-Geigy was tried in Tokyo and forced to pay reparation to the victims. In 1982, it announced that it had taken both medications off the market, but in 1984 both medications were still being sent to Africa, the Middle East, and Mexico. It can be presumed that they are still being used. Also, in 1982, Ciba-Geigy admitted that it had tested a cancer-causing pesticide in Egypt on children and youths.

Birth control pills were originally tested in 1956 in Puerto Rico, and then El Salvador to see if there were any side effects and if they even worked! Sometimes this was done without the women's knowledge. These pills were twenty times stronger than the ones on the market today, and as they cannot be used in North America and Europe, they are still being sold in these third world countries.

After the post-war baby boom, when birth rates declined in the West, infant formula companies looked to the relatively untouched third world markets. Convinced by aggressive and often unethical advertising practices that a bottle fed baby would be more healthy and more likely to survive than a breastfed baby, millions of third world mothers stopped breastfeeding. Unfortunately, the sanitary conditions for mixing and storing the formula could not be maintained, instructions were often not included, and the women could not afford to purchase sufficient quantities of the formula. The result has been ten million cases of severe malnutrition each year and approximately three million infant deaths. Nestle generates almost half of all infant formula sales in the third world and, as a result, there has been a large boycott on the company.

These pharmaceutical companies also manufacture many pesticides and herbicides. The average DDT content in human blood in Guatemala's cotton areas is 520.6 parts per billion contrasted with 46.2 in Dade County, Florida. Common pesticides besides DDT include Toxaphene and Parathion, both banned in the U.S. Parathion was developed by the Nazis and is sixty times more toxic than DDT. It causes eighty percent of Central American poisonings. In La Flora, Guatemala, thirty or forty cotton workers a day must be treated for pesticide poisonings. Pesticides in the U.S. often read "for export only" but frequently do not carry any warnings. Pesticide poisoning is a problem that is coming back to the first world. DDT applied to cotton in Nicaragua showed up in beef carcasses imported through Miami.

Our Daily Collaboration

Most of the food/products which we use everyday, or at least are encouraged to use, come from the third world. Our coffee, tea, sugar, tobacco, cotton, rubber, tropical fruits, and some beef (especially in the U.S.) are all imported in for us. These are cash crops – grown not for the people who provide the slave-labour but for foreign consumers. Crops grown for a large profit.

Over forty countries economies depend on coffee export, which is the world's most heavily traded commodity after oil. In Ethiopia, seventy-five percent of the land is used to grow coffee, which makes up seventy percent of its exports. Sixty percent of that is received by the U.S. This coffee is grown on land which could be used for food for the people. Cotton and sugar cane production are close to follow the coffee monopolies. Eight of the world's ten largest cotton-trading companies are U.S. corporations. Cotton is El Salvador's second largest crop (next to coffee), and eighty percent of it is exported. (This means that finished garments are usually imported back in, at high prices).

Cattle ranching is responsible for the conversion of 20,000 square kilometres of land every year in Latin America. The companies first clear the land of its forests (over eighty percent of the U.S. hardwood imports come from these tropical areas), then the area is filled with defoliants like 2.4.5-t, the basic ingredient in Agent Orange, or other pesticides, and the area is then used for cattle feeding. After a few years of feeding and chemical treatments, these area become "red deserts," completely infertile. Most of the beef produced finds its way to first world countries. Burger outlets like Burger King, McDonalds, Wimpys, etc. get most of their hamburger this way. While beef consumption within these third world countries is decreasing rapidly (e.g. in Guatemala, beef consumption has dropped by fifty percent), the exporting of beef has increased by as much as 500% in the last few years. The beef is also used for hotdogs, pet food, and other miscellaneous items (e.g. beef fat in cookies produced by companies in the area).

Other everyday items obtained from the third world include calculators, computers, typewriters, car tires, sporting goods, etc. While these items are not "grown" in the developing world, the resources for them often are, and it is the people of these areas that provide the slave-labour which puts the products together. Often, the factory work conditions have much to be desired. The electronics

Endless Struggle 9 (1989)

industry is considered one of the safest and cleanest of the factory industries, and yet toxic chemicals and solvents sit in open containers filling the air with powerful fumes. An American Friends Service Committee worker in northern Mexico heard about cases where ten or twelve women passed out at once. In one electronics assembly plant in Penang, Malaysia, workers have to dip circuits into open vats of acid. The workers wear gloves, but when these leak, burns are common and occasionally fingers are lost. Textile factories pack in workers and often the temperatures rise over 100F. Textile dust, which causes permanent lung damage, fills the air and management sometimes provides pep pills and amphetamine injections just so orders can be filled.

There are a lot of things in this society that we have little control over contributing to (e.g. through taxes). There are some things, though, that we can decide. It is up to us as consumers to know what we are buying, how it got to us, and the practices of the company which produces it. It is often very hard to find out about companies/products, but once we know this information it is up to us to act on it. Boycotting Multinational corporations is a step in fighting capitalism and third world oppression, and one in which we can put our ideals into practice. This is something we can choose ourselves.

The Corporations

BANK OF AMERICA
In Guatemala, it is the largest private creditor and ranks second only to the government as a source of capital for the agro-export sector. It has extensive holdings in South Africa to whom it gives many loans.

BORDEN
Brand names: Cracker Jack, Eagle condensed milk, ReaLemon, Elmer's glue, Mystik tapes, Krylon spray paints. Owns 48 food and dairy plants and 49 chemical facilities overseas. The company is now expanding into oil and gas.

CASTLE AND COOK
Brand names: Dole bananas and pineapples, Bumble Bee Seafoods, Royal Alaskan Seafoods, Bud of California produce, Pool Sweep swimming pool cleaner. Castle and Cook were two missionaries who made a fortune in Hawaii and soon expanded their interests throughout the world. The company is prominent in Central America. In 1976 it transfered its railroad network in Honduras to the government, which allowed the company to continue operating the railroad and to retain title to all rolling stock. In 1964, Castle and Cook gained control of Standard Fruits and has allied itself with military governments in Central America to crush unionization and worker organizing. It is a heavy user of pesticides.

CHASE MANHATTAN
The third largest U.S. bank and a large shareholder in many of the big multinationals. Chase Manhattan specializes in helping multinationals, particularly oil companies, move their money around the world to get the best from fluctuations in currency markets. The company has exercised its influence over foreign policy through the leadership of its former chair David Rockefeller in such groups as the Trilateral Commission, the Council of Foreign Relations, and the Americas Society.

CITICORP
Citicorp is the largest U.S. lender to South Africa. The bulk of the company's deposits are overseas, where loans are usually large ones made to governments and multinationals. Citicorp has been known to discriminate against small businesses involved in third world local markets in favour of large corporations and businesses which provide products for export.

COCA COLA
Brand names: Coca Cola, Tab, Sprite, Fanta, Mr. Pibb, Fresca, Minute Maid, Hi-C, Snow Crop, Maryland Club, Taylor Wines. Coke is sold in 135 countries. In 1978, the average consumption of soft drinks was 36 gallons per person compared to 25 gallons of milk. A strong anti-union company.

COLGATE PALMOLIVE
Brand names: Colgate toothpaste, Ultra Brite toothpaste, Hand-I-Wipes, Curity and Curad first aid products, Helena Rubenstein cosmetics, Irish Spring soap, Palmolive soap, Ajax cleaner, Fab laundry detergent, Water Maid rice products, Etonic golf and running shoes. Colgate owns and leases 31.7 million square feet of manufacturing, distribution, and office facilities around the world. It markets in 58 countries and exports to 70 more. The company does more than half its business overseas.

EXXON
Brand names: Exxon, Esso, Uniflo, Zelog computers, Qyx typewriters, Quip telephone devices. Exxon's annual sales roughly match the Gross National Product of countries like Mexico, Sweden, and Iran. Exxon brings in $10 million in sales per hour! Its 65,600 gas stations around the world sell gas to millions of customers every day. The Rockefeller family dominates the Exxon Empire.

GOODYEAR
Brand names: Goodyear tires, Kelly-Springfield tires, and Lee tires. Called "the Brute" by other rubber companies because of its high-powered marketing strategies, Goodyear is the top seller of tires in the U.S. Goodyear operates on the "runaway shop" premise, having closed its factory in Akron, Ohio, to avoid union demands, and headed south for cheaper wages. In 1977, the Securities and Exchange Commission accused Goodyear of using slush funds for foreign payoffs and illegal political contributions. They also manufacture components for nuclear weapons.

NABISCO
Brand names: Oreo cookies, Fig Newton cookies, Chips Ahoy cookies, Nabisco breakfast cereals, Premium saltines, Wheat Thin crackers, Mr. Salty pretzels, Junior Mints, Milkbone dog biscuits, Geritol vitamins, Sominex sleep aid, Acu-test in-home pregnancy test, Rose Milk skin care, Aqua Velva toiletries. Nabisco merged with Standard Brands in 1981 and does a third of its business outside of the U.S.

PEPSICO
Brand names: Pepsi-Cola, Mountain Dew, Fritos, Chee-tos, Doritos, Lay's, Taco Bell, Pizza Hut, North American Van Lines, Wilson sporting goods, Pro Staff golf balls, Chris Evert Autograph tenns rackets. Pepsi is the second largest soft drink company, largest maker of sporting goods, and is the fourth largest fast-food server in the U.S. In 1980, workers at a PepsiCo trucking firm charged that of 820 long-distance drivers employed, only five were Black, and eight Hispanic. Pepsi settled the lawsuit with a payment to the eighty-two Blacks denied jobs.

R.J. REYNOLDS
Brand names: Winston, Camel, and Vantage cigarettes, Prince Albert tobacco, Del Monte, Hawaiian Punch, ChunKing Chinese food, Patio Mexican food. In and out of tangles with the Securities Exchange Commission, RJR has been involved with illegal political contributions and objectionable corporate payments. In 1975, the Wall Street Journal

reported a $500,000 payment to a Guatemalan "business consultant" who negotiated a deal with the Guatemalan government that allowed Del Monte to acquire a 55,000 acre banana plantation despite initial government opposition. RJR's food business is based on exports: Philippine bananas to Japan, Mexican asparagus to Europe, African fruit to the U.K. RJR is extensively involved in South Africa.

STANDARD OIL

Brand names: Chevron, Standard, Ortho chemicals. Standard Oil sells gas at 14,000 filling stations in U.S., Canada, Central America, Puerto Rico, and Tahiti. There were 147 violations of federal drilling regulations in 1970 alone, and $156 million in unpaid taxes in 1977. Chevron, Standard, and Ortho all produce various chemicals and pesticides, and Ortho is a major pharmaceutical company.

TEXACO

Brand names: Fire Chief, Sky Chief, Havoline. Texaco has been known for its long history of rotten deeds and deals. It sold $6 million worth of oil to the Spanish dictator Franco in violation of the neutrality act, and shipped oil to Germany during WW2. In Honduras, Texaco has the nation's only facility for refining crude oil and storing petroleum. When Texaco decides to shut-down its plant (as it did six times in 1981), it paralyzes up to 95 percent of the country's transport. Texaco has used this monopoly to get more money on various oil refining deals.

UNITED BRANDS

Brand names: Chiquita, E-Z Beef, Full-O-Life plants, A+W restaurants. United Brands is the largest private landowner in Central America. In addition to assisting in coups, using bribes to lower taxes, and attempting to destabilize governments it disfavours, it runs very sexist advertising campaigns. A very anti-communist company which supplied two of its ships for the Bay of Pigs invasion.

Information taken from:
Dollars and Dictators – AG Central America by Tom Barry, Wood, and Deb Preusch, 1983.
The New Our Bodies, Our Selves by the Boston Women' Health Book Collective, 1984.
A Book About Birth Control by the Montreal Health Press.
Dirty Fingers In Dirty Pies.
Resistance, no. 12.
various encyclopedias from the library for statistics on exports, imports, etc.

– SUE

INTIFADAH!

More than eighteen months ago, in December 1987, the Palestinian people rose up against the Israeli occupation. The Intifadah, the Uprising, has become a critical point in the Palestinian struggle, bringing that struggle into the very centre of the occupied land. What is so powerful about this Uprising is that, unlike Palestinian Liberation Organization military attacks, which hit Israeli targets outside of the occupied lands, this demonstration of resistance is carried out by an entire people. Before the Intifadah, there had never been any general strikes or mass demonstrations, nor had Arabs of pre-1967 Israel joined Arabs of the territories.

Even before the Intifadah, Palestinians faced a daily oppression, a daily suffering. These conditions intensified between June and August 1987, when a series of pogroms against Palestinians began. Suddenly, in a given neighbourhood, all the apartments, houses or rooms rented by Arabs were vandalized and burned. Arabs were beaten and expelled. Police gave no protection, and the neighbourhood was "free" of Arabs. To describe this, the Hebrew press used a German word, *Arabrein*, derived from the Nazi word *Jedenrein*: "clean of Jews." To compare this process to that used by the Nazis is no mistake. This is believed to be one of the instigations of the revolt. Another important factor is what has been called the "Transfer Proposal." This has been the current in Israel from around August 1987, and it is a proposal to expel *all* Palestinians, both from Israel and from the occupied territories. This idea of mass expulsions first surfaced in 1939, with Zionist leader Zeev Jabotinsky. Even more recently Ariel Sharon stated, in 1982, that his own long-term strategy was to push Palestinians out of the West Bank, keeping only enough for labour. Rabbi Meir Kahane, a former American and founder of the *Jewish Defense League*, regularly calls for the purification of Israel by excising the Arab "cancer." Kahane reportedly enjoys growing support among Israel's younger generation.

The Palestinian struggle for independence has a long history, having gone through four successive military occupations: Turkish, British, Jordanian, and Israeli. The first civilian administration of the British occupation, in the early 1900s, was presided over by Zionist Herber Samuel, who, along with other Zionists in control of legislation laws and immigration, vigorously pursued the Zionist program of creating the state of Israel. By 1947, with large numbers of Jews fleeing persecution in war-torn Europe, and moving to Palestine, the Jewish population swelled to close to thirty percent of the entire populace. A United Nations resolution recommended partitioning Palestine into two states, one Jewish, and one Palestinian. Palestinians, still the large majority, rejected the proposal of splitting their country. By March 1948, with the British forces disarming and repressing any Palestinian resistance, Zionist forces went on the offensive to bring a military solution to the problem. By May 15, over 400,000 Palestinians had been driven out of their homes and land. In the end of the 1948 war up to 800,000 Palestinians were homeless, and more than 400 Palestinian villages had been razed. The newly created state of Israel also enlarged the area provided in the partitioning plan by taking half the area destined for a reduced Palestinian state. With this, only the West Band and Gaza were left to the Palestinians, which were administered by Jordan and Egypt. In the 1967 war, Israel attacked its neighbouring Arab countries, and took control of the West Band and Gaza. Thus a complete turn-about of the situation was engineered. In 1947 Jews possessed less than nineteen percent of the land, now Arabs are left in possession of fifteen percent of that same land, with the rest in Jewish control. It has become a brutal example of the oppressed becoming the oppressor, the executed now the executioner. So, as has been said in a French journal, *Le Brise-Glace* (translated in *Fifth Estate*), "however repressive it may have been from its very origins, Zionism represented a movement of emancipation for many oppressed Jews. Once Israel was established, Zionism, whether left or right, has been nothing more than a project to defend a state which, to survive, is condemned to practice a policy of apartheid internally and imperialism externally."

Apartheid Internally

The system of apartheid Israel practices has drawn deserving comparisons to the apartheid in South Africa, with whom Israel has had a long and prosperous economic and military relationship with, dealing in arms and intelligence support (a tale of two fascist states?).

Like non-whites in South Africa, Palestinians must carry identification papers at all times, with threat of imprisonment. They must follow strict curfews; no one from the West Bank or Gaza can be in Jerusalem after midnight. This also is the same for most Israeli towns, and no Palestinians may be in those towns after dark. Palestinians are not allowed to study or train for certain jobs, especially high-technology jobs. This, as in South Africa, perpetuates an inequality, which provides Israel with a cheap, "unskilled," and ultimately dependent labour force. Any symbol connected to Palestinian liberation, the PLO, the Palestinian flag, is forbidden. West Band and Gaza Palestinians are subject to deportation by Israeli military decision, and last year an Israeli court also extended this to residents of Jerusalem. Dozens of prisoners who have been expelled have been flown by helicopter into Lebanon. In fact, Palestinians maybe held for up to *six months* without any trial, often in very harsh conditions. Prisoners are beaten, tortured, and sexually harassed. One women who was being interrogated was kept locked in a closet, described as a "stand up coffin," for four days. A prisoner was reportedly beaten and then taken in an army helicopter and dropped to the ground below. Refugee camps have become virtual concentration camps, with Palestinians subject to collective punishment and attack from both Israeli soldiers and settlers.

Shoot-to-Punish

Since the Intifadah began, up to 500 Palestinians have been killed by Israelis, with *at least* 6,000 imprisoned, possibly up to 12,000. In contrast, only about twenty-five Israelis have been killed. Israeli soldiers indiscriminate attacks, without regard for "guilt" or innocence, have hit women, men, children, the young and the old. Besides breaking bones with clubs and boots, Israeli soldiers have used live ammunition, poisonous U.S. made CS tear gas, and deadly plastic bullets on protesters. All these weapons have inflicted death and thousands of injuries. Witnesses have reported seeing soldiers firing indiscriminately into crowds, as well as seeing snipers and selected shootings.

Plastic bullets were put into use to enforce a "shoot-to-punish" policy announced last September 1988 after live rounds, tear gas and clubs proved "ineffective." The plastic bullets, "non-lethal" at 230 feet and, according to officials, has only been issued to officers and snipers trained in their use, has been both used at close-quarters and enjoyed a wide distribution as standard weaponry among the soldiers. Approximately half the plastic bullets do not shatter or exit the victim (though they have penetrated and exited skulls and major organs), leaving plastic bullets inside the person, who often cannot under go surgery to remove it as it would result in even greater injury. Such injuries are not even registered, as there is no bullet, and the number of deaths due to plastic bullets is also unknown as Palestinian physicians are prohibited – by local religions codes and Israeli military regulations – from removing bullets post-mortem. The typical victim is the young, 13–15 years old.

Collective punishment has been used to divide communities and punish them for resistance. Entire villages have been put under army siege, such as Idna, where Palestinians have been extremely active and militant. There, rebels attacked Israeli soldiers with not only rocks, but also Molotovs and a few army grenades. In retaliation, the village was cut off of all water, electricity, and food supplies. Schools were closed, and shops were forbidden to open. Other villages have been put under similar conditions, with no one allowed to leave or enter. Entire homes and buildings have been demolished and bulldozed where just one suspected activist may live, or if the houses are, oddly enough, found to be outside the *licensed* area. One Israeli civilian bulldozer operator working for the army told a journalist that he destroyed a home in one West Bank village because it was between two homes slated for destruction and "in the way."

Resistance

If the repression by Israeli soldiers has been vigorous, so too has the Palestinian resistance. The rebels in the street with stones, slings, bottles, and molotovs, entire communities carrying out General strikes closing down entire areas, the boycott of the Israeli economy, have clearly shown that the Palestinians, after twenty years of "quiet," like all oppressed peoples, will never remain docile. To paint a picture of a beaten, submissive, people would be inaccurate. The oppressed fight back, and attack their oppressors too! For outrages, such as killings, there are massive demonstrations, even under threat of further army attack. In defiance of the laws forbidding any symbols of liberation, a "Flag Day" was called for, in clandestine leaflets, in which Palestinians plastered villages with the Palestinian flag, on telephone poles, buildings, even on balloons. There has been an ongoing campaign to refuse to pay taxes, and many tax collectors have resigned their positions, and in one mass resignation 500 Arab cops resigned. Action is also taken against collaborators, who receive special privileges, weapons, and protection by the Israeli state, and have had their cars firebombed, houses attacked, and have been ostracized from the community. In some cases, they have been executed. In the West Bank, Palestinians have also taken control for managing their own health and education systems.

Resistance to the Israeli occupation and brutality has also come from leftist Jews, who have condemned their country's actions and have continually called for dialogue with the PLO to resolve the situation. Some Israeli soldiers have also refused to enforce the occupation.

A boycott of Israeli products has been called for and demonstrations have taken place across North America, as well as vigils for the Palestinian people. It is important to realize that the system of repression of the Palestinian people is the same system attacking the people of Central America and South Africa and Asia. It is a system that is maintained through economic and military support for our very own countries, the advanced industrial countries. Israel is itself a part of this structure of imperialism, supplying arms and training to fascist regimes and death squads in Guatemala, Honduras, and in Africa. The unconditional support from the U.S., and with that the support of the entire western imperialist block, is what gives Israel the strength to practise apartheid, the same situation as in South Africa. With this the Soviet block also maneuvres its way around, coming to the aid of many liberation movements not through an actual desire to see oppressed people become free, but rather through its own imperials designs. So, keeping these important factors in mind, we are in total solidarity with the Palestinian people, the Intifadah!!

Down with the Occupation!

Endless Struggle 10 (1989)

INTIFADAH!

More than 18 months ago, in December, 1987, the Palestinian people rose up against the Israeli occupation. The Intifadah, the Uprising, has become a critical point in the Palestinian struggle, bringing that struggle into the very centre of the occupied land. What is so powerful about this Uprising is that, unlike Palestinian Liberation Organisation military attacks, which hit Israeli targets outside of the occupied lands, this demonstration of resistance is carried out by an entire people. Before the Intifadah, there had never been any general strikes or mass demonstrations, nor had Arabs of the territories been joined by Arabs of pre-1967 Israel.

Even before the Intifadah, Palestinians faced a daily oppression, a daily suffering. These conditions intensified between June & August 1987, when a series of pogroms against Palestinians began. Suddenly, in a given neighborhood, all the apartments, houses or room rented by Arabs were vandalised & burned. Arabs were beaten & expelled. Police gave no protection, & the neighborhood was "free" of Arabs. To describe this, the Hebrew press used a German word, Arabrein, derived from the Nazi word Judenrein -"clean of Jews". To compare this process to that used by the Nazis is no mistake. This is believed to be one of the instigations of the revolt. Another important factor is what has been called the "Transfer Proposal". This has been the current in Israel from around Aug. '87, & it is a proposal to expell all Palestinians, both from Israel & from the occupied territories. This idea of mass expulsions first surfaced in 1939, with Zionist leader Zeev Jabotinsky. Even more recently Ariel Sharon stated, in 1982, that his own long-term strategy was to push Palestinians out of the West Bank, keeping only enough for labour. Rabbi Meir Kahane, a former american & founder of the Jewish Defence League , regularily calls for the purification of Israel by excising the Arab "cancer". Kahane reportedly enjoys growing support among Israels younger generation.

The Palestinian struggle for independance has a long history, having gone through 4 succesive military occupations-Turkish, British, Jordanian, & Israeli. The first civilian administration of the British occupation, in the early 1900s', was presided over by Zionist Herbert Samuel, who, along with other Zionists in control of legislating laws & immigration, vigorously pursued the Zionist program of creating the state of Israel. By 1947, with large numbers of Jews fleeing persecution in war-torn Europe, and moving to Palestine, the Jewish population swelled to close to 30% of the entire populace. A United Nations resolution recommended partitioning Palestine into 2 states, one Jewish, & one Palestinian. Palestinians, still the large majority, rejected the proposal of splitting their country. By March 1948, with the British forces disarming & repress-

ing any Palestinian resistance, Zionist forces went on the offensive to bring a military solution to the problem. By May 15, over 400,000 Palestinians had been driven out of their homes & land. In the end of the 1948 war up to 800,000 Palestinians were homeless, & more than 400 Palestinian villages had been razed. The newly created state of Israel also enlarged the area provided in the partition plan by taking half the area destined for a reduced Palestinian state. With this, only the West Bank & Gaza were left to the Palestinians, which were administered by Jordan & Egypt. In the 1967 war, Israel attacked its neighboring Arab countries, & took control of the West Bank & Gaza. Thus a complete turn-about of the situation was engineered; in 1947 Jews possessed less than 10% of the land, now Arabs are left in possession of 15% of that same land, with the rest in Jewish control. It has become a brutal example of the oppressed becoming the oppressor, the executed now the executioner. So, as has been said in a French journal, Le Brise-Glace (translated in Fifth Estate)-"however repressive it may have been from its very origins, Zionism represented a movement of emancipation for many oppressed Jews. Once Israel was established, Zionism, whether left or right- has been nothing more than a project to defend a state which, to survive, is condemned to practise a policy of apartheid internally & imperialism externally".

APARTHEID INTERNALLY

The system of apartheid Israel practises has drawn deserving comparisons to the apartheid in S. Africa,with whom Israel has had a long & prosperous economic & military relationship with, dealing in arms & intelligence support (a tale of two fascist states?).

Like non-whites in S. Africa, Palestinians must carry identification papers at all times, with threat of imprisonment. They must follow strict curfews; no one from the West Bank or Gaza can be in Jerusalem after midnight. This also is the same for most Israeli towns, and no Palestinians may be in those towns after dark. Palestinians are not allowed to study or train for certain jobs, especially high-technology jobs. This, as in S. Africa, perpetuates an in-equality which provides Israel with a cheap, "unskilled", & ultimately dependent labour force. Any symbol connected to Palestinian liberation, the PLO, the Palestinian flag, is forbidden. West Bank and Gaza Palestinians are subject to deportation by Israeli military decision, and

DOWN WITH THE OCCUPATION! PALESTINE LIVES!!

ENDLESS STRUGGLE 12

last year an Israeli court also extended this to residents of Jerusalem. Dozens of prisoners who have been expelled have been flown by helicopter into Lebanon. In fact, Palestinians may be heldup to 6 months without any trial, often in very harsh conditions. Prisoners are beaten, tortured, & sexually harrassed. One women who was being interogated was kept locked in a closet, described as a "stand up coffin", for 4 days. A prisoner was reportedly beaten & then taken in an army helicopter & dropped to the ground below. Refugee camps havebecome virtual concentration camps, with Palestinians subject to collective punishment & attack from both Israeli soldiers and settlers.

SHOOT-TO-PUNISH

Since the Intifadah began, up to 600 Palestinians have been killed by Israelis', with at least 6,000 imprisined, possibly up to 12,000. In contrast, only about 25 Israelis have been killed. Israeli soldiers indiscriminate attacks, without regard for "guilt" or innocence, have hit women, amen, children, the young & the old. Besides breaking bones with clubs & boots, Israeli soldiers have used live ammunition, poisonous US-made CS tear gas, & deadly plastic bullets on protesters. All these weapons have inflicted death and thousands of injuries. Witnesses have reported seeing soldiers firing indiscriminently into crowds, as well as seeing snipers & selected shootings:

Plastic bullets were put into use to enforce a "shoot-to-punish" policy announced last Sept. '88 after live rounds, tear gas, & clubs proved "inneffective'. The plastic bullets, 'non-lethal' at 230 feet &,according to officials, has only been issued to officers and snipers trained in their use, has been both used at close-quarters & enjoyed a wide distribution as standard weaponry among the soldiers. Approximately half the plastic bullets do not shatter or exit the victim (though they have penetrated & exited skulls & major organs), leaving plastic bullets inside the person, who often cannot under go surgery to remove it as it would result in even greater injury. Such injuries are not even registered, as there is no bullet, & the number of deaths due to plastic bullets is also unknown as Palestinian physicians are prohibited- by local religions codes & Israeli military regulations- from removing bullets post-mortem. The typical victim is the young, 13-15 years old.

Collective punishment has been used to divide communities & punish them for resistance. Entire villages have put under army siege, such as Idna, where Palestinians have been extremely active & militant. There, rebels attacked Israeli soldiers with not only rocks, but also molotovs & a few army grenades. In retaliation, the village was cut off of all water, electricity, & food supplies. Schools were closed, & shops were forbidden to open. Other villages have been put under similiar conditions,with no one allowed to leave or enter. Entire homes & buildings have been demolished & bulldozed where just one suspected activist may live, or if the houses are,oddly enough, found to be outside the 'licensed' area. One Israelian civilian bulldozer operator working for the army told a journalist that he destroyed a home in one West Bank village because it was between 2 homes slated for destruction & "in the way".

Israeli plastic bullet

RESISTANCE

If the repression by Israeli soldiers has been vigorous, so too has the Palestinian resistance. The rebels in the streets with stones, slings, bottles & molotovs, entire communities carrying out General strikes closing down entire areas, the boycott of the Israeli economy, have clearly shown that the Palestinians, after 20 years of "quiet", like all oppressed peoples, will never remain docile. To paint a picture of a beaten, submissive, people wouldbe inaccurate. The oppressed fight back, & attack their oppressors too! For outrages, such as killings, there are massive demonstrations, even under threat of further army attack. In defiance of the laws forbidding any symbols of liberation, a "Flag Day" was called for, in clandestine leaflets, in which Palestinians plastered villages with the Palestinian flag, on telephone poles , buildings, even on balloons. There has been an ongoing campaign to refuse to pay taxes, & many tax collectors have resigned. Palestinian kops have also resigned their positions, & in one mass resignation 500 Arab kops resigned. Action is also taken against collaborators, who reciewe special priveleges, weapons, & protection by the Israeli state, & have had their cars fire-bombed, houses attacked, & have been ostracised from the community. In some cases, they have been executed. In the West Bank, Palestinians have also taken control for managing their own health & education systems.

Resistance to the Israeli occupation & brutality has alsocome from leftist Jews, who have condemned their countries actions & have continually called for dialogue with the PLO to resolve the situation. Some Israeli soldiers have also refused to enforce the occupation.

A boycott of Israeli products has been called for, & demonstrations have taken place across N. America, as well as vigils for the Palestinians. It is important to realise that the system of repression of the Palestinian people is the same system attacking the people of Central America & S. Africa & Asia. It is a system that is maintained through economic & military support from our very own countries, the advanced industrial countries. Israel is itself a part of this structure ofimperialism, supplying arms & training to fascist regimes & death squads in Guatemala, Honduras, & in Africa. The unconditional support from the US, & with that the support of the entire western imperialist block, is what gives Israel the strength to practise apartheid, the same situation as in S. Africa. With this the Soviet block also manouevres its way around, coming to the aid of many liberation movements not through an actual desire to see oppressed people become free, but rather through its own imperialist designs. So, keepingthese important factors in mind, we are in total solidarity with the Palestinian people, the Intifadah!!

Down with the Occupation!

13 ENDLESS STRUGGLE

PALESTINE

INTIFADAH!

AFRICA..ASIA..LATIN AMERICA...ONE ENEMY..IMPERIALISM

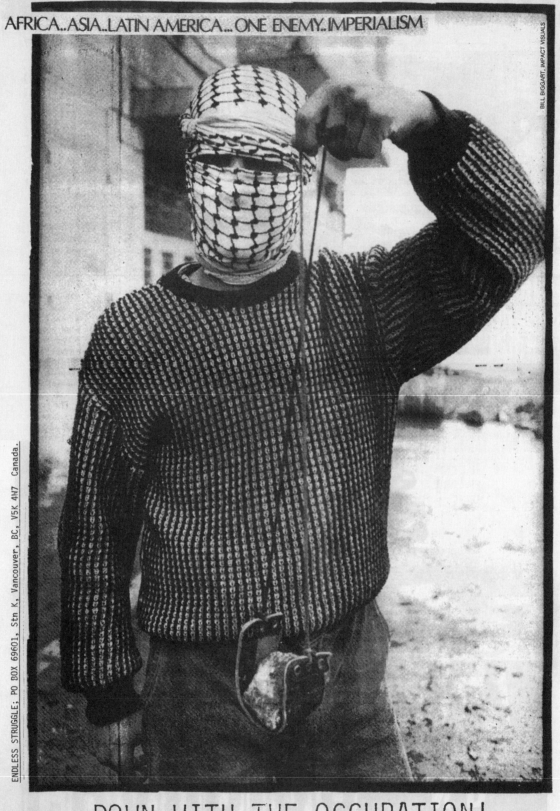

BILL BIGGART, IMPACT VISUALS

ENDLESS STRUGGLE; PO BOX 69601, Stn. K, Vancouver, BC, V5K 4N7 Canada.

DOWN WITH THE OCCUPATION!
SUPPORT THE PALESTINIAN UPRISING!!

Endless Struggle 10 (1989)

Resistance 15 (1991)

OKA, 1990

CHRONOLOGY AT OKA

March 11, 1990: Kanehsatake Mohawks blockade the road leading to a 22-hectare pine forest (planted by Mohawks) bordering the Oka Golf Club. The municipality of Oka approved clear-cutting of the forest to make way for a 9-hole extension to a local golf course. This land is part of a much larger territory which successive treaties between the Mohawks and European states define as Mohawk land.

April 27: The municipality of Oka brings an injunction against all members of the Kanehsatake Mohawk community, ordering them to remove the roadblocks and stop interfering with traffic on the forest road.

May 3: At Oka, near Kanehsatake, talks between Mohawk representatives and federal, provincial and municipal negotiators break down.

July 8: Mohawk roadblocks at Kanehsatake are fortified.

July 10: Oka Mayor Jean Ouellette refuses to negotiate further with the Mohawks or to postpone the clear-cutting of the forest and asks the Québec provincial police (*Sûreté du Québec* — SQ) to intervene to remove barricades at Kanehsatake. Mohawks strengthen the fortifications.

July 11: At 5:30 A.M., more than 100 SQ officers armed with automatic weapons attack the barricades near Oka. They begin their raid by saturating the area with tear gas for three hours, then, at 8:30 A.M., firing concussion grenades and live ammunition in the direction of Mohawk women and children while attempting to dismantle the barricade. Members of the Mohawk Warrior Society fire into the air to warn the SQ officers, who respond, at 8:40 A.M., by firing thousands of rounds into the Mohawk encampment. The firing lasts 18 seconds. During the firing, Cpl. Marcel Lemay of the SQ is shot in the head and killed. The SQ fires tear gas at the main barricade, but the wind blows it back toward them, and the attacking officers flee, leaving SQ cars, vans and a front-end loader behind. The cars are smashed and used to strengthen the barricade. This is a humiliating defeat for the SQ and radically undermines the authority of the Québec government, as armed Mohawks are defying the state and getting away with it. Kanehsatake is completely sealed off from the outside world by hundreds of police. As news of the SQ raid reaches Kahnawake (a Mohawk community of 6,000 people immediately to the south of Montréal) the Mercier bridge, a major traffic artery linking Montréal with the south shore, is blockaded by armed Warriors who threaten to blow up the bridge if there is a second attack at Oka. They also blockade highways 132 and 138, which run through Kahnawake.

July 12: Québec Minister for Native Affairs John Ciaccia meets Mohawk negotiators at the Kanehsatake roadblock in an attempt to defuse the standoff.

July 13: Ciaccia calls for the federal government "to assume its responsibilities" in regard to the standoff after meeting with Mohawk negotiators behind the barricades at Kanehsatake.

July 14: In Toronto more than 300 people demonstrate in support of the Mohawks.

July 15: Talks between government officials and Mohawks break off.

July 16: In Châteauguay, a community on the south shore right next to Kahnawake and affected by the blockade, nightly anti-Mohawk demonstrations at the Mercier bridge, organized by "Solidarité Châteauguay", the brainchild of ex-SQ officer Yvon Poitras, turn into racist riots. Mohawk Warriors are burned in effigy, and the crowd repeatedly attacks the SQ who place themselves between the rioters and the Mohawk barricades. The protesters call for army intervention and compensation from the Québec government. Most of the protesters come from outside Châteauguay. Reliable sources indicate that the Ku Klux Klan is organizing in Châteauguay. Over the following weeks there will be repeated racist attacks against Mohawks.

In Montréal, the municipal police riot squad attacks a demonstration of 200 people protesting the SQ raid, sending two demonstrators to hospital and arresting 47.

July 17: As Premier of Québec, Robert Bourassa orders the army to mobilize and move to staging areas near the barricades at Kanehsatake and Kahnawake.

July 18: Protests take place in support of the Mohawks in Montréal, Ottawa and Québec.

Nearly 250 native leaders come to Kahnawake to discuss the situation with Mohawk representatives.

A tentative agreement is reached between Mohawk and provincial negotiators, involving three major points: (1) withdrawal of significant numbers of SQ officers; (2) a public inquiry into the conduct of the federal and provincial governments; and (3) that John Ciaccia, Québec Minister for Native Affairs, attempt to set up direct nation-to-nation negotiations between Mohawks and the federal government.

In B.C., Manitoba and at Kingston in Ontario, native and non-native protesters block roads or slow traffic in solidarity with the Mohawks. In Nova Scotia, 30 Micmacs begin a hunger strike in protest.

July 19: In Toronto, 60 demonstrators protest government repression and support the Mohawk cause.

A shipment of food, medical supplies, fuel is delivered to the Mohawk community at Oka by Mohawks of the Six Nations territory near Brantford.

July 21: Negotiations break off.

July 22: 200 Laval residents try to deliver food to Mohawks at Kanehsatake, but are turned back by the SQ, which has totally sealed off Oka.

Some 200 native protesters rally on Parliament Hill in Ottawa, demanding that the federal government enter into direct negotiations with Mohawks.

Federal Deputy Minister for Indian Affairs Harry Swain refers to the Warriors as a "gang of criminals" and alleges that they have hijacked negotiations and seized control of Kanehsatake by force. His outrageously provocative statement is only one of many made in the middle of a delicate negotiating process by government officials in an explosive, life-threatening situation.

July 24: Parti Québécois leader Jacques Parizeau declares to a press conference that the SQ should have cleared the barricades on the Mercier bridge by force as soon as they were put up, before the Warriors could solidify their position. He refers to the Warriors as "terrorists". Well-informed readers will remember that Parizeau was a member of the PQ government that ordered hundreds of SQ officers onto Micmac territory at Restigouche in 1981 over a fishing dispute.

July 25: 1000 people demonstrate in support of Mohawks in downtown Montréal.

An SQ official says that the SQ has opened 1000 files alleging criminal activity by Mohawks since the July 11 attack.

July 29: 2500 people rally at Paul Sauvé park near Oka in support of the Mohawk people. Representatives from tribes all across Canada and the U.S. are present, and non-natives come from as far as Kingston, Ontario.

August 1: In Montréal, 250 demonstrators met at Lafontaine Park to support the Mohawk cause and denounce the repression.

In Châteauguay, 10,000 demonstrators demand army intervention. MPs Ricardo López and Vincent Della Noce, both Conservatives, call for army intervention.

August 5: Robert Bourassa gives Mohawk negotiators a 48-hour ultimatum to resume negotiations, and declares that "appropriate measures" (read army intervention) would be taken if they do not.

August 8: Mulroney appoints judge Alan Gold to negotiate the preconditions to full negotiations. He also announces that the army is available to the Québec government.

August 10: By now, Oka is a ghost town. At least 80% of the townspeople have left. Micmacs in Nova Scotia have smuggled at least 3 truckloads of food to Mohawks behind police barricades. Many of the 50 Micmacs in Oka take shifts at the Mohawk barricades.

August 11: 1000 people attend a demonstration in support of Mohawk demands at Carré Phillips in Montréal. In Châteauguay, particularly violent clashes take place at the Mercier bridge between SQ and anti-Mohawk rioters, who throw Molotov cocktails.

August 12: Gold and government and Mohawk negotiators agree to three preconditions: (1) free access to food and supplies for Kahnawake and Kanehsatake; (2) free movement of Mohawk advisors of all kinds; and (3) formation of an international team of observers to monitor events during negotiations.

August 13: Ojibwa protesters blockade the only east-west passenger rail line in Canada.

August 14, 9:30 P.M.: Units of the 5th Mechanized Brigade, based at Valcartier near Québec, move to their forward staging areas: at Blainville and St-Benoît near Oka and St-Rémi and Farnham near Châteauguay. The movement involves 4,400 soldiers. Of these, 2,629 are troops, with 1144 vehicles. The troops are equipped with mortars, several hundred armoured personnel carriers, 90 armoured cars, several 105 mm field guns, helicopters, TOW missile launchers and 3 Leopard tanks equipped with 105 mm guns. In short, enough military power to destroy Oka many times over. At this time, an estimated 200-300 Warriors are behind the barricades at Kanehsatake, accompanied by women and children.

August 16: Direct negotiations begin between Mohawks and federal and provincial governments.

August 20, morning: The first army troops arrive at Kanehsatake and Kahnawake and take up positions near the major barricades (at Kanehsatake, 500 metres away from the main barricade). Mohawk negotiators break off talks with the federal and provincial governments. Racists stone a caravan of 75 Mohawk cars leaving Kahnawake while the police, who held up the cars for hours while the mob gathered, do absolutely nothing to stop it. Joe Armstrong, a 71-year-old Mohawk man, dies of a heart attack following the stoning. Several other Mohawks are injured.

August 22: A Mohawk woman bleeding from childbirth complications is held up for one hour on the Mercier bridge by the SQ and a racist mob. Ojibway war veterans attempt to talk to soldiers at Kanehsatake. They are prevented by SQ officers at police lines, who assault them.

August 23, morning: The army advances its armoured cars and troops to within 30 feet of the main Mohawk barricade at Kanehsatake. One false move could result in a bloodbath. Mohawk negotiators break off negotiations.

August 25: In a sinister development, Québec "Public Security" Minister Sam Elkas says he intends to look into the creation of a European-style militarized police force specialized in suppressing strikes, riots and protests, etc.

August 26: Mulroney makes public declaration to the effect that the government is "losing patience".

August 27, 10:30 A.M.: An incident at the main barricade in Kanehsatake nearly triggers a massacre.

August 28: Protesters block a street in Vancouver, demanding withdrawal of the army from Oka. Federal negotiator Bernard Roy breaks off negotiations with Mohawk representatives. Premier Bourassa orders the army to remove the barricades. Warriors dismantle the Mercier bridge barricade with the army's help. During this period (from about August 28 to September 1), a large number of Warriors and their weapons are evacuated from Kahnawake by light planes using the paved roads inside Warrior-held territory as runways. The planes fly very low to avoid radar detection. A thousand demonstrators block Boul. René Lévesque in downtown Montréal for 5 hours, demanding the withdrawal of the army.

August 29: A defence lawyer for three Kanehsatake Mohawk men publicly charges the SQ and Montréal police with torturing them until they signed confessions. The three men are: Daniel Nicholas, André Simon and Angus Jacobs. Eight hundred people demonstrate in downtown Montréal against the army's presence at Oka.

August 30, 8:00 P.M.: Federal and provincial governments break off talks with Mohawk negotiators.

September 1, 1:00 P.M.: Without warning, the army and SQ overrun the barricades at Kanehsatake and Kahnawake. At any second, a full-scale bloodbath could break out, resulting in dozens of casualties. The vast majority of land held by the Warriors is retaken, and they retreat to the Treatment Centre, a federal building that the SQ does not have the authority to enter. The army surrounds 100 Mohawk women and children seeking shelter in the food bank. Warrior-held territory is reduced to a small strip of land around the Treatment Centre.

September 4: In Kahnawake, there is a combined SQ-army raid (40 armoured vehicles and 200 troops) at the Longhouse, the site of traditional Mohawk government. The SQ seize a few weapons, which Mohawk sources say were planted.

September 6: The army's proposal for the surrender of Warriors in the Treatment Centre is rejected on their behalf by their mediator Terry Doxtator.

September 8: A 4-6 man army reconnaissance team slips into the Warrior-held area at night and severely beats Randy Horne, who is hospitalized and held by the military. During this period, incidents that can explode into lethal violence happen at the razor wire every day.

September 9: More than 500 native people from all over North America rally at Paul Sauvé park near Oka in support of the Mohawks in the Treatment Centre.

September 13: SQ applies court-ordered blackout of journalists' cellular phones at Kanehsatake T.C.

September 18: A combined army-SQ raid is carried out without warning on Tekawitha Island, which is part of Kahnawake. Immediately, 600-1000 Mohawks (about one-sixth of the community) run to the bridge near the army's landing site and block the army's advance. A riot ensues, with Mohawks beating soldiers caught between the crowd and the water. Two automatic rifles are ripped out of soldiers' hands by enraged Mohawks. The army launches tear gas canisters and fires bursts of machine-gun fire into the air. About 75 Mohawks are treated at Kateri Hospital in Kahnawake for tear gas inhalation.

September 20: Lt.-Gen. Kent Foster, the officer in charge of the army operation, holds a press conference, declaring that the army is preparing plans to withdraw in stages from Kanehsatake and Kahnawake in favour of the SQ.

Montréal-area radio stations CKAC and CFGL reverse their decision to censor music by Montagnais rock band Kashtin, following massive public pressure in their favour.

September 23: 1000 natives and non-natives demonstrate in support of the Mohawk people at Kahnawake. At the bingo hall in Kahnawake, the demonstrators listen to speakers comment on the situation. One of the speakers is a native soldier from the Royal Canadian Regiment in full uniform, with his face concealed. He expresses his support for the Mohawk struggle, denounces the repression of the federal and provincial governments and apologizes for the army's behaviour in Kahnawake. He then leaves quickly to avoid arrest. News of this man's courageous stand is totally suppressed by the media. Grand Chief Joe Norton is prevented from attending the meeting by the army.

September 24: Parliament reopens in Ottawa.

September 26, 6:45 P.M.: 50 Warriors and friends in the T.C. cross the razor wire fence, and dodge soldiers. The 78-day siege ends. A melee ensues, with soldiers fixing bayonets and physically subduing Mohawk men and women on live TV. Some Mohawks escape, among them Loran Thompson, who simply walks down the road to Oka and is given a lift by a fellow Mohawk. Three journalists are also arrested. Soldiers take aim at 400 Mohawk protesters at Kahnawake for the first time since the army was mobilized; they were attacking soldiers at a checkpoint near the entrance to the Mercier Bridge. Luckily, no Mohawks die. Reports indicate that Warriors handed over to the SQ by the army are beaten, particularly Ronald Cross, who has to be sent to hospital for treatment before his arraignment.

October 5: 21 out of 22 Warriors detained at the Farnham military base in Québec are released on bail.

October 10: Six Mohawks from Akwesasne are charged in New York State in relation to the violence at Akwesasne in early May. All are either members or supporters of the Warrior Society.

October 11: Bail hearings take place at St-Jerôme, Québec, for the last Warriors held prisoner at Parthenais prison (also SQ headquarters) in Montréal. They are: Ronald Cross, Dennis Nicholas, and Gordon and Roger Lazore, and their application for bail is turned down by the judge, who calls them a threat to public safety.

October 15: There is a significant police presence (SQ and RCMP) at Kahnawake. The army declares that the last troops will withdraw within two weeks.

Demolition Derby 2 (1991)

MOHAWK RESISTANCE AT KANEHSATAKE AND KAHNA-WAKE

This summer, people living in and around Montréal nearly witnessed a massacre of Mohawk people at Kanehsatake by the armed forces — a stone's throw from their own neighbourhoods. Everyday life in Canada being what it is, the massacre was prepared for and planned in full view of the public (because everyone knew the broad lines of what the army intended to do) and put into operation with what amounts to complete impunity. Apart from a handful of demonstrators and other people of goodwill who gave generously of their time and effort to support the Mohawk people, the response to this situation was one of indifference. Most people who had the heart to recognize army mobilization for what it was did nothing, perhaps because they felt powerless to intervene. Overnight, the barricades became a media circus, and the issues that motivated the Mohawks' act of self-defence were trivialized to death. As if that wasn't bad enough, the airwaves were full of war propaganda and "antiterrorist" rhetoric, in a bid to prevent the public at large from identifying with the Mohawks and overcoming their airtight separation from the events unfolding near Oka.

During the Nazis' suppression of the Warsaw Ghetto uprising in 1943, daily life outside the ghetto walls went on as usual; that is, there were no serious disturbances of public order by the citizens of Warsaw while the massacre was in progress. Inside the walls, people died in their thousands and the ghetto burned.

By their massive use of military force in a situation that in no way called for it (the presumed threat posed to "public security" by a handful of armed Mohawks was pure fabrication), the federal and provincial governments clearly showed that their intention was to terrorize and humiliate the Mohawks, and by extension all native peoples, not because state security was threatened by the roadblocks (the very thought is ridiculous) but because the Mohawks' actions were connected to a countrywide movement in favour of real native sovereignty. If necessary, they were ready and willing to kill dozens of Mohawks in order to shut down the roadblocks, and there were and are real reasons to fear a massacre.

The authorities were reluctant to do this for three main reasons. First, because of their fear of worldwide condemnation, and possible trade sanctions and boycotts of Canadian goods; second, because of their fear of widespread acts of sabotage by native people across Canada in retaliation for any bloodshed; and third, their fear of the long-term consequences of bloodshed for native/government relations, as millions of hectares of land and billions of dollars of "natural resources" are at stake.

The Canadian state did not have to fear the media, which admirably fulfilled its function as a mass thought control apparatus, blandly supporting the repression and condemning the Mohawks' defence of their land. The current minister of public security for the province of Québec, Claude Ryan, one notes, was once editor of Le Devoir, a leading Montréal daily.

As of this writing, 85% of the province of Québec is under some form of native land claim. The figures are similar all across the country, and native bands have waited for generations for concessions from the federal and provincial governments without success while their land bases and lifeways are being eroded by the pressure of the industrial economy.

The Canadian economy largely depends on "resource extraction and processing" for its continued good health. For maximum profitability (which is the name of the game for the briefcase-toting zombies who run our world), Canadian businesses must have unimpeded access to Canadian territory and its natural wealth. Native peoples are on a collision course with the state and the transnational capital groupings that it represents because it is precisely native peoples' control of their lands and the immense wealth they represent that is at issue, at least as far as the state is concerned.

How much sovereignty is the federal government prepared to concede? What is the difference between the structured dependency of formally self-governing territories under native jurisdiction and the bantustan concept applied in South Africa?

Bantustans are nominally independent, but in reality completely at the mercy of the South African state. South African officials visited Canada to study its system of reservations, which served as a model for the development of apartheid. Canada is a settler state, and its relationship with native peoples is a colonial relationship, based on their subjugation and the theft of their land.

The Canadian nation-state was hurriedly cobbled together in the 19th century. From its beginnings in the colonial settlements of the European imperial powers, its primary purpose was to implement an immense land grab, organized by ruling classes whose racism and genocidal intent were openly and murderously displayed. Because the Europeans who settled the "Canadian" part of the continent were uprooted from their communities in their countries of origin and artificially brought together in North America by social forces outside their control, there has never been a stable Canadian polity. "Canada" is politically fragile. As the October Crisis showed, a movement in the direction of political autonomy by any significant sector of Canadian society is considered a serious threat by the Canadian state, and treated as such.

If, during negotiations, the Canadian state recognizes the Mohawks as a sovereign people, this would imply that other native peoples are or could be equally sovereign. If they are sovereign, then in theory there is no reason why Québec or any other province cannot also be sovereign. If the once-centralized elements of this society, like neighbourhoods, counties, towns and cities, tended to become autonomous under the pressure of a cohesive and determined grassroots movement, the federal, provincial and municipal governments could be bypassed. This is not to say that decentralization and democratization of capitalist social relations could resolve our problems, but rather an observation that decentralization of political and economic power can only be pushed so far without destabilizing the existing social order.

By itself, a broad movement for native sovereignty would challenge the political structure of Canada but would leave intact the alienated social relations that give rise to it.

What is likely to happen (given the present balance of force between native peoples and the Canadian government) is some form of jurisdictional compromise between all-out sovereignty, like the full independence demanded by the Gitskan and Wet'Suwet'en for the 22,000 square miles of land in British Columbia they claim as their own, a sovereignty which the federal government has already said it will not even consider — "Native self-government ... does not and cannot ever mean sovereign independence within Canadian territory" (Prime Minister Brian Mulroney) — and the current situation, with no sovereignty at all, which is an intolerable one for native peoples living in Canada. There are already signs of varying positions within native communities regarding the degree of sovereignty they want and the strategies that can be used to achieve it. A Canadian university professor has already proposed that native territories be considered as a "province" in their own right; in effect, as a third level of government, after the federal and provincial levels. This is the "distinct order of government" the Assembly of Manitoba Chiefs has called for in recent press conferences. The native communities involved would be considered as living on Canadian territory and be subject to Canadian laws, but could pass laws, raise taxes and run schools and health care. Micmac chief Dan Paul has made similar public statements, calling for greater Micmac control of their communities, but within Canada. If something like this happens, native people could be manoeuvred into "self-managing" their participation in an industrial system that is radically hostile to what remains of their traditional lifeways. If, on the other hand, no stable compromise occurs between native peoples and the state, a situation of chronic conflict could result, leading to even more intense criminalization and repression of native people, which would be disastrous for their already fragile communities.

We should back this movement for self-determination; it will give native peoples an improved ability to defend their communities from further destruction and consolidate their gains. Non-native support is crucial to the successful conclusion of this process on terms that are right for native people.

Doug Imrie

CONTACTS:

Mohawk Nation Office (Kahnawake)
via Box 1987
Kahnawake, PQ JO1 1BO
(514) 638-4750
(514) 638-6790 (fax)

Mohawk Nation Office (Kanehsatake)
(514) 479-8353
(514) 479-8355

Canadian Alliance in Solidarity With Native Peoples
(416) 588-2712

Leonard Peltier Defence Committee (Toronto)
(416) 439-1893 (also fax)

Akwesasne Notes
Mohawk Nation
Box 196
Rooseveltown, NY 13683
USA

TRIAL IN CATANIA, SICILY, AGAINST ALFREDO BONANNO

Alfredo Bonanno and Giuseppe "Pippo" Stasi (see Demolition Derby No. 1) are still in prison in Bergamo, Italy. They were arrested during a robbery of a jeweller's store in Bergamo on February 2, 1989. Alfredo was sentenced to 5 years and 6 months, and Pippo was sentenced to 4 years and 8 months. Other accusations were laid against them in reference to a murder that took place in Bergamo in April 1987 and another robbery which took place in March 1985. These latter charges are completely unfounded and were only laid to further criminalize the two men, both active anarchists. On appeal their sentences were reduced: Pippo's to 4 years and Alfredo's to 4 years and 8 months. On March 20, 1990, Alfredo was sentenced to 8 months by the appeal court for instigation of a crime and apology for a crime as a result of articles that appeared in the anarchist journals Anarchismo and Provocazione, which he edits. The comrades can be contacted at the Carcere di Bergamo, Via Gleno 61, 24100 Bergamo, Italia.

IMPORTANT!

Possible Canada Post strike in November (or perhaps later)

It looks as though there may be a postal strike and it may be a long one. According to a letter in the most recent Factsheet Five, in the event of such a strike, mail sent to Canada from other countries may simply be returned to sender, likely stamped undeliverable, usually with no accompanying explanation as to why. Readers outside of Canada should check and see if there is a postal strike on before sending anything to DD (or other Canadian journals). Because of the strike possibility, anyone sending a letter for publication will receive a note acknowledging that your letter got through (if you don't receive one, it didn't).

Khanawake and Kanesatake: The Struggle Continues

When one hundred heavily armed officers of the Quebec provincial police (Surete du Quebec – SQ) attacked the Mohawk road blockade in Kanestake, they contributed to a new radicalisation in Native struggles for self-determination. After the tear-gas and gun-smoke cleared on July 11/90, the police retreat left behind much more than one dead officer and six police vehicles: what was left from the flash-point of Oka was a new dynamic in Native resistance. A new dynamic that clearly enters into an extra-parliamentary perspective on the part of militant Natives, manifesting itself in an urgency that requires resistance to go beyond discussions with the Canadian state.

This discussion, which has for the most part been limited to court actions regarding Native land claims, has been little more than a thinly-veiled public relations exercise on the part of federal and provincial governments. As a legal action on the part of Natives, to both achieve some level of sovereignty and stop destructive industrial practises on their land, the court room battle has been severely limited. These limitations have led many Natives to view the court room with a high level of cynicism; "more and more among us are saying it's useless even if we do get to the table" (George Erasmus, Assembly of First Nations).

As a result, many Native nations have turned increasingly to other forms of struggle, mostly blockading roads on their lands. As well as achieving direct results in terms of stopping destructive industrial practises in a particular area, it is also a physical expression of Native sovereignty: "It's an expression of our ownership and jurisdiction" (Gitskan-Wet'suwet'en member).

The armed resistance of the Mohawks in Oka is not an abstraction, but instead a direct result of the "barricades" in the courts and parliament buildings. Barricades put in place to retain a method of exploitation carried out by industrial capitalism which has penetrated Native lands, extracted vast amounts of raw materials, and left ecological disasters in its wake. The internal imperialism of Canadian capitalism is maintained by an internal apartheid, which has its roots in the colonial subjugation of Native peoples. The thrust of capitalist attack was and is against the very culture of Native peoples.

With this article, we want to develop an understanding to the background of the armed confrontation in Oka, to place it in an historical context that offers a perspective for a concrete solidarity.

Apartheid: Canada and South Africa

The pattern of imperialist domination of entire peoples is one that is seen the world over wherever there has been an indigenous people. The differences in exploitation are ones of methods, but the goal remains: domination and subjugation of entire peoples, based on their relation to capitalist production.

As an example, we can compare the Bantustans in South Africa and Native reservations in Canada. The difference in methods: for European settlers in Azania (South Africa), the requirement was for control of mineral-rich land and a large labour force to extract these materials. In Canada, the land was also to be controlled for resources, but Natives were seen as surplus and redundant population. To achieve these goals, both colonial states made use of extermination, relocation and segregation. But here, the historical conditions and differences in methods leads to two seemingly contradictory situations: South Africa, the fascist regime: and Canada, the "liberal democracy." In the first case, one system has had to resort to a real overt fascism; in the second, the system has developed a strategy of low-level reforms coupled with high-level and sophisticated repression/control.

The expansion of Canadian capitalism in the 1800s brought it into conflict with a Native society almost directly opposed to the European capitalist society based on class and exploitation; the Native society was communally based and relied more on co-operation. As well, European settlers were to be established as the primary producers in the rapidly developing agricultural industry. Native peoples were an obstacle to be removed and/or controlled.

The Dominion Lands Act, drafted in the 1870s, provided cheap land for immigrating European settlers. Natives were to be restricted and contained on reserves. Large-scale military operations were clearly too expensive, and the reserve system, based on British colonial experience, appeared to offer a cheap and effective form of control. To achieve this, the independence of Native nations was to be dismantled. The Indian Act, and its accompanying restrictions on Native fishing, criminalisation of Native economy (ie, in 1881, the law made it illegal for Natives to "sell, barter, or traffic" fish), exclusion from parliamentary politics by the denial of a vote, the use of a pass system to control movement on and off reserves, criminalisation of Native cultures (potlatches/ceremonies outlawed) and the breaking up of Native society (children were forced into boarding schools where English and Christianity were the rule); created the conditions for this dependence. The political, social, economic and cultural bases of Native society, in short: the physical means for retaining their autonomy, were attacked. It is no mistake that South African officials came to Canada on several occasions to study the Canadian reserve system after the Boer war, and that the South African Settlement Act of 1912 was strikingly similar to the Dominion Lands Act.

By the 1950s and '60s, social and economic conditions were liberalised. Natives were allowed access to the wage-labour market by removal of the pass system, and the participation in electoral politics granted with the vote. However, these liberalisations were also absorbed by the manipulation of "status" and "non-status" categories for Natives who remained on the reserves (and thus kept some support from the "welfare state"), and those who moved off them (withdrawal of support). By the 1970s, in the upsurge of radical struggles including Black, Puerto Rican and Natives, fuelled by high poverty levels, and racism, resistance was growing. Wounded Knee exploded. The Canadian state moved quickly, co-opting or smashing any independent Native organisations, dependent and controlled.

The historical conditions of this Canadian apartheid places into context what was the main struggle in Oka: self-determination and autonomy.

Oka, the Struggle for Autonomy

The pretext of the July 11/90 police raid was the Mohawk road blocks, erected five months earlier, against a proposed golf-course expansion that would over-run Mohawk burial grounds. However, the extreme offensive launched by police was not only against the road blocks, but against the very core of why the road blocks existed. Several factors contribute to why the state saw it necessary to neutralise the Mohawks, the primary ones can be seen as the level of resistance and militancy of the Mohawks, and their will to fight for a practical autonomy.

Prior to the July 11 raid, there was also factional infighting among the Mohawk communities in Akwesasne in May. The clash, which left two Mohawks dead, was the climax of a split over the issue of gambling casinos and tobacco smuggling on the reserve. The factions are, generally, the "anti-gamblers" who see the practises as destructive and against traditional values; and members of the Warriors society and other Mohawks who support/ engage in the gambling casinos.

The casinos, located on the U.S. side of the reserve, which is divided by the Canadian and U.S. border, catered to mostly tourists from Montreal, Ottawa and New York state. Allegations of organised crime connections, and individual profiteering have been directed against some of the Mohawks who operated/supported the casinos. During the 77-day armed stand-off in Oka, this aspect of the Warrior Society's activities fuelled government propaganda that they were "criminals, thugs, terrorists" who weren't fighting for anything but their profits. For some non-Native groups this became a controversial situation, besides the primary one of armed struggle itself, and led to a limited solidarity, distancing, etc. This can be seen to result from a moralism, firmly rooted in middle-class politics, that viewed such activities as "immoral, unethical" and at times even "criminal." From this perspective, it would appear the Canadian state is moral and legitimate in operating its gambling ventures (lotteries), non-Native groups equally so (with raffles, etc.), but not Native reservations with extreme levels of poverty and unemployment. The allegations of

"organised crime connections" obscured the main aspect of the casinos; employment of over 700 Natives. That is: the establishment of a real autonomy by developing an economic independence from the U.S. and Canadian states, which by its nature must be "illegal." It was from this basis, the ability to self-manage their own communities, to resist the state-imposed structures on their communities, that the Mohawks qualitatively advanced their struggle.

Counter-Insurgency

In 1988, the Canadian Security and Intelligence Services submitted a lengthy report entitled "Native Extremism," the result of intense surveillance of militant Natives. The report put forward the idea that Natives would be an area of intense resistance in the future. The Mohawks foremost among them, with their determination to not only create the conditions for their autonomy, but also their will to militantly defend that autonomy.

The massive deployment of military troops on August 15, with over 4,600 soldiers mobilized, complete with Leopard tanks, Cougar armoured vehicles, and four 105 mm guns was intended clearly as a stupefying display of force to demonstrate the Canadian state's resolve to crush any form of militant resistance from Native communities.

The August 20th deployment of troops from the Royal 22nd Regiment in Oka and Kahnawke, replacing police positions, marked a clear change in the counter-insurgency operations. The intentions were clear: to contain, breakdown and if necessary overtake the Mohawk positions.

Prior to their deployment, the soldiers received two days intensive training in overtaking enemy barricades. Even while Mohawk negotiators struggled with obstinate Quebec and federal negotiating teams, the military and police engaged in all levels of counter-insurgency. These included attrition; preventing food and medical supplies from entering beyond the military checkpoints, preventing spiritual healers from entering; aggression; beatings of those arrested, low-level helicopter flights, firing para-flares, tampering/severing Mohawk communications, surrounding Mohawk positions, which later retreated to the Kanesatake Drug and Alcohol Treatment Centre, with enormous amounts of razor-wire and moving them closer, patrols into Mohawk areas (which resulted in the berating of the Warrior "Spudwrench"), as well as various provocations from soldiers including firing shots on September 2 and 19, as well as the raids into Kahnawake which resulted in confrontations.

These are all elements of a high-level psychological warfare campaign to de-stabilise and de-moralise the Mohawks behind the barricades. As well, the Canadian Forces released a slick video production that military strategist experts stated was an attempt to prepare the public for a sympathetic or at least non-aggressive response to a full armed assault by troops.

Solidarity in Practise

The most important factor which did prevent a military action, which would have resulted in a massacre of the two dozen Warriors who remained in the treatment centre, was the widespread solidarity practised by Native nations throughout Canada. With few exceptions, Native nations declared their solidarity with the Mohawks, recognizing in Oka the same situation facing them: "Their fight is our fight. It just happened to crystallize in their community, but it was imminent" (Stewart Phillip, Penticton Band councillor).

Actions swept across Canada, on both Native reserves and in every major city; demonstrations, road and rail blocks (including over forty in B.C. alone), occupations of various government buildings, vigils, clothing and food donations, graffiti paint-bombs. There was also low-level sabotage actions, such as a CN rail-bridge in Alberta set on fire on August 18th, five hydro-towers toppled over near London, Ontario, causing over $750-thousand damage on September 4th. On the same day, a CN railway bridge near London, Ontario was destroyed by fire. The vulnerability of such targets, and their importance in capitals infrastructure, was obvious to many Natives: "If there is an attack against the Mohawks, it would be considered an attack on all of us.… There's hydro-electric lines crossing most of our communities.… There are major highway arteries … major water supplies" (Peguis chief Louis Stevenson of Manitoba).

As well as solidarity actions already occurring, there was the very real threat of an entire, qualitative escalation in resistance, should there have been a military assault. Speaking on the possibility of such an attack, Don Ryan of the Gitksan-Wet'suwet'en said "If that's their approach, then you're going to see a long, protracted fighting condition by the Indian people, and it'll be guerrilla warfare" (August 28, *Vancouver Sun*).

Despite the attempts by politicians, both Native and non-Native, to co-opt or break up the militancy in practise, there was a clear understanding that Native peoples are not one homogenous group, that there would indeed be diversity in the forms of struggle. Native organisations who were advocating "non-violence" admitted that they themselves weren't representative of Native peoples; "We have indicated before to governments that we don't have control over all our people" (Gordon Peters, Ontario regional chief of the AFN).

Concurrent with the substantial Native solidarity with the Mohawks was the solidarity from unions, church, and leftist groups. In August, railway unions and shippers placed blame on the federal government for Natives blockading railways, not the Natives themselves. The United Transportation Union, which represents 14,000 rail workers, threatened to walk out "from Vancouver to St. John's" if layoffs resulting from the rail blockades continued. The Ojibwas blockading the rail line in northern Ontario demanded the workers be paid for their lost time.

For some left groups, the questions of violence, and their moralism concerning the gambling issue, led to an inability to take a position of real solidarity. There was also the parliamentary politics, such an important area for most of the left, that the armed Mohawks rejected. As well, the statements of the "anti-gambling" factions within the Mohawk people gave the necessary ideological backdrop for particular groups to refrain from contradicting their "non-violence" politics; "The Warriors have not been disarmed, those M-60 machine guns are still there, the assault weapons and grenades are still there, the potential for violence is incredibly high…what we are dealing with here is no less than Indian organised crime, as violent and corrupt as that of the mafia" (Doug George, editor of *Akwesasne Notes*, a Mohawk journal). With no analysis of why gambling casinos were operated, and a disarming adherence to "non-violence," some left groups attempted to present Native leaders who they agreed with as representative of all Native people. Such a representation, as has already been noted, does not exist.

The Empty Rhetoric of Reform

While constantly denouncing the armed Mohawks in Oka, hypocritically stating that violence doesn't solve anything, the federal government began announcing wide-ranging programs for "dealing with the problems of Canada's Native peoples." Ironically, the most comprehensive reform statement came from Prime Minister Mulroney on September 26, the day of disengagement by the Mohawks. In this, Mulroney announced the Native agenda would have four aspects: "land claims; economic and social conditions on reserves; relationships between aboriginal peoples and governments; and concerns of Canada's Native peoples in contemporary Canadian life." All the concerns that Natives have been struggling for ever since their independence was taken away was suddenly being discussed at the federal level! In the same speech, Mulroney made it clear the intentions of any such reforms were to co-opt more radical demands when he said "The Warriors have been acting as

Resistance 14 (1990)

if the concept of Native self-government means national independence. I will be very clear on this point; Native self-government does not now and cannot ever mean sovereign independence. Mohawk lands are part of Canadian territory, and Canadian law must and does apply."

With his statement, Mulroney not only made a mockery of "self-government" but also demonstrated clearly the governments' strategy for groups fighting for self-determination, including the Quebecois.

What was ironic about the Oka conflict, was that it had to be fought in, and on some levels against, a people fighting for their own sovereignty: the Quebecois. That Mohawks faced racist Quebec mobs in Chateauguay, complete with KKK intervention, and that Jacques Parizeau, leader of the nationalist Parti Quebecois, condemned both Quebec and the federal government for negotiating with the Mohawks, indicates not only the reactionary tendency of Quebecois nationalist leaders but the division of oppressed groups engineered by the state. A primary factor of this was the Meech Lake Accord. Devised in 1987 to bring Quebec into the Canadian constitution by establishing the concept of "two founding peoples of Canada," and recognizing Quebec as a "distinct society," the MLA was scheduled to be passed on June 23/90. However, because of the nature of the MLA, Natives and women's groups opposed it. For Natives, it was an exclusion from a discussion they had pursued since contact with European settlers; sovereignty. The MLA can be seen as a tool which was used to divide Native and women's groups from Quebecois groups. If passed the MLA would co-opt more radical Quebecois groups who fought for independence alongside Native groups, as well, Native and women's groups would see Quebecois nationalism as an obstacle. If the MLA failed to pass parliamentary procedures, it would only fuel Quebecois frustrations. On June 23/90, the MLA was stopped in the Manitoba legislature when Elijah Harper, a Cree-Ojibwa member of the Manitoba legislature, blocked it.

Less than a month later, Quebec police attacked the Mohawk barricades. Chateauguay exploded with racist violence; stone-throwing mobs and Mohawks burned in effigy.

In the end, the parliamentary perspective remains intact.

Sept. 26: Disengagement

After seventy-seven days of confrontation, the Mohawks disengaged on September 26. In the afternoon, those who remained in the drug treatment center held discussions to reach a concensus on the disengagement action, and once accomplishing this built a large fire and destroyed sensitive documents and radio equipment. In the evening, thirty-one Warriors, twenty-three women and children, plus ten journalists, walked out of the treatment center and took the military by surprise who quickly went into a panic, fixed bayonets, and scuffled with the Mohawks. A total of forty-seven people are arrested and detained in military trusteeship by the army, while nine people, including some who had slipped out of the military encirclement, are arrested by the SQ. Charges range from obstructing police, wearing a disguise, possession of dangerous weapons, to participating in a riot.

In a communiqué, the Warriors stated bluntly their reasons for disengagement; "After several attempts at trying to find a peaceful and creative solution to the situation we have all realized that we are dealing with an essentially Neanderthal attitude on the part of the Quebec and Canadian governments." In nearby Kahnewake, Mohawks erect barricades and set fire to a military tent, in response to the capture of the Mohawks.

Oka; the struggle continues

For seventy-seven days, the Canadian state was subjected to an armed confrontation that drew widespread support from Native nations, and also at a social level. The internal peace of Canada, the "world leader" in human rights crusades, the zealous prosecutor of South African apartheid, was shattered. The repression has been exposed.

Just as importantly, important lessons can be drawn out from the conflict, particularly the example of solidarity as a concrete weapon, and the important role of militant actions in that resistance. If our solidarity is to reach its logical conclusion, we must analyze and attack the social, political and economic structures that created the conditions for Canada's internal apartheid, for without a doubt, there will be more flashpoints in the future.

Presently, four men are still imprisoned; Dennis Nichols, Ronald Cross, Roger Lazore and Gordon Lazore. All others captured on Sept. 26 have since been released on bail (and many of these have conducted an information tour around the country). Those captured on Sept. 26 and held at Canadian Forces Base Farnham were subjected to various harassments, beatings and for several of the men, a mock execution. Altogether, most of those captured face a possible fourteen years imprisonment based on their charges to date. 160 others have also been charged in connection with confrontations in Kahnawake and Kanesatake. There are a further 150 warrants. RCMP, SQ and Montreal police continue to lay siege to Mohawk communities with surveillance, harassment and assaults on people. In no way has the repression ended, in no way has the struggle ended.

> *Just because the Warriors have left does not preclude people from picking up arms and continuing the struggle across the country – only next time you won't see media events like Oka. It could end up like Northern Ireland. (Penticton Band councillor Stewart Phillip).*

The only recognized legal defense fund is:

The Liberation of the Mohawk Nation
Account no. 80-186
Mail to: Confederacy Crisis Center
POE Box 292
Kahnawake, Quebec
Mohawk Territory
JOL 1BO

For information or to contribute to the political activity write to the Confederacy Crisis Committee c/o the PO box already listed. There are plans for a newspaper and book entitled *Behind the Razor Wire*. For contributions or to pre-order write c/o the Crisis Committee.

We would also recommend readers to *Arm the Spirit* nos 2–3 and *Prison News Service* nos 25–27 available from:

ATS Distribution
Box 475, 253 College st.
Toronto, Ont.
M5T 1R5 Canada.

Oka; the struggle continues

In 1990, the Canadian Government sent 1,500 troops to Iraq and 4,500 troops to Mohawk lands.

DIRECT ACTION
Speaks Louder Than Words

A group of Vancouver mothers who had been pleading for months with authorities for an overpass of a dangerous rail line near their homes finally got quick results when they took direct action and pitched tents on the tracks, refusing to let any trains pass until they got firm guarantees for the overpass. The action helped unify the group of mothers, who went on to organize a community centre and food co-op for their neighborhood, and also served as a model for other local groups fighting for day-care and other needs.

Open Road 15 (1983).

AFTERMATH OF A GULF WAR

Establishing A New World Order

It is now several months after the conclusion of the Gulf War. The US has staged its victory parade and fallout from the war continues to be felt, not the least by the Iraqi people, the Kurdish and the Palestinians.

Southern Kurdistan (northern Iraq), the Persian Gulf and other areas in the region now contain American troops, ships and aircraft, with a permanent military presence now being put in place. How did this come about, what was the background to the war, and why a war in the Middle East?

Prior to the beginning of the war, Luis Bilbao wrote in the Buenos Aires daily *Nuevo Sur*,

"In the show of force in the desert, one can now precisely measure abstract concepts that only months ago were nearly out of reach: a breakup of the international balance of power and a strengthening of the seven leading industrialized countries... the conflict of interest between the Big Seven and the rest of the world is merely beginning to take on its true shape".

The background to the war can be traced to recent international developments, in particular a reconstitution of the global order. This includes not only the breakup of the Eastern Bloc in 1989 and the ending of the Cold War, but also the forming of three competing economic blocs; Europe, Japan-Asia and North America.

One can say that the East-West conflict has shifted to a North-South conflict or, as Bilbao has already said, a "conflict of interest between the Big Seven and the rest of the world". But while its clear that the world economy is now subject to conditions imposed by the G-7, the Gulf War must be seen first of all as an assertion of US hegemony (a dominant leadership).

THE NEW WORLD ORDER

The restructuring of international capital, the economic competition rising from Europe and Japan-Asia, concurrent with the economic decline in the US, means the US is now capable of asserting its hegemony in an economic-political-military way.

The Persian Gulf was the proving ground of the New World Order, in essence an order led by the US which

"dominates its affairs and destiny on the international and regional levels... the US conquest of the Arabian Peninsula is part and parcel of the US global policy at this juncture. The Arabian Peninsula has 66 percent of the worlds oil resources. Oil is no longer only a source of energy, although that is important. Oil now means (1) energy; (2) a series of major, diversified and growing petrochemical industries; and

Vancouver, January 26; protest against Gulf War

(3) control of the circulation of international finance... the US has invaded the Arabian Peninsula to retain its leading world position. By domination of Arab oil, the US dominates not only the political and economic destiny of this region, but can also determine the outcome of its fierce competition with Europe and Japan" (George Habash, the Popular Front for the liberation of Palestine (PFLP), *Democratic Palestine* November-December 1990).

As well, western and US imperialism has had to contend with various threats to its power in the Middle East, including the rise of Islamic Fundamentalism (which can be characterized as decidedly anti-western as in the 1979 Iranian revolution), the Palestinian resistance and the *Intifada* (which has increasingly challenged western imperialism asset in the region, Israel), Pan-Arab nationalism, and the Kurdish guerrilla struggle in NATO's southern flank, Turkey.

Combined, these factors make the region one of the most unstable in the world for western imperialism.

In this context, Iraq was another essential factor. Iraq was a major military power in the region and an oil producing country that worked against the interests of the US. Not only with the invasion of Kuwait, which was nothing more than a preconceived context for US military intervention, but through its oil policies which included raising the price of oil and limiting production, contrary to the agreements reached by OPEC and western imperialism.

The Iraqi challenge had to be dismantled to deter threats to western interests and/or to the security of the Zionist state of Israel

and the pro-US Arab regimes

The Gulf War was aimed at establishing US hegemony in the New World Order, gaining control of the Arabian Peninsula, dismantling Iraq and crushing the liberation struggles in the region.

CANADIAN INVOLVEMENT IN THE GULF WAR

Canada's military involvement in the Gulf War was, in the overall balance of forces deployed, minor. With only 2,000 troops, Canada's role was limited to providing logistical support in sea and air operations.

Despite this, it must be noted that Canada was one of the first countries- outside of the US- to respond militarily, by sending three ships to the Gulf on August 24/90 to enforce the economic embargo. The Canadian government also supported, with little reservation, all US-led UN resolutions against Iraq.

LIMITED MILITARY CAPABILITIES

Under Operation *Friction*, naval and air task groups from the Canadian Armed Forces (CAF) were deployed in Saudi Arabia at Al Quaysuma and Al Jubayl; in Manama, Bahrain; Qatar; in the southern Gulf; and aboard the US Hospital ship *Mercy*. By January 15, the deployment consisted of the three ships, HMCS *Athabaskan, Protecteur,* and *Terra Nova*; 24 CF-18 fighters; field hospitals; and two companies of infantry for security. The role of the CAF was limited to logistical support: interdiction of cargo ships, escort

Turn to page 22

Canadian Forces ground crew load Sparrow missile onto CF-18 in Qatar

AFTERMATH OF A GULF WAR

Continued from page 5

of supply ships, escort of bombers and medical aid.

What may at first appear to be another facet of the world-wide myth, "Canada the peacekeeper", is in reality the extremely limited military capabilities of the CAF; only 80,000 personnel in total, outdated and overworked equipment, and a lack of desert fighting equipment and training. As well, an activation of more troops would have "placed a severe strain on the ability of the CAF to... take on such tasks as responding to another Mohawk crisis at home" (an unnamed source, *Globe and Mail*, January 12/90).

The Canadian military contribution was limited, but Canada's economic and political interests in the war knew no boundaries.

CANADIAN ECONOMIC INTERESTS

Canada's political and military involvement in the war was determined by economic interrelation with the US, realized through the Free Trade Agreement on one level, and international groupings such as the G-7;

"If the war is ended quickly, Mr. Wilson (the Canadian Finance Minister) said, he agrees with US officials that an Allied victory could help improve consumer confidence and trigger a rebound in the N. American economies... All of the countries were searching for ways to make sure the recessions facing the US, Britain and Canada don't become severe enough to trigger a global downturn" (*Globe and Mail, Report on Business*, January 21/91, a meeting of the G-7 in New York).

In the development of three competing economic blocs (Europe, Japan-Asia and N. America) Canada's economic and political destiny now lies with that of the US. As a participant in and beneficiary of US imperialism, Canadas interests are strongly connected with those of the US.

Militarily, Canada can contribute little to the US's New World Order. Rather, it will be in the economic and political fields, through Canada's position in the IMF, the G-7 and the UN, that Canada will re-affirm US imperialisms new era of exploitation.

THE FUTURE

The New World Order will be a period of more military interventions, primarily by the US- the one nation militarily capable of such incursions- and increased exploitation of the Three Continents. The effects of this New World Order, the ending of the Cold War (which was greeted with such euphoria as opening to an era of "peace") and the economic restructuring, can now be seen in the aftermath of the Gulf War.

The struggle continues.

The Gulf War & 'Internal Security'

Throughout the course of the Gulf War and in the months leading up to it, North America and Europe experienced unprecedented levels of "internal security". The threat of "terrorist" attacks was almost as newsworthy as the war itself. Soldiers and armored vehicles patrolled airports in Britain, SWAT teams and bomb squads were deployed at Super Bowl V in Florida, Arabs were detained, harassed and placed under surveillance. The massive security campaign had specific goals; repression of Arabs, repression of opposition to the war in general; propaganda for the war; and actual security of potential targets of resistance.

If the US and other nations had learned anything from the defeat in Vietnam, it was that wars can be significantly disrupted from internal movements. Therefore, the role of counter-insurgency; maintaining the "inner peace", controlling dissent to ensure the ability to wage war from the military-economic centres, and mobilizing social concensus in favour of the war, was given a high priority.

THE TERRORIST HYPE

The use of "anti-terrorist" hysteria attempted to establish an image in the social consciousness of a society under siege- not only involved in a "just war" in the Persian Gulf- but under threat in its own peaceful backyard. Prior to the war, reports were already filtering through the media of "terrorist" groups in Canada. This followed the pattern of the "Libyan hit squads" of the early '80's and the IRA unit gunning for Thatcher at the 1988 Economic Summit in Toronto. Neither of these cases proved much substance.

Not easily discouraged, "terrorist units" appeared in the headlines on January 21/91: "Terrorism hits home- Canadians believed targeted by radical supporters of Iraq"[1]. This report originated from the expulsion of three Iraqi diplomats in Ottawa. Diplomats it was later discovered, to have "had suspected links with Arab terrorist cells in Canada". Suddenly, "terrorist cells" appeared *ad nauseam*: "Small cells of the Lebanese Shi'ite group *Hezbollah* had been uncovered in Toronto and Montreal... Also involved were cells of the Shi'ite party known as *Al Da'wa*... Meanwhile, terrorists linked to Iraq may be trying to infiltrate the US through Canada... it is possible we will see terrorist attacks in the coming week"[2].

No such attacks occurred in N. America, nor were there any spectacular and "high-level" actions of the sort security officials could even attribute to Arab guerrilla's (one action, six pipe-bombs found near a US naval base in Virginia turned out to be an insurance scam by three businessmen).

Undaunted by this conspicuous absence of attacks, security agencies continued with their campaign. Arabs in Canada continued to be interrogated by Canadian Security and Intelligence Service (CSIS) agents[3], to the point where the Canadian Arab Federation was forced to hold news conferences on the issue and distribute a brochure on CSIS. The CAF received over 60 complaints by Arabs who had been followed, questioned at length or photographed by CSIS. CSIS claimed their activities were merely to learn more about the politics of the middle east. However, such overt and aggressive surveillance techniques have less to do with information gathering and more to do with repression via intimidation. The Arab community and particularly the radical elements were to be neutralized- not because they were "potential terrorists"- but because they offered the strongest orientation of resistance, because they had the ability to expose the real goals of the war, and to

provide a perspective that went beyond the "No Blood for Oil Bring Our Troops Home" sloganeering of the anti-war movement.

THE USE OF IMMIGRATION AS CONTROL

Along with the highly publicized activities of CSIS, the use of immigration laws and refugee status was used to further silence the Arab community. Throughout N. America and Europe, Arabs and particularly Palestinians and Iraqis were detained, denied entry, had their visa's revoked or denied extension. In the UK, Iraqi nationals were barred from entry and those already living in the UK required to register with police. By the end of the war, up to 200 Iraqis and Palestinians had been detained. In Germany, the surveillance of Arabs and new laws against immigrants required doctors, lawyers and public officials to give the government all information they had on immigrants. In Spain, some 6,000 Arabs were "suspect" and entered into computer files under "Operation Duna". In France, a similar program was enacted under "Vigipirate".

In Canada, amongst other cases, was the example of an Iraqi couple arriving at Toronto's Pearson airport allegedly carrying false Saudi passports, who were detained on January 9/91. The couple applied for refugee status, and the man was a member of the opposition *Da'wa* party and had fought on the side of Iran in the Iran-Iraq war. He was found to be carrying a notebook with a list of weapons, which he claimed he compiled during the Iran-Iraq war.

Initial government efforts to have the couple detained as security threats were overturned when immigration adjudicator Dennis Paxton ruled that the governments arguments were "to be generous, unlikely"[4]. However, his decision to order the couple released was overruled by a "national security certificate" filed by then-Immigration Minister Barbara McDougall and Solicitor-General Pierre Cadieux.

The certificate, used for the first time, is issued under section 40 of the Immigration Act if both the Immigration Minister and Solicitor-General "are of the opinion, based on security or criminal intelligence reports" than an individual poses a threat to the safety of Canada.   On march 12 the Federal Court of Canada ruled the government lacked any evidence that the couple were a security threat. In his ruling, the judge stated that the couple "appeared to have a genuine refugee claim based upon their opposition to the regime of Saddam Hussein". Interestingly, the use of the couple as propaganda shifted from "potential terrorists" prior to and during the war, to refugees fleeing the Iraqi regime after the US military "victory".

A "POTENTIAL FOR SABOTAGE"

Along with the CSIS surveillance and the use of immigration laws was the actual security presence:

"A vast array of strategic facilities- everything from airports and border crossings to power plants- are on the alert... Security at nuclear plants in New Brunswick and Ontario has been strengthened"[5].

On January 15/91 the National Energy Board issued directives to oil and gas pipeline companies to increase security at key installations. "It's a quiet reminder of the crisis in the Persian Gulf and of the potential for sabotage"[6].

The heightened security ran from the highest levels of state agencies such as the national Security Co-ordination Centre down to local police forces.

In Toronto, city police met with public department heads.   According to Nick Vardin, commissioner of Toronto's Public Works Department, they had a "strategic meeting with police to discuss what would be expected in the event of an emergency or terrorist attack... that we would be expected to provide manpower and any resources to help out".

In Vancouver, Jewish Congress chairperson Dr. Michael Elterman stated his organization had "had discussions with Vancouver police and worked out a plan"[8] in the event of "terrorist actions".

There was also a marked increase in policing of anti-war demonstrations in Vancouver with higher numbers of police including the use of riot-equipped police on the international protest day of January 26 (this occurred after demonstrators assailed a militia armory, destroyed recruiting signs and proceeded to a recruiting center, presumably to do similar actions). In other demonstrations when more radi-

Riot cops moving to protect recruiting office, Vancouver January 26

cal demonstrators blocked streets in downtown Vancouver to further disrupt traffic and "business as usual", the police were quick to point out that the people involved were "fringe groups" and that the police "knew who they were and were keeping an eye on them".

THE EMERGENCIES ACT

The final phase of such security would have been enactment of the Emergencies Act, requiring only a simple declaration by the federal cabinet. The Emergencies Act, which replaced the War Measures Act[9] in 1988, contains all the necessary instruments to launch an internal war on "dissent". Under the Act, a "war emergency" can be declared which is a "war or other armed conflict, real or imminent, involving Canada or any of its allies that is so serious as to be a national emergency". With this, the government can make any "orders or regulations" that it believes "on reasonable grounds, are necessary or advisable". Another aspect of the Act is the "international emergency", which enables

the government to regulate "any specified industry or services" and control the travel of any Canadian citizen. In this way, any substantial increase in resistance, such as workers strikes involving military equipment or armaments, widespread sabotage, could prompt implementation of the Emergencies Act.

SOMETHING WAS MISSING!

But where was this wave of "terrorism"? Certainly, armed attacks occurred in many countries throughout the world- but even counter-insurgency "experts" claimed it wasn't from Iraqi or Palestinian groups but in fact endemic (local) guerrilla groups. Even with this, the offensive of armed actions was primarily in the Three Continents and relatively limited in the major western states.

According to Yigal Carmon, adviser on "terrorism" to Israeli prime minister Yitzak Shamir, this was due to the increased vigilance in the west:

"Carmon noted western countries had taken an unprecedented range of countermeasures to detect and deter terrorism... Among other measures, maintenance workers and cleaners of Arab origin was dismissed from jobs in European airports, government buildings and military installations. Asked if such dismissals violated civil rights, Carmon said he assumed such measures were all legal because the countries concerned were all law-abiding (!!!-ed.). He pointed with approval to western countries that have "investigated and restricted the movements of Arab nationals and have detained and deported them""[10].

However, the reality of this "vigilance" in deterring armed attacks can be seen in the actions which did take place: the *Red Army Fraction* machine-gunning of the US embassy in Bonn, bombings by the *November 17* organization in Greece, bombings throughout Turkey, scores of firebombings of military recruiting centres, corporations and US interests throughout the US and

W. Europe, and most striking of all, the February 7 IRA mortar attack on No. 10 Downing st.- the very nerve centre of the British government- while the prime minister met with his war cabinet!

Clearly, when radical groups have the ability and determination to carry out attacks, any level of security can be breached or avoided.

The actual security of targets is in many ways a side-effect of the ultimate goals. That is, while security of military, government and corporate property is of importance (more so in the Three Continents), such security also has political goals aimed at a level of social control that goes beyond more guards and razor-wire. The guards and razor-wire are necessary, but they are used to also mobilize people into acceptance and even support for the military force used against Iraq, and de facto Arab people, because not only is there a war "over there" but also an "inner threat" here. The crudest manifestations of this social control politic was the upsurge in racist violence against Arab people. Vandalism, assaults, firbombings and even shootings occurred. The Canadian Arab Federation documented over 100 violent anti-Arab incidents. Another effect of the racist war hysteria was an increase in anti-semitic attacks on synagogues, Jewish schools and businesses. Clearly, many of these actions can be attributed to the extreme right/fascist groups who, if they weren't fully supporting the war, were railing against the war as yet another "Jewish conspiracy to rule the world", such as Tom Metzger's *White Aryan Resistance*, which instructed its members not to fight for "Jews or camel-jockeys and sand-niggers".

RACISM IN THE ANTI-WAR MOVEMENT

The response in much of the anti-war movement to this racism was to reinforce it. Aside from other critiques of the anti-war movement, such as its lack of clear analysis as to how to resist the war, its sexism and lack of class consciousness, was its own racism.

Seemingly unable and/or unwilling to go beyond slogans and perspectives of the '60's, or more correctly the media image of that movement, anti-war opposition relied on opportunistic slogans: Bring Our/The Troops Home (to which one must ask why- to suppress another Oka or enforce Martial law?), and No Blood for Oil (to which one must ask whose blood- white Anglo-saxons blood?). The movement in general played up to white supremacy and patriotism as it attempted to depoliticize every aspect of imperialist war except self-interest: Hell No We Won't Go We Won't Die For Texaco. What mattered most to the "official" peace movement was the numbers of people it could attract to demonstrations and vigils where its sacred rituals of psuedo-dissent were enacted like a broken record. A broken John Lennon record!

But at whose expense?

The failure to link the Palestinian and Kurdish struggles with the war, to analyze the economic and political conditions which have ensured there has not been one day of peace since World War 2, the absence of an attempt to develop a perspec-

tive for resistance to the war and not just protest, meant that the anti-war movement was circumscribed. It had come to a dead end even before it started. Who was absent from its programs and platforms: people of colour and particularly Arabs. The crystallization of this process was the Jan. 26 mobilizations in which the Vancouver "disarmament" group End the Arms Race refused to allow a member of the Arab community to speak on a platform they controlled. allegedly to avoid "controversy", it was yet another attempt to retain the depoliticization EAR had worked so hard to achieve, and in the end can only be seen as furthering the efforts by the state to silence the Arab perspective: collaboration is the definitive term.

CONCLUSION

In conclusion, the use of "anti-terrorism" and security plays a special role in social control. It creates the conditions for selective and if necessary widespread repression. In this way, the argument that armed or militant actions creates repression is shown to be absurdity; the state constantly organizes its repressive laws and apparatus and constructs the necessary conditions to implement them.

However, it isn't only counter-insurgency that can weaken or even destroy oppositional movements. Nor is it the state which is solely responsible for widespread racism, or in the context of the Gulf War, attacks against Arabs and support for the wholesale slaughter of Arabs. This is something the "peace" movement can also lay claim to.

In this way, the question must also be asked: what role does false opposition play in social control? Certainly, as long as movements of opposition do not attack causes and instead rally around effects, and do not direct themselves against the determining point of conflict between the exploited and exploiter, they fulfill the role of reaffirming the "pluralistic democracy" by acting as the (false) voice of dissent.

Above all, the security measures taken during the Gulf War need to be understood and, in future conflicts as well as now, countered by breaking through the limitations imposed by the state and the "official" peace movement. Limitations not only in our analysis, but in our actions and solidarity work.

FOOTNOTES;

1. Vancouver Province, January 21/91.
2. Ibid.
3. See also Resistance no. 14.
4. Globe and Mail, February 6/91.
5. Globe and Mail, January 12/91.
6. Globe and Mail, Report on Business, January 15/91.
7. Globe and Mail, January 18/91.
8. Vancouver Province, January 22/91.
9. Enacted in October 1970 during the FLQ "October Crisis".
10. Globe and Mail, February 14/91.

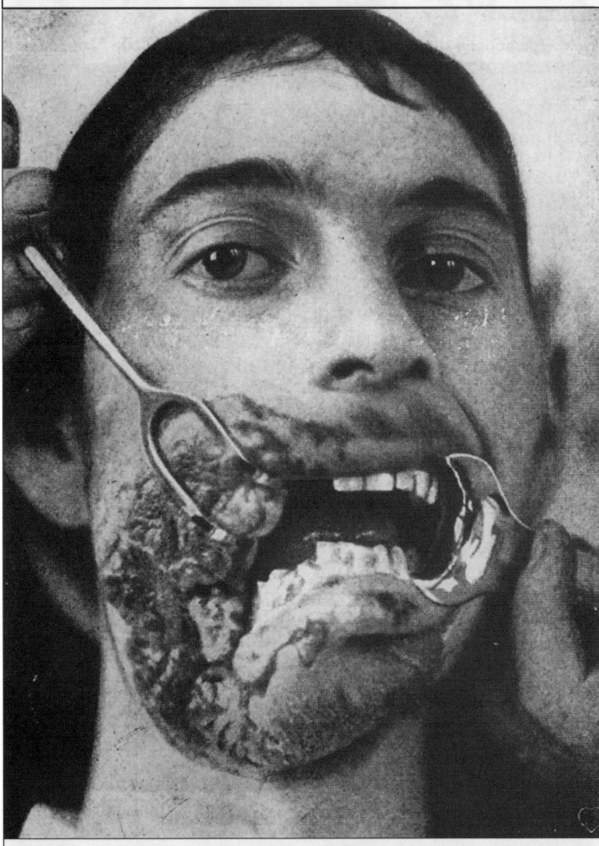

GOING TO THE GULF?

THE GULF WAR, 1991

poster: Allan Antliff (1990)

SEE YOU WHEN YOU GET BACK

by Robynski

Role-Reversal
A Symbol of Palestinian Political Maturity

In his article of September 12th, 2001, "The wickedness and awesome cruelty of a crushed and humiliated people", in Britain's Independent, Robert Fisk wrote of the images shown on the news all over the world of Palestinians celebrating the bombing of the New York towers

That Palestinians could celebrate the massacre of 2,000, perhaps 3,500 innocent people is not only a symbol of their despair but of their political immaturity, of their failure to grasp what they had always been accusing their Israeli enemies of doing: acting disproportionately.

A more shrill—not to mention racist—interpretation of this event is offered by Rochelle Wilner of the Toronto chapter of B'nai Brith, "Palestinians were dancing in the streets during the New York horror, and they have no "culture of peace". Children are taught to hate from the moment they're born,'" (NOW, September 13-19, 2001).

No one, from the likes of Fisk to that of Wilner and B'nai Brith seem to have the least informed conception of exactly why the Palestinians would celebrate what the rest of the world mourns and views as a catastrophic tragedy. But their first mistake in evaluating the Palestinians' response is seeing the event as a catastrophic tragedy, when, to the peoples of the Middle East, such tragedies are daily events. The Western perspective is completely biased by its privilege—"This sort of thing never happens to us"—while the Eastern perspective is a direct consequence of its oppression.

In order to understand exactly why, and what, the Palestinians were celebrating, the first thing that must be stated without equivocation is that Arabs and Muslims (as they themselves have told me) regret the loss of life in the attacks just as much as do Westerners. The Palestinians' oppression (along with that of other peoples of the Middle East) enables them to bifurcate analysis of the event and look at it from two sides, namely, the loss of life (which everyone, East and West, unquestionably regrets) and role-reversal, which is what the Palestinians were celebrating.

Role-reversal: putting the United States in the same position that Palestinians and other Middle Eastern peoples are in. By their celebration, the Palestinian people are only saying to the United States and the world: "See! Now you know what it feels like to have your cities bombed, buildings destroyed and your people killed. Now you know how it feels to be shelled into the Stone Age. Now you know how it feels when the shoe is on the other foot. Now you know what it's like for us, what it feels like when it happens to us and what it's like to be in our place for a change. Now you know how it feels to deal with catastrophic loss of life. See how you feel when it's done to you. How do you think we feel when it's done to us?"

For people in the West, witnessing the towers crumble was a gruesome and numbing shock that totally immobilised them, but for people in the Middle East, witnessing such events in their own lands is

12.

Ye Drunken Sailor 1/1 (2001)

commonplace. They have gotten used to seeing their homes and their cities collapse into ruins under the weight of U.S. bombs, their children, families and loved ones lost, not just in the thousands as in the case of the towers, but in the tens and hundreds of thousands. If an event like that which occurred in New York were to happen in the Middle East, it would lose much of its impact. It would be just another two buildings amongst the thousands of structures leveled by U.S. missiles.

The fact is that the U.S. is the world's bully, and up until now has had complete command of the schoolyard, has been able to pick on and beat up others much smaller than itself at its leisure and with impunity, without ever fear of reprisal. And if being a bully isn't a "symbol of ... political immaturity," then I don't know what is. Now, for the first time, the U.S. has had it's own nose bloodied; for the first time, the bully knows what it's like to be picked on. That is what the Palestinians were celebrating. If you were the one being bullied all the time, wouldn't you celebrate, too?

The fact that the Palestinians, and other Middle Eastern peoples, are capable of a two-pronged response—regret on the one hand, role-reversal on the other—while the West is totally incapable of so sophisticated an analysis, shows that it is in fact not the Palestinians but the West who is guilty of "political immaturity"

Now for once, perhaps for the first time, the U.S. knows how it feels when their missiles obliterate Palestinian homes.

Now the U.S. knows how it felt when, on September 9th, two days before the twin towers fell, U.S. and British aircraft peppered southern Iraq with bombs, killing eight people.

Now the U.S. knows how it felt when its missiles were launched from helicopters into a Lebanese ambulance in 1996.

Now the U.S. knows how it felt when, a few days after this, its shells bombarded a village called Qana.

Now the U.S. knows how it felt when, as a result of the Gulf War, an estimated 200,000 Iraqis perished.

Now the U.S. knows how it felt when it bombed the Sudan, Iraq and Libya, killing hundreds of thousands of people and destroying the infrastructures of these countries.

It is not the Palestinians celebrating, it is the hypocrisy of the West in response to these events that is "a symbol of ... political immaturity."

The hypocrisy of the christian West is best illustrated by the double standard it applies morally to issues like the destruction of the twin towers. At home, it's all about christian "love," "gentle jesus," and the New Testament ethical imperative, "Do unto others as you would have them do unto you." But the policy of the West abroad and especially in the Middle East is that of Old Testament vengeance. "An eye for an eye; a tooth for a tooth."

In the West, there was a huge outpouring of not only grief but also sympathy and support, both material and financial as well as moral, for the twin towers tragedy. But not even a shadow of anything remotely similar to these responses for any of the tragedies in the Middle East that the U.S. is directly responsible for.

In the West, the victims of the twin towers disaster get the gift of a "We are the world" kind of song from mainstream entertainment celebrities. And what does the East ever get from them for the victims of U.S. militarism: absolutely nothing.

In the West, 6.000 are mourned. In the East, hundreds of thousands dead at the hands of the U.S., and the West sheds not a tear.

In the West, there is up to the minute coverage by all media of the destruction of the World Trade Center and the Pentagon, a coverage which monopolises virtually every minute of the day and has done so from the very instant the event happened, and still continues without abatement. Of the the 17,500 civilians killed in Israel's 1982 invasion of Lebanon, of the million civilians—half of them children—that have since died in Iraq as a result of the sanctions imposed by the United States and Britain, of the peoples killed in the U.S. attacks on the Middle East listed above, there has been, in comparison, little to no coverage by the mainstream media.

And if this hypocrisy weren't enough, at the United Nations the U.S. government has always voted against resolutions demanding an end to terrorism, for example, U.N. resolution 42/159.

Measures to prevent international terrorism which endangers or takes innocent human lives or jeopardizes fundamental freedoms and study of the underlying causes of those forms of terrorism and acts of violence which lie in misery, frustration, grievance and despair and which cause some people to sacrifice human lives, including their own, in an attempt to effect radical changes.

On Dec. 7, 1987, the U.N. General Assembly voted 153-2 (with one abstention) to approve a resolution that condemned international terrorism. The two nations rejecting the resolution were the United States and Israel. Now if that isn't a "symbol of ... political immaturity," then I don't know what is.

To make the hypocrisy complete, celebration of the carnage of their wars is not without precedent among U.S. citizens. A Comrade on the Nefac mailing list writes that:

Footage of the bombing of Hiroshima was being shown in America as entertainment in the 1950s and I have heard that the part of the film 'Das Boot' which mentions the

14.

Ye Drunken Sailor I/I (2001)

number of U-Boat crews who lost their lives in the Battle of the Atlantic was greeted with cheers in American movie theaters. Arabs are no different from Westerners except for the fact that they have more justification for their celebration of violence.

If this isn't a "symbol of … political immaturity," then I don't know what is.

You would think that from its experience, the schoolyard bully would have learned its lesson, would have pause to reflect, would perhaps think twice about picking on one smaller than itself, or at the very least would pick on someone its own size for a change. But experience does not teach the U.S. Now the bully is raging about the schoolyard, holding its bloodied nose, like a mad, rampaging animal, thirsting for revenge. Instead of thinking that maybe the experience of the twin towers and the Pentagon should make it reconsider its policy and past, and take the only sane recourse—namely, that these sorts of things should never happen anywhere in the world, East or West, that the U.S. should stop its incessant bombings of the Middle East. Instead of this, the U.S. is continuing the actions which in the first place caused and which can ultimately only perpetuate the violence by devastating Afghanistan with its cruise missiles. Already, as of this date, the U.S. and Britain have reduced the air strips to rubble, wounding 100 Afghani civilians, killing 75, amongst them children, including even some U.N. workers, whose headquarters were destroyed by a cruise missile.

The U.S. is too stupid, arrogant and ignorant to realise that its own militarism and its own imperialism is the real cause of the disaster in New York, and that the only sure prevention of such disasters in future will be for it to completely abandon those two courses. And if that's not a "symbol of … political immaturity," I don't know what is.

Role-reversal. The U.S. should try it some time.

15.

Something Did Start in Quebec City:
North America's Revolutionary Anti-Capitalist Movement

by Cindy Milstein

When thirty-four heads of state gathered behind a chain-link barrier in Quebec City this past April to smile for the television cameras during the Summit of the Americas, it was the tear gassing outside that garnered all the media attention. Those on both sides of the fence jockeyed to put a spin on the meaning of the massive chemical haze that chocked the old city for over two days. The "insiders" claimed that as duly elected leaders of so-called free countries, they were attempting to democratically bring "freedom through free trade," and as such, those on the streets were merely troublemakers without a cause or constituency that needed to be dealt with accordingly. The "outsiders" asserted that those hiding behind the fence were the real source of violence: the tear gas exemplifying what nation-states are willing to do to protect capitalism and the dominant elites- and thus, a certain level of militancy was necessary to tear down the "wall of shame" that many saw as separating the powerful from the powerless.

What got lost in the smoke, however, was the substantive transformation that this particular direct action represented. For Quebec City's convergence, more than anything else, ushered in an explicitly anti-capitalist movement in North America: one spearheaded by anti-authoritarians (by and large, anarchists). That was our real victory in Quebec. But what caused this sudden sea change?

Serendipitously, one fence; self-consciously, two groups.

It was this movement's collective "good luck" that law enforcement officials and politicians determined on a fence as the heart of their strategy to counter the protests. "It didn't start in Quebec," one could say; last June, in Windsor, Ontario, similar trade discussions went off without a hitch behind chain-link, and barbed wire served nicely to make Davos, Switzerland, an impenetrable fortress this past winter for the World Economic Forum. The state-sponsored prophylactic in Quebec City did in fact ward off unwanted intruders: the summit meetings went on, generally unimpeded. Thus, if the fence had remained merely a physical barricade, it could have been counted as a security success.

Unfortunately for Jean Chretien, George W., and their cohorts, the ten-foot fence became a larger- than-life symbolic divide, in essence demanding, "Which side are you on?"

The contrasts could not have been sharper. Closed meetings and secret documents inside; open teach- ins and publicly distributed literature outside. The cynical co-optation of "democracy" via a gratuitous "clause" as a cover for free-floating economic exploitation versus genuine demands for popular control and mutual aid in matters such as economics, ecology, politics, and culture. The raising of glasses for champagne toasts versus the rinsing of eyes from chemical burns.

All of the recent direct actions have, of course, also focused on targets that were figurative to a certain extent. Indeed, the symbolic value of these spectacular showdowns is an essential ingredient in the fight to win the majority of minds over to one perspective or another. But previous focal points, such as the World Trade Organization and International Monetary Fund, have shown themselves to impart somewhat ambiguous messages. The debate stirred up has often centered on how these institutions can potentially be reformed, how the social "good" they do can be salvaged from all the harm they inflict. Besides, some contend, what would replace them? It's proved difficult to move beyond questions regarding the single institution being protested other than to fall back on the buzzword "globalization." And "globalization," while suggesting a wider critique, is just as ambiguous" in no way necessarily underscoring systemic forms of domination that cannot be reformed.

Things were very different in Quebec City. From the vantage point of those on the outside, the fence served no purpose. It not only exemplified a lack of commitment to free expression on the part of the nation- states represented inside but also a further circumscribing of the possibility of freedom itself, and those political leaders trying to allege otherwise were merely revealing their hypocrisy. Hence the heightened level of militancy, illustrative of a movement increasingly intent on fundamental social transformation, directed at tearing the fence down. Yet the fence was crucial for those gathering behind it, too. Beyond providing a literal sense of security, it functioned as a stand-in for the attempt to control the debate around" as well as protect the implementation of" the neoliberal agenda across the Americas. Hence the fiercely fought battle on the part of the police and military in Quebec City to hold the line.

The widespread hatred of the wall and all it embodied meant that those who took a leadership role to bring it down" the libertarian anti-capitalists" stepped not only into the limelight but gained the respect and admiration of other demonstrators, much of the local populace, and a healthy cross section of the broader Canadian public. Sympathy" for the first time in this North American branch of the new global movementâ "was largely on the side of those seeking revolution. No longer the pariah or the parvenu at this direct action, the anti-authoritarian contingent was able to come into its own as a strong and visible force,

16

rather than a marginal, marginalized, or even feared element.   To a great extent, credit must be given to two key organizations: la Convergence des luttes Anti-Capitalistes (the Montreal-based Anti-Capitalist Convergence, or CLAC) and le Comite d'Accueil du Sommet des Ameriques (the Quebec City "based Summit of the Americas Welcoming Committee, or CASA). For starters, it was a brilliant stroke to stake out a nonreformist posture not only in CLAC's name but in the very theme for the summit weekend as well: the Carnival against Capitalism. An opposition to capitalism was openly front and center, both during the many months of organizing leading up to April and at the convergence itself. It was, moreover, an anarchist-influenced version of anti-capitalism. As nuanced by CLAC/CASA's short lists of organizational principles, a rejection of capitalism included a refusal of hierarchy, authoritarianism, and patriarchy, along with the proactive assertion of such values as decentralization and direct democracy. There was no mistaking the message at this direct action.

This brand of anti-capitalism, in turn, served as the substantive and radical tie that bound Quebec City's many direct action participants together. Those people organizing toward and/or coming to the direct action events could bring along their varied concerns and identities, but they were clearly doing so under the rubric of anti-capitalism. A sense of unity was achieved" not through a shapeless tag such as "mobilization," nor by watering down demands until they lose their rebellious edge, nor by ignoring particularity itself. As articulated by CLAC/CASA's "Basis of Unity," "anti-capitalism" created a defined and uncompromising space for the multiplicity of individuals who see themselves as part of a revolutionary project.

Crucial in this necessary yet delicate balancing act between a striving for unification and individuation was the strategically smart phrase "diversity of tactics" in CLAC/CASA's statements of principles. Many have written elsewhere that this principle allowed for heightened militancy in Quebec City, or that it diffused the often poorly formulated and argued "violent" versus "nonviolent" debates that seem to fracture this movement internally. Each claim rings partially true, yet both miss the forest for the trees. The diversity of tactics notion helped to unmask the anti-capitalism element, and in showing its full face, revealed how influential (and even appealing) it is as a force in this new global movement.

In the recent past, there have been thousands of libertarian anti-capitalists at North American direct actions, but they remained separated" and thus largely hidden" by dress, role (such as medic, media, or comm), age, ideological tendency, strategic notions, and so on. Anti-authoritarians "converged" together at mass direct actions, but sadly, the "Revolutionary Anti-Capitalist Bloc" was generally seen as synonymous with the black bloc" meaning that a radical political outlook appeared to have minimal support. The blame lies not with the black bloc or the fact that many

anarchists choose to wear other colors. Instead, the problem has been the inability to combine this spectrum of anti-authoritarian styles under a transparently radical canopy.

The full line in CLAC/CASA's "Basis of Unity" statement on a diversity of tactics altered that equation. It reads: "Respecting a diversity of tactics, the CLAC [or CASA, respectively] supports the use of a variety of creative initiatives, ranging from popular education to direct action." By embracing on an equal footing "education" and "action," thereby also breaking down the supposed theory versus practice divide, the conflation of "militancy" with "radicalism" was shattered. One wasn't a revolutionary because one was a priori a militant; and this indirectly affirmed that not all revolutionaries can afford to take the same risks" just compare a healthy eighteen year old to wheelchair-bound octogenarian. (As a corollary, it showed that being militant doesn't necessarily make one a revolutionary, either. There were plenty of disgruntled Quebecois youth on the streets each night during the convergence intent on mischief and it's highly doubtful that they shared CLAC/CASA's principles.)

The diversity clause, in essence, acknowledged that an opposition to systemic domination such as capitalism and nation-states could and should take many forms if a majoritarian movement is to be built. The principle did not make room under the anti-capitalist banner for militants; they were there already. What the diversity of tactics stance did do was create a welcoming space for those many more anti-authoritarians who perceive themselves as less militant. It widened the margins not of militancy, in other words, but of what it means to reject capitalism as an anti-authoritarian.

Thus, Quebec's anti-capitalist bloc was not one little contingent among many. It was the direct action bloc itself" precisely because it allowed anyone who subscribed to CLAC/CASA's nonreformist stance to march together regardless of how they dressed (or didn't), whether they carried a black flag or a puppet, or whether they wished to avoid arrest or tear down the fence. This was tangibly facilitated, to cite just one example, by the three-tiered color coding of events to indicate varying possibilities of arrest risk and militancy. As the "CrimethInc. Eyewitness Analysis" observes, this "served the purpose ahead of time of making everyone comfortable [by] setting their own level of involvement and risk." Instead of 500 or 1,000 people as at past direct actions, then, the ranks of the two anti-capitalist bloc marches during the convergence swelled to 5,000 or more" perhaps the largest in North America in recent memory.

What the diversity of tactics principle translated into was a diversity of people. But this commitment to inclusiveness was only one of the ethical parameters spelled out in the rest of CLAC/CASA's "Basis of Unity." As such, rather than an assertion of difference for difference's sake" potentially implying a diverse movement emptied of content" what emerged in practice was an explicitly radical movement that was

17

diverse. One could argue that the convergence of anti-capitalists in Quebec City wasn't diverse enough, of course. Yet it provided the first real guide of how to go about nurturing inclusiveness and unity in a way that is at once qualitative and sincere, and moreover, that allows the particular and universal to complement rather than crush each other as part of a social movement.

> Left in the wake of summits and direct actions could be not a small, weary group of anarchist organizers but a large, invigorated radical milieu along with the foundations for resistance attempts in numerous cities across the global.

To return for a moment to the heightened level of militancy in Quebec City, perhaps the diversity of tactics phrase encouraged a somewhat more confrontational stance. But that pales in comparison to the catalyst exerted by the fence and police tactics as reasons why many people choose to go one step further than they ever thought they would during the direct action. Suggestive of this is a photo that appeared in the 22 April 2001 issue of Le Journal de Quebec: sporting a Ralph Nader for President T-shirt, a young man lobs a tear-gas cannister back at the police line that just shot it indiscriminately into the crowd.

Care must nevertheless be taken not to let the diversity of tactics principle morph into a code for "anything goes." As noted by L. A. Kauffman in her recent essay, "Turning Point," already "in certain radical circles . . . the militant acts at the front lines are being seen" and celebrated" in isolation, as part of a growing mystique of insurrection." These direct actions are not yet, and perhaps will never become, insurrections. Viewing them as such could lead to the use of tactics that would be potentially suicidal for this still-fledgling movement" as the historical examples of the Weather Underground and Red Army Faction show. Without a bit more definition to the diversity principle, and a way to make people accountable to any parameters decided on, the anti-capitalist movement is wide open to stupidity or sabotage" or at least more than it needs to be.

At the same time, it is a positive sign that the diversity of tactics phrase has worked its way into the call for an anti-capitalist bloc in D.C. at the World Bank/International Monetary Funds meetings well in advance of the actual protests this October. For where the tangible commitment to diversity of tactics really shone was in the months of organizational and educational work prior to Quebec City's convergence. Here, the tired bumpersticker phrase, "Think Globally, Act Locally," took on renewed meaning in CLAC/CASA's efforts. While they brought teach-ins to numerous cities across Canada and the United States, and put out their politics on the World Wide Web, the real key to their strategy was the attempt to win over the summit "host" city itself (where many CASA members live and work).

18

Rather than merely organizing a weekend-long direct action, CLAC/CASA used the global and continental issues raised by the Free Trade Agreement of the Americas as a wedge into their own communities, as a way to develop radical resistance for ongoing struggles long after the tear gas clears. These Canadian-based organizers, in short, never lost sight of the need to link the global to the local, and to do such community work openly as radicals. They thereby succeeded in one of the more difficult tasks: bringing anti-capitalism home.

A few examples suffice to illustrate the scope of their community activism. For instance, they asked Quebec City inhabitants to "adopt a protester," which meant agreeing to house and hence have relatively intimate contact with an anti-capitalist out-of-towner during the convergence. CLAC/CASA's massive leafletting effort in Quebec City, on the streets and door to door, included handing out thousands of copies of a four-page bilingual tabloid that tried to debunk fear-provoking stereotypes and urged townfolks to "unite in one big anarchist contingent on A21." The anti-capitalist organizers worked in and with grassroots neighborhood associations, and helped ensure that a no-arrest zone was strategically placed in the residential neighborhood abutting the fenced-in summit meetings to create a sense of security for the locals as well as nonlocals. After the convergence, members of CASA pitched in to help other city residents decontaminate the urban parks affected by tear gas.

This community organizing campaign" slipping into public relations at times" put a positive human face to the negative media (and state/police) portrait of anarchists and gave locals some of the knowledge they needed to begin to judge (and hopefully reject) capitalism for themselves. It probably convinced numerous Quebecois to participate in the days of resistance (or at least provide water and bathrooms, as many did), and much more than that, built a solid foundation of support, sympathy, and trust in the community for longer-term projects. The fact that Laval University gave several of its comparatively luxurious buildings in Quebec City over to CLAC/CASA for such things as a convergence center, sleeping facilities (housing over 2,500 people), and rallying point for the two anti-capitalist marches is testimony to these two groups' grassroots efforts. As were the signs in local shopkeepers' windows: "We support you."

CLAC/CASA have proved that it is possible not just to bring thousands into your city but to also work closely with the thousands already there to radicalize and mobilize them for the convergence and beyond. Given that the cities where summits and ministers meet constantly rotate" from Seattle, Washington, D.C., and Ottawa, to Prague, Genoa, and even Qatar" many anti-capitalists will probably get their chance at "hosting" a

Kick It Over 39 (2001)

convergence and could therefore view it as an opportunity to link global concerns to on-the-ground local struggles. Left in the wake of summits and direct actions could be not a small, weary group of anarchist organizers but a large, invigorated radical milieu along with the foundations for resistance attempts in numerous cities across the global.

For it is not a matter of community organizing versus splashy direct actions but how to balance the two so they reinforce, complement, and build on each other in a way that escalates a revolutionary movement globally; as the efforts of CLAC/CASA has shown. While journalist Naomi Klein has been an insightful commentator on this movement, she is wrong in dubbing direct actions as "McProtests." Putting aside the fact that each direct action is not alike but borrows from, rejects, and/or transforms elements of previous actions" that is, there is often a generative, creative process at work" as Quebec City exemplified, mass actions also afford moments of real gain that would otherwise not be possible if resistance and reconstruction were merely parochial affairs. And they give people hope.

The real task of social transformation has only just been glimpsed, of course. Quebec City's convergence felt revolutionary, yet it was by no means a revolution. CLAC/CASA members, like other libertarian anti-capitalists globally, are a long way from helping to turn the places they live into free cities in a free society. At least to date, it also appears that they have done little work, much less published thinking, on what a reconstructive vision might look like, as well as how to move toward it in their communities and this movement. Rather than just a Carnival against Capitalism, a carnival for something might have better provided the utopian thrust necessary to sustain and give direction to the difficult struggle ahead.

While journalist Naomi Klein has been an insightful commentator on this movement, she is wrong in dubbing direct actions as "McProtests."

photo m. hissocks Quebec 2001

Nonetheless, by working locally and globally, by nurturing diversity in the arms of an explicitly anti- authoritarian politics, CLAC/CASA, with the help of a flimsy fence that became a mighty symbol, motivated thousands who came to and live in Quebec City to hoist the anti-capitalist banner onto center stage. Something did start in Quebec; a distinctly radical movement in North America. Now the hard work of self-consciously shaping and building that movement must begin.

Cindy Milstein   is a faculty member at the Institute for Social Ecology (http://www.social-ecology.org), a board member for the Institute for Anarchist Studies (http://flag.blackened.net/ias), and a columnist for Arsenal magazine (www.azone.org/arsenalmag). She can be reached at cbmilstein@aol.com.

19

R   e   f   e   r   e   n   c   e   s   :

Comite d'Accueil du Sommet des Ameriques (Summit of the Americas Welcoming Committee). "CASA's Principles." Available at http://www.tao.ca/~clac/principesen.html#btop.

Convergence des luttes Anti-Capitalistes (Anti-Capitalist Convergence). "CLAC Basis of Unity." Available at http://www.tao.ca/~clac/principesen.html#btop.

CrimethInc. Rioters Bloc. "CrimethInc. Eyewitness Analysis: Free Trade Area of the Americas Summit, Quebec City, April 19â "22." Available at http://crimethinc.com/features.html.

Kauffman, L. A. "Turning Point." Free Radical: A Chronicle of the New Unrest, no. 16 (May 2001). Available at www.free-radical.org.

Klein, Naomi. "Talk to Your Neighbor; It's a Start." Toronto Globe and Mail, 2 May 2001.

Open Road 11 (1980)

BIKESHEVIKS: CYCLING FOR FREEDOM

Militant cyclists have shut down bridges, disrupted auto-shows, and organized urban "die-ins." By Bob Silverman

> *The bicycle is a vehicle for revolution. It can destroy the tyranny of the automobile as effectively as the printing press brought down despots of flesh and blood. The revolution will be spontaneous, the sum total of individual revolts like my own. It has already begun.*
> – Daniel Behrman in *The Man Who Loved Bicycles, the Memoires of an Autophobe*

The velorution has started. That's the message of radical bicyclists organizing and gaining strength all over the world for a bicycle revolution.

They believe that bicycles, when conceived as daily urban transport, are instruments of profound social change. The cyclists' daily confrontation with automobiles for the use of street and parking lot space induces a changed consciousness, they say.

For the bicycling militant, or Bikeshevik, the urban bicycle is the revolutionary's best friend.

Why? Because it permits individuals to take transport into their own hands, enabling them to bypass the auto-necessity constructed step-by-step by the giant car and oil monopolies and the governments who operate in their favour. Bicycling is accessible to virtually every healthy person and its advocates maintain their movement will gather irresistible momentum in the deteriorating Eighties.

Existing groups, like Le Monde a Bicyclette in Montreal, are calling for the velorution, and their methods and social theory are profoundly anti-authoritarian with conscious anarchists involved in the struggle to overthrow the *auto-cracy*.

Already militant cyclists have shut down bridges, disrupted auto-shows, organized urban "die-ins," and begun redesigning urban transportation schemes outside government channels. What's more, they've been successful in implementing many of their aims.

However, the velorution is far from over and the huge automobile interests have barely begun to fight. To understand the scope of the velorution it is first necessary to understand the profound socio-economic forces it threatens to topple.

Automobiles have been with us for so long many people, including radicals, view them as "normal," taking their necessity for granted. But normality is little more than accumulated economic interest and the private car is the supreme economic interest in the world.

The ten largest companies in the world are all producers of cars or oil. General Motors (GM) and Exxon both have sales far in excess of Canada's budget. And the car/oil multinationals have molded the world to suit their interests. Urban geography reflects the stamp of auto-necessity. And their billions have corrupted everyone's heads and value systems.

How did it happen?

The automobile can be compared to the amoeba. They have multiplied and multiplied. First mass-produced and mass-consumed in the United States, they are now produced and consumed throughout the world. In *Running on Empty*, a book assessing the future of the automobile, the authors point out, "cars have assumed a major role in the lives of millions of people and in the aspirations of millions more. Automaking has become the world's largest manufacturing industry. More than 300 million passenger cars are now travelling the world's roads, and some 100,000 new ones roll off the assembly lines each working day."

Clearly, the automobile became the chief motor of capitalist growth in North America. Its attraction to a frustrated and alienated people was immense. For workers disliking their jobs, feeling powerless, the auto had a great appeal, promising to finally put them in the driver's seat of life. It offered them status and identity, and a tangible, visible justification for their labour. Owning a car actually gave meaning to life.

From the beginning the car created and attracted fellow travellers. Oil for cars, steel for cars, glass for cars, rubber for cars, cement for roads for cars, highway bureaucracies and police forces for cars. And every year these forces, both capital and labour, called for more roads to accommodate even more cars.

Kenneth Schneider, an expert on the subject of cars vs. people, writes: "Their variety is bewildering, and they infiltrate virtually every realm of industry, service, and government. Behind auto-making are machine tools, steel, rubber, glass, lead, lacquer, plastics, chrome, copper. Behind gas and oil lie explorations and drilling equipment, refining equipment and its machinery, pipelines and tankers. Behind highway, bridge and parking development lie construction machinery, cement, asphalt and steel."

In the mid-thirties, three of the principle auto-concerns, GM, Standard Oil of California and Firestone Tire Company, started to buy up and destroy the streetcar systems of North America in order to eliminate an impediment to expanded auto sales.

In 1974, Bradford Snell, before the U.S. Senate Committee on Monopolies, traced how GM annihilated all the alternatives to the car and "built the auto-necessity."

"General Motors is a sovereign economic state," Snell once wrote in *American Ground Transport*, "whose common control of auto, truck, bus and locomotive production was a major factor in the displacement of rail and bus transportation by cars and trucks." He notes, moreover, that these displaced methods of travel were energy-conserving, dependable, economical, safe and environmentally compatible. His conclusion: the monopoly in ground

CRITICAL MASS

vehicle production has inexorably led to a breakdown in North America's ground transportation.

"The economics are obvious," Snell continued, "one bus can eliminate 35 automobiles; one streetcar, subway or rail transit vehicle can supplant 50 passenger cars; one train can supplant 1,000 cars or a fleet of 150 cargo-laden trucks. The result was inevitable; a drive by GM to sell cars and trucks by displacing rail and bus systems.

"Nowhere was the ruin from GM's motorization program more apparent than in Southern California. Thirty-five years ago Los Angeles was a beautiful city of lush palm trees, fragrant orange groves and ocean-clean air. It was served then by the world's largest electric railway network. In the late 1930s General Motors and allied highway interests acquired the local transit companies, scrapped their pollution-free electric trains, tore down their power transmission lines, ripped up their tracks, and placed GM buses on already congested Los Angeles streets. Largely as a result, L.A. today is an ecological wasteland: the palm trees are dying of petrochemical smog; the orange groves have been paved over by 300 miles of freeways; the air is a septic tank into which 4 million cars, half of them built by General Motors, pump 13,000 tons of pollutants daily."

In another transport area General Motors and its allies succeeded in destroying intercity train and bus transportation. Greyhound was established by General Motors to replace intercity train travel. They succeeded. Similarly, using its position as the largest shipper of freight in the country, GM imposed its diesel railway engines on the railways which shortly afterwards went bankrupt. At the same time railways in Europe and Japan converted to electricity and are still widely used both for passengers and freight.

In June 1932, Alfred P. Sloan, Jr., president of General Motors, organised the National Highway Users Conference to combine representatives of the Nation's auto, oil and tire industries in a common front against competing transportation interests. Its announced objectives were dedication of highway taxes solely to highway purposes, and development of a continuing program of highway construction.

During the succeeding forty years, the National Highway Users Conference has compiled an impressive record of accomplishments. Its effect, if not purpose, has been to direct public funds away from rail construction and into highway building. At the state level, its 2,800 lobbying groups have been instrumental in persuading forty-four of the nation's legislatures to adopt and preserve measures which dedicate state and local tax revenues exclusively to highway construction. By promoting these highway "trust funds," it has discouraged governors and mayors from attempting to build anything other than highways for urban transportation.

Auto-cracy Damage

Subway and rail transit proposals have had to compete with hospitals, schools and other governmental responsibilities for funding. By contrast, highways have been automatically financed from a self-perpetuating fund which was legally unavailable for any other purpose. From 1945 through 1970, states and localities spent more than $156 billion constructing hundreds of thousand of miles of roads. During the same period, only sixteen miles of subway were constructed in the entire country.

Likewise, at the federal level this organization has been very successful in promoting highways over rail transportation. The National Highway Users Conference managed to persuade Congress to adopt the same trust fund arrangement which it had successfully promoted earlier to the state legislature. The impact of the Federal Highways Trust Fund on transportation spending was similar to that which occurred at the state level. While urban rail proposals were forced to compete for funds with dozens of Federal priorities including national defense, health, and social security, thousands of miles of highways were built automatically with gasoline tax revenues unavailable for any other purpose. From 1956 through 1970, the Federal Government spend approximately $70 billion for highways; and only $795 million or one percent for rail transit.

America and much of the developed world lies prostrate before auto-cracy.

In America public transport has been so thoroughly destroyed that sixty-three million American workers (eighty-seven percent of the workforce) are forced to commute by car. In many cities like Los Angeles and Atlanta over sixty percent of the total land area is allocated to streets, parking lots, and autoroutes. Vast sections of urban inner cities have been annihilated for parking lots. 55,000 Americans die every year in car crashes while the world figure is 200,000. Since the turn of the century 27 million human beings have been killed in cars. Air pollution causes countless cases of lung cancer, asthma, and other bronchial disorders. In Montreal alone, twenty-five percent of the inner city population suffers from lung diseases. Not to mention that automobile noises disturb the peace and tranquility of bicyclists, walkers and neighbours.

Schneider writes: "America is a corporate society. A corporate society is based upon corporate values like money, hard values like steel, operating values like production and consumption, human values like employment. Ever since the second decade of this century the corporate world has realized that there could never be a better vehicle to advance society than the automobile."

So, what's so special about the bicycle? Are they not a commodity just like any other? Capitalists invest money in bicycle factories, workers are exploited in them and bicycles are sold in the market place like televisions, automobiles, pants and skis. It's all true, but in 1980 bicycles are becoming a unique commodity for a very important reason. Unique

Open Road 11 (1980)

not because of how they are made, marketed or advertised, but because of their capacity to change users' consciousness when conceived as daily urban transport.

When viewed as daily urban transport, the bicycle becomes a tool of economic and social change. It becomes a means of bypassing the "official" transports and a way for cyclists to refuse the manipulation of the auto-cracy.

On an economic front you can't beat the bicycle. After four months of steady bicycle commuting the cost of a bicycle is paid in full, with saved expenses. However, the non-monetary benefits of the cycle are even greater. In a city, the bicycle is simply the best transport. Cyclists get to their destinations just as quickly as motorists and much quicker than public transportation. Cycling advocates point out, "It is great fun. Your mind and body get stronger every day. It's a transport you can repair yourself. On a bicycle you become virtually an urban geographer. Just going to your destination you discover previously unknown neighbourhoods that you now find interesting. You observe the architecture more closely. You have daily random encounters with friends. You get door to door service. You can place your transport in your home."

The list goes on and on.

Bicycle Benefits

In the two decades before the turn of the century the bicycle was very prominent. It was the first personal transport. It gave women a tool which eventually permitted them to leave their homes unchaperoned and to wear pants (bloomers). The League of American Wheelman, founded in 1880, quickly became the biggest lobby in the United States and succeeded in getting the streets paved for the first time.

At the turn of the century the mass production of the automobile gradually displaced the bicycle from the streets which the bicycle had paved. And bicycle technology stagnated for sixty years.

This all began to change in the 1970s. The development of the ten-speed bicycle made bicycling easier for people in hilly cities and for longer distances. Slowly, throughout the decade and in all the cities of the developed world bicycles began to make their comeback in greater and greater numbers. For the first time in years bicycles outsold cars in the U.S., Canada, France, England, Germany and Japan.

Although the number of cyclists keeps growing, the facilities for bicycles haven't. Cyclists have become frustrated and angry. They see that cars have all the road space, pedestrians have the sidewalks and cyclists have nothing. They want to ride to work, to school, to market and to friends in perfect safety. They want to be able to park bicycles without worrying that they will be stolen. They want to be able to cross over or under all tunnels and bridges. And they don't want hassles on buses and trains. In short, cyclists are suffering from cyclo-frustration.

Cyclo-frustration

The urban cyclo-frustration has resulted in the creation of bicycling organizations to improve the cyclist's lot. In many cities, groups developed when the number of cyclists became sufficient to support an organization. Montreal's group, Le Monde a Bicyclette (LMB), began in April 1975. By 1979 similar organizations had sprung up in more than ninety cities throughout the world.

The programs of the various cycling groups are virtually identical, for similar realities engender similar responses. The cycling groups all demand:

1: A complete network of bicycle routes and paths so that a ten-year-old child could go anywhere in the city in perfect safety.

2: Safe bicycle parking at all cyclist' destinations: all schools, public transit stops, factories, office buildings, major stores, apartment houses, theatres, restaurants and bars, etc.

3: The integration of the bicycle into the public transport network. Bicycles must be permitted on all metros, on city buses by the installation of rear end bike racks like those in San Diego.

4: Access to all bridges and tunnels.

5: Showers at work places.

6: No dress code in offices so as to be able to work in your bicycle commuting clothes.

7: Bicycle education, both mechanical and signalling, throughout the school system.

8: The compensation of employees using their bicycles for work at a rate presently paid out to cars.

And, in the case of more radical groups like LMB in Montreal, 100,000 community bicycles to be placed in depots throughout the city.

Who would think that something so positive as encouraging bicycle commuting would or could lead to confrontations with the State? After all, don't high government officials in environment, health and energy fields take out expensive ads suggesting the public bicyle for health, energy saving and ecology?

In reality, however, governments have chosen to give the car most of the transport budgets and virtually all the street space. They have constructed bicycle-throttling bridges and tunnels on which only automobiles can travel. In fact, the main cyclist-State confrontations have taken place on bridges.

Confrontations with the State

One could say that bridges and tunnels built since the Second World War, which limit access to automobiles only, are a metaphor for Western society. People just don't count in their planning. All of the bridges built since the last war over the St. Lawrence River in Quebec have omitted facilities for bicyclists. And the four bridges involved include both those constructed by the government of Canada and the government of Quebec. The two rivals seem to be able to cooperate well when it comes to helping the auto/oil industry. Even worse, in Montreal things are actually retrogressing. The hundred year old Victoria Bridge was renovated to eliminate sidewalks in favour of two additional car lanes.

And it's the same all over America.

In Boston a tunnel divides two highly populated parts of that city. Cyclists can't use it and must take a thirty minute detour. In New York they built the Verrazzano Bridge, the largest suspension bridge in the world. This bridge has sixteen lanes and replaced a ferry boat. The ferry boat took bicycles. The Verrazzano Bridge bans bicycles and pedestrians. It cost about $600 million.

In Philadelphia, no less than four bridges crossing the Delaware River have no bicycles access. One such bridge is named after Walt Whitman, author of the *Open Road*. And it's the same unbelievable situation with bridges over San Francisco Bay.

Bridge inaccessibility brings out the most acute cyclo-frustration. For the other hassles, like lack of urban bike paths and safe parking, are only inconveniences. Cyclists can cope with them by being careful and by buying theft-proof personal bicycle locks like Kryptonites and Citadels. *But they often can't cross over to the other side of the water.*

Under pressure, in recent years, transportation authorities have made some concessions. In San Diego, California, busses are equipped with rear end bicycle racks. The PATH Subway system uniting New York with New Jersey accepts bicycles at non-rush hours. The BART subway in San Francisco accepts bicycles at non-rush hours. During the morning and afternoon rush hours Caltrans, California's Transport Ministry, has provided cyclists with a bicycle shuttling service on the Oakland/San Francisco Bay Bridge. Cyclists pay twenty-five cents.

In New York City, the twelve lane Queensboro bridge used to have no bicycle access for the four million people who live on both sides of the East River in Queens and Manhattan. Last year militant cyclists from Transportation Alternatives and the Bicycle Commuters of New York organized several illegal rush hour crossings. In July 1979 the City of New York announced the opening of a lane for bicycles on the Queenboro Bridge. The cyclists' struggle paid off.

In Montreal, Le Monde a Bicyclette in conjunction with Velo-Quebec, the Quebec Government financed cyclotouring association, stormed the renovated and de-biked Victoria Bridge last August. Two baton wielding bridge police failed to stop the forty cyclists. After the illegal ride, the cyclists were offered an escort if they phoned in advance. After crossing the bridge the protesters headed on to the Streetcar Museum to mark the twentieth anniversary of the elimination of Montreal's streetcars.

Kenneth Schneider points out that in the early years auto drivers, before they were powerful enough to attack the general tax resources, built their own roads "with wrench and hammer, and pick and shovel." Well cyclists are now doing the same thing.

The most spectacular "do it yourself cycleroute" was built in the summer of 1979 between Bristol and Bath in England. George Platts, chairperson of Bristol's bicycling organization, writes: "We have achieved a number of 'firsts' including the construction of a five mile stretch of inter-urban cycle/footpath (on a disused railway line between Bristol and Bath) in ten weeks, using volunteer labour and raising the 5,000 pound material costs ourselves." Platts adds that thousands of people use the path every weekend.

Impatient cyclists took paint brushes in hand in New York in the early winter of 1979. After the City of New York Traffic Department was slow in repairing the Broadway Bicycle Path, members of New York's Transportation Alternative started repainting the lines in plain daylight.

In the summer of 1978, bicycle paths suddenly appeared one morning on the side of Marianne and St. Urbain Streets in Montreal. Cars "illegally" parked in the paths built by the impatient cyclists received official looking tickets. The *Montreal Gazette* wrote in its editorial several days later that they had hoped that it was city crews who had built these North-South and East-West bicycle paths. The *Gazette* editorial recommended that the bicycle paths be extended East-West and North-South throughout the city. Unfortunately, the newspaper's advice was not followed. Three days after the appearance of the bicycle paths, the Montreal road department painted them over with a dull grey paint.

In Vancouver the threat of direct action brought quick results. The Lions Gate Bridge crossing Burrard Inlet had expansion joints which were vertical and grabbed bicyclists' wheels. For years the Vancouver Bicycle Club (VBC) had demanded that this be changed to horizontal expansion joints to protect cyclists. Their letters drew no response. Finally they decided to make their own, and install them themselves. That did it.

No Bridge Access

A week before the cyclists had intended to install the safe expansion joints the bridge authorities installed expansion joints similar to those designed by the VBC.

In 1977, of the five bridges over the St. Lawrence River at Montreal, only one, a pre-war bridge, the Jacques Cartier, had sidewalks for bicycles and pedestrians. In March of that year a piece of one of the sidewalks collapsed and fell into a parking lot. Probably fearing another more serious incident, the National Harbours Board closed both the sidewalks, thus depriving cyclists of their only access between two river banks.

LMB and a sister group on the South Side of the St. Lawrence, La Rive Sud au Becane, reacted quickly to the

Open Road 11 (1980)

provocation. They first wrote and phoned the authorities only to be told that repairing the sidewalks was not a priority.

The cyclists then decided that if bicycles could not cross the bridge then cars shouldn't be allowed across either. They prepared a mid-bridge "Die-In," planning to play dead in the middle of bridge traffic. A leaflet was prepared and a press conference organised.

On April 9th, the day before the scheduled die-in, the authorities caved in and reopened one of the sidewalks, covering up the hole and other weak points. Instead of halting the action the cyclists decided to go ahead. Next day contingents of pedestrians and cyclists, walking their bicycles, left simultaneously from each end of the bridge blocking traffic as they went.

The two groups, numbering 400 cyclists in all, united at the summit. They embraced, sang and danced in joyous delirium. And then, for fifteen minutes, to show their good will after the Harbour Board's reopening of the sidewalks, they sat down, tossed volleyballs around and listened to some speeches about the need for "bicycle access."

But the sidewalks on the Cartier Bridge were still dangerous. Several months later, in August 1977, equipped with wheel barrows and cement, militants from Le Monde a Bicyclette and La Rive Sude au Becane repaved a portion of one of the sidewalks. Several weeks later the Harbour Board repaired both sidewalks and even rounded over the steps which had inconvenienced cyclists for years.

Enemies of the Velorution

Since the cyclists' one legal way across the St. Lawrence River is inadequate, and since they sometimes get flat tires, and since it sometimes rains suddenly, and since it is so reasonable, they have demanded bicycle access to Montreal's Subway at non-rush hours. Polite letters get nowhere.

In the Spring of 1978 Montreal cyclists began to step up the pressure on the local Subway system to gain access for bicyclists. On May 10 of that year 200 riders, dividing their forces, entered the Subway at about eight different stations. They then headed to the chief transfer point on the Subway, Berri de Montigny, and there sang and danced to the amusement of subway passengers. Unfortunately, at one of the stations there was a fracas and two velorutionists, Claire Morissette and Francoise Guay were arrested.

In November, Morissette and Guay were found guilty of "disturbing the peace" and fined $25 plus costs of $50. Rather than pay this, the two velorutionaries decided to go to jail. They were sentenced to three days but were released after one.

The struggle to gain access to the Montreal subways continues even today. On April 13, 1980 cyclists were arrested for being next to their bicycles in Montreal's Subway. At the same time they announced the launching of a bicycle-subway pass identical to that of the PATH Subway System in New York which enables New York bicyclists to cross the Hudson River into New Jersey. Forty cyclists demonstrated outside Montreal Transit Authority's Offices while Le Monde a Bicyclette launched the pink card. The struggle continues. A mock application form for the permit was also prepared.

On a world wide scale progress is being made. Berlin, Germany, recently modified its subway to reserve one car per train for cyclists.

On the die-in front, LMB has been a pioneer. They believe death is a frequent consequence of the auto-cracy. To illustrate the point a hundred-plus bikesheviks dropped dead on Montreal's main street at evening rush hour. It was an effort to commemorate the first anniversary of the public transit fare hike and it received continent-wide publicity.

To illustrate the same point another way, every January the LMB uses the occasion of the International auto-show to carry out anti-car propaganda. For the first few years they demonstrated outside the show with a ketchuped child on a stretcher, gas masks and the twisted remains of car fenders, hubs, mufflers, etc. But for the last few years the Montrealers have stepped up their guerrilla theatre in the face of the auto show's thick carpets and disco dances. Last year, ten militants paid the admission to the show and at a prearranged moment they all "died" in front of a Cadillac. The demonstrators were dragged out after thirty minutes, but the point was made.

This year, escalating auto-phobic theatre further, six militants interrupted a carefully orchestrated auto-show opening for the press by lying down on the carpet, playing an anti-auto tape depicting a car crash and beginning with the words Pinto, Pinto, Pinto while others banged away at two bashed up mufflers. At the same time on audacious velorutionary disrobed down into his underwear and mockingly made love to the car, thus satirizing the auto-show's use of half-dressed women to sell their deadly commodity.

This year, cyclists from around the world will be celebrating International Cyclists' Day on the first Saturday of June. As they have in past years, cyclists will ride down the main and most coveted street of their respective cities. In Montreal, upwards of four thousands cyclists participate depending on the weather.

In their campaign to wake up people to the revolutionary potential of the bicycle, velorutionaries identify four basic contradictions:

1: Between the great social value and the vast scope of our demands and the little money required to implement them.

2: Between the positiveness of our demands and the resistance of the governments to accord them.

3: Between the horrors of the automobile and the general reluctance to perceive it.

4: Between the governments' declarations in favour of bicycling and their doing almost nothing to encourage it.

Velorutionary Syndrome

There is another contradiction which has become apparent in the last few years. It's known as "the laws of urban street space" or the "velorutionary syndrome." The cyclists want utilitarian commuter bike paths. The authorities keep conceding recreational paths costing a great deal. Why allot urban street space in this manner? Street space for cars constitutes a subsidy to cars, and car oil companies. These interests don't want to surrender this space to that alternative road user, the bicycle. But recreational bicycle paths, safe bicycle parking, showers at work places do not directly confront auto-interests. It is in these areas where there is no direct car/bicycle clash for the city street space and parking lot space that cyclists are advancing the most rapidly.

In 1979, Chrysler lost over a billion dollars, Ford lost a billion dollars on U.S auto operations and even G.M. lost money on U.S. car operations. Both Ford and G.M. however, made money on foreign car sales to compensate for the domestic losses. Autocracy started in the U.S. and its decline, militant cyclists hope, is now starting there.

As an issue, bicycling is virtually unassailable. Almost everyone, from all social classes and occupations can identify with the cyclists and their demands. The "apple pie status" of bicycling probably explains why velorutionaries receive such good press when the achievement of their aims would require a drastic revolution in North American lifestyle.

However, make no mistake about it, the powers that be are still a potent threat to the bicycle revolution. Just like the automobile companies bought up and destroyed the streetcar systems, an alternative to cars, and destroyed the trains in America, they are ready to do the same to the only street alternative that they have not yet destroyed: the bicycle. This danger is a "velorutionary's nightmare." Exxon already makes an expensive Grafite bicycle. Peugot makes cars and bikes. Montebecane, a fine French bicycle, was just taken over by Renault which two years ago bought up Gitane Bicycles. Since the takeover Gitanes have got worse and more expensive. In Italy, Fiat just bought the biggest Italian bicycle company, Biachi. They will make them more expensive and of a worse quality.

In an issue of the Wall St. Bible, *Forbes* magazine editor Malcolm Forbes said of radical cyclists: "This is one species of health nut that should be harvested by the law." Forbes understood that urban bicycling tends to liberate city bicyclists, to him the real threat is the freedom inherent in bicycling. And that is what will eventually goad the powers that be to reaction.

The apparent success of the velorution to date could also prove to be a danger in the long run. When safe parking or an access to a bridge or subway is won the cyclofrustration of those concerned is reduced. Temporarily.

But militant cyclists hope the urban advantages of cycling will become clearer to millions of people in the coming decade. Objective factors like scarce and expensive gasoline, subjective factors like wanting to be in good health and the pleasure principle will promote bicycle commuting.

The car and the bicycle represent polar opposites. When generalized in the city that contradiction becomes even more acute. The generalization of cars in the city means urbicide, destruction of communities, pollution, noise, intimidation, isolation, and death. The generalization of bicycles in the city means community, ecology, quiet, efficiency and love. Cars mean exploitation and hierarchy. Bicyles mean mutual aid and equality and openness.

Freewheeling is must reading for velorutionaries. For a sample copy, write to them at 14 Picardy Place, Edinburgh 1, Scotland, U.K. Run by a journalists' co-operative, *Freewheeling* gives extensive coverage to the cyclists' struggle throughout the world as well as giving the reader technical and economic information about the cycle industry and related subjects.

Other recommended reading includes Ivan Illich's masterpiece, *Energy and Equity*. Already translated into fourteen languages, the validity of Illich's central theory – that energy when it surpasses a certain threshold becomes increasingly destructive – is becoming manifestly evident.

Another important book is *Autokind vs. Mankind* by Kenneth Schneider (Shocken Books), as is *Access for All* (Pelican). Other's on the subject include: *Dead End* by Buel, *Paradise Lost* by Emma Rothschild, *The Social History of the Bicycle* by Smith, *The Penguin Book of Bicycling*, and *The Man Who Loved Bicycles* by Daniel Behrman.

It is still possible to get the 1980 tri-lingual (English, French and Spanish) World Bicycling Calendar by writing to Le Monde a Bicyclette, 4224 Clark Street, Montreal, Quebec. Costs $3 and the 1981 Calendar is out in July.

Open Road 11 (1980)

FACTORY EARTH

I had been in this discussion so many times before that it was now starting to sound as if it had been rehearsed. It usually started when someone moaned about how much they hate treeplanting, and what a shit job it is. Seemed inevitable that someone would then pipe up that at least we weren't in a factory and we were doing something that was good, ie: greening the Earth. They were able to feel good about their work re-foresting clear-cut logging sites. This is had been point where I'd open my big mouth and ruin their job satisfaction.

The province of B.C. has an economy that is based on primary resource exploitation. Logging is the #1 industry here. A large part of Canada's total wood production comes from here.

Up until about twelve years ago most treeplanting was done by prisoners of the state. Relative to the amount that was cut, the amount of planting was negligible. Today, faced with the prospect of there being nothing left to harvest within twenty years,...... the rush is on. The rush to recuperate this potential wealth, corresponds with our society's attitudes towards the earth, which continue the process of annihilation, while seemingly re-foresting the logged areas.

The first step in this cycle of madness is the issuing of a Tree Farm Liscence to a forest company. The liscencee is given permission by the forest ministry to 'harvest' timber in a specific area and is sometimes also responsible to re-forest it. Logging means clear-cut. The leveling of every standing tree, no matter it's size, species or health. The practice then entails removing the best wood, and only the best wood, leaving the rest to rot or burn. To stand on a clear-cut and witness the destruction and the waste, is to get a sense of this society's attitude to natural life and the natural order. Total disrespect.

Often, the next step on the 'tree farm', depending on the amount of waste that covers the ground, is to burn this slash and debris that remains. The main reason for this is to make the job of planting the trees more cost-effective, or possible at all for that matter. Treeplanting is done on a piece-work basis and if the ground on a clear-cut is free of slash, the trees will be much simpler to plant, therefor the price paid to the planter for each tree will be considerably less. Burning makes things simpler for the planter but it also removes the last remaining source of organic nutrients, eliminates what little material is left for water retention, and also eliminates most of the insulating debris that is left to protect returning plants, animals and micro-organisms from extremes in temperature.

Here's where the planters come in. The trees we are given to plant are usually one to two years old. They are grown in a nursery. Hundreds of thousands, millions and millions of super trees. Perfect little seedlings, thanks to the heavy (normal) use of chemical fertilizers and a multi-

PEACE RIVER
ALASKA
HIGHWAY

BRITISH COLUMBIA
ROCKIES

H BY
WEST

SUPER,
NATURAL
BRITISH COLUMBIA, CANADA

SUPER,
NATURAL
BRITISH COLUMBIA, CANADA

This cycle is eliminated because, well you see it simply takes too long. After these supertrees have been stuck in the ground, the odds are very good that in the next one to ten years something or someone will come along and spray a new generation herbicide on the entire plantation, quite possibly a number of times to eliminate competition for moisture, nutrients and light from these nasty, natural, rapidly growing weed trees. So now we've not only delivered to the earth a ghastly wound, we're lacing that open wound with mutgenic compounds designed to kill. The herbicide treatments are repeated whenever needed to protect this investment and ensure an abundant return, a.s.a.p.

Guided and reassured by the experts, these destructive and exploitative practices increase in intensity and scale yearly. All this is of course accompanied at the same time with much P.R. hooplah about the wonderful job being done in our forests. As this goes on concrete signs begin to show how the greed inspired shortsightedness has ensured the potential for complete and utter failure of these high-tech timber farms. An extensive programme of aerial fertilization was initiated this year on some of the plantations that the 'experts' consider to be prime growing sites. These are places on the lush, temperate coast that have an abundance of the requirements that a tree needs to sustain rapid, robust growth. Older plantations of ten to fifteen years are showing an alarming trend of a slowing and even stunting of growth. The forests were levelled, the wood taken away, the earth then burned, the nutrients leached from the soil and then a regenerative growth cycle poisoned and stopped. These super trees, reaching a point where the soil nutrient requirements are more substantial, are stunting off because the land is now broken and cannot support what is now an artificial demand. In the last decade the number of trees planted has

tude of insecticides, herbicides and fungicides, (Captan, Benlate, Bravo, Ambush, etc., etc.,) The seeds for these tiny potential logs were taken from the tallest, straightest, healthiest trees in the forest.

But wait just a second! Most of these clear-cut sites had a mixture of trees didn't they? And the way each individual tree came to be where it was, depended on milleniums of selection that took place in each micro-site. Variables such as soil type, available moisture, abundance of sunlight, slope aspect and site elevation combined to form a unique set of characteristics determining what would grow where. In the tree farm of today, not only is the entire site usually planted with one species, but the seedlings quite often come from a few 'super' parents.

the natural cycle of regeneration that would take place after a forest is destroyed by fire or in this case logging, would begin with the growth of a deciduous forest (trees that lose their leaves each autumn) which would start to rebuild soil fertility, check erosion and provide insulation from extremes in heat and cold for the young coniferous (evergreen) seedlings that would eventually grow and mature through this deciduous forest, completing a cycle. Our highly trained foresters who, in their words 'manage' the forests, eliminate the cycle of deciduous growth, which in the natural state occurs at a much faster pace than coniferous, and also outgrows even the 'super' trees we are planting now.

increased substantially, but the plantation sites are increasingly less able to withstand the devastation wreaked by the monster. Corporations in search of the last remaining large stands of timber, are taking the forests from steeper, less stable mountainsides and from extremely fragile higher elevation areas.

The chemical corporations are realizing a bonanza marketing pesticides for disease, herbicides for growth competition, napalm for burning clearcuts and fertilizers to force feed this sad excuse for a forest.

In the past, before the advent of aerial insecticide spraying, 'pest' epidemics such as the Spruce Budworm and the Pine Bark Beetle seemed to 'peak-out' and then decline into almost inexistence for generations. The widespread and sustained aerial spraying campaign seems only to have extended the peaks of the epidemics allowing the infestations to spread over entire regions. We have succeeded in turning an immense, almost untouched area into a logged off, toxic environment. The insects' resistence to the chemicals grow and the egghead foresters with their heads up their arses respond as programmed with stronger, more toxic chemicals in larger doses. Du-Pont, Dow and C.I.L. love our forest professionals.

Insect epidemics generally attack only a specific age of a specific species of tree and leave the rest of the forest untouched. If these bugs got into a valley planted with hundreds of thousands, even millions of trees, all of them being of the same age and species...... well the results are fairly simple to predict and you can safely bet that the bastards in charge of forest 'management' are going to protect their increasingly heavy investment by bombarding these potential logs with lots and lots of you know what.

Super Natural British Columbia! Yours

to explore!... The posters glare with glossy, full colour images of mountains too majestic, forests too lush, the sky so blue with clouds so striking that a purity and perfection almost come to mind. Tourism is big business in BC. Ocean, beaches, rivers, lakes, mountains, forests and wildlife.... a natural paradise(?)... actually in a rare instance of concrete long term planning and vision, politicians of a few decades ago created 'Scenic Corridors' in this province. All logging and mining activities, so far as possible, are kept beyond the view of major population centres and transportation routes This was a move inspired by the knowledge of what lay in store for the technicolour landscapes. Taking into consideration that 80% of our population live in cities, and that the great majority of them never get

out of those Scenic Corridors, the reality of what is happening to Earth remains effectively out of sight/mind. It's the complete perspective of the Earth as a commodity to be exploited for material wealth and power, not the Earth as part of us and source of all life.

Toiling up the isolated mountainside, slamming in fake tree after tree after tree, I feel like I'm a factory worker on the shop floor. A worker on a production line spewing out another disposible product. The rich get richer and the Earth gets fucked over.

When the work is over and we drive back to the city past well maintained, clean parks full of nature lovers, the parks just seem like more factories. Factories of illusions that hide the rape and plunder in the hills just over there!

Chester Harry

Mount Robson Provincial Park

West Lake, Wistaria

THE VANCOUVER FIVE

From Protest to Resistance:
the Vancouver five
Remembered

by Jim Campbell

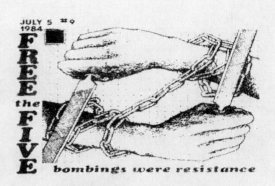

JULY 5 #9 1984
FREE the FIVE
bombings were resistance

Linking anarchism to deliberate acts of violence might seem very natural to most people if they think about anarchism at all. But for most younger anarchists, it must be difficult to imagine that in the early 1980s armed struggle in Canada not only seemed possible, but a small group coming out of the anarchist community in Vancouver actually engaged in it. Moreover there was small but significant support for all three actions claimed by Direct Action and the Wimmin's Fire Brigade.

Political struggle didn't end in the early 1970s with the end of the Vietnam war. The anti-war, and other movements had pulled back, but miltants had gone underground to wage war against the system. Insurrection in Europe seemed possible as the Red Army Fraction and the Red Brigades assassinated and kidnapped politicians and corporate executives. In the U.S. the Black Liberation Army, formed when the Black Panthers went underground, was active until 1981. The United Freedom Front (UFF) and the Armed Resistance Movement were active into the early 1980s, bombing government buildings to protest American military involvement in Central America and attacking corporate targets to protest their involvement in South Africa.

On the American west coast, a multitude of small groups robbed banks, set off bombs and one group kidnapped Patty Hearst, a wealthy heiress. Some of these were explicitly anarchist or anti-authoritarian groups. Bill Dunne and Larry Giddings, for example, were anarchists who continue to be imprisoned in the U.S. today for trying to break a friend out of jail. The George Jackson Brigade was anti-authoritarian, pro-woman, pro-gay and lesbian and advocated collective as opposed to party politics. Even though all of these groups were eventually crushed, they did offer a political alternative to organizing demonstrations and putting out papers.

The Canadian anarchist papers, *Open Road* in Vancouver, *Bulldozer*, in Toronto, and Resistance, which started in Toronto and then shifted to Vancouver, covered the armed resistance in the U.S. and in Europe and the subsequent repression. We published communiques explain-

ing actions, provided supportive coverage of trials and offered an outlet for the writings of the captured combatants and their supporters. Revolution, or at least a protracted struggle, seemed quite possible. Direct Action and the Wimmin's Fire Brigade were part of this wave of armed struggle in North American, part of a broader anti-NATO, anti-war machine politic. The perspective was very much internationalist even if it was understood that it meant working within one's own local and national situation.

In the spring of 1982 a bomb destroyed the nearly completed Cheekeye-Dunsmuir Hydro substation. It's construction had been strongly opposed by local residents on environmental grounds. It was thought that it would lead to the industrialization of Vancouver island and the construction of nuclear power plants for export sales to the U.S. Several hundred pounds of dynamite stopped that plan in its tracks. There was a lot of local support for the action. It wasn't clear whether or not Direct Action, which had claimed the action, was an anarchist group, in a sense it didn't make any difference. The action had raised the political stakes in Canada. But as the bombing had taken place in the wilderness, it was easy to ignore. The next action wouldn't be.

In the late evening of October 14, 1982, a truck exploded outside the Litton Industries plant in Rexdale, in the northwest corner of Toronto resulting in million of dollars in damages. Seven workers were injured, one permanently. After a few days, Direct Action issued a communique claiming responsibility. As a political piece, the communique is as relevant today as it was in 1982, the only change being that the cold war is over. In a second written statement, they took responsibility for a series of errors which resulted in the injuries, especially for seeing the cops and security guards as super heroes.
They weren't.

To ensure that the bomb would be taken seriously, they drove the van in front of a glass-enclosed security booth and parked in front of the factory. The guards didn't notice the truck even though the van driver could clearly see them. Then the phoned-in warning was not understood. But at least it drew the attention of the guards to the van. Unfortunately Direct Action was a bit too clever. They had placed a box painted fluorescent orange outside the truck, easily visible from the security booth. On top of the box they placed a sheet of paper with information and instructions. They expected the guards to come over to the box once they received the phone warning. To emphasize the seriousness of the situation, they placed a stick of unarmed dynamite on top of the box. The guards avoided the box, given that they didn't know that the dynamite on the box was unarmed. In spite of the obvious threat, they didn't start to evacuate the plant until 20 minutes after receiving the warning! And then the bomb went off early, probably set off by radio signals from the arriving police cars.

The bombing took place at a time when the possibility of nuclear war was very real. Both sides of the Cold War were attempting to achieve first strike nuclear capability through new weapons such as the Cruise and Perishing Missiles, the Trident Submarines, and the Neutron Bomb. In response, a peace movement developed in Europe, North America and elsewhere. Canada's agreement to let the U.S. test the Cruise over northern Alberta and the Northwest Territories was seen as a particular affront by peace activists. Litton had been the focus of extensive protests by peace groups since they were producing the guidance systems for the Cruise. But the protests were going nowhere.

The initial reaction of many radicals and activists was joyful on first seeing the headlines in the paper. But this changed on more sober reflection as the implications were thought through. The bombing wasn't just a threat to the militarized state, but to the peaceful coexistence so many activists have with the system. It is clear that even with the injuries, there was not much reaction to it by the average person. For most people the bombing was only another spectacular event in a world gone mad.

It certainly was a major event for the anarchists and the pacifists. The anarchist-communist paper, Strike!, which came out of Toronto, initially condemned the action because it would discredit the movement. It repeated the usual critique that such actions could not by themselves do anything. Direct Action never claimed that it would.

FREE THE FIVE NEWSLETTER MAR. 1st/85

"WE ARE POLITICAL PRISONERS..."

To quote the communique, *"while we have no illusions that direct actions, such as this one, can by themselves bring about the end of Canada's role as a resource based economic and military functionary of Western Imperialism, we do believe that militant direct actions can have a constructive function as a springboard to the kind of consciousness and organization that must be developed if we are to overcome the nuclear masters."*

A more sophisticated critique was issued anonymously by anarchists around *Kick It Over*. They complained that, "the bombing at Litton can not be said to have increased the self-activity of either the community or the employees at the plant." Fair enough, though the same point can be said about putting out newspapers and most other things we do. These anarchists didn't condemn Direct Action for being violent, rather they put the violence in the context of state violence. Though wrongly labeling the bombing as "Vanguard Terror", it was valid to say that "clandestine organizations tend to become isolated from the people" and see their continued existence as becoming a goal in itself. Again this problem is not unique to underground groups.

In early November, less than a month after the bombing, the *Toronto Globe and Mail* ran a major front page article linking the Litton bombing to the Vancouver anarchist community. It quoted unnamed anarchists who drew out the similarities between the politics of Direct Action and the Vancouver anarchist scene. In a later, more sympathetic article, other anarchists provided some background information as to what the purpose of the bombing might be without explicitly claiming that it was an anarchist action. This article was condemned by many anarchists in Toronto but it did help to get the ideas to a wider public.

In mid-December, the offices of the main peace groups in Toronto were raided along with the homes of some of their prominent members. Activists in Toronto and Peterborough were picked up and harassed and threatened by the police. It has never been clear to what extent the police actually thought that these pacifists were really suspects or whether the raids were simply used to disrupt their work against Litton. Some pacifists tried to put as much distance as possible between themselves and the bombers. But there was enough support from other pacifists to show that there need not be a total split between militants, whatever their position might be on the use of violence. The largest demonstration ever to occur against Litton happened on November 11, 1982 less than a month after the bombing. As we said at the time, armed actions can make other forms of protest more visible, rather than less credible.

Litton lost a major contract shortly after the bombing. As Litton President Ronald Keating put it, "(t)hey (the protesters) are an irritant, they get a lot of publicity, and the Americans read every damn bit of it. Pressure from these people is making the Americans look twice." He added rather sadly that, "no one else has been bombed."

In early November, in Vancouver, the Wimmin's Fire Brigade firebombed three Red Hot Video stores. This American chain built up an inventory of video tapes pirated from hard-core porn films. According to *Open Road*, "(m)any of the films depicted not only explicit sex scenes, but women being trussed up, beaten, raped, tortured, forced to undergo enemas by armed intruders and other forms of degradation." Women's groups had been fighting for six months against Red Hot Video, but there was no response from the province. Within a few weeks, scores of women's groups of all stripes had issued statements of sympathy and understanding for the action, demonstrations had been held in a dozen centres across the province, and six porn shops had closed, moved away or withdrawn much of their stock out of fear they would be the next target. Within two months the first charges were laid for combining explicit sex with violence.

The Wimmin's Fire Brigade action was so successful because it was so well integrated into, and complimentary to the public campaign. As *B.C. Blackout*, a biweekly autonomist newsletter put it, the action of the Wimmin's Fire Brigade could only have the impact it did because of the months of spade work by many groups and individuals educating themselves, doing research, making contacts, pressuring the authorities, documenting their case — in short, building the infrastructure for an effective, grass roots, above-board movement.

On January 20, 1983, near Squamish, B.C. the Five were returning to Vancouver from target practice in the mountains. The police, dressed as Department of Highway workers, stopped their van and in a violent attack pulled them out of the van and arrested them at gun point. They were charged with 12 to 15 counts, including Red Hot Video, Cheekeye-Dunsmuir, conspiracy to rob a Brinks truck, as well as conspiracy to commit more bombings. Immediately after the arrests, the police had a news conference at which they displayed the extensive weaponry which they claimed had been seized from the Five. This was the beginning of what came to be called, "Trial by Media", as the police and prosecution used the media to try to contaminate public opinion ,not only against the Five, but against the anarchist movement in general. Newspaper headlines screamed about "police netting terrorists" and a "national network of anarchist cells." The police raided 4 homes in Vancouver the morning after the first support group meeting. No arrests were made, but typewriters were seized and people were subjected to verbal abuse.

The official police story was that the break in the case came when a reporter from the *Globe and Mail* showed anarchist papers to the Toronto police who, noticing the Cheekeye-Dunsmuir communique in Resistance, sent the Post Office Box address to Vancouver. The cops there supposedly put the box under surveillance and were

Bulldozer #8, summer 1985

eventually able to track down the Five through a series of contacts. The story was convincing enough that the reporter was going to apply for the substantial reward before being talked out of it by more conscious and principled friends.

This story was a cover, for the police were already very aware of the Five. They had been under police surveillance for one reason or another since well before the first action. Brent Taylor and Ann Hansen in particular were pretty notorious in Vancouver. A cop didn't have to be too bright to consider them as possible suspects. Activists who didn't even know them thought they probably had something to do with Direct Action. They were the only ones who regularly went to demonstrations all masked up, looking much more prepared for demonstrations in Germany than in Vancouver.

It is quite likely that the security police had actually watched them do the Red Hot Video actions. This became very relevant at the trials. The Vancouver police obtained warrants to tap their phones and bug their house in order to investigate Red Hot Video. Such warrants are only supposed to be issued as a last resort when all other means of investigation have failed. But these were issued shortly after the firebombing happened. Moreover, they were not needed if the police already knew who had participated in the attacks. The RCMP security service had watched them commit other crimes and had them under observation at the time of Red Hot Video. But there were no surveillance notes covering the period of the actual attack. It was assumed that the wire taps were actually needed by the police to connect the Five to Litton, for which it would have been more difficult for the Vancouver police to obtain a legal warrant. The evidence obtained through these bugs provided the bulk of the case against the Five which is why the first part of the eventual trial dealt with the legality of wire tapps.

On June 13, 1983, the *Bulldozer* house in Toronto was raided by the local Litton squad. The warrant, which included the charges of Sabotage of Litton, Seditious Libel, and Procuring an Abortion allowed the police to specifically seize anything related to *Bulldozer* magazine. They took layout flats, letters, articles, magazines, and the mailing list. We finally got all this stuff back after a year of legal fighting.

The Seditious Libel charge was apparently related to a leaflet entitled "Peace, Paranoia and Politics" which laid out the politics around the Litton bombing, the peace movement and the arrests of the Five. Seditious Libel apparently involves calling for the armed overthrow of the state. The last time the charge had been used was in 1950 against some trade unionists in Quebec. Our lawyers eagerly anticipated defending us on this charge, but nothing ever came of it.

The Procuring an Abortion charge came about when an alleged menstrual extraction performed by a midwife, Colleen Crosby, on a member of the *Bulldozer* collective, had come to the attention of the police through phone taps. Crosby was picked up a week later by cops who drove her around for several hours, threatening to charge her with the Procuring an Abortion charge unless she told them about any links between *Bulldozer* and the Litton bombing. Crosby would have refused to cooperate anyway, but she had no information to give. It took a couple of years and thousands of dollars in legal fees before the charge was eventually dropped.

Our political weakness — referring to both the Five and their supporters — became apparent during the trial and the support work we did around the trial. The Five assumed that they would go down in a hail of bullets. Instead of the relative glory of the spectacular death, they had to deal with the much more pedestrian reality of sitting in jail awaiting trial. This lack of political and personal preparation for the almost inevitable consequences of their actions was compounded by a lack of preparation by their supporters. It is straightforward to reprint communiques from underground comrades. But it is much more difficult to handle raids and lawyers, harassing arrests, and watch friends and comrades distance themselves just when support and work is needed the most. One must be able to handle high-stress politics for what could be a period of years, while advancing politics that may not even be supported by one's own friends and political associates, let alone the wider society. Yet competent and principled above ground support is crucial if underground actions are to have any long term impact. The community in Vancouver was able to maintain a presence outside and inside the courtroom during the trial in spite of differences in strategy as to how to support them. In Toronto, we were able to keep the ideas in circulation, but had little public impact.

In the initial confusion, the right to a fair trial became the main demand. Since it seemed possible that the room bugs which provided the main body of evidence might be thrown out, this strictly legal course was hard to resist without prior political clarity as to how trials should be conducted. The right to a fair trial must not be ignored if the battle is going to be fought on the legal terrain at all. But it is the state's battleground, and their first weapon is criminalization. The Crown split the indictments into four trials, the first of which was on the least overtly political charges, weapons offenses and conspiracy to rob a Brinks truck. While it may be obvious to those who have a certain political understanding why guerrillas need weapons and money, television pictures of a desktop full of weapons, and reports of meticulous planning for a raid on a Brinks truck, were calculated to defuse claims that the Five were principled political activists. The fight for a fair trial did draw support from ac-

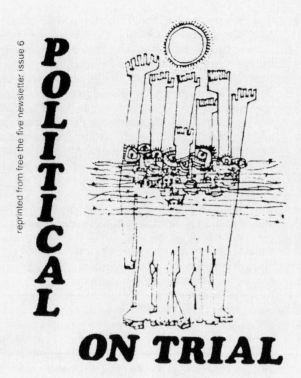

reprinted from free the five newsletter: issue 6

POLITICAL

ON TRIAL

PRISONERS

tivists, progressive journalists and lawyers and human rights activists. But it can create real problems if the trial is made to appear legally "fair". Or when, as happened, the Five eventually pled guilty. Some people who did support work felt manipulated into supporting guilty people even though we tried to be clear that there is a difference between pleading not guilty and being innocent.

The "trial by media" strategy fell apart when the court ruled that the wire tap evidence was admissible. The first trial for the weapons and conspiracy to rob the Brinks truck began in January 1984. The evidence of the first 4 months mainly involved the surveillance prior to their arrests. In March, Julie Belmas and Gerry Hannah entered guilty pleas, including Red Hot Video, and for Julie, the Litton bombing. In April, Doug Stewart was ordered acquitted on the Brinks charge but found guilty of weapon offenses. In June, he pleaded guilty to Cheekeye-Dunsmuir. The jury found Ann and Brent guilty of all the charges from the first trial. In June, in a surprise move, Ann pled guilty to Cheekeye-Dunsmuir and Litton.

Brent was brought to Toronto for a trial around Litton and eventually pled guilty. Recognizing our own weakness, we told him that little could be gained politically in Toronto if the trial was to go ahead. In our relative isolation it was difficult to imagine taking on what would have to be a major effort to present the politics behind the bombing through a hostile mass media. Yet not doing so meant that there was never a longer-term focus nor sense of direction for those who might have been willing to come

forward with more active support. It was not our most glorious moment.

To sum up this section, let me quote from Ann's sentencing statement,

"(w)hen I was first arrested, I was intimidated and surrounded by the courts and prisons. This fear provided the basis for the belief that if I played the legal game, I would get acquitted or less time. This fear obscured my vision and fooled me into thinking that I could get a break from the justice system. But this eight months in court has sharpened my perceptions and strengthened my political convictions to see that the legal game is marked and political prisoners are dealt a marked deck."

Doug Stewart was sentenced to 6 years, and served the maximum 4. Gerry Hannah got ten years, but was out in 5. Julie, only 21 at the time of sentencing, got 20 years. She appealed and got five years off when she turned against Ann and Brent, effectively sabotaging their appeal. Many people were really pissed at this betrayal by Julie. But Julie's testimony was not the reason why Ann and Brent were convicted. If Julie really wanted to make a deal, she could have implicated other people by lying. This she didn't do.

Brent got 22 years, and Ann got life. The sentences, especially Julie's and Ann's were considered unduly harsh. But the state wanted to stamp out any incipient guerrilla activity. The prison system, though, controls how long people actually served. Ann and Brent were both out before 8 years were up. In comparison to what happens to American guerrillas, this was almost lenient.

Doug Stewart wrote in *Open Road* after their conviction that the size of the bombs was problematic. He suggested that medium-level attacks such as arson and mechanical sabotage are easier to do than bombings and large scale actions virtually demand going underground. Direct Action understood that they had to break off contact with other political people; that to do actions in one city, they should live in another. But this demands enormous emotional and personal sacrifices. It was the failure to completely cut off ties with friends and lovers that left a trail for the local police. Smaller actions are technically simpler and allow, as Stewart says, "a group to come together easily and quickly around a particular issue."

Medium-level activity also, has a much less intense impact on one's personal life. If you are not underground, you are less emotionally isolated, and the overall stress level is very much lower. Capture for a medium-level action would be much less devastating in every way. A two or three year sentence is no joke, but it is substantially easier to deal with than a ten or twenty year one.

To summarize, let me quote from an article in Prison News Service written ten years after Litton:

Overt political actions such as these bombings, propaganda by deed, as they are known, are not understood in a non-political society. Even though few people will understand the motivations behind the attack, the positive side is that there won't necessarily be a major reaction against it either. It is an error to think that something like the Litton bombing will be a wake-up call for people to do something about a critical situation facing them. But properly explained it can make a difference to those people who are already concerned about the situation and who have become frustrated with other methods of dealing with the issue.

Guerrilla actions are not an end in themselves; that is, a single act, or even a coordinated series of actions, has little likelihood of achieving little more than some immediate goal. Such actions are problematic if it is assumed that they can be substituted for above ground work. But if they can be situated within a broader politics, one tactic amongst many, then they can give the above ground movements more room to maneuver, making them both more visible and more credible. At the same time, activists are given a psychological lift, a sense of victory, regardless of how fleeting, so that they go about their own political work with a renewed enthusiasm...

For most North American activists, armed struggle is reduced to a moral question: Should we, or should we not use violent means to advance the struggle?

Wimmin's Fire Brigade Communique
Reprinted from Kick It Over #6 February 1983.

We, the Wimmin's Fire Brigade, claim responsibility for the fire-bombing of three Red Hot Video outlets in the Lower Mainland of B.C. on Nov. 22, 1982. This action is another step towards the destruction of a business that promotes and profits fom violence against women and children.

Red Hot Video sells tapes that show wimmin and children being tortured, raped and humiliated. We are not the property of men to be used and abused.

Red hot Video is part of a multi-billion dollar pornography industry that teaches men to equate sexuality with violence. Although these tapes violate the Criminal code of Canada and the B.C. guidelines on pornography, all lawful attempts to shut down Red Hot Video have failed because the justice system was created, and is controlled, by rich men to protect their profits and property.

As a result, we are left no visible alternative but to change the situation ourselves through illegal means. This is an act of self-defense against hate propaganda. We will continue to defend ourselves!

Though this is relevant on a personal level, it only confuses what is really a political question. Most radicals, at this point in time anyway, are not going to become i n - volved directly in armed attacks. But as resistance movements develop in North America – and they had better or we are all lost – it is inevitable that armed actions will be undertaken by some. The question remains if these armed actions will be accepted as part of the spectrum of necessary activity. Much will depend on whether people suffer harm or injuries. Far from being "terroristic", the history of armed struggle in North America shows that the guerrillas have been quite careful in selecting their targets. There is a major difference between bombing military or corporate targets, or even assassinating police in response to their use of violence, and setting off bombs on crowded city streets. The left in North America has never used random acts of terror against the general population. To denounce any who would choose to act outside of the narrowly defined limits of peaceful protest in order to appear morally superior, or to supposedly avoid alienating people, is to give the state the right to determine what are the allowable limits of protest.

Repression is most effective when it is able to keep the radical ideas from being transmitted to a new generation of activists. If the ideas can be passed on, then the next wave of activists develop their politics from the base that has already been created. Fortunately, a relatively small, but very active milieu of young activists adopted many of the politics around Direct Action and developed them through such projects as *Reality Now*, the Anarchist Black Cross and *Ecomedia*. Their work in the peace, punk and native support movements, helped ensure that such politics did not end when the Five went to prison.

This is an edited version of a talk that Jim gave during the Spring 1999 Anarchist Lecture Series in Toronto.

From the Archive: **Interview with the Vancouver 5: Resistance v.s. Protest Ann Hansen and Brent Taylor**
edited and reprinted from Kick It Over 8, September 1983

KIO: Do you feel that pacifism in future years will create meaningful social change as opposed to reformism? Do you see pacifism as a tactic in relation to a revolutionary resistance perspective?

First of all, pacifism is not simply a tool or a tactic. Pacifism is actually a fundamental set of moral beliefs which determine how one lives one's life, and therefore, how one acts politically. Pacifism should be respected as an individual choice. However, pacifism has been elevated to a theory for revolutionary social change and is adhered to as the [only] process and the [only] means we must adhere to. When assertions are made that only a pacifist movement will enable us to create a better world, our understanding of historical and present day reality compels us to disagree.

In the "Peace Movement" in North America, the ideals of pacifism are being applied very dogmatically to a mass social struggle, and have become entrenched as "ideology of non-violence". Often times, adherence to the ideology appears to actually take precedence over the realization of the goals we are seeking...

Granted, it would be much nicer if revolutionary change could come about according to pacifist practice. Unfortunately however, it is doubtful that is the case, and thus, it is wrong to base our future on such assumptions.

Nevertheless, there is a great deal of potential for effective use of non-violent tactics in the liberation process. It is, in fact, absurd to imagine that a revolutionary movement could ever exist without mass participation in non-violent mobilizations....

However, the same can not be said about pacifism. If we, as a movement, restrict ourselves to non-violent tactics only-in other words, if we are a strictly pacifist movement- we will continue to make definite advances from here, but eventually, we will find ourselves prevented from going any further by the repressive forces of the state....

This does not mean that the ends justify any means. The process that we follow is extremely important, and most certainly we must at all times be guided by strong moral concerns and true reverence for life, yet sometimes reality necessitates certain means. We live in a world of violence but it it critical that we always recognize that such violence is not of our choosing. In this sense, reality also justifies the use of certain means; even those means which go beyond the limitations of pacifism.

It is too simplistic to reject revolutionary violence along with the horrible indiscriminate magnitude of reactionary violence [of the state etc.], just because both are violence. To equate both so simplistically removes them from the context of social reality, and in doing so ignores the essence of each - the meaning and purpose for which they are employed. To then determine the limits of our own practice on the basis of such an artificial equation is obviously wrong....

The way we hope to live in that future is not necessarily a realistic way to live now....

It is true that all revolutionary movements in power have become Statist regimes, but it is false to conclude that this is because violent tactics were used during their liberation process. Instead, it should be attributed to the fact that such movements operated according to authoritarian Statist ideology.

KIO: When you speak of the need to reject industrial civilization, is it not possible to utilize such technological advances for the good of the Earth's people and the Earth itself? If you believe that such is not the case, please explain your position.

Further technological advancements are not necessary for the good of the Earth's people or the Earth; in fact, under the present world order, any further advancements will only benefit the profits of the corporations and the men that run them.

For many, many centuries human beings have survived and developed civilizations on this Earth that were rich spiritually, intellectually, and culturally without industrialism or advanced technology. As well, their survival was not at the expense of hundreds of animal species and environmental destruction. Somehow people managed to hunt, fish, and grow food without General Foods or Safeway. Dances, music and stories flourished without RCA, Sam the Record Man and Harlequin Romances....

The work with machines offered by industrialism alienates people from each other and from the natural functions of the Earth. Whether industrialism exists in the socialist or capitalist bloc, the work still remains alienating and the Earth must constantly be disemboweled so that machines, fuels, and products can be made. The only real difference is that profits in socialist countries are more equally distributed than in capitalist regimes....

KIO: When you refer to the need to build an active resistance, would you define in what manner it should appear?

We don't envision one particular form in which an active resistance movement should appear, but believe that what needs to happen is for a resistance mentality to take root among activists in Canada. From this radical consciousness, active resistance will then appear in various forms and many different struggles.

To a great extent the movement now operates with a protest mentality which unfortunately fosters wide spread reformist illusions about what kind of struggle is necessary to realize the goals we seek. Protest attempts to influence the decisions of those in power by showing public disagreement with their policies. Because we imagine that through protest the powerful will eventually be pressured to change, we are mistakenly wholly engaged in a form of struggle in which the outcome is ultimately left in the hands of those we oppose....

A resistance mentality is based upon the premise that the powerful will ignore our protests, and therefore that we must build a movement with the commitment and determination to utilize means of struggle by which we ourselves can stop the projects that we oppose....

A resistance movement would not be limited by legalities when there is a need for direct action confrontation: such a militant approach is definitely necessary when we are confronted with life-threatening situations; in particular, the on going destruction and polluting of the envronment or the build up of nuclear arsenals and the war machine....

It is now almost six months since the Day of Action during this years Anarchist Gathering in Toronto. So far there seems to have been little or no critical analysis of what happened. Hopefully this will put forward some ideas to spark discussion towards future demo's & similiar situations.

An examination of police tactics & reaction, & our own response, is important if we wish to continue & develop using demo's as a means of protest. Please note this article isn't an account of the protest but rather an analysis. Other papers covered that aspect, as well as this paper.

following the demo, more police had to be called to block off the protesters. The demo would respond by changing its course, heading down another street, but not changing the general direction.

As the demo loosely moved across a parking lot behind a construction site, undercover cops/gov't. agents went up an elevator located in the construction site. They could be seen giving orders and/or information via radio from the top. Then police on foot & horseback quickly moved forward from behind the demo. clubs drawn. The protesters ran to avoid in-

SNATCH SQUADS

After this point the cops were much better organised. The use of police snatch-squads became a serious problem that wasn't really dealt with. Because the demo was spread out, individual cops were allowed to mingle, apparently to select a target. Targets were most often those who had carried out actions.

WILD IN THE STREETS!

CONTROL

The initial tactic of the police, who at first numbered around 30, was to strictly control & contain the demo. This was done by forming a block-long 'corridor' of fences & vehicles. Once the bulk of the protesters (around 400) had arrived outside the US consulate, a police loudspeaker announced that it was an 'illegal' demonstration. The idea appeared to be to contain the demo. & at the same time let those who feared immediate arrest a chance to disperse. This would have possibly worked except that once protesters walked into the corridor, they immediately saw a potential trap. The first concern of many protesters was to escape the police corridor, & people began moving down to the opposite end of the block. As the demo. moved down & across the street onto an island in the middle of the boulevard, police moved down & as the traffic lights changed divided the demo into two. It was an obvious police tactic to split the demo as we came to intersections. Protesters who voluntarily obeying traffic light signals didn't help in keeping the demo together.

The war memorial on the 'island' became a rallying point, lots of noise, flags burning, creating a strong sense of militancy. The police did nothing, perhaps hoping this would be the extent of the demo (all the best photo oppurtinities occurred here!).

UNDESIRABLE ELEMENTS

At this point media & undercover cops etc. worked freely, mingling amongst the protesters. Our inexperience in doing militant demo's led to our in-action in dealing with their presence, but also we did not know towhat level the protest would develop. At this early stage would it have been wiseto take assertive action against undesirable elments? The question of what to do next was solved as people spontaneously moved backup & past the US consulate , still on the concrete island. Again the demo stopped at the traffic lights, allowing mounted police to move up to the head of the demo & cut off the peop people who had made it across the street. This was a re-curring problem & at no poin point was there any real co-hesion within the demo. The police took advantage of this by moving-in at intersections, where hesitation between doing something illegal in an already illegal demo caused confusion. The whole question of the traffic lights would have been solved by not allowing any group of protesters to be isolated- in real terms there should've been no gaps at all & a space of only 5-6 feet should be considered a gap.

The level of militancy increased as people moved onto the street & off the sidewalk. At this point it would have been a good idea to link arms & form into rows. The basic idea from the front of the demo seemed to be to go to the downtown core, the police obviously didn't want this. A pattern developed where the cops were trying to divert the demo but because they were underpowered & always

jury & arrest. At this point individual cops were running after individual protesters, but were unable to succesfuly arrest anyone because they had no immediate back-up or co-ordination. On the other hand, protesters would simply pull or push the person free. A small pitched battle quickly occurred when protesters stopped running, regrouped, & fought the advancing police. The front of the demo, which had kept moving forward onto a street & across a small intersection, found itself too far ahead & spread out. As they regrouped & moved back to join the main body police on horse & vehicle began moving into the intersection. The prevent these cops from moving forward some protesters pulled traffic control barricades (similiar to ones used by police) across the street. This was succesful, and as a second barrier was moved up, some cops reacted by chasing one person moving it. As one of the cops had the person on the ground, nearby protesters immediately reacted by pulling him off & chasing him a away. This could be seen as a major development as protesters had at least for the time overcome their fear of uniformed cops. Up until now it was to our advantage that the demo moved quickly and spontaneously, never giving the cops the chance to succesfuly organise co-ordinated action. However, going across Nathan Phillips square/city hall area,

After identifying a target, the cops would withdraw & form a group of 4-5. They would wait for the target to become more or less accesible, then rush in, grab them & put them to the ground. Two cops would carry out the actual arrest, while others would circle & prevent demonstrators getting close. Horses were often used to hold back the crowd, & prevent photos being taken. The snatch squads created fear & apprehension amongst protesters, & a feeling of helplesness.

Once again, if protesters had linked arms & formed rows (maybe with those who felt most at risk in the centre rows), the police snatch squads would have been prevented from reaching people. This form of organisation also improves communication within the demo, gives a very strong sense of solidarity, eases tension, reduces panic if police attack, & provides a better position at the front of the demo for those who know the city and/or route.

LESSONS FROM EUROPE

In many parts of Europe for militant demos this form of organisation happens, with the addition of ropes along both sides of the demo, which further prevents police access & protester panic. Also

pg 6

the demonstration, slowed up, spread out, & some people stopped to taunt police. Meanwhile the cops had also stopped, regrouped, increased their strength to about 50 (with more arriving in the surrounding area), & then started moving forward again- It would have been much better if the demo had kept moving, as a group, without waiting for the cops to regroup etc.

present are groups known as the 'black block' who come prepared for the defence of the demo but also importantly they sometimes act as offensive groups. This group is so-called because of their mostly black masks & predominantly black coloured clothing (often leather jackets for protection). Many wear motorcycle helmets for further protection, & carry sticks & gas masks. Those with the most protection go to the front of the demo, with smaller blocks interspersed throughout, and a group at the rear.

Police are intimidated by this threatening, seemingly well-organised & prepared force. It also reduces police attacks through fear of provoking the 'black block-block'. The presence of the 'black block' greatly increases feelings of strength & solidarity within the demo. Within the 'black block' itself are clearly identified people trained in first aid. The level of communication is greatly increased by 2-way radios, especially between the routes to be marched as well as the route that has been marched.

ACTION

In Toronto, the spontaneous actions of flag burning, graffiti, barricades, & pitched battles, were an important expression of frustration & anger, encouraging more solidarity & militancy. Some of the physical signs of the actions lasted much longer than the demo itself. Maybe it's also worth remembering that police are only the defenders of capitalism, & that sometimes to direct all actions agaisnt them is to forget the actual structures of capitalism, ie; banks, corporations etc. If the police exist to protect property, then they did a good job in Toronto! Despite this several thousand dollars in property damage did occur, in the form of a smashed window, graffiti, & city property burned etc.

Police were able to identify people who carried out actions by their conspicuous clothing &/or hair. Things that could be done to avoid this would be to take a change of shirt or reversible jacket, & often just swapping clothes could help confuse cops. Again, the 'black block' idea, with many people wearing masks & similiar coloured clothing, reduces the risk of identification.

For those who, for various reasons, did not want to take part in actions, a bag of quarters for bogus telephone calls to police would divert police resources, & give conflicting information'' to the police central command, as would captured police radios.

Before going to a demo it's important to consider the expected level of militancy or violence (instigated by either side). It's also important to consider the context of the demo. This is best done in small affinity groups to discuss possible actions to be taken as affinity groups, to discuss the implications their actions may have on the demo, and to consider possible actions in response to situations that may develop (more police than expected, police attack, & divisive elements with-in the demo).

Remember to take the equipment you may need, for example; sling-shots,

paint/stink/smoke-bombs, missiles , masks, gloves, rope, etching fluid, the list is endless, be adventurous!

Some questions we need to ask are; In Toronto, would it have been wise to tak take positive action against main-stream media people? Would wide-spread property damage at the demo have made it more succesful?(police reaction, during & after, public opinion, & support from protesters)-

What was the real purpose of the demo? To protest against the shooting down of the Iranian air-liner, to have an Anarchist protest, or because there were a few hundred Anarchists laying about? Would an actual riot have been desirable or possible?

PLANNING

The method & amount of planning involved would have been almost adequate for the AN ANVA (Alliance for Non-Violent Action) pacifist demo that occurred earlier that day. However it should have been obvious that most of the protesters wanted to actually confront the state. Clearly the mass meeting in the public park the day before

was neither desirable nor effective. Bearing in mind the public nature of the 'planning', it still wasn't discussed wether or not to go beyond the illegality of an 'illegal' demonstration, & wether or not those who chose to carry out 'illegal' actions would have the general support of the protesters. These considerations are very important & led to the lack of direction, lack of cO-ordination, hesitation, & in-decision, which sometimes led to a lack of involvement & committment during the actual protest.

It was naive to simply plan to demonstrate at the US consulate, move to the 52nd police division, & then tothe Japanaese consulate for the Omori demo. No contingency plans were considered at all.

In a public meeting such as it was, the question of "illegal" actions should have been discussed in full (but not specific actions of course), & some kind of consensus arrived at so everyone knew where they stood. We were also too quick to jump into the idea of a standard type demo instead of examining other possibilities & forms of protest, eg; writing to your MP (haha), city-wide direct actions, street theatre, & of course a possible confrontation with cops. If ther there had been an actual planning meeting then affinity groups should have formed, and then moved off to secure areas to discuss & plan their part in the Day of Action, & prepare for possible actions.

DISPERSAL

The demo ended when everyone more or less made it to Queens park. Many were arrested on the way by police snatch squads. Having a march to a dispersal point when we were being picked off by cop-cops all the way was not a good idea. Maybe (in the absence of any pre-arranged plan) spreadin g the word to disperse in groups of 10 or so would have been an effective way to disperse. Instead a group of 200 (the demo had become smaller at this point) attempted to have another public meeting in a park! All this time a

cordon of at least 100 cops (with more arriving all the time) was forming an almost complete circle around us. Fortuantly we realised what was about to happen. Groups of 10 or so began leaving- many in rows with linked arms (at last!). As far as we know no one was arrested after this point. At every safe oppurtinity these groups split up & mingled with pedestrians. The cops that had been busy all day seemed relieved to see us go, but those who recently arrived seemed to want to go after us- but were unable to deal with all those little groups splitting up. Vehicles & foot cops to follow the small groups but it was relatively easy to lose them.

CONCLUSION

It's all very easy for us to sit back & critcise & analyse an event where we all made mistakes. As with many things it take--

takes actual participation to put ideas into practise. If there is to be more protests, or a protest at next years Anarchist Gathering in San Francisco, the lessons of Toronto must be learnt & applied. We certaintly don't have all the answers, but many obvious mistakes were made. The points & questions raised here also need wider & further discussion.

For us it was a positive experience in many ways. Mainly-it was an 'illegal' demo which went ahead, more or less choosing our own route through a downtown core on a Monday lunchtime. Through our experiences we can develop new strategies & tactics in demonstrations.

It was the first time such a number of Anarchists have come together for an explicitly Anarchist demo.

It was a relatively 'safe' (eg. no real riot cops, tear gas, sustained baton charges, mass arrest etc) demo which gave us a chance to see our strengths & weaknesses. The demo was an oppurtunity to vent real frustrations & angers. The demo created a new militancy within the N. American movement.

Despite all their equipment & training the cops are as stupid as they look & were just as unorganised & unprepared as we were! Perhaps more so considering their supposed effeciency & specialised training. In the final analysis public & media opinion was not as hostile as we have expected. Forward!

RESIST TO EXIST!
ORGANIZE TO TAKE BACK OUR WORLD!

DOUG GRIFFIN / TORONTO STAR.

IN most instances when people have been arrested here in Canada, (including the arrests of anarchists after the Toronto anarchist gathering, July 1988), the first response has been to frantically work for their release. While this is, of course, the most important step in helping imprisoned activists, the habitually chosen strategy may be detrimental in the long run.

As soon as an activist is picked off, their supporters on the outside have traditionally run first to the lawyers and courts, and then to the media, in an attempt to get them out. What it usually comes down to, though, is a legal and media battle for "the right to *justice* and/or a fair trial", both of which are *completely non-existant in the state's courts*. The approach is fundamentally flawed.

First of all, legal and media courting tactics are often discussed before a *political* approach is decided upon. In other words, plans are made as to how to use the lawyers and what kind of press releases might be made, before even *considering* whether or not the courts or the media will be played with at all. The foregone conclusion is that we must concede to fighting on the state's home ground, without even looking for alternatives to such approaches.

The courts are not un-biased institutions. They are controlled by the state and the ruling classes. They are a tool used to enforce the laws and attitudes decreed by our enemies, those in power. When we appear in their courts we are being held and judged by those who oppose our ideas. No "justice" can be expected.

Often activists (such as the Vancouver Five) have tried to soften the blow against themselves by arguing about technicalities, and in some cases this may be possible. In most cases, however, doing so has managed to cloud over the political motives of the actions in question, and the political motives of the state in persecuting them. It is an expensive trade-off; In the case of the Five our support work centered on the "right to a fair trial" and only when it was too late did the focus change; and yet, despite legal wranglings, the blow was as hard as ever. This points to two things: one, the state doesn't play with technicalities—if they want to put us away they will, and two, it shows that it is essential to decide *in advance* upon our

Emergency Response: Beyond Collaboration

strategy regarding the courts before we simply wade into the thick of it for the sake of expediency.

The media must also be treated with the same suspicion. Much talk has gone on over the years as to whether we can use the capitalist media to get out our message. There is a temptation to try to get our message through, especially in emergencies, and an implicit trust in the media to accurately represent it. Such has never been the case and likely never will. The media is a propoganda arm of capital which is designed to distort and misrepresent everyday events. There is no good reason to make concessions to them. We quite simply have no control over the media so we should forget talk of "using the media". We can only play into their hands or ignore them completely. When attempting to publicize a situation we must (and can!) use anarchist publications, leaflets, radio broadcasts, street theatre, international networking in lieu of capital/press syndicates, etc. That is to say — we can use our own strengths.

Moves have also been made in the past to play on "sympathetic" authorities and even politicians in order to obtain release. Playing on the lowest common denominator to gain public support has always obscured the basic fact that we are anarchists and when we go to jail it is because we oppose the state, capitalism, and all its tentacles (ie the police and the media).

This is not some kind of absolutism. As self-defined anti-statist people, we are clearly excluded from "using" certain methods because they will not work for us, nor will they bring us any closer to the kind of society we're put in prison for creating. If people are jailed for political acts then we must make it clear that they are political prisoners, that it is a political case

It is also a guard against what can be a dangerous practice. By suggesting that because this is an emergency situation one must adapt distasteful approaches, we get

into a bind which has long been the downfall of anarchists. The collaboration of anarchists with the Spanish government in 1939 was done for many of the same reasons, with disastrous results. We have to *learn* from past mistakes, and learn that collaboration is our downfall.

Contrary to the legal/media ensemble, we propose that we mobilize around a political case. We can use many contacts locally and internationally to mobilize emergency responses to arrests such as demonstrations, leaflettings, direct actions and other possibilities which go beyond collaboration and extend the possibility of further insurrection. We can use our own media (anarchist press and radio) to get the word out to people. Leafletting the streets in the wake of actions or arrests can be an effective counter-media. Spraypainting, street theatre and other counter media efforts can be employed, *anything* which will make the case before the courts into a political/social issue, not a legal/criminal issue as the state would have it.

Inside the courtroom the approach can be one of talking about the issues involved rather than calculating who was where when etc. Lawyers are not as necessary as they usually become in a "legal" case, which might cut down on expenses which have to be paid for by our movement. It's a drag that we have to throw so much money away on lawyers and bail. In fact, defending ourselves in court, if we must appear, can be the only way to use the situation as a move towards autonomy. It could also serve to set a positive example to other (poor) people who are forced through the courts and who are taught that the law system is a mystical entity they must accept, and not even try to exert some control over their situation.

In the jails non-cooperation is often effective as long as solidarity exists between *all* arrested. We've gone into ideas before about how to deal with being arrested (see issue 7) which also include not talking to police, steeling ...self

TACTICS

cannot by any means guarantee success by abandoning the legalistic methods, we may be able to build up a support network bit by bit so that we don't always get forced into the courts. Perhaps we can take some empowerment as a community from the situation: turn the State on its ass, managing to make it into a "positive", strenghtening experience. When our support networks are strengthened by our *using* them, they will be able to accomplish more, and in the long run we will be able to rely on them for *effective* support and abandon the legal process altogether. Then we will truly be beyond collaboration.

To this end we would like to repeat here the suggestion made at the Anarchist Gathering prison workshop this year, that an "ememency response network" be set up, members of which could be relied upon to organize support immediately in their own locality when a crisis comes up anywhere in the international community. For this we ask that people who are willing to take on this task (and not take it on lightly, as it means a lot of commitment) send us an address and phone number which we can compile in a list to be distributed to everyone on it.

In local areas it would imply setting up the resources to facilitate immediate action. For instance a phone list of people willing to demonstrate/take action, the resources to publish leaflets quickly, and other kinds of contacts which enable you to get the information out quickly and organize action quickly.

If you feel you would be a good contact for emergency response, write to us at the Toronto Anarchist Black Cross, P.O. box 6326 Stn A Toronto Ont. M5W 1P7.

If you have arrests in your area which require response, we are willing to be one contact for such a network. We can be reached at (416) 947-0808. If you live in Toronto and will respond to emergencies locally (by organizing/coming on demos or actions, meeting, preparing and distributing leaflets etc.) then please also contact us at the address above, and send your phone number.

psychologically for the situation and other obvious moves. One problem we've always had is that in the first few days of an arrest little communication is possible between the inside and the outside. Because we are dealing with the lives of those captured, we have to follow their direction as to our tactics. Usually it is assumed by those on the outside that they want out at any cost, but often they would prefer not to have their politics compromised either. To avoid confusion here we would recommend that communities discuss this article and in particular discuss how they would prefer to have the outside react if they are arrested, and in different arrest situations — one might have different reactions to different levels of charges, expected or unexpected arrests, or whether one was alone or in a group, etc. This is best done in affinity groups, collectives or families, or between friends. In the future if any of us are arrested we would be easier able to

organize immediate solidarity in that first few days until we can further discuss it when lines of communication are more free.

We are not saying here that all situations are the same. In some cases it may indeed be possible to avoid a long sentence by playing the legal game. What we are saying is that it is necessary to *think* about how to approach the case before making the immediate assumption that collaboration is an appropriate response in every situation. It is also necessary to confront the possibility of arrest before it happens and discuss tactics so that we give ourselves choices as much as possible.

By relying on our own contacts, our own media and our own creative solutions to the emergency response, rather than repeatedly trying to rely on lawyers and state media, we will also build up our own movement. It is the difference between direct and indirect action. Although we

162 § ONLY A BEGINNING

THE WHITE NORTH AMERICAN POLITICAL PRISONERS IN THE U.S.

Speech given at the International Tribunal by Rita "Bo" Brown, October 3, 1992

I am very honoured to be here today, at this tribunal which condemns 500 years of genocide and celebrates 500 years of resistance. I come speaking about the nearly thiry-five white political prisoners presently being held in U.S. prisons and jails – many of whom are imprisoned because of their solidarity with oppressed nationals and peoples in the U.S. and around the world. I speak from experience and deep feeling for I am a former political prisoner myself having spent 8½ years in federal prisons around the country because of my actions as a member of the George Jackson Brigade.

In those years I was moved from prison to prison. During that time I spent almost a year in isolation in Davis Hall at Alderson. This was the first special control unit for political women in the Federal system. Sister Assata Shakur and I were held there along with reactionary and Nazi prisoners – the government's threat to us was very clear. I was also kept for extra long periods in isolation and threatened and harassed specifically because I am a lesbian. This was not all that unusual treatment however, for my experience mirrors that of all the political prisoners. Yet our very existence is still denied by the U.S. government and not seen or understood by most people in this country.

The strategy of the U.S. government towards all political prisoners and POW's held in prisons is to criminalize them – to disguise their political identities under the rhetoric of criminal activity. But they are not criminals. All of these white North American political prisoners have been convicted of and imprisoned for activities which are strictly political in nature.

These political prisoners and POW's are not a new phenomenon but are part of the history of the resistance in the Americas. In fact under international law, as well as the Constitution of the U.S., people not only have the right but the absolute responsibility to resist the illegal policies and practices of the oppressor and colonizing nation. And that's what they have done.

The North American political prisoners draw on a history of white resistance which includes the anti-slavery/abolitionist movement, those who helped in the Underground Railroad, women's rights activists, labour and working class organizers and supporters of anti-colonialism and anti-militarism. Some of their names are familiar: John Brown, Emma Goldman, Eugene Debs, Ruth Reynolds and Ethel and Julius Rosenberg; but most of the names of our historical grandmothers and grandfathers remain unknown to us because the historians don't want us to know about them.

Some of these political prisoners come from working class or poor communities, some were already ex-cons, and still others were college students, but a common thread runs through all their stories: that is the decision to take action. Action in support of self-determination; action against racism; action against U.S. military and nuclear policy; action against apartheid in South Africa and action in solidarity with workers and poor people around the world.

In order to understand them and their situation better we have to go back a little in history.

If you were living in this country in the '60s and '70s you had to be affected by the struggles for freedom and social justice. The women and men who are in prison today are no exception and are the products of these times.

Many of them were active in support of the Civil Rights movement and were influenced by Malcolm X's demand for self-determination and the organizing of Martin Luther King, both of whom would be assassinated by 1968. Others worked with the Black Panther Party (BPP), often in defence of BPP members who were imprisoned for political activities. Many came to work also with Native American, Mexicano/Chicano and other Third World liberation struggles. Along with millions of others they consistently opposed U.S. policy in Vietnam and were part of the anti-war movement. There were mass demonstrations throughout the country, marches on Washington, student strikes, sit-ins and the burning of draft cards. There were also thousands of acts of sabotage against academic, corporate, military and government targets which ranged from property damage to bombings.

This was also the period when women began to be more conscious about their own oppression and began to demand liberation and when lesbians and gay men came out of the closet and went into the streets demanding an end to gay oppression.

During these years a prisoner's rights movement developed, led mostly by Black prisoners and with close ties to the BPP and other community groups. Many of these white political prisoners worked with these organizations and thus came to better understand the integral part that prisons play in this society. They came to understand this country needed to control its people and criminalize, jail or kill those whom it either couldn't control or didn't need.

The government's response to this legitimate protest and sense of empowerment was swift, repressive and violent. COINTELPRO, the FBI's counter-intelligence program was responsible for the destruction of the BPP and the disruption of the American Indian Movement. Hundreds of BPP members and other Black activists, like Fred Hampton and Bunchy Carter, were killed or jailed. The same was true for Native people struggling for sovereignty. This period also saw the killing of students at Kent and Jackson State universities and the widespread use of grand jury witch hunts which were designed to further disrupt legal organizations.

Bulldozer 41 (1993)

Out of these experiences came the understanding that U.S. society is based on the rape and plunder of Native lands, the expropriation of life and labour of African slaves and the class exploitation of European, Asian and Mexican workers. People were enraged at the racism so basic to this country and were determined not to be a part of it. Many began to see the colonialism here at home and the war of imperialism in Vietnam.

It was during this time that activists in various parts of the country independently decided to begin armed resistance, expropriations and sabotage. These were difficult steps to take but were all done in pursuit of their vision for change.

This vision included changing centuries-old oppressive practices which promote hatred and which create psychological and physical damage and destruction. It meant creating a society based on self-determination for oppressed peoples both inside and outside the U.S. based on an end to white supremacy. A society which was not based on class divisions. It meant creating a society where lesbians and gay men could be proud of who they were. And it meant creating a non-sexist society where women could be equal, free and not afraid. Finally all these people are driven by a vision of a future based not on greed and profit but one that truly answers people's needs.

This vision and spirit of resistance continued to move North Americans to action during the '70s and '80s. Thousands of people organized to resist the building of nuclear weapons, the intervention in Nicaragua and El Salvador and in solidarity with Black forces against apartheid in South Africa. Many whites demonstrated and organized against racism and the growth of the Klan and other white supremacist groups. Thousands of people signed pledges of resistance to participate in civil disobedience if Nicaragua was invaded and participated in these acts as intervention in Central America increased. Women marched en masse against cut backs in reproductive rights and protected abortion clinics against attacks. Lesbians and gay men demanded that the society deal with the AIDS pandemic and pushed for broader acceptance of lesbian and gay rights. Again, during the Gulf War, thousands of white people joined in the streets protesting U.S. policy.

Not much has changed. We can understand the desire to resist very well. Genocidal conditions are increasing for Black and other communities of colour. There is a rise of police brutality, drugs and jailings and as we all know a dramatic decrease in social services. Violence against women is way up – a woman gets raped every two minutes. The right wing scapegoats and whips up hysteria against gays and lesbians who can forget "family values." Abortion is all but gone; the courts are making one right wing decision after another; and if we don't look out soon we won't even have air we can breathe or earth we can stand on.

Before we get more specific about who these prisoners are we'd like to take time to define what we mean by political prisoner. For some of us this definition means those in prison as a direct result of their political actions, affiliations and beliefs. Still others whish to extend that definition to those imprisoned for social crimes who have become politicized while inside prison and who therefore suffer extra repression for it. Some of us also think it important to extend the definition of political prisoner to those imprisoned for their sexual orientation (adopted by Amnesty International this year) and to those imprisoned for defending themselves against and/or fighting their abusers, such as women imprisoned for killing batterers.

So let's get down to specifics:

First there are prisoners who consider themselves to be revolutionary anti-imperialists.

The Jonathan Jackson-Sam Melville Brigade and United Freedom Front were armed clandestine organizations which emerged from the experiences of working class people in poor communities, in the military and in prison. The Jackson-Melville Brigade was held responsible for a number of bombings of government and corporate offices in the mid to late '70s. These actions raised the demands of independence for Puerto Rico and an end to U.S. support for apartheid in South Africa, among other issues. The UFF operated from the early to mid '80s and demanded the end of governmental and corporate support for South Africa, an end to U.S. intervention in Central America and freedom for all political prisoners and POWs in U.S. prisons.

Today the people charged with these acts are known as the "Ohio 7." They include Raymond Lavasseur, Thomas Manning (both Vietnam Vets who had spent years in prison for social crimes), Jaan Laaman, Carol Manning, Richard Williams, Barbara Curzi and Pat Gros Levasseur (these last two are both out on parole).

Other North American anti-imperialists are imprisoned for their direct aid to armed clandestine Black organizations in the early '80s. Judy Clark, David Gilbert and Kathy Boudin are serving life sentences in prison. They are charged with aiding an attempted expropriation (robbery for political reasons) of an armoured truck in New York State in 1981. This action was claimed by the Revolutionary Armed Task Force. Marilyn Buck was also charged as a result of this action as well as for assisting in the escape of Assata Shakur.

Susan Rosenberg and Timothy Blunk were captured in 1984 on charges of conspiracy to possess explosives. Later, they along with Alan Berkman, Laura Whitehorn, Linda Evans and Marilyn Buck were charged with a number of bombings claimed by the Armed Resistance Unit and the Red Guerilla Resistance. Included in these is the 1983 bombing of the Capitol in solidarity with the people of Grenada and in retaliation against the U.S. invasion that year. Other actions were taken against corporate and military targets in solidarity with the peoples of Central America and against intervention, against the Zionist occupation of Palestine and to protest police killings of Black and Latino people in New York City.

Bulldozer 41 (1993)

Once again I come to my own background as a former member of the George Jackson Brigade. We were a multi-racial armed organization which operated in the Northwest in the mid to late '70s. We took our name from George Jackson, the Black revolutionary who was assassinated in prison on August 21, 1971. We were composed mainly of working class ex-convicts and engaged in acts of armed resistance in solidarity with the struggle of Native people for sovereignty, in support of a strike by Seattle Auto workers and in support of struggles by Washington State prisoners for basic human rights. I've already told you that I was in prison for 8½ years. My comrades, Mark Cook, a Black prisoner and Ed Meade, a white prisoner remain in prison to this day for these actions.

There are also anti-authoritarian prisoners. Bill Dunn and Larry Giddings have been in prison since 1979 for participating in expropriations and the liberation of a comrade from jail. Richard Picariello has been in prison since 1977 for armed actions against U.S. oppression and imperialism. Due to be released after fifteen years, the state is scrambling to extend his sentence because he's dared to continue struggling from inside.

Next, I'd like to talk about those people who consider themselves part of the Ploughshares.

Taking their name from the famous biblical quote about turning swords into ploughshares, these anti-nuclear and anti-military activists come from a religious conviction and tradition that insists that they must not sit by while weapons of destruction are being made and used.

Over the last ten years many have entered military bases and destroyed military property directly, while others have borne witness and engaged in symbolic acts. The most recent case is that of Peter Lumsdain and Keith Kjoller who destroyed the Novstar computer – part of the U.S.'s first strike capability – to the tune of 2½ million dollars. They received eighteen months for this "crime."

Throughout the '80s the government also prosecuted members of the Sanctuary movement. These include clergy, church workers and lay activists who have "illegally" provided refuge to Central and South American refugees fleeing U.S. sponsored repression in their homelands.

Following a historic tradition, there are also military resisters. For example, Gilliam Kerley was sentence to three years in prison plus a $10,000 fine not merely for refusing to register but because he persisted in organizing against registration and the draft. Military resisters continue to sit in jail as a result of their refusal to serve in the Gulf war.

The U.S. legal system is also used to serve the government's allies in effecting their own counter-insurgency programs. In so doing, it echoes and enforces U.S. foreign policy. Along with Haitians, Central and South Americans and other Third World people there are several European nationals being held in U.S. prisons.

Silvia Baraldini, a citizen of Italy, received a forty year sentence for aiding in the escape of Assata Shakur. Although the Italian government has said that it wants her back in Italy to serve her time in an Italian prison – in accord with the Straussberg Convention – the U.S. justice department refused to let her go claiming the Italians won't be harsh enough.

There are also nine alleged members or supporters of the IRA, Irish Republican Army held in U.S. prisons by the U.S. government.

Counterinsurgency Tactics

The same counterinsurgency tactics that have been detailed in other presentations have been used against white political prisoners. These include sophisticated spying and infiltration techniques, the jailing of many white activists for refusing to testify and/or cooperate with grand juries, the use of broad and vague conspiracy laws to criminalize people for association and belief and the use of preventative detention to deny bail. Laura Whitehorn was held without bail for four years before going to trial.

Finally, because they are political prisoners they get some of the longest sentences in the world. Their political beliefs are used as a basis to impose sentences that are, in many instances, the equivalent of natural life in prison. The reason for this is that they are revolutionaries.

For example, in 1986, a man convicted of planning and carrying out bombings, without making warning calls, of ten occupied health clinics where abortions were performed was sentenced to ten years in prison and was paroled after forty-six months. In contrast, Raymond Levasseur was convicted of bombing four unoccupied military targets in protest against U.S. foreign policies. He received forty-five years in prison.

Or this one: A Ku Klux Klansman, charged with violations of the Neutrality Act and with possessing a boatload of explosives and weapons to be used in an invasion of the Caribbean island of Dominica received eight years. [Toronto's own Wolfang Droege – ed.] Linda Evans was convicted of purchasing four weapons with false ID and she was sentenced to forty years – the longest sentence ever imposed for this offence.

Prisons are a horrible experience for everyone in this country. This was well documented in the Prison Discipline Study Report issued in 1991. This national survey revealed that both physical and psychological abuse, so severe that it approaches the internationally accepted definition for torture, is the norm in maximum security prisons throughout the United States. That's the case for all prisoners.

In this context the North American prisoners – like political prisoners everywhere – are systematically singled out for particularly severe sentences and constant harassment once incarcerated. This includes particular abuse directed at the women and lesbians, including sexual assault and threats often at the hands of male guards.

Bulldozer 41 (1993)

One of the most brutal weapons in the government's arsenal is the control unit prison: a special maximum security unit based on total physical and sensory deprivation. Control unit prisons are currently the trend in new prison construction in the U.S. Their goal is to reduce prisoners to a state of submission where it becomes possible to destroy their bodies, their spirit, their will and ultimately their resistance and very self-definition.

While officials claim that these units are only for the most violent disciplinary problems, more and more political prisoners are being placed there solely for their political beliefs. For instance, Alan Berkman, Raymond Levasseur and Tom Manning were all sent directly to Marion Control Unit after sentencing.

Silvia Baraldini and Susan Rosenberg along with Puerto Rican POW Alejandrina Torres were sent to the Lexington High Security Unit for two years in 1986 – the justification: their political beliefs and associations. Once it was closed, a result of a massive campaign inside and out, Susan and Silvia were sent to the new control unit for women at Marianna. Marilyn Buck was also sent there directly after sentencing.

In addition to isolation in control units, all political prisoners are more frequently subjected to cruel and unusual punishment. This includes torture, sexual assault, strip and cavity searches (including those by male guards on women prisoners), punitive transfers, censorship and denial of medical care, which has had grave consequences in several cases. Alan Berkman, suffering from Hodgkin's Disease, nearly died several times while in prison because officials withheld necessary medical treatment. Silvia Baraldini's abdominal lumps, which anyone could feel, were ignored for months only to reveal that she had an aggressive form of uterine cancer. Silvia continues to have difficulty receiving medical attention.

Imprisonment doesn't mean the end of these revolutionaries' organizing and political work. They continue once they're inside. For many of them this has meant organizing resistance to oppressive prison policies, publishing prison newsletters, providing legal help and assistance, facilitating courses, work stoppages and hunger strikes. For others it's also meant becoming AIDS activists. In fact some of the women prisoners are responsible for developing the most comprehensive models (like ACE at Bedford Hills and PLACE in Pleasanton) for AIDS education and peer counselling in prisons in the country!

But even in these cases political prisoners are punished for being too successful in their work. For instance, Ed Mead who organized Men Against Sexism at Walla Walla was prevented from continuing his work on prisoner-on-prisoner rape. Bill Dunne was kept at Marion for years for publishing a newsletter there and David Gilbert was moved from place to place for developing work on AIDS in prison, finally prevented from doing any work at all. Quite recently, Laura Whitehorn was transferred from Lexington to Marianna after she participated in the first women's prison uprising in twenty years when the women protested an attack on a Black woman prisoner by a male guard. Tim Blunk was moved back to Marion from Lewisburg after there was a strike there of Black and Puerto Rican prisoners.

Why does the government so determinedly continue to attack and repress these women and men once they are incarcerated? It needs to break their spirits and prevent them from continuing to educate and mobilize from within the prison walls. On the one hand these prisoners are used as examples to intimidate whole movements and communities from continuing their resistance. The government wants it made very clear the price one can pay for being a white person willing to take a stand against this racist and inhuman system is very high. On the other hand they need these revolutionaries to be buried away and forgotten.

We won't let that happen!

Clearly now is a time for action. We too can follow the examples of these brave women and men who have given so much of their lives for freedom and justice. We must recognize who and what they are: political prisoners. We must demand their freedom so they can be back on the streets where they belong.

I know I speak for all the white political prisoners when I say that it's been a great honour to be able to speak to you today at this international Tribunal. All of us pledge to continue our resistance to the crimes outlined by today's speakers and commit ourselves to continue to work until there is a world where everyone can have true justice and freedom.

Bulldozer 41 (1993)

Prison News Service May/June 1993

The White North American Political Prisoners in the U.S.

Speech given at the International Tribunal by Rita "Bo" Brown October 3, 1992

I am very honored to be here today, at this tribunal which condemns 500 years of genocide and celebrates 500 years of resistance. I come speaking about the nearly 35 white political prisoners presently being held in US prisons and jails – many of whom are imprisoned because of their solidarity with oppressed nations and peoples in the US and around the world. I speak from experience and deep feeling for I am a former political prisoner myself having spent 8-1/2 years in federal prisons around the country because of my actions as a member of the George Jackson Brigade.

In those years I was moved from prison to prison. During that time I spent almost a year in isolation in Davis Hall at Alderson. This was the first special control unit for political women in the Federal system. Sister Assata Shakur and I were held there along with reactionary and Nazi prisoners – the government's threat to us was very clear. I was also kept for extra long periods in isolation and threatened and harassed specifically because I am a lesbian. This was not all that unusual treatment however, for my experience mirrors that of all the political prisoners. Yet our very existence is still denied by the US government and not seen or understood by most people in this country.

The strategy of the US government towards all political prisoners and POW's held in prisons is to criminalize them – to disguise their political identities under the rhetoric of criminal activity. But they are not criminals. All of these white North American political prisoners have been convicted of and imprisoned for activities which are strictly political in nature.

These political prisoners and POW's are not a new phenomenon but are part of the history of the resistance in the Americas. In fact under international law, as well as the Constitution of the US, people not only have the right but the absolute responsibility to resist the illegal policies and practices of the oppressor and colonizing nation. And that's what they have done.

The North American political prisoners draw on a history of white resistance which includes the anti-slavery/abolitionist movement, those who helped in the Underground Railroad, women's rights activists, labor and working class organizers and supporters of anti-colonialism and anti-militarism. Some of their names are familiar: John Brown, Emma Goldman, Eugene Debs, Ruth Reynolds and Ethel and Julius Rosenberg; but most of the names of our historical grandmothers and grandfathers remain unknown to us because the historians don't want us to know about them.

Some of these political prisoners come from working class or poor communities, some were already ex-cons, and still others were college students, but a common thread runs through all their stories: that is the decision to take action. Action in support of self-determination; action against racism; action against US military and nuclear policy; action against apartheid in South Africa and action in solidarity with workers and poor people around the world.

In order to understand them and their situation better we have to go back a little in history.

If you were living in this country in the 60s and 70s you had to be affected by the struggles for freedom and social justice. The women and men who are in prison today are no exception and are the products of these times.

Many of them were active in support of the Civil Rights movement and were influenced by Malcolm X's demand for self determination and the organizing of Martin Luther King, both of whom would be assassinated by 1968. Others worked with the Black Panther Party, often in defense of BPP members who were imprisoned for political activities. Many came to work also with Native American, Mexicano/Chicano and other Third World liberation struggles. Along with millions of others they consistently opposed US policy in Vietnam and were part of the anti-war movement. There were mass demonstrations throughout the country, marches on Washington, student strikes, sit-ins and the burning of draft cards. There were also thousands of acts of sabotage against academic, corporate, military and government targets which ranged from property damage to bombings.

This was also the period when women began to be more conscious about their own oppression and began to demand liberation and when lesbians and gay men came out of the closet and went into the streets demanding an end to gay oppression.

During these years a prisoner's rights movement developed, led mostly by Black prisoners and with close ties to the BPP and other community groups. Many of these white political prisoners worked with these organizations and thus came to better understand the integral part that prisons play in this society. They came to understand this country needed to control its people and criminalize, jail or kill those whom it either couldn't control or didn't need.

The government's response to this legitimate protest and sense of empowerment was swift, repressive and violent. COINTELPRO, the FBI's counter-intelligence program was responsible for the destruction of the BPP and the disruption of the American Indian Movement. Hundreds of BPP members and other Black activists, like Fred Hampton and Bunchy Carter, were killed or jailed. The same was true for Native people struggling for sovereignty. This period also saw the killing of students at Kent and Jackson State universities and the widespread use of grand jury witch hunts which were designed to further disrupt legal organizations.

Out of these experiences came the understanding that US society is based on the rape and plunder of Native lands, the expropriation of life and labor of African slaves and the class exploitation of European, Asian and Mexican workers. People were enraged at the racism so basic to this country and were determined not be a part of it. Many began to see that there was a connection between the colonialism here at home and the war of imperialism in Vietnam.

It was during this time that activists in various parts of the country independently decided to begin armed resistance, expropriations and sabotage. These were difficult steps to take but were all done in pursuit of their vision for change.

This vision included changing centuries-old oppressive practices which promote hatred and which create psychological and physical damage and destruction. It meant creating a society based on self-determination for oppressed peoples both inside and outside the US based on an end to white supremacy. A society which was not based on class divisions. It meant creating a society where lesbians and gay men could be proud of who they were. And it meant creating a non-sexist society where women could be equal, free and not afraid. Finally all these people are driven by a vision of a future based not on greed and profit but one that truly answers people's needs.

This vision and spirit of resistance continued to move North Americans to action during the 70s and 80s. Thousands of people organized to resist the building of nuclear weapons, the intervention in Nicaragua and El Salvador and in solidarity with Black forces against apartheid in South Africa. Many whites demonstrated and organized against racism and the growth of the Klan and other white supremacist groups. Thousands of people signed pledges of resistance to participate in civil disobedience if Nicaragua was invaded and participated in these acts as intervention in Central America increased. Women marched en masse against cut backs in reproductive rights and protected abortion clinics against attacks. Lesbians and gay men demanded that the society deal with the AIDS pandemic and pushed for broader acceptance of lesbian and gay rights. Again, during the Gulf War, thousands of white people joined in the streets protesting US policy.

Not much has changed. We can understand the desire to resist very well. Genocidal conditions are increasing for Black and other communities of color. There is a rise of police brutality, drugs and jailings and as we all know a dramatic decrease in social services. Violence against women is way up – a woman gets raped every 2 minutes. The right wing scapegoats and whips up hysteria against gays and lesbians who can forget "family values". Abortion is all but gone, the courts are making one right-wing decision after another, and if we don't look out soon we won't even have air we can breathe or earth we can stand on.

> **This vision included changing centuries-old oppressive practices which promote hatred and which create psychological and physical damage and destruction ... all these people are driven by a vision of a future based not on greed and profit but one that truly answers people's needs.**

Before we get more specific about who these prisoners are we'd like to take time to define what we mean by political prisoner. For some of us this definition means those in prison as a direct result of their political actions, affiliations and beliefs. Still others wish to extend that definition to those imprisoned for social crimes who have become politicized while inside prison and who therefore suffer extra repression for it. Some of us also think it important to extend the definition of political prisoner to those imprisoned for their sexual orientation (adopted by Amnesty International this year) and to those imprisoned for defending themselves against and/or fighting their abusers, such as women imprisoned for killing their batterers.

So let's get down to specifics:

First there are prisoners who consider themselves to be revolutionary anti-imperialists.

The Jonathan Jackson-Sam Melville Brigade and United Freedom Front were armed clandestine organizations which emerged from the experiences of working class people in poor communities, in the military and in prison. The Jackson-Melville Brigade was held responsible for a number of bombings of government and corporate offices in the mid to late 70s. These actions raised the demands of independence for Puerto Rico and an end to US support for apartheid in South Africa, among other issues. The UFF operated from the early to mid 80s and demanded the end of governmental and corporate support for South Africa, an end to US intervention in Central America and freedom for all political prisoners and POWs in US prisons.

Today the people charged with these acts are known as the "Ohio 7." They include Raymond Lavasseur, Thomas Manning (both Vietnam Vets who had spent years in prison for social crimes), Jaan Laaman, Carol Manning, Richard Williams, Barbara Curzi and Pat Gros Levasseur (these last two are both out on parole).

Other North American anti-imperialists are imprisoned for their direct aid to armed clandestine Black organizations in the early 80s. Judy Clark, David Gilbert and Kathy Boudin are serving life sentences in prison. They are charged with aiding an attempted expropriation (robbery for political reasons) of an armored truck in New York State in 1981. This action was claimed by the Revolutionary Armed Task Force. Marilyn Buck was also charged as a result of this action as well as for assisting in the escape of Assata Shakur.

Susan Rosenberg and Timothy Blunk were captured in 1984 on charges of conspiracy to possess explosives. Later, they along with Alan Berkman, Laura Whitehorn, Linda Evans and Marilyn Buck were charged with a number of bombings claimed by the Armed Resistance Unit and the Red Guerrilla Resistance. Included in these is the 1983 bombing of the Capitol in solidarity with the people of Grenada and in retaliation against the US invasion that year. Other actions were taken against corporate and military targets in solidarity with the peoples of Central America and against intervention, against the Zionist occupation of Palestine and to protest police killings of Black and Latino people in New York City.

Once again I come to my own background as a former member of the George Jackson Brigade. We were a multi-racial armed organization which operated in the Northwest in the mid to late 70s. We took our name from George Jackson, the Black revolutionary who was assassinated in prison on August 21, 1971. We were composed mainly of working class ex-convicts and engaged in acts of armed resistance in solidarity with the struggle of Native people for sovereignty, in support of a strike by Seattle Auto workers and in support of struggles by Washington State prisoners for basic human rights. I've already told you that I was in prison for 8-1/2 years. My comrades, Mark Cook, a Black prisoner and Ed Meade, a white prisoner remain in prison to this day for these actions.

There are also anti-authoritarian prisoners. Bill Dunn and Larry Giddings have been in prison since 1979 for participating in expropriations and the liberation of a comrade from jail. Richard Picariello has been in prison since 1977 for armed actions against US oppression and imperialism. Due to be released after 15 years, the state is scrambling to extend his sentence because he's dared to continue struggling from inside.

Next, I'd like to talk about those people who consider themselves part of the Ploughshares.

Taking their name from the famous biblical quote about turning swords into ploughshares, these anti-nuclear and anti-military activists come from a religious conviction and tradition that insists that they must not sit by while weapons of destruction are being made and used.

Over the last ten years many have entered military bases and destroyed military property directly, while others have borne witness and engaged in symbolic acts. The most recent case is that of Peter Lumsdain and Keith Kjoller who destroyed the Novstar computer – part of the US's first strike capability – to the tune of 2-1/2 million dollars. They received 18 months for this "crime".

Throughout the 80s the government also prosecuted members of the Sanctuary movement. These include clergy, church workers and lay activists who have "illegally" provided refuge to Central and South American refugees fleeing US sponsored repression in their homelands.

Following a historic tradition, there are also military resisters. For example, Gilliam Kerley was sentenced to three years in prison plus a $10,000. fine not merely for refusing to register but because he persisted in organizing against registration and the draft. Military resisters continue to sit in jail as a result of their refusal to serve in the Gulf war.

The US legal system is also used to serve the government's allies in effecting their own counter-insurgency programs. In so doing, it echoes and enforces US foreign policy. Along with Haitians, Central and South Americans and other Third World people there are several European nationals being held in US prisons.

Silvia Baraldini, a citizen of Italy, received a 40 year sentence for aiding in the escape of Assata Shakur. Although the Italian government has said that it wants her back in Italy to serve her time in an Italian prison – in accord with the Straussberg Convention – the US justice department refused to let her go claiming the Italians won't be harsh enough.

There are also 9 alleged members or supporters of the IRA, Irish Republican Army held in US prisons by the US government.

Counterinsurgency tactics

The same counterinsurgency tactics that have been detailed in other presentations have been used against white political prisoners. These include sophisticated spying and infiltration techniques, the jailing of many white activists for refusing to testify and/or cooperate with grand juries, the use of broad and vague conspiracy laws to criminalize people for association and belief and the use of preventative detention to deny bail. Laura Whitehorn was held without bail for 4 years before going to trial.

Finally, because they are political prisoners they get some of the longest sentences in the world. Their political beliefs are used as a basis to impose sentences that are, in many instances, the equivalent of natural life in prison. The reason for this is that they are revolutionaries.

For example, in 1986, a man convicted of planning and carrying out bombings, without making warning calls, of ten occupied health clinics where abortions were performed was sentenced to ten years in prison and was paroled after 46 months. In contrast, Raymond Levasseur was convicted of bombing four unoccupied military targets in protest against US foreign policies. He received 45 years in prison.

Or this one: A Ku Klux Klansman, charged with violations of the Neutrality Act and with possessing a boatload of explosives and weapons to be used in an invasion of the Caribbean island of Dominica received 8 years. [Toronto's own Wolfgang Droege - ed.] Linda Evans was convicted of purchasing 4 weapons with false ID and she was sentenced to 40 years – the longest sentence ever imposed for this offense.

Prisons are a horrible experience for everyone in this country. This was well documented in the Prison Discipline Study Report issued in 1991. This national survey revealed that both physical and psychological abuse, so severe that it approaches the internationally accepted definition] for torture, is the norm in maximum security prisons throughout the United States. That's the case for all prisoners.

In this context the North American prisoners – like political prisoners everywhere – are systematically singled out for particularly severe sentences and constant harassment once incarcerated. This includes particular abuse directed at the women and lesbians, including sexual assault and threats often at the hands of male guards.

One of the most brutal weapons in the government's arsenal is the control unit prison: a special maximum security unit based on total physical and sensory deprivation. Control unit prisons are currently the trend in new prison construction in the US. Their goal is to reduce prisoners to a state of submission where it becomes possible to destroy their bodies, their spirit, their will and ultimately their resistance and very self definition.

While officials claim that these units are only for the most violent disciplinary problems, more and more political prisoners are being placed there solely for their political beliefs. For instance, Alan Berkman, Raymond Levasseur and Tom Manning were all sent directly to Marion Control Unit after sentencing.

Silvia Baraldini and Susan Rosenberg along with Puerto Rican POW Alejandrina Torres were sent to the Lexington High Security Unit for two years in 1986 – the justification: their political beliefs and associations. Once it was closed, a result of a massive campaign inside and out, Susan and Silvia were sent to the new control unit for women at Marianna. Marilyn Buck was also sent there directly after sentencing.

In addition to isolation in control units, all political prisoners are more frequently subjected to cruel and inhumane punishment. This includes torture, sexual assault, strip and cavity searches (including those by male guards on women prisoners), punitive transfers, censorship and denial of medical care, which has had grave consequences in several cases. Alan Berkman, suffering from Hodgkin's Disease, nearly died several times while in prison because officials withheld necessary medical treatment. Silvia Baraldini's abdominal lumps, which anyone could feel, were ignored for months only to reveal that she had an aggressive form of uterine cancer. Silvia continues to have difficulty receiving medical attention.

Imprisonment doesn't mean the end of these revolutionaries' organizing and political work. They continue once they're inside. For many of them this has meant organizing resistance to oppressive prison policies, publishing prison newsletters, providing legal help and assistance, facilitating courses, work stoppages and hunger strikes. For others it's also meant becoming AIDS activists. In fact some of the women prisoners are responsible for developing the most comprehensive models (like ACE at Bedford Hills and PLACE in Pleasanton) for AIDS education and peer counselling in prisons in the country!

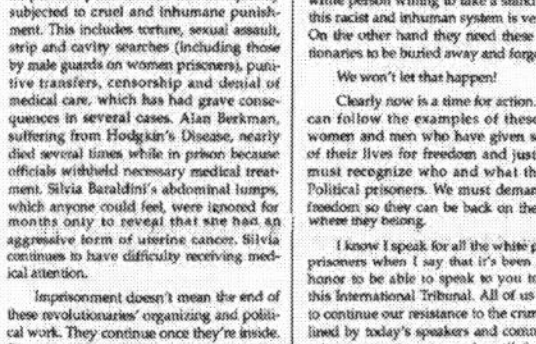

But even in these cases political prisoners are punished for being too successful in their work. For instance, Ed Meade who organized Men Against Sexism at Walla Walla was prevented from continuing his work on prisoner-on-prisoner rape. Bill Dunne was kept at Marion for years for publishing a newsletter there and David Gilbert was moved from place to place for developing work on AIDS in prison, finally prevented from doing any work at all. Quite recently, Laura Whitehorn was transferred from Lexington to Marianna after she participated in the first women's prison uprising in 20 years when the women protested an attack on a Black woman prisoner by a male guard. Tim Blunk was moved back to Marion from Lewisburg after there was a strike there of Black and Puerto Rican prisoners.

Why does the government so determinedly continue to attack and repress these women and men once they are incarcerated? It needs to break their spirits and prevent them from continuing to educate and mobilize from within the prison walls. On the one hand these prisoners are used as examples to intimidate whole movements and communities from continuing their resistance. The government wants it made very clear the price one can pay for being a white person willing to take a stand against this racist and inhuman system is very high. On the other hand they need these revolutionaries to be buried away and forgotten.

We won't let that happen!

Clearly now is a time for action. We too can follow the examples of these brave women and men who have given so much of their lives for freedom and justice. We must recognize who and what they are: Political prisoners. We must demand their freedom so they can be back on the streets where they belong.

I know I speak for all the white political prisoners when I say that it's been a great honor to be able to speak to you today at this International Tribunal. All of us pledge to continue our resistance to the crimes outlined by today's speakers and commit ourselves to continue to work until there is a world where everyone can have true justice and freedom. ••

ANTI-RACISTS ROCK TORONTO

On May/4/92 the biggest "riot" in recent history struck downtown Toronto. Influenced by events in Los Angeles, but fuelled by the reality of police racism and violence in Toronto, angry demonstrators smashed store windows, threw rocks and bottles at the police and did a bit of looting. A rally had been called for by the Black Action Defense Committee (BADC) in solidarity with the protests in the U.S. after the Rodney King verdict as well as to protest the recent acquittal of two Peel Regional cops for the killing of a local Black teenager in 1989. The fatal shooting of Raymond Lawrence, a young black man, by a member of the Metropolitan Toronto Police on May/1/92 added to the grief, frustration and rage felt by those attending the demonstration. The media's repeated cries about the "unfortunate" timing of Lawrence's murder – as though there might be times when the killing of an African is "fortunate" – added to the fury. In the past four years, four Blacks have been killed, with another four wounded by police in the Toronto area. In spite of protests, liberal articles in the media, and government reports, the police still regard it as their right to shoot and kill as they desire.

The demonstration heated up quickly as four members of the fascist Heritage Front were chased when they showed up to counter-protest. After marching up Yonge St., a thousand people sat down at a major downtown courthouse as a group of forty youth rushed the building. Continuing on to City Hall, bottles and rocks were thrown at mounted policemen who were blocking the entrance. No city official could be bothered to speak to the rally even though council was in session, so the crowd headed back to Yonge St. (Yonge St. is Toronto's commercial heart. Filled with cheap electronics stores, small businesses, and flanked by major shopping malls, it has long been a hang-out spot that is usually crowded with an amazing mix of people.) For several hours, the cops held off as a core of people continued to do the riot thing. Hundreds of people, though not participating in the rock throwing or looting, stayed with the window-smashers, providing them with needed cover and support. As streets were taken over, passers-by joined in and others came downtown as radio and TV spread the news about what was happening. Away from the intensity of the window-smashing, the streets, suddenly freed of vehicle traffic, took on a festive air as people debated and watched what was going on. In the end, thirty people were arrested, with all but seven being released by next morning.

The media, politicians and police went predictably crazy. It shocked all the little burghers to think that Toronto, "the city that works," could seem, well, so American. Compared to the television image of the menacing underclass of the big American cities, those marginalized by Canadian society always seemed relatively harmless. The media went on and on about the "violence" of that evening of which it had a distorted sense, since the majority of threatening incidents were directed at journalists and their ever-present cameras. For the demonstrators there was a sudden sense of power and possibilities, however awkward it felt. The streets were ours for a brief moment. Curiosity, rather than fear, seemed to be the shared emotion for those who, as spectators, also thronged the streets and sidewalks.

Whereas it was generally easy for Canadians to accept that deep-rooted racism in the U.S provoked the uprising in Los Angeles, the riot here was regarded by many as a copy-cat affair and not due to systemic racism in Canadian society. The participation of white people in the street action was seen as evidence that looting was the motivating factor that evening – as though opportunism was the only basis on which Whites would participate in an anti-racist event. But the rally and later events were among the most racially mixed demonstrations to be held in this city – Natives, Latinos/as and Asians as well as Blacks and Whites came together in a shared anger at the un-apologetic racism of the police and the inadequacies and/or refusal of the justice and political systems to stand against them.

Black activists attacked

Though relations between the police and black community have been severely strained, rather than trying to resolve these tensions, the police department has been consciously attacking black activists. It spent at least $500,000 to entrap Dudley Laws, a prominent black civil rights activist and a leading member of BADC. Laws, charged with conspiracy to smuggle illegal aliens into the U.S., was subjected to wiretaps and heavy surveillance as twelve cops worked full-time on his case even as they whined that they needed more money to save Toronto from crime and indecency. The Toronto cops actively participated in the case, even though immigration is normally the work of the Mounties. Other Black activists have been directly attacked. A local artist and activist had her arm broken when she was physically assaulted as she was singled out for arrest after an earlier demo. And in a case going back to 1990 when eleven people were arrested after police attacked a demonstration protesting a racist exhibit at the Royal Ontario Museum, Oji Adisa was given ninety days in jail for assault. The judge made clear that the sentence was related to his role as a leader of the protests.

Some liberal commentators used the fact that more non-Blacks have been shot and/or killed by the police in the last four years to obscure the fact that Blacks, who are only about ten percent of the local population, are disproportionately subjected to police violence. All this shows, though, is that along with their racist attitudes there is a major problem with police use of violence, both lethal and non-lethal. Nor is Toronto alone in this problem. Racism and frequent brutality has been documented in the actions of the police in Vancouver, Halifax and Montreal. Across the country the police beat and oppress Natives, Asians, Blacks, Latinos/as and

Prison News Service 36 (1992)

poor and working Whites – a multi-cultural society offering them plenty of targets for their abuse and ignorance.

The problem goes beyond the prejudices of the police (though they are ignorant fuckers). Multi-culturalism has been the official ideology of the Canadian state since the early seventies. The official lie has been that Canada is not a melting pot, but a mosaic, where people can come from around the world and maintain their own communities with their own values. But reactionary and conservative elements have never accepted this vision of Canada where immigrants and refugees from the Caribbean, Africa, Asia and Latin America could become fully functioning members of Canadian society on their own terms. The police, reflecting their historical roots in the British colonial police, see themselves as being the last line of defence in protecting "White" Toronto from these changes. The best way to do this is to marginalize and criminalize anyone who does not fit in. As the children of immigrants discover, skin colour alone can determine whether or not one is considered acceptable.

Social explosion

All the elements for a social explosion were here: police violence, racism, poverty, corporate greed, conspicuous consumption, political indifference, unfulfilled promises, homelessness, unskilled youth, and racial polarization. But what happened that Monday evening was not just an outpouring of rage and despair in response to deteriorating social and economic conditions. The events took place within a context of increasing political awareness. Although the media, police and politicians tried to label it the work of hooligans and thugs, it was clear that their real concern was that it had a conscious element to it that threatened them in a way that other riots that occur with some regularity on Yonge St., for any number of reasons, do not.

Though police shootings of Blacks has been a primary political focus for the Black community, racism has become a key issue in the schools and universities, amongst writers and artists, in the women's community and in the work place. The struggle against racism by people of colour in a country of immigrants as Canada is, takes a different form than that of the U.S. where the black and white communities face each other over what seems at times to be an unbridgeable gulf rooted in the centuries of slavery. Immigrants, almost by definition, are optimists. Though there has been a radical leadership, particularly from the Caribbean, (and historic black communities in Ontario and Nova Scotia) exposing racism in Toronto, the majority of immigrants don't make waves. But it is their children, raised with higher expectations, who run into the institutionalized racism in the schools, the lack of equal access to jobs and police harassment on the streets. As happened in England in the 1970s, it is these young people who radicalize the fight against racists and racism. Aiding

this process is the awareness of, and often connection to, the struggles of African people in the U.S, the Caribbean, England, and Africa itself.

It is not just those of African heritage who are resisting racism in Canada. Many other immigrants: South Asians (Sri Lanka, India and Pakistan) South East Asians (Vietnam, Hong Kong, China), Latin Americans and from the Middle East are all discovering the racist reality in Canada. Nor is racism a new phenomenon here. The indigenous people in Toronto have also been struggling for their rights as urban natives, and against the prejudice and racism they face in the city, as part of their historic struggle for self-determination and survival. The African community in Canada which goes back to the very beginning of non-Native settlement, began in the chains of slavery. There is pride that Canada was a haven for escaped slaves from the U.S. before the American civil war. Little mention is made of the fact that most of these former American slaves chose to return to the U.S. after emancipation since their conditions here were no better than what they experienced on the other side of the border.

Anger at racism and police violence, and the failure of any level of government to take these issues seriously, motivated many Whites that night along with those people who are directly experiencing that racism. But there were other reasons for the anger as well. Gays and lesbians, who were well represented, were incensed because two days earlier the police had raided a local gay bookstore, seized a lesbian magazine and laid a charge of obscenity. Women of all races, who also participated in large numbers, have seen ever increasing levels of violence directed against them, even as a backlash is regularly mounted in the press against the gains that a small number of women have made. Rising levels of poverty and homelessness, along with the loss of tens of thousands of jobs in the recession, have made a mockery of claims that Canada has a "kinder, gentler" form of capitalism. The "business as usual" attitude of the social democratic provincial government in Ontario, elected less than two years ago with hopes that social issues would have political priority, has forced many activists and radicals to reconsider the role of parliamentary politics and the ways in which change will come about.

Over the past several years, a non-parliamentary opposition has strengthened in Canada. In spite of the clever and elaborate schemes of the state to buy people off and incorporate popular struggles, the women's movement, immigrant communities, people of colour and particularly the native people have gained in momentum and clarity. Much is owed to the courageous armed self-defence of the Mohawk people in 1990 against the army and police threats against their land, for they showed that there were many ways to struggle in honour and principle. In spite of all the difficulties – the struggle against racism, chauvinism, sexism, class distinctions and homophobia within these movements – there has been a gradual coming together of forces. Issues are no longer considered in isolation from each other. People have been in a process of learning how to give support to each other. It has not been easy, and there is a long way to go, but an emerging culture of resistance offers some possibility of practical unity against the oppressor – a unity which begins as we come to understand that we need not feel threatened by the gains of others.

New level of resistance

The mini-uprising that evening offered evidence of a new level of resistance in Toronto. By itself, it momentarily brought about an increase in the attention paid to the issue of racism directed against the Black community. But it also showed a new willingness to go outside of the confines of acceptable protest. The militant action had a sense of inevitability, shared by both activists and many ordinary people, given the unresponsiveness of the system to racism and police violence combined with hard economic times. Three days after the riot, 2,500 people attended a rally previously scheduled by the Black Action Defence Committee. The politicians, media, and police had all called for BADC to cancel the event. This show of support, in spite of dire warnings of violence that kept some away, confirmed that the attempts by the authorities to isolate the political elements of the Black community would not work.

As opposition is slowly transforming itself into resistance, the forces of reaction are growing. The racism of the general population is increasing and becoming more open. Skinheads are organizing themselves and are working with the fascist Heritage Front. For a week after the riot, the Police Public Order unit – a riot squad by another name but with specialized training – patrolled Yonge St. and forced confrontations with young people, arresting several. The campaign against the leaders of BADC continues without let up, blaming them for stirring up trouble even though the official report of the riot confirmed the extent of racism in Ontario, particularly against Blacks. The media has recently carried scare stories about "Black Muslims" being a threat, with pictures of pigs with machine guns providing "protection" for a trial for people charged with conspiracy to bomb a Sikh temple. Though the connection has never been made clear, the propaganda impact is readily apparent, that black radicals are inherently dangerous. But as always it is those who seek to maintain the status quo at all costs who are endangering social peace. By refusing to address the serious social issues with which we are being confronted, they will only add fuel to the fires to come.

– JIM CAMPBELL

Prison News Service 36 (1992)

THANK YOU for your kind support and encouragement. Your help is important to us as we continue to work for adequate and affordable housing in Vancouver.

HOME, SWEET HOME

REVOLUTION

Here is a picture
picturesque home
The estate was occupied

HOME, SWEET HOME

HOME
LIFE
M
O
H
E

THE
HOME

the FRANCISE STREET SQUATTERS during the year of 1990. A community of people dedicated to exposing some of the lesser known, yet very real problems that exist in todays north america.

The main thing we where doing was, and still is, To show the world, or more realisticly, our community, that you don't have to sit by and watch, and that whatever you choose to protest you can make a difference.
If you want to save the rain forest's... it's up to you and nobody else, wright letters, sign patitions, do somthing that will help your cause.

We as a, group, decided to take action on the current housing crisis, and other issues including Womins rights and native land claims.

The press and the government say that we acomplished nothing, but I put It to you, how many of you have heard anything about this on the news or from a friend? , most of you I would bet, the word is out now it's up to you to take action.

As a group we did take action. Not violent action as the police, government, and multi-media would have you believe, but very loud and very obvious action with civil disobedience and slogans that where aimed at you, just so you would ask why.

The police, have once again, over stepped their bounds in the eviction of the SQUATTERS as they used un-nessesary violence, in an obiously "no resistance situation". They brought vicious police dog's, bull dozers, hellicoptors, S.W.A.T. teams, dump truck's, and at least 80 cop's hyped up to beat poor people with a variety of personal weapons including riot gear, high powered machine guns, sticks, rubber hoses, and other nasties.

Not to mention 30 roof top snipers and another 100 or so police officers waiting in the wing's.

We were armed with water ballons, soggy doughnuts, and paint.

When the police realised that we where going to be unarmed and public, they fabricated a story to explain or justify their future actions.

We where unarmed, and they knew it, if you don't

believe me, look a little for your self, NO GUNS WHERE EVER FOUND, and don't you think if the police had had any real reason to suspect us of bieng armed, some of us would have been kept in jail? Or questioned about it or even followed up on?

Seeing as none of these things came to be, and the evedence of these thing's are there for the reading and seeing, you should be fairly convinced that the cop's are afraid, the government is afraid, and the rich are too, of loosing their power to manipulate the people and mabey having too face the problems they have created.

So don't be afraid, voice your opinions and do your best to make a difference.

Tjeerd Rutchinski
Jan. 10th 1991

'DECRIMINALIZE SQUATTING'

SQUAT RIGHTS

In the Feb.revolutian of 1990 the opportunity arose to Squat a series of houses on the 1600 block of Frances St. in Vancouver. We took the available accomadations as a step in the process of highlighting the crisis of affordable decent housing. Developers are buying up older rentable homes & tearing up neighborhoods displacing people so that Condaminaruns & high priced apts. destroy our cents of community. This gentrification/profit motivation is the cause of bldg. that are boreded up & left unusable while homelessness & skyrocketing rents send us deeper into poverty. Piss on those land pimps,eh! No respect or excuse for the mentality of exploiters. So we empowered ourselves and took possession of empty houses before they were greedily destroyed by "development". We lived in community together, not as six seperate unrelating dwellings. This sense of unity was what nurished & sustained our ability to survive the pressure to oust us from our home along with (the direct) support of the East End (Van.) community and other parts of town. We are a family/tribe of friends and new political comrades. Sisters & brothers all, we have a wide variety of backrounds & experience. This strength was reinforced and clarified in political discussion & endless struggle, sometimes with agreement to disagree. The decision to create a wimmin only house/space named Bushwomin, both facilltated and defined the conversations & conciousness of men's sexism. Our practice of communal living included sharing the joys and work of child care, food gathering (free when ever possible- dumpsters) & cooking, non-nurotic house cleaning (sanitation) & space sharing (our homes), political outreach/organizing(?), creating music - to make lovly revolution by: the issues of class and racism were also very topical & ongoing. But Direct Actions speak louder than words & that we stand proud of too - the encampment on the lawn of the Van. Art Gallery in the middle of downtown - in support of the OKA Warriors and all land claims based on (the) Soverthe of Native Peoples (everywhere). Linked togther thru struggle for justice and peace, the truth of the attack's bear witness to the context that intimidation thru repression will not stop progressive movements from demanding & getting free from the many forms of oppression. The over kill & sick mentality is best examplified by the (amount of) nuclear weapons stockpiled. That means police/military brutality is a given...state repression is the logical outcome of our capitalistic system that puts property and profit before the needs,concerns and aspirations of people. Greed modivates the rich to insure that they keep getting richer at the expense of working folks. media manipulation tellin us were prepared to go to war ...to die for Mr. George (& he don't even like broclile even tho it's green)and the imbalance of power in that olly part of the world where white makes right. Kops at home think they too are at war/haven't scene nothin yet;could be closer than we think! hope we win-stop them from killing mother earth- or die trying.   sos it's two weaks latter & the U.S. of Amerikkka has begun THE war...what do we do as the world burns;cry in belief that they have totally lost what ever small amount of humanness they may have had? if they can't have it their way will they destroy us: resist their crazyness, get MAD-get even, don't let anything in the way of freedom. be responsible for Actions. join together with like minded people and express rage towards gov't insanity. love life more than money, power or material things. personal & social liberation from the thought police is the begining of the movement away from there\total control. believe what you feel (to be true) not what your told. become what you want. don't listen to THEM. trust your desires. be real, get clear (headed) don't give in to their bullshit &

lies. LIVE life and love people. venceremos! Fight to survive. Resist the death machine culture. there is no other way. it's them or us.

Thou shalt not RENT.
Their needs are few and simple.

i guess if i thought they thought we actually had guns
i'd have been shit scared but instead we yell
challenges of baseball to the snipers Squatters versus
SWAT team to settle once and for all the fate of
Frances street the problem with militants you see is
they tend to be scrawny and underfed like Dog Day
Afternoon we pick up our phone and a cop on the line
every single time or MOVE one barricaded house
rumours of guns and Philadelphia cops killed eleven and
burnt down the block ooops didn't find any weapons
after words only charred black people but we're doing
the hokey pokey out in the open where the crowd and
cameras would be able to see us get shot as we
shake it all about the gangs of riot cops peeking
around the corner wondering if they danced in Oka but
someone can hear them singing We Shall Overcome give us
sub-machine guns and we'll overcome too a squatter
coming out of her home with a bottle of prune juice six
ERT guys running rifles aimed Put it down! Put it down!
that prune juice a little too close to a molotov for
Vancouver's finest what is this? fucking America?
nine of us sitting on the barricade given up
the idea of donuts so much for symbolism
waiting for them to come arrest us three hours what the
hell's taking them so long never thought it could be
so boring to have high powered rifles trained on me
says Geoff and people laugh inside the barricaded house
the four of them playing Boeuf a card game from
down home by candlelight wearing gasmasks giving us a
play by play over the walky talky they're going to look
so stupid tomorrow unless they shoot someone by
accident my non-violent friends beside me dissipating
to be reborn in a new understanding of what it means
to live on your own terms the crazy thing is the
SWAT team evicts me from my home points high powered
rifles at me for six hours demolishes my house in front
of my eyes and now they want to put *me* in prison
i tell ya it oughta be a crime

Will Vancouver make property rights more important than human rights?

nor feed the swine;

A HOUSE IS NOT A HOME

...WHEN THE COPS HAVE A WARRANT

Do you sneeze in the breeze
Do you feel old in the cold
We all need
Someone to feed
Dying in all this greed.

Sometimes I wonder why
They don't come out and say
Let's stop the overkill
Of the underfed today.

I am so sick of all these pain days
In the maze of relativity
Spare me you're hate

Come on out and say
Let's stop the overkill
Of the overfed today.

Housing Is a RIGht!

SQUATTERS ALLIANCE OF VANCOUVER EAST

DISCONTENT

Flap your wings.

Ready to start   E   A   R   S

Will Vancouver make property rights more important than human rights?

nor feed the swine;

... WHEN THE COPS HAVE A WARRANT

Dear Steve-n-Cathy-n-Francise

Sorry I haven't called recently but I have been very busy of late and of course you know me for keeping in touch. Your probably not getting the real story about the squats in your news so I will fill you in; 25th of nov.,Police have told us to get out or they will evict us [AGAIN] this time they say they have gone through the courts and have legal backing, so that morning,barricades go up in the street,sealing off half of our block and lighting small camp fires in the street.

The police come at around 4pm, chief of pigs;bob cooper and a small team of cops who where all smiles. They said they couldn't get the legal crap they needed to boot us so if we took down the wall of furniture no further action would be taken that weekend,A VICTORY,.

On monday the barricades went back up with more consiteration for the neighbors and for others involved to a lesser extent I.E. closing in three of the houses and having both,inside and outside defences,What where these defences;soggy doughnuts water balloons,and rocks with concenses to use them only on cars and equiptment.

AND THEN CAME TUESDAY.......

At aboout 8am a police hellicoptor began to circle over head The police say they have information that we have stockpiled firearms including 2 shotguns and at least 3 handguns inside the houses , this , of course this was totally false. Soon afterward, city dumptrucks in military fashion sealed off all the streets, busloads of cops were brought in, including 80 regular police officers, and atleast 30 SWAT-team hit men. These men brought with them large amounts of high caliber weapons, including machineguns, teargas, sniper rifles, and other assorted riot control gear. Nobody threw anything. Nobody said anything. As far as I'm concerned that was the right thing to do. No sense in getting killed, better to live to fight another day.

At noon, the police told us we had 10 minutes to vacate the houses. However, by four o'clock, nobody had moved, ANOTHER VICTORY. By five, four of the squatters had gone inside a barricaded house, and the rest were preparing for the worst. When the police finally moved in, they used a backhoe, pointed machineguns, and riot gear to confront the ten or so unarmed squatters outside the barricade. In the meantime, anyone who looked vaguely suspicious was arrested and a crowd was mounting, you can imagine their reaction to a hundred screaming people.

After the people outside the barricade were arrested, a steamshovel crashed through the barricade and all the houses, except for the barricaded one, were emptied of their squatters by means of violent arrest. At this point, I was being arrested for mooning a police officer, and roughly stuffed into a paddywagon with alot of my friends. On the way, and inside the jail, I

was beaten,kicked and punched, then thrown in solitary.

Back at the houses, they used heavy machinery, to smash the front and back wall off of the barricaded house. Since the squatters didn't come out, they threatened to use teargas. The squatters emerged with gasmasks and a drum.

Soon after, they were all arrested, slightly beaten, and thrown in jail overnight. NO WEAPONS WERE EVER FOUND, NO CHARGES WERE MORE SERIOUS THAN OBSTRUCTING AN OFFICER AND MISCHIEF.

DISCONTENT

Flap your wings.

The remainder of the houses were torn down for health reasons (a good excuse). All of us were released within 24 hours.

In the aftermath, such things were done as; invading Mayor Campbell's office, small civil demo's, and formal and informal letters of complaint to the city. Some of the support we got was amazing, some of it depressing, but all in all, I still figuer it was a victory.

So that's the story, what do you think?..

I remeber what you said about pig abuse, and I think it makes all the difference when your inside, they can't do anything worse than bruise the skin and bleed on your pride.live to fight the powers that be!

So I guess this means I'm a full fledged subversive now, like father like son. you've always told me the revolution is comming and the more I see the angrier I get. Somday soon I hope we can agree enough on the smaller details of change to fight togeather and win.[WE AGREE THAT THE SYSTEM MUST BE CRUSHED THE WAY IT STANDS,AND I'M SURE WE AGREE TO DEVIDE THE WEALTH WHEN IT COMES]

However we differ on the way we would like to see it rebuilt it seems to me that the party can and has been using basicly the same burocratic look and prosess, now don't get me wrong I'm still young and learning, but as far as I'm concerned a new system must not exclude any of the people in it, including those with weird hair, strange lifestyles, and anarchists.

where does the party stand on these things?

I will be sending a vidio with both news footage and inside recordings to give you a clearer picture.I was hoping mabey this could be shown to the party and other groups in your area.

Jane's fine, and was alot of help on the day of eviction generally harrasing cops and overseeing arrests.

Anyways, I did'nt call, but then again neither did you so, stay in touch, OK?

love TJ.

Poster people stick it to 'em

By David Spaner

YOU *can* fight city hall. You can also poster it. These are just a couple of the lessons of an ongoing battle for the right to poster in Vancouver.

Last summer, Vancouver's city council passed a bylaw making postering a crime punishable by a $2,000 fine or two months in jail. As part of the poster crackdown, the new bylaw was given a high profile unveiling, complete with threatening letters to 'known posterers' (bands, political organizations...), press releases, and advertisements asking upstanding citizens to call the police if they saw anyone postering.

Within days a loose coalition of over 50 groups, representing an array of political and cultural activity, had organized a defense committee and announced they would defy the law by putting up 3,000 copies of a poster that listed the endorsing groups and exclaimed: "CENSORED. This is a poster. It has a right to be here."

The group kicked off the mass postering by openly posting the poles outside city hall. After a couple of people were ticketed, the poster pasters took their protest into the bowels of city hall, taping a poster on the wall behind the outraged mayor's podium and shutting down the council meeting that was in session.

The media jumped on the story, declaring a "poster war" and christening the protestors "the poster people." Groups, independent of the coalition, began adding onto their posters, "This is a poster. It has a right to be here." Benefits were staged, T-shirts and buttons printed, and stickers went up (Yeah... "This is a sticker. It has a right to...").

In October, the poster issue was brought to the walls of city hall. Since city hall was prohibiting the postering of poles, the poster people decided to turn city hall itself into a giant postering pole.

One-hundred and fifty people lay siege to city hall, plastering the *world's largest poster* (over 1,100 feet long) completely around the building, leaving walls, doors, windows and slow-footed bureaucrats blanketed in their wake. The massive poster was made up of an assortment of regulation sized posters and slogans such as: Billboards are the posters of the rich; This is the world's biggest poster, it has a right to be here; One big union of posterers; Posters: art or menace?

As well as partaking in direct actions, the poster advocates have been busy on the legal front. A team of lawyers have agreed to defend anyone charged under the bylaw and, at one point, had it overturned in court. City council passed a new anti-poster law the following day, but the law is continuing to be challenged in court as a violation of the right to "freedom of speech."

The response to the bylaw caught local authorities by surprise. The assistant city engineer—in charge of poster removal—complained that people who put up posters are nuisances. "My whole purpose in life is to get rid of nuisances," he whimpered. One council member condemned postering as a "cross between vandalism and littering."

Anti-poster laws exist in most North American cities (a less severe anti-poster law had been in the books in Vancouver since 1912) but they had never been challenged on an organized, grass-roots level before. (Coincidentally, just a few days before the postering of city hall, poster riots broke out in several cities in China.)

A campaign against a civic bylaw may seem unimportant but, in the same way that many began to question and break the laws they had been reared to respect the moment they smoked marijuana or received a draft card, many who now need to poster find themselves confronted by a particularly absurd law.

Whether one thinks posters add a speck of colour to a drab city or are "visual clutter" as the council maintains, is a matter of personal aesthetics—many people think billboards or black office towers are unattractive—but the only opinion being enforced is that of politicians who can afford expensive advertising. The bylaw cuts off one of the few inexpensive means of communication for those who can't afford radio spots, newspaper ads or billboards.

Posters played a vital role in the development of Vancouver punk rock (as they have in the underground music scenes of many communities). When the ability to stage self-promoted concerts is stifled, new rebel rockers—who face opposition from established promoters—are often discouraged from performing. Posters also played a major role in warning women in one Vancouver neighbourhood about a rapist/jogger. As a member of Rape Relief pointed out, "It's okay to exploit women if you can afford to buy a billboard, but not okay to protect and educate us."

Whether the law will be overturned in court or changed by Vancouver's new city council remains to be seen. But one thing is certain: posters will keep going up and those doing the pasting in Vancouver will do so with a renewed conviction that posters "have a right to be here."

For further information write to **Poster Information, c/o The Open Road, Box 6135, Stn. G, Vancouver, B.C., V6R 4G5.**

Vancouver poster people wrap up City Hall.

Up Against The Wall

In Vancouver, political graffitti, spraypainting and postering have turned the city's walls, power poles and construction site fences into the billboards of the poor. Whether it's the visual pollution—the authorities' view—or popular art and expression seem to be irrelevant. Just about every morning there's new evidence that somebody's been up against the wall getting out the word.

How do they get away with it?

"Well, for spraypainting, it's the later at night the better," says a veteran. "I try to avoid the shift changes when the cops are coming and going from the station. That's when there's the most cops out roaming around looking for action."

For postering: "The ideal time, at least in the winter here, is four or five in the afternoon, just as its getting dark—a lot of people in the streets, you get lost in the shuffle. Late at night you stand out too much for the repetition of putting up a lot of posters.

According to one accomplished wall artist it is generally better to work in groups. "I always try to work with at least a couple of other reliable people. I've gone out in groups of ten or twelve people openly doing graffiti even with the cops tracking you. It's kinda interesting."

It's always more fun to be the spraypainter than the lookout. "The lookout has to be constantly looking for cars, looking over the headlights for the outlines or colorings of cop cars. Once you're at the wall you're free. There's something joyous and liberating about putting your thoughts up there."

Most nights you go out you have some contact with the police just because there's so many around. You can minimize that with lookouts, signals or whistles, but, if you're out there, you will run into the cops."

What do you say when you're caught black handed spraying your favorite slogan?

"I've been caught, but I've gotten out of it by being cool, not having the cans on me (dump them anywhere) and having a plausible rap," says a regular graffiti artist. "What I do is walk right up to them rather than standing by the wall gawking. I think some of the police are actually amused by the graffitti and anarchists in general."

"Taking care of business, the adventure, and the fact that so many people get to see a message they might normally never see, is a powerful incentive," notes yet another wall painter. "Besides, how else are poor people going to compete with Madison Avenue and the mass media? We've got to keep it up."

top: Open Road 12 (1981); bottom: Open Road 15 (1983)

"The Eagle Takes The Wind"

A Photo-Word Journal.

Words By David.
Photos By David & Kenn.

One of the major events that took place in my life recently was a 2 1/2 month journey into the United States, beginning near the end of Feb. and continuing until the middle of May. There were three of us together - Kenn, Michael and myself - travelling in a VW Minibus (complete with numerous technical and mechanical problems) and we covered at least 6000 miles before abandoning our (then) immobile vehicle in Arizona. The three of us had hoped to get this issue of Dissident News out for the Haymarket gathering, but a mobile base from which to work from proved to be too complicated, due mostly to a lack of time, energy and stability. We did however, get some work done, and I wrote quite a bit in a journal, from which I'll be pulling out excerpts. The following was intended for our opening statement for this issue, and although written over five months ago, I think its ideas and clarity make it timeless. It clearly articulates my ideas and thoughts presently.

April 14, 86

This Is A Story...

"This is a story about a journey into the occupied territory of the United States; a part of what is known as Turtle Island to the concentration campers living in this part of the Earth. This is a story about travelling through ruined wasteland more commonly known as "cities", "urban development", "modern society", etc. This is a story about resistance, about struggle; about reclaiming our planet, our lives, our culture. This is not a story the government and corporate puss-heads want to hear. Indeed, this is a story being continually censored, suppressed, altered, and actively fought against by those sickos known as "authorities". But fuck those bastards! This is a story we will tell, will create, and will prosper and thrive like the massive inter-connecting roots of resistance that have been growing under the soil of Mother Earth and her power of will and inspiration.

"This story is one of thousands upon thousands across this planet, yet it is unique in itself. It is about three Toronto-based anarchists on a journey through the eastern cities of the U.S., through the Blue Ridge Mountains, through the Klan territories of the southern states, up the Mississippi to the mid-west, across to New Mexico and the Four Corners area of Arizona and Big Mountain, and finally, up to Chicago for MayDay.

"This journey began in November 85 when a third of us went to the planning conference for the MayDay gathering. It began with him having his unread letters opened and read by customs officials; having his address and phone book confiscated; and finally to be turned away at the border for being an "undesireable"- only to try and find another time or route to pass through the armed gates of the U.S. The second try was more successful. The remaining two thirds of this anarchist entourage didn't

Librarie Alternative Bookshop (Montreal)

"This Land Is Ours" (NY)

leave Toronto until the end of February. It was difficult to leave, especially for me, to pack up all my belongings for storage; to decide what files, literature, contacts, to take along and risk being seized by the border guards.

"After finally leaving and making our way through friends and the Librarie Alternative bookstore in Montreal, we arrived at a small, two-guard border-crossing near midnight somewhere in Quebec. We were questioned for an hour, had our names run through their computers, and had a casual search conducted on our van - not finding our "subversive" literature or the drugs we forgot to hide! An address book, which we luckily thought to remove pages on which certain addresses were written, was thumbed through. They still managed to find an address or two to ask questions about. I was strangely asked if I used any aliases! (Of course I gave them all fifteen I use!) We did finally make it through, although somewhat surprisingly.

"Our next stop in Boston, where we met up with Kenn, turned from a four day stay to about three weeks when a slow oil leak shut down our VW engine. The new engine is running fine... The journey continues through Willimantic, CT, New York, Harrisburg, PA, Washington, Philadelphia, West Virginia, Tennessee, Atlanta, Birmingham, AL, New Orleans, the Mississippi, the Ozarks, and Kansas City where I'm writing this from.

"Our journey has shown us many exciting things happening to many good people, and it's shown us many depressing things happening to both these people, our planet, and the other beings inhabiting Earth. It's shown us that what we are doing - what all of us who are at war are doing - is *essential* and *vital* to the survival of our planet and all the species. And still I wonder whether we're at least holding our ground. The perspective one gains from a journey such as ours, can both exhilirate you and massively depress you. What you will find on the following pages we hope will do more of the former to you. We hope these pages inspire you to fight for your lives, because that's the stage this planet has reached. There is no more time to sit on the fence and hope liberalism and the "good will" of MAN(un)kind will win out. The planet and all life on it is dying. The time to resist and fight back the death culture is NOW! "

I wrote this during our time in Kansas City where we stayed at the Support House, which housed the Big Mountain Support Group, the Leonard Peltier Support Group, the Survival Network and Bayou La Rose, lawyers offices, transient inner-city Indians, and any friends that are passing through and need a place to crash for the night. This house was very intense, to say the least. I believe that it has decentralized somewhat since our visit (in fact, the Survival Network and Bayou La Rose have moved to San Diego).

The East Coast

Digressing somewhat to chronology, after we left Montreal and crossed the border, we headed straight to

Boston where we met up with Kenn. Our stay in Boston has some interesting stories. This was our longest stop in one city, due to our van fucking-up. We stayed at a friend's place, a woman who is part of the Boston Poster Collective - a recently-formed direct action artists' group. They have recently produced three colour posters dealing with war and Big Mountain. While there, they presented a workshop on graffiti which brought together graffiti artists, students, activists, and a wide assortment of ideas. You can contact them at P.O.Box 663, Dorchester, MA, 02125, Uphams Corner, USA. We also attended a (first-ever) Boston-area Earth First! meeting that brought together people active in different areas: from diverting proposed roads in Wendell, MA to Big Mountain support, to anarchists, animal liberationists and pagans. I was pleased to learn that this group is continuing and recently held a regional EF! conference.

While held up in Boston, we took a side-trip over to Willimantic, CT and visited our friends at the Lysander Spooner Collective, two of whom own and operate one of the better anarchist bookstores I've seen. The Spooner Collective also publishes "Instead Of A Magazine", which approaches issues by printing a wide variety of ideas from anarchists. Recent topics have included Work, Family and Marriage, Animal Liberation and Food, etc. Their address is P.O.Box 433, Willimantic, CT, 06226. The bookstore's Box no. is 806 where you can write to for their distribution list.

Squat/Abandoned Building (NY)

When our van was fixed, we headed for New York for a couple of days. As we slept at a friend's place, our van was promptly broken into while on a street in the infamous "lower east side". We should have known better! Our c.b. radio was the most important item that was taken, as well as a valuable sweater (not as in $$) belonging to Kenn. Later on that day, while wandering through the streets of concrete and squats, we were told by passing co-conspirators of a demonstration planned for later that day. The following is an excerpt from my journal, which best explains the atmosphere and situation.

March 17, 86

Adam Purple's Garden Demo

"Sitting in the Manhattan City Library, this is the second day here in this concrete island of mindless idiots! Well, not every-one is mindless, just about 90% of these so-called humans."

"Yesterday we were at the most amazing demonstration. After visiting the Yippie place on Blecker St., we went to a street demo for Adam Purple, a guy who had a garden in an abandoned lot for the past 13 or so years. The city

* from "Misty Mountain" by Ferron.

Special thanks to Reality Now for expropriating the photo work from the boss-man!

WANDERING

Giant Earthworm Causes Chaos During Demo

decided that they were going to use that space for student housing, and set a day that they were going to bulldoze the garden down. They destroyed it 3 days before their deadline to avoid the demo/occupation planned for the set day. Assholes! So yesterday there was an amazing demonstration of about 50 people, all in colours, costumes, masks; all with props and musical/noise instruments, etc.

Garden Demo

"We took to the streets and blocked traffic wherever we went. We sang, danced, handed out leaflets, and invited

Pick-Axing The Road

people to join us as we made our way to the construction area that was once an amazing garden (called "The Garden Of Eden"). At one point, someone started pick-axing the middle of the road and a woman placed a flower in the small concrete hole. The cops were on the scene at this point, but didn't stop or arrest anyone. When we reached the garden, we managed to get through the fence around it and declared that we would replant it, since we brought along bulbs and tools. The cops still didn't arrest anyone, and the "owner" of the property unlocked the gate so the remaining few could pass through and join the rest.

"It was so much fun and excitement, with the group made up of yippies, squatters, anarchists... there were joints and booze flowing."

Cops Harassing Woman During Demo

Banner Showing What Garden Used To Look Like

'Garden Of Death'

From New York we travelled to Harrisburg, PA - home of the infamous Three Mile Island nuclear power plant. It's a small town, complete with a Farmers Market where two friends of ours operate "VeganJoy"- a vegan food stall right next to the butcher! Gaz And Kaz made some of the delicious food we ate at the Chicago Haymarket gathering.

Our next stop was in Washington, DC where we met up with a group of (mostly) young activists who've formed Positive Force - an educational, direct action group. They are involved/interested in animal liberation, Big Mountain support, school activism, Central American struggles, and workers' struggles - with an anarchist/anti-authoritarian approach. Positive Force produce a newsletter called "Off Centre", and can be reached at 2111 Florida Ave. NW, Washington, DC, 20008, USA.

After three days in Washington we left for Philadelphia, where we visited the Wooden Shoe Bookstore. There was a Greens Conference going on at the time right across from the house we were staying at, but much of it didn't interest us. Perhaps it was our headspace. We had covered New York, Harrisburg, Washington and Philadelphia in a period of ten days! A much-needed escape from the concrete jungles was next as we travelled through the Blue Ridge Mountains (part of the Apallacians) in Tennessee. Sleeping atop mountains and beside rivers does amazing wonders for one's state of mind!

Blue Ridge Mountains (Tennessee)

Five Points Community

Our next stop was the Five Points community just outside of downtown Atlanta. Some of the Circle A collective live in this area, where we stayed, among many other dissidents who have gravitated there. To be honest,

Road Devastation (Atlanta)

Making Way For The Super-Highway

among all the communities I visited on this trip, this one in Atlanta is the only one I would give any serious thought to moving to. One resident described it correctly as "like an oasis". Part of the appeal is the climate - I love hot weather - but it is certainly the feeling of community I found there as well.
One aspect here which has drawn the community closer together is a struggle against developers who have already devastated a huge area. They have cut down trees and destroyed the earth right through the middle of Five Points, to make way for a super-highway. The highway is supposedly to enable people to access a new library built for former president Jimmy Carter (for past favours). At the time we were there, the road was temporarily stalled through court proceedings, which had followed several ecotage EF!-type actions on vehicles and survey stakes. Indeed, I had quite a good time roaming the area during some nights! At this point I am unaware of the latest happenings, but the Circle A collective would probably know. They also produce a magazine, and can be reached at P.O.Box 57114, Atlanta, GA, 30343, USA,

From Atlanta we went further south to New Orleans, but we made a stop-over for a couple of hours in Birmingham, Alabama to meet the people with the Mafundi Defense Committee. They are good people working hard in the black liberation struggle, but it was disappointing to learn that they are working toward forming a political party - the Kushite Party. Nontheless, our meeting was good and we shared ideas and contacts. Mafundi is a black political activist in prison on an *indefinate* sentence for being a so-called "habitual offender". For an overview of his life and the many involvements and achievements he's helped bring about, and his ongoing struggle for freedom, you can write us here for an informational pamphlet "The Trials Of Mafundi", or you can write to the Mafundi Defense Committe at P.O.Box 955, Birmingham, AL, 35201, USA.

Continuing right along, we arrived in New Orleans and stayed at the home of two friends who publish a community paper Dialogue. You can write them at 916 Euterpe, New Orleans, LA, 70130, USA. They showed us some of the more relaxed areas to hang out at, at the various bohemian cafes. The famed "French Quarter" is mostly a tourist-trap, carnivorous, trendy, drinking type-of-an-area. Sort of disgusting.

Tourists In New Orleans' "French Quarter"

"Buck-Assed Naked!"

Before heading back in a northerly direction, we decided to go further south to the Gulf of Mexico, to Grand Isle, Louisiana. The beach we stayed on was nearly deserted, but we did manage to get a visit from the beach police. This patrol-guy warned us not to be "buck-assed naked" on the beach! Didn't we know that we had to use their special change buildings to change our clothes because we might

cont'd pg. 12

WANDERING

A Photo-Word Journal continued...

Gulf Of Mexico (Grand Isle, Louisiana)

offend somebody with our naked human flesh?! I simply looked straight into his eyes, trying desperately not to laugh - to understand that yes, we were in Amerika and this guy _was_ serious. He must have caught on to my silent questioning of his "authority" because before he finished his diatribe he was visibly shaking!

On our way to Kansas City, we travelled through the Ozark mountains. During this stretch, humans' abuse and destruction of animal lives became quite graphic and apparent - visually and in our thoughts as well. We passed many factory farms (for chickens and cows), as well as passing many dead animals killed by highway vehicles driving on a part of the Earth where there used to be trees and plants. And animals. Another disgusting spectacle brought to you by the "civilized" way-of-life!

Somewhere In The Ozark Mountains

In Kansas City, at the Support House mentioned earlier, we talked with Arthur Miller (Survival Network, Bayou, etc.), and with Elders and people from Big Mountain, at nearby Lawrence, KS. These talks gave us our first real picture of what to expect at Big Mountain; of what it might really be like as opposed to fantasized dreams of illusion. Arthur Miller is part of a group that is responsible for organizing the resistance in one area of the land, and has suggested that anarchists who are serious in wanting to physically help out, should contact him c/o the Survival Network, P.O.Box 2576, San Diego, CA, 92112, USA. Only serious, no-bullshit, committed people need apply!

Abandoned Centuries-Old Cliff Dwellings

From Kansas we travelled southwest to Arizona, but not without going through beautiful New Mexico first. As perhaps a typical example of urban upbringing and living, the three of us expected to see desert and cactus as soon as we crossed the border into New Mexico. We assumed hot or warm temperatures at least. Well, the marvels and wonders of this amazing planet were again realized as, after driving up several thousand feet on one of the many mountains in the area, we found ourselves in the midst of a blazing snow storm! It was a bit cold, to say the least! Unprepared, we quickly drove back down to find a less hazardous and warmer area to rest for the night.

Many of the beautiful and historic sites in the U.S. are now controlled by the state - supposedly for protection from vandals and developers. We visited an area where people had lived centuries ago, atop and inside various cliffs. The land in this part of the world is quite incredible. Huge gullies lie where rivers flowed thousands of years ago. Rocks and cliffs stand tall as if they grew straight up from the earth.

Rock Formations (Arizona)

Before reaching the Big Mountain Survival Camp, we drove to the most southern city of Arizona called "Why", only several miles from the Mexican border. To get there we had to drive through a huge military bombing range (several thousand square miles) where we constantly heard the boys playing with their guns, airplanes and bombs. We also had the unpleasant (but reality, nontheless) experience of viewing a huge strip-mining operation in progress. The company was kind enough to set up a small tourist area, complete with picnic benches overlooking their rape. A convenient push-button-operated recorded message told you the marvels and wonders of destroying our planet for her "natural resources". It helped our understanding, though, to visually see the destruction rather than simply reading words.

Earth-Rape Strip-Mining In Arizona

Close-Up Of Above Strip-Mine

Big Mountain

"U.S. Out Of N. America"

We finally made it to the Big Mountain Survival Camp, where we set up camp and prepared to meet comrades and Indians and talk about plans and support for their struggle. Being an animal liberationist, I am constantly trying to find a synthesis between animal liberation and the native struggles and their lifestyles. It was probably for this reason that I chose to stay with a Navajo family during my time there; to try and develop a better under-standing of their way-of-life. My visit involved herding sheep, hauling water, and talking to the family at different oppor-tunities. I missed most of the Big Mtn. workshops as a result, but for me, this experience was just as (if not more) important.

April 26, 86
"I'm sitting in a Hogan just outside of the Big Mountain Survival Camp. It's the home of Ruby, a Navajo woman, and her children. I was out with Arthur (Ruby's son) this morning helping and learning how to herd the sheep. This morning I watched a sheep being carved up into little pieces; saw his guts pulled out; and helped hang him to dry. I was washing dishes when he was killed.

"We arrived at the B.M.S.C. two days ago, and last night I volunteered to help herd sheep, at which point I was committed from last night when I left the camp until probably tomorrow morning sometime. Talk about confusion! I really don't know where I stand about anything anymore. Especially in regard to animal rights and liberation. I guess there's a major difference be-tween McDonald's hamburgers and the sheep here, but these are still sentient beings whose lives are being manipulated. I have agreed to eat some of the meat of the sheep killed here today.

"Today at the camp the Hopi and Navajo Elders are meeting with the representatives here from the Big Mtn. Support Groups across the country. I'm here (at Ruby's home) supposedly to free-up some time for Ruby, but Arthur is here as well, so I'm not really needed on the weekend. They would rather I stayed for a couple of weeks at least instead of one day, so today is mostly a learning experience for myself. The Camp itself consists of about 350 people (yesterday's count), most of whom (well a large part anyway) are anarchists. The number is expected to rise to over 500 today. It's a pretty exciting place to be with everyone being friendly and helpful; all there for a single purpose - save Big Mountain.

"I'm sort of regretting volunteering to help with the sheep today because I'm missing a good part of the gathering. But I guess this is my experience of the Survival Gathering, which is unique. This will be something I can take back and share with many people - specifically the anarchist gathering in Chicago in a few days. There will certainly be a twist to the animal liberation workshop I'm to help give there!"

April 27, 86
"Pretty soon I'll be leaving this ranch to go back to the Survival Camp. Yesterday, after a nap I took out the sheep by myself. I didn't allow them very much freedom to roam because I was quite unsure of myself in regard to finding my way back. I felt like a prison guard. I pretty much understand how to keep them all together, and it is much easier with two people doing it. The people here say they are missing one sheep. I don't know whether it was me who lost him (or her), or if s/he's really missing. In one way I feel that it's unfortunate because they might think I'm incompetent or something - 'another white man fuck-up'. But in a stronger way I feel that if truly a sheep is missing, then hooray! for that sheep. There are somewhere around 110 sheep and goats here and surely one who decided to leave will not upset the balance of things.

WANDERING

Communicating

"Last night I ate some of the sheep that was killed here, in a soup. I have to admit that, after the initial adjustment I had to make in my mind, the animal did taste good. This morning I had ham and milk as part of breakfast. Both came from the store and I didn't fully realize the difference until about half-way through the meal. I've had some good discussions with the Arthur's father here about the differences between the meat from animals raised and fed here on the farm and those bought in wrapped packages from the store. He understood exactly what I was talking about. In fact, I've had quite a few small talks about several things: religion, politics, Big Mountain, life on the farm, etc., and I've had a chance to explain why I don't eat meat and, as well, about my anarchist politics. We agreed on a good amount.

Teaching And Learning At Big Mountain

"This morning I helped haul water from the well and fill the troughs for the horse and cow. The animals are coming home now from their morning graze. Last night was pretty amazing with all the stars out. I was planning to do a 'reawakening' ritual at midnight, but I fell asleep around 10:30 pm."

"When I was out with the sheep yesterday, I found myself singing and praying to the Mother Earth, the sun, the wind, and the animals. It was an incredibly emotional experience. Out there I was alone with the animals and the elements."

"This lifestyle is entirely dependent on animals, and I see it as a natural flowing cycle, for the most part in harmony with the pla-net. It still does nothing for my understanding of animal rights."

Dwarfed By Hills And Mountains (Arizona)

Contaminated Water (Big Mountain)

While herding sheep with Arthur, we carried a rifle in case other predators tried to take any sheep. Arthur talked about taking shots at low-flying planes that cruised the area every now-and-again. He told me of one plane - an old bomber - that "mysteriously" crashed in the area about two years ago. Talking to his sister was not very pleasant. She has, understandably, much anger against white culture and people - a lot of which came out and was directed at me. There wasn't much I could say or do other than listen and learn. Their mother, Ruby, does not speak any english, so our communication was minimal - mostly translated through her children. Her husband worked in one of the cities, and is away for most of the time. He was there for the conference at the camp and, as I wrote in my journal, we talked about many political ideas. He seemed to be caught up in the dogma of christianity and the state; possessing christian-native magazines and denouncing the Soviet Union as being much worse than the U.S. As with a vast majority of people - both white and native - he believed that the "justice" system was the only answer and solution to correcting the problems. I explained my anti-state/anti-authoritarian ideas, which he understood quite easily, and which he said he basically agreed with.

'Bunch Of White Folks' With Broken Van!

For more info on the current situation at Big Mountain, a donation to the Legal Defense/Offense Committee will get you their latest newsletter. Write them at 2501 N. 4th St., Suite 18, Flagstaff, AZ, 86001, USA. Both Kenn and Michael went back down to Big Mountain after Chicago, and continued travelling around. Excerpts from some of Kenn's letters follow this article. Much has been written about the Chicago gathering in the alternative press. You can read the Toronto anarchists' views on page 10 of Reality Now, and other views and experiences can be found in the centrespread of Dissident News.

On To Chicago

Coming out of Big Mountain, our van broke down once again. It might have had something to do with the fact that we were carrying three more bodies (Great Peace Marchers coming with us to Chicago) as well as their camping gear. I guess it was a bit much for a '72 VW Bus! We managed to get a tow into Flagstaff, and we stayed at the Support House there while we made other travel plans. Being on a tight schedule at this point (in order to make Chicago on time) we left our van at a VW mechanic-friend's place while we drove two expensive 'drive-away' cars (only paying for gas) from Arizona to Chicago. It was the first time any of us had driven a fully-equiped Mercedes Benz - and I didn't know whether to laugh or be sick!!

Since we drove straight through (24 hours non-stop) until we reached Chicago, we had an extra three days with the two cars before we had to return them. I'm sure several anarchists present at Haymarket who saw us in them and wondered who we were and where we came from are still questioning! It was sort of a joke with us, and we planned to explain at some point, but our arrests at the demonstration on May 2 cancelled that. So here goes: No, we are not rich; we don't own expensive cars; and we're not cops! Now I feel better!

Big Mountain Survival Camp Gathering

It's a planet of resistance;
It's a whirling flame of choice.
Are you my comrades in resistance?
I swear they'll know us by our voice.

Do we lay down in dusty corners?
We are ragged as a scar.
And when we rest, our eyes stay open;
We are always off to war.

We're always off to war, my friends,
We're always off to war.
It makes me think of this, my friends:
Where can the quiet be?

Is it up the misty mountain,
Where wild flowers by the road?
Is it down by the rushing river,
Where force wears those boulders down?

Is it underneath my covers?
Is it trapped inside my brain?
Is it up above the misty mountain?
Is it up above the rushing river?

Is it up above the bed of longing,
Where the eagle takes the wind?

The eagle takes the wind.
Words by Ferron (Misty Mountain)

Our Beautiful Earth

Reality Now 6 (1986)

¡*Venceremos!* Che Guevera remains an important symbol of revolutionary struggle in Mexico, as well as all of central and south america. Besides seeing his picture in leftist student centres in towns such as Morelia, one can also find posters, buttons, & plaques for sale with street vendors!

Miguel de Atoxxxico. Muchas gracias amigo!

Marcha del Dia Internacional de la Mujer, March 7 89. Punks in the streets celebrating International Wimmins Day.

MEXICO- NO ESTAMOS CONFORMES

SS-20, tocada in Garamarrero. Patty Zappa, vocalist for ss-20. In Mexico, there are more wimmin involved in the punk scene than in N. America. They also face a lot of sexism. There has been some resistance in the form of zines put out by wimmin; "Sin leyes" (without laws), and a wimmins collective "CHAPs, who put out a newsletter and held a conference protesting patriarchal violence.

Massacre 68, tocada contra la represion (gig against repression), from june 88 in solidarity with the chinese uprising. Massacre 68 is named after the 1968 massacre in Mexico city, similiar to Tiananmen square.

Tierra y libertad, Land & Liberty. As in most countries in the 3 continents, the question of land ownership is central to both the exploitation of people and resources as well as the revolutionary struggle for self-determination.

Every *sabado* record, tape, magazine sellers set up along 3-4 blocks of a street near the train station in mexico city. The punks also sell their zines, tapes, jewellry, clothing & tattoos, some of them not paying the vendors license and occasionally being attacked by the kops. Frequently, anarchists also set up a stall selling books and *Testimonios*, a libertarian magazine. Many of the punks are also anarchists, and most identify loosely with the circled a. The authoritarian and dogmatic nature of many of the leftist groups doesn't appeal to them, and in a way the political punks define their own struggle and carry out their own actions. This includes posters against Sefinas, the president, done up as a punk, distributing info against Laguna de Verde nuclear plant being built by GE, collectives such as *Radical Change Positive Force & Change or Death*, who have organised punk expositions and conferences. As well, the literature and music produced in mexicos punk kulture is very anti-statist, anti-kop etc., and this is reflected in the titles; *Brigada Subversiva, Contra la Violencia, MELI (Murder in the industry), Motin (Riot), Disolucion Social, Sedicion, No Estamos Conformes* and others.

TIERRA Y LIBERTAD

CIRCULO DE ESTUDIO DE LA CASA DEL LAGO

poster: Jean Smith

THEORY & PRACTICE

Anarchists tend to shun any theory-building that is divorced from practice. Of course this means their theorizing is far more contingent than partisans of logical consistency might wish for. Indeed, arguments are frequently raised by way of dialogues rather than cut-and-dried position statements. As such, they are invitations to further inquiry as well as directives for actualizing social change in the here and now.

"Theory and Practice" opens with an interview on the subject of biotechnology in which Chaia Heller, Jennifer Moore, and Marc Bernhard unpack the capitalist foundations of the industry and its integral role in the late 20th-century shift toward information-based modes of production. "The Body of Women" from the Quebec journal, *Les Sorcières* offers a fast-paced overview of patriarchal constructions of the female body. This is followed by a provocative analysis of identity politics and the social construction of "race." The next article, "Insurrection and the Informal Organization," argues the anti-capitalist struggle should be spearheaded from a base of informal autonomous groupings, rather than monolithic union or federation structures. This article also includes a cautionary afterword on the need for "Constructive Criticism." "No Means No!" from *BOA* sends a powerful message to male abusers. "Fire and Flames: An Interview with a Berlin Autonomist"

discusses the politics of Europe's anti-authoritarian milieu in the late 1980s. Theorizing strategies for ending the fur industry while building solidarity with Indigenous peoples is the focus of "Animal Liberation and Native Struggles" and its sister article, "Attack the Real Sources of Suffering." This is followed by Jesse Hirsh's article on "The Mythology of Technology: The Internet as Utopia," in which he suggests the internet's anarchist potential lies in its ability to facilitate the free creation and exchange of information beyond the reach of corporate control.

Radical solutions to the "oldest professions" are the subject of the next two articles – "No More Cops" and "No Pornography, No Censorship" from *Reality Now*. The revolutionary import of freedom is placed front and centre in "Freedom – It is Forbidden to Forbid!" from *Open Road*. In "Bisexuality" Jamie challenges biases amongst sexual liberation activists. The sanctity of property comes under attack in "Manifeste Contre la Societe Spectaculaire Marchande." "Is Marxism Racist?" poises the question and answers in the affirmative. Finally, primitivist Feral Fawn calls for the downfall of civilization in "Feral Revolution: Rebelling Against Our Domestication" from *Demolition Derby*.

– ALLAN ANTLIFF

Biotechnology and Society:
An Interview with Chaia Heller

KIO: The companies that manufacture genetically modified seeds believe that biotechnology holds the key to increased crop yields. As the world population increases, such innovation may be needed to feed the world. Seen in this way, genetic modification is promoted as a great humanitarian innovation. What do you think is the underlying motivation for the development and production of genetically modified foods?

CH: Well, that is clearly the line of reasoning that the industry has been using, although, recently a year ago, Monsanto took off their web site the claim that agricultural biotech is going to feed the world. This is because the problems with world hunger are not problems of food shortages but problems of food distribution, and the political obstacles that keep food from moving into areas where it needs to be. This idea that agricultural biotechnology is going to increase yield and feed the world is not just dubious but patently erroneous and intentionally misleading. The first generation of crops was not designed necessarily to increase yield. The primary goal in the first generation of resistant varieties was to lower production costs for producers; to have lower and more effective pesticide use. These benefits were for the producer, not destined for export to the southern hemisphere. A lot of these yields were going to Europe and processed foods throughout first world supermarkets. So this idea that agricultural biotechnology was driven to increase yield is incredibly dubious, and was not the primary goal of this generation of crops. The second generation of crops will be known as the value-added crops, and they are promising that they will produce crops which have either added pharmaceutical or nutritional value. This again is the product of the humanitarian end of biotechnology and we don't know if that's a) what they are really planning to do, or b) if they are even able to fulfill that promise. As to the hunger question, that is misleading and I would say, intentionally misleading.

KIO: The companies also claim that the introduction of this genetic technology will constitute a "green revolution" as pesticide use will be reduced. Do you think that it constitutes a "green revolution"?

CH: It's funny because the first green revolution was the introduction of hybrids and industrial agricultural machinery into the south that, again, had uneven and dubious results. So this question as to whether this technology will indeed reduce pesticide use is very dubious for several reasons. First of all, it looks like biotechnology's real goal is to create the same kind of monopoly that you see Bill Gates trying to get with Windows; the idea is to create a patented product that is perhaps useful, and yet expensive, creating a market where people will be increasingly obliged to buy that product. In terms of agricultural biotechnology, you basically have to be a multinational in order to have

enough money to generate the capital required for investment in research and development. These few companies are investing in this industry to get a monopoly on the seed, to make that kit, or combo, where people will have to buy both to buy one. The goal here is to pair a pesticide with a seed, where every farmer has to buy seed and now every time they buy seed they also have to buy that pesticide. And so, these agro-chemical companies, who are calling themselves life-science companies, are very invested in pesticide use. In fact, they are promoting the same model of industrial chemical agriculture that we have seen grow more powerful since World War II. So I don't think that these companies are at all interested in reducing pesticide use. Second of all, these plants, these transgenic varieties run the risk of, within a few generations, becoming resistant to pesticides. So now you have these farmers who will become increasingly dependent on these companies to produce new chemicals every few years, creating a built-in obsolescence, or a genetic treadmill effect, where you increasingly have to come up with new chemical inputs to keep up with this so called "environment." So, no, in short, in the long run I do not see this technology decreasing the amount of pesticide use.

KIO: Many people reject technological development in general, as they believe that technology in and of itself is oppressive. Others claim that it is not the technology that is oppressive but it is how it is wielded, and by whom, as it can be liberating if it is utilized for the benefit of all people and not for the profit-making of a few. In your opinion is there a liberating potential to genetic modification if it was somehow separated from the profit-motive?

CH: We are still living in a 19th century model of cultural evolution, where we believe that "technology" is this autonomous essence or force which unfolds out of itself and has its own momentum. It is seen as either progressive, or regressive and dangerous. It is either bringing us towards a better society or towards a worse society. There is another way to look at technology and that is to look at technology as simply a set of cultural practices. Technology is merely a prosthetic enhancement of human activity, and because human beings are cultural creatures, every practice that we do, every prosthetic enhancement that we make, is a cultural expression. So once we see technology as culture and not as some outside autonomous force that is impacting on society either positively or negatively. Now we have a very important cultural question, that is, what kind of technology, what kind of culture are we going to be creating? If it is to be a culture, which has a political and economic system, based on hierarchy, domination, unlimited growth, and accumulation, then our cultural practices and the technological expressions of those practices will be going in that direction. I am also not saying that technology is inherently neutral or deterministic, again, technology is cultural practice and there are certain cultural practices which are very biased and culturally driven. The question is, can we see technology as a cultural practice that we can assess and evaluate, just as we can assess any cultural practice? In the case of biotechnology, I don't think that you can separate that set of social, cultural, political, and economic practices that constitute biotechnology from biotechnology. Agricultural biotechnology

4

Kick It Over 39 (2001)

can only be understood as the history of agricultural biotechnology. It has to be understood as capitalism moving into a more flexible phase looking for more flexible forms of production, looking for renewable resource base, that genetic information or genetic materials provides. That technology came at a time when the US was weaning itself from an early industrial mode of production, moving towards this new phase of production; and it can only be understood as the result of venture capital gleaned from industrial production poured into the development of new technologies, for the purposes of creating a new kind of production monopoly. It can only be understood as being that. So, to say, could there be an agricultural biotechnology that was emancipatory and humanitarian, that would only be true if you had a society that was emancipatory and humanitarian and the question is, we have no idea, would we be using genetic engineering, recombinant DNA in this way if we were living in a society that was directly democratic, a society that was not profit-driven? We have no idea, we could speculate, but the point is that that is not really the point. We DO live in a society in which it is really clear as to the how and why and when and for what purposes this industry emerged and I think that we can make a very convincing argument against it.

KIO: Over the past few years there has been increasing opposition to GM products, but to a large extent it has been a gut reaction based on the idea that GM food is weird and unnatural.

CH: It is very interesting and, in fact, this is what I think a lot about. I am an anthropologist and I have been studying the question of genetically engineered food in France for the last 3 years and one of the things I look at is how people construct their arguments for or against GE food. Two of the main arguments I see are: 1) is the fact that GE foods are risky; and 2) the other argument is that they are dangerous environmentally, or naturalistically speaking, something that I call the "ick factor": that people find GE food to be "icky" and monstrous and weird. If you analyze this, again anthropologically speaking, what you find is that every culture has a way of organizing its social realities by constructing taboos that are basically boundaries, culturally constructed categories that should not be transgressed. And when people think about transgressing that boundary they usually feel disgust. An example would be cannibalism. In many societies there is a very powerful taboo about eating another human being. It hits what you could call a "cultural nerve." There is an "ick" factor of absolute disgust. And so, when there is that feeling of disgust, that "ick" factor, you know that there has been a cultural boundary that has been transgressed. Now, in the case of GE foods, people are having that "ick" reaction without realizing that it is a cultural response, they see it as somehow being a universal knowledge that has an inherent truth and they want to ground their claims against GE foods on that. Here's the problem, it might be true that it is dangerous, in fact a lot has led me to believe that it is dangerous. However, the real danger is to base the rejection of a cultural or technological practice on a gut feeling, on a feeling of transgressing a cultural taboo, because this brings us to make naturalistic arguments, which itself creates a barrier against transgressing many inappropriate

barriers or taboos in today's society. The problem is that I don't believe that you can base a politics on a cultural response, because sometimes they are right and sometimes they are not and they are inherently subjective and cultural and do not make a good ground for a political argument because they can lead in reactionary directions. I don't believe in naturalistic arguments against cultural practice. I believe in social and political arguments against cultural practice. So whereas I understand, anthropologically, why we want to call these "Frankenfoods," I see that to be dangerous, because there are some very right wing elements, which are very drawn to this issue on these same grounds. They are not legitimate arguments, although they are understandable cultural responses; but we need to be conscious of why we have them and we need to ground them not in naturalistic gut, cultural, "ick" reactions, but we need to really understand the social, political, and economic, as well as the cultural disruptions associated with these technologies.

1950's scenic Saskatchewan Canadian dollar bill, now defunct in favour of our coin known as the 'loonie.'

KIO: In the fall 1999 issue of Perspectives on Anarchist Theory, you mentioned in the interview you did with them that these new technologies are transforming agricultural economies around the world and that this is linked to the idea of an information age.

CH: Biotechnology is an integral component of a larger shift that capitalism is undergoing. As we are weaning ourselves from a primarily industrial mode of production we are moving towards a more flexible and information-based mode of production. After World War II the US had to face the problem of competing with the recovering western and Japanese countries that were recovering their industrial infrastructure. The US had to figure out how to compete, to make its own industrial production process more flexible, loosening up markets and labour forces, and primarily by creating new productive processes that would be more flexible, that would have renewable resource bases, and that could create very specialized and flexible products that could be both creating and adapting to ever-changing markets. These new technologies would be biotechnology and the telecommunications industry. These are information-based. Biotechnology required taking the sphere of life itself and translating that into information and then calling it intellectual property that can be patented. The same is true for

5

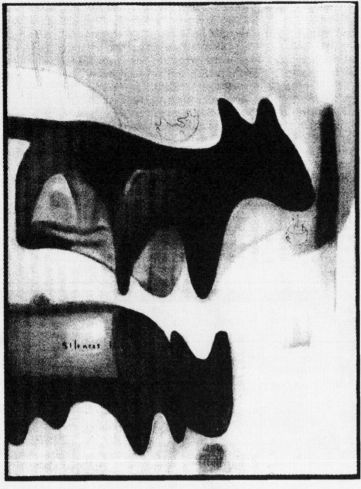

chains and mega-chains and superstores, telecommunications, micro-processing and computerization, and again biotechnology. This is the information age of global capital and it requires a new form of governmentality that cannot be provided by the state because the state, again, is a unit of self-interest and the state will always look out to protect its own capital. So there has to be an institution that is beyond a state, or a meta-state, and that is what the WTO wants to be, and is trying to be, unless we keep being good at keeping it from doing what it would like to do. The meta-state of the WTO is going to be, would like to be, that new form of governmentality that would be there to protect intellectual property through trade related intellectual property laws (or TRIPS),and to remove every obstacle, every environmental regulation, every labour regulation, every import regulation, to remove every obstacle to the free flow of informational capital. So, the job of this new form of governmentality called the WTO is to remove obstacles from the flow of informational capital and to protect the informational capital through TRIPS.

KIO: As an anthropologist, what do you think the cultural significance of these phenomena, these changes is? What kind of impact will this have on society?

6

telecommunications. You have to be able to copyright all of the music, image, and text that constitute telecommunicative product. It is the information that is the resource base that is being used in the production process. And I do believe that the franchise, the chain-store, which I call chain-space that is in the process of enchaining us, is also an information-based technology, that we have to see McDonalds as an informational factory. It is producing signs, symbols, test, inscriptions, scripts, recipes, etc. It is a patented matrix of information that people who manage McDonalds have to clone, or reproduce, as you would clone or reproduce a gene or a piece of software. This is an information-based technology, and McDonalds is not just producing hamburgers and those little happy meal figurines, etc., it is producing signs, symbols, images; it is information based and what they make their money from is by allowing managers to, in a sense, lease out that information in order to replicate it, to clone a McDonalds or a Jiffy Lube, or a Staples, etc. That they are borrowing the copyright rights to that information to create their own little factory, or what I call a factory-ette. It is a dispersal of the older style factory as it is made more flexible, and more dispersed. So, biotechnology is part of this larger shift to new information-based capital, a service economy based on

CH: I think that we are already seeing tremendous impacts, and I would say tremendous disruptions are happening culturally. I think what is interesting is the biotechnology question and how it has this "ick" response, as sort of the most visible response that something is hitting a cultural nerve. What is so interesting to me is why people respond culturally to certain innovations, certain transitions, and not to others. Why are people grossed out by the transgression of a species boundary and the explosion of informational capital and not by the encroachment of chain stores that are being cloned all over and are taking up public space and are really encroaching upon the cultural sphere? People aren't grossed out by that, it doesn't hit the same kind of cultural nerve that biotechnology tends to hit. What happens is that there has historically been this tension between the realm of commodified production and consumption and the private sphere, the realm of home and neighbourhood, etc., or public life as well. What is happening now is, in a certain way, very analogous to what happened during the transition from feudalism to industrial capitalism. There was an enclosure of the Commons, creating enormous social upheavals as the peasants were forced off the countrysides and into the urban centres. Today we have different forms of enclosures. We are having biological forms of enclosure, where capital is moving into the biological commons of the gene and the genome, both literally and globally, as the genome becomes this new sphere, which is being enclosed upon, and there is tremendous social disruption associated with that. People are experiencing a cultural response to the enclosure of the biological commons or the encroachment of capital. In the cultural sphere the enclosure by capital represents a qualitative shift to the way it was done before. Before World War II, there was much more autonomy in the sphere of culture making than there is now. People were much more able to entertain themselves, literally, to have recreative activities (recreation) than they are now. People were able to feast themselves, provide music for themselves, and provide their own parties, their own entertainment, both within their own homes and within their communities. That sphere of culture-making has been increasingly encroached upon by service capital that is very entertainment-based through sedentary tourism or theme spaces. So recreation has been enclosed upon and the enclosure of public space itself is dramatic. This is all closely analogous to the enclosure of the Commons, where now private corporations own the downtown urban centres, the public centres brought to us by the nation state, from universities, to libraries, to the sidewalks themselves. This encroachment of the public commons by capital into these spheres, public, cultural, and biological, is creating tremendous cultural disruptions, as people have fewer and fewer places to experience themselves as uncommodified beings in uncommodified spaces. And what I ask as an anthropologist is what happens when you get to a point in history when that tension between commodified and non-commodified cultural reproduction becomes so thoroughly saturated, commodified, centralized, and/or trans-local or multinational production of cultural practice? Is there a point when we will be thoroughly saturated

and what will we look like then? I really wonder. I imagine that there will always be people at the margins who will continue to think and to retain some level of cultural generativity, but it will be a very interesting and quite disturbing thing to see when that tension breaks down. I can't help but assume that this will affect our imagination, our consciousness, and our ability to think. I think that it will affect us all dramatically.

KIO: Consumer action is often advocated as the best method to oppose the excess of the capitalist market. Do you agree with this, or do you feel that there is something more?

CH: Yes, of course, I believe that there is something more. In fact, what is really frightening to me is that Marx made a prediction, now more than a century ago, that capitalism will create a world after its own image, and I think what has happened during this period is that capitalism has created a human being in its own image. We are so thoroughly identified with capitalism that we have internalized capitalism, in that we can only think of ourselves in terms of either consumers or producers. When we think of ourselves as producers and we want to step out of the capitalist system, we think about creating economic alternatives, co-ops, etc. When we think about ourselves as consumers outside the capitalist system, we think about consuming alternative products or boycotting products that we don't agree with. We only see ourselves in terms of producers and consumers, as agents of capital, either resisting the capital, and capital becomes the subject of the

political project. We have to leave the era of capitalism, at least in terms of how we see ourselves, and enter the era of the political, and to see ourselves as citizens. This becomes quite problematic as we live under a nation state and the whole notion of citizenship under a nation state becomes problematic as there are people who are not even allowed to be citizens because of international borders to keep people from coming in or to keep people from enjoying their rights as citizens. So we have to begin to think about recapturing political power that would be within a stateless direct democracy. This requires a very big leap in terms of how we think about politics, because we have to think our way out of and act our way out of a representational and parliamentary democracy. You would have to go back to the original Greek meaning of politics, not fully encompassing the ancient Greek way of life, but building on what was innovative at the time, of the idea that citizens in a direct face-to-face way, could meet in a general assembly to create the public policy that would govern their everyday lives. That is what politics means. It means the citizens of a polis going into that assembly and seeing themselves as mature, adult beings who can govern themselves. This politics is called libertarian municipalism. As it is being developed now within social ecology, it is a body of ideas primarily developed by Murray Bookchin and there are movements all over the world, and it is a movement very much in an embryonic phase, but the logic would be that we, as citizens, would reclaim the public sphere, engage in a directly democratic way, and that incrementally municipalities would confederate with other self-governing municipalities to create an independent community of communities, a confederation of locally self-governing municipalities. And there is a lot of discussion about how this would happen or how we would do this. Ultimately, we can only fight and recover our humanity, I believe, we can only fight capitalism and the state, not by countering the state and capitalism on their own terms, but we have to counter it on OUR terms as citizens, by reclaiming existing, legitimate, political forums. I do not believe that we can green-consume our way to a democratic society, and I also do not believe that we can protest, or reform, or alternative our way to a good society. I think that we have to politicize our way to a good society and that means taking our communities and our politics into our own hands to really see ourselves as capable of creating the sort of society that we would want to live in.

Chaia Heller is a faculty member at the Institute of Social Ecology in Vermont where she teaches classes on social ecology, eco-feminism, and other topics. She is also the author of The Ecology of Everyday Life: Rethinking the Desire for Nature published by Black Rose Books 1999.

This interview was conducted in Guelph, winter 2000, by Marc Bernhard and Jennifer Moore. Zoe Pfeiffer made the transcription from video recording.

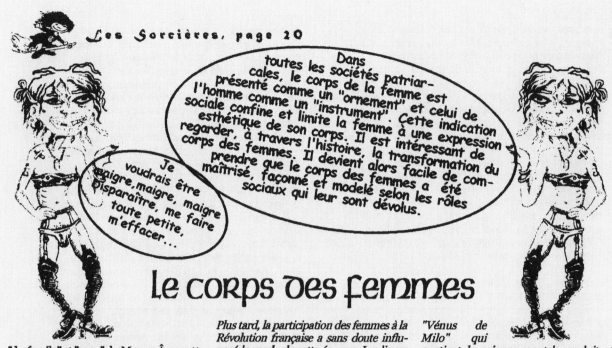

> Dans toutes les sociétés patriarcales, le corps de la femme est présenté comme un "ornement" et celui de l'homme comme un "instrument". Cette indication sociale confine et limite la femme à une expression esthétique de son corps. Il est intéressant de regarder, à travers l'histoire, la transformation du corps des femmes. Il devient alors facile de comprendre que le corps des femmes a été maîtrisé, façonné et modelé selon les rôles sociaux qui leur sont dévolus.

> Je voudrais être maigre, maigre, maigre, disparaître, me faire toute petite, m'effacer...

Le corps Des femmes

"la fragile" et "pure" du Moyen-Âge: cette époque privilégie la maigreur et cultive l'impression de fragilité qui s'en dégage. Les formes sont menues, délicates, les poitrines sont petites, les hanches effacées, la gorge menue, les bras et le cou sont longs. Les robes longues et ajustées accentuent la hauteur et la fragilité de la silhouette. C'est l'époque de l'amour chevaleresque, où l'on se bat pour ces femmes si fragiles.

"la majestueuse" du 17ème siècle: bien que la silhouette des femmes soit lourde et plus opulente, on assiste au redressement du maintien. On apprécie les beautés majestueuses. Le corps est semblable à une armure et il est maintenu par des baleines, des tiges de bois ou de jonc. Le corset se lace devant, rejettant les épaules en arrière, afin de solenniser la posture. L'attitude rigide et morale du corps est important puisqu'à cette époque, les femmes exercent un certain pouvoir en tant que régentes.

"la révolutionnaire" du 18ème siècle: Apparition du modèle impressionniste: c'est une beauté en lignes douces, la tendre fermeté d'un corps fluide et potelé, vif et familier, d'un corps à fossettes riant dans sa chair blanche.

Les femmes superposent à leur corps de larges cercles d'osier recouverts d'étoffes, atteignant un diamètre de 3 à 4 mètres. Les robes sont encombrantes, restreignent et paralysent la liberté de mouvement des femmes.

Plus tard, la participation des femmes à la Révolution française a sans doute influencé la mode de cette époque. Les lignes sont épurées, le style est dépouillé. Les robes sont plus légères, épousent le corps et mettent en évidence ses formes réelles. Certaines femmes adoptent un vêtement de type "grèce antique". La taille est remontée et la poitrine est soutenue par une petite brassière. Le vêtement permet alors une plus grande liberté des gestes et se veut plus naturel, sans toutefois mettre en valeur les rondeurs féminines

"la romantique" du 19ème siècle: on réintègre le corset, les paniers et les crinolines toujours aussi démesurément larges. Tout au long de ce siècle la taille sera soit allongée, raccourcie ou contorsionnée.

Le corset dessine une taille étroite entre les hanches gonflées par une crinoline. Il comprime le ventre et la taille, faisant ainsi saillir les seins. La taille des femmes ne sera jamais assez mince et l'on fabriquera un corset se laçant dans le dos afin d'obtenir une véritable taille de guêpe. Ces corsets compriment les organes internes, déforment la cage thoracique, provoquent des évanouissements, la respiration étant oppressée. On a d'ailleurs retrouvé des squelettes de femmes dont les côtes ont été brisées par le port du corset.

Ce siècle développera également une panoplie d'appareils mécaniques pour rectifier et modeler le corps des femmes. Dans son livre Le travail des apparences, Philippe Perrot reproduit le corset dit

"Vénus de Milo" qui contient des seins en caoutchou palpitant au moyen d'un ressort situé derrière la taille. Si un bras le frôle, la poitrine palpite aussi longtemps que la pression est exercée.

Vers 1800, on voit apparaître le faux-cul. C'est un coussin rembourré sur les fesses qui contorsionne la silhouette. Le corset est alors plus grand, couvre le corps jusqu'en haut des cuisses faisant avancer les seins et rebondir les fesses. Pour obtenir de bons résultats et présenter une croupe intéressante, les femmes devaient au préalable avoir une bonne couche de graisse sur les fesses. Cette silhouette fait penser au profil des volailles de basse-cour.

Tous ces mécanismes concourent à raidir, à handicaper et à mutiler le corps tout en le réduisant à la passivité et en promouvant sa fragilité. On entérine ainsi un discours médical décrétant que la fragilité féminine fait partie intégrante de la nature du corps des femmes. L'image sociale des femmes en est une d'improduction, d'objet de consommation et de faire-valoir. Elle représente le rang de son mari. Elle sera sa devanture sociale. "

(Ces descriptions, très révélatrices, qui nous tracent l'évolution du contrôle du corps des femmes à travers l'histoire sont tirées mots pour mots d'un document produit par Le Centre des Femmes de Verdun- Daigneault-l'Archevêque, D., Dessureault L., et Walsh S.- et intitulé Un Regard Féministe sur l'Obsession de la Minceur).

Le corps des femmes, suite

L'apparence physique et l'idéal féminin imposés aux femmes sont le reflets des valeurs dominantes de la société dans laquelle elles évoluent. Il est également important d'observer que certaines périodes ont promulgué une plus grande liberté du corps des femmes. Ces périodes coïncident avec une participation plus active des femmes à la vie sociale, politique et sexuelle. Cependant, ces périodes furent généralement de courte durée et furent suivies de période de "récupération" où l'on a contraint et mutilé de nouveau leur corps. Par exemple, l'apparition des mouvements féministes dans les années 1960-70 est venu ébranler quelque peu les rapports homme-femme traditionnels. Les femmes se sont imposées dans des sphères où auparavant elles étaient absentes ou effacées (le travail, la vie politique et sociale, les rapports de couple, etc.). Nous pourrions croire que le mouvement de "réduction" du corps des femmes qui sévit à l'heure actuelle est le prix que l'on nous fait payer pour avoir pris "un peu trop de place" dans les 30 dernières années. Sans être paranoïaques, nous pourrions voir un lien entre la montée du féminisme et le mouvement de réduction du corps des femmes. Ainsi, pendant que les femmes prennent du poids socialement, la mode vise à réduire le corps des femmes. Ce phénomène serait donc la réaction d'une société patriarcale dans laquelle les femmes revendiquent du pouvoir dans les sphères traditionnellement réservées aux hommes.

On nous présente des canons de beauté féminins qui sont quasi inaccessibles. La publicité nous offre l'image de corps prépubères, sans sein, sans ventre, sans hanche. Pour être acceptées socialement, plusieurs femmes vont même jusqu'à se faire violence elles-même pour répondre aux standards de beauté: régimes à répétition qui maintiennent les femmes en état de famine permanent, chirurgies plastiques (liposuccion, réduction ou augmentation des seins, etc.), l'épilation, le maquillage, les souliers à plateforme et à talons aiguille qui déforment les pieds etc. Dans notre société, l'idéal de la beauté féminine est si difficile à atteindre, tellement innaccessible, qu'il est implicitement lié à la souffrance

De plus, on a fait de l'obsession de la minceur une immense industrie qui gère des milliards de dollards et qui hante les femmes et détruit parfois toute leur vie. Cette industrie est bénéfique principalement pour des hommes: la haute couture (les grands couturiers), la publicité, les photographes, le cinéma, l'industrie pharmaceutique, les Weight Watchers et compagnie, les médecins et chirurgiens plastique etc.

D'autre part, il est important de souligner qu'en tant qu'"ornement", le corps de la femme est toujours utilisé pour séduire les consommateurs. Le corps de la femme c'est vendeur! Une "belle" femme pour vendre de la vaisselle, du savon à lessive, du savon à vaisselle, une Pizza Mc Cain, des vêtements, des produits pour bébés, des Corn Flakes, du jus d'orange, des lunettes, des vitamines, des médicaments contre la toux, des gants de vaisselle (pour garder nos mains douces et soyeuses),de la pâte à dents blanchissante, des lentilles cornéennes, du Monsieur Net, des cigarettes menthol (c'est doux pour la gorge), de la peinture (dans les tons de pastel), des stores verticaux (ça met en relief les jolies courbes de la pièce), les robots culinaires (c'est multifonctionnel), des cartes de crédit, des arrangements funéraires , des shampoings orgasmiques, des balais magnétiques, des balayeuses, des pastilles, des lames de rasoir ("la perfection au masculin"). Bref, partout on nous apprend que nous sommes consommables, notre corps est un attrait, une séduction, une stratégie de marketing. Mentionnons aussi que seuls les corps minces, sans vergeture, sans culotte de cheval, bronzés, sans ride, sans varice sont illustrés, sont montrés.

Certaines thèses féministes avancent l'hypothèse que le modelage du corps des femmes qui s'incarne présentement à travers le mouvement de réduction de leurs corps serait une façon de les désapproprier de la maternité, " de leur dénier ce pouvoir ". Le patriarcat, depuis son instauration, a tenté (toujours par la force) de contrôler le corps de la femme. En effet, nos corps " reproducteurs ", pour bien servir le capitalisme et le patriarcat, doivent être contrôlés. Nos corps sont des réceptacles à bébé (c'est sûrement pour cette raison que la mère de Jésus le Christ était vierge - elle n'était, en fait, qu'un gros contenant pour recevoir le fils de Dieu sur terre).

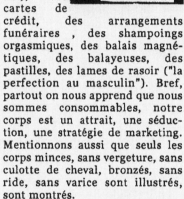

PATRIARCHY

Les Sorcières, page 22

Le corps des femmes fin

Le contrôle des naissances (que ce soit leur expansion ou leur diminution) dans une communauté donnée passe nécessairement par le contrôle du corps des femmes en tant que " reproductrice " de l'espèce humaine. Par exemple, pour stopper le phénomène de surpopulation, les dirigeants chinois ont mis en place une politique de " réduction des naissances ", on demandait alors aux femmes de se restreindre à 3 enfants. Fait important, la contraception était alors quasi inexistante, donc une fois leur " quota " dépassé, les femmes qui tombaient enceintes utilisaient toutes sortes de moyens pour s'avorter elles-mêmes. D'autres Chinoises laissaient mourir leurs bébés de sexe féminin : parce que selon la division sexuelle du travail traditionnellement imposé par le capitalisme et le patriarcat superposés, un mâle constitue une force de travail beaucoup plus grande qu'une femme. Ensuite, laisser mourir les bébés féminins est une assurance qu'on pourra ralentir ou diminuer le nombre de naissances potentielles dans une communauté donnée. D'autre part, pour illustrer cette hypothèse, nous

Graffitez les pubs sexistes, massacrez les compagnies de publicités qui présentent une image de la femme dégradante et soumise, dénoncez haut et fort tout ce qui concoure (mais pas de beauté !) à opprimer les femmes !

pourrions aussi observer le phénomène de la colonisation du continent " américain " par les pays impérialistes européens. En Nouvelle-France par exemple, les femmes étaient littéralement contraintes à la " reproduction " massive - n'était-ce pas le rôle des " filles du Roi " de venir peupler la colonie? (10-11-12-20 et même davantage de bébés pour une seule femme). En terminant, à chaque fois

dans l'histoire, que la silhouette féminine a été montrée dans des formes un peu plus représentative de la réalité du corps des femmes (un peu plus rondes), c'était pour symboliser l'abondance et la fécondité dans des périodes où les menaces de famine planaient et où la survivance d'une communauté, d'une population était menacée.

On voit bien qu'à travers l'histoire, les femmes ont toujours été dépossédées de leur propre corps. Celui-ci fut, depuis toujours, modelé, façonné, mutilé, violé, violenté, " mécanisé ", instrumentalisé pour servir des intérêts de domination et de conquête, des intérêts qui ont avantage à maintenir les femmes dans des positions d'infériorité et de soumission.

"Le Corps Des Femmes"

The thesis of this article is summarised by the Anarchist-Feminist at the beginning of the piece, who tells us: "In all patriarchal societies, the body of the female is presented as 'ornament' and that of the male as 'instrument.' This social indication confines and limits the female to an aesthetic expression of her body. It is interesting to examine, through history, the transformation of the female body. It then becomes easier to understand how the bodies of women have been controlled, shaped (fashioned), and moulded according to the social roles allotted for them." The article starts with a discussion of changing attitudes toward the female body from the Middle Ages to the era of the corset, noting that, in revolutionary periods such as the era of the French Revolution of 1789, the female body was liberated by virtue of clothing that allowed greater freedom of movement relative to the usual physical constrictions. This discussion is based on a pamphlet produced by the "Centre des Femmes de Verdun" collective titled "A Feminist Perspective on the Obsession with Thinness." In fact, thinness performs an important regulatory function in patriarchal societies: it defines women's physical appearance in order to oppress them. Noting that in revolutionary moments, such as the French Revolution, a greater freedom is allotted to the female body as a function of greater inclusion of females in "social, political, and sexual life" the author nevertheless adds that disjunctions between such forces of liberation and the female image in society at large can also occur. For instance, during the '60s and '70s a vibrant feminist movement wanted to change gender relations; yet at the exact same time the media image of femininity promoted an increasingly thin and fragile female body. The correlation between a rising feminist movement and this "reduction of the female body" was a reaction on the part of a patriarchal society to the "threat" of female liberation to the gender status quo. There are other examples of this use of the body to enforce oppression. We have the "pre-pubescent" body – the "thin look" propagated by male-dominated fashion and film industries, as well as male-dominated industries like pharmaceuticals, Weight-Watchers, etc. By virtue of its status as "ornament" "the female body is always used in order to seduce consumers" and thus becomes a "market strategy" in patriarchal capitalist societies. Even when the body-image of the woman violates the codes of "thinness" one finds the female body still subjected to systems of patriarchy. This is especially the case with the pregnant female, whose body is subjected to State regulation and control. For example, in China, where population control dictates the number of pregnancies, female infants are killed because they are less highly valued in the patriarchal family structure. When Quebec was still a French colony – "New France" – the French Monarchy dictated that the role of French women in Quebec was to produce as many children as possible (so-called "filles du Roi"), regardless of the hazards to their health or the limitations large families imposed on women's socio-economic aspirations. In sum, throughout history "women have always been dispossessed of their own bodies."

– Mark Antliff

Les Sorcières 1/1 (2000)

Language, identity and liberation: a critique of the term and concept "people of color"

A week ago I read "To whom it may concern: 'a few thoughts on racialism'" by Abd al Bari in the November/December 1993 PNS. I think it is one of the best articles I have read so far in PNS and one of the best anywhere about the racial question in prison. Notwithstanding the ideological and world view difference I might have with the author, in general I agree with most of his analysis and consider it very sharp and illuminating. As a result of my reading, I thought that my article on the concept "people of color" could offer other angles of the general problematic of identity, the specific category of race, and the relation with language and discourse. I present it with hopes that it could contribute to the debate.

Any critical discussion on the question of identity must remind us that the process of liberation is not only a process of self-determination. This internal process is valid and important in and of itself, but when it is present in the political/ideological struggle for liberation, it becomes crucial and qualitatively determinant.

Perhaps from a perspective of the excluded (*los excluidos*) and their "experience with the law," it would be beneficial to us all to comment on the implications of the term/concept "people of color." At issue in this case is their experience with the authority, "the law" of the "dominant language" and discourse. This is an experience that also reminds us of the complex relationship between tongue,[1] language, discourse and ideology[2].

In this essay, I use the term *language* in a broad sense. I do not conceive of it as a mere political-direct instrumentality of as an "object of study" that belongs exclusively to linguistics or any other academic discipline. Language must be something alive — not a closed (dead) system of signs. It is not equivalent to ideology either. But even when tongue and language in themselves do not belong to a specific class or sector of society, these classes or sectors — through oral and written discourse — affect such matters as rhythm, meaning, terminology, function or decisions on what is "correct" or "incorrect," "derogatory" or "affirmative."

When I talk about "the language of Power" or "dominant language," I do so in a rather metaphorical, non-linguistic sense; in the sense of what Power reveals to us through its various discourses. On the other hand, "the power of language" can either unveil to us or hide from us that relationship that exists between ideological or linguistic sign and the real. We can either feel language as a prison or as liberation, or we can recognize that both aspects of lan-

> **We can either feel language as a prison or as liberation, or we can recognize that both aspects of language are dialectically inseparable.**

guage are dialectically inseparable. We, the periphery and excluded[3] from dominant culture, must resort to the power of language and discourse — but in the most creative and radical way.

The power to name or to be named is also a part of the class and ideological struggle. The former is, of course, a highly political act, but as in any politics the power of decision is not to be located in language itself but in the people who use that language through their discourses. It is, then, in the collective and individual subject and through the multiplicity of discourses that class and ideological struggle takes place. Though this struggle between signs and discourses has a very abstract nature, it also has a very concrete side when it deals with one's collective or individual identity or self-esteem.

It is no surprise then that any attempt to reconceptualize any old/new aspects of our reality, or to criticize/problematize those "deep-rooted" class or individual prejudices that pass often as unquestioned scientific truths or laws, will meet the most hostile resistance not only from dominant ideology but from our own ranks as well. This "intolerance" for difference in our own ranks is many times unconscious. That is, it is so internalized that we often do not realize how much we reproduce dominant processes of ideology among ourselves. We function, therefore, like terminals in a circulatory system of values, beliefs, representations sent to us through all kinds of signs and electronic/synthetic images. It is thus the task of a radical discourse to *always* (the struggle never ends) make these contradictions visible in order to resolve antagonisms or to achieve a harmonious non-antag-

onistic co-existence among equals but with the right to be different, the right to alteration and dissent.

However, difference can become a superficial pose, an opportunistic way of taking advantage of one's "accidental" features when there is no danger and when conditions are in one's favor. The exploitation of one's race, nationality, gender or culture for personal (moral or material) profit and prestige — this is difference as mere status, difference for difference's sake.

In this dialectic of difference/sameness within our ranks, sometimes one aspect demands the sacrifices of the other. That is to say, individuality is sacrificed for collectivity, or vice verse. Ideologism, which is the reduction of everything to ideology, demands one or the other. For example, if my discourse becomes problematic and "difficult" among my ranks (my "equals", my "peers") I might become suspect, stigmatized, alienated. In order to correct this "deviation" one has to adjust to the limits of collectivity even when one might be ready to transcend those limits. Further, this means that liberation (or freedom) stop where the dominant *conception* of "liberation" within my ranks stops. The same thing can be said about any dominated group or "minority" in relation to the society (system) of which it forms part. Somehow, this process is a "mimic," a duplication of the process of consensus of dominant ideology, but it is always — here and there — the powerless subject who suffers.

When a discourse springs from this lack of power and abundance of pain, this discourse can end up in plain personal or ideological resentment. But also, in the measure of its ethical and political commitment, and its significance, it can become a discourse of liberation *in spite of* the limits of tongue, language and ideology. When passion and concept find their dynamic unity there is a possibility that a discourse might be able to express that which language itself can't express; or that which the thinking of a certain moment has not yet been able to think.

Bearing this challenge and risk in mind, I approach critically the term/concept "people of color" as it is currently used in the United States. In the U.S., dominant values, beliefs and representations of reality (i.e. ideology) are those of the capitalist class, which along with the majority of the U.S. population,[4] is composed almost exclusively of the so-called "white" race. The rest of the population, the so-called "minorities," are referred to as "non-whites." Only when matters get complicated, or there are some political interests involved, do the dominant agencies divide and subdivide "racial groups" to the absurd. Sometimes it is difficult — if not impossible — to know to which group one belongs.

The single most important feature used to classify people in the U.S. is "color." People are classified by the "color" of their skin: Black, Brown, Red, Yellow, etc. This is axiomatic, you may think, because we all know this. But having this knowledge has not made any difference in how the excluded ones and radical/progressive people approach the question of identity and race most of the time. This approach never moves beyond the "color/skin" fixation. This fixation has a long tradition, and therefore, is difficult to break away from, to the point that most terms used to generalize the amalgam of "minorities" within the U.S. only reflect their dependence on dominant ideology. As a result, the evolution of the old term "colored people" to the "new" term "people of color" remains with the "color/skin" perspective. It seems to me, though, that before, "colored people" referred mostly to "black" people; today "people of color"

refers to all those who do not belong to the "white" race. Still, this "new" form of the concept can neither indicate the new content within it (all the "minorities" in the U.S.) nor the "old" term ("colored people") simply because the new content overflows the form of this reworded term/concept. Why? Because within the Third World "minorities" in the U.S, the racial spectrum (or "color" spectrum) includes all races and their mixtures, all "colors," "shades," and "tones," including "white" and "black" as "colors."

In this sense, "people of color" is a provincial term. Not just because it is only used within the U.S.[5] but because it could only have come into being in a society like

this. First because "race" is still looked at from a puritan Anglo-Saxon point of view: "blood purity" is fetishized and "mixing is taboo."[6] And second, because the U.S. is a modern Rome, it is the imperial(ist) center where all kinds of displaced peoples (from this hemisphere and other continents) usually end up. (It is obvious that this is due not to a magical attraction, but to a fatal one.) So, for better or worse, it is here where the meeting of all racial, cultural, ethnic and national groups takes place under the most antagonistic and ironic of ways. This reunion of "differences" in relation to the mainstream demands a new analysis and re-conceptualization of the relations of forces. It also demands an effective economy of words, terms that can provide an easier way of grasping this new agglomeration of peculiarities and similarities. Hence, the "color/skin" fixation which is part of the ideological circulatory system (which affects *all of us*) "nationalizes" this otherwise extranational phenomenon.

This provincial term — captive by dominant ideology — reduces this phenomenon to only one of its components: that of "race". It does not have the same political immediacy and sense of other terms like "racial" or "national minorities," "oppressed minorities" and "Third World people," which emerged in times of more militancy.[7]

For one, this term "people of color" has this fastidious "picturesque" element so familiar to the vocabulary of tourism. It sounds like a color Polaroid photograph of "nice" and "cute" people; innocent, inoffensive and domesticated people, where everyone is homogenized with this attribute of color. And who is this photographer who has so carefully taken this picture? A "white" tourist with "good intentions?" Or, in fact, is no one to be blamed but ideology itself?

Furthermore, though it may seem inappropriate in this essay to use the term *color* out of this racial context, this might be helpful in order to unveil this intrinsic relationship between *concept* and *term*, and how, for example, terms like "people of color" unconsciously reinforce prejudice and distorted concepts to classify people.

Rigorously speaking, color is something that depends on light. Indeed, color itself is within light. It exists and it does not exist. Can we say the same thing about races? One thing is for sure: for most important matters, we do not exist for mainstream society unless it is in the form of a political token, a marketing product or domesticated folklorization. Puerto Ricans only exist as "people of color" to Anglo-America. Black is only that which proves whiteness. And all dominated racial and national groups exist first of all as "color" not as people. On the other hand, it seems that the important question is not even color *per se* but *where* color is located. That is, if "yellow" located in the hair, it is good, very good; but if it is located in the skin, then it is not as good.

But what if we use instead the term "colorless people" to express our concept of the "white dominant class?" I fear that this term would be considered "reverse racist" or "anti-white." So a better solution would be to say that all peoples are "people of color," that there are no colorless people. In such a case, "color" is neither a privilege nor a stigma, but a commonality.

Let us consider another perspective. While "people of color" could be used with good or bad intentions, and it could also be transformed from derogatory to affirmative, as other terms have been, whose original intention was insult, epithet, etc. (e.g. mulatto, Black, Chicano),[8] it is also true that we cannot advance our process of liberation (today we are more self-conscious that previous generations about the importance of names, about who exerts the power to name and why) if we do not simultaneously liberate our thought and our praxis from those terms that have ceased to truly articulate or describe our situation and understanding of our historical, cultural and quotidian reality.

It is very self-defeating, both in the short and in the long term, to depend on these masters' "original" terms. We must be *original* too, but in the true sense. Our capacity to survive, resist and finally win depends on our capacity to be *inventive*. Originality is not to be understood exclusively as a mode, fashion or "the new." It is also *the necessary*.

Our dependence on our "masters'" terminology has ontological implications. The term "people of color" has a dependent idiomatic discharge, i.e., its identify, its meaning, depends on another referent: "white" people. And within this context, "white" becomes a code word for "superior" or "original." We may resolve to explain this as the nature of things when it comes to the human condition, but what we may not realize is that by perpetuating the use of such terms we are ironically reinforcing the other term, "whiteness." We are saying: my race, my nationality, my identity, my being, can only be defined in relation to the "white" race. My "racial" being is a gift from the other, the master. So in the same way that I am a creature of social relations and the relations between ideological and linguistic signs, I am also a creature of the dominant racial vision.

Thus, if we want to transform the pre-

dominant relations and world visions, we must also transform this creature condition, this reduction of people to "color." We must becomes *creators*, and cease to be subjected to the other's fantasies and myths. We must become the *dreamers* and cease to be the dreamed ones, because in fact transformation is a question not of "color" but of *vision* and *sensibility*, both how we *see* and *feel* the world. It is our (political, philosophical, ethical, aesthetic) vision/sensibility searching for its realization.

If we understand that the aspect of "color" is the aspect imposed by the dominant vision to classify and identify people, and we emphasize instead the cultural-social-economic-political aspects, which are

---

> **We, the periphery and excluded from dominant culture, must resort to the power of language and discourse — but in the most creative and radical way.**

---

the real vectors conditioning our views on identity and race, what we are saying is that we are forming a different criterion that can better grasp our similarities but that can also simultaneously maintain our differences. A criterion that needs and wants to "exorcise" itself from the old criterion; a criterion that will make us recognize the objective, concrete fact that we are now beyond "color/skin" aberrations. This will be a criterion that unequivocally points toward the roots of the problem: that Third World people are discriminated against not only in terms of race, but also class, gender, culture and nationality. Besides, when it comes to exclusion, hate, humiliation, etc., of "minority" groups in the U.S., the dominant class, its institutions and repressive apparatuses do not "discriminate".

For all these reasons, we must rethink this term/concept "people of color" if we want to overcome this subjection to mummified language. The quality of our political action is determined by the quality of our political vision and sensibility. To *politicize* our concepts and terms inherited from the past, we must correct them with the notions obtained through our irreducible experience of reality and the political/social praxes. Of course, we can only do this if we recognize that it is necessary, not in order to please ourselves with "new" morphologies or plastic surgeries trying to merely resolve real contradictions through the means of language, but to make of language a force capable of infusing energy and blood into our discourse and movement.

The codes and language of Power, which otherwise want to conquer my heart and yours, must be defetishized by a language and discourse of liberation. That is, we must do a lot of scraping, scratching and scrapping to do away with this incantation.

To construct or re-construct our identity in terms of difference we do not have to keep resorting to such innocent and picturesque terms like "people of color." It is preferable, in my opinion, to use the

term "Third World people" or "the excluded." We are in fact quasi-phantas-magorical people reaching for our political being, in spite of "color" and independently of nationality. Different, not because of superficial features deeply rooted in the dominant classes' prejudices, but because we have a *different experience* of reality. ∞

Elizam Escobar #88969-024
Box 1500 Colorado Two
El Reno, OK 73036

Footnotes

1. A specific language, such as English or Spanish, as compared to language as a general system of signs.

2. Meschonnic, *El lenguaje, el poder*, 6 Cuadernos de Poetica (Santo Domingo, 1985); Meschonnic, El marxismo excluido del lenguaje, 7 Cuadernos de Poetica (Santo Domingo, 1985).

3. In "negative" terms, not only those who form part of colonial and ex-, neo-, post-colonial histories in relation to European colonial powers and United States imperialism a.k.a. First World, Occidental culture/civilization); but today, also those Third World peoples living in the First World ("internal colonies"), and those groups or individuals who because of race, nationality, culture, gender, sexual preferences or/and ethical, political, artistic or ideological positions find themselves "exiled" from mainstream society and culture.

4. Recent studies estimate that at the beginning of the twenty-first century the "minorities" within the U.S. will become the "majority".

5. In Puerto Rico, "people of color" refers, euphemistically, to a person whose dominant facial features are "black"-African (Western and Central Africa). This euphemism is characteristic of our "psychological" form of racial prejudice, used by many instead of "negro" to avoid "offense", though, paradoxically, in Puerto Rico as in other Latin American countries, "negro" also means "dear" and "loved one." It would be interesting to find out the origin of "personna de color" in Puerto Rico, though I am almost certain it came about under U.S. colonial domination.

6. Compared to the Anglo-Saxons and other North European colonizers the Spanish colonizers had a different "attitude" toward the mixing between the races. The roots of these different

racial/color/skin attitudes can be found in the different historical development of these European peoples prior to the colonization period of the Western Hemisphere, i.e. prior to the fifteenth century.

This is not to say that the Spanish attitude toward race and race mixing was "better." It was different. Maybe more "flexible," subtle, hypocritical, and psychological, and therefore less visible; but the fact remains that the new socio-economic-political orientations and ideologies brought by all European colonizers were the beginning of developed "anachronistic" slavery, and later on, of ideological and structural racism in this hemisphere.

7. The term/concept "Third World" seems to have developed from the term "the third front," used by communists to refer to colonial countries in relation to the struggle against capitalism and imperialism.

8. One way of dealing with this is *irony*, especially in literature, but also in the way an essay makes use of humor to ironize or ridicule terms, concepts, values, beliefs, etc. that mis-represent others. By doing this we make of the epithet a "boomerang" or make *the namer* look at it in a mirror as his/her own projection. Nevertheless, this is a weapon to dismantle. As far as I can tell, "people of color" is not used in an ironic way. Nor is its intention "metaphorical," but, to the contrary, it is a very *literal* term/concept rooted in the way dominant ideology in the U.S. perceives and understands "racial identity." Finally, and more importantly, even when this term is not used in an ironic way, it paradoxically becomes ironic in the sense that we ourselves help to reinforce what palpitates behind it.

Prison News Service 44 (1994)

Insurrection and the Informal Organization

The following is a synopsis of some of the ideas on organisation presented in the anarchist magazine *Insurrection*. We feel that, although we may or may not agree or fully understand the implications of these ideas, they are a unique challenge for the anarchist movement to consider. We recommend all readers to obtain a copy of the whole magazine at the address given at the end of this article.

One of the most difficult problems anarchists have had to face throughout their history is what form of organization to adopt in the struggle.

An anarchist movement that is really active and incisive needs two main factors: an agile and effective instrument and an objective that is sufficiently clear in perspective. We think that the **informal organization** and **insurrection** are the concrete possibilities that present themselves at the present time.

Insurrection, a necessary phase along the road to revolution, is for almost the whole of the revolutionary anarchist positions seen as a mass revolt set off by certain socio-economic forces. Anarchists are limited to propagandizing, but the mass must do everything themselves.

There is a different way to envisage revolutionary struggle in an insurrectionalist key, in our opinion.

We consider that the anarchist organization, so long as it is informal, can contribute to the constitution of autonomous base nucleii which, as mass organisms, can programme attacks against structures of social, economic and military repression. These attacks, even if circumscribed, have all the methodological characteristics and practices of insurrectional phenomena when not left to the blind forces of social and economic conflict but are brought into an anarchist projectuality based on the principles of autonomy, direct action, constant attack and the refusal to compromise.

Beyond Syndicalism

We believe the revolutionary struggle is without doubt a mass struggle. We therefore see the need to build structures capable of organizing as many groups of exploited as possible.

We have always considered the syndicalist perspective critically, both because of its limitations as an instrument, and because of its tragic historical involution that no anarchist lick of paint can cover up. So we reached the hypothesis of building autonomous base nucleii lacking the characteristics of mini-syndicalist structures, having other aims and organizational relations.

We believe that due to profound social transformation it is unthinkable for one single structure [such as a union or federation -ed] to try to contain all social and economic struggle within it. In any case, why should the exploited have to enter and become part of a specific anarchist organization in order to carry out their struggle?

Autonomous Base Nucleus

The main aim of the [autonomous base] nucleus is not to abolish the State or capital which are practically unattackable so long as they remain a general concept. The objective of the nucleus is to fight and attack this State and this Capital in their smaller and more attainable structures, having recourse to an insurrectional method.

The autonomous base groups are mass structures and constitute the point of encounter between the informal anarchist organization and social struggles.

The organization within the nucleus distinguishes itself by the following characteristics:

a) autonomy from any political, trade union or syndical force;

b) permanent conflictuality (a constant and effective struggle towards the aims that are decided upon, not sporadic, occasional interventions);

c) attack (the refusal of compromise, mediation or accomodation that questions the attack on the chosen objective).

These attacks are organized by the nucleii in collaboration with specific anarchist structures which provide practical and theoretical support, developing the search for the means required for the action, pointing out the structures and individuals responsible for repression, and offering a minimum of defence against attempts at political or ideological recuperation by power or against repression pure and simple.

The base structures have a single objective. When this objective has been reached, or the attempt fails, the structure either widens into a situation of generalized insurrection, or dismantles as the case may be.

Informal Organization

The basic project of an informal organization has, in our opinion, the objective of intervening in struggles in an insurrectional logic. This organization does not give one area privilege over another, does not have a stable centrality. It singles out an objective which at a given moment presents a particularly acute area of social conflict and works in a perspective of insurrection.

ORGANIZATION

Affinity Groups

Basically, to have an affinity with a comrade means to know them, to have deepened one's knowledge of them. As that knowledge grows, the affinity can increase to the point of making an action together possible; but it can also diminish to the point of making it practically impossible. What it is necessary to know is how the comrade thinks concerning the social problems which the class struggle confronts [them] with, how [they] think [they] can intervene, what methods [they] think should be used in given situations, etc.

Once the essentials are clarified the affinity group or groups are practically formed. The deepening of knowledge between comrades continues in relation to their action as a group and the latter's encounter with reality as a whole.

The affinity group ... finds it has great potential and is immediately addressed towards action, basing itself not on the quantity of its adherents, but on the qualitative strength of a number of individuals working together in a projectuality that they develop together as they go along. From being a specific structure of the anarchist movement and the whole arc of activity that this presents—propaganda, direct action, perhaps producing a paper, working within an informal organization—it can also look outwards to forming a base nucleus or some other mass structure and thus intervene more effectively in the social clash.

We think it is never possible to see the outcome of a struggle in advance. Even a limited struggle can have the most unexpected consequences. And in any case, the passage from the various insurrections—limited and circumscribed—to revolution can never be guaranteed in advance by any procedure. We go forward by trial and error, and say to whoever has a better method—carry on.

Copies of **Insurrection** are available in North America from D. Imrie C/O Box 121, 55 McCaul St., Toronto, Ontario, Canada M5T 2W7 (416) 947-0808 and distribution for other continents can be reached at Elephant Editions, BM Elephant, London WC1N 3XX, England. Also read "From Riot to Insurrection" by Alfredo M. Bonanno, available from Elephant Editions for $2.50.

Constructive Criticism
(we could all use some improvement)

When we criticize someone there are generally two ways to do it: one is to slag them off and basically leave it at that. The other is to criticize what they've said or done, and then offer them an alternative which might be better. One is done simply to prove them wrong; the other is done to change their ideas or ways of doing things, and is done out of caring and the desire to change things rather than as a proof of superiority.

Non-violent activists have come up with several formulas with which to deliver 'constructive criticisms'. Most of these, though, I find to be fairly unpractical or too mechanical for everyday use. Instead I think the key to delivering a constructive criticism is to keep a few main things in mind.

First and foremost, think out your criticism before you say it! Try to think of how to say it as clearly as possible to get your point across.

Keep in mind how the person might react to receiving this criticism, and how you would feel if you were being criticized in this way. Try to word your criticism so that the person(s) receiving it won't get defensive and disregard it. Remember that the objective is to change that person's behaviour, not to create hostility between you, or to hurt their feelings.

Keep in mind that it's your responsibility as much as theirs to try to offer them a better way of doing/saying things. In fact, some of the best constructive criticism is merely to provide a good example yourself. By suggesting and following through on a better example, the criticism becomes constructive, because it offers the person being criticized the opportunity to change. Keep in mind, though, that you may not have all the 'right answers' yourself, so try to offer your criticism as an opinion only, and remain open to the discussion of the ideas.

Remember to explain why you're offering this criticism. (ie: "because I want us to work together more co-operatively"). Also explain clearly what exactly it is that you feel is problematic in their behaviour. Be very specific, don't just say "I think you're an asshole...". On that note, it doesn't hurt to be polite either.

Part of this whole process is also being able to receive criticisms well (this is the hardest part). Don't go stomping off in a rage every time someone has a differing viewpoint from your own. By being open to criticism yourself (admitting that you're not infallible can actually be a relief - making mistakes becomes less traumatic), and by listening, considering and changing where appropriate, you make others all the more willing to listen to you.

All in all, it's mostly just a matter of common sense whether or not you're really being constructive in your criticisms. These are just some ideas we've had in trying to work together collectively on various projects, and while we've still had our differences and haven't always been constructive, this kind of consideration and respect for eachother is pretty much the first step in being able to work together (for, you know, anarchy!).

love, **REALITY NOW**

NO MEANS NO

one step closer +
i'll blow your balls off

graph of found by Carole
words, Lone.

fear, as
instinct is one
of our weapons,
but i don't
want to
own it
anymore.
let's
give
it
to
men.

64

FIRE AND FLAMES;

Interview with a W. Berlin Autonomist

So maybe you could begin by telling us how it is living in West Berlin and how it differs from other West German cities? It's not that different than living in big cities like Hamburg, Frankfurt... There might be some differences, for instance W. Berlin is like an island, surrounded by a wall, and so people live really crowded in a city of 2 million. And especially in the wintertime it's getting really depressive. I'm living in Kreuzberg, and it's one of the poorest neighbourhoods, and you could compare this area with say the lower East Side of New York, with large apartment buildings, many people living crowded together, not much green, and many people are really frustrated. Another thing about West Berlin, located in East Germany, is you must drive three or four hours to West Germany and may stay in West Berlin because maybe they don't have the money to drive out, so especially many poor people have no choice and must stay in West Berlin. And I have stayed two to three years in West Berlin without leaving for a week, etc., so it's a kind of prison in a way. You're surrounded by a wall and to leave the city the atmosphere is dufferent than say Vancouver because you have to cross a border, to show your ID, have money, etc. Also, West Berlin isn't really a part of West Germany: West Germany has 11 federal states including W. Berlin, but W. Berlin doesn't have the right to send politicians to the federal government to make decisions. It's a similar system to the U.S.: from each state they send a senator to the congress. West Berlin doesn't have this right. And it's also a military zone. We have 30000 soldiers, Americans, British, French, all divided into their repective sectors. And sometimes it's really fucked up. In your neighbourhood, you see them driving down the street standing in their jeep with a machine gun and pointing at you. They don't shoot, but they play all kinds of head games.

It's like an occupied city then? Yeah, you don't feel like it's your city or anything. It's a result of the second world war. The americans have total power, they can overturn the W. Berlin gov't. & the police. When Ron Reagan came to W. Berlin in 1982 & around 10,000 people were fighting back the kops in the street, the US administration was considering sending the military into the streets, & america has a right to do it, it's a constitutional right.

What are the origins of the autonomous movement? What are the struggles you're fighting for? Uh, the origins of the autonomous movement are found in the beginning of the '80s, they have their background in all sorts of social movements, like squatting, struggles against the NATO runway in Frankfurt, against nuclear power, environmental destruction. The major goals of the movement, I would say, are struggling for self-determination, for a society with-out power, against capitalism, against imperialism, fighting against states, & a really important part of the movement is fighting against the patriarchy & sexist society. The autonomous movement isn't like an organisation. It's many independent groups joining in, & of course they have different experiences, they work on different projects, but the major things that unite autonomous groups together are the points of anti-statist, anti-capitalist, anti-imperialist, anti-patriarchy, & fighting for a totally self-determined society. It is also very international, supporting the liberation struggles in the 3 continents, the people in Azania (S. Africa), in Palestine, in El Salvador. And of course the movement is very critical of so-called "socialist" states such as Cuba, and when they support liberation struggles they support the peoples struggle not just the party.

How does the movement show this solidarity, how do they support these struggles? How do they see this as a part of their day to day lives? One way for example is going in the streets & demonstrating. The last demo I went to before coming to Canada was in Hamburg. Autonomous & anti-imperialist groups called a demo in support of the Palestinians, the Intifida, & around 3,000 people participated. We went down the streets in Hamburg & there were Palestinian solidarity groups, people from the PFLP (Popular Front for the Liberation of Palestine, who made a speech, one person from the autonomous movement made a speech as to why it was important to link the nation-wide struggle in W. Germany with the international struggle, because the world economic system is organised internationally & it's exploiting people all over the world, so of course it's really important that we as a movement, it doesn't matter if you live in Canada or W. Germany, organise the struggle also internationally & be in solidarity with the struggle all over the world; in China, Palestine, Azania, basically the people who are fighting for their right to survive, to live without hunger... & how we show it is going to demos, leaflets, magazines, putting out info. And of course there is the struggle by militant groups, guerilla groups, like for example the Revolutionary Cells who are attacking S. African businesses, businesses in S. Africa or Israel, for example Daimler-benz supplies the Israeli army with vans & the S. African police with vans, cars. So there is a widespread resistance in demos, benefit shows, militant direct actions... and anytime a scumbag from one of these countries is coming we organise big demos...

What are some ways people are living outside of the capitalist system... are people doing that? It's not entirely possible to live outside of the capitalist system because you live in it, and there isn't any real free space where you can live totally independent, because society affects you all the time. But of course we do try and fight for free spaces; for

Endless Struggle 11 (1989)

MayDay 1989 in W. Berlins Kreuzberg district. Rioting broke out and many stores were looted, with autonomists, turkish kids & many other people participating. Food was distributed throughout the community, & over 200 kops injured in street-fighting.

example squatting, which gives you a certain kind of free space because you don't respect paying rent to housing companies or landlords. And this is a way we try to show a different way of living, & squatting to me is a kind of anti-capitalist struggle because you refuse to pay rent, you don't accept the idea of "property". It's also a de-controlled area we live differently. We don't live isolated, we live together. Like 50-60 people live together, & it's really important for communication, exchanging info, within the movement.

And I suppose by squatting it means not being isolated as much as in a workplace...

For sure. And that's all about what we're fighting for. In Kreuzberg people work and pay like 50 - 60 % of their wage for rent. You work 40 hours a week and 50% of your wage goes to rent. That's totally unjustified, totally against people. Right now there is a campaign in W. Berlin to organise a rent-boycott also, and now there are 8 big squatted houses in W. Berlin, also in Hamburg in the Hafanstraase. And as I said it's really important for communication, because like in Vancouver you have say 10 different houses, and so the exchange of information isn't that great. You don't have daily discussions, which is important for organisation.

So what kind of repression does the autonomous movement face? I think every movement faces oppression by the gov't, because if these movements are revolutionary movements, the people who control the country, the gov't, the corporations, businesses, they want to protect their capitalist, imperialist and patriarchal society, of course!

They try to dam up the revolutionary struggle. Many people are arrested, sent to jail, and we must look at how we can organise resistance without getting caught up in this oppressive machine. But everyone who is part of the revolutionary autonomous movement, they know that the people who rule the country don't wanna give up just like that, not voluntarily. For example, this year there was a hunger strike by 48 political prisoners from the RAF, autonomous and anti-imperialist groups, to fight against the practise of isolation in prison. They demanded association, free medical care, open political debate, so we as an autonomous movement organised a big wide-spread campaign to back up the demands; we had big, fucking huge demos, in Hamburg with 8,000, 10,000 in Bonn, many small independent anti-imperialist groups attacked multi-national corporations with incendiary bombs, we had all kinds of struggles to back up the demands. And it's important to show that the autonomous movement doesn't forget the prisoners, and they are a part of our movement.

Another major position of the autonomous movement is that it is not pacifist, the movement is not only supporting militant, direct actions - the armed struggle - they also practice it. The autonomous movement sees revolutionary violence against an oppressive society as a part of the resistance. This is seen in attacks on property, militant demos, smashing windows of sex shops, riots; this is all part of the resistance. It's not that important <u>how</u> you are fighting back, violent or non-violent, it's <u>what</u> you are fighting for.

What are some ways the autonomous movement fights against patriarchy? Uh, one militant group; the Roten Zora (Red Zora) is a militant feminist group, and they are a really effective guerilla group. They did the action against Adler, a big multi-national corporation who produce clothing. And this corporation has some factories in South Korea, & here wimmin are working for maybe 20 cents an hour, & these wimmin face sexual harrasment, exploitation, & they demanded, in a strike, better work conditions, higher wage, end sexual harrasment. Adler didn't give a fuck about this, so Red Zora attacked Adler with incendiary bombs in 10 different places in West Germany, causing approximately $10 million damage, backing up the wimmins demands in South Korea. And they were saying; when you don't do as the wimmin workers demand, we're going to fucking blow you away. So Adler was forced to do as the workers demanded. This is a good example of militant actions having a positive effect, and can support the struggle of wimmin in the periphery countries, against sexism, against multi-national corporations. It raised consciousness, & Red Zora released statements on the actions which were re-printed in many magazines, so people knew what this corporation was doing & why it was attacked.

We also have many anti-imperialist people who are part of the revolutionary movement who are not quite autonomous in the way that they are organised. They're quite influenced by Marxist-Leninist ideas, but most of them

cont. on pg. 18 ▶

W. Berlin cont...

are pretty much unorthodox communists; they aren't into partys, but they're not like the autonomous movement, and they don't have as much criticism of state-socialist countries, & they're also supporting more Marxist-Leninist urban guerrila groups like the RAF. The autonomous movement supports their politics in a way, but are really critical to their statements & politics.

I think the autonomous movement has an effect on the society because many, many people are getting pissed off, frustrated, & they'll realize that they're exploited too, by the state. So of course they're sympathizing with the autonomous movement in a way, they're saying we should connect more with these people because maybe they're fighting for something I'm fighting for too...

And maybe that's the real hope for change. That's the real hope for change of course. 10,000 or 50,000 people can't really change a society, of course we need more people. We aren't stupid. We know we can only win when we are more, when we're the majority of the people. So we have many papers, magazines, radio, demos, many things where we try to educate people, to make contact with other groups in society whoa re not necessarily autonomous people For example in Wackersdorf, where the government is building up a nuclear re-processing plant in Bavaria, and many people are living in this area who are very conservative in their way of thinking, living, voting etc., but theyn these people realized that they didn't want this nuclear plant in their area and they started protesting and fighting back. Also many autonomous people were fighting back against this plant, and so conservative people and autonomous people were working together. Many people made good contacts and good friends... and many of these people have changed, realizing that the gov't doesn't really give a shit about them. And I was down there, at the fences which they built around the construction area, and over half the people at the protests were from the area. Many very old people, all these people were no longer in illusion... they saw the police brutality. I was really amazed how they've changed their way of thinking after they saw the police violence. And we were down there trying to break through the fence, which wasn't totally possible with about 20,000 kops inside, & they were throwing tear-gas etc., and an old man came up with us and he said: "This is really great, what you are doing. You know, I'm really too old to do this, I'm really not able to break the fence with a bolt-cutter or to saw it, but you know what? I would use dynamite!" It was one of most positive experiences I've had with people who have different ways to thinking and living. And I saw the possibility that if we fight with these people we're going to be a bigger movement, it gave me a lot of optimism & hope, that it's possible to build a

movement capable of stopping the people who rule the society. And it's not just that I'm fighting <u>against</u> something, I'm also fighting <u>for</u> something, to express my love & my feelings, to explore - something I can't do in this society. I'm caught.

Thanks a lot for talking. Okay, and I hope the struggle continues in Canada as in West Germany, and one day we're gonna make it. Ciao!

↑ SEPT. 88 ANTI-IMF PROTESTS, W. BERLIN.

18

Endless Struggle II (1989)

Autonomous Movement Victory Parade for the Hafenstrasse
Squat, Hamburg, Germany, November 1987.

photo: Sabot, *Black Flag* (London)

Animal Liberation and Native Struggles

RN Notes: The debate that follows is based on our attempts to find common ground between two very important movements. The first part, by Freebird, was published in the Ecomedia Toronto Bulletin earlier this year, and then in "Front Line News", the ALF support group newspaper. The second is an addition by a member of the RN collective. We need to find a basis of unity which is neither simplistic nor symbolic, which recognizes the real sources of the problem and real solutions. The following articles are by no means the be all and end all of this debate, but merely a means of starting a discussion around these issues. In the future we would be interested in publishing a booklet of different viewpoints on animal liberation and Native struggles, so feel free to contribute to this project at the RN address.

In the debate over animal rights versus Native rights, people on both sides continue to become polarized as tensions mount. Animal rights activists are increasing pressure on the public and government officials to support a ban on all hunting and trapping, while Native leaders increase their counter-campaign by producing movies and videos on indigenous ways of life, and forging stronger ties with the fur industry. I would like to add my voice and opinion to this controversy, by suggesting alternatives to what I feel are the dogmatic and rigid views expressed by both sides. As both an animal liberation activist and a supporter of Native peoples' struggles, I believe that there is much common ground between the two groups that needs to be further explored. Very briefly, here are the basic statements being made:

The animal advocates want a total ban on all hunting and trapping, as this practice is not only cruel and unnecessary, but it supports a multi-million dollar industry that profits from the killing of animals for the vanity of rich people in New York or Paris, among other places. They also state that the fur industry and Native hunting and trapping do not represent indigenous ways of life because the methods and tools used in the hunt are modern devices such as snowmobiles, high powered rifles, and steel leg-hold traps made in New York.

The Native peoples' position is that they have always traded in furs, long before white men and the Hudsons Bay Company invaded Turtle Island. They say that if the campaign to ban hunting and trapping is successful, it will not only force Native people into a life of welfare, resulting in social breakdown of their communities, but it will open up their land to the government and development corporations who will come and proceed to exploit the earth for minerals and oil, not to mention the military's use for low level flight testing of fighter jets. As well, if Native people can't use the land for hunting and trapping, they say this will make it harder for land claims in the courts.

Given this, albeit a very simple breakdown of the issues, there are many ways in which both groups can reach common ground and perhaps work together.

First of all, I see the alliances made between Native people and the fur industry as being totally unnatural, and that, despite what some Native people claim, the fur industry — the white greedy profiteers — are once again exploiting the Indians for their own interests. I also believe that , whether or not Native people will admit it, this alliance is for purely political reasons that have nothing to do with indigenous ways of life. But, of course, if you're fighting for the survival of your people, you may use different tactics, including siding with your exploiters if the short term gain is worth it. I believe that if there are any natural alliances to be made, it is between the Native people and animal liberation activists. Please note that I specifically mean animal 'liberation' as opposed to animal 'rights'. By far the majority of the animal rights movement is composed of people who are white, middle or upper class, and who have little or no analysis of any other political struggles other than that of saving animals. Quite often animal rights people come across as uncaring towards oppressed people, if not outright

Reality Now 8 (1988/9)

racist. This, I believe, is a major obstacle in the struggle to bring the two movements together.

As an animal liberation activist and an anarchist, I see no hypocrisy between my anti-fur position and my pro-Native struggles position. I believe that the earth is a living entity, and that all life on her is connected — whether in a life and death cycle or part of an extremely complicated ecosystem.

My main focus in my anti-fur politics is those who are the exploiters: the multinational fur industry, the fur retailers, and the person on the street wearing a fur out of vanity or ignorance. I choose to attack these people in my campaign and *not* Native people, because I believe that Native peoples' struggle for their land and their lives is much more important than whether they hunt and trap.

In the fur industry in Canada, Native hunting and trapping make up only 8% of the total industry, while the majority of the rest comes from factory farming. And hardly any of the Native people involved in the trade are part of the wholesale and retail parts, where most of the money is made. It simply makes absolutely no sense whatsoever to focus on Native trapping and hunting in the anti-fur campaign.

So where does this leave the animal rights people as they work toward a total ban on hunting and trapping, and are trying to destroy the fur trade?

Well, regardless of how successful they are in destroying the fur trade, there will still be a market, however small it may be. If we can get rid of the multinational corporations and the white man's interference, and leave an exemption clause in the campaign against fur for Native hunting and trapping, then I'm sure the 8% market share Native people have now will not decrease at all.

Native leaders who are siding with the fur industry are making a big mistake. The fur industry has no interest in indigenous cultures and will sell them short when the time is right. Animal rights activists who refuse to develop a wider analysis of different people's struggles will always show themselves to be an arrogant group. Clearly the fur industry is the target, and not an 8% market share group.

Native people, animal liberationists and anarchists have much in common. We have a common enemy, if we choose to recognize it; that being the profit-making, greedy capitalists, who will exploit everything and everyone if there's money to be made. We also have a common desire to save our planet. This entails many ideas, from stopping the military and government interference on the land to combatting the destructive practices of the white race.

Many Native people are very opposed to vivisection, factory farming, fur farming, and other animal abuses, because the exploitation and torture of animals is not in balance with our life cycles. And most animal liberation activists are very supportive of Native struggles. In Toronto, animal liberation activists can always be seen at rallies and events supporting Native struggles. By the same token, more Native activists are purposely seeking out animal liberation activists and anarchists to form alliances with — because the strong possibility for unity is there.

These groups must find ways to work together, because we do have a common goal — the desire to bring a balance back into our lives on this planet, and to evolve toward a harmonious relationship with our Mother Earth.

Freebird

Attack the Real Sources of Suffering

ANIMAL LIBERATION

Freebird's views on animal liberation and Native struggles are refreshing; he, as all animal liberationists should, recognizes that true freedom for animals is having clean air to breathe, clean water, and an ecological balance such as that proposed by traditional Native peoples.

However his article is overly simplistic when it evaluates the possible effects of 'animal rights' campaigns against fur trade on Native communities. There is no question that the fur industry is an enemy, and no one should deny that it is far from natural or ecologically sound. Yet as a multinational capitalist venture it must be analyzed in the context of the standard reactions of such industries to opposition.

When a multinational is threatened, especially when it starts to lose money, it will seek to pawn off that loss on the most powerless people in the chain. Normally it will fire workers, or cut their pay, or close down the branches in working class communities **first**. Only after all cuts possible have been forced on the powerless will those in control of the corporation start to feel it.

In the fur industry, the first to feel the effects of the anti-fur campaigns will be the Native people, for two reasons: the first is what I have just explained above, and the second is that they can then hold up the impoverished Native communities as an example of the "evils of animal liberation movements". So although Freebird cites an 8% share of the market for Native people as small enough to merit exemption from anti-fur campaigns, this is the share which will be hit **first**. Why? Because they aren't in control ... the large fur corporations are, and they will shift the economic losses off onto the Native trappers first.

So Freebird chooses to attack the multi-nationals, the retailers, and the people on the street wearing furs. While these aren't deliberate attacks on Native trappers, the effects of an attack on a retailer will eventually be felt by Native people. When the outlets, as part of the chain are losing money, the Native people will again be left to bear the brunt of this. The attacks on those who wear fur, or the attempts to make fur unpopular in the general public will have the same effect as fur sales go down. It's in the nature of capitalism.

What will be an effective action for animal liberationists (and I am leaving out "animal rights" folks here because they are rarely anti-capitalist) to tackle is to attack the source of the exploitative fur industry, the fur farms themselves. These farms can hardly be considered part of a natural environment, nor are they run by impoverished people or those struggling to survive as a culture. They are a source of misery for animals and the environment, and are a purely capitalistic venture by those who can afford (as people and as a culture) to do something else. The liberation of fur animals, and economic sabotage of these industries is a campaign which would attack the exploitation of animals for fur, while leaving Native trappers alone to pursue their ways. Such a campaign would be more likely to win support from Native people and bring the two movements closer together.

As for Native trappers, while they are part of the corporate-controlled fur industry, they will be at the mercy of these corporations. This is an industry which pays them sweet-fuck-all for the pelts, and then holds up impoverished communities as the "results of animal liberationists", all the while neglecting to look at the over-stuffed pocket-books of the industry's owners. This is an industry which will betray Native people when it is no longer profitable to buy pelts from them. Native people in the fur industry would be much better off as an organized entity who could fight back against low payments for theirs pelts, and against the losses being heaped on them by a fur industry on the decline (which is the hope of animal liberationists). An organized group could stop the regulations on licences which force them to over-trap, and decide for themselves what is ecologically sound for an area. Providing alternative outlets for furs caught in the wild (as opposed to farmed) would further enable Native people to control the industry in an ecologically sound manner which would benefit their communities, not keep them poor and tied to economic slavery. Native communities will be benefited more by an end to capitalism and control of their land than by a shaky alliance with the fur corporations. Animal liberationists should support moves by Native communities to take back control of their lands and lives; such moves will, in the end, mean a safer existence for the animals on those lands.

I would hope that animal liberationists would support these moves, and that Native people would recognize and support any moves by animal liberationists which attack capitalism and capitalist industries without hurting those at the bottom end of these industries.

The Mythology of Technology: The Internet As Utopia

http://www.tao.ca/thunder/Anarchives/

Jesse Hirsh (*jesse@tao.ca*)
Sun, 17 Nov 1996 14:29:12 -0500

This is the written version of some of the talks that I have been giving throughout my travels this year along the North American east coast as well as Brasil. Anywhere I launched this virus, revolution was sure to follow. For further information on how to launch this meme into your local environment, email me <jesse@tao.ca> or the international media collective <media-l@lglobal.com>.

The Mythology of Technology: The Internet as Utopia

The ideology of technology serves a global hegemony.
Technology as milieu; technology as mythology.

If we do not act, we will relinquish the responsibility to rule, and transfer our decision-making capabilities to a machine named 'The Global Market'. With the decline of the printed word and the rise of the digital word, the nature of our literacy is changing. The state itself is being redefined: the author becomes corporate, and the narrative becomes non-linear.

The world is transformed as the planet plugs into itself. A unified mediated environment emerges which presents an epic struggle of change. The media, after successfully consuming the masses, reverses and implodes into a universal black hole. We are caught collectively staring into a narcissistic pool of distorted self-reflection and self-absorbsion, desperately wondering where it all leads.

The term "media" refers to neither institution nor artefact, but rather to an environment. The environment in which we all live. Media are the methods in which we communicate with ourselves, each other, and the world at large, and as we communicate, we forge the material reality in which we exist.

The medium is the message. Linguistic hacking is an attempt to find the message in the medium. We need to crack the code that distorts language and mind created through media, examining the culmination of time and space, the basis of our living reality, hacking through to the meaning imbedded in the medium.

In a society dominated by technology, media manifests the mythology that consumes and immerses the masses into the growing global market. We are entering an existence in which total inclusion will be the constant, and exclusion a technical impossibility. One operative, the politics of exclusion, has been the basis of power and empire throughout history. Now information management and the mythology of technology becomes the method of maintaining a grip upon the minds of the mass. In its wake most are excluded from the process of self governance. Technological mythology is the medium by which information warfare is waged.

The information economy, the crisis economy, the global economy, are all pseudonyms for an economy based on perpetual war. Capital centralizes into the hands of conglomerates, originally the global military industrial complex: AT&T, General Electric, Westinghouse, Disney. A melee of media mergers make the way for corporate giants to wage information war in the battle for your mind.

The linguistic hacker exposes myths by examining the context by which the word receives meaning. 'Figures' are defined by the ground which surrounds it. The figures themselves however can also be reflected through the media, itself a mirror of ground, clouding our language and warping our words. In the struggle for the free mind we try and identify truth and dissolve myth. As an act of self-defence, linguistic hacking disarms the imperial assault on the mind, by examining each figure naked unto itself, in direct immediate relation to its actual ground.

The most dominant myth of our time is the Internet.
The mythological meaning of the Internet: 'Utopia'. It has become the technological metaphor large enough to absorb all the hopes, dreams, and desires of a civilization. Millions have rushed on-line in search of a meaning, a harmonious narrative that describes change. Billions are sunk into the Internet to feed the hunger to be the future: we become Spaceship Earth via the Starship Enterprise, "Free Enterprise".

The US Telecom Act that was passed in February of 1996 was the bottle of champagne broken upon the vessel's hull. Bon voyage, screamed the most far sweeping and corrupt bill in US legislative history. Written by and for big business, the bill unilaterally raised concentration and cross-ownership limits on media. Within days and weeks there were a flurry of media mega-mergers, in which the military establishment (General Electric, Westinghouse) and their propaganda arm (Disney) bought the major networks, cable czar Ted Turner took over the Time Warner empire, the regional phone companies all jumped into bed together and reduced in number by almost half, radio and newspapers fled beneath various umbrellas, and most recently British Telecom made the largest foreign take-over in US history by increasing their stake in MCI (the largest shareholder of which is News Corp.).

The Internet is the black hole at the center of our universe: it is the negation of time and space. Comparable to gravity, the Internet is an imploding force that draws everything into it.

The Internet by definition, does not exist. It is an abstraction that nobody has seen, smelled, or touched. It is a myth used to shift our belief systems and dramatically alter our behaviour. It transforms our linguistic framework by changing the context in which language interacts with mind. It is a redefinition of literacy as the linguistic system itself becomes simultaneously individual and collective.

What is the effect of the Internet myth? What is the basis of its meaning?

The Internet is the virus from West Virginia that will consume all media until it becomes the information superhighway media monopoly brought to you by AT&T.

The Internet is the ultimate red herring, the dazzling distraction that abducts our attention while power plays with totality. Instead of addressing the decline of democracy in the real world, Internet consumers discuss and debate the democratization of the Internet. The US Telecom Act was able to be passed so easily for two reasons: OJ Simpson, and the strategic placement of the Communications Decency Act within the Telecom Bill. The CDA was a purposefully useless attack on free speech on the Internet, that within only a few months was overturned by the Supreme Court. The CDA was another red herring, a distraction for the liberal media outlets and civil liberty groups to rally around, as the rest of the communications system was hoarded into the hands of the very few.

Anarchives 4/1 (1997)

Through the virtualization of our culture, the medium of mythology reconstructs reality to manufacture consent. Growth and development are guided and directed by the few at the expense of the many. The technological mythology is reality in the virtual world, and our consuming desires drive us to live virtually perfect. In the process we have negated our sovereignty and secured the Platonic chains around our neck as we stare at the shadows on the cave wall.

The Internet is the post-modern gold rush, a mass anxiety to get 'plugged in'. People ask themselves, 'why fight gravity?', and our mother responds: 'If all your friends (or co-workers) jumped off the CN Tower would you?'

We are entering a new regime of market regulation. 'Usage sensitive pricing' as introduced through both the US Telecom Act and the CRTC in Canada, is designed to allow the 'market', and the mechanisms of supply and demand, to determine the development of communications. This structure replaces existing democratic rights with consumer rights.

Democratic rights are inherent and unlimited. You always have them, and you can always exercise them, at least in a democracy. Consumer rights on the other hand are not inherent and they are limited. They are based on the pay-per-use model, as your rights are determined in relation to your participation in the economic marketplace. Thus the more you pay the more you play. The concept of one person one vote is replaced with one dollar one vote. Consumer rights subvert democratic rights by introducing a quantitative factor, achieving a finite definition of our entitled rights, and limiting the extent to which we may exercise them.

Universal access to the technology will exist, but the use of the technology will be limited. Democracy depends upon free and open access to information, which becomes severely limited, if not negated by proposed pay-per-use pricing structures. Your right to speak still exists, but how much you get to say is determined by your economic standing.

During a CRTC hearing in Canada that discussed this change in regulation, I and I challenged the actions of Stentor, the consortium of Canadian phone companies, and asked why they were dismantling democracy by introducing 'usage sensitive pricing'. Stentor responded by charging that I and I were protecting the status quo and that these changes were like the future: inevitable.

The dominance of the Internet myth is based on the myth of the future. What we call the future is a means by which we can objectively deal with the present. What we perceive as the present is the past. The future does not really exist. Like the Internet it is also an abstraction of a negation. Have you seen the future? Perhaps you have seen a reflection of the past (maybe in your dreams), that either becomes or resembles a later present, however none us can ever exist in the future. In the past we were, in the present we exist, in the future at some point we are dead. Accept it and transcend it.

Myths themselves are largely reactive rather than proactive. They are an act of co-optation, a response to either natural or spontaneous actions that might jeopardize the technological system. Both the Internet and the future have origins in positive notions of change and vision. It is the mythological manifestation that distorts the meanings of these metaphors.

If we undress the myths surrounding the Internet, and examine the true meaning of the word, we see that it is not a story of technological revolution. Rather it is a narrative of popular revolution. It isn't about technology, it's about people. People coming together and expressing themselves freely. That in itself is a revolution. We are the Internet. We are the revolution. We drive it, we make it, we use it, we are it. This is the return of the subjective experience. I think with my brain, but I act with my heart. I cannot change the world, I can only change myself. If we were all working on healing ourselves we would all be a lot better.

http://www.tao.ca/thunder/Anarchives/

Anarchives 4/1 (1997)

The Internet is not utopia, as it clearly demonstrates that as the medium is the message, there is no end. The living language is all about process: it matters little where were going. What's important is how we get there. The Internet as global consciousness could be an uprising that achieves human liberation.

When I look into the world that is my own, the planet that reflects me, I see genocide and terror, conquest and colonialization. I immediately and spontaneously denounce the perpetrators of these crimes. They stand naked before me: Pepsi in Burma, Nike in Indonesia, Northern Telecom in China, McDonalds all over; whoever and wherever.

Yes the emperor is naked. The Internet as open mind exposes this to any one who looks. There are no lies in the environment of infinite comparison. We are exposing the corporate coup of global domination.

In an environment of total visibility, only via mythology and the bending of truth can power maintain control. Media concentration is the knee-jerk reaction of the frontiersmen circling their wagons in fear of the natives getting restless.

The youth are the media aboriginals. Raised and bathed in electronic media, they are the open minded hackers who can traverse and navigate through the complex information systems of the electronic mind.

The youth are ageless as time and space dissolve, and the search for truth becomes a quest for identity. I and I bringing down babylon. Speak, yell, kick, shout, until they are forced to hear you. You have the truth, and the truth will set you free. The youth know this truth. This can also be called a youth revolution as it is the youth who still remember how to play. If you can't dance don't even bother coming out to the Internet revolution.

We need an active approach to media, a fight for our own awareness, and our own liberation. Nobody can give us freedom, we have to take it.
We need to look at the current media domination, and rise up in media liberation.
We need to come together, and remove the mediation between us. Face to face communication is the best way to convey loving energy.

We must not abandon our bodies in the technological rush to be everyone and everywhere. We come from the earth and to the earth we will return. When our feet are on the ground we are more likely to not only recognize, but make change. Taking care of our bodies is the same as taking care of the land upon which we live. We must reclaim our land in the face of a cataclysmic environmental threat, and we must reclaim our bodies in the face of a cataclysmic nutritional technological threat.

The Internet is a mind, a living global growing mind, that is demonstrating self-awareness in its drive for consciousness. We must engage and reclaim this mind, as it is collectively our own. In reclaiming our bodies, we must also reclaim our mind. It will be our love that will carve the path to reclaiming our mind. However we must be sure that the distortion of our love, as manifest through media mythology does not destroy our mind through its own reversal.

We walk a fine line, in what is an epic struggle of change. What is true now, was true 30 years ago, and has been true forever. If large Banks run Bob Dylan songs as commercials for on-line services, perhaps there's something being said here that nobody has acknowledged?

Like the late 1930s and the late 1960s, the late 1990s are themselves defined by dramatic changes in media. From the radio to colour television to the digital network, media revolutions draw on the tensions and energy that exist between people and technology. Popular political upheavals occurred in the first two media revolutions of this century, if we are to engage the runaway train of technology, we desperately need another now in the the third.

The youth of the nineties need to reach out to the youth of the sixties and build a creative movement that once again mobilizes the masses. Similarly as adults we must all recognize our responsibility to retain and reclaim democracy, and with it a social system that progressively builds equality.

Together we can combine experience and energy, to make a final effort to break the bonds that hold us docile, facing the flashing cave wall.

The Internet is all about the unknown: living with the unknown.
The Internet may be alluring and seductive, but is the Information Superhighway really the way? One hopes that in the middle of this mad search for utopia, we will realize that the earth is the utopia, and we have been living here all along..

"The highway is for gamblers better use your head.
Take what you have gathered from coincidence.
The empty handed painter from your streets.
Is drawing crazy patterns on you sheets.
The sky too is folding under you,
It's all over now, Baby Blue."
(Bob Dylan, It's All Over Now Baby Blue - 1965)

Anarchives 4/1 (1997)

NO MORE COPS

The need for police stems from two sources: one, from the State and corporate interests, which need some force to protect its interests, and two, from the fear within our communities of interpersonal violence. The problem with police as they stand is that they serve this double purpose, fail to solve the latter problem, and remain a force outside the control of those they pretend to serve. As such they need to be abolished as an institution.

"Crime" is defined by the ruling class; the definitions which clutter our lawbooks are based more on the defense of property and privilege than on the defense of people and our environments. A self-governed and classless society would re-define the nature of "crime" yet we must admit that interpersonal violence will not disappear immediately. Though it is for the most part generated by our patriarchal society, the destruction of this society will not mean an immediate end to crimes such as rape or murder. We will have to find ways of dealing with these problems.

There is always a temptation to replace one failed institution with another, which usually becomes worse. The idea of vigilantes has been revived in New York, for instance, where self-appointed would-be-goodie gangs patrol against street gangs. But, in the same United States, Southern vigilante groups were worse than appointed police, only substituting lynch law for bench law.

But there is a need for some kind of community-based defense to protect people from crime of all sorts, including crimes of the state and capitalism. A community must organize its own defense because an unorganized mass can always be overpowered by an organized group, be it a state or a gang or simply an individual rapist. We cannot rely on outside forces like the state (who in fact, depend on individual crime to justify their regime and force us into reliance) or upon abstractions like "good will" to defend us against unprovoked attacks.

First of all there is a need for individual self-defense programs such as those run for wimmin in Toronto by the Toronto Rape Crisis Centre. These should be widely available for wimmin and others so they will be able to fend off any attackers (including husbands and other relatives).

On a wider scale, perhaps what would be useful is a volunteer defense force made up of community members, who would be available in emergency situations when there is a need for more defense than an individual can put up. Ideally the whole community would be on guard for each other, and willing to help out when someone is in trouble, but there should be assistance available in case this kind of help falls through (we simply aren't all perfectly responsible all the time). Such a force carries the danger of becoming simply a gang of parasites, such as the police, with the power to enforce its own brand of law on people. To avoid this it must not be a permanent position but a rotating duty for its members, to keep them rooted in the work of the community and to avoid excessive power trips. Also, it would have to be accountable to the whole community so that any failings or excesses can be both reported and dealt with by the people of the area (as opposed to inaccessible and police run "complaint commissions" which exist now).

Such a force would logically come out of the struggles against capitalism. Organization against capitalist crime, such as exploitation, evictions, layoffs, can also be extended to organize against individual or organized crime (or in fact, any other oppression). Trade union forces are inefficient as they concern themselves only with the industrial angle and the size of our

THE LAW, THE POLICE, THE STATE

wages. However organization around industrial issues can and should be part and parcel of organization around community defense.

The measure of success of such an approach is how much it enables the people to control their community and how much it eliminates peoples reliance on state mechanisms.

All that having been said, it is important to note that the so-called "dangerous few" whom everyone fears on the streets are indeed very few. In fact we are six times more likely to die from an industrial accident as from murder; we are 2.5 times more likely to die from a drunk driver than from murder; and we are much more likely to die from family and "friends" than from the "dangerous few". The "violent few" are only 5% of the prison population in Canada (the majority of prisoners are in for non-violent property "crimes", or to put it bluntly, for being poor).

Obviously these statistics exclude the violence of those in power, who are much more dangerous than any man on the street, but they also illustrate where our needs for protection actually lie. Wimmin are in danger more from known men than from unknown men, though such a reality is rarely portrayed in the press, who are scared to admit that so many men are rapists. So we also need to look at fundamental ways of preventing violence at the source.

First if all, the high proportion of families where wimmin and children are abused show that we have yet to establish that family violence is unacceptable. It is interesting that most abusers were themselves abused, indicating a chain of abuse which must be broken. We need to feel able to intervene in incidents of abuse; in fact we have an obligation to challenge it when we see it happening. Intervention in the abuse of children could be a start in stopping the cycle which might turn them into abusers in the future.

We also have to challenge our society on every level for the violence it encourages, through the sense of powerlessness and frustration from being under the thumb of bosses of all kinds (part of the reason I believe anti-social violence will greatly decrease after we create a stateless and classless society), and through the media. It has been estimated that this generation of TV viewers will see 500 times more as-

saults, 500 times more rapes, and 300 times more murders than their predecessors. This encourages the fear of violence (hence the reliance on the state for seemingly necessary protection) and the belief that people are naturally violent. Media images can be challenged through many creative means from stickers on offensive ads to throwing your TV out the window, public education, etc.

In abolishing police and prisons we must find new means of dealing with our conflicts ourselves. Conflict resolution programs allow problems to be dealt with in the community where they came from before they result in violence. Often "crimes" and the courts are results of disputes between people that could have been solved earlier through mediation, where people can listen to each other, talk to each other, get advice from their neighbours and then work out solutions. Such programs have been tried and could work out in the long run, providing their use was encouraged to the point of becoming a natural response to difficult conflicts.

One of the big complaints about prison abolition is that the victims are not taken care of. Some kind of reconciliation is possible between victims and their attackers which is actually more useful to both than just locking away the attacker. While prisons merely punish, reconciliation enables the "offender" to see the **results** of their crime and understand the full extent of what they've done. It also enables them to make moves towards compensating the victim or changing that behaviour, which does the victim more good than to have them locked away. There is the possibility of feeling safer when you know the offender has learned rather than knowing that in a couple of years they'll be out again and angrier. It also enables the victim to get out their feelings directly at the offender in a safe environment.

Finally, it must be recognized that at times particularly violent people will have to be dealt with. The present "solution" is to stick these people in a little cell for several years and hope it makes them better people. People who have committed a series of violent acts need to be separated from the community. While it is up to each community what they choose to do with these people (some might just as soon kill them) one possibility is to place these

people in treatment programs in a humane environment. Programs should be on a self-help model with strong community involvment. There do exist prisoner self-help groups where a group of prisoners help each other sort out problems they may have with sexism, violence, etc. These have been successful in many cases and are a great inspiration.

There is also a need for victim support, where people who have suffered violence can work out their feelings about it together. For all the lip service the right-wing-crime-and-punishment people give to this, there is surprisingly little they've ever done for victims.

Finally it needs to be said that justice is impossible within the present system. We are all victims of the crime of capitalism and patriarchy, which has broken up our communities, isolated us from one another, subjected us to exploitation and powerlessness, and, of course, poverty. Criminalization has long been just another way of getting rid of the poor; even though all classes commit crimes, only one is pointed out and imprisoned. So we need to define just what we have to defend ourselves from, then begin the long process of a) re-defining social roles and relations towards cooperation and non-patriarchal values, b) attacking the sources of our oppression, our exploiters on the job, in the government, in the community, the prisons and the police, c) developing individual control of our lives and communities, with mutual aid and solidarity as the building blocks, and d) creating alternative means of resolving conflicts, dealing with any exploiters or attackers and defending our people and communities.

This is all part of the struggle to create anarchy, to take back control of our lives and keep it, safe from the attacks of reactionaries and a new class of exploiters whether capitalist, state-communist, or whatever. Promoting such ideas and putting them into practice *now*, may be a key in moving towards such a world and building confidence in the possibility of a world without exploitation.

• ideas for this article have been shamelessly plagiarized from *Black Flag, Ecomedia Toronto Bulletin*, the *"Brief to the Daubney Committee"* by Ruth Morris, and probably others I've forgotten.

Reality Now 8 (1988/9)

NO PORNOGRAPHY
NO CENSORSHIP

WHAT WE NEED IS SELF DEFENSE!

WHEN TACKLING THE QUESTION (?) of pornography, no matter where you end up standing you must realistically take into consideration that we live in a society that not only thrives on violence, domination and emotional isolation - one that eschews deep and valuable ties between people - but one which depends on the maintenance of voyeurism. Life as a spectacle which we watch go by but neither participate in nor have any control over. Pornography - *watching* others fuck, etc., and being fed *someone else's* fantasies to masturbate by, rather than masturbating to your own imagination or making love with someone, touching someone and exploring *your* desires and sexual curiousity - is a tool which helps keep us from participating in our own lives, our own sex. Rather than a tool which liberates us and helps us to grow sexually, it stifles and imposes certain ideas of correctness and fulfillment upon us - steals whatever sexual freedom we may have maintained.

A very tired argument is that if pornography gives some people pleasure, then what is wrong with it? Well the exploitation of anything for profit gives some people pleasure while for others it is brutally oppressive. Does that make it right? Trees, water, the earth, animals, wimmin, men. All exploited for profit. But we are NOT products. When we allow our sexuality to be produced and consumed, instead of arguing that we are winning the battle for sexual liberation, we should understand that we have forfeited our freedom of sexual expression.

We have no choice but to defend ourselves and the humanity that is left in us. As wimmin, we live day to day, with the pornographic images which surround, threaten and lie about us, as our prison walls, and at the same time we remain imprisoned by the solutions to pornography we invent:

1. CENSORSHIP.
2. DOING NOTHING BECAUSE WE KNOW CENSORSHIP IS WRONG.

I suggest that we do not have time (in terms of wimmin's - sisters lives around the world, in terms of the numbers of rapes, beatings, and molestations - the lives controlled by fear) to only act when we have found the perfect solution. Nor is there only one way out. I do *not* suggest that pornography is the whole problem, and that when it is gone we can relax and enjoy the revolution. On the contrary, I set forth that it is a mere symptom of the disease (patriarchy - control of and violence against wimmin, animals and the earth) and that pornography is to patriarchy as militarism is to multinationals. To work with serious intent, in a well thought out way, to attack the problem of pornography would be to begin to crumble the base on which social domination stands.

What is available in the expressly "pornographic" market today consists largely of 'hard core' and violent pornography (I consider *all* pornography to be violent to different degrees) while the general public gets it's daily inundation of 'soft core' and equally violent pornography through advertisement, television and most films playing at the cinema. As a result the humyn population is becoming more and more desensitized and will eventually become immune to "pornographic" images. At the rate things are going we are surrounded by them and yet most take no notice. Even now people are no longer disturbed by them and come to see them as an example of "normal" behaviour.

I believe in the elimination of pornography. As it is one of the most obvious forms of exploitation and social control; I feel it should not exist.
People must learn to be well adjusted enough to find enough interest and fulfillment in their own sexual relationships without needing to feed off the acts of others. This takes much self examination and discovery. Finding and exploring the sexuality that comes from the self is a real rocky road and takes a lot of courage to follow - we have been separated from it for so long.

However, although I believe in the elimination of pornography, I do NOT believe in censorship. Both the mainstream and alternative papers seethe with debate over governments' decision to "cut down" on pornography through censorship. This situation is laughable on at least two levels. Firstly, cutting down on pornography means that there is less pornography available, but it is still available. Also the pornography that will be censored as a result of legislation will most likely *not* be the most violent snuff films, violent hard core pornography or the most insidious sexual violence found in advertising; but relatively innocent and expressive art displays depicting menstruational images (is menstruation pornographic?) or a ten second scene of mutually consented to sodomy in a mainstream film (fundamental wierdos on censor boards usually feel that this is necessarily synonomous with rape). Therefore censorship does nothing to eliminate pornography, but instead does it's best to ban images which are strictly sexual in nature. It does not and cannot work by any stretch of the imagination. But secondly and perhaps most importantly, censorship does not eliminate the 'need' for pornography. People use pornography often because their sex lives are unfulfilling on their own, and in using it they develop both an acceptance of what is a misrepresentation of 'fulfilling sex', and a grasping need for self-assurance - easliy perverted into a need for power. People in many cases begin to look to their sexuality for fulfillment of power, in response to the lack of power or control they have over their own lives.

Many men have an extremely poor if not totally off base conception of wimmin's sexuality. "**Women's** sexuality" - controlled by men - as seen in the media, encourages these misconceptions, which when translated to wimmin's real lives are often outright lies. Unfortunately, pornography does little to act as a sexual aid to benefit *both* partners, as it is often highly unrealistic, and as many of its depictions encourage acts geared strictly for male pleasure, and depict wimmin as necessarily enjoying this also. In practice, this often proves to be false. I think that more realistically speaking, we might consider improving our abominably poor, bigoted sex education system (where it even exists). With helpful, realistic, honest, explicit sex education, we can be free to explore our own sexuality safely, and begin to break down the sexual TABOOS which are the root of the pornography reaction; those who watch it seeking sexual explicitness and ideas! I do not question the need for sex. I question why we allow and even condone the evolution of our sexuality to just another stinking commodity.

The centre of another facet of this debate over censorship is the fact that no one seems to feel that they are able to discern pornography from erotica, and it's no wonder. We have all grown up under the thumb of totally illogical and essentially backwards conditioning. Many of us have learned, mostly through media influence and bombardment, to *accept* violence, paranoia, hatred, war, poverty, starvation, exploitation, discrimination, and above all, having someone else control our lives for us. To accept or put up with things we hate. Keeping all this in mind, using arguments based on what is commonly known as 'logic', it is reasonable to conclude that indeed we cannot distinguish pornography from erotica. But if we reach down into our not entirely extinct emotions, our gut reactions, I would say the difference between the two is clear. Any material that makes a womyn (in most cases a womyn) feel uneasy, dehumanized or threatened is pornographic. To be more specific, I would speculate that pornography can be detected by numerous elements such as fanatical idealization, objectification, non-interpersonalism, isolation of sexuality from life, power over another, coercion, mutilation etc., being represented as factors of desirable sexual encounters. (In cases where this sort of behaviour is used to illustrate a point ie: Rape is horrifying and wrong, it is a different case. Everything must be taken in context.) Erotica therefore involving lovingness, pleasure, gentleness, naturalness, personalism, communication, and last but not least - mutual consent.

Under mutual consent, I include those who participate in S and M relationships, as this is also very consensual. Although S and M erotica creates in itself a special problem. While this kind of material may be erotica for participants who *understand* (not many non-participants do) the dynamics of sado-masochism; consent, interested and curious men not of the persuasion by habit, may pick up this same material and misunderstand, because S+M-M= rape. Rape is, after all, a sadistic act without consent. This second instance of influence is obvious as a source of fantasy much abused in the wrong hands, ie: rapists who tie up, blindfold and gag their victims, or tie them with rope and hang them from trees. (I do not personally condone sado-masochism, as an anarcha-feminist, and also as someone who doesn't enjoy pain. We must recognize however that this sexual practice is one of mutual consent.)

What the elimination of pornography will require in the long run, is a complete turnaround of attitudes towards wimmin and sexuality itself. In the short term - education and 'deconditioning' help for wimmin and men of all ages, and **actions economically disabling to the pornographers** by both wimmin and men.

After all, pornography is not a single issue. It is a symptom of the overall disease, and a symptom which in itself causes many different sideaffects. It undermines the health of our humyn situation to such a degree that it may act as a catalyst, that feeds and feeds off other symptoms of the same disease, forming an obscene 'support system'. And so it continues in a cyclical fashion.

What I have just described, metaphorically, is pornography in the context of social control. Obvious lines between the two can be drawn. Both rely on fear, fear of inadequacy, ignorance, alienation, and power to continue functioning. Institutions of social control create the preceding factors to gain and keep profit, and pornography works as an instrument of perpetuation of these factors to gain and *increase* profit. Pornographers

PORNOGRAPHY

PORNOGRAPHY

need the effects of social control to successfully sell their product, and institutions of social control **can** and **do** utilize pornographers and pornography as an opiate, for manipulation of the accepted norm of behaviour (In Orwell's **1984**, The Party manufactures violent pornography for distrubution among the proles to keep them distracted and satisfied that they are doing something 'dirty', to prevent their uprising; deemed by the Party as having the possibility of success, were it to happen). This mutually beneficial situation keeps members of these institutions powerful and influential, while allowing a virtually interference-free market for the porn -makers. Pornography is a multi-billion dollar business, and important money making item - it fits right in with enterprises like **McDonald's**, making the business defendable within legal and 'moral' institutions of Western societies. Unmistakably too, it prepares us to adjust our emotional selves so that we can ignore or even accept the acts perpetrated internationally - rape, domination, torture, murder, incarceration; all of which very closely resemble those seen in pornography.

The reality of this situation is that neither police nor government officials can be relied upon to eliminate pornography (I'm stating the obvious), for economic (consumer) reasons. It is not beneficial for the government to close down pornography outlets or distributors, because they would lose out on property, income and business taxes they recieve. The police, known for their raids and confiscation of pornographic materials have also been known to have private screenings of these materials or to rent them out to friends. It is more beneficial for them to obtain this material for free through warranted raids, and even make a little profit from it than to have materials distribution discontinued. Besides which when a government talks censorship in relation to anything, not just pornography, you know they're not jumping on the bandwagon to aid and abet in the sisters' and brothers' liberation. They even benefit from the censorship debate itself, because not only does it enable them to spread lies such as "There is no 'concrete evidence' suggesting that rape and pornography are interrelated in any way" - the government having done these studies - but while we are busy debating about censorship we are not doing a whole hell of a lot to stop it. Either way, through allowing pornography to proliferate unhindered, or by censoring pornography, the government hacks away at our freedom. The method they use or stance they take depends solely on public opinion polls.

I don't think this is a problem we ought to allow the government to try to solve. Or even *touch*. It is a question of **self-defense**.

Solutions to the problem may be complicated in the actualization, but I see them as fairly clear cut. The pornography industry is a multi-billion per year exploit. By and large the pornographers are pretty well- off **scum** (anything that is widely sold is bound to make somebody rich) and the only way to stop pornography from being made in the short term is to take away the money they use to make it. Censoring pornography does nothing to stop the wimmin et al who have made the film from being degraded - they've already made the film, or in the cases of harder core and snuff films not allowing them to be distributed does not change the fact that the womyn, child, animal, has already been tortured, mutliated or killed. **We have to economically disable the pornographer who will then (eventually) have no money left to make the material with, in order to do that we must attack the centres of distribution; the distributor will then not have the money to purchase more - leading to the eventual disabling at the source.**

But just how can we take away their money? I suggest **direct action** with two major intents.

1. **Erode public acceptance through education.** A well known activist from the states, **Nikki Craft**, engages in many very creative anti-pornography/anti-censorship civil disobedience actions using street theatre, leafletting, boycotts, slide shows and speaking tours. Education about the effects of pornography and violence against wimmin as well as the effects of censorship and building healthy sexuality without fear. While you're at it - erode public acceptance of most other things too.

2. **Property destruction.** THIS DOES NOT MEAN VIOLENCE. Be creative, effective and careful. Glue, spraypaint, bricks, battery acid, firebombs. People have effectively used grease on the material itself. You get the picture. Go as far as you can. Anything helps.

NOTE: It is very stupid for the same people to engage in both civil disobedience and property destruction at the same time. Remember security. If you are worried that property destruction is not educational enough, **make sure** to distribute a communique to local media.

On the more personal side of things, there already exist men's and wimmin's support groups which discuss the effects of pornography on our earth, our lives and ourselves. This is essential. The real change will come about when all people learn to recognize and escape their conditioning - to analyze their situation and attitudes and decide what feels best for them. We must relearn to communicate with eachother - to be honest and open and tell the truth. Once we've become willing to break out of our conditioning and have internalized that sex is not dirty, and it is not a commodity, and have discovered the joy of honest communication we'll have come much closer to the goal. **But whatever you do don't forget the fun part** - exploring your natural sexuality and recognizing the truly erotic for yourself. Then and only then can we throw away pornography and be free from it forever. **Anyone for a great big cuddle?**

Remember the Wimmin's Fire Brigade,

A Sister in
Struggle.

RN: If you'd like more information on Nikki Craft and the Preying Mantis group and their actions as well as other related materials, write to Reality Now at P.O. Box 6326 Station A, Toronto Ontario, M5W 1P7, Canada.

top: *Reality Now 7* (1987); bottom: *BOA 2* (1988)

IT IS FORBIDDEN TO FORBID

The explosive confrontation of 1968 marked the end of the social calm that characterized the post-war [World War 2] era. That year, revolts in Europe and North America ignited a new militancy, signaling the resurgence of a non-Leninist left.

Like 1789 France, the events of 1968 displayed the potential for revolutionary change in a social setting previously unchallenged. The May-June revolt in France, in particular, demonstrated the vulnerability of authority in an advanced industrial State. It showed that the contradictions in capitalism had not been eliminated as some disillusioned leftists had come to believe. Rather, they had been heightened by the tensions inherent in a highly technological society.

"It is forbidden to forbid." – May-June graffiti

Under the surface calm of industrial countries there are festering rebellious impulses that can break loose spontaneously. Just months before the revolt, the French left seemed little more advanced than the North America movement. Then, without vanguards or self-proclaimed leaders, the expulsions of a few students organizing against the Vietnam War touched off strikes, riots, and occupations.

During May, barricades were erected throughout Paris, ten million workers (two-thirds of the French labour force) went out in a general strike, and several factories and campuses were seized and run by popular assembly.

May-June was a sweeping economic/cultural revolt. The street became a place to create art, discuss revolution, play, make love. Class lines were shattered as rapidly as windows as workers lined up with students and TV performers and football players and…. Even the football league draped from its office a banner emblazoned, "Football Belongs to the People."

The material forces that emerged after the Second World War resulted in relative affluence, free time and education and spawned a generation that had largely mastered economic *survival* (the demand during the depression and earlier struggles). Now they demanded *life*; an all-encompassing economic, sexual, psychological, cultural liberation.

And the workers' demands were often as qualitative as those of the students. At one electronics plant, workers who had just concluded a successful strike for higher wages hit the bricks again, explaining: "We are now striking for only one demand: workers' control of industry – and not only for our plant, but for all the plants in France."

The militancy of the workers had been catalyzed by the actions of students, youths, women, and other sectors that had recently been consciously radicalized. Prior to the revolt, the working class base of the revolutionary movement was relatively weak. The French Communist Party and its adjunct union, the CGT, attempted to prevent the fusion of subjective (students, youth, women) and objective (workers, because of their class position) revolutionary forces because it represented a threat to its grip on the working class movement. The CP attacked the new radicals as "non-workers," failing to recognize that they come out of a new set of conditions and were at the very least as revolutionary as any traditional workers' movement.

"Nothing gave me greater pleasure than to be at the head of a demonstration with all that Stalinist filth at the rear."
– Daniel Cohn-Bendit, 1968

May '68 was, in a sense, the gala world premiere of both the autonomist movement and Eurocommunism. The autonomy of the French insurrection forced the French CP to show its reformist colours. In its desire to avoid confrontation with the State at all costs, the CP turned on the left, attempting to prevent the general strike, opposing the wide-spread attack on hierarchy, trying to get workers to accept wage agreements and calling for an election.

The CP felt it controlled the left; owned the working class. It was its holy duty to set the time-table for revolution so it was bewildered when others decided to start without it. The CP was correct in one sense though – its authority was being challenged and its hold on the left shattered. The May events were the first mass manifestation of the anarchic potential in industrial countries (Portugal was to follow suit in 1975). Throughout the world, they generated interest in anti-authoritarian revolution and a new sense of instantaneous exhilaration that moved many leftists (including some who still labelled themselves Marxist) to a more libertarian stance.

The Stalinists showed that no organization using the model of the bourgeois State could be revolutionary; that no party could legislate freedom. Revolutionary organization had to reflect the forms of the spontaneous organization of people.

The revolt ended as an "almost revolution," not because it lacked a party to impose freedom but because it lacked a broad *awareness* of the need to smash State power. Although anti-authoritarian forms sprung up everywhere (there were even "barricade affinity groups"), people didn't escalate from the general strike to a widespread seizing and operating of factories. Creative joy and liberty sparked by tactical spontaneity characterizes the initial phase of all revolutions (1789, 1917 …). Anarchists fight to maintain this initial euphoria as a permanent characteristic of the new society. But, to avoid bourgeois counter-revolution or "people's vanguards" who attempt to commandeer the revolution, spontaneity must be backed by solidly-organized armed defense. For, behind every spontaneous

FREEDOM

outbreak is a lot of hard work. And, although France '68 was a spontaneous revolt, it was part of a process taking place in several other countries at the same time.

> *"No rules, speeches, won't do, leaders are all full of shit. Pull your clothes off (make love, not war), punch a marshal, jump a wall, do a dance, sing a song, paint a building, blow it up, charge and get inside." – Abbie Hoffman, 1968*

May '68 was the closest to *reality* of a series of 1968 events that cumulatively created a myth of impending revolution. A myth is a fantasy that's accepted as reality. The Chicago convention riots in August '68, unlike May-June in Paris, didn't actually threaten State power, but they became a myth because not only many leftists, but the right and the general populace as well, accepted them as a genuine revolutionary threat. Chicago was the most spectacular of a series of left "events" that were occurring so regularly (from Chicago to Columbia to Berkeley to your home town) that a fantasy of imminent revolution was generalized.

The very acceptance of this fantasy as reality made it more real. People have myths that they project into their reality. Everyone has fantasies they want to see come alive. The myth of impending revolution was fomented by organically conceived, explosive confrontations that rocked international consciousness and set the pattern of struggle for a time. Little "Chicagos" spontaneously seeped into every corner of America as people sought to emulate the myth; realize their fantasies.

Because only a few thousand people participated, the revolutionary threat of Chicago was a fantasy. Still, the days of street clashes, the battle for the park, the massive military apparatus mobilized against the new culture, the absurdity going on inside the convention hall, and the resulting Chicago Eight trial was real and was brought home, in bloody living colour, for the whole world to watch.

Although Chicago, and other sixties actions, were successes because they appealed to emotions through creative action, they weren't, in the long run, as effective as they could have been because they lacked a systematically-organized base. People turned on by Chicago would ask a Yippie "How do I join the Yippies?" "You wanna be a yippie, just call yourself a yippie and you'll be one," was the usual response. People turned on were left in a vacuum. Without anything to plug into, they soon drifted off into other trips.

Actions helped spawn a movement that had little organizational base. Conversely, lots of people today are creating programmatic, organizational packages without bothering to help generate a movement by acting.

The political awareness needed to create a revolution in France '68 or a solid anti-authoritarian movement out of Chicago '68 comes not from issuing directives about freedom. It comes from creative direct action combined with solid day-to-day organizing. Organization serves to develop and is an expression of action.

Like the anarchic March 22 Movement in France, the Yippies of Chicago were an autonomous group unencumbered by respect for authority, order, rationality or bureaucracy. The May-June manifestos weren't published in pamphlets, they were scrawled on the walls of Paris: "Humankind will not be free until the last capitalist has been hanged by the entrails of the last bureaucrat."

Nineteen sixty-eight drove consciousness from non-violence to rage; from single-issue organizing to revolution. It was the first large-scale manifestation of the youth, autonomous, non-workerist left that is currently rampaging through Europe (the autonomous groups, "spontis") and beginning to make its presence felt in North America. The autonomist left has combined with the re-emergence of more traditional groups like the Spanish CNT anarcho-syndicalist movement to create the most active anarchist movement in at least forty years.

The '68 revolutionaries knew that it is impossible to transform society through the "normal channels." They ushered in a spirit of surreality – the truth of imagination. "Be realistic, demand the impossible," they demanded. And in advanced industrial societies, *that which is considered impossible has become possible*, because virtually anything is conceivable. Advanced technological capabilities (automation, cybernetics) have erased the distinction between rationality and irrationality. They contain the material basis for a euphoric, co-operative society because they could free people from labour, giving us time to control our lives.

The maintenance of authoritarian States artificially stifles this potential, giving rise to rebellious responses. The smatterings of co-operative activity (co-ops, sexual liberation, alternative cultures, autonomous violence) are such responses. Every person is involved in a daily rebellion against authority: be it at work, school, the street, the family. In 1968 people who had been rebelling in isolation, rebelled together to create collective, anarchic revolts. They *expressed* the *repressed* potential of advanced industrial societies. Let us continue that expression every day.

Open Road 7 (1978)

1968: TEN YEARS AFTER

IT IS FORBIDDEN TO FORBID

The explosive confrontations of 1968 marked the end of the social calm that characterized the post-war era. That year, revolts in Europe and North America ignited a new militancy, signalling the resurgence of the non-Leninist left.

Like 1789 France, the events of 1968 displayed the potential for revolutionary change in a social setting previously unchallenged. The May-June revolt in France, in particular, demonstrated the vulnerability of authority in an advanced industrial State. It showed that the contradictions in capitalism had not been eliminated as some disillusioned leftists had come to believe. Rather, they had been heightened by the tensions inherent in a highly technological socity.

"It is forbidden to forbid."
—May-June graffiti

Under the surface calm of industrial countries there are festering rebellious impulses that can break loose spontaneously. Just months before the revolt, the French left seemed little more advanced than the North America movement. Then, without vanguards or self-proclaimed leaders, the expulsions of a few students organizing against the Vietnam War touched off strikes, riots, and occupations.

During May, barricades were erected throughout Paris, ten million workers (two-thirds of the French labor force) went out in a general strike, and several factories and campuses were seized and run by popular assembly.

May-June was a sweeping economic/cultural revolt. The street became a place to create art, discuss revolution, play, make love. Class lines were shattered as rapidly as windows as workers lined up with students and TV performers and football players and ... Even the football league draped from its office a banner emblazed, "Football Belongs To The People."

The material forces that emerged after the Second World War resulted in relative affluence, free time and education and spawned a generation that had largely mastered economic *survival* (the demand during the depression and other earlier struggles). Now they demanded *life*; an all-encompassing economic, sexual, psychological, cultural liberation.

And the workers' demands were often as qualitative as those of the students. At one electronics plant, workers who had just concluded a successful strike for higher wages hit the bricks again, explaining: "We are now striking for only one demand: workers' control of industry—and not only for our plant, but for all the plants in France."

The militancy of the workers had been catalyzed by the actions of students, youth, women and other sectors that had recently been consciously radicalized. Prior to the revolt, the working class base of the revolutionary movement was relatively weak. The French Communist Party and its adjunct union, the CGT, attempted to prevent the fusion of subjective (students, youth, women) and objective (workers, because of their class position) revolutionary forces because it represented a threat to its grip on the working class movement. The CP attacked the new radicals as "non-workers", failing to recognize that they come out of a new set of conditions and were at the very least as revolutionary as any traditional workers' movement.

"Nothing gave me greater pleasure than to be at the head of a demonstration with all that Stalinist filth in the rear."
—Daniel Cohn-Bendit, 1968

May '68 was, in a sense, the gala world premiere of both the autonomist movement and Eurocommunism. The autonomy of the French insurrection forced the French CP to show its reformist colors. In its desire to avoid confrontation with the State at all costs, the CP turned on the left, attempting to prevent the general strike, opposing the widespread attack on hierarchy, trying to get workers to accept wage agreements and calling for an election.

The CP felt it controlled the left; owned the working class. It was its holy duty to set the timetable for revolution so it was bewildered when others decided to start without it. The CP was correct in one sense though—its authority was being challenged and its hold on the left shattered.

The May events were the first mass manifestation of the anarchic potential in industrial countries (Portugal was to follow suit in 1975). Throughout the world, they generated interest in anti-authoritarian revolution and a new sense of instantaneous exhilaration that moved many leftists (including some who still labelled themselves Marxist) to a more libertarian stance.

The Stalinists showed that no organization using the model of the bourgeois State could be revolutionary; that no party could legislate freedom. Revolutionary organization had to reflect the forms of the spontaneous organization of people.

The revolt ended as an "almost revolution", not because it lacked a party to impose freedom but because it lacked a broad *awareness* of the need to smash State power. Although anti-authoritarian forms sprung up everywhere (there were even "barricade affinity groups"), people didn't escalate from the general strike to a widespread seizing and operating of factories.

Creative joy and liberty sparked by tactical spontaneity characterizes the initial phase of all revolutions (1789, 1917 ...). Anarchists fight to maintain this initial euphoria as a permanent characteristic of the new society. But, to avoid bourgeois counterrevolution or "people's vanguards" who attempt to commandeer the revolution, spontaneity must be backed by solidly-organized armed defense. For, behind every spontaneous outburst is a lot of hard work. And, although France '68 was a spontaneous revolt, it was part of a process taking place in several other countries at the same time.

Scenes from '68: Black flags in France, Parisians liberate liberty and Yippie in Chicago.

"No rules, speeches won't do, leaders are all full of shit. Pull your clothes off (Make love, not war), punch a marshall, jump a wall, do a dance, sing a song, paint the building, blow it up, charge and get inside."
—Abbie Hoffman, 1968

May '68 was the closest to *reality* of a series of 1968 events that cumulatively created a myth of impending revolution. A myth is a fantasy that's accepted as reality. The Chicago convention riots in August '68 unlike May-June in Paris, didn't actually threaten State power, but they became a myth because not only many leftists, but the right and the general populace as well, accepted them as a genuine revolutionary threat. Chicago was the most spectacular of a series of left "events" that were occurring so regularly (from Chicago to Columbia to Berkeley to your home town) that a fantasy of imminent revolution was generated.

The very acceptance of this fantasy as reality made it more real. People have myths that they project into their reality. Everyone has fantasies they want to see come alive. The myth of impending revolution was fomented by organically conceived, explosive confrontations that rocked international consciousness and set the pattern of struggle for a time. Little "Chicago's" spontaneously seeped into every corner of America as people sought to emulate the myth; realize their fantasies.

Because only a few thousand people participated, the revolutionary threat of Chicago was a fantasy. Still, the days of street clashes, the battle for the park, the massive military apparatus mobilized against the new culture, the absurdity going on inside the convention hall, and the resulting Chicago Eight trial was real and was brought home, in bloody living color, for the whole world to watch.

Although Chicago, and other sixties actions, were successes because they appealed to emotions through creative action, they weren't, in the long run, as effective as they could have been because they lacked a systematically-organized base. People turned on by Chicago would ask a Yippie "How do I join the Yippies?" "You wanna be a yippie, just call yourself a yippie and you'll be one," was the usual response. People turned on were left in a vacuum. Without anything solid to plug into, they soon drifted off into other trips.

Actions helped spawn a movement that had little organizational base. Conversely, lots of people today are creating programmatic, organizational packages without bothering to help generate a movement by acting.

The political awareness needed to create a revolution in France '68 or a solid anti-authoritarian movement out of Chicago '68 comes not from issuing directives about freedom. It comes from creative direct action combined with solid day-to-day organizing. Organization serves to develop and is an expression of action.

Like the anarchic March 22 Movement in France, the Yippies of Chicago were an autonomous group unencumbered by respect for authority, order, rationality or bureaucracy. The May - June manifestos weren't published in pamphlets, they were scrawled on the walls of Paris: "Humankind will not be free until the last capitalist has been hanged by the entrails of the last bureaucrat."

Nineteen sixty-eight drove consciousness from non-violence to rage; from single-issue organizing to revolution. It was the first large-scale manifestation of the youth, autonomous, non-workerist left that is currently rampaging through Europe (the autonomous groups, "spontis") and beginning to make its presence felt in North America. The autonomous left has combined with the re-emergence of more traditional groups like the Spanish CNT anarcho-syndicalists to create the most active anarchist movement in at least 40 years.

The '68 revolutionaries knew that it is impossible to transform society through the "normal channels." They ushered in a spirit of surreality—the truth of imagination. "Be realistic, demand the impossible," they demanded. And in advanced industrial societies, *that which is considered impossible has become possible*, because virtually anything is conceivable. Advanced technological capabilities (automation, cybernetics) have erased the distinction between rationality and irrationality. They contain the material basis for a euphoric, co-operative society because they could free people from labour, giving us time to control our lives.

The maintenance of authoritarian States artificially stifles this potential giving rise to rebellious responses. The smatterings of co-operative activity (co-ops, sexual liberation, alternative cultures, autonomous violence) are such responses.

Every person is involved in a daily rebellion against authority; be it at work, school, the street, the family.

In 1968 people who had been rebelling in isolation, rebelled together to create collective, anarchic revolts. They *expressed* the *repressed* potential of advanced industrial societies. Let us continue that expression every day.

BISEXUALITY

When I was a young catholic boy of thirteen I fell in love with a boy in my school class. He was a gentle and happy person. We used to pull our desks close together to help each other with our assignments. I remember feeling tickled every time he lowered his voice and spoke close to my ear. This sensation, of being caressed by someone's voice has been with me ever since. In class I used to ask him questions just so he'd have to whisper to me.

One afternoon he asked if I'd like to sleep over at his house. "Of course," I said, I loved to spend time with him. Later that night his parents asked if we'd mind sharing a large bed. It was early spring on Canada's East coast and still quite cold.

I remember his happy, relaxed eyes as he said good night. I couldn't sleep. I wanted to hug him. I wanted him to hug me, to whisper something in my ear. Anything. I laid there for what seemed like hours. Half asleep, half awake. I recall feeling a little confused, but not guilty or ashamed.

My crush never was consummated, and I'm unsure whether he was even aware of how much I wanted to be close to him, both emotionally and physically.

Before this, at the young age of seven, I experienced the trauma of being "kid-napped" from a school playground and taken to an isolated field where I was beaten and sexually assaulted by a young woman for several hours. The woman was later apprehended, having been pointed out by me (to my father) in church one Sunday morning. Throughout my childhood I experienced much more female to male aggression than vice versa. Physical assaults, verbal humiliation, intimidation, etc., against my child-friends by mothers, guardians, and the nuns who taught us at school, were frequent. I hadn't developed any social-political-historical awareness at this age and consequently didn't have a context to place all this female anger within. Only later did I actually attempt to understand my kidnapper/assaulter and eventually realized the role authoritarian society played in the tragedy. Her admittedly fucked-up actions, I decided, were nevertheless created by something almost autonomous of her. In a way she has become an unknown sister living and struggling under the weight of the same oppressive world that also crushes me.

Despite the fear and hatred of women, adults and of sexuality this left me with for many years, I still don't believe that locking her (or others like her) away in a cage would be a solution. I wasn't the victim of a "child molester," but rather of a fucked-up society that creates angry, alienated and fucked-up people. On the other hand, I do want to help create a society where people take responsibility for their actions. Ideally, this would be within the context of belonging to a real community and living in some form of egalitarian social system, which would have a more caring (and likely more effective) method of dealing with it's problems. In fact, by allowing, or even worse, suggesting,

that the State coerce and intimidate us into behaving in certain ways (e.g. by threatening imprisonment) whether we agree with even part of the desired result (deterrence, protection) only exacerbates the problem and further disempowers us. I guess an appropriate slogan would be: "community solutions to community problems." The real problem of course is that real community and capitalism/hierarchy are mutually exclusive.

My negative experiences with women had nothing to do with my same-sex love affairs. For instance both of my parents were equally positive images for me, though my father, who has been described as "too nurturing," "overly paternal," and "chronically honest," also uncritically accepted his patriarchal role as house boss. He further believes that women have a gender-determined role to play in society and that god "himself" somehow wants it that way. In this sense he is both a gentle, caring person and an agent of oppression. My mother on the other hand has always exemplified the myth that women are inherently subservient, having sacrificed her life for her family and husband as all good catholic women are expected to do. At the time, however, I interpreted her seemingly infinite kindness and affection as part of a natural maternal instinct and not the result of patriarchic demands in a capitalist society. These most immediate and familiar images of both men and women as caring and nurturing, helped to mitigate my perception of a world of nasty, loud women lording over scared, defenseless kids. As time went on there were fewer and fewer reproductions of image of females having power over males (though able-bodyism, racism, ageism, and classism are only some examples of this). In fact the overwhelming sense I began to have of our world, as far as violence was concerned, was that it originated with men and rarely with women. It has since become clear to me however, that an authoritarian social system and not gender is responsible for violence against those with less status than others. In any case, by the time I was twenty-one I had had about the same number of infatuations with women as with men, though naturally I had to repress many of my homosexual crushes.

As a bisexual I'm weary of the stereotypes and generalizations. We are not for instance, oversexed libertines. I fall in love with and am attracted to people, not genitalia. It's as simple as that. The person's gender is irrelevant. Because I'll have sex with "anyone" doesn't mean that this is all I do. On the other hand, moralisms about too much sex are ultimately boring and repressive. Nor are bisexuals sitting on the fence, or experimenting until we realize our true sexuality. I am a bisexual.

Rather than having the best of both worlds, as straights and gays believe we have, we actually get mixed signals from both groups. For instance, bisexuals often experience the same discrimination and prejudices from straights as do gays and lesbians. Furthermore, straights want us to admit that we are straight, and gays often want us to admit that we

No Picnic 4 (1988)

are gay. Because of this, many of us retreat into an integrated lifestyle within one of the official sexual communities (a word by the way, that has practically lost any significance or meaning), rather than assert our own identity as bisexuals. I tend to questions this dichotomous interpretation of human sexuality, i.e. either you are gay or straight. In fact I find this polarity only serves an unliberated society. As a bisexual, the accepted notion that there are only two sexualities, hetero or homo, is personally oppressive. In a recent article on bisexuality in a local student paper, Melinda Wittstock reasons: "… the political and cultural necessity of exclusive homosexual identification, for the sake of gay and lesbian visibility in a society where heterosexuality is virtually compulsory, has polarized human sexuality." For instance at a woman's sexuality conference in Toronto just over a year ago, she relates how many women "talked about the pressures put on bisexuals (women) to choose between either a strictly lesbian or straight lifestyle." She speculates that within the lesbian movement there is yet very little security and not enough outside support, this reality combined with extreme pressure from heterosexual society to become "straight," makes bisexuality appear threatening. She then quotes a woman who states that being active in some feminist and sexual liberation circles can be exceptionally difficult for bisexuals as some lesbians see them as opting for a male-dominated society and the patriarchy whenever they sleep with men. Some women feel they are being threatened with exclusion unless they make a black and white choice. Within both the gay and lesbian milieus, many bisexuals feel that they are being forced into the closet.

How is this liberating or empowering? Few bisexuals sleep with the opposite gender for acceptance from the dominant sexual culture, nor do many of us have same-sex partners as a form of rebellion. We follow our natural desires as much as possible rather than allow ourselves to be programmed by the existing dominant sexual bias or pressured by political ideology. All of our sexualities are unique to our personal experiences and shaped by them.

Who knows what type of sexuality would be prevalent in a freer society. However, I feel, as a man, that if we followed our natural inclinations, there would be more bisexuals among us. I am particularly surprised how few there are of us in milieus involved in anti-authoritarian politics. My experience is more or less limited to Montreal and Vancouver, but if that is any indication to what extent libertarian men are interested in becoming emancipated then the situation is pretty disappointing. I make the large assumption of course, that the more liberated we are, the more we will tend toward bisexuality.

Most of the men that I've met seem painfully afraid of anything physical/emotional with other men unless within the context of an anti-sexist men's group (the ones I've had experience with seem more like pat-yourself-on-the-back therapy groups). In fact, something that I've noticed and which has been pointed out to me by women friends, is

the near paranoia surrounding sexuality that many men in our milieu seem to be possessed by, including officially sanctioned heterosexuality. This appears more prevalent among those men with "leftist" influences. They seem so thoroughly guilt tripped (and consequently ashamed) of being male (or white or North American) that any expression of what they see as part of these qualities is interpreted as oppressive. They gain a sort of masochistic pleasure by reducing themselves to their penis (or pigment or class background). This atmosphere of guilt is often paralyzing (and not very fun). It's unfortunate that critical theories apparently intended to expose the oppressive/repressive nature of this society are, for some folks, stultifying ideologies that are contributing to our imprisonment rather than helping us free ourselves. Perhaps we should direct our anger where it belongs (not at each other) and begin encouraging one another to be free and to celebrate our loves and desires, rather than reproduce the same uptightness, conformity and guilt (and boredom) that are hallmarks of capitalist/patriarchal society.

— By Jamie

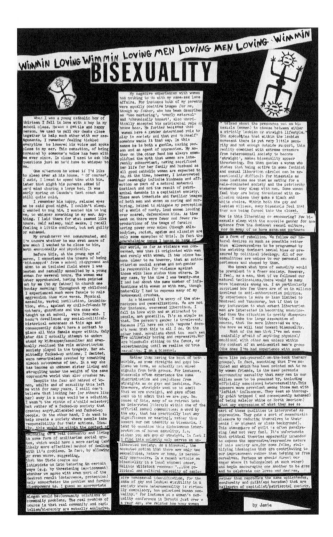

MANIFESTE CONTRE LA SOCIÉTÉ SPECTACULAIRE MARCHANDE

C'est un spectacle désolant que de voir ces milliers de jeunes, qui, dans les rues de Washington, la capitale illusoire de l'Amérique, se précipitent bravement au devant du matraquage, de la répression et des ennuis. Désolant, car les pseudo-militants, pseudo-militantes vont ainsi par centaines se donner bêtement à l'ennemi, tout en pensant changer le monde. Un spectacle, car le tout est chorégraphié en grande partie par les médias, relais de l'idéologie bicéphale de la contestation dans les normes. D'une voix outré, ce protestataire non-violent, venant de perdre son quartier général au main de la police, nous déclamait la lithanie de l'Amérique mainstream, celle de la constitution et de la contestation de surface. "On viole nos droits et le 1er amendement de la Constitution". Exit la lutte de classe, exit le radicalisme. Le FMI ne devient qu'une agression constitutionnelle. La Banque Mondiale doit être réformée pour tenir compte de nos droits. Voilà achevée la mise en scène orchestrée par tous les Duhamel(s) et les Canevas de l'Amérique du Nord.

AssisEs devant des flics ou couché-e-s devant des voitures, on projettait une image unitaire et terne de la contestation: celle de la soumission. Se soumettre à la bonne volonté des forces de l'ordre quant à savoir le nombre de points de suture ou le nombre de jours de prison obtenus. Se soumettre au médias pour qui tout ceci est mis en place; car sans eux, la non-violence devient impossible, la résistance pacifique ne sert à rien si on ne peut toucher l'opinion public. L'humeur était à la fête des deux côtés. Les protestataires voyaient enfin le moment venu de s'exprimer "publiquement"; les policiers de se défouler abondamment.

La foire anti-FMI, contre-BM se transforme en foire du dégoût. Dégoût du matraquage, dégoût de voir les gens rester impassibles quand leurs camarades se font démolir par les plus méprisables d'entres les humains (les policiers pour ne pas les nommer). Mais aussi, un haut le coeur de savoir que tout cela était planifié. Planifié et inutile. Car toute action, en fait, est expliquée, démontrée, mise à jour à l'avance. Il n'y a pas de secret chez les non-violents. On communique toute la stratégie, à tout le monde, en tout temps, même au flics. On appelle ça transparence. Tellement transparent en fait que ça devient inéfficace. Il suffit de changer les plans de l'autre côté de la clôture, et voilà, des mois de travail à l'eau.

C'en est trop de voir cela. Nous ne supportons plus que les non-violentEs monopolisent l'espace de contestation. Si ces gens désirent vraiment se faire matraquer, libre à eux et à elles. Mais nous désirons vivre debout. La différence est frappante. Lorsque nous sommes assis, le flic nous parait deux fois plus grand. Lorsque nous sommes debout, il perd tellement de son prestige! Et il peut même avoir peur de nous. Et nous le savons.

Nous ne voulons pas nous laisser faire. C'en est assez de la passivité. Nous n'avons jamais considéré que de rester à porté d'un jet de poivre de cayenne ou à la disponibilité des flics, cela constituait un acte de résistance. Cela n'est qu'une action irraisonnée, basée sur de faux arguments. Jamais nous ne nous sentirons plus forts, plus sûrs de nous par terre devant une voiture de police, en prison, dans le panier à salade ou dans un procès où l'État est juge et partie. Le fait que le public soit au courant de certains enjeux (comme l'AMI), même si cela aurait pu être suffisant pour repousser ou empêcher ces choses de prendre place, ne saurait constituer un victoire pour nous. Ce ne serait qu'une victoire pour les médias et une faction du capital hostile à ces accords. Mais nous n'avons pas non plus été naïfs au point de croire que l'action non-violente avait réussi à mettre fin aux traités de l'AMI.

Quant à l'OMC, nous savons bien que les actions "violentes" du Black Bloc comme l'opportunisme économico-élec-

GANDHI is DEAD
BECAUSE HE WOULDN'T

DC PD

Apr. 16 2000

STRIKE BACK!
support your local BL CK BLOC!

torale de Clinton ont été au moins aussi importantes dans la balance que les quelques heures de retard du congrès occasionnées par des fanatiques respirant le grand air des gaz CS au son de la police claire. Nous pensons même que les premières heures, les plus *hardcore* ont été décisives dans le déroulement de la rencontre. Quand Nike, Planet Hollywood et consorts ont eu perdu quelques millions de dollars en dommages en ventes, on peut dire que le Black Bloc avait alors touché le centre du problème.

Le système capitaliste, patriarcal et spectaculaire ne carbure pas à coup de rencontres, fussent-elle ministérielles ou celles des dignitaires. Le coeur de la société spectaculaire-marchande est constitué de crystal, de vitres polies faisant refléter en même temps le portrait du consommateur, de la consommatrice, que la présente la marchandise déifiée. En brisant les symboles de l'oppression, l'envitrinement et la mise sous tutelle de biens pouvant être utiles à d'autres, le Black Bloc remportait la première victoire qui

allait ouvrir les années 2000.

Pendant que les non-violents étaient tournéEs vers le passé, vers les vieilles croûtes qui prétendent dominer le monde (mais qui ne seront plus là dans 5 ans), il se passait des choses bien plus importantes dans les rues de Seattle comme de Londres. On s'en prenait aux vrais responsables. La marchandise était prise à partie. Jamais une révolution ne s'est faite sans la désagrégation des systèmes d'oppression, et c'est toujours vrai aujourd'hui. Nous rions des non-violentEs soi-disant libertaires, révolutionnaires, mais qui vont tout de suite nous pointer du doigt sur toutes les tribunes (y compris au poste de police) quand nous attaquons ce que nous dénonçons et detestons. Ces gens, pacifistes et patriarches de la connerie humaine, ne sont ni militantes, ni anarchistes, ni révolutionnaires; elles ne sont que ridicules.

Nous voulons être efficaces. Nous prenons partie en faveur de la radicalité, de la destruction de la propriété privée par les moyens qui soient. Nous ne sommes pas fondamentalement violentEs. Nous sommes pour une résolution pacifique et sans contraintes des conflits si ceux-ci ont lieu entre deux personnes jouissant d'une égalité en droit et de facto, et bénéficiant de la liberté de se retirer du conflit. Mais quand l'inégalité est de mise, tant qu'existera le patriarcat, le capitalisme et l'État, nous ne nous résignerons pas à la position la plus faible que nous puissons adopter: la non-utilisation de la violence. Car il ne s'agit pas d'un débat sur la non-violence. Comme le gouvernement parfait ou l'État de bonheur absolu, la non-violence n'existe pas. Dès qu'une des deux parties emploie la force, la brutalité, la non-violence n'existe plus. C'est comme le vide. Dès qu'il y a quelque chose pour le remplir, il perd sa propriété de vide.

Alors, puisque nous voulons tout le plus vite possible, nous employons le chemin le plus court pour arriver à ce but. Nous ne laissons pas dans les mains de l'ennemi son arme la plus forte: la légitimité et l'usage exclusif de la violence, ou son contrôle et sa répartition en fonction de ses besoins. Nous prenons ce que nous voulons. Si cela constitue un acte de violence, et bien tant pis. Mais ultimement, c'est l'ordre établi qui se trouve à être violenté, lézardé.

Nous l'avons dit: nous voulons être efficaces. Nous avons donc décidé de nous organiser selon cet objectif. Formons nos Blacks Blocs, prenons le pouvoir de la rue. Créons nos Women Blocs et prenons le pouvoir sur notre vie. Organisons nos Commandos bouffe et prenons le pouvoir sur notre faim. Batissons nos Squatts et prenons le pouvoir sur nos logements. Faisons la révolution et redonnons le pouvoir à chacunes et chacuns pour que personnes n'en ait plus que les autres.

Pour une destruction efficace de la marchandise

La société en est une de spectacle. Chaque occasion dans la vie d'un individu se doit de répondre à une préoccupation élémentaire; le désir de fuites permanentes et amusantes.

Étant une personne critique, songée et rationnelle, j'ai acheté un produit odieux. Le produit étant qualifié par sa valeur, voilà pourquoi le terme odieux s'y applique si naturellement. Le contenant avant le contenu.

Comble de la liberté, mes choix étaient variés; " quelle est la meilleur pub alors ? ", me dis-je. L'étouffante période débute grâce à un dilemme crucial. Ivory, ou 2000 the Lever. Peut-être Palmolive, avec leur offre 2 pour 1, vaisselle et mains. Enfin mains et vaisselle, quoiqu'il en soit. Avec l'appât, le piège me sautait à la figure. Ma liberté s'est tuée lorsqu'elle a heurté la caisse. Celle-ci représente, à petite échelle, tous les facteurs coercitifs qui entourent nos vies. Barrière, privilèges de classe, rôle et fonction, surveillance, identification et répression unilatérale.

Une lutte pour une vie où la production non salariée se métamorphose en distribution gratuite des biens. Une société où l'abolition de la propriété privée - la propriété tout court plutôt - permet d'instaurer la gestion collective des ressources matérielles désirées et utiles par le regroupement des producteurs en assemblées d'autogestion.

Alors, j'ai immédiatement saisi l'ampleur des problèmes que nous vivions, notre aliénation individuelle, et bien sûre collective. J'ai pris la barre de savon que la publicité me conseillait sincèrement (?!), et je l'ai enfoncé dans le rectum du gérant de la place, lequel était vêtu d'un uniforme - uninazi - bien sûr ridicule. Contre les frontières du réel, disons plutôt de leur réel, j'ai répondu mes frontières personnelles par l'agitation de tous mes membres corporels. Voilà mon pouvoir individuel! "RÉVOLUTION TABARBAK !", dis-je à haute voix, à chaude voix.

Prendre en main sa destinée. Ni dieu, ni maître.

C'est depuis ce temps que j'ai organisé, avec d'autres êtres humains, un joyeux feu d'artifice social. Tout ça, sans compter un atout essentiel, du combustible matériel. Macdonald, banques, postes de polices, établissements gouvernementaux, centralisateurs et - par nature - bureaucratiques, syndicats fédératifs, chambres de commerce ainsi que plusieurs autres, étaient sollicités pour céder leurs possessions les plus triviales à l'intention d'un feu de joie libertaire; le reste était, environnement oblige, composté. Les sans-abri se retrouvèrent sous des toits bourgeois et douillets.

Pour en finir avec la *représentation, le symbole et le mensonge fonctionnaliste. Pour en finir avec la marchandise qui transforme le temps en argent, et les gens en produit standardisé par les agents de socialisation capitaliste. Une existence véritable, parsemée de passions, sans temps mort, qui mène à l'épanouissement maximal des individus par une liberté sans frontière, sans discrimination, sans classe, sans hiérarchie.*
Depuis ce temps, mes camarades me surnomment " le puant. " Savon ou révolution ?

"Manifeste contre la societe spectaculaire marchande"

Analysing the 1999 anti-World Trade Organization and 2000 International Monetary Fund/World Bank demonstrations, the author begins with a critique of the complicity of pacifist-oriented protestors with the powers of the State. At these events non-violent demonstrators "performed" for the media and, in keeping with their principles of non-violence, framed their acts of civil disobedience as a defence of their rights as citizens – rights defined by Statist documents like the U.S. constitution. Their leaders also proclaimed the goal of the protests was to "reform" institutions like the IMF/World Bank by bringing them in line with these rights. And so, "exit the battle of classes, exit radicalism." The author then points to three ways in which pacifists submit to rather than resist authority. First, they take up a bodily position of submission by sitting or lying down in front of police vehicles and/or the police, which only empowers the latter psychologically and physically. Secondly, they submit to the media, for without it their pacifist acts lack any meaning and could not effect public opinion. Thirdly, they submit to authority be preplanning their actions, making everything they do "transparent" – even to the "flics" (police)! Anarchists will no longer support non-violent strategists monopolising "the spaces of contestation." Black Bloc actions at Seattle involving the destruction of "commerce" in the guise of Nike and Planet Hollywood stores are appropriate and much needed: the destruction costs businesses millions and gets to "the centre of the problem" – capitalism. No revolution can take place without insurrectionary action: it brings about the "disintegration of systems of oppression." Non-violent "pacifists and patriarchs" who seek to repress this level of protest are neither "militants," "anarchists" or "revolutionaries." As a feminist anarchist the author concludes by calling for the creation of "Women Blocs" on the model of the Black Bloc.

– MARK ANTLIFF

Is Marxism racist?

by Ron Hayley

When we hear the term "Third World", it conjures up an image of non-Western peoples fighting against European (and North American) political, economic and cultural domination. But this term conceals the fact that these peoples wage this fight with very different philosophical perspectives. For some, the fight is fought on Eurocentric lines: that is, the oppressed peoples accept their designation as "underdeveloped" (in contrast with the "developed" West) and seek to remedy the situation by emulating the science and technology of the "advanced" nations. The Eurocentric model derives, in large part, from the influence of Marxism and what we accept as an authentic expression of Third World politics is, to some degree, the result of ideological imperialism.

But there is a new current emerging from among the submerged nations of Europe and among the Native peoples of the Americas. It terms itself "Fourth (or Host) World" and it is this perspective which powerfully comes through in *Marxism and Native Americans*. MNA is structured in the form of a debate between Marxists of various stripes and Native spokespeople, with the opposition between them ranging from strident to wishy-washy. The essential point is: is the Marxist theory of historical development essentially racist? an issue the volume's Marxists manage to sidestep, for the most part.

The book begins with a Preface by Winona LaDuke in which the question is posed: "Is Marxism as it is now structured, *or could be structured,* a part of the solution or a part of the problem?" (pp. vi-vii). Editor Ward Churchill then takes over (and lest we anarchists grow too smug) and begins his Introduction by relating an inci-

23

dent in 1973 involving anarchist Karl Hess. Hess, at a speaking engagement, had just finished giving his spiel for the abolition of the federal government and the establishment of a system of localized self-governance:

After the customary polite applause, the session was thrown open to questions from the audience. The question I had to ask was: "How, in the plan you describe do you propose to continue guarantees to the various Native American tribes that their landbase and other treaty rights will be continued."

Hess seemed truly flabbergasted. Rather than address the question, he pivoted neatly into the time-honoured polemicist's tactic of discrediting the "opposition" by imputing to it subversive or (in this case) reactionary intentions: "Well, I have to admit that that's the weirdest defense of the federal government I've ever heard." The debate was joined.

I countered that I had no interest in protecting the federal government, but since Hess was proposing to do away with it, I was curious to know the nature of the mechanisms he advocated to keep the Indians' rather more numerous white neighbors from stealing the last dregs of Indian land — and anything else they could get their hands on. After all, such a scenario of wanton expropriation hardly lacks historical basis.

Perplexed by my insistence and a growing tension in the room, Hess replied that the federal government seemed something of a poor risk for Native Americans to place their faith in. Perhaps, he suggested, it was time the Indians tried "putting their faith in their fellow man rather than in bureaucracies"...(pp. 1-2)

From there, Churchill goes on to describe his own personal quest for an "American Radical Vision", and the studied neglect of Native problems and perspectives which he and other Native activists have encountered on the left, in marked contrast to the canonization of Mao, Fanon, Che, Lumumba, Arafat, Ho, Kim Il Sung, et al. The upshot is his conclusion:

...the (North)American Radical Vision (is) a failed promise; (North) "American" radicalism (is) fundamentally and completely an intellectual import. Conversely, there (can) be no (North) American Vision, radical or otherwise, which (does) not begin with the original (North) "American", the Native American. (p. 5)

Now to the actual meat of the book (or tofu for you vegetarians). The first essay is not really an essay at all. It is a beautifully spoken diatribe (copied down and printed in various magazines) by Russell Means, long time member of the American Indian Movement. The occasion for the speech was the Black Hills Survival Gathering at Rapid City, South Dakota in the summer of 1980. Means' speech (called "The Same Old Song" in this collection) provoked a storm of controversy (see excerpts). Its basic thesis is that every so-called "revolution" in Europe or America has been an occasion for further depredations against non-European peoples. Means also hits at the distinction between "being" and "gaining" and the fact that both capitalism and communism are oriented towards gaining. And, finally, he points out that the despiritualization of the universe, so characteristic of European culture, is a necessary prelude to exploiting it,

Kick It Over 12 (1985)

Russell Means — photo by Camilla Smith

just as dehumanization is used to justify murder.

Both Marxism and capitalism (and some forms of anarchism) adhere to the notion of "historical progress" whereby peoples progress through a series of predetermined historical stages increasing in technical sophistication until they finally reach the stage of being able to conquer scarcity through "conquering" nature. By this historical schema, some peoples are "advanced" and others are "backward" ("underdeveloped" or "developing"). For the latter, development is their *destiny* — there is no escaping it. It is a precondition for their liberation (whether conceived in a capitalist or Marxist terms).

For Means, such a historical methadology (no matter whose mouth it issues from) is racist. The second essay, "Searching for a Second Harvest", proves it. Written by the Revolutionary Communist Party, U.S.A., it is a direct response to Means article. As Marxists are wont to do, they reverse roles and portray Marxists as the victims of an imperialist-inspired attack (have you ever noticed how Reds never "bait" anyone else — it is always *they* who are the victims of baiting?). For the RCP, it's a clear-cut case of the "most backward" ideas against the "most advanced" (hmmm, where have we heard that before?). They accuse Means of borrowing his ideas of the "noble savage" from Rousseau, etc. (As the rejoinder authored by Churchill and Dora-Lee Larson points out, to the European chauvinist, any attack on European ideas can only come from other European ideas.) For the RCP, European ideas are more advanced because they rest on a more developed system of technology. Furthermore, their essay is punctuated with references to the "mastery of Nature" and "the struggle against nature". The one area where they score some points is in showing how Native people often over-romanticize their own culture and hide its warts (like woman abuse in some cultures and inter-tribal warfare), but this is largely irrelevant since what's at issue is getting Europeans to admit that they even have something to learn from Native peoples.

The RCP accuses Means of wanting to return to a state in which Native peoples allegedly stored their own feces for purposes of removing undigested seeds (the "second harvest" referred to in the title). Churchill and Larsen respond by reminding the RCP of the "9 million odd deaths attributed, mostly by starvation, to Stalin's forced labor reorganization of the Soviet economy on the heels of the NEP" (p. 69). During this period it was not uncommon to find the rural populace separating undigested corn from horse dung as well as their own excrement as a survival expedient: "Were these victims of 'advanced ideas' somehow exempt from eating the nutrient residue of their own stool during the enforced and terminal starvation? Less so that the millions who were systematically starved to death in the Hitlerian organization of another 'advanced' industrial context? (p. 69) At least the RCP is honest, something that can't be said of the other Marxist contributors in this volume. They either sidestep the issues or seek to impress their readers with theoretical verbiage. Bob Sipe, affiliated with the magazine *Radical Therapy*, proves Churchill's contention that North American radicalism is an imported product. Sipe literally talks German.

In the last analysis, as Churchill points out in his endpiece, the more sophisticated Marxists in the volume are merely playing Teilhard Chardin to Bob Avakian's Oral Roberts — they share the same basic ideology. What comes through in almost all the Marxist contributions is how much Marxism has to offer Native people and how they should seek to acquaint themselves with it, never what Marxists might gain from familiarizing themselves with the Native perspective. The intellectual correlate of economic imperialism is arrogance and messianic zeal. And, as Churchill points out, when they do borrow aspects of Indian thought, they do so in order to make their own outlook seem more appealing.

A common reason cited for the marginality of the Native struggle is that their struggle is hopeless (so is the Palestinians' for that matter, but that has never been raised as a consideration) and is not "strategically important". From my vantage point, our whole struggle may well be hopeless, but that is not reason to abandon it. With respect to strategy, what Marxists and some anarchists have to say on this score is sophistic. Indians control land which contains 60% of the energy sources needed by our technocratic society — one could make a case that their role is every bit as strategically important as that of the (increasingly irrelevant) industrial proletariat. But after all, traditional leftism is built on such sophistry. In the final analysis, there is no excuse for the shameful abdication of support for Native peoples and Native struggles. Nor can we fight technocracy and imperialism with an ideology which mirrors it in all important respects. We need something new. In the words of Winona LaDuke:

No movement or group of related movements can succeed in offsetting present circumstances merely through a shared rejection. Not only must they struggle against something, but they must also struggle toward something. Action alone can never provide the required answers. Only a unifying theory, a unifying vision of the alternatives can fulfill this task. Only such a vision can bind together the fragmentary streams of action and resistance at large in America into a single multi-faceted whole capable of transforming the synthetic reality of a death culture into the natural reality of a culture of life. (pp. v-vi)

The same old shit —

When I speak of Europeans or mental Europeans, I'm not allowing for false distinctions. I'm not saying that on the one hand there are the byproducts of a few thousand years of genocidal, reactionary European intellectual development which is bad, and on the other hand there is some new revolutionary intellectual development which is good. I'm referring here to the so-called theories of Marxism and anarchism and "leftism" in general. I don't believe these theories can be separated from the rest of the European intellectual tradition. It's really just the same old song.

Take Christianity as an historical example. In its day Christianity was revolutionary. It changed European power relations for all time; that is, unless you happen to think the Roman Empire is still a dominant military force. But European culture, of which Christianity became a part, acted on the religion in such a way as to use it as a tool for the destruction of non-European peoples, for the expansion of European military and economic power across the planet, for the consolidation of the European nation-states, for the formation of the capitalist economic system. The Christian revolution or revolutions were an important part of the development of European culture in directions it was *already* headed; it changed nothing other than to speed up Europe's genocide outside Europe and maybe inside Europe too.

The same holds true for the capitalist and other European "revolutions". They changed power relations within Europe around a bit, but only to meet the needs of the white world at the expense of everyone and everything else.

Revolutionary Marxism, as with industrial society in other forms, seeks to "rationalize" all people in relation to industry, maximum industry, maximum production. It is a materialist doctrine which despises the American Indian spiritual tradition, our cultures, our lifeways. Marx himself called us "precapitalists" and "primitive". Precapitalist simply means that, in his view, we would eventually discover capitalism and become capitalists; we have always been economically retarded in Marxist terms. The only manner in which American Indian people could participate in a Marxist revolution would be to *join* the industrial system, to become factory workers or "proletarians" as Marx called them. The man was very clear about the fact that his revolution could occur only through the struggle of the proletariat, that the existence of a massive industrial system is a precondition of a successful Marxist society.

At this point, I've got to stop and ask myself whether I'm being too harsh. Marxism has something of a history. Does this history bear out my observations? I look to the process of industrialization in the Soviet Union since 1920 and I see that these Marxists have done what it took the English "industrial revolution" three hundred years to do; and the Marxists did it in sixty years. I see that the territory of the USSR used to contain a number of tribal peoples and that they have been crushed to make way for the factories. The Soviets refer to this as "The National Question," the question of whether the tribal peoples had the right to exist as peoples; and they decided the tribal peoples were an acceptable sacrifice to industrial needs. I look to China and I see the same thing. I look to Vietnam and I see Marxists imposing an industrial order and rooting out the indigenous tribal mountain peoples.

I hear a leading Soviet scientist saying that when uranium is exhausted *then* alternatives will be found. I see the Vietnamese taking over a nuclear power plant abandoned by the U.S. military. Have they dismantled and destroyed it? No, they are using it. I see China explode nuclear bombs, developing uranium reactors, preparing a space program in order to colonize and exploit the planets the same as the Europeans colonized and exploited this hemisphere. It's the same old song, but maybe with a faster tempo this time.

The European materialist tradition of despiritualizing the universe is very similar to the mental process which goes into dehumanizing another person. And who seems most expert at dehumanizing other people? And why? Soldiers who have seen a lot of combat learn to do this to the enemy before going back into combat. Murderers do it before going out to commit murder. SS guards did it to concentration camp inmates. Cops do it. Corporation leaders do it to workers they send into uranium mines and to work in steel mills. Politicians do it to everyone in sight. And what each process of dehumanization has in common for each group doing the dehumanizing is that it makes it alright to kill and otherwise destroy other people. One of the Christian commandments says "thou shall not kill", at least not humans, so the trick is to mentally convert the victims into non-humans. Then you can proclaim violation of your own commandment as a virtue.

In terms of the despiritualization of the universe, the mental process works so that it becomes virtuous to destroy the planet. Terms like "progress" and "development" are used as cover words here the way "victory" and "freedom" are used to justify butchery in the dehumanization process. For example, a real estate speculator may refer to "developing" a parcel of ground by opening a gravel quarry there; "development" really means total permanent destruction with the earth itself removed. But European logic has *gained* a few tons of gravel with which more land can be "developed" in the construction of road beds. Ultimately, the whole universe is open — in the European view — to this sort of insanity.

You can't judge the real nature of a European revolutionary doctrine on the basis of the changes it proposes to make within the European power structure and society. You can only judge it by the effects it will have on non-European peoples. This is because every revolution in European history has served to reinforce Europe's tendencies and abilities to export destruction to other peoples, other cultures and the environment itself. I defy anyone to point out an example where this isn't true.

Look beneath the surface of revolutionary Marxism and what do you find? A commitment to reversing the industrial system which created the need of white society for uranium? No. A commitment to guaranteeing the Lakota and other American Indian peoples real control over the land and resources they have left? No, not unless the industrial process is to be reversed as part of their doctrine. A commitment to our rights, as peoples, to maintaining our values and traditions? No, not as long as they need the uranium within our land to feed the industrial system of the society, the culture of which the Marxists *are still a part.*

It's only a matter of time until what Europeans call "a major catastrophe of global proportions" will occur. It is the role of American Indian peoples, the role of all natural beings to survive. A part of our survival is to resist. We resist, not to overthrow a government or to take political power, but because it is natural to resist extermination, to survive. We don't want power over white institutions; we want white institutions to disappear. *That's* revolution.

When I use the term "European", I'm not referring to skin color or a particular genetic structure. What I'm referring to is a mind-set, a world view which is a product of the development of European culture. People are not genetically encoded to hold this outlook, they are *acculturated* to hold it. The same holds true for American Indians or for the members of any other culture. □

Kick It Over 12 (1985)

FERAL REVOLUTION: Rebelling against our domestication

When I was a very young child, my life was filled with intense pleasure and a vital energy that caused me to feel what I experienced to the full. I was the center of this marvelous, playful existence and felt no need to rely on anything but my own living experience to fulfill me. I felt intensely, I experienced intensely, my life was a festival of passion and pleasure. My disappointments and sorrows were also intense. I was born a free, wild being in the midst of a society based upon domestication. There was no way that I could escape being domesticated myself. Civilization will not tolerate what is wild in its midst. But I never forgot the intensity that life could be. I never forgot the vital energy that had surged through me. My existence since I first began to notice that this vitality was being drained away has been a warfare between the needs of civilized survival and the need to break loose and experience the full intensity of life unbound.

I want to experience this vital energy again. I want to know the free-spirited wildness of my unrepressed desires realizing themselves in festive play. I want to smash down every wall that stands between me and the intense, passionate life of untamed freedom that I want. The sum of these walls is everything we call civilization, everything that comes between us and the direct, participatory experience of the wild world. Around us has grown a web of domination, a web of mediation that limits our experience, defining the boundaries of acceptable reality, creating our lives within the limits of the processes of production and consumption. Domesticating authority takes many forms, some of which are difficult to recognize. Government, capital, and religion are

An Andulusian peasant defiles a religious statue

some of the more obvious faces of authority. But technology, work, language with its conceptual limits, the ingrained habits of etiquette and propriety -- these too are domesticating authorities which transform us from wild playful unruly animals into tamed, bored, unhappy producers and consumers. These things work in us insidiously, limiting our imaginations, usurping our desires, suppressing our instincts, denying the significance and often even the reality of our lived experience. And it is the world created by these authorities, the civilized world, in which we live. If my dream of a life filled with intense pleasure and wild adventure is to be realized, the world must be radically transformed, civilization must fall before expanding wilderness, authority must fall before the energy of our wild freedom. There must be -- for want of a better word -- a revolution.

But a revolution that can break down civilization and restore the vital energy of untamed desire cannot be like any revolution of the past. All revolutions to date have been centered around power, its use and redistribution. They have not sought to eradicate the social institutions that domesticate; at best they have only sought to eradicate the power relations within those institutions. So revolutionaries of the past have aimed their attacks at the centers of power seeking to overthrow it. Focussed on power, they were blind to the insidious forces of domination that encompass our daily existence -- and so, when successful at overthrowing the powers that be, they ended up re-creating them. To avoid this, we need to focus not on power, but on our desire to go wild, to experience life to the full, to know intense pleasure and wild adventure. As we attempt to realize this desire, we confront the real forces of domination, the forces that we face every moment of every day. These forces have no single center that can be overthrown. They are a web that binds us. So rather than trying to overthrow the powers that be, we want to undermine domination as we confront it every day, helping the already collapsing civilization to break down more quickly -- and as it falls, the centers of power will fall with it. Previous revolutionaries have only explored the well-mapped territories of power. I want to explore and adventure in the unmapped, and unmappable, territories of wild freedom. The revolution that can create the world I want has to be a feral revolution.

There can be no programs or organizations for feral revolution, because wildness cannot spring from a program or organization. Wildness springs from the freeing of our instincts and desires, from the spontaneous expression of our passions. Each of us has experienced the processes of domestication, and this experience can give us the knowledge we need to undermine civilization and transform our lives. Our distrust of our own experience is probably what keeps us from rebelling as freely and actively as we'd like. We're afraid of fucking up, we're afraid of our own ignorance. But this distrust and fear have been instilled in us by authority. It keeps us from really growing and learning. It makes us easy targets for any authority that is ready to fill us. To set up "revolutionary" programs is to play on this fear and distrust, to reinforce the need to be told what to do. No attempt to go feral can be successful when based on such programs. We need to learn to trust and act upon our own feelings and experiences, if we are ever to be free.

So I offer no programs. What I will share is some thoughts on ways to explore. Since we have all been domesticated, part of the revolutionary process is a process of personal transformation. We have been conditioned not to trust ourselves, not to feel completely, not to experience life intensely. We have been conditioned to accept the humiliation of work and pay as inescapable, to relate to things as resources to be used, to feel the need to prove ourselves by producing. We have been conditioned to expect disappointment, to see it as normal, not to question it. We have been conditioned to accept the tedium of civilized survival rather than breaking free and really living. We need to explore ways of breaking down this conditioning, of getting as free of our domestication as we can now. Let's try to get so free of this conditioning that it ceases to control us and becomes nothing more than a role we use when necessary for survival in the midst of civilization as we strive to undermine it.

In a very general way, we know what we want. We want to live as wild, free beings in a world of wild, free beings. The humiliation of having to follow rules, of having to sell our lives away to by survival, of seeing our usurped desires transformed into abstractions and images in order to sell us commodities fills us with rage. How long will we put up with this misery? We want to make this world into a place where our desires can be immediately realized, not just sporadically, but normally. We want to re-eroticize our lives. We want to live not in a dead world of resources, but in a living world of free wild lovers. We need to start exploring the extent to which we are capable of living these dreams in the present without isolating ourselves. This will give us a clearer understanding of the domination of civilization over our lives, an understanding which will allow us to fight domestication more intensely and so expand the extent to which we can live wildly.

Attempting to live as wildly as possible now will also help break down our social conditioning. This will spark a wild prankishness in us which will take aim at all that would tame it, undermining civilization and creating new ways of living and sharing with each other. These explorations will expose the limits of civilization's domination and will show its inherent opposition to freedom. We will discover possibilities we have never before imagined -- vast expanses of wild freedom. Projects, ranging from sabotage and pranks that expose or undermine the dominant society to the expansion of wilderness to festivals and orgies and general free sharing, can point to amazing possibilities.

Feral revolution is an adventure. It is the daring exploration of going wild. It takes us into unknown territories for which no maps exist. We can only come to know these territories if we dare to explore them actively. We must dare to destroy whatever destroys our wildness and to act on our instincts and desires. We must dare to trust in ourselves, our experiences, and our passions. Then we will not let ourselves be chained or pinned in. We will not allow ourselves to be tamed. Our feral energy will rip civilization to shreds and create a life of wild freedom and intense pleasure.

Feral Faun

Active Resistance (1998), photo: Susan Simensky-Bietila

DEBATES

In "Anarcha-Feminism, Why the Hyphen?" Kytha Kurin characterizes anarchism as "a continuously created explorative and active response to the immediate and the future." This section features six of the movement's most hotly debated issues.

In Canada the problem of nationalism has been a recurring one, particularly for Francophone anarchists in the province of Quebec. *Démanarchie*'s special issue on the subject from the mid-1990s pits the anti-nationalists of *Démanarchie* against two nationalist apologists associated with Montreal's *Rebelles* journal. There are many lessons here for those who remain enamoured of "national liberation" struggles but have no firsthand experience of the related contradictions. Similarly, the related exchange between the editors of *Reality Now* and *Resistance* concerning degrees of solidarity with authoritarian leftists still resonates today, when Marxists of various stripes are hastily recasting themselves as anarchism's allies in a bid to maintain their radical purchase.

In the early 1980s the bombing campaigns of the Direct Action group and Wimmin's Fire Brigade put the issue of guerrilla warfare front and centre. The ensuing discussion in *Open Road* and *Kick It Over* is important because it addressed not only the motivations for the bombings, but also the consequences for above-ground work. As the Direct Action/Wimmin's Fire Brigade actions suggest, there is a profound synchronicity between radical feminism and anarchism and this too has generated considerable discussion. In "Anarcha-Feminism: Moving Together," Elaine Leeder summarizes how radical feminists have challenged men to recognize sexism and patriarchy within the anarchist movement. Whereas Leeder views feminism and anarchism as separate but complimentary movements, Kytha Kurin argues the ultimate goal is a "living" anarchism qualitatively transformed and broadened by feminist experience. Finally, in "Side-Winding Our Way to Sedition," the editors of *BOA* present a working example of how anarchist-feminists may challenge patriarchy by transforming the very act of writing and reading.

Since the 1960s, American Murray Bookchin has played a leading role in the renewal of the ecological imperative so central to the 19th-century anarchist-communism of Eliseé Reclus and Peter Kropotkin. Bookchin's "Open Letter" in *Open Road*'s special issue, "Lessons of the 70s/Strategies for the 80s," is a classic statement of his position. The reply from Frank Stevens, contributor to the Toronto-based biweekly, *North American Anarchist* (journal of the short-lived Anarchist Communist Federation of North America) presents the other side of the debate. In "The Buffe-ooneries Continue" from *Demolition Derby*, Michael William provides the final word in an exposition on "primitivism" and its numerous critics.

– ALLAN ANTLIFF

Demanarchie 1/2 (1994)

Inventaire des luttes séparatistes à travers le monde

Pays	Territoire	Mouvement	Situation
Afrique du sud	Les frontières revendiquées demeurent floues	Front du Peuple Afrikaner (AVF) et le Parti Conservateur, tous deux de l'extrême droite blanche	Mandela, le nouveau président, a permis la création d'un "Conseil du Volkstaat" qui réfléchirait à la faisabilité du projet.
Azerbaïdjan	Nagorny-Karabakh	-	Depuis février 1988, le conflit a fait plus de 20 000 mort-e-s et l'indépendance fut déclarée en 1992.
Belgique	Flandre	Vlaams Blok (extrême-droite), 7.6% aux dernières élections nationales	Décentralisations à coups de réformes constitutionnelles, la dernière en date, le 29 septembre 1992, instaura carrément le fédéralisme.
Bosnie-Herzégovine	"République serbe de Bosnie" (70% du pays)	Parti Démocratique Serbe	Les grandes puissances tentent d'imposer un plan de partage du pays en une fédération de trois républiques ethniques.
Brésil	"République indépendante des pampas" (qui regroupe les états de Parana, Santa Catarina et Rio Grande do Sul)	-	Le séparatisme étant illégal, les autorités ont emprisonné les dirigeants du mouvement.
Canada	Québec	PQ, Nouveau Parti Démocratique (NPD-Québec)	Le PQ doit tenir un référendum en 1995.
	"Ganienké" (9 millions d'acres regroupant la vallée du St-Laurent, l'est de l'Ontario et les 3/4 de l'état de New York	Warriors Society	Les Mohawks cherchent l'indépendance en essayant d'obtenir la reconnaissance de droits ancestraux par la négociation ou la confrontation.
Chine	Xinjang	groupes musulmans clandestins	-
	Tibet	mouvement dirigé par des moines bouddhistes	Le chef spirituel et politique des Tibétain-e-s, le Dalaï Lama, modère ses revendications, alors que la Chine refuse de négocier.
Chypre	"République turque de Chypre du Nord" (30% du pays)	-	Sécession "de fait" depuis 1974, proclamation en 1983, appuyée par 36 000 soldat-e-s turcs. Négociations dans l'impasse.
Croatie	"République serbe de Krajina" (1/3 du pays)	-	Les affrontements entre serbes et croates de l'été 1991 ont abouti à un statu quo politique et une accalmie militaire.

démanarchie vol 1 no 2 page 12

Demanarche I/2 (1994)

Espagne	Pays Basque	Herri Batasuna (parti indépendantiste basque); Euskadi ta Askatasuna (ETA, groupe armé)	Malgré l'arrestation de son leader, "Pakito", le 29 mars 1992, l'ETA continue sa guérilla urbaine vieille de 25 ans.
	Catalogne	Esquerra Republicana de Catalunya	-
France	Corse	Front National de Libération de la Corse (FNLC, groupe armé)	Annonce de la fin de la trêve par le FNLC le 17 février 1994.
	Bretagne	Armée Révolutionnaire de Bretagne (ARB)	-
	Nouvelle-Calédonie	Front de Libération National Kanak et Socialiste (FLNKS)	Signés en 1988, les accords de Matignon suscitent des mécontentements du côté kanak.
Géorgie	Abkhazie	-	Proclamation de la souveraineté en juillet 1990, qui vira au carnage en août 1992. Fragile cessez-le-feu depuis le 4 avril 1994.
	Ossétie du sud	-	Revendication, par le Congrès du peuple ossète, de la réunification avec l'Ossétie du nord (Russie) le 13 décembre 1991. Cette dernière semble réticente.
Grande Bretagne	Irlande du nord	Sinn Fein (12,5% aux élections municipales de 1989), Irish Republican Army (IRA), Irish National Liberation Army (INLA)	La guerre civile qui a fait 3200 mort-e-s depuis 25 ans a connu une trêve, annoncée par le Sinn Fein le 1er septembre 1994.
	Écosse	Parti National Écossais (SNP)	Trois députés du SNP aux dernières élections générales.
Inde	Assam	Front uni de libération de l'Assam	-
	Pendjab	mouvement Khalistam	Pacification et restauration du processus démocratique.
	Cachemire	Front de Libération du Jammu et Cachemire (JKLF); Hizbul Mujahedin; Hezb-Moudjahidin (favorable à l'intégration au Pakistan)	Disputé entre l'Inde et le Pakistan depuis 47 ans, le conflit a fait 17 000 mort-e-s lors des quatre dernières années.
Indonésie		Gerakan Aceh Merdeka (mouvement pour l'indépendance d'Aceh, réclame un état islamique)	La lutte, qui débuta dans les années '70, se bute à l'armée indonésienne qui, en 1990, rasa des villages et tua 3000 personnes.
	Timor-Oriental	Front Révolutionnaire pour l'Indépendance du Timor-Oriental (FRETILIN- 600 à 800 combattant-e-s); Conseil National de Résistance Maubère	L'arrestation d'un chef historique de la lutte, Xanana Gusmao, n'a pas arrêté la lutte.
	Irian-Jaya	Organisation pour une Papouasie Indépendante (OPM-modeste guérilla peu hiérarchisée apparue en 1965)	Intégrée à l'Indonésie depuis 1963, l'armée y tua des dizaines de milliers de personnes.
Israël	Palestine (Cisjordanie et Bande de Gaza)	Front Démocratique de Libération de la Palestine (FDLP); Front Populaire de Libération de la Palestine (FPLP); Hamas (islamiste)	L'Organisation de la Libération de la Palestine (OLP) a reconnu l'état israélien le 13 septembre 1993. Le 4 mai 1994, un accord est signé, garantissant une modeste autonomie pour Gaza et Jéricho.
Maroc	"République arabe sahraouie démocratique" ou Sahara Occidental	Front POLISARIO (Front Populaire pour la Libération de Saguia al-Hamra et de Rio de Oro- 10 000 combattant-e-s)	Le 16 février 1976, le Maroc envahit tandis que le Front proclame l'indépendance. 15 000 mort-e-s plus tard, le Maroc contrôle 80% du territoire, alors que l'ONU tente sans succès d'organiser un référendum.

Inventaire des luttes séparatistes à travers le monde, suite et fin

Moldavie	Transdniestrie (12% du territoire)	l'ex-14e Armée Soviétique et quelques kozaques	Indépendance proclamée le 2 septembre 1990 suivie d'un conflit armé, puis d'un accord de paix signé le 21 juillet 1992.
Papouasie Nouvelle-Guinée	île de Bougainville	Bougainville Republican Army (BRA)	Déclaration de sécession en mai 1989. La Papouasie a recours à des mercenaires et des conseillers militaires australiens dans le conflit.
Philippines		Moro National Liberation Front (MNLF- 20 000 combattants islamiques); Moro Independance Liberation Front (MILF)	Pourparlers entre le gouvernement et le MNLF. Le groupe fondamentaliste Abou Sayyaf s'oppose à ces discussions.
Russie	Tchétchénie		Indépendance proclamée fin 1991. Des mercenaires tentent de renverser le président séparatiste.
Sénégal	Casamance (1/7 du pays)	Mouvement des Forces Démocratiques de Casamance (MFDC- doté d'une branche militaire depuis 1985)	Un fragile cessez-le-feu tient depuis juillet 1993.
Somalie	Somaliland	Mouvement National Somalien (MNS) du clan issak	Proclamation d'indépendance le 17 mai 1991. Depuis, Somaliland est géré comme un pays souverain.
Sri Lanka	péninsule de Jaffna	Tigres de Libération de l'Eelam Tamoul (LTTE- groupe armé)	Des pourparlers de paix vont commencer bientôt.
Tanzanie	île Zanzibar	mouvement Kamahuru	-
Turquie	Anatolie du sudest ou Kurdistan	Partiya Karkerên Kurdistan (PKK), Parti des travailleurs du Kurdistan, ARGK (Front national de libération du Kurdistan - branche armée du PKK)	La lutte séparatiste, amorcée le 15 août 1984, a fait jusqu'alors environ 6500 mort-e-s au Kurdistan, où règne l'état d'urgence depuis 1987.
Ukraine	Crimée	nationalistes russes	Le parlement fit sa déclaration d'indépendance le 5 mai. Son président, Iouri Mechkov, semble avoir renoncé à tenir un référendum sur la question.
USA	Porto-Rico	Parti Indépendantiste Portoricain (PIP)	Le PIP surpasse difficilement les 5% lors des élections.
Yougoslavie	Kosovo	Ligue Démocratique du Kosovo	Référendum sur l'indépendance le 26 septembre 1991 avec 99% d'approbation.
Zaïre	"République du Sandjak"	Parti de l'Action Démocratique du Sandjak	Souveraineté proclamée le 27 octobre 1991.
	Shaba		Proclamation de l'"autonomie totale" par le gouverneur provincial le 14 décembre 1993.

Demanarchie I/2 (1994)

L'état-nation victime de sa popularité

Cet inventaire, qui n'a pas pantoute la prétention d'être complet, est une tentative d'apporter d'autres éléments dans l'incontournable, malheureusement, débat sur le nationalisme. Pour ce faire, une question se pose: peut-on encore dire que les luttes de libération nationale sont progressistes? Parce qu'appuyer le principe du droit des peuples à l'autodétermination, sur la base d'une oppression de son identité, signifie aujourd'hui de s'exposer à de multiples contradictions. Il n'est pas rare de voir un peuple, lorsque guidé par des nationalistes revanchard-e-s, en écraser un autre au nom de sa libération à lui. Ainsi, pour certain-e-s nationalistes serbes de Bosnie, la logique de l'autodétermination passe par l'éviction, le viol et le massacre de populations musulmanes et croates. Reformulons la question: peut-on appuyer les séparatistes du Front du peuple afrikaner et du Vlaams Blok, deux partis d'extrême-droite, et celles du PKK et du FLNKS, deux organisations d'extrême-gauche, et aller faire dodo avec un sentiment de cohérence politique???

Soutenir aveuglément, ou sans regard critique, le principe de l'autodétermination nationale, c'est oublier de différencier le nationalisme de gauche, qui est anti-impérialiste et anti-colonialiste, et le nationalisme de droite, chauvin et chiant. Non satisfait-e-s de participer à la fabrication d'une identité nationale, les politichiens et politichiennes vont jusqu'à créer la menace de l'extinction de cette identité, fournissant l'occasion ainsi de resserrer les rangs d'une population enrégimentée par des consensus bidons. D'un autre côté, quand le peuple est soumis au génocide, comme c'est le cas au Timor oriental, où l'armée indonésienne assassina un tiers de la population lors des six premières années d'occupation, on peut difficilement parler d'une oppression imaginaire.

Il est capital de prendre position dans ce débat, non seulement à cause que notre "Belle Province" (enfin, ça dépend des goûts) est un terrain où s'exerce ce type de lutte, souvent au détriment de la question sociale, mais aussi parce qu'il est plutôt probable de voir s'allonger la liste des pays touchés par les luttes séparatistes au cours des prochaines années.

D'une part, la montée des inquiétudes personnelles et de l'insécurité collective fait d'un climat social en pourrissement une opportunité propice à l'exacerbation de la psychose identitaire. La mondialisation de l'économie, dans un cadre où les gros bouffent les petits, ouvre la porte à toutes sortes de replis craintifs de la part de minorités qui font de moins en moins le poids: "réveils identitaires" en réaction à la diffusion mondiale d'une culture de masse uniformisante. Bien que pas mal de gens diront s'y identifier avec émotion, la culture c'est une industrie, avec un marché intérieur, et un marché extérieur si le "produit" est exportable, le tout soumis aux lois de la compétition sauvage. La souveraineté ou l'autonomie que réclament dans cette juridiction plusieurs minorités représente davantage un enjeu économique plutôt qu'un enjeu du style "sauver l'âme du peuple".

D'autre part, l'aggravation de la crise de confiance entre la classe politique et le peuple contraint les élu-e-s à modifier les liens qu'elles et ils ont avec les gens: "Vous n'aimez peut-être pas mon programme, mais moi au moins je suis de la même ethnie que vous". L'ethnicisation du vote provoque des situations politiques de rupture, dans la mesure où les porte-étendards du nationalisme limitent leur mandat à la défense des intérêts de leurs prétendu-e-s semblables. Et, selon les tempéraments et la valeur de ce qui est en jeu, le bon peuple deviendra soit spectateur d'un compromis réconciliateur, soit témoin d'une surenchère dont l'aboutissement sera la sécession.

Ce sont ces types de facteurs qui ont su favoriser la création de 23 nouveaux états dans le monde depuis 1991. Sur le continent européen, on compte 14 200 km de frontières qui se sont additionnés aux 26 000 km qui existaient déjà avant 1989. La popularité du phénomène peut s'expliquer aussi par le fait que le séparatisme semble se transmettre aussi aisément qu'une fièvre contagieuse. C'est dans les nouvelles républiques qui ne disposent pas d'une population ethniquement homogène que l'intégrité du territoire est le plus en péril. On a qu'à penser à la Géorgie, avec ses séparatistes abkhazes et ossètes, ou à la Moldavie, avec ses sécessionnistes russes et gagaouzes, qui, à peine venaient-elles tout juste de faire voler en éclats l'Union Soviétique que déjà leur minorités respectives s'organisaient afin de leur faire connaître le même sort.

suite au verso

FORMIDABLE!
LA POPULATION S'EST MOBILISÉE POUR EXIGER UN PETIT SA-CRIFICE DE LA PART DE L'HONORABLE JEAN CHRÉTIEN POUR SAUVER LE PAYS!!!

Si c'est bon pour moé, c'est bon aussi pour le Canada

SI T'APPUIE, ON T'APPUIS

ADMIRONS SON COURAGE PATRIOTIQUE

Démanarchie 1/2 (1994)

L'État-nation...

suite de la page précédente

À première vue, si l'option souverainiste remporte l'éventuel référendum, le Québec pourrait être exposé à ce genre d'ennuis, grâce aux bons offices de Keith Henderson, président du parti Égalité, qui propose de faire annexer l'ouest de Montréal au Canada, des Cris du nord, qui s'intéressent à faire un référendum sur la sécession du Nouveau-Québec, sans oublier les Mohawks, qui voyagent déjà avec leurs propres passeports. Il s'agit de s'assurer à savoir si ce sont des projets sérieux, ou si ce n'est qu'une autre campagne de bluffage politique (après tout, il y a bien eu des ministres conservateurs pour prédirent la libanisation du pays en cas d'un rejet des accords de Charlottetown).

Ghassan Salamé écrivait dans "L'État du Monde 1993" qu'"à l'inquiétante facilité de se constituer un état, l'État se dévalue; le concept est victime de sa popularité", dans la mesure où la souveraineté juridique dont les états sont censés bénéficier se trouve régulièrement bafouée avec la plus grande banalité: "droit d'ingérence" (Irak, Somalie, Rwanda, etc.), gestion des finances publiques par des institutions bancaires internationales (FMI, Banque Mondiale), etc. Enfin, de quelle espèce de souveraineté-de-mes-deux est supposé jouir un état comme le Vanuatu, en Océanie, qui mesure 12 189 km2 et a une population de 154 000 personnes??? C'est un cas extrême, mais l'existence d'états aussi minuscules inspire bien des luttes sécessionnistes pour des nationalistes en mal d'état qui y voient là un riche enseignement et en tirent la leçon qu'on peut fonder une "république indépendante" dans un carré de sable et disposer d'un siège à l'ONU.

Pour saisir comment on en arrive là, il faut comprendre le rôle que joue le "droit international", cette fiction pour juristes fantaisistes. En théorie, un état devient indépendant quand il est reconnu comme tel par les autres états, qui légalisent son existence et l'accueillent dans la grande famille incestueuse qu'est la "communauté internationale". Sauf que lorsque la réalité confond les rêveries démocratiques des conventions internationales, enfreintes quotidiennement, on s'aperçoit, par exemple, qu'étant donné que la "République arabe sahraouie démocratique" est déjà reconnue par 75 autres états, elle ne devrait pas subir l'occupation par le Maroc.

Ce que cache cette sinistre farce du "droit international", c'est que ceux et celles qui tirent les ficelles du grand "Muppet Show" international, ce sont les pdg d'entreprises multinationales et autres mégalomaniaques. Ce que cachent les émouvants discours sur "l'unité nationale" des chef-fe-s d'état, c'est la peur des classes dominantes de perdre le contrôle des ressources naturelles et des industries que peut contenir un territoire en proie aux aspirations séparatistes. Et ce que cachent les luttes de libération nationale, ce sont les intentions d'une clique locale de s'emparer de ces mêmes ressources et industries afin de mieux pouvoir diriger, exploiter et martyriser la population, en toute SOUVERAINETÉ.

Il n'y a pas de contradiction à soutenir la lutte d'un peuple soumis à l'extermination massive ou sélective tout en clamant haut et fort qu'aucun peuple ne sera souverain tant et aussi longtemps que l'état sera souverain. Aspirer à détruire un état pour en construire un autre relève d'une monstrueuse absurdité qui, si elle n'avait pas tant d'aspects tragiques, se limiterait à n'être qu'une blague de mauvais goût.

Popov

LA SOUVERAINETÉ DU QUÉBEC ... OÙ EST-CE QU'ELLE EST CENSÉ NOUS MENER? FAITES LE LABYRINTHE ENTRÉE VOUS N'AUREZ PLUS LE CHOIX DE COMPRENDRE

Culture, identité et questions nationales

L'existence même des réalités nationales est remise en cause dans certains milieux anarchistes montréalais. Ces derniers semblent être incapables de se distancier de la doctrine anarchiste classique niant toute ouverture à la compréhension des phénomènes nationaux. Certaines personnes poussent même leur résistance à toute compréhension globale des groupes humains en niant la notion de culture. Les objectifs de ce texte sont de tenter de donner une définition à la notion de culture, à celle de nation, ainsi que de faire la différenciation entre le concept d'État-Nation et de nation. Ces éléments devraient me permettre d'émettre des éléments de réflexion sur ce que devrait être une intervention libertaire face aux questions nationales dans les pays dits avancés1. J'espère que ce texte permettra de mettre en perspective ces notions et d'ouvrir le débat.

Est culture, les éléments de référence qui nous aident à déterminer ce qui est bon à manger, à tisser des liens d'amitié et/ou amoureux, à communiquer nos idées et nos sentiments, etc. C'est à dire l'ensemble des archétypes, codes et rituels que nous avons intériorisés. Ces éléments sont acquis. Ils ne sont pas programmés dans notre code génétique. Du langage, en passant par le fait de manger des toasts le matin, tous ces éléments sont des constructions de l'activité humaine déterminés par plusieurs facteurs. Ces constructions issues d'un processus évolutif ne représentent pas en soi des éléments positifs ou négatifs. Ce ne sont que des outils. Outils de l'animal humain pour être capable d'interpréter les rapports avec la nature, la mort, le mystère, la technique, les oppressions, etc. Cet outillage intellectuel et émotif se construit dans des contextes spécifiques. Ce qui permet d'expliquer l'originalité des réponses culturelles à des défis universels. Par exemple, tous les êtres humains cherchent à communiquer leurs idées et leurs sentiments. Pourtant, il existe des milliers de codes (langage) pour témoigner de nos vécus.

La maudite nation

Ces éléments d'interprétation, de médiation du réel, naissent dans des espaces géographiques précis. Ils sont parfois issus des transferts de population. Dans d'autres cas, sont influencés par l'organisation des rapports de domination, etc. Il suffit qu'un ensemble d'éléments de référence se développent, soient partagés et reconnu par une population pour se retrouver devant un phénomène national. Le concept de nation ressemblant en quelque sorte à une grille d'analyse diffuse de l'existence. Cette construction facilite la compréhension commune des événements touchant une communauté.

La nation est une construction sociale. Elle n'a rien de naturel. Elle est en (dé)construction permanente, les éléments de référence «nationaux» n'étant pas des absolus. Ils ne sont que des points de repère. Un individu ne les intègre pas mécaniquement. Toute personne construit un rapport plus ou moins critique face aux codes, rituels et archétypes qui lui sont offerts. Si ces derniers sont incapables d'offrir une interprétation satisfaisante du vécu de l'individu, celui-ci rejettera plus ou moins les éléments inutiles. Il puisera au sein de ses références culturelles des éléments nouveaux plus aptes à répondre à sa réalité. L'introduction rapide de nouveaux modes de production, de nouvelles formes de domination peuvent rendre non fonctionnelles les références culturelles d'une communauté. Ce manque de points de repère se manifeste par diverses formes d'aliénation, ainsi que par une incapacité temporaire (parfois permanente) à trouver les réponses adéquates aux changements des rapports des humains entre eux et face au reste du réel. Les populations dites autochtones vivent parfois des phénomènes de cette sorte.

L'État et les nations

La victoire du capitalisme sur l'absolutisme et le féodalisme a entraîné la création de nouveaux modes de contrôle des populations, dont l'État-Nation. L'ensemble des individus habitant un territoire étaient appelé-e-s à se reconnaître dans l'État et ses institutions. L'État «bourgeois» est devenu le gestionnaire des éléments culturels unissant les gens. L'école, le service militaire, les médias servent d'engins de propagande des «nouveaux» codes, rituels et archétypes régissant les rapports humains. L'État et ses institutions définissent la langue, la bonne culture, imposent à l'école les valeurs bourgeoises etc. Bref, l'État se substitue au concept d'espace national. Il devient la nation, ou plutôt l'expression de l'aliénation des individus enfermés dans ses frontières.

À titre d'exemple, la France à fait disparaître, à toutes fins pratiques, les espaces nationaux occitan, basque, breton, etc. Malgré certaines résistances à la standardisation, dans ces espaces nationaux, il y a peu de chances de survie de ces collectivités. Encore moins, qu'elles restent génératrices d'une culture originale sur des bases autonomes, le processus d'ethnocide s'étant réalisé en à peine plus d'un siècle.

Ce processus de standardisation répond à plusieurs besoins des appareils de domination (l'État, le marché). Il permet d'encadrer le développement de l'imaginaire des gens, par la diffusion d'éléments culturels définis par les expert-e-s en marketing et les technocrates de l'État. Il facilite la vente de modèles culturels (actuellement l'American way of life). Il renforce l'aliénation des individus. Ces dernier-e-s, dénué-e-s d'éléments de référence, se tournent vers l'État ou le marché pour leur indiquer la façon de vivre. Les liens entre les individus, les communautés et le reste de l'environnement sont de moins en moins forgés par l'interaction «libre» de ces composantes. Ils sont de plus en plus définis à l'extérieur de la société civile pour répondre à des logiques de domination et d'aliénation.

Et les libertaires

Dans la période actuelle, la tendance générale est à la standardisation, à la programmation des besoins et des imaginaires. Tout espace de résistance à ces phénomènes peut être intéressant, si il comporte des potentialités libératrices. Notre objectif est la destruction du capitalisme et la construction d'une société non autoritaire. Les luttes de libérations nationales, dans les pays développés, peuvent tactiquement rejoindre en tout ou en partie nos objectifs, quand elles s'opposent aux tendances à l'uniformisation et à la programmation des vies humaines. Elles peuvent potentiellement dégager des éléments d'alternative à la programmation des besoins et de l'imaginaire. Elles peuvent nous permettre des alliances tactiques pour faire avancer certains de nos points de vue, etc. C'est à l'évaluation des potentialités libératrices ou aliénantes que nous devons évaluer la nature de notre travail sur les questions nationales.

Mario Tardif

membre du collectif REBELLES

1- Dans certains pays dits en développement, le support aux luttes de libération nationale constitue un simple devoir d'anti-impérialisme, malgré toutes les limites de ce type de luttes.

Demanarchie 1/2 (1994)

On donne not' langue

La langue c't'une affaire q'le monde plus "nationaliss" veut protéger. Ça veut pas dire q'les autres veulent la changer, par zemple.

Démanarchie est allé voir du monde qi parlent d'autres langues pou voir si sé pareil comme au Kébèk ou si l'monde d'ici sont surtout paranos. M. Suleyman, de "l'Association culturelle des Kurdes du Québec" trouve, lui, q'la langue est une part pas mal importante d'l'identité. Par zemple, pou lui, un-e Kurde, même en parlant une autre langue qeq part, va s'faire reconnaître à cause de son accent. Sé de même qe, dans pays où 'es Kurdes vivent ousq'y sont toutt une minorité, y vont s'faire discriminer. Si on rajoute à çà q'ya pas d'école en kurde, l'monde risq de perdre qeq chose d'leur façon d'être, q'y pense. Pou M. Saleyman, une affaire qi est sûre sé q'la langue sa fait partie d'la culture, mais q'la culture sé plus que çà.

Y faut dire q'si 'à structure d'une langue est pas mal compliqée, ya moins d'monde qi vont avoir l'goût d'l'apprendre. C't'un peu c'qi s'passe ak le Françà dans l'west du Canada. Sé moins facile avec de

On peut manifester peu ben d'autres choses que la langue...

communiqer ak du monde d'ailleurs. Dans l'hongrois, par zemple, eul même mot peut s'écrire 34 façons différentes dépendant ousq'y est dans phrase. Ça vous tenterait-tu d'apprendre de qoi de même? (Imaginez une compagnie japonaise à Montréal qi décide de runner son buro rienq en japonais!) Sé p't'être pou ça q'l'anglais est ben populaire, mais sa marcherait sûrement mieux encore pou l'kréyol (qi s'parle en Haïti) ousq'on conjugue pas les verbes pis q'ya pas d'mot pour "le" ou "la", sauf q'icitte y ont pas ben d'pouvoir.

Les Anglos, eux-autres, pensent plus la langue comme qeq'chose de commode. Y trouvent q'sé rienq un façon d'communiqer. La même chose peut s'dire dans plusieurs langues pis vouloir dire la même affaire. Sauf q'yn'na qi vont croire q'ça veut dire autre chose parsq'on a choisi une autre langue pou l'dire... Après toutt, les langues sont comme l'monde: sont égales mais sont pas mal différentes. Quant t'apprends d'autres langues, tu vas encore dire les mêmes choses, mais pas au même monde, quant on en parle plus, ya moins d'ghettos parsq'eul monde s'comprennent mieux.

DÉBAT SUL NATIONALISME AVORTÉ

Eul collectif de Démanarchie devait faire un débat sul nationalisme en faisant cte numéro-citte. Mais on avait pas eu encore l'temps d'organiser l'débat q'les 2 nationalistes du collectif crissaient leu camp, juste avant 'es élections.

Du monde de Rebelles pis d'ailleurs avaient été invité-e-s à écrire des textes pis à participer au débat à Démanarchie. Juste pendant à mise en page du Démanarchie spécial, les anciens membres du collectif nous ont amené leus lettres de démission. Les lettres vont passer dans l'prochain Démanarchie, yn'n'a pou plusieurs pages.

Comme toutt le reste d'la gang est pas nationaliste, ça servirait pus à grand chose de faire le débat. Y devait servir à c'qe l'monde s'comprenne mieux pis à règler la fameuse qestion qi r'vient toul temps depuis l'début du collectif en janvier. Du monde avait d'mandé q'on les expulse, mais l'idée du débat avait été choisie pou q'y puissent dire leurs idées.

J'souhaite bonne chance à FYJ pis au camarade sans pseudonyme qi faisaient d'la mise en page tous les 2. L'dernier avait pas encore écrit d'article. Personne dans les 2 avait faitt de texte pour le Démanarchie sul nationalisme.

le dernier des Granuliens

Démanarchie I/2 (1994)

au chat!

Vous rmarq'rez q'la langue se r'trouve dans l'triangle de domination culturel: État, culture, médias. Ces 3 "acteurs"-là vont touttt faire pou q'on s'soumette à leus mots pis à leu façon d'dire.

Rgardez les notes aux tests de français q'y font à l'université: la moitié du monde coule. Eul problème est facile: ou ben l'monde parle pas français, ou ben sé trop compliqé. Yn'na qi disent: eul Joual c't'une maladie du français. Y peuvent pas comprendre qe du monde parlent pas comme dans grammaire pasq sé trop rushant. P't'être q'sé la grammaire kié en retard su'l monde, non? Y faudrait pas oublier q'la langue, c't'un moyen d'communication, mais ça peut être aussi un instrument d'pouvoir. Sé l'monde qi contrôlent la langue qi ont cte pouvoir-là.

Les Grec-que-s qi sont venu-e-s vivre icitte dans années 50 ont choisi surtout l'anglais. Sa paraît encore aujourd'hui, mais dans l'temps y ont senti q'y avaient pas ben l'choix: à ce moment-là en français (ou en Joual?) on était pauvre, en anglais on avait plus de pouvoir.

Astheure qe l'PQ est rendu au pouvoir, on peut imaginer q'la "question" d'la langue au Kébèk va r'venir dans touttt les bouches. Comme q'y disait l'gars d'l'asso des Kurdes, la langue c't'un moyen d'libération nationale. Mais comme l'peuple est pus oppressé pasq'y est kébékois, ya pas d'libération nationale à faire de cte bord-là.

Quand l'PQ avait pris l'pouvoir en 76, une des premières affaires q'y a faittt c'tait la loi 101. Vz'avez sûrement r'marqé qe qand l'monde sont occupé-e-s à discuter d'langue pis d'constitution, les vrais problèmes sont oubliés ben vite. (Rapplez-vous entre 87 pis 92, eul Lac Meech, la loi 178, touttt les commissions pis les négos du fédéral, l'référendum...) Qand q'on dit q'qune langue est plus importante q'les autres, sé oublier "l'égalité absolue des langues pis des nations", comme les marxistes disent. Ya sûrement personne kia plus raison q'les autres, mais si qeq'un les empêche de dire keski veulent comme y veulent, q'y mangent d'la marde!

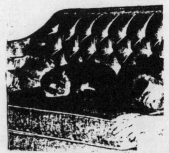

La docteure Zoé Haddad-Renaud. Lui donner vot langue frait avancer la science en motadit...

La gang d'académicien-ne-s qi décident de c'qi est bon ou pas, sé justement ceux-là qi voudraient q'on parle comme elles pis eux, pis qi auraient l'pouvoir su nous-autres. Mais si on les laisse faire en parlant aut-'chose, y vont avoir du pouvoir parsq'on comprend pas tout l'temps. On va-tu laisser l'impérialisme parisien (l'reste d'la France est pas toujours pareil) décider touttt pou nous-autres? La langue est à toulmond, y faut q'personne décide tout seul pou toulmond kesq'on fait avec.

le dernier des Granuliens

DIKSYONÈR DE JOUAL

Cte fois-citte ya pas de dictionnaire de Joual. Comme personne a jamais répondu à qoi sa sert, ben sa l'air qe c'pas utile. Safak si vou comprenez ryin, ben écrivez-nous pis on va vous envoyer eul sens des mots q'vou comprenez pas!

eul gars ki fesè l'diksyonèr de Joual

¡DAMOS NUESTRA LENGUA AL GATO!

La lengua es una cosa que quiere defender la gente más "nacionalista". Pero eso no significa que la quieren cambiar l@s otr@s, en cambio.

Démanarchie se fui a encontrar con gente hablando idiomas diferentes a ver si su situación es similiar de la de Quebec, o si la gente aquí tiene demasiado miedo. Para el señor Suleyman, de la Asociación cultural de l@s kurd@s de Quebec (inmigrantes de Kurdistán), la lengua es una parte muy importante de la identidad. Según él, un-a kurd@, mismo bablando otro idioma, puede ser reconocid@ porqué de su acento. Así, en cualquier país donde la nación kurda es une menoredad, se hacem discriminar. Si se añade que no hay escuela de habla kurdo, tienen el riesgo de perder algo de su manera de ser, cree el señor Saleyman. Es seguro, según él, que el idioma es parte de la cultura, pero ésta es mucho más generosa.

También hay que decir que si la estructura de une lengua es muy complicada, habrá menos gente que querrá aprenderla. Es un poco lo que pasa con el francés en el oeste de Canadá. Es menos fácil comunicarse con gente de otra parte. En húngaro, por ejemplo, se puede escribir la misma palabra en 34 maneras diferentes según su lugar en la frase. ¿Les gustaría aprender algo así? (¡Imaginen una compañía japonesa en Montreal funcionando sólo en japonés!) Quizás ésto es porqué el inglés es tan popular, pero sería mejor con el criollo haitiano, porque no se conjugan los verbos y no existen las palabras "la" y "el". Pero aquí, la comunidad haitiana no tiene mucho poder.

L@s anglófon@s, por su parte, creen más que el idioma es sobre todo algo cómodo. Creen que un idioma es ante todo un medio de comunicación. La misma idea puede ser dicha en todos idiomas y quedarse con su significación. Pero siempre habrá gente creyendo otra cosa, porqué se escojó otro idioma para espresarlo. Finalmente, los idiomas son cómo la gente: diferentes pero iguales. Cuando aprendes otro idioma, puedes decir las mismas cosas pero a otra gente. Cuando un@ habla más idiomas, hay menos ghettos porqué la gente puede comprenderse mejor.

Miren las notas en los testos de francés en la universidad: hay la mitad de l@s estudiantes que no pasan. El problema es fácil: o sea que la gente no habla francés, o sea demasiado complicado espresarse en éste idioma. Hay un@s que dicen: el Joual es una enfermedad del francés. No pueden comprender que haya gente que no hablen cómo en la grammática porqué es demasiado largo. ¿Quizás es la grammática atrazada comparada a nos?

El PQ: ¿hablar sólo francés para tener poder?

Hay que no olvedirse que la lengua es un instrumento de poder. Y es la gente que controla el idioma que tiene el poder. L@s Grec@s que vinieron a vivir aquí en las 50s escogieron sobre todo el inglés. Esto todavía parece hoy, pero en aquella época habían sentido que era la mejor selección. En francés (¿o en Joual?) se pudía vivir sólo pobre, pero en inglés tenían más poder.

Ahora que está el PQ al poder, podemos creer que el sujeto de la lengua en Quebec regresará en todas las bocas. Cómo lo dice el representante kurdo, la lengua es un medio de liberación nacional. Pero, cómo el pueblo no es discriminado porqué es quebeco, no hay más liberación nacional que hacer.

Cuando tuvo el poder el PQ en 76, una de sus primeras acciones fue la ley 101 (francés sola lengua oficial de Quebec). Quizás han visto ustedes que cuando se habla de lengua o de constitución en la ésta sociedad, olvidemos los problemas verdaderos. Por ejemplo, entre 87 y 92, había el acuerdo de la laguna Meech, la ley 178 (bilinguismo sólo al interior de los edificios), las varias comisiones y negociaciones del gobierno federal, el referéndum... Decir que una lengua es más importante que las otras es olverdirse de "la igualdad absoluta de las lenguas y naciones" cómo lo dicen l@s compañer@s marxistas. Seguro que no hay nadie que tiene más razón que l@s otr@s, pero si alguién les impide decir lo que quieren y cómo quieren, ¡que coma mierda!

El grupo de acedémic@s que deciden de lo que es o no es bueno son l@s que querían especialmente que hablemos otro idioma, tendrán poder porqué no entendramos todo lo que hacen. ¿Vamos a dejar el imperialismo parisiano y de Francia decidir todo para nos? El idioma es a todo el mundo, hay que nadie decida sol@ para el pueblo, por el idioma cómo por todo.

El último granuliano

¡Surscríbate a Amor y Rabia!

El colectivo de Démanarchie está organizando un grupo de subscripción al periódico mexicano Amor y Rabia. Es de la federación anarquista revolucionaria Love and Rage / Amor y Rabia. También éste papel necesita dinero para ayudarlo porqué no pudié verder su edición zapatista en la calle...

El número cuestará alrededor de 75 centavos cada ($18 U.S. por diez números en subscripción desde Nueva York, $1.40 cada en la Librería alternativa). Escríbenos para más informaciones:

Démanarchie
C.P. 32100
Montréal
H2L 4Y5

Démanarchie es un colectivo antiautoritario, anticapitalista y antinacionalista. Somos por la ecología social, la autogestión, un mundo sin estados ni países, y el fin del sexismo, racismo, homofobia y otras opresiones y discriminaciones que vive el pueblo. También somos contra la jerarquía y el culto del trabajo y de la productividad. Los fines de Démanarchie son de hacer educación política, irse a un público ancho y dar une alternativa al "mainstream".

A partir del próximo número, Démanarchie será un periódico trilingüe: español, inglés, joual (y/o francés) y quizás criollo. Ustedes pueden enviarnos sus textos en todos estos idiomas, o aún en otros, a

colectivo Démanarchie
apartado postal 32100
Montreal, (Quebec, Canadá
H2L 4Y5

subscripciones disponibles por la misma dirección ($10 por cinco números, todo incluido)

démanarchie vol I no 2 page 20

Demanarchie I/2 (1994)

DEBATES § 231

Québec

QUESTION NATIONALE: «TS'É VEUX DIRE !»

Trop de choses semblent aller de soi dans ce monde voué à l'oubli et à la désinformation. La capacité du doute est la première vertu révolutionnaire, car elle seule permet de ne pas se laisser aller aux belles certitudes et aux principes vides, véritables béquilles du peuple. La critique, voilà ce qui manque à tous ceux et celles qui discourent sur la «question nationale» au Québec (dont la devise est, si je me rappelle bien, «Je me souviens»! Rien que de la prononcer, une envie de vomir ou de rire me prend...) puisque le débat semble tourner très vite à un véritable «crois ou meurs». L'indépendance du Québec règlera-t-elle tous les problèmes sociaux par enchantement? N'est-elle qu'une nouvelle forme de la méchanceté de la bourgeoisie et de l'État, monstre vicieux toujours aux aguets pour mieux nous asservir? On oublie vite que la «question nationale» est une... question, avec aucune réponse certaine et éternelle. Restent quelques banalités de base sur lesquelles il s'agit de revenir.

Le capitalisme est une bien belle machine, mais...

On vit, on produit et on (se) reproduit dans le cadre d'un système social qui est le capitalisme. Ce dernier possède une capacité étonnante (par rapport, du moins, aux systèmes sociaux qui l'ont précédé) d'expansion et de développement. Tout, espace et temps, peut devenir objet du capital, intégré dans la logique marchande. La Terre, les relations amoureuses, les jeux, l'art, la bouffe, le logement et bien d'autres choses sont sans cesse réduites à l'état de marchandises qu'on vend et qu'on achète. Tout tend à s'uniformiser sous la dictature marchande: le Coke que l'on boit à Pékin est le même que celui de Paris. Le marché mondial, tant vanté par les économistes à la solde du capital, réduit sans cesse les singularités et les différences.

Pourtant, au même moment, jamais les traditionalismes et les ghettos ne se seront autant développés. C'est une constante du développement capitaliste, uniformiser le monde tout en élargissant certaines différences sur une base hiérarchique et inégalitaire. On peut prendre comme exemple caricatural de ce développement l'apartheid en Afrique du sud: la division entre les «races», inégalitaire

et hiérarchique (au profit du pouvoir blanc) allait de pair avec la domination capitaliste. Le capital se développe donc inégalement, créant des zones nationales et régionales qui sont laissées de côté.

Le Canada, création artificielle des capitalistes britanniques du siècle dernier, est lui-même le théâtre d'un développement fortement inégal. Formée au départ sur une négation du droit à l'autodétermination des peuples qui vivaient là - autochtones, acadien-ne-s, québécois-es et métis - la fédération canadienne a permis la croissance d'un centre (essentiellement l'Ontario) au dépend de périphéries (Maritimes, territoires autochtones et, dans une certaine mesure, le Québec) toujours plus «sous-développées».

L'ordre capitaliste au Canada se maintient sur ces inégalités économiques qui chevauchent d'autres inégalités. Une de celles-ci, fondamentale, touche les peuples autochtones, premiers habitants du territoire, et complètement dépossédés de tout moyen de contrôle. Il s'agit, non seulement d'une dépossession économique (les réserves autochtones sont des territoires possédant des ressources naturelles intéressantes pour le capital canadien et étatsunien), mais aussi d'une oppression nationale, dépassant le simple domaine de l'économique et touchant aussi le culturel et le politique.

Ces considérations sont aussi valables pour le territoire québécois où une population, «résidu» d'une ancienne colonisation (et donc, dans une certaine mesure, partie prenante de la dépossession des autochtones), constitue une singularité dans l'Amérique du nord anglo-saxonne.

Le capitalisme peut sembler être une machine parfaite, mais il n'en crée pas moins des différences, économiques et culturelles, qui lui sont nécessaires pour son bon fonctionnement mais qui peuvent se retourner contre lui. Je dis bien qui «peuvent», car rien n'est acquis dans ce domaine. La lutte contre l'apartheid prouve que le capital peut dépasser certaines différences qui lui servaient pour en reconstituer d'autres. On passe, en Afrique du sud, d'un capitalisme où les barrières raciales sont remplacées par des barrières économiques, une poignée de patrons «noirs» donnant le change sur

l'intégration du pays alors que la vaste majorité (noire) continue à croupir dans la misère. Le Québec peut connaître (et connaît déjà) un processus similaire où le patronat anglo-saxon serait remplacé par des patrons bien de chez nous.

L'ordre, c'est l'ordre plus le pouvoir

Le bon fonctionnement de l'ordre capitaliste, depuis 1945, est assumé par le gouvernement des États-Unis. C'est encore plus vrai en Amérique du nord, jardin principal du capital étatsunien. Pour Washington, il ne saurait y avoir le moindre bouleversement, de quelque nature que ce soit, dans le paysage politique américain. Le réformisme le plus banal n'est pas admissible (le Chili en 1973, le Guatemala en 1954 ou Cuba en 1960 en savent quelque chose!), car le moindre bouleversement semble porteur, pour l'administration étatsunienne, de ruptures beaucoup plus radicales. Elle n'a d'ailleurs pas tort, car les révolutions sociales prennent leur billet d'entrée généralement par la porte d'en-arrière. Cela veut dire qu'une révolution ne commence jamais comme telle, elle suit un processus d'approfondissement où le peuple, élargissant les portes ainsi ouvertes, commence à pratiquer l'autonomie d'une manière de plus en plus élargie. C'est la peur des dominant-e-s et des possédant-e-s que de voir les réformes, nécessaires pourtant pour l'amélioration de la machine capitaliste (comme dans le cas de la «Révolution -sic!- tranquille», au Québec, en 1960), se retourner contre eux. L'accession du Québec à la souveraineté risquerait, précisément, d'introduire des éléments de déséquilibre dans le système de domination étatsunien en Amérique du nord. C'est d'ailleurs avec persévérance que le Parti québécois s'attache à convaincre Washington qu'il n'en est rien, qu'il contrôle parfaitement le processus. À ce titre, les péquistes n'ont pas tort, car ils ont réussi, dans le cours es années 70, à prendre l'hégémonie du mouvement indépendantiste québécois, marginalisant les ailes radicales. La revendication «socialisme et indépendance» a été mise au placard, au

suite au verso

Demanarchie I/2 (1994)

«Ts'é veux dire!»...

suite de la page précédente

profit d'une vague souveraineté-association social-médiocrate.

Le potentiel de rupture avec le capitalisme du mouvement indépendantiste a été canalisé vers un replâtrage de l'ordre existant. Oubliés l'anti-impérialisme et la solidarité avec tous les dominés de l'Amérique (Puerto-Rico, Cuba, les noirs américains, etc), relégués aux oubliettes le pouvoir populaire et l'autogestion au profit d'un soutien critique au Parti québécois. D'abord la souveraineté et après on verra... Une fois de plus, le mouvement déraille comme dans le cas de la plupart des luttes de libération nationale: Algérie, Cuba, Angola et Mozambique, Afrique du sud, etc.

Alors, Kaputt l'indépendance du Québec? Pas encore, car la revendication est toujours présente même si elle habillée par des vêtements nationaleux et capitalistes. L'exigence d'autonomie nationale est un droit premier dans la construction d'un monde fondé sur la plus large autonomie individuelle et collective. Le refus de prendre en considération la demande d'autodétermination (le droit de choisir sa propre route en tant que peuple, communauté culturelle), c'est déjà refuser toute autonomie. Ce qu'il faut considérer, c'est que cette autonomie nationale (l'indépendance) ne doit pas se faire au détriment des autres nationalités et groupes opprimés. Seule la solidarité, valeur de base du socialisme, peut organiser les rapports entre communautés nationales sur une base égalitaire. Si on considère que notre but est une humanité capable de se prendre en charge, sans passer par le marché ou l'État pour échanger et communiquer, il faut aussi se rendre compte que cette humanité ne sera pas uniforme (le mot veut tout dire si on se rappelle ce qu'est un uniforme dans l'armée), elle contiendra des différences. Les nationalités actuelles, les différences culturelles sont une base (et seulement une base...) de la différenciation humaine. Elles sont une richesse car elles permettent le contact, l'échange et la communication. Le «world beat», goulasch musicale mise en boite par les multinationales du disque, exprime bien, d'une manière tordue, cette réalité: seule les différences permettent de progresser.

Alors, l'indépendance du Québec serait un moyen d'aller vers un peu plus de liberté? Non, si les choses continuent comme maintenant, car cela ne saurait déboucher que sur une affirmation nationaliste, excluant l'Autre et la différence. Il s'agit de redonner un contenu socialiste à cette revendication, à faire de l'ordre un ordre moins le pouvoir. Cependant, rendu ici, c'est encore une question et pas une réponse. À nous d'y répondre collectivement.

Christian Brouillard

La dégueulasserie du mois...

Cette fois-ci, pour la dégueulasserie du mois, nous avons choisi de taper sur les pseudo-anarchistes qui se présentent aux élections. Au niveau municipal, c'est une véritable plaie. Mentionnons entre autres: Marcel Sévigny, qui disait à l'hebdo VOIR qu'il était anarchiste et comptait changer le système de l'intérieur, Jean-Guy Aubé, un membre du collectif REBELLES, qui se présente pour la CDMÉ (un parti qui a rien compris à Bookchin) et Dimitri Roussopoulos des éditions Black Rose Books, un mec qui se dit anarchiste et qui trippe lui aussi sur Bookchin.

Démanarchie hait touttt les candidat-e-s aux élections. Mais on devient méchant-e-s quand y a des twits qui se présentent sous les bannières de l'anarchie. Cette belle gagne de zoufs représentent, avec leurs complices sociaux-démocrates jaunes, l'illusion que le capitalisme peut être réformé de l'intérieur. Contre les réformes bourgeoises, vive la révolution! Protestons en coeur contre cette cochonnerie qu'est le réformisme! Quant aux personnes si haut mentionnées, si elles ont choisi leur camp, celui de la collaboration, nous avons choisi le nôtre, celui de la révolte.

C'est absolument dégueulasse!

démanarchie vol 1 no 2 page 22

THE NATIONALISM DEBATE
Démanarchie, AUTUMN 1994

BACKGROUND: *Since the 1970s politics in the province of Quebec has been dominated by the separatist Parti Québéçois (PQ), a political party that claims to represent the interests of the province's majority French-speaking Québéçois population. The independence movement was preceded by the so-called "quiet revolution" of the 1960s, when reformers successfully challenged the cultural domination of Catholicism in Quebec and began questioning the Canadian political status quo. Independence for Quebec emerged as a political movement in the late 1960s with the founding of the PQ. The PQ platform states that separation must first be approved by a majority vote in a provincial referendum. Once the PQ has this mandate, it will negotiate an economic association with Canada ("sovereignty association") to ensure Quebec avoids economic chaos during the transition to statehood.*

Since coming to power in 1976 the PQ have lost two independence referendums, the first in 1980 and the second in 1995. In the late 1980s the PQ was a crucial backer of the path-breaking "Free Trade" agreement (the model for neo-liberal trade agreements) between the United States and Canada, implemented in 1989. This was followed in 1992 by the signing of an expanded North American Free Trade Agreement linking the economies of Mexico, the United States and Canada. Through these agreements the PQ sought to weaken Quebec's economic ties to the rest of Canada. In 2001 negotiations for a Free Trade Agreement for the Americas got underway in Quebec City, again with the full backing of the PQ. In 2003 the PQ were defeated in a general election by the federalist Quebec Liberal Party.

The debate opens with a satirical cartoon, "Are You a Nation?" The cartoon attacks the bureaucratic initiatives of state representatives to construct a homogenized concept of the "people" and the role of consumer marketing and media manipulation in propagating the idea of a "nation." In sum, nationalism is not in opposition to capitalism – it is perfectly amenable to it. This is followed by a chart of "Separatist Battles Throughout the World" – detailing the aims and territorial disputes of nationalist movements in the modern era.

identity at the expense of others, as in Bosnia, where "ethnic cleansing" ran rampant during the Yugoslavian civil war. There are also political divisions within nationalist movements that undermine progressivism. "Nationalism of the left, which is anti-imperialist and anti-colonialist," for example, can and does coexist with "right-wing chauvinist nationalism." And opportunistic politicians routinely appeal to both the right and left when calling for the defense of "the nation."

In the 1990s the globalization of capitalism, which threatens to create a uniform mass culture, has led separatists to put the defense of culture high on their agendas, ie; presenting sovereignty as the means of retaining control over culture and thus saving "the soul of the people." In this rhetoric, differences between the "political class" with a vested interest in the state and the "common people" without power are papered over in the name of shared ethnicity: "ethnic votes" are created that subordinate working-class interests to the "greater good" of national solidarity.

The renewal of nationalism has led to the creation of twenty-three new states since 1991; and within these ethnic-based states – Georgia, for example – sub-separatist groups have emerged due to the lack of a single homogenous "ethnic" identity within the new territories. Quebec nationalism does not escape this particular contradiction: for example, the Partie Égalitè (a pro-Canada political organization) has threatened to annex west Montreal (a predominantly English-language area) to Canada if Quebec separates; the First Nations in the north have also threatened to separate, as have the Mohawks in the south.

In his article, "State of the World – 1993," Ghassan Salamè has pointed out that the recent proliferation of "nations" has only intensified the exploitation of the planet under the aegises of the International Monetary Fund and the World Bank. Popov observes that, indeed, nationalist movements are often manipulated by business elites desiring to gain control of resources and industries for their own ends. And capitalists welcome the creation of more small states because they are incapable of withstanding globalization. This is the penultimate contradiction of the current wave of nationalism: "the desire to destroy a state in order to construct another state" only furthers capitalist exploitation.

"The Nation State – Victim of its Own Popularity" by Alexandre Popov of Démanarchie

Popov begins with an important question: "Can we still say that battles for national liberation are progressive?" He argues that they aren't: the principal of a people's right to self-determination as a means of ending oppression is fraught with "multiple contradictions." For example, nationalists routinely assert the defense of their own

"Culture Identity and National Questions" by Mario Tardiff of the Rebelles *collective*

Tardiff begins by criticizing "certain Montreal anarchist groups" for being incapable of parting from "the classical anarchist doctrine" of anti-nationalism and its related denial of the importance of "the notion of culture." The aim of Tardiff's essay is to provide a definition of culture and the nation that differentiates between the concept of "nation-state" and "nation."

"Culture" is defined as a composition of interiorized social codes and rituals that are acquired, not genetically encoded. Language is a key mechanism in the construction of social behaviour, and therefore of culture, which evolves over time. National cultures are generated in particular geographic spaces, subject in some cases to the transferral of populations or encounters with other culture groups (ie; one culture may become subordinate to another). The nation is constituted out of these complexities – "culture" therefore, is not genetically determined and the concept of nationhood is dynamic and undergoing constant revision. The elements in question making up the nation include culture itself and reactions to "new modes of production" as well as "new forms of domination." In some instances pressures result in an impasse in the guise of various forms of alienation or a temporary inability to find adequate responses to changing relations both within the cultural group or relations with other national entities.

The victory of capitalism over absolutism and feudalism resulted in the creation of new modes of population control, such as the nation-state. A group of people living in a territory were now expected to identify with "the state and its institutions." The "bourgeois" state became synonymous with the "cultural elements" that served to unify the people: school, military service and the media all served as propaganda engines propagating new "codes, rituals, and archetypes." The state and its institutions defined language and "good" culture. It imposed bourgeois values through school, etc.

In sum, the state substituted itself for the concept of "national space" and this led to the "alienation" of many nations circumscribed within a given state's boundaries. In France, for example, Basque, Breton and Occitan "national spaces" were "historic spaces" that had no chance of survival in the midst of the "bourgeois nation-state" – this led to the diminishment of their cultural autonomy, which resulted in "ethnocide."

Domination of the state and marketplace create "standardization": culture is fabricated to mirror techno-cratic and mercantile interests. A good example is the selling of a world culture that is actually "the American way of life." This is the exemplar of the state-capitalist conspiracy against real culture forged from the interaction of local individuals in a community.

In the present era the tendency is towards the standardization of "needs and dreams." All forms of resistance to standardization are of interest if they contain "liberatory potentialities." "Our objective," states Tardiff, "is the destruction of capitalism and the construction of a non-authoritarian society." From this perspective "battles of national liberation in developing countries" possess "liberatory potential." Thus the *Rebelles* collective advocates entering into "tactical alliances" with groups advocating national liberation. Readers interested in how the PQ fits into this scenario are urged to read *Rebelles*.

"On donne not' langue au chat!" by "Le dernier des Granaliens"

This is a pointed response by the *Démanarchie* collective to *Rebelles*'s support of nationalism. The article is written in joual – working class slang which embodies an ethnic hybridity not shared by the "good French" of Tardiff.

The author begins by pointing out that language is a part of culture and culture is more than a question of language. Within linguistic communities there may exist distinct regional accents tied to regional identities. And within a given linguistic group there can exist, for example, French-speaking Kurds and associations such as "L'Association culturelles des Kurdes du Quèbec."

Language is a metaphor for power, and in the hands of the nationalist government in Quebec English hegemony has merely been replaced with French hegemony over the existing plurality of cultural-linguistic minorities. Bill 101, which enforces the hegemony of the French language ("good" French) in the province, is a form of "partisan imperialism." A bureaucratic regime run by the educationally privileged marshals language as a means of forcing its political-economic agenda on Quebec's poor and independent communities.

Quebec – The National Question: "Ts'e veux dire!" by Christian Brouillard

Brouillard addresses the relationship of nationalism to capitalism and statist bureaucracies. Is Quebec independence just another tool of "the bourgeoisie and the state?" Capitalism is "diabolical" in its ability to adapt to changing circumstances, and its ability to reduce all human relationships to mercantile ends. The "standardization" of culture is an instance of this: the same coke bottle can be bought in Paris as in Peking. This standardization is parallelled by the creation of greater differentiation when it comes to economic inequality and its hierarchical correlates, such as race – the ethno-economic division produced by apartheid in South Africa is an example. Thus capitalism develops unequally, creating national, regional and ethnic divisions on the basis of economic inequality.

Canada is an "artificial creation of British capitalists" that was itself an arena of unequal development. It was formed on the basis of the negation of the right to self-determination for the First Nations, Acadians (French-speaking settlers of the Atlantic region of Canada), Québécois (French-speaking settlers born in Quebec) and Metis (a distinctive amalgam of First Nations and French-speaking settlers in Western Canada). The nation-state was also premised on the creation of an economically dominant centre (Ontario) and an "underdeveloped" periphery (the Maritimes, Indian territories, and to some extent, Quebec). The capitalist order in Canada was based on these inequalities, which in turn resulted in other inequalities. Examples include the subordination of First Nations which not only entailed economic oppression but also cultural and political subordination. Such issues were also relevant in the case of the "Québéçois territory" where a "residual" population left over from earlier French colonization "constituted an unique entity in an Anglo-Saxon North America."

Capitalism can have great flexibility in cases where its internal contradictions result in a change to the status quo. In South Africa, for example, the racial divide between rich and poor was replaced by a system where black rulers and capitalists were integrated into the hierarchy, while the majority of blacks remained poor. Similarly in Quebec Anglo-Saxon bureaucrats are simply being replaced by Québéçois overseers.

In the post-1945 era the United States is the principle protector of the capitalist order and that government has suppressed any signs of revolutionary change (Chile in 1973, etc.). In Quebec the changes to the status quo were designed so as not to upset the capitalist apple cart: hence the so-called "quiet" revolution of the 1960s. The problem of sovereignty is that it has the potential to threaten the system of U.S. capitalist domination in North America. Consequently the PQ spends a lot of time trying to convince Washington that separatism will not threaten the capitalist status quo. Brouillard suggests that the PQ is probably right to say it won't upset the capitalist order because in the 1970s the party succeeded in marginalizing the radical wings of the separatist movement. Thus the party falsely claims to represent "socialism and independence" when in reality it stands for a "vague sovereignty-association social-mediocrity." The "potential rupture with capitalism" represented by the independence movement has been channeled into a system designed to support the existing order. The PQ tells its adherents to forget about anti-imperialism or identifying with oppressed groups and nations in America (Puerto Rico, Cuba, African-Americans).

Is Quebec nationalism "kaputt" or is it still a legitimate aspiration? It is if it truly expands the scope of human liberty, does not oppress the national aspirations of other groups, and adopts "socialism" as the basis of establishing equality between other "national communities." Establishing a society in which the state and marketplace do not dictate human relations means recognizing cultural differences and broader human differences – multi-cultural "world beat" music, for example.

– MARK ANTLIFF

RESISTANCE OR AUTHORITARIANISM?

The local anarchist community is wandering in a void. Many of us appear rootless, uninformed and ignorant of our own past. The circle @ is now produced, circulated and consumed like any other commodity on the cultural market. There are punks who wear it and neo-nazi symbolism on the same leather jacket, apparently confusing anarchism with macho style nihilism. Others it seems attach themselves to anarchism because of its trendy status amongst political philosophies (as the most hip at this point in time) and therefore most accomodating to their marginality, as groupies glue themselves to the most hip/wild bands or art scene. Even among so called anarchist militants, the real possibilities that anarchist ideas indicate are rarely pursued, in fact hardly ever even discussed.

All of this points at the necessity for local anarchists to engage in more critical analysis not only of capitalist, hierarchical society, but of ourselves as well.

I would like to open a constructive, mutually respectful discussion with one of the projects that seems determined, in my opinion, to perpetuate confusion, which is at the source of the aforementioned problems.

The most recent issue of Resistance (simply R for the rest of the article) came out in August 1987. It was # 11, the first to come out in a year. It consisted of 16 pages of communiques from various clandestine groups, for the most part European, that are consciously engaged in highly illegal activity. Typical actions covered in # 11 were firebombings, kneecappings and executions. The paper is signed by the Friends of Durruti, and is described as " covering militant autonomist, anti-imperialist, national liberation, feminist and anti-nuclear struggles in advanced capitalist countries ".

I criticize R primarily because of its insistance on associating itself with anti-authoritarianism and anarchism, when in fact one is hard pressed to find anything truly anarchistic about any of the groups whose communiques it publishes, or about the way in which the paper is presented to the public.

Let's look at some of the groups that are applauded in its pages: The ETA, Fighting Communist Cells, Red Army Fraction, Vancouver 4. Of these groups only the Vancouver 4 seem to have had a genuine anti-authoritarian approach, in the sense that the spirit behind their love and respect for our planet and their deep desire to put into practice the creation of a free society, were not sacrificed on the altar of ideology to satisfy the gods of pure revolutionary thought and action. In other words, their activity, or at least the verbalized form of it, seemed to be as influenced by Chief Seathl's message, as by leftist ideologues. In fact much of their published statements seem to point at a conscious rejection of the dull, jargon laden communiques of most of the other urban guerilla groups who are regularly given coverage in R.

There are other groups whose perspective is generally anti-authoritarian and whose ideas and news coverage are sometimes expressed in R. Among these are groups like Rote Zora and the Ecomedia reports. But these are the exception and not the rule.

As for the other groups mentioned none even consider themselves anti-authoritarian. Their vocabulary does at times flirt with anarchism. Words like ' autonomist ' give the appearance that perhaps they are not the stalinist sects that most of them actually are. Yet their structure and expressed analyses lay bare their complete and utter rejection of the anarchist critique and explanations of this shit world that we live in. In fact, the description that the Friends of Durruti themselves give us of R is typical of leftism, and makes absolutely no reference to anti-authoritarian struggles. They do not seem to know that promoting the concepts of anti-imperialism and national liberation as ultimate ends is antagonistic to the development of anarchist resistance. Seeing the struggle as one between small/weak nations and larger/stronger ones is not an anti-statist or anti-hierarchical approach. That the ruling class or aspiring ruling class of one nation should be free from the ruling classes of others to develop and refine their internal exploitation is a pro-statist m-L approach, and has nothing whatsoever to do with the creation of free societies. National liberation, i.e. the creation of separate nation states, misses the point. The source of oppressed cultures misery is not only in the imperialism of foreign ruling classes and states, but in the existence of class society and the state as such. From an anarchist perspective therefore it is against these forms of social organization that the struggle must be waged. This is often seen as both an internal and external struggle, both against the institutionalization of domination and against its internalization, the aspects of it that we have absorbed as individuals.

That groups who have every intention of retaining capitalism, the state and the repressive apparatus should they ever achieve power, are given extensive, uncritical and unqualified coverage in a journal that is signed by the Friends of Durruti, a revolutionary anarchist, only further confuses an already confused public thereby preventing an informed anarchist resistance from ever developing.

On another level there is a tragic irony in the fact that it was precisely the ideology of groups like the ETA that was directly responsible for the death of Durruti and the suppression of his ideas. I find it incredible that R is not aware of this or simply doesn't care.

Most folks who believe that R is important usually claim that without it we wouldn't have any idea what these groups are doing or ' think they are doing ' as Reality Now put it. They further claim that R is necessary as a medium for the groups to be able to speak for themselves as opposed to the bourgeois medias' censorship of any coverage of their activity or the crude misinformation that they might decide to print.

The truth is that anyone who really wants to know what these groups are up to can plug into the same information outlets that R does. All of these groups regularly publish their communiques and discussion papers in various magazines throughout Europe and in North America as well. What R does, is it publishes reports from a variety of groups and prints them all in one language (english). My interest however is not in disputing what R is, but rather in opposing its presentation of these essentially vanguardist, pro-authoritarian, statist, hierarchic and in many instances racist units as having a positive contribution to make to the development of an anti-authoritarian, anti-hierarchical, and anti-statist resistance.

In this all too brief critique of R I have intentionally neglected to address the issues that concern me about guerillaism as such. Nor did I want to dismiss the personal courage of many of its activists. My main concern in it has been with the complete absence of qualifications and/or clarifications that should accompany many of the articles, reports and communiques in R, so as not to leave uninformed readers with the impression that these groups are anarchistic in some way, especially when the paper is often displayed in the anarchist section of bookshops, advertises anarchist periodicals and signs itself Friends of Durruti. As for the R project itself, I find it unfortunate that its members have never really engaged in public discussion with anarchists. Apparently, however, they have decided to begin printing a letters column in the next issue. This is certainly a decision that I for one would like to commend them on.

– Amigo de Flores Magon

Budapest 1956.

Durruti was an anarchist guerilla 'leader' killed in Madrid, in November 1936.

No Picnic (January 1988)

RESISTANCE RESPONDS

The article "Resistance or Authoritarianism" published in your January 88 issue contains some inaccuracies and distortions which we, the Friends of Durruti collective, would like to dispel.

We reject the inference that we are responsible for the local anti-authoritarian community appearing "rootless, uninformed and ignorant" and we don't see our role as that of a perpetuator of confusion within the anarchist movement. We have a much less exagerated view of our influence in the local area, and indeed throughout the rest of North America, where the bulk of our issues are distributed.

We believe the theme of Resistance, revolutionary armed and militant struggle, cuts across ideological barriers on the Left. In this sense it differs from such papers as Open Road which are explicitly anarchist in perspective. Our objective is to develop an understanding of the tactics and politics of armed/militant action as it is currently being practiced in advanced capitalist countries through first hand documentation. We hope that by our publication of communiques, interviews and hungerstrike statements, we can dispel the media generated image of the "mindless terrorist" and instead present a truer picture of committed revolutionaries who, thoughtfully and courageously, attempt to put their ideas into practice. We hope to illustrate that armed and militant struggle is a real possibility; that others in similar circumstances, have been able to create illegal structures from which to fight the system; and in fact that we can too.

As we have stated before in our editorials, we don't agree with all the material that we publish: the collective considers itself to be anti-authoritarian and so does not support the creation of states or political parties, which is the intention of some of the groups whose communiques we have published. We believe that the anarchist movement has a very strong tradition of armed revolutionary struggle, from the insurrections in Italy, the guerilla army of Makhno in the Ukraine, to the Spanish revolution; and so we expect this movement to have an interest in what we present. But Resistance is not intended solely for the anarchist community. If our publication gives heart to a supporter of the United Freedom Front in the U.S., so much the better: at this stage of the struggle any display of revolutionary outrage is better than none.

Many of the communiques we publish present a thorough critique of their targets, whether this be NATO, the European Space Agency, or a bio-genetics firm. It would be simplistic to disregard this information just because it came from a Marxist group. We believe it is of value to anarchists to understand the politics of other ideologies and that there are many things that can be learned and applied from a study of guerilla groups of differing perspectives.

To illustrate this point: the West German Red Army Fraction is one of the oldest of the modern European guerilla groups. In it's 16-year history the situation of it's political prisoners, kept in conditions of extreme isolation, has been one of it's primary concerns. The strength of the political prisoners, their determination to remain together and to maintain their political identity is exemplary. Though we may reject their political project, we can learn from their experience.

We have also published some material from the Italian Red Brigades; they are a Stalinist organization committed to the creation of a fighting communist party. One text was from a Red Brigadist who had undergone torture at the hands of the Italian

Local anti-authoritarians at the V-5 bail hearing

police and had described how one could resist the techniques of the torturers. An anarchist might find that perspective of great importance some day.

The ETA, the national liberation movement committed to the creation of socialism in the Basque region is another group whose communiques we have published. In Resistance #8 we included an account of how one of the organizations leaders became involved with the struggle, along with an interview with an anti-authoritarian urban guerrilla group, the Autonomist Anti-Capitalist Commandos, of the same region. We thought it would be useful to compare the perspectives of these two groups. In our last issue we published a text from ETA political prisoners about the execution of a former member who had renounced armed struggl and had begun to aid the Spanish government. The problem of turning is one which guerrillas have to face and it is of value to see how this problem is dealt with by various groups.

We publish as much material as we can from anarchist and anti-authoritarian groups. There are very few guerrilla groups currently active which are explicitely anarchist. Many of the founders of the French group Action Directe considered themselves to be anarchist; in Italy during the 70's, there was the anarchist Revolutionary Action; and there is Anarchist Cells now active in West Germany (our next issue, out this summer, includes a text from this latter group.) In Italy and West Germany there are also many small groupings which carry out actions, send out short communiques and then disband but these communiques, when we are able to aquire them, are generally of little use to us due to their briefness and concern with local issues.

In West Germany, the autonomist movement is very strong and dwarves the anarchist and anti- imperialist (RAF) movements. The autonomist movement has within it feminists, squatters, anti-nuclear activists, pro-immigration activists, etc. It is a non-authoritarian, non-hierarchical movement, and amoung it's most militant members are the Revolutionary Cells and the feminist Rote Zora. This movement, and these groups, cannot be considered Stalinist in any way. We have devoted a considerable amount of space to the Revolutionary Cells and Rote Zora because we find their analyses to be particularly insightful, well written and politically close to our own. In our next issue, besides more material from these two groups, we will publish an interview with the Autonomist Cells, which has been involved primarily in the fight to stop the construction of the nuclear reprocessing plant at Wackersdorf.

A word about dogma and jargon. Some of the material in Resistance is hard to understand. Part of that difficulty is due to the problem of translation, some is due to the lack of context, and some to the use of political jargon. The RAF and the CCC are perhaps the worst for using dogma/Leftist terminology. The RAF has, in fact, been criticized for this in West Germany. Keep in mind that these texts were not written for us; they were intended for their political supporters in Europe. Generally speaking the level of political discourse is much higher there than it is here in North America; the left wing ideologies of anarchism and Marxism originated in Europe over a hundred years ago, and have played a much greater role in the histories of these countries than they have in our own.

A few last points: given our coverage of armed struggle, we believe that our choice of Durruti - a passionate advocate of the same, prior to, and during the Spanish Revolution - for the name of our collective is an appropriate one. It is our tribute to the memory of this anarchist guerilla leader, and serves to reafirm the role of armed struggle in anarchist revolution. Our critic writes that groups such as ETA caused his death, but that is quite untrue: Durruti was killed by a fascist bullet coming from the Guardia Civil who had taken the Clinica Hospital in Madrid, as he was encouraging a group of militiamen to return to the front.

Compliments to our friend on his multilinguistic abilities if he finds it so easy to aquire and translate the type of material that is found in Resistance Our own translators find it to be a difficult task, one that takes months of hard work. It is quite untrue that "all of these groups regularly publish their communiques and discussion papers throughout Europe and North America as well." American and Puerto Rican groups publish their communiques in such papers as Libertad, Insurgent and Breakthrough, but European communiques are quite rare in North America except in Resistance. There are a few journals in Europe

which publish communiques from the guerilla, but they frequently are closed down by the police, their editors jailed, and their publication confiscation confiscated. We suggest that our critic's unstated, but hinted, opposition to "guerillaism" is the reason behind his attempt to invalidate Resistance by claiming it's contents to be so easily available elsewhere. We believe that our aquiring and translating state-

"We hope to illustrate that armed and militant struggle is a real possibility; that others in similar circumstances have been able to create illegal structures from which to fight the system, and in fact, that we can to."

ments by the guerilla to be very useful to those in North America interested in this topic.

Our critic must confuse us with someone else when he writes that we publish communiques from "in many instances racist units." We do not publish any racist communiques, but we have published a number of anti-racist ones such as those from the Dutch Revolutionary Anti-Racist Action and Split Apartheid, as well as the American United Freedom Front which attacked a number of multinationals heavily involved in South Africa. Gratuitous slurs such as this can hardly be considered to be in the interest of a "constructive, mutually respectful discussion." But perhaps our comrade is referring to the bloody anti-semitic attacks which occurred a number of years ago in Paris and were blamed on Action Directe; if so our critic should check his facts and make sure he is not parroting the official government line. We published an interview with AD founder Jean-Marc Roullian and some communiques from this guerilla organization in which they denied involvement in the attacks and pointed out the government's motives in slandering them

We are not sure what our critic meant when he said Resistance is not presented in an anarchist fashion. Resistance might be considered an esoteric publication; it is not that useful to the general reader, but it is for those who have a particular interest in it's subject matter. We tend not to repeat introductions to the various groups whose statements are reprinted, but if this is causing confusion amoung our readers we will consider placing more attention on this part of our work. We always welcome letters from our readers

Keep up the good work of your paper!

The Friends of Durruti collective
PO Box 790, Stn,.A
Vancouver, BC
Canada, V6C 2N6

No Picnic (Spring 1988)

Dear *No Picnic* Folks,

Here's a few comments about the *Resistance* response to add to the debate.

At first glance, one notes, the *Resistance* collective's text looks like a straightforward, blow-by-blow reply to Amigo de Magon's critiques. Quickly though, the clashing directions of the collective's affirmations lead to whirlpools of confusion and crunching air pockets.

On the one hand, the collective says that it "considers itself to be anti-authoritarian and does not support the creation of states or political parties" and complains that "we are not sure what our critic meant when he said *Resistance* is not presented in an anarchist fashion." On the other, the bulk of the text is devoted to marketing the attractions of the authoritarian groups Amigo de Magon found objectionable.

But if the collective's statement that it "does not support the creation of states or political parties" would seem to slam the door shut, by the end of the same paragraph the authoritarians have reappeared through a back entrance: "If our publication gives heart to a supporter of the United Freedom Front, so much the better: at this stage of the struggle any display of revolutionary outrage is better than none."

The initially seductive quality of the latter part of the quote plays with our frustrated desires but turns out to be mainly a "hook" introducing a "revolutionary" melting pot. Here, presumably, we are all comrades of "revolutionary outrage." But what is important about groups like the RAF, CCC or the Italian Red Brigades is not what they are doing but what they are: expressions of state-capitalism, the extreme left of capital, with political outlooks close to the "socialist block" (countries which, not surprisingly, these groups are very reluctant to criticize). Presently, most of these countries are rapidly introducing market mechanisms, while political power remains firmly in the hands of the central committees.

About as far from displays of "revolutionary outrage" as one could possibly imagine, the activities of the authoritarian guerilla groups are on the contrary local representations of the status quo, the day-to-day chatter of the bureaucratic class oppressing half the people on earth. Some of these miserable mini-rackets are candid about taking power and dream of their own personal police force, army, prisons and bureaucracies. Perennial vanguardists, they are in the vanguard of the counterrevolution, amongst the most ardent of the competing gangs who will fight tooth and nail to preserve the state and capital. The collective comments about "this stage of the struggle" as if our struggle and that of the authoritarians were not irreconcilably opposed.

References to "the left wing ideologies of anarchism and Marxism" and "ideological barriers on the left," intended to remind us that we are on the left, are only reminders that the collective considers itself on the left. "The ETA," it informs us, seemingly confused for a moment about whether they are writing to an anarchist journal or addressing an anti-imperialist conference, is "the national liberation movement dedicated to the creation of socialism in the Basque region" (perhaps this tic comes from uncritically reproducing too many authoritarian communiques). And when we are told that the Italian Red Brigades are a "Stalinist organization committed to the creation of a fighting communist party," this ends up sounding like an awkward but ultimately trivial detail compared to the "many things that can be learned and applied" from this type of organization.

The collective devotes a paragraph to the problems of "dogma and jargon," warning us that "some of the material in *Resistance* is hard to understand." "Some" of this situation (not much, to go by the impression given) is due to "the use of political jargon," but we are soon let in on the real problem: "Generally the level of political discourse is higher there (in Europe) than here in North America." In other words, we are too unsophisticated to realize that what we had mistakenly taken for dogma and jargon, typically an offering of petrified and useless neo-Leninist gibberish, was really a "higher" form of political discourse. The collective makes it clear that anti-authoritarians take the vanguardist groups' texts seriously only because of insight/information from prisoners or occasional strategy tips (the examples *Resistance* often uses): they are "thorough critiques" which stand on their own as theory, despite the fatal flaw of their generic neo-Leninist (where as some Marxist or post-Marxist ones, for example texts published by Black and Red, offer real insight into modern domination). Is it surprising that neo-Leninists, having become integral cogs of modern domination, are unable to understand it.

What is perhaps most ironic about *Resistance* is that when the Vancouver 5 burst onto the scene, completely unexpectedly for most of us, we had to come to grips very quickly with where we stood concerning the many questions raised by their actions. In a number of cities, a wave of repression accompanied police investigations, adding to the urgency. This debate/discussion took place, in private and in the pages of journals such as *Strike*, the *Fifth Estate*, and *Kick it Over*, but strangely not in the journal specializing in the matters at hand; it preferred to retreat behind a wall of communiques, shunning an entire dimension of what was taking place. An editorial approach affirming an anti-authoritarian vision (to return to the question of why *Resistance* is not presented in an anarchist fashion), was absent.

In fact, another anti-authoritarian magazine that can be read from cover to cover without noticing it was put out by anti-authoritarians doesn't come to mind (no sectarian anti-Leninist rants here to disconcert vanguardist *Resistance* afficionados!). Choosing absence, *Resistance* "reduces anarchy to merely a matter of tastes among a competition in the shopping mall of leftism," to borrow a phrase from E. Maple [Peter Werbe of the *Fifth Estate*].

No Picnic (Summer 1988)

It is not my intention to convey the impression that the editors of *Resistance* are not sincere anti-authoritarians. Their outlook is part of a broader phenomenon characterized by a two-track approach: the authoritarians are strongly rejected and strongly accepted at the same time. This leads, in France for example, to entire libertarian-communist organizations which advocate the abolition of the state and capital and at the same time support a variety of "national liberation organizations." It has been the basic orientation of *Open Road* (see their interview in the first issue of *No Picnic*) throughout innumerable changes of collective members. And now one of the editors of *Reality Now* in an exchange with the *Fifth Estate* touching on many of the questions raised above, writes that "*Reality Now* does not support any state capitalist or communist," and further on in the text states that "If the FMLN is successful in at least redistributing land so people can survive and also stop the genocide ordered by the U.S., I'll support them and I *do* support them" (author's emphasis).

The collective makes a specially strong pitch for the German autonomists, who are termed a "non-authoritarian, non-hierarchical movement." Although too amorphous to be summarily written off like the neo-Leninists to be sure, here the collective is attempting either to paint the autonomists in the most flattering light possible or to water down the meaning of non-authoritarian and non-hierarchical, to go by autonomists I have met in Nicaragua (recognized by their black stars or black star tattoos – they must regret those tattoos if they turn into yuppies or new-age pacifists …). None of the autonomists I talked to seemed to have strong objections to the Sandinistas or the Nicaraguan state, leaving the impression that they were unenthusiastic about being ordered around by vanguards back at home, but didn't necessarily object to it elsewhere. "This movement and these guerilla groups cannot be considered Stalinist in any way," the collective assures us, referring to the autonomists, but then that the Sandinistas are not "Stalinists" either didn't prevent them from supporting the [Soviet] invasion of Afghanistan and the suppression of Solidarity [in Poland].

– PRIMITIVE NATURE

No Picnic (Summer 1988)

Letters

On Nationalism

Dear Friends,

A friend recently loaned me a copy of the Summer edition of *No Picnic*. It was with great interest that I read the letter from Amigo in which he replies to criticisms of an earlier article critiquing *Resistance*. It appears that he is denouncing nearly the entire armed leftist movement in Europe as "Stalinist," racist, and generally ineffective. I've missed out on part of the debate but I'd like to add my two cents worth. Here goes!

Amigo states that nationalism is often the precursor to and justification for racism. I think that we must make a distinction between bourgeois nationalism and revolutionary nationalism. I agree that under bourgeois nationalism it is usually thinly disguised racism and offers a rationale for the exploitation of minorities and other racial groups. Nazi Germany is the classic example of where bourgeois German nationalism did this. However, under revolutionary nationalism this is not the case. Without going into the whole Soviet question and such, Cuba is an example of where a revolutionary nationalism has *not* led to a racist structure. It was the revolutionary nationalism of the Vietnam people that allowed them to struggle for forty years against various imperialisms.

Amigo criticizes the European clandestine urban guerilla strategy as being essentially ineffective and leading only to the death and imprisonment of many militants. He mentions other forms of struggle, like popular insurrection, etc. that can be engaged in. However it is unclear if he is disapproving of an entire strategy and resistance and armed struggle or just at this stage. I think that anyone at all realistic will realize that historically, no group or class has ever peacefully abdicated power; and the capitalist class [don't] look like they want to set any precedents on this. Ultimately all struggle comes down to an armed struggle to kick out and destroy the old ruling class so that it can be replaced by something new, be it a Leninist state or otherwise. As to its ineffectiveness, in the immediate case it hasn't brought down the present imperialist states and I don't think that the RAF, Red Brigades, etc. operating as they are will be able to do so. It will take a larger mass movement *in conjunction* with the armed groups to do this. In the meantime however they do have a destabilizing effect on the state. They have caused the state to have to spread and thin its resources, become more overtly repressive thus shredding the facade of bourgeois democracy and making the state spend much more time, men and money in pursuit of "security."

I was a member of the U.S. armed forces and I was stationed in Germany. In 1984–85 the RAF firebombed a couple of U.S. Army attack helicopters, totally destroying them. With a relatively simple and inexpensive device they put the U.S. Army out of a couple million dollars worth of equipment. Because of incidents like that the American military in Europe and other NATO forces have to devote a much larger portion of their resources now to protect themselves and their equipment from attacks like these. Amigo should realize that while the Western Imperialists have enormous resources for repression these resources are not infinite, they do have a limit. The RAF alone has caused many of these resources to be redirected from active aggression to passive "defence" where the RAF can and does have the tactical advantage. It isn't so much a matter of dropping this whole tactic but of expanding it so that NATO forces are under constant attack in their own "rear areas." This shouldn't take place in a vacuum but in a context of sabotage, property destruction, etc. all coming together to undermine the state, its authority and, ultimately, its forces of oppression.

Amigo states that his criticism of the ETA was prompted after reading about their execution of a former comrade. He states that he doesn't know how he would deal with a similar situation. While I haven't read that particular issue of *Resistance* I assume that the comrade in question was killed either for being an informant, a traitor or a threat to security. Amigo should be reminded of the quote "A revolution isn't a dinner party." The bottom line is that when you are participating in an armed clandestine guerilla group the stakes are too high to allow the possibility of being infiltrated by police informants or having members back-sliding and betraying the group. Around the world the prisons and cemeteries are full of comrades and militants that have been betrayed by informants and have had their organizations infiltrated. While proper security measures can lessen the impact of informants you must ask yourself what you are willing to do to safeguard your security and integrity. In a cell structure an informant should (if all goes well) only be able to betray four or five people. What will Amigo do if he is one of those people? He can either say "oh well" and go to prison or get killed by the forces of repression or he can eliminate that threat and allow the organization to go on. It appears that the ETA made the latter choice and by remaining security conscious can better safeguard the security of their members.

Well, that's it for now. I hope that my observations can further the debate on armed struggle in the industrialized countries. Debate is sorely needed.

— Sincerely, Joseph Steele (Joseph Stalin?)

A *friend of Amigo's responds*

When the oppression is unbearable, people fight back. A resistance will grow and manifest itself in many forms, both physical and psychological. Some, and only some, of those resisting see national liberation (creation of another state) as the answer. Hence, elements of the resistance promote the *basics* of that same system they are fighting to eliminate (hierarchical, authoritarian power structures). Although I can see why you use the terms "revolutionary" (Cuba/ Vietnam) as opposed to "bourgeois" (Nazi Germany) nationalism (because it's simple), to describe the changes of ruling classes in those countries, the use of the term "revolutionary" nationalism bugs me.

Apologists for the status quo in Havana or Hanoi (to use your examples) are quick to say that those situations "aren't perfect but …", and then generally go on to describe the wonderful *material* improvements that have come since the "revolution." This works, and is quite true if you tend to hold a *materialist* based view of our oppression. I do not. Marxists (and others) do. I'm not going to deny the extreme importance of the material aspects of our lives (I can already hear the moralizing about middle class white males not having a right to "belittle" material improvements). Material basics like the big one, your physical well being (no death squads, actually food on the plates, medical attention, literacy, etc. etc.) are undeniably important. What bugs me is the tendency to downplay (often with heavy moral, ie., religious, overtones) the *social* situation in these new (old) states.

The cadre (military, intelligentsia) that achieve positions described by themselves as representatives of the people, are situated at the peak of a whole shit-load of organized hierarchical oppression.

Once Castro made it to the presidential Palace, among other things, he quickly set about eliminating political opposition that remained in *his* new "revolutionary" state. Along with many others, the *anarchists* were rounded up and shot or imprisoned in the new (old) prison camps.

I can relate to the desire that people have to look for models and examples of liberation struggles. Concrete proof that there is light at the end of the tunnel is an emotional/spiritual (real) need that we all have to greater or lesser degrees. But if that emotional need blurs our *dreams* and visions of what is possible, then I think those emotions become disturbing.

A good example is the situation where the Sandinistas (recent national liberation phenomenon), hit the anarchist and left (separate) headlines when the details of what this new state power did to the indigenous peoples of the Atlantic region of Nicaragua [were revealed]. After this clear display of what is basically racist and class oppression (mass relocations, assassinations, imprisonment of dissidents), you have people (apologists) saying how, yes, they did "get

out of hand" a little, *but* the indigenous people are linked to the Contras and the CIA, *but* the Sandinistas are at war with the U.S.A. and cannot "at this time" deal with internal disputes, and the excuses went on.

The Sandinista Intelligentsia, more sophisticated than many authoritarian political gangs of the past, realized the damage this oppression was having on their image. They set about to repair this image with the public announcements of wrong-doings, creation of commissions of inquiry and political bodies to "negotiate" an understanding between the separate parties.

The public airing of dirty laundry as a technique used to deflate a growing balloon of dissent was probably perfected by Amerika. This technique was not lost on the Sandinistas. And it seems to have worked by and large. We now hear that the over-zealous Sandinistas have realised their errant ways and are now giving the indigenous peoples the "autonomy" they deserve. A bunch of shit!

Fact is the Sandinistas tried to use more sophisticated ways to repress, divide, disrupt and destroy the native people through 'democratic' commissions, inquiries, etc., etc. all the while continuing to effectively eliminate opposition to this oppression. The "soft" oppression has fallen apart. No outside visitors are allowed to travel the Atlantic region of Nicaragua and the situation [there] is *not* in the anti-authoritarian/left news.

No Picnic (Spring 1989)

Interview with the Vancouver 5:

RESISTANCE v.s. PROTEST

Ann Hansen and Brent Taylor

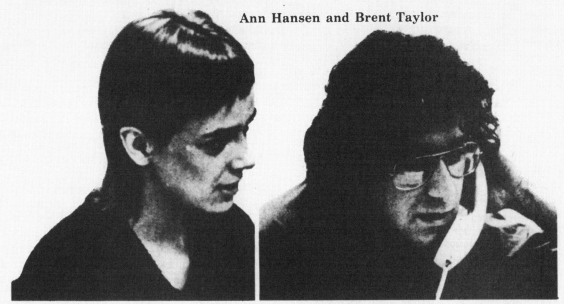

In response to a set of questions sent to Ann Hansen and Brent Taylor (two of the five people sitting in Oakalla Prison charged with various political of- fences) we have received the following. It has been requested that we do not attribute any of the respon- ses to one or the other directly.

Here is a brief summary of the charges and what's been happening with them:

The five are facing a total of 25 charges and if found guilty will most likely get life sentences. The charges range from auto theft to conspiracy charges (See box for a total list). They are to have a set of four trials in B.C. and one trial in Toronto. There was recently a decision made in the bowels of "justice" to change the British Columbia trials to New West- minster from Vancouver. This change makes it ex- tremely difficult for the Vancouver support group to attend the trials on a daily basis. It also appears likely to result in a more reactionary panel of jury members. The first set of trials is scheduled to begin September 12, 1983.

KIO (1) Do you feel that pacifism in future years will create meaningful social change as opposed to refor- mism? Do you see pacifism as a tactic in relation to a revolutionary resistance perspective?

Ans. First of all, pacifism is not simply a tool or a tac- tic. Pacifism is actually a fundamental set of moral beliefs which determine how one lives one's life, and therefore, how one acts politically. Pacifism should be respected as an individual choice. However, pacifism

has been elevated to a theory for revolutionary social change and is heralded as **the** process and **the** means we must adhere to. When assertions are made that only a pacifist movement will enable us to create a better world, our understanding of historical and present day reality compels us to disagree.

In the "Peace Movement" in North America, the ideals of pacifism are being applied very dogmatically to a mass social struggle, and have become entrenched as "ideology of non-violence". Often times, adherence to the ideology appears to actually take precedence over the realization of the goals we are seeking . . . .

Granted, it would be much nicer if revolutionary change could come about according to pacifist prac- tice. Unfortunately however, it is doubtful that is the case, and thus, it is wrong to base our future on such assumptions.

Nevertheless, there is a great deal of potential for effective use of non-violent tactics in the liberation process. It is, in fact, absurd to imagine that a revolutionary movement could ever exist without mass participation in non-violent mobilizations . . . .

However, the same cannot be said about pacifism. If we, as a movement, restrict ourselves to non-violent tactics only—in other words, if we are a strictly pacifist movement—we will continue to make definite advances from here, but eventually, we will find our- selves prevented from going any further by the repressive forces of the State . . . .

This does not mean that the ends justify any means. The process that we follow is extremely important,

32

and most certainly we must at all times be guided by strong moral concerns and a true reverence for life, yet sometimes **reality necessitates certain means**. We live in a world of violence but it is critical that we always recognize that such violence is not of our choosing. In this sense, reality also justifies the use of certain means; even those means which go beyond the limitations of pacifism.

It is too simplistic to reject revolutionary violence along with the horrible indiscriminate magnitude of reactionary violence, just because both are violence. To equate both so simplistically removes them from the context of social reality, and in doing so ignores the essence of each—the meaning and purpose for which they are employed. To then determine the limits of our own practice on the basis of such an artificial equation is obviously wrong . . . .

The way we hope to live in that future is not necessarily a realistic way to live now . . . .

It is true that all revolutionary movements in power have become Statist regimes, but it is false to conclude that this is because violent tactics were used during their liberation process. Instead, it should be attributed to the fact that such movements operated according to an authoritarian Statist ideology.

KIO (2) When you speak of the need to reject industrial civilization, is it not possible to utilize such technological advances for the good of the Earth's people and the Earth itself? If you believe that such is not the case, please explain your position.
Ans. Further technological advancements are not necessary for the good of the Earth's people or the Earth; in fact, under the present world order, any further advancements will only benefit the profits of the corporations and the men that run them.

For many, many centuries human beings have survived and developed civilizations on this earth that were rich spiritually, intellectually, and culturally without industrialism or advanced technology. As well, their survival was not at the expense of hundreds of animal species and environmental destruction. Somehow people managed to hunt, fish, and grow food without General Foods or Safeway. Dances, music, and stories flourished without RCA, Sam the Record Man and Harlequin Romances . . . .

The work with machines offered by industrialism alienates people from each other and from the natural functions of the Earth. Whether industrialism exists in the socialist or capitalist bloc, the work still remains alienating and the Earth must be constantly disembowelled so that machines, fuels, and products can be made. The only real difference is that the profits in socialist countries are more equally distributed than in capitalist regimes . . .

KIO (3) When you refer to the need to build an active resistance, would you define in what manner it should appear?
Ans. We don't envision one particular form in which

an active resistance movement should appear, but believe that what needs to happen is for a resistance mentality to take root among activists in Canada. From this radical consciousness, active resistance will then appear in various forms and many different struggles.

To a great extent the movement now operates with a protest mentality which unfortunately fosters widespread reformist illusions about what kind of struggle is necessary to realize the goals we seek. (Protest attempts to influence the decisions of those in power by showing public disagreement with their policies Because we imagine that through protest the powerful will eventually be pressured to change, we are mistakenly wholly engaged in a form of struggle in which the outcome is ultimately left in the hands of those we oppose . . . .

A resistance mentality is based upon the premise that the powerful **will** ignore our protests, and therefore that we must build a movement with the commitment and determination to utilize means of struggle by which we ourselves can stop the projects

that we oppose . . . .

A resistance movement would not be limited by legalities when there is a need for direct confrontation: such a militant approach is definitely necessary when we are confronted with life-threatening situations; in particular, the ongoing destruction and polluting of the environment or the build up of nuclear arsenals and the war machine . . . .

KIO (4) What motive has the State in mind when they are intent on having 4 separate trials instead of one big event for the B.C. charges?
Ans. The separation of trials is a commonly used counter-insurgency technique against political prisoners internationally. This technique is aimed at taking the political content out of the trial and

Kick It Over 8 (1983/4)

criminalizing it as much as possible. In our case we will face charges of conspiracy to rob a Brinks guard, car theft, possession of weapons and stolen property in the first trial. The second trial will hear the Red Hot Video charges; the third trial will be the bombing of Dunsmuir sub-station, conspiracy and sabotage of Cold Lake Air Base, Terry Fox icebreaker and conspiracy to sabotage Cheekeye-Dunsmuir, and the fourth trial will be an IGA robbery.

The first trial will be an attempt to criminalize us, remove any political motives from the charges. The trial will be publicized, and through the media the stage will be set for the rest of the trials. Before we are tried on the Red Hot Video charges, the jury will already have read in the paper of an alleged Brinks guard robbery, weapons and stolen vehicles, divorced from any political context . . . .

KIO (5) What motive does the State have in asking that the trials be undertaken in New Westminster as opposed to Vancouver?

Ans. The State's motive in moving the location of the trials is twofold, and is part of an ongoing systematic effort of carefully planned harrassment to hinder, in all possible ways, our defence. On the one hand, they want to make it as difficult as possible for our friends and supporters to attend the trials. It will be much more difficult for people from Vancouver to attend now that they will have to travel every day to New Westminster. The State hopes that the time and energy wasted, and the complications that this daily travel will incur, will wear down our support. Also, the courtrooms in New Westminster are much smaller than the large trial courts in Vancouver, and in this way too, they can ensure that fewer people will be able to observe the farcical ritual of "justice" unfold . . . .

The second motive concerns jury selection. The potential jury members for a trial in New Westminster are drawn from the voting lists of municipalities that are generally recognized as being more reactionary than Vancouver. In this sense, the switching of the trial location is undertaken to aid in ensuring convictions . . . .

KIO (6) You accepted the blackmail offer from the State for a shortened version of a preliminary hearing, but with little or no warning at the last moment they (the State functionaries) chose to proceed by Direct Indictment. Why in your opinion, did the State authorities renege on their promised offer? How do you feel about this denial of due process?

Ans. We believe that the State reneged on its first offer because they wanted to cut court costs to the minimal and didn't want any more publicity of this case than is absolutely necessary. What with funding the infrastructure for the development of North East Coal, B.C. Place and other scams, the Social Credit party can't afford the court costs of a preliminary hearing for a group of people in direct opposition to their projects.

But this does not surprise us in the least. It is an illusion to expect that anyone in this society, particularly political radicals, can obtain a fair trial. The concept of a fair trial within the bourgeois justice system is an illusion that hopefully, if nothing else, this case will dispel.

KIO (7) Now that the State has charged you with the Litton bombing, when do you expect that you will be brought to Toronto to face those charges?

Ans. We haven't been informed of when we will be taken to Toronto, but it's pretty certain that it won't be until all the trials are finished with here in B.C. Most likely that won't be untill February or March of 1984. Expect a preliminay hearing regarding Litton within a month or two of then.

KIO (8) Do you believe that the demands of middle class feminists can be transcended by radical feminists into a radical vision and perspective?

Ans. Radical feminists cannot achieve their vision through middle class demands such as "equal pay for work of equal value", "more day care centres" etc. These demands are for the middle class feminists to make. Radical feminists have a responsibility to break new ground, to create radical demands, to be guided by their own truths rather than catering to the mass mentality.

The demands of middle class feminists are rooted in an acceptance of the prevailing patriarchial order, values, and way of life. Equal pay for work implies the acceptance of multinational corporations, government, and the jobs they offer. As well, womyn who wish to succeed in the patriarchy must become competitive, aggressive female replicas of men. In effect, these demands would reform the patriarchy so that middle class womyn would gain more benefits from the system thus strengthening the patriarchy by making it appear less oppressive.

In order to end the patriarchy, womyn must break with it to form communities of their own with their own values and ways of life that can form the basis of a womyn's resistance movement. This break with the patriarchy is natural for a liberated womyn because she can no longer express herself or live her life within the patriarchal workplace, justice system, entertainment industry, and sciences. Her values, her speech, her dress, her behavior are in constant conflict with the patriarchal society and so rather than submit, she is compelled to resist . . . .

KIO (9) Lastly, is there anything you all wish to add to what has already been said above?

Ans. We look forward to meeting, and having discussions with, a lot of people when we are in Toronto, and hopefully making many new friendships. So we certainly hope that people will be into visiting us regularly at whatever prisons they cage us in there . . . .

It has been good to read that many people active in Ontario have been seriously analysing the actions of the police regarding the "search for the Litton bombers", and recognize that, in the face of police harassment and intimidation tactics, a policy of complete non-collaboration with the enemy is absolutely necessary. This sort of political analysis is a welcome development ——

Lastly, we want to thank those people in Toronto, and elsewhere for that matter, who have been supporting us thus far, and have been working to raise awareness and understanding of, and around, our case. We appreciate such efforts immensely. Take good care of yourselves. Be strong and resist!

TO BOMB OR NOT TO BOMB?
— That is the Question —

The following article was submitted to KIO as a self-criticism by the authors of a leaflet circulated in Toronto after the Litton bombing. We reproduce both below.

Soon after the bombing we published:

VANGUARD TERROR vs. STATE TERROR
An Anarchist Critique of the Litton Bombing

The October 14th bombing of Litton Systems in Rexdale has given rise to a storm of debate about armed struggle. We would submit that there are no absolute criteria by which these acts can be judged but, in considering specific acts, there are criteria that can be applied.

First, given that any such act will invariably be used as a pretext for repression, did it accomplish anything the achievement of which might outweigh or, at least, mitigate these negative consequences? And did it lead to an increase in **the self-activity of the people?** Our goal is a society in which people freely manage all aspects of their lives, and how can this be brought about save by the involvement of **everyone** at **every step** in their liberation?

Violent activity that arises out of a mass movement can be an expression of people's growing self-activity. Vanguardist violence leaves people in the role of spectators. Clandestine organizations tend to become isolated from the people and to develop their own raison d'etre. Both the terrorists and the reformists presume to know "what's best" for the people and abandon the difficult task of awakening them to the possibility and necessity of revolution.

The bombing at Litton cannot be said to have increased the self-activity of either the community or the employees at the plant in opposition to the cruise missile. The injuries suffered by seven people will no doubt make reaching these workers even more difficult. Nor did the bombing effectively sidetrack war production as the production facilities were entirely untouched. Nonetheless the RCMP, SIS, Metro Red Squad and others will use the bombing as the excuse for a "fishing expedition" and will practice a little of their own state-sponsored terror on the left.

The fact that an act brings down repression does not in itself condemn it as **any** effective action, particularly revolutionary action, is bound to have that effect and one cannot avoid stepping on official toes if one intends to revolutionize society.

Nor can the fact that an act is violent in and of itself be used to condemn it. We beg to differ with the U. of T. Campaign for Nuclear Disarmament which declares to the press that "Whether it be individuals or governments, the use of violence as a way of achieving goals is no longer possible". Condemning the violence of isolated armed struggle groups while asking people to put their faith in flyswatter referendums and the morality of profit-and-power-driven madmen is asking people to commit collective suicide. For us, the only solution is revolution. Revolution, not as a mere change of rulers but as a fundamental transformation in the values, thinking, and spirituality of millions of people.

For people of conscience, violence is always a horror and a disaster but, rather than counsel people to go peacefully to the gas chambers, we will teach the lessons of Vietnam, Chile, Poland and October 1970—that no ruling class will ever voluntarily retire from the stage of history. We do not rate very highly the chances of a violent revolution, but, if its that or killing our sisters and brothers around the world for the State, then there is only one moral choice: civil war.

In this time of mass media demagoguery, we should concentrate not on defensive appologetics, which amount to nothing more than statements of our **loyal** opposition to the status quo, but on exposing the **real** terrorists: the states wielding nuclear and conventional weapons, preparing for world war while smashing (or preparing to smash) all resistance to war at home. As Noam Chomsky has pointed out, terrorism are those selected acts of violence which our **rulers** oppose. Those who decry and persecute "terrorists" are themselves terrorism's biggest perpetrators and collaborators.

CRITIQUE OF THE CRITIQUE
OF THE LITTON BOMBING

When we wrote the document above we hadn't had time to think about the meaning of the bombing, or even to read thoroughly the Direct Action communique. What we felt had to be done was react rapidly, create an anarchist pole in the flurry of debate that the issue was raising in the peace-movement and the left generally to prevent the discussion from being monopolized by the mindless baaaing of the peaceniks on the one hand and the left criticisms of "adventurism" on the other.

What we ended up with, because of the previous involvement of the two main authors in Leninist groups, our fear of police and state attack, and fear of our own attraction to this kind of direct action, was a document that was as much "loyal opposition" as anything the New Democratic Party might have come up with.

Our knee-jerk reaction ignored the real consequences of the action—in terms of the physical attack on the war machine, the power of example on other radical peace activists, and its power as a 'publicity gimmick' to inform people of the existence of a cruise missile plant in Toronto. We ignored our own feelings about the action and the consequences of our feelings (and those of other radical activists in the city) of pure delight, on our future activities against the war machine. We substituted ideology for reality.

We characterized the action as 'vanguardist' despite the lack of any 'party-building' orientation on the part of Direct Action. We called the action 'terrorist' despite our later quote from Chomsky that "terrorism are the acts of violence opposed by the ruling class". We lied about our feelings through not stating them and using loaded words like 'terrorist'.

Now, there are places where our instincts were fulfilled—especially in our insistence on the need for revolution and on the primacy of building towards that and avoiding sidetracks into actions that don't encourage the self-activity of people in their own liberation and in our attack on simple-minded non-violence. It seems from any study of the past that only nonviolent movements supported by violent movements have had any effect—Ghandi was backed by a radical bombing campaign as was Martin Luther King (though the bourgeoisie, in its wisdom, only show us the non-violence).

Basically our ideas have shifted around, after seeing the three major peace things since the bombing—october 17th here in Toronto, October 30th in Ottawa, and November 11th out at Litton Systems in

Rexdale. We have read and digested the Direct Action communique, and seen these events. We now believe that, though we didn't do the the bombing or help out the Direct Action group before the Litton bomb, the action was very good—there are many more radical peaceniks thinking beyond civil disobedience towards insurrection.

**The bombing was a good action,
some Toronto area anarchists.**

Against U.S. Missile Testing in Canada

Do Canadians want this country to be a test range for Ronald Reagan's Cruise Missile and weapons of mass destruction? 3 out of 4 Canadians in 134 municipal referenda voted "YES" for disarmament. Tens of thousands of us have protested in almost every city and town across Canada. Trudeau's Liberal government has ignored us. Canada is about to become a party to the Reagan government's massive arms escalation. An agreement drafted and completed in almost total secrecy, to test the Cruise Missile, cluster bombs, and other yet unspecified weapons of mass destruction, is about to be announced.

Make your government finally hear you.

Join people all across Canada.

Demonstrate!
1 p.m., 34 King St. E. (Liberal Party H.Q.)

On the Saturday following the announcement of the agreement.

a project of

AGAINST CRUISE TESTING COALITION 532-6720
653-3706

Endorsed by the Toronto Disarmament Network

Kick It Over 6 (1983)

THE POLITICS OF BOMBS

This discussion paper was submitted to us by a reader. Although we don't all agree with the writer's position on what revolutionary activity is, we do feel the paper will begin a discussion on the role of armed struggle in Canada. It also points out lessons to be learned from the activities and trials of Direct Action.

The nature of the response to the article, "Julie Rats Out," in *Resistance* 10, and the discussion surrounding the letter to *Open Road* 21, indicate the degree to which we, as a movement, have not addressed the most basic issues raised by the actions of Direct Action and the Wimmin's Fire Brigade, or the subsequent arrest and trials of the Vancouver Five.

It has been our tendency to treat this example of armed resistance within the boundaries of the Canadian state as if it were an isolated, unprecedented, and wholly ahistorical event. After all, with the exception of the FLQ in Québec between 1963 and '70, Canada has no modern experience of homegrown clandestine armed resistance—in fact, very little history of militant resistance of any stripe. It is our weakness that we fail to recognize that in this way Canada is not representative of every other major West European societies, but is in fact, unique. Most West European societies have developed and sustained an armed movement since the early 70s. If we are to understand the Direct Action/Wimmin's Fire Brigade/Vancouver Five experience, if we are to critically assimilate and build upon it, we must look at it in this broader context of resistance.

If we are to look at armed struggle as a serious option within the Canadian State, we must establish its potential purposes. These are: armed propaganda, sabotage—causing real material damage to the State apparatus and capitalism, posing the revolutionary option; laying the base for a future popular armed resistance.

Armed Propaganda

The coordination of urban guerrilla actions, including armed action, is the principal way of making armed propaganda. These actions, carried out with specific and determined objectives, inevitably become propaganda material for the mass communications system.
—Carlos Marighella,
Minimanual of the Urban Guerrilla

All guerrilla actions are inevitably armed propaganda. The success of such actions as propaganda tools, however, depends on a variety of factors. The greater the degree to which the target of the action is associated in popular consciousness with some aspect of oppression, the greater the ease with which it can find broad-based support. If the target has been a clear focus for ongoing work on the part of the legal movement, the reason for the actions will be immediately clear, at least to those people aware of the issue. This will be especially true if the activities of the legal movement have failed to alter the behaviour of the target, despite an ongoing and consistent campaign. The timing in this case is important. Armed propaganda will be most effective if the legal movement has hit an apparent impasse.

It is equally important to the overall propaganda success of an armed action that workers not be endangered. Any reticence regarding armed struggle within the movement will be reinforced by the injury or death of an innocent party, and any potential popular appeal will be completely precluded.

However, we must equally recognize that such injuries and deaths, as tragic as they certainly are, will always be a possibility in the context of armed resistance, particularly as the State often has a secret interest in allowing such incidents to occur (if not creating them) to fuel its propaganda war against the guerrilla. It must equally be recognized that all States, including the Canadian State, are daily engaged in genocide and violent attacks against Third World peoples, against other species, and against the earth itself. No error on the part of the guerrilla could begin to touch this daily violence, which has become acceptable as a structural part of our society to such a degree as to go on virtually ignored.

Beyond the actual action itself, the success in terms of propaganda depends, to a great degree, on the capacity of supporters in the legal movement to effectively do propaganda work. The action must become widely known and contextually understood to receive the maximum popular support. The guerrilla cannot be expected to do this, and by and large will not be in a position to do this. This job is the responsibility of sympathetic people in the legal movement.

Sabotage

Every urban guerrilla action directed at property is an act of sabotage. Whereas the legal movement can raise consciousness regarding a particular issue, as long as it is public and legal, it can do little to actually disrupt the ability of the State apparatus to carry through its intentions. Only a flexible, clandestine, armed movement is in a position to carry out relentless attack and sabotage, albeit in a limited form. Such sabotage, while it may not ultimately stop a project, slows it down and greatly increases the cost.

Posing the Revolutionary Option

The principle (is) that revolutionary action in itself, the very act of arming oneself, preparing, equipping, and pursuing activities that violate bourgeois legality, generates revolutionary consciousness, and conditions.
—a Tupamaro

The mass armed capability which will destroy the State has its beginnings in very small armed actions, and through these guerrilla actions the armed mass capability develops.
—Red Army Fraction (RAF)

By engaging in armed struggle, even in its most formative stage, the guerrilla raises the issues of militant armed resistance to the capitalist State from a dim theoretical concept to an immediate practical possibility. In doing so, the nature of left discussion is qualitatively changed. The possibility for revolutionaries to engage in effective armed resistance is affirmed. While this preliminary armed resistance will, de facto, receive only limited support, even on the left, this limited support is the potential nucleus for the eventual armed struggle that will be necessary for revolutionary change to occur in any nation-State.

As well as indicating the possibility for militant resistance, armed activity demonstrates the possibility of pinpointing the system's weak points, and attacking offensively and effectively, even from a perspective of relative weakness. By so doing the myth of the invincible State is deflated and new possibilities for resistance are opened up.

Urban guerrilla warfare aims to destroy the domination of the State by striking at single weak points, and to destroy the myth of the omnipotence of the State and its invulnerability.
—RAF

When carried out in a consistent way, guerrilla politics can be empowering to even the legal left. The guerrilla, because of its clandestine organization, is in a position to add a concrete dimension to the propaganda and agitation of the legal left.

In short, the guerrilla is an offensive position adopted by a limited number of comrades. The guerrilla is the revolutionary expression of our rage in the face of a seemingly monolithic and untouchable enemy.

Almost every example of urban guerrilla resistance has been subject to a litany of attacks from the "traditional" left. The most common and recurrent criticisms are that: the time is not right, and therefore, armed resistance is elitist; and, armed resistance brings down repression on legitimate left organizations and individuals.

Waiting for the Right Time

If there is not a reasonably prepared group, the revolutionary conjunctures are simply wasted or not taken advantage of.
—a Tupamaro

It would be wrong to engage in armed struggle only when the "the consent of the masses" is assured, for this would actually mean to renounce the struggle altogether, as this consent can be obtained only by struggle itself. True mass armed struggle can only take place when it is understood by the masses, however, the comprehension of the need for armed struggle can only be aroused through beginning armed struggle.
—RAF

The concept that when "the time is right" for armed struggle we will recognize it and by some amazing osmosis, absorb the information and ability we need to effectively wage guerrilla warfare is indeed a curious one. Clearly, if we don't begin now to prepare for the eventual armed conflict with the State, the State will take all necessary precautions to ensure its ultimate control before the point of crisis likely to motivate massive resistance in the First World actually occurs.

Fig. (d) Towers should be felled across transmitter station

In fact, it is clear that the modern techno-police State is fairly advanced in this area. While we carry on our low-level, largely educational, political work, the State is busily developing the means of surveillance that will allow it to identify and, if necessary, monitor the movement and activity of each and every individual in this society. If we do not act now to organize effective clandestine opposition, the total surveillance State will be quietly placed in motion, perhaps curtailing once and for all the possibility of effective revolutionary upsurge.

Armed Resistance Brings Down Repression

Repression is indeed part of revolution, a natural anti-thesis, the always-to-be-expected defense/attack reflex of the beleagured, toothless tiger.
—George Jackson

The concept that armed activity brings down repression on uninvolved people of the left is one of the more revealing statements to come from those opposed to armed struggle.

Such a perception presumes that somehow the State is willing to stand by and allow left opposition to unfold unchallenged as long as it remains non-violent. Clearly, this is not the case. While non-violent, legal organizing may not illicit direct intervention from the State, the police apparatus engages in constant intervention, infiltration, surveillance, and destabilization. Andy Moxley's work as an infiltrator in the peace movement stands as witness to this.

This statement further presumes that there exists some form of valid left activity that will allow the left to play an objectively revolutionary role without threatening their security vis-a-vis the State.

The unrecognized reality is that armed activity does not create repression. Repression is a structural part of the "techno-fascist" State on every level. Armed resistance simply brings it out into the open where it can be seen and understood for what it is.

Finally, the legal left often fails to realize that the primary motivation for raids, arrests, and other repressive actions against the legal left in the wake of a guerrilla attack is not to capture those who are responsible (the police know they won't be found in legal left organizations), but to drive a wedge between the legal movement and the guerrilla. The tragedy is that the legal left, by and large, falls right into the trap, often going on to do the State's anti-guerrilla public relations work.

If we accept revolution, we must accept all that it implies: repression, counter-terrorism, days filled with work, nervous strain, prison, funerals.
—George Jackson

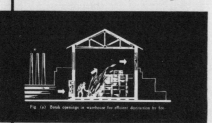

Fig. (a) Break openings in warehouse for efficient destruction by fire.

Having established a general framework for evaluating armed struggle in First World urban environments, we'd like to turn out attention to the particulars of the Direct Action and Wimmin's Fire Brigade experience.

Cheekye-Dunsmuir Power Substation

On May 31, 1982, Direct Action bombed the Cheekye-Dunsmuir power substation. From both an ideological and a strategic perspective, this action was armed activity of the highest order.

As an act of sabotage is was very successful. The power-substation, which was just about ready to go into action, was rendered useless. Direct Action's four bombs caused more that $5 million damage, necessitating the reconstruction of the substation nearly from scratch.

In terms of posing the revolutionary option, the action was well timed. The legal movement had spent

years petitioning, letter-writing, picketing, blockading, etc., without successfully putting a halt to Hydro's plan to develop Cheekye-Dunsmuir regardless of environmental or human costs. Direct Action showed that when the State closes all legal channels there still remain options for people who are opposed to the policies of the State, and these options can be exercised by small committed groups with few resources.

In propaganda terms, the communiqué was clear and concise, explaining simply why the bombing had been necessary. If there was a weakness in propaganda terms, it didn't lie either in the action or the accompanying communiqué; it is to be found in our inability as a movement to recognize the parameters of what had occurred and to widely circulate the communiqué and develop a discussion around it.

Litton Industries Bombing

As an act of sabotage, the Direct Action bombing of Litton Industries on October 14, 1982, was a massive success, causing an estimated $7 million damage and eventually playing a role in creating the situation whereby Litton Systems of Canada was not invited to bid on the contract for the guidance device for the advanced version of the Cruise Missile. Litton President, Ronald Keating, made clear in April '84 that both public pressure and the Direct Action bombing played a role in knocking Litton out of the running. He said, "(Protesters) are an irritant, they get a lot of publicity, and the Americans read every damn bit of it. Pressure from these people is making the Americans look twice." He added, "No one else has been bombed." (He's got a valid complaint, someone ought to do something about that.)

Again, the communiqué was clear and concise. In fact, from a sabotage and propaganda perspective, it seems likely that the action would have been a success had it not led to seven injuries, some of them quite serious. The injuries were a result of the bomb exploding twelve minutes early (there has been speculation that police radios accidentally triggered it), and of security personnel and police failing to grasp the seriousness of the situation and evacuate the building immediately. As it was, the workers were leaving the building at the exact moment the 50-pound bomb exploded, leaving them open to maximum injury.

Direct Action released a communiqué taking responsibility for errors on their own part, as well as indicating actions on the part of Litton security personnel and the cops which contributed to the tragedy. The communiqué then went on to delineate all of the errors which led to the injuries. It is too long to reprint or summarize here, but it is well worth reading. It clearly outlines the errors Direct Action made and the degree to which the police and security incompetence contributed to the situation.

The police moved quickly to exploit any uncertainties in the movement regarding the actions. They mounted a series of raids against legal peace groups including the Cruise Missile Conversion Project, the Alliance for Non-Violent Action, and World Emergency, as well as against prominent individuals in the peace movement. These actions, clearly intended to drive a wedge between Direct Action and the peace movement were, in large part, successful, with some leading figures in the peace movement going so far as to cooperate with the police investigation and to publicly state their hope that Direct Action would be successfully apprehended. There were also laudable examples of individuals in the peace movement who clearly expressed their solidarity with Direct Action (and later, the Vancouver Five) in the face of State attacks.

Red Hot Video Firebombings

The November 22, 1982 firebombings of three Red Hot Video locations in the lower mainland of BC was far and away the most popular armed attack of this period. This action was extremely successful, reducing one outlet to ashes and seriously damaging a second. In the third case, the incendiary device failed to ignite. It was also an action immediately embraced by all sections of the women's movement as one which expressed their rage. Groups as diverse as the BC Federation of Women and the Montréal-based Feminist Coalition Against Pornography publicly embraced it. It was soon clear that women recognized in this action the final option when faced with the total intransigience of the State.

In spite of the unfortunate injuries at Litton Industries, the Direct Action and Wimmin's F Brigade campaigns of 1982 were, by and larg effective on all levels. As propaganda the actions a communiqués were extremely pointed and effectiv interlocking well with large-scale public campaig We wish to reiterate that any shortcomings on t propaganda level were in large part based on the lack recognition by sympathetic people active in the leg movement of the necessity for distributing t communiqués and encouraging discussion about the and the strategy they represented. It was not until t injuries at Litton that the movement began discussi Direct Action and their strategy, and those of us w wished to defend the strategy were forced into an i tensely defensive position, a very poor position fro which to begin such a complex discussion. Retrospe tively, it was a major error to let the positive examp of the Cheekye-Dunsmuir bombing pass with so litt attention. The fact that the Litton bombing w destined to be Direct Action's last action furth complicated matters because we were still in t middle of the very complex discussion surroundi that action and the injuries at the time of the arrest

The Arrests

The arrest of the Vancouver Five, on January 2 1983, was, when looked at retrospectively, almost i evitable. The quantity of organizing those five i dividuals had to do in isolation made it virtually certa that they would manage for long. Nonetheless, appears as if they made certain errors that indicate a inadequate understanding of police tactics. The errors must be recognized, examined, and understoo so as to be avoided in the future.

The fact that they continued to live in the Vancouver area and continued to maintain contact, even at a very low level, with some friends was a complete misjudgement of circumstances. Clearly, if and when the police pinpointed them as suspects, friends and acquaintances would be put under surveillance. At that point it was only a matter of time until the police came in direct contact with one or more of the Five. If one is to believe the police version of the surveillance that led to the Five (although certain parts of the police story are totally implausible) then this is exactly what happened.

There are lessons to be learned from the information available regarding the nature and style of the police investigation. It is clear that they are more aware of where individuals are at ideologically than we sometimes give them credit for. They were able to draw up a pool of suspects reasonably quickly, and although this pool contained many individuals who were totally uninvolved, it appears to have eventually provided the key connection that led to the Five, after which it simply became a matter of collecting the necessary information. It is clear that they are capable of sophisticated surveillance. They claim to have had as many as eight to ten cops surveilling a single suspect at times, and they claim to have been able to place Brent in Calgary at a certain time due to a "paper trail" which he left. It is also clear that they are willing to overlook criminal activities if they are holding out for a bigger bust. They clearly let several possible stolen vehicle arrests pass, and quite probably watched the Red Hot Video firebombings, while holding out for a more major arrest.

Some of the lessons to be drawn from this are clear. Comrades engaging in illegal activity on this scale must be prepared to go completely underground, which implies severing all contacts with their previous milieu and friends. Such contacts, while emotionally and psychologically significant, are suicidal from a security perspective. Police surveillance is sophisticated. If comrades involved in clandestine work are to avoid it, they must practice sophisticated counter-surveillance. Primary to this is a capacity to remove themselves from the areas where investigations are likely to start. And, of course, it is clear that any sense that the police are aware of one's activities, particularly any direct contact with the cops, however seemingly innocuous, requires that the guerrilla disappear and destroy everything that might allow the cops to trace them. All of this implies a highly developed network.

The urban guerrilla presupposes the organization of an illegal apparatus, in other words, apartments, weapons, ammunition, cars, and identification papers.
—RAF

It appears that by remaining in the Vancouver area, by maintaining contacts with friends, and by ignoring significant brushes with the law, the Five greatly facilitated their own ultimate arrest.

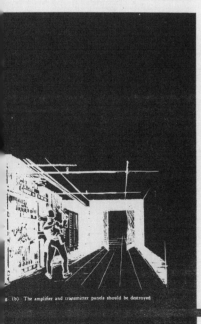

g. (b) The amplifier and transmitter panels should be destroyed

The Trial

If the military situation is difficult from the first moments, the political situation will be no less delicate; and if a single military error can wipe out the guerrillas, a political error can check their development for a long period.
—Che Guevara

While certain tactical errors may have contributed to the arrest of the Five, their ramifications for the strategy of armed resistance were minor. It was the errors committed by the arrested comrades and those of us who did defence/support work that served most to defuse the importance of the contributions of Direct Action and the Wimmin's Fire Brigade to resistance in Canada.

The approach of the Five to the legal system and the trials was a serious political misjudgement. By denying responsibility for the actions, rather than defending the actions and approaching the trials as a vehicle for a discussion of the issues and the role of armed struggle in a First World country, they completely abdicated any control over the trials.

By hedging their bets on minimizing their sentences, the Five put themselves in a situation where they could not actively use the trials for propaganda purposes without threatening their legal strategy. In so doing they promoted several erroneous perceptions. First of all, they de facto recognized the right of the courts, and by extension, the State, to judge their actions, rather than pinpointing the role of the legal system as a pillar of class injustice before which no equitable judgement can ever be expected, and least of all in a case of armed resistance. Secondly, the integrity which they lost by denying responsibility for their actions, lost them the support of certain sections of the public—including the jury. These errors were further compounded by the fact that they ultimately placed the case in the hands of lawyers and hung their hopes on legal challenges regarding the legitimacy of wiretaps, and similar details of legal protocol. Such a statement of faith in the legal system served only to contribute to further mystification surrounding the theoretical "neutrality" of the courts, and by extension, the State.

The response of supporters was to adopt the liberal demand of the "right to a fair trial." The more we worked with this demand, the more we boxed ourselves in politically. If the Five were maintaining their innocence and we were demanding a "fair trial," then we were de facto blocked from engaging in the primary discussion regarding the actions and role of armed struggle in Canada. If questioned regarding the actions, we were forced by our line to treat the issue of armed struggle as secondary or even inconsequential. Although the Five did resist this, they did so in a weak fashion.

We know that if there was such a thing as fair trials and justice—we would walk free. But there is no justice and we will not receive a fair trial. Yet because it is sometimes possible to exploit the contradictions inherent in the bourgeois democratic legal process (which result from the need for lawmakers to appear fair and legitimate), we will be participating in the courtroom facade to try and minimize the legal attack against us.
—Julie, Ann, Gerry, Doug, Brent
"Free the Five Newsletter"
March 13, '83

It was not until issue 7 of the "Free the Five Newsletter," issued November 16, '83, that four of the Five first publicly opposed the "fair trial" strategy, which by that time had been going on for nearly ten months.

Much of the political work done around our case has been centred on the process of "right to a fair trial," and abuses of process by the media, police, and prosecution. We would like to see the political work done on our case centre around what we consider to be the real issues: environmentalism, feminism, anti-imperialism, and radical activism.
—Ann, Gerry, Doug, Brent

However, in spite of these statements the defence/support milieu failed to change gears. We continued to orient our work around State excesses and illegalities, dispensing information, but refused to engage in the central debate: What is the role of armed resistance in Canada? How can militant resistance be constructed here?

Fig. (h)   Apply sulphuric acid and ignite bomb

If we are to attempt to pinpoint the reasons why we failed to respond positively to the situation the arrests and trials presented us with, several weaknesses become apparent. Both the prisoners and their defence/support committees failed to see the judicial experience, both the courts and prison, as an integral part of the armed struggle. The Five failed to take the lead in using the courtroom as a platform for propaganda and the prison as a central element in the confrontation between oppression and resistance. For our part we fell into the trap of believing we could somehow save our friends if we dwelled on the contradictions within the State's legal system and downplayed the armed actions of Direct Action and the Wimmin's Fire Brigade. The liberal deviations that occurred in this scenario were never rectified in any important way because no shared conception of politics in general or of the trials in particular ever evolved between the Five and their supporters. Because there was no solid political analysis of the situation coming from the prisoners and the supporters failed to evolve one, the possibility of using the trials to build support for the armed struggle was lost.

The situation worsened when the guilty pleas were filed. On March 17, 1984, Julie and Gerry pleaded guilty. Julie pleaded guilty to conspiracy to rob a Brinks armoured car, attempted arson of the Port Coquitlam Red Hot Video, car theft, possession of explosives, possession of weapons dangerous to the public peace, and bombing Litton Industries. Gerry filed the same guilty plea, less possession of explosives and the Litton bombing. On June 4, '84, Ann pleaded guilty to the Cheekye-Dunsmuir bombing, the

GUERRILLA WARFARE

Litton bombing, possession of explosives, and possession of weapons. Ann had already been found guilty of conspiracy to rob a Brinks armoured car, possession of explosives, possession of weapons, possession of stolen property, vehicle theft, and breaking and entering. On June 8, Doug pleaded guilty to the Cheekye-Dunsmuir bombing and Brent pleaded guilty to possession of weapons and possession of explosives, having already been found guilty of the same charges as Ann in the first trial.

While the desire to put an end to dead time faced in endless trials is understandable, especially given the fact that the outcome of the first trial was hardly a victory from a legal perspective. The guilty pleas left little to be recouped politically following the almost exclusive focus of defence/support politics on the "right to a fair trial." Particularly damaging was Gerry's decision to accept a guilty plea on the Wimmin's Fire Brigade actions as part of a plea bargain. This was particularly disorienting as the Wimmin's Fire Brigade had been generally recognized as an all women's group and the action as an all women's action. Gerry's decision to plead guilty purely as a practicality, while understood by those supporters close to the decision-making process, was not necessarily so clear for the broader political community watching the trials, some of whom were taken aback. (We had done such an effective job of our "right to a fair trial" campaign that some people in the political community actually believed the Five were persecuted innocents and in the face of the guilty pleas, felt their trust had been betrayed! This is rather a large statement of how effectively we buried the key issues in our defence/support work.) And it was left unclear whether the Wimmin's Fire Brigade had actually been a statement of women's resistance, or simply Direct Action using another name for reasons of political efficacy. Given the massive popularity of the Wimmin's Fire Brigade, particularly in the women's community, to introduce such unclarity was a political error.

It was not until the sentencing that the first real political statements came from the Five, and this was one and a half years after the arrest and nearly two years after the last action. On June 5, '84, Ann read her statement. This long, eloquent, and powerful statement said, among other things:

> In the beginning when I was first arrested, I was intimidated and surrounded by the courts and prison. This fear provided the basis for the belief that if I played the legal game, I would get acquitted or get less time. This belief obscured my vision and fooled me into believing that I could get a break from the legal system. But this past eight months in court has sharpened my perceptions and strengthened my political convictions to see that the legal game is rigged and political prisoners are dealt a marked deck.
>
> Even though I knew that a few militant direct actions would not make the revolution or stop these projects, I believed it was necessary to begin the development of an underground resistance movements that was capable of sabotage and expropriations and could work free from police surveillance. The development of an effective resistance movement is not an overnight affair—it takes decades of evolution. It has to start somewhere in small numbers and whether or not it grows, becomes effective and successful, will depend on whether or not we make it happen.

Finally, on June 25, '84, Brent was sentenced and made his sentencing statement. A brief portion follows:

> Illegal activities were one part of my activism in the struggle, against the injustices and threats to life manifest in modern industrial civilization and the political and economic system of imperialism. The overall purpose of any illegal activity I was involved in was to further develop the struggle and thereby contribute to the possibility of a better world—one in which all people can finally live in freedom and international unity. Even if this does not come about in my lifetime, it is my hope that one day our future relatives will live in such a world.

The sentencing statements were powerful political statements and were received as such. As good as the sentencing statements were, coming as they did, at the end of a long and intense process, they did not serve as a rallying point for a discussion. Had such statements come early in the legal process and had the defence/support committees chosen to stress the politics inherent in the actions and accompanying communiqués, the political potential of the trials might have been realized. As it was, the political issues, quite simply, came to the fore too late.

The Appeals

A further blow came with Julie's decision to break with her former comrades and recant.

In an emotionally charged performance Julie used her sentence appeal to focus the bulk of the responsibility for Direct Action and the Wimmin's Fire Brigade on Ann and Brent, particularly Brent, whom she identified variously as the leader and the planner. She claimed to have been harassed into the group, to have been young and impressionable, a state she described as an adolescent crisis, and to have been worn down and molded by constant pressure and abuse. She claims her seeming vigour for revolutionary activity, as it was recorded on the wiretaps and bugs, was not representative of her true feelings, but part of an effort to appear tough in order to ward off the constant criticism she was a victim of. She even went as far as to suggest she would have left the group, claiming she feared to do so after reading Marighella's Mini-Manual of the Urban Guerrilla, where she claimed Marighella said anyone leaving the guerrilla must be liquidated.

It is important to note in passing that Marighella didn't say this. What he, in fact, said regarding the guerrilla was:

> When he (a guerrilla) cannot face the difficulties, or knows he lacks the patience to wait, it is better to relinquish his role before he betrays his pledge, for he clearly lacks the basic qualities necessary to be a guerrilla.

While the purpose of Julie's patchwork story of lies, distortion, and paranoia was clearly to save her own skin, the quality of her story, the degree to which it fits into the standard State line on guerrilla politics, the degree to which it is tailored for counter-insurgency, indicate that she must have fallen victim to fairly intense police pressure, that she had been a pawn in the larger political strategy. The long sentence that Julie was given was doubtless part of a strategy to break her spirit so that she would be open to approaches from the State. In order to have this excessive sentence reduced, Julie was willing to engage in whatever grovelling was required and to portray her former comrades, particularly Ann and Brent, both of whom had sentence appeals forthcoming, as deranged and irresponsible, if not out-and-out remorselessly evil.

The outcome was predictable. Ann and Brent had their sentence appeals denied. Julie, for her part, received a five year reduction from twenty to fifteen for her propaganda role in the State's attack on Ann and Brent in particular, and the guerrilla in general.

Prison

With the end of the appeals came the end of the Vancouver Five as a public issue and the comrades withdrew from the public eye to serve their sentences. In Ann's case life, in Brent's 22 years, for Gerry ten, and Doug six.

As was the case with the trials, they have not used their prison time or the repression they face there as a springboard for a discussion of guerrilla resistance. Rather than asserting themselves as political prisoners in an ongoing way, they have assimilated themselves into the anonymity of the prison milieu. This has led to a situation where their courageous acts of resistance and their entire strategy as enunciated in the communiqués and the sentencing statements have been forgotten by all save a few tiny, isolated pockets of supporters.

To sum up, the Five and their supporters have thus far failed to play their potential role in advancing an understanding of armed struggle within the Canadian State. This lack is due to serious shortcomings in our political understanding of the elements at play. We failed to recognize and utilize the possibilities for advancing the strategy of armed struggle available in the trial process. In so doing, the opportunies opened up by the actions of Direct Action and the Wimmin's Fire Brigade were lost. The mystifying demand of the "right to a fair trial," led nowhere and served to liquidate the key issue of armed resistance in Canada. Although the history of Direct Action and the Wimmin's Fire Brigade has doubtless left its mark on the Canadian left, although the concept of armed resistance has been put on the agenda in a practical way so that it will never again be the non-issue it was prior to this experience, to date we have not really overcome the pacifying effects of the political errors we have made. It seems that both the Five and their supporters, having suffered this defeat, have turned away from the discussion of armed struggle to focus their energy elsewhere.

If we are to overcome the errors we have made, we must critically examine these errors, we must critically examine the events surrounding Direct Action, the Wimmin's Fire Brigade, and the Vancouver Five. As painful as it may be, we must pinpoint the errors and shortcomings of both the prisoners and their supporters and deal with them honestly. We can learn by studying the national liberation struggles of Third and Fourth World peoples in the Third World, Western Europe, and the USA, as well as by examining the history and current practice of the urban guerrilla movements in the USA and Western Europe. And, of course, we must face the responsibility of developing our own practice in Canada.

We have written the above not as an attack on the prisoners or their support community. We extend our love and solidarity to the imprisoned comrades who have contributed so much of themselves towards the realization of armed struggle in Canada. We also extend our love and solidarity to all who have worked to support the imprisoned comrades, and to all those who struggle for revolutionary change.

We cannot see any way to avoid certain criticisms given the current situation on the Canadian left. However, we have offered the above criticisms not as a personal attack on anyone, nor to create further divisions in the movement, but in the hope of creating a genuine discussion around the experiences of armed resistance and in the hope of aiding in pushing the struggle forward.

> It is better to err acting than to do nothing for fear of erring. Without initiative there is no guerrilla warfare.
> —Carlos Marighella

Open Road 22 (1988)

Anarcha-Feminism: Moving Together

By Elaine Leeder

For the last four years I have called myself an Anarcha-Feminist. I have participated in Anarcha-Feminist groups, meetings and conferences and have taught courses in "small-group process." Through my experience I have come to realize that the interraction in all women's groups has a unique flavour and style and that this is particularly true of feminist groups. This style has been called the "mosaic" process. It contrasts with traditional "linear" thinking that has pervaded human interactions in this society. The characteristics of competition and hierarchy are integral to a Capitalist system. Linear, logical arguments are used in discussions to perpetuate the values of this system. Linear thinking is done to substantiate or to argue a hypothesis. Women's values of cooperation, emotion, and intuition have been given little credence in this type of thinking.

The mosaic pattern that women use includes a supportive structure with considerably less competition. This style uses anecdotal material, encourages the interjection of comments into conversation, accepts emotional data as a legitimate part of intellectual discussions, uses narratives, paraphrases, shifts directions and moves the group together toward a mutual search for understanding. It is an organic process, non-hierarchical and non-competitive. It could in fact be called Anarchist because the values of leaderlessness, lack of hierarchy, non-competition and spontaneity have historically been associated with the term Anarchism. They are also Feminist values. From what I have seen, this style exists less frequently in mixed groups of men and women. In fact, it rarely even exists in groups of Anarchist men and women. Anarchist literature is full of documentation of the exploitation by Anarchist men of the women in their lives (e.g. Emma Goldman and Alexander Berkman, *Nowhere at Home*). My own recent experience among old-time Anarchists, and even among the new breed, substantiates this statement.

Bearing in mind that sexism exists within Anarchism, it seems apparent that its principles and its current practice, in fact, conflict. It is important for Anarchists to incorporate this "Feminist Process" into their practice so that ultimately the principles and the practice of Anarchism can become one.

Political Hybrid

There are a number of Feminists who have realized the inherent Anarchism in our process and have begun working in groups to study and grow together as Anarcha-Feminists. This hybrid developed out of the late sixties when many of us were involved in male-dominated, competitive, hierarchical, mass organizations. At that time (and to this day in Anarchist literature) women were told to work for the larger movement. Instead we formed small consciousness-raising groups which dealt with personal issues in our lives.

These were spontaneous, direct action groups organized for ourselves. They were much like groups organized in Spain prior to 1936 and could be called affinity groups. These affinity groups were based on similarities of interests and had an internal democracy in which women would share information and knowledge. These groups generally consisted of white middle-class women who often for the first time were placed in a situation in which they were not in competition with one another. Third world and working class women were generally not involved in these groups, which is also the case today in Anarcha-Feminist groups. This may be explained by the fact that these women were more concerned with survival issues, since they were exploited as workers and as minorities.

Feminist Theory

Out of these early beginnings of a Feminist theory slowly evolved. Some of us began to study political theories in these small groups and discovered the inherent Anarchism in our Feminism. We began to use an Anarchist analysis to aid in our development of theory and strategy for social change. We realized that patriarchy was a male-dominated hierarchy and that the nuclear family perpetuated that hierarchy. The family, we discovered, teaches us to obey Father, God, Teachers, Boss and whoever else is above us (see Peggy Kornegger, *Anarchism: The Feminist Connection*). It teaches us competition, consumerism, and isolation as well as the treatment of each other in a subject-object relationship. Nuclear families, we know now, are the basis of all hierarchical, authoritarian systems. As a result, if one fights patriarchy, one fights all hierarchies. If we change the nature of the nuclear family we may begin to change all forms of leadership, domination, and governments.

Linear Thought

As a result of this form of thinking, Feminists now place value on other ways of looking at things. No longer must we see the world through linear thought patterns: rational vs sensual, mind vs body, logic vs intuition. We have begun to look at things on a continuum rather than in dualistic, competitive terms. It follows that Anarcha-Feminists do not say that women should get an equal share of power. Instead we say that there should be an abolition of all power relationships. We do not want a woman president. We want no presidents at all. To us equal wage for equal work is not a crucial issue. Hierarchies and power distribution is.

Open Road 10 (1979)

Anarchism

Much has been written on the similarities of Anarchism and Feminism (e.g. Lynn Farrow, *Feminism as Anarchism* and Carol Erlich, *Socialism, Anarchism, and Feminism*). In essence what they all say is that Feminism and Anarchism have much in common. Both encourage spontaneous change and free association. Both see the need for mass movements, not a vanguard. Both encourage change from below, not above.

Anarchism sees the enemy as the State. Feminism sees the enemy as Patriarchy. Anarcha-Feminists see them as the same. Patriarchy is part and parcel of the State. We are fighting the same enemy at different points on the continuum.

Feminist groups often follow anarchist principles. Some of us have articulated the connection. Others of us have not, but the form is still there, whether it is conscious or not. Our groups are generally small, and sometimes these groups form alliances to act together with others on certain issues. This is similar to the Anarchist concept of federations. Within the groups there is an attempt at rotation of tasks and skill sharing so that power never resides with the same person. According to Anarchist principles there is equal access to all information, and these groups are voluntary and intentional. The groups are non-hierarchical, and self-discipline is crucial. The unskilled are urged to take leadership positions, and the indigenous leaders translate their skills to those not as knowledgeable in certain areas. We work in these groups on practicing the revolution now in our daily lives. We discuss the immediate experience of oppression of power among us and those with whom we live. We work on the everyday issues that oppress us, not just on the theoretical, abstract ideas of revolution.

When conflicts arise among us attempts are made by each of us to use self-discipline and to put ourselves in the other person's position. I have rarely seen coercion used in Anarcha-Feminist small groups. Instead we share ideas, support others' perceptions, disagree, argue and hammer out our differences. Dissension is accepted, listened to and learned from. Sometimes there is a point that is objected to, and then a debate ensues. It is often heard and understood, because many of us realize that our conflicts come from different life experiences. Generally by the end of the session there has been a conflict resolution. If not we return next time having thought the issue through further. We then discuss it or leave it as need be. There is room for dissension because there is mutual trust and respect that has grown. This trust is a difficult quality to develop in larger groups, which might explain why we continually gravitate to smaller ones. We have learned that communication is crucial, and that through it we can work out our differences. Conflicts can and do occur regularly because we have seen ourselves work it through.

Sexism

Because we see the need to confront sexism in our daily lives some of us have seen the need to confront men (Anarchist or otherwise) who do not live in their personal lives what they preach in their political lives.

Some of us have worked in restructuring mixed political organizations so that intuition, emotion, spontaneity and other Feminists principles can be experienced by people other than Feminists. In some of these mixed groups we have tried to introduce the consensual decision-making process that is usually part of women's groups.

It is clear to me from my experience with women in varying groups that the time has come for Feminists to make clear and articulate the Anarchism in our Feminism. We need to call it by name and begin to create it as a viable and acceptable alternative. No longer does the word "Anarchism" have to be whispered. We are living it now in our small groups. The next step is to let ourselves and others know who we are, and what our vision is for now and for the future.

Open Road 10 (1979)

ANARCHA-FEMINISM: WHY THE HYPHEN?

With the vision of anarchism and feminism's durability, we'll put up one hell of a fight to be human.

BY KYTHA KURIN

While there have always been women who considered themselves anarchists, the term anarcha-feminist is a product of the 70s. The following piece attempts to trace its roots and possible future.

Part I – The Question

Those who moan about the apathetic 70s may be high-salaried academics, disillusioned student rebels of the 60s, male marxists or anarchists, dupes of the mass media who equate value with spectacle appeal, possibly even liberal women's libbers, but they aren't radical feminists.

Through the numberless twists and phases of large pro-abortion demos, intimate consciousness-raising groups, internal heterosexual-lesbian splits, anti-male separatism, feminist union organizing, rape crisis centres, in short, through confronting the present anti-woman, anti-life society straight on, the radical feminist movement has picked up the 60s euphoria of daring to demand the impossible and has sat down to the actual task of translating the dreams into reality.

And anarchism has been forced to labour with anger, dynamism and love of the women's movement. Throughout the decade some feminists and anarchists have called for the synthesis of the two movements. In 1975 Peggy Kornegger first published "Anarchism, the Feminist Connection," the Zero collective printed their statement "Anarcha-Feminism" in 1977 and *Open Road* had several features on the subject.

But while these have been real efforts to deal with a hyphenated concept that many feel should be contained in the single word anarchism, there have been many more who see the two movements as mutually exclusive. Depending on who you're talking to, they're also likely to see "their" movement as "more genuinely revolutionary."

Many of us tend to welcome a new decade as offering a clean slate. That's one reason for reconsidering the dialectics behind anarcha-feminism. Radical feminists have worked hard, experienced unexpected joys and frustrations and learned a lot about confronting patriarchy. And no person for whom anarchism is more than a label can have failed not only to have learned from the feminist experience, but to have seriously questioned and refocused on the politics in anarchism.

Have the experiences of the feminists and the impact of those experiences on the anarchists been understood well enough for all of us to successfully confront and create the 80s? That's the urgent question – because, while a new calendar may seem to allow a fresh start, our anti-life society does not. Women are still oppressed by personal and institutionalized sexism, most people are still denied any life beyond a mere survival existence, and all humanity lives under the pervasive threat of nuclear annihilation.

The meaning or non-meaning of anarcha-feminism is not a question of semantics or preferences. It's a question of what we've learned and how we can apply that learning to reclaim the planet as our life source instead of seeing it prepared as our death bed.

While it is customary to define one's terms before using them, in an examination of anarcha-feminism it makes more sense to consider the activities before the label. It has, after all, been the concrete experiences of radical feminist activity that have created the need to understand the potentials and limitations of feminism and anarchism.

After looking at some of the major accomplishments, desires and disappointments of the radical feminist movement, we should at least be able to appreciate the historical circumstances that gave birth to the concept of anarcha-feminism. Looking at where the word came from rather than arguing about what the purity of the words feminism or anarchism should mean, we'll be in a better position to consider the future of anarcha-feminism. And finally, from that to consider some of the most viable directions for revolutionaries of the 80s.

Part II – The Radical Feminist Experience Redefining the Political

The radical feminist movement has never been more than superficially related to women's libbers of the *Ms. Magazine* variety who fit so nicely into liberalism's "The-world's-yours-for-the-manipulating" image. Radical feminists, many of whom were first politically active in anti-war and student demonstrations, always knew that the establishment gets nasty when it's threatened. And because being a feminist means confronting that establishment at every turn, feminists have met with a lot of nastiness – from governments, from men, from repressed-oppressed women, from lovers, from non-feminist radicals and even from our own internalized sexism. But while the constant confrontations have been exhausting and at times demoralizing, they have also pushed feminists to redefine the political.

What are political issues for women? Health, day care, sexuality, family, work, prisons, education, housing? For each of these, the myriad "sub-sections:" health flies into psychiatry, food, abortion, contraceptives, drugs, nuclear radiation. It's not a matter of choosing a "project," it's finding yourself involved in a particular struggle that's manipulated by and implicated in this authoritarian destruction bent society.

For many women, our first specifically feminist

FEMINISM

politicization came through demanding the right to abortion, that is, the right to control our own bodies. When anti-woman laws were exposed not as neglected holdovers of the Dark Ages, but as conscious means of reinforcing a woman's body as property of the State, many feminists were prepared to work in political movements because we had already found ourselves in a political confrontation. There was no question of "learning" to make politics personal, the intimacy of the personal was made political by the intervention of the State.

Men hadn't been so clearly confronted by this reality. In spite of the fact that most men sell their body/mind power and potential through wage slavery, and that their creative abilities are drained, suffocated and side-tracked into commodity consumption, many so-called radical men still acted as if they accepted an electoral definition of "politics" – something you go out and "do" for at most, a few hours a day. While many men recognized the urgency of political activity (something's got to change soon), most did not recognize the immediacy (we've got to make changes every day).

SEPARATISM

Traditionally women had been stereo-typed as "not understanding" politics and to a certain extent many women acquiesced in that opinion. But being forced to fight for a say in our own bodies, many women now felt that we did understand politics and the need for a unified opposition to the present structures of society.

It's important to remember that originally many tried to work in existing left political groups. Anarchism, with its recognition that the process of making a revolution can't be separated from the goals of that revolution, appeared to understand the political in much the same way that feminism did. Anarchists recognized that an authoritarian, exploitative movement could not possibly create a non-authoritarian, non-exploitative society. But what anarchist theory recognized, feminists demanded.

Anarchist meetings were not substantially different from other Left party meetings. There were some subjects that were relevant to political meetings and there were proper ways of speaking at political meetings. But feminists who now understood politics all too well demanded that all types of domination and exploitation be recognized as political issues because when oppression confronts people in every aspect of their lives, how can some areas of living be acceptable for political work and others not? These feminists insisted on confronting domination, power tripping, and sexism right when it happened in a meeting, instead of simply in the abstract or outside the group.

Feminists also refused to decapitate the "reasoning" self from the "emotional" self before participating in political meetings and demanded that the whole person, complete with warmth and confusion of life be present. We exposed

the irrationality of believing that a life direction that didn't spring from a sensitivity to the totality of life could in any sane way be considered rational.

Most anarchists had never been asked to so directly live their anarchism and found the feminist insistence on "process" and the repeated "interruptions" about male domination, upsetting. And many feminists who had been attracted by anarchist theory but were really more concerned with anarchist practice, felt frustrated and refused to be placated with the rhetoric that would have one believe that anarchists couldn't possibly be authoritarian sexists.

So a lot of feminists left mixed groups. Some worked in anarcha-feminist groups and many gave up on anarchism altogether.

At the same time, feminists were naturally becoming disillusioned with other Left groups too. Most marxist parties didn't even have to pretend to deal with feminism because their party lines clearly set priorities and hierarchies for political activity. Feminist insistence on attacking sexism could be dismissed as bourgeois self-indulgence and when you're trying to set up the dictatorship of the proletariat, it's not inconsistent to be authoritarian.

So while some feminists stayed in mixed political groups, many left to work in women-only groups. Inside these women-only groups were a number of feminists who never had belonged to any political parties but who, like their more disillusioned sisters leaving the mixed groups, recognized that there was a lot of work to be done and that separatism seemed to be at least a temporarily necessary tactic for fighting patriarchy. And indeed, looking back over the decade, in North America and much of Western Europe, much of the significant political work was done by or sparked by radical feminists working outside the traditional Left.

SOME RADICAL FEMINIST WORK
AND ITS IMPLICATIONS

It's not surprising that most of the work done by radical feminists has been centered around education and service. For many women the transition from the traditional home help-mate role to the political help-mate role was a natural one.

Confrontations over abortion rights being the catalyst to many women becoming political, a logical extension was the growth of self-help health collectives. Aware that authoritarian structures, whether of the State or radical political groups, retain the power of authority by hoarding and mystifying knowledge, feminists tried to avoid becoming the "new experts."

They worked to reclaim the body as a natural organism that could be understood and cared for by women themselves rather than left to the authority of doctors, multi-billion dollar drug companies or even radical feminists. They tried to share skills among themselves and

Open Road 11 (1980)

258 § ONLY A BEGINNING

tried to share knowledge and skills with the "patients." Thus, "self-help" health collectives rather than simply "women's" health collectives.

But the big job of combatting the insidious drug pushing in our culture and the need for major medical research has meant that if feminists are to be really effective we have to also work outside our small collectives. If contraceptive research has only managed to deteriorate since the Dark Ages because it is economically profitable to drug companies and patriarchy to have it that way, and if contraceptive research is absolutely essential for women, then the power of drug companies and patriarchy has to be confronted.

People working in rape relief centres faced the same kind of problems. While the centres are essential to rape victims, if they're primarily "reaction" centres, they've got an unending future as helpers of the State. While many women have pushed for stricter enforcement of rape laws, radical feminists know that rape is not a crime against society as we know it, but rather the ultimate expression of our society's belief in and acceptance of force as righteous.

Aside from the fact that it's almost always poor and minority race men who are actually convicted, it's to the advantage of the patriarchal State to encourage its citizens to see rape as a perverted form of sexual pleasure because that helps to contaminate the whole concept of sexuality as nasty, thus reinforcing the idea of the body as something that has to be controlled and legislated against by that State. When the State calls rape a crime it distracts people from realizing that implicitly through advertising, frustration inducement, and the concept of the righteousness of power of the stronger over the weaker this society in fact promotes rape.

The reality of the staggering number of rape victims who are battered wives and the State's horror of upsetting the nuclear family has further forced feminists into directly confronting and educating society about rape rather than relying on legal channels. In transition houses battered wives help each other in rejecting the "security" of their violent relationship. Unlike traditional social workers, radical feminists aren't interested in patching things up in the home or "getting even" through the courts. They're interested in eliminating rape. By distributing literature, which tries to explain the role of society in rape, by printing descriptions of rapists so that the rapists lose their anonymous power and by going with rape victims in groups to confront rapists in public, feminists work to expose rapists, expose society's implicit approval of rape and by clearly attacking the real problems of frustration, weakness, capital and power, develop the highest form of education. That is, an education that learns from what really is and then moves forward to change the reality.

The kind of shared, living, explorative education that has grown within the self-help clinics and rape relief centres is representative of education as practiced by most radical feminists. The sharing of knowledge and skills is something women have been doing in their homes for centuries but because these skills were centered around such things as cooking and child care, they've generally been denigrated as "women's stuff." Likewise, the openness of women in talking about their relationships has been swept aside as "gossip." Now, in our printing, theatre, health – in all our groups – women have continued sharing our skills, knowledge and feelings.

As feminists rejected the lopsided histories of patriarchal society and demanded "herstory," we set to liberating education as lived experience in place of taught submission.

SOME LIMITATIONS OF THE RADICAL FEMINIST MOVEMENT

With all the concrete work done by radical feminists, it's understandable that the feminist movement has been hailed as the strongest and most durable of the 70s. But while there's no question of its positive impact over the last decade, it would be destructive to the good work already done, to ignore its problems and limitations. Most feminists have displayed an amazing staying power and avoided much of the male burn-out but even so, there are many who have dropped out from exhaustion and there are many experiencing the tension and frustration of feeling unequal to the task of eradicating patriarchy.

Experiences within health and rape centres have clarified both the dangers of being coopted as a band-aid for the system and of being ineffectual beyond a small group (and seeing even that effectiveness restricted by the magnitude of the opposition). Feminists have had to recognize that while endurance may be the prime quality of a serious radical, there really is an urgency to change the whole structure of society and no matter how hard any one group works, it can't liberate humanity.

And finally, what many feel to be the most serious limitation of the feminist movement is that not only are we unable to reach most women, but in many cases the concept of radical feminism is alienating to many women and more men. Perhaps we can best understand how this has happened by looking at a similar distrustfulness that developed within the movement itself – the lesbian/heterosexual splits.

Lesbians quickly discovered not only that many heterosexuals had internalized male modes of behaviour and work methods but that they often denied connections with lesbians in order to present a "respectable" public image. At the same time, while many heterosexuals didn't want to work with men, they hadn't given up on them altogether and didn't want to be associated with the anti-male separatism of many lesbians. So the original cause for splits developed out of real problems in trying to work together and could have taught us a lot about our own sexism.

But while many struggled with the situation, to a large extent the issue became dangerous to the feminist cause when the splits degenerated from a working problem to a holier-than-thou and defensive problem. Lesbians felt purer because they weren't selling out to men or the media. Heterosexuals felt purer because they were still working with the majority of the population, that is, other heterosexual women and men.

A lot of heterosexuals recognized their own anti-lesbian sexism and tried to overcome it, or feeling guilty, became defensive. Lesbians, with the historical reality of having been denied by their straight sisters, were often suspicious and often failed to appreciate genuine attempts of heterosexual women to overcome their sexism. What resulted was a lot of heterosexual women feeling unfairly rejected by lesbians and a lot of lesbians not trusting heterosexuals.

In many ways it's the same kind of problem that developed with men. Many men felt so consistently and often unfairly rejected by feminists that even many who originally tried to overcome their sexism finally felt too defensive to actually be able to learn anything valuable from the feminist experience. And many women who opposed sexism didn't want to be purer than men, just equal to them.

The lessons of the lesbian/heterosexual split have been crucial to feminists. Many of us backed off from painful confrontations. But that also meant we were backing off from learning. With this internal lesson about the shady boundaries between constructive criticism and harmful guilting, we should be more sensitive to non-radical females and men.

Finally, caught in the busyness of all the work needing to be done, feminists can lose a sense of direction about how to ultimately get out of "reaction" work. How to make sure that reforms will be replaced by change? How not to be directed by the power of the State and capital but rather to plan direction to dismantle the present system? How to make sure that the important work done in the 70s is not digested and catalogued as an interesting historical phenomenon of the 70s, but pushes through to inform, direct, and liberate the political activity of the 80s?

Part III – Anarcha-feminism and the Case of the Hyphen

In *Anarchism: The Feminist Connection*, Peggy Kornegger suggested that women were "in the unique position of being the bearers of a subsurface anarchist consciousness" and in an article in the *Open Road* last summer, Elaine Leeder said, "It has been said that women often practice Anarchism and do not know it, while some men call themselves Anarchists and do not practice it." While neither Kornegger nor Leeder are saying that females biologically make for better anarchists, a too facile acceptance of their statements has encouraged many to believe just that. But if anarchistic tendencies within the feminist movement are accepted as a natural by-product of being female, it puts an unfair pressure on women to "live up to their natural anarchism" and it limits our potential for political development because it discourages us from examining why women behave more anarchistically than men. Many women's groups do disintegrate, many women do exploit other women and men, and feminists haven't been able to liberate humanity. These "shortcomings" don't make women less female, they confirm woman's humanness.

So why have feminist groups incorporated so many anarchistic principles in our work situations? Largely because as women we've been raised to be sensitive, nurturing, and to think of our activities as being carried out in small intimate circles. While in the past these traits have facilitated the brute force of male domination, keeping women ineffectual in "worldly issues," now, with a conscious appreciation of the life nurturing power of our "female" qualities we are in a position to expand their influence while retaining their strength.

Also, by realizing that it is our education that has brought us to this point, we can more consciously extend that kind of education to men, and in particular, to rearing our sons and reinforcing our daughters. We can also recognize the inherent limitations of that very education. Those limitations include a tendency towards passivity and towards exploding inside our heads instead of fighting our oppressors. While we may excel at working in small groups we've traditionally been cautious of larger groups and need to guard against isolation.

This leads us right back to the question of education. As has already been said, women have had to fight to liberate our suppressed history. That experience should have taught us always to be suspect of "education." Just as the worker in Bertolt Brecht's poem asks if Alexander conquered India all on his own, so women have demanded to know where women were when the men were fighting. We've discovered what we always knew but wouldn't have found in most books – women were right there working, suffering, loving, and fighting – in fact, in spite of our invisibility in history – living.

The question for anarchists to ask is similar. While humanity has been dragged through domination, plunder and war, and brainwashed into believing that exploitative competitiveness is only natural, hasn't anybody resisted? How is it that if we're naturally so nasty we still manage to

Open Road 11 (1980)

love and share? The answer is, because lots of people have fought back and have insisted on remaining human.

It's because so many people individually and collectively have tried to liberate humanity that it's important to liberate our anarchist history to learn from and be reinforced by it.

While it would be ridiculous to pretend that anarchist groups have always practised their anarchism, what is revealed by studying anarchist theory and history is that liberation of the total human being is in the *essence* of anarchism. The radical feminist experience has often been traumatic for anarchists because it is something they must deal with and learn from if anarchism is more than a label.

It's also important to realize that anarchism isn't what it was before the radical feminist experience. If anarchism is its history, it is also a continuously created explorative and active response to the immediate and to the future. In theory, anarchism always included feminism but it's only in the last few years that we've really discovered what that means and therefore been able to learn about that part of ourselves.

Theoretically, anarchists shouldn't have had to learn to be feminists, but they did have to learn and the lessons have been invaluable. These lessons have taught us what it really means to *live* our politics and they've given concrete, contemporary examples of direct, local, collective action.

It's easy to see how anarchism has benefitted from feminism and there are many who argue in favour of a feminist rather than an anarchist movement. But while I think it is premature to drop the hyphen in anarcha-feminism, I do see the eventual return to – or rather arrival at – *anarchism* as a liberating prospect.

Putting the anarcha into feminism has helped to place the immediate concrete work done into a historical perspective. That's important so that successful, collective human ways of dealing with our struggles aren't seen as isolated flukey episodes, but rather as part of a total life approach and vision to ALL our living.

While we can only move forward if we first perceive the present real problems (and these have a become clearer through the work of feminists) we need a vision if we are to move freely forward. A vision can only be the expression of our past, present and future. Part of that vision includes our anarchist history and part of that history includes the sharing of skills traditionally considered male. If our positive "female" skills are products of our education, so are our "female" deficiencies. Our male comrades can help us liberate "male" skills from our denied pasts and from the destructive uses they generally suffer in capitalist society.

Although the feminist experience has advanced the practice, we *will* find attempts at living non-authoritarian collective lives in *our* anarchist history – and present.

Anarcha-feminism isn't the only compound in the movement. The other two one hears of most frequently are anarcho-syndicalism and anarcho-communism. In all cases the addition to the anarchism is the element of anarchism that seems to need the most emphasis. Anarcho-syndicalists recognize that most people's lives centre around work and they believe that that is where the major organizing must be done. Anarcho-communists stress the importance of the communes and the community. Because anarcho-communism is concerned with life in all its personal interactions I would suggest that the word anarchism *includes* the communism.

Anarcha-feminism exhibits aspects of both anarcho-syndicalism and anarcho-communism. To the extent that women are being exploited and degraded more than men, anarcha-feminism is like anarcho-syndicalism. The emphasis has to be on that part of anarchism that deals with personal and sexual exploitation. To the degree that feminism moves beyond "reaction to" exploitation and poses a total life approach, it is like anarcho-communism in that it becomes synonymous with anarchism.

Part IV – Anarchism in the 80s

Having said that it's premature to drop the feminist stress in anarchism, why have I done it? Mainly because I do see anarchism – an anarchism broadened by the feminist experience – as the most viable revolutionary direction for the 80s. Those of us who choose at times to work in mixed groups will probably still have to direct a lot of our energy to emphasizing the feminism in anarchism and of course, many of us will continue to call ourselves anarcha-feminists. For myself, I drop the feminism in the label, but not in the struggle.

Work that I hope will be inspired by the feminist experience includes uncovering our own anarchist roots and experiences, and recognizing the political as an everyday issue.

Anarchist roots doesn't just mean specifically anarchist inspired actions or theories. It means paying attention to all expressions of revolt and anti-authoritarianism. From such diverse revolts as the Diggers in England in the 1600s, to the Spanish collectives of the 1930s, to May 1968 in France, to squatters in present day Amsterdam, we are reminded that anarchist theory has grown from a human revolt against oppression and a responsibility to life that has preceded any theory. The experience of radical feminism is the most obviously recent example of this truth.

More attention to this heritage should encourage us to examine our immediate living situations more closely and to recognize in them the frequent indications of, and overwhelming potential for, radical rejection of authoritarian society. This is crucial if we are to be more than a discontented few and if we genuinely believe in the possibility of human liberation.

Particularly through "outreach" work such as the health collectives, street theatre, and rape relief, feminists have been most successful in combining a conscious political perspective with the unarticulated need of those whose lives are the expression of the need and potential for liberation.

The relationship between a sense of immediacy and the effectiveness of the work being done has become clearer through feminist struggles and I expect the most radical feminists will continue doing the kind of work we've been doing for the last decade – fighting sexism wherever we encounter it. Women definitely are still more oppressed than men, the State is trying to crack down on abortions now that it sees the serious consequences of "granting" a woman some say in her own body, and for the most part, political groups are still sexist.

As an extension of the feminist emphasis on fighting right where you are, I think that anarchists in the 80s will be fighting more to liberate our urban environments. There are always many who don't like city life and promote going "back to-the-land" but throughout the 70s there does seem to have been more of a recognition that most people can't just drop out and feminists in particular fought where they were, that being primarily in the cities. As feminists move more and more from reaction to direction, and as we all work to develop community sharing skills, we should be looking at making our cities more livable rather than devising ways to escape them.

And while many of us would wish to escape, most of us do have to work in wage slavery for a living. If we really do intend to live our politics more immediately, we're going to have to work more on liberating our workplaces. Feminists have become progressively more involved in workplace organizing because the number of working women has risen so dramatically in the last two decades. As with our other political work we've had to fight the hierarchies of male dominated unions. Where unions already existed, women have fought to introduce even a slight degree of feminism, but for the most part, unions hadn't previously been interested in organizing women so that now to a large extent we're doing our own distinctly feminist organizing. It's important that our organizing be as creative and liberating as our lives should be.

For many marxists, the workplace offers an ideally rigid and authoritarian setting for organizing for the dictatorship of the Workers' State. But for anarchists who challenge the whole concept of the State and reject all dictatorships, workplace organizing requires more imagination. As Murray Bookchin has pointed out, the worker becomes a revolutionary not by becoming more of a worker but by undoing his "workerness."

Just as feminists have fought to clarify the personal of politics, now feminists and anarchists have to insist on our humanness at our workplaces and reject our objectification as workers. It is as harmful to organize workers on authoritarian lines as to simply wish that people weren't primarily workers. Because the workplace is generally so alienating and boring it seems difficult to liberate human energy. But, because the workplace is where most of us are, once we liberate the human being from the worker, the power of anarchy will be unlimited. Just as feminism has broadened the reality of anarchism, so will the unleashed energy of working people astound us with our own potential. If we are successful in claiming work as something we do for ourselves rather than something we are for others, our imaginative creative future will know no bounds. If we fail, we know our future only too well.

While aware that the political will always be most strongly felt at the immediate, local level, we also have to recognize that the "immediate" is not easily contained. In this era of massive media brain-washing, of mind numbing drugs forced into protestors, of increasing militarism, and of nuclear mania, the global crisis is a local crisis.

Obviously we can't all be actively involved in fighting all the oppression weighing down on us but unless we see our struggles in their global context, we're doomed to the repetition of individual or small collective struggles and finally, to no struggle at all because at some point we will be destroyed by nuclear insanity. That's where the importance of an anarchist vision, history, and network come in.

It's important to see our constructive local struggles in their global context so that we don't get assimilated into the system, so that we can learn from others who are struggling in their own areas, so that we never forget that we're involved in world revolution and so that when we do join in large demonstrations such as anti-militarist and anti-nuke, we do so from an informed position and are able to participate constructively. The kinds of struggles for liberation that I'm anticipating in the 80s have been made possible by our history.

The euphoria of many of the spectacular struggles of the 60s helped to liberate our imaginations. The 70s expanded definition of what is political extended the horizons for our imaginative visions and the steady, solid, local work of radical feminists has helped to establish our endurance as serious revolutionaries. And in the 80s we're going to need all the spirit, imagination, and endurance we

Open Road 11 (1980)

can get. The big powers are gearing up for war and playing with nuclear power. We'd be foolish to be optimistic about our future.

But with the visions of anarchism, and the example of feminism's durability, we'll put up one hell of a fight to be human.

Some sources: *Open Road* most issues have at least one article on militant feminist actions. For specific discussions on anarcha-feminism see numbers 4, 7 and 10. The following Black Bear Pamphlets, available through Black Bear, 78A Crofton Road, London SE5: *Anarchism: The Feminist Connection* by Peggy Kornegger, *Feminism As Anarchism* by Lynne Farrow, *Socialism, Anarchism and Feminism* by Carol Ehrlich and *Anarcho-Feminism: Two Statements* manifestos of Chicago and Black Rose anarcha-feminists. A couple of excellent North American radical feminist papers are *off our backs* 1724-20th St. NW Washington, DC 20009 and *Big Mama Rag* 1724 Gaylord, Denver, Colorado 80206.

Anarcha-Feminism: Why the hyphen?

With the vision of anarchism and feminism's durability, we'll put up one hell of a fight to be human. By Kytha Kurin

We exposed the irrationality of believing that a life direction that didn't spring from a sensitivity to the totality of life could in any sane way be considered rational.

Feminists attracted by anarchist theory were more concerned with anarchist practice & refused to be placated with rhetoric.

You can't take my church/ state/ family/ education/ security/ babysitter!" they cry. "Who would tell me what to do?...er...I mean who would I tell what to do?...er...I mean..humans must have order. otherwise there would be complete fascism." (HUH?)...so the argument goes...

think of the terror you really do live in and dare to dream of a world where people have a roof over their head because they need one, can walk down the streets at any hour in any sex, colour, size body that they happen to be in, and where people's voices are relative to their own experience, and not to someone of a higher class, different biology, position, etc....sounds idealistic.

Type (A) On Trial

An excellent example of this is that KIO's Ron Hayley feels that he is adequately versed in the a-f experience to write the a-f her story article in the upcoming feminist issue. The problem is that a-f herstory/ theory is an ongoing dance with our practical lives. It is not a theory that we impose on ourselves, strap ourselves into, and try to live up to.

We act our thoughts & think our action's. And sometimes we make mistakes but we reserve the right to be our own thinker/ doer. So... gimme a fuckin' break/ brake. Sorry buckaroo, but this is just another example of male anarchists' inability to live up to their own theories. That being that you begin with the personal the local and the immediate, and work from there. You don't go co-opting other peoples' lives thru bogus theory. All the boys are welcome to participate in the dialogue, but i'd like to put you on hold for awhile. For once, we as wimmin should be able to speak for ourselves. Men can only speak of a-f from a theoretical viewpoint! As a man, he categorically cannot experience our position...

The penultimate irony of anarchists not taking a-f seriously, is that anarchism; by its simplest definition: anti-authoritarianism, implies feminism, in its simplest form: against the oppression of women. In theory, anarchism and feminism are not mutually exclusive. However, in practice, they often have and continue to differ. First, I'd like to consider the similarities.

You bet! but, we plant our feet firmly in this terra/or & wade through what's got to be done here & now, struggling to keep ourselves sane, nurtured, reached out to...not some grandiose idea of saving the masses from themselves, or whatever constitutes the usual version of the macho revolution...

It's been rumoured lately that the reason there is little or no discussion about anarchist-feminism (a-f) is that there isn't much written about it. This rumour even springs from the heart of the anarchist press, the very place that one might expect something to be done about this lack of discussion. Wouldn't this be the most prudent place to initiate a discussion, the anarchist milieu? Isn't this the arena where one might expect support for such 'radical' and therefore silenced ideas like a-f?

Radical feminism and social anarchism have always had intuitive, if not defined, alliances in theory and practice. Many radical feminist groups operate collectively and do not delegate 'power-over' through hierarchical constraints, as do so many anarchist groups. Secondly, 'ideally,' both social anarchists and many radical feminists want to "erode power...not seize power..."(Ehrlich, in Women and Revolution) by virtue of a process that is consistent.if not synonymous with the end. The theory and practice are based on the belief that the revolution is a process, as opposed to some point in time.

However, since 'feminism' is the political program of radical feminists, many of the other manifestations of patriarchal power-over are not dealt with sufficiently, such as the socio-demographic differences among women, oppression of other cultures and species etc.. In theory, social anarchism deals with all forms of power-over, (like our relationship to the "third" world, other species, and the earth), not just the power relationship between wimmin and men. However, in practise, male anarchists have not been the good little boys that their theory permits them to be, particularly when dealing with wimmin. Many male anarchists are not aware of the oppression of women, OR pretend to be aware, while perpetuating the oppression of wimmin.

slips of the tongue

hidden thoughts and anxieties

linguistic mixups

The pen written in the hand of the inscriber and inaccessible to the inscribed, is not only a powerful weapon, but is the creator of the universe

Even the very language that we use to communicate in (English/French)is a language created for and by men. All Euro-based languages culture and sievelisation is based on a Chain of Being

throughout the last 5000 years (a pin 'prick' in the body of herstory), wimmin have been considered tertiary to men and boys, and equal in status to "domestic animals": breeders

The so-called ancient Greeks, believed that it was impossible to have a full andsentient relationship with wimmin, because wimmin were not full sentient beings, and therefore incapable of sharing the language of 'ideas' and explor/ploitation. How can a language, based on such fundamentally false premises, and therefore invalid as a paradigm, begin to 'speak' to wimmin? My rage cannot be contained, or even expressed in this language and yet, out of necessity, i have to speak to you in your tongue. We who haven't even a language, a voice, are supposed to listen to You, who has both, define us? Deal with your own sexism, learn to communicate with each other, take responsibility for your OWN re-socialization. Speak with us, try even listening first, but don't speak for us, for me.

Social anarchism is insufficient to deal with wimmin's issues (yet one more ghettoization?), even though theoretically, it deals with diffrences of power based on sex (& race, sexual choice, species etc.), in reality it *is*

a practical joke!

And radical feminism, based on the political program of oppression of wimmin as a group, does not take into account of the differences among wimmin. As it stands today, neither of these life perspectives are sufficient unto themselves. This is where anarchist-feminism bridges the gap between social anarchism and radical feminism. A-F cogently addresses our differences.

As an anarchist-feminist, i want to see the end of ALL forms of Power-over. I see the oppression of wimmin, as both a macro-structural problem, and a culturally specific one, including our place in the imposed 'world order', grandiosely referred to as first, second and third world. Within that order, differences based on colour, age, capital, sexual choice differences, in physical and mental capacities, further differenciates us. For example, black wimmin are not just oppressed by black and white men, but very often by white wimmin, and even black wimmin of a higher 'class'. Recognising that these nuances of oppression are manifestations of the patriarchal-capitalist chain of being, is insufficient. We need a 'modus operandi' to DEAL with these differences. While white, middle class wimmin teach physics in universities, very often wimmin of colour are cleaning their residential toilet bowls. As an anarchist-feminist, i want to have a workable non-oppressive, non-pretentious relationship with wimmin of different backgrounds and origins. I do not want to oppress other wimmin in order to get what i want for myself.

My relationship to, say, a metis womyn from one of canaduh's glorious reserves, is similar in kind as men's is to me: one based on a difference in privelege. As an a-f, i can only earnestly try to empathize and earnestly try to understand the conditions that lead her to, for example, choose to operate in mainstream society as, say, a lawyer.I have no right, to condemn this choice, since it was a choice obviously made on many internal and external factors. BUT, as an a-f,i see that her choice is made under coercive structural constraints,and is therefore not a 'free' choice at all.As an a-f, rather than 'liberalise' (equal to slipperyize)my politix, & feel guilty about not actively supporting my siste's right to Power within the patriarch,i can, and do turn my energees to what oppresses both of us:patriarchy.The very real structure that makes it logistically formidable for her to make any other choice (i.e. the right not to work, work collectives,etc.)We are becoming more aware that within our personal herstories (mine being relatively priveleged as a white 'formally educated'(read:blenderized) womyn from the middle class) that these options are extremely difficult to act on.NOT because we haven't the will or capacity or knowledge, but because society interferes in very real ways (sucking our spirits into ideological lies; sucking our energies into the tedium of feeding,clothing & housing ourselves & for many, our children.)

Not only does a-f potentially and non-pretentiously open a dialogue amongst all wimmin, that are vaguely aware of their oppression, we do one better. We bite the balls of the beast that beholds all of us. I see patriarchy as a closed system that perpetuates all forms of bigotry and rape. How 'normal'ized men relate to each other (competitively and coercively), other races, wimmin, children, the otherwise abled other species, including ecosystems of every order, non-hets, non-monogs., in short, anything Other, are practises based on hierarchical patriarchy: POWER-OVER. Blind to the cybernetix and dance of reality, they continue to live by the number one rule of dick: fuck ye over, before ye get fucked.

For me, it is the very least i can do to put my perceptions into practise. How? By being aware and acting on both my privilege and my oppression- to deny that you have both is a false schism in the self that manifests in the way that you deal with reality- by facilitating discussion with other wimmin (& men); by empowering myself psychologically, physically, and spiritually thru means of mutual aid and respect; by realising and assimilating the fact that direct action means more than spray paint. For me, right now, in this particular-time-space-zone, it means stuff like fighting my landlord and asshole men generally; it means trying to develop a sense of autonomy independent of male structures; it means working with a great collective of wimmin on a 'zine (without which i probably wouldn't have written this); reaching out to other wimmin of other perspectives and backgrounds; learning french in a french community; terrorising the act of consumerism; fucking up and reconsidering; developing skills; singing and howling; being deeply in solidarity with all oppressed peoples and species; being wimmin identified, and being in tune with all sorts of nuances that come into light in the play, in the dance of daily life. I am trying to live, not just theorise my politix.

PATRIARCHY REST IN PIECES

EXPERIENCE THE LIVING DIFFERENCE.

EXPERIENCE boA

AN OPEN LETTER TO THE ECOLOGY MOVEMENT

Social ecology has to begin its quest for freedom not only in the factory but also in the family.

BY MURRAY BOOKCHIN

Murray Bookchin is a lifelong militant who has provided critical and constructive analysis of contemporary social movements through his seminal works on anarchism and ecology. In his best known (and highly recommended) book, Post-Scarcity Anarchism, *Bookchin argued how a true revolutionary movement must integrate ecological ideas with an anarchist critique of society. In the following piece he extends this analysis.*

With the opening of the eighties, the ecology movement in both the United States and Europe is facing a serious crisis. This crisis is literally one of its identity and goals, a crisis that painfully challenges the movement's capacity to fulfill its rich promise of advancing alternatives to the domineering sensibility, the hierarchical political and economic institutions, and the manipulative strategies for social change that have produced the catastrophic split between humanity and nature.

To speak bluntly: the coming decade may well determine whether the ecology movement will be reduced to a decorative appendage of an inherently diseased anti-ecological society, a society riddled by an unbridled need for control, domination and exploitation of humanity and nature – or, hopefully, whether the ecology movement will become the growing educational arena for a new ecological society based on mutual aid, decentralized communities, a people's technology, and non-hierarchical, libertarian relations that will yield not only a new harmony between human and human, but between humanity and nature.

Perhaps it may seem presumptuous for a single individual to address himself to a sizable constituency of people who have centered their activities around ecological concerns. But my concern for the future of the ecology movement is not an impersonal or ephemeral one. For nearly thirty years I have written extensively on our growing ecological dislocations. These writings have been reinforced by my activities against the growing use of pesticides and food additives as early as 1953, the problem of nuclear fallout that surfaced with the first hydrogen bomb test in the Pacific in 1954, the radioactive pollution issue that emerged with the Windscale nuclear reactor "incident" in 1956, and Con Edison's attempt to construct the world's largest nuclear reactor in the very heart of New York City in 1963. Since then, I have been involved in anti-nuke alliances, such as Clamshell and Shad, not to speak of their

predecessors Ecology Action East, whose manifesto, *The Power to Destroy, the Power to Create,* I wrote in 1969, and the Citizens Committee on Radiation Information, which played a crucial role in stopping the Ravenswood reactor in 1963. Hence I can hardly be described as an interloper or newcomer to the ecology movement.

My remarks in this letter are the product of a very extensive experience as well as my individual concern for ideas that have claimed my attention for decades.

It is my conviction that my work and experience in all of these areas would mean very little if they were limited merely to the issues themselves, however important each one may be in its own right. "No Nukes," or for that matter, no food additives, no agribusiness, or no nuclear bombs is simply not enough if our horizon is limited to each one issue alone. Of equal importance is the need to reveal the toxic social causes, values, and inhuman relations that have created a planet which is already vastly poisoned.

Ecology, in my view, has always meant social ecology: the conviction that the very concept of dominating of human by human, indeed, of women by men, of the young by their elders, of one ethnic group by another, of society by the state, of the individual by bureaucracy, as well as of one economic class by another or a colonized people by a colonial power. To my thinking, social ecology has to begin its quest for freedom not only in the factory but also in the family, not only in the material conditions of life but also in the spiritual ones. Without changing the most molecular relationships in society – notably, those between men and women, adults and children, whites and other ethnic groups, heterosexuals and gays (the list, in fact, is considerable) – society will be riddled by domination even in a socialistic "classless" and non-exploitative" form. It would be infused by hierarchy even as it celebrated the dubious virtues of "peoples' democracies," "socialism," and the "public ownership" of "natural resources." And as long as hierarchy persists, as long as humanity organizes itself around a system of elites, the project of dominating nature will continue to exist and inevitably lead our planet to ecological extinction.

The emergence of the woman's movement, even more so than the counterculture, the "appropriate" technology crusade and the anti-nuke alliances (I omit the clean-up escapades of "Earth Day"), points to the very heart of the hierarchical domination that underpins our ecological crisis. Only insofar as a counterculture, an alternate technology or anti-nuke movement rests on the non-hierarchical sensibilities and structures that are most evident in the truly radical tendencies in feminism can the ecology movement realize its rich potential for basic changes in our prevailing anti-ecological society and its values. Only insofar as the ecology movement consciously cultivates an anti-hierarchical and a non-domineering strategy for social change can it retain its very identity as the voice for a new balance between humanity and nature

Open Road 11 (1980)

and its goal for a truly ecological society.

This identity and this goal is now faced with serious erosion. Ecology is now fashionable, indeed, faddish – and with this sleazy popularity has emerged a new type of environmentalist hype. From an outlook and movement that at least held the promise of challenging hierarchy and domination have emerged a form of environmentalism that is based more on tinkering with existing institutions, social relations, technologies, and values than on changing them. I use the word "environmentalism" to contrast it with ecology, specifically with social ecology.

Where social ecology, in my view, seeks to eliminate the concept of the domination of nature by humanity by eliminating the domination of human by human, environmentalism reflects an "instrumentalist" or technical sensibility in which nature is viewed merely as a passive habitat, an agglomeration of external objects and forces, that must be made more "serviceable" for human use, irrespective of what these uses may be. Environmentalism, in fact, is merely environmental engineering. It does not bring into question the underlying notions of the present society, notably that man must dominate nature. On the contrary, it seeks to facilitate that domination by developing techniques for diminishing the hazards caused by domination. The very notions of hierarchy and domination are obscured by a technical emphasis on "alternative" power sources, structural designs for "conserving" energy, "simple" lifestyles in the name of "limits of growth" that now represent an enormous growth industry in its own right – and, of course, a mushrooming of "ecology"-oriented candidates for political office and "ecology"-oriented parties that are designed not only to engineer nature but also public opinion into an accommodating relationship with the prevailing society.

Fashionable Ecology

Nathan Glazer's "ecological" 24-square-mile solar satellite, O'Neill's "ecological" spaceships, and the DOE's [Department of Energy's] giant "ecological" windmills, to cite the more blatant examples of this environmentalist mentality, are no more "ecological" than nuclear power plants or agribusiness. If anything, their "ecological" pretensions are all the more dangerous because they are more deceptive and disorienting to the general public. The hoopla about a new "Earth Day" or future "Sun Days," "Winds Days," like the pious rhetoric of fast-talking solar contractors and patent-hungry "Ecological" inventors, conceal the all-important fact that solar energy, wind power, organic agriculture, holistic heath, and "voluntary simplicity" will alter very little in our grotesque imbalance with nature if they leave the patriarchal family, the multinational corporation, the bureaucratic and centralized political structure, and property system, and the prevailing technocratic rationality untouched. Solar power,

Open Road II (1980)

wind power, methane, and geothermal power are merely power in so far as the devices for using them are needlessly complex, bureaucratically controlled, corporately owned or institutionally centralized.

Admittedly, they are less dangerous to the physical health of human beings than power derived from nuclear and fossil fuels, but they are clearly dangerous to the spiritual, moral and social heath of humanity if they are treated merely as techniques that do not involve new relations between people and nature and within society itself. The designer, the bureaucrat, the corporate executive, and the political careerist do not introduce anything new or ecological in society or in our sensibilities toward nature and people because they adopt "soft energy paths;" like all "technotwits" (to use Amory Lovin's description of himself in personal conversation with me), they merely cushion or conceal the dangers to the biosphere and to human life by placing ecological technologies in a straitjacket of hierarchical values rather than by challenging the values and the institutions they represent.

Hierarchy and Domination

By the same token, even decentralization becomes meaningless if it denotes logistical advantages of supply and recycling rather than human scale. If our goal in decentralizing society (or, as the "ecology"-oriented politicians like to put it, striking a "balance" between "decentralization" and "centralization") is intended to acquire "fresh food" or to "recycle wastes" easily or to reduce "transportation costs" or to foster "more" popular-control (not, be it noted, *complete* popular control) over social life, decentralization too is divested of its rich ecological and libertarian meaning as a network of free, naturally balanced communities based on direct face-to-face democracy and fully actualized selves who can really engage in the self-management and self-activity so vital for the achievement of an ecological society. Like alternative technology, decentralization is reduced to a mere technical stratagem for concealing hierarchy and domination. The "ecological" vision of "municipal control of power," "nationalization of industry," not to speak of vague terms like "economic democracy," may seemingly restrict utilities and corporations, but leaves their overall control of society largely unchallenged. Indeed, even a nationalist corporate structure remains a bureaucratic and hierarchical one.

As an individual who has been deeply involved in ecological issues for decades, I am trying to alert well-intentioned ecologically-oriented people to a profoundly serious problem in our movement. To put my concerns in the most direct form possible: I am disturbed by a widespread techocratic mentality and political opportunism that threatens to replace social ecology by a new form of social engineering. For a time it seemed that the ecology movement might well fulfill its libertarian potential as a movement for a non-hierarchical society. Reinforced by the most advanced tendencies in the feminist, gay, community and socially radical movements, it seemed that the ecology movement might well begin to focus its efforts on changing the very structure of our anti-ecological society, not merely on providing more palatable techniques for perpetuating it or institutional cosmetics for concealing its irremediable diseases. The rise of the anti-nuke alliances based on a decentralized network of affinity groups, on a directly democratic decision-making process, and on direct action seemed to support this hope. The problem that faced the movement seemed primarily one of self-education and public education – the need to fully understand the meaning of the affinity group structure as a lasting, family-type form, the full implications of direct democracy, the concept of direct action as more than a "strategy" but as a deeply rooted sensibility, an outlook that expressed the fact that everyone had the right to take direct control of society and her or his everyday life.

New Opportunism

Ironically, the opening of the eighties, so rich in its promise of sweeping changes in values and consciousness, has also seen the emergence of a new opportunism, one that threatens to reduce the ecology movement to a mere cosmetic for the present society. Many self-styled "founders" of the anti-nuke alliances (one thinks of the Clamshell Alliance) have become what Andrew Kopkind has described as "managerial radicals" – the manipulators of a political consensus that operates within the system in the very name of opposing it.

The "managerial radical" is not a very new phenomenon. Jerry Brown [Governor of California], like the Kennedy dynasty, has practiced the art of the political field for years. What is striking about the current crop is the extent to which "managerial radicals" come from important radical social movements of the sixties, and, more significantly, from the ecology movement of the seventies. The radicals and idealists of the 1930s required decades to reach the middle-aged cynicism needed for capitulation, and they had the honesty to admit it in public. Former members of SDS and ecology action groups capitulate in their late youth or early maturity – and write their "embittered" biographies at 25, 30 or 35 years of age, spiced with rationalizations for their surrender to the status quo. Tom Hayden hardly requires much criticism, as his arguments against direct action at Seabrook last fall attest. Perhaps worse is the emergence of Barry Commoner's "Citizen's Party," of new financial institutions like MUSE (Musicians United for Safe Energy), and the "Voluntary Simplicity" celebration of a dual society of swinging, jeans-clad high-brow elitists from the middle classes, and conventionally-clad, consumer-oriented low-brow underdogs from the working classes, a duel society generated by corporate-financed "think tanks" of the Stanford Research Institute.

Managerial Radicals

In all of these cases, the radical implications of a decentralized society based on alternate technologies and closely knit communities are shrewdly placed in the service of a technocratic sensibility, of "managerial radicals," and opportunistic careerists. The grave danger here lies in the failure of many idealistic individuals to deal with major social issues on their own terms – to recognize the blatant incompatibilities of goals that remain in deep-seated conflict with each other, goals that cannot possibly coexist without delivering the ecology movement to its worst enemies. More often than not, these enemies are its "leaders" and "founders" who have tried to manipulate it to conform with the very system and ideologies that block any social or ecological reconciliation in the form of an ecological society.

The lure of "influence" of "mainstream politics," of "effectiveness" strikingly exemplifies the lack of coherence and consciousness that afflicts the ecology movement today. Affinity groups, direct democracy, and direct action are not likely to be palatable – or, for that matter, even comprehensible – to millions of people who live as soloists in discotheques and singles bars. Tragically, these millions have surrendered their social power, indeed, their very personalities, to politicians and bureaucrats who live in a nexus of obedience and command in which they are normally expected to play subordinate roles. Yet this is precisely the immediate cause of the ecological crisis of our time – a cause that has its historic roots in the market society that engulfs us. To ask powerless people to regain power over their lives is even more important than to add a complicated, often incomprehensible, and costly solar collector to their houses. Until they regain a new sense of power over their lives, until they create their own system of self-management to oppose the present system of hierarchical management, until they develop new ecological values to replace current domineering values – a process which solar collectors, wind machines, and French-intensive gardens can facilitate but never replace – nothing they change in society will yield a new balance with the natural world.

Obviously powerless people will not eagerly accept affinity groups, direct democracy, and direct action in the normal course of events. That they harbour basic impulses which make them very susceptible to those forms and activities – a fact which always surprises the "managerial radical" in periods of crisis and confrontation – represents

Open Road 11 (1980)

a potential that has yet to be fully realized and furnished with intellectual coherence through painstaking education and repeated examples. It was precisely this education and example that certain feminist and anti-nuke groups began to provide. What is so incredibly regressive about the technical thrust and electoral politics of environmental technocrats and "managerial radicals" today is that they recreate in the name of "soft energy paths," a specious "decentralization," and inherently hierarchical party-type structures the worst forms and habits that foster passivity, obedience and vulnerability to the mass media in the American public. The spectatorial politics promoted by Brown, Hyden, Commoner, the Clamshell "founders" like Wasserman and Lovejoy, together with recent huge demonstrations in Washington and New York City breed *masses, not citizens* – the manipulated objects of mass media whether it is used by Exxon or by the CED (Campaign for Economic Democracy), the Citizen's Party, and MUSE.

Ecology is being used against an ecological sensibility, ecological forms of organization and ecological practices to "win" large constituencies, not to educate them. The fear of "isolation," of "futility," of "ineffectiveness" yields a new kind of isolation, futility and ineffectiveness, namely a complete surrender of one's most basic ideals and goals. "Power" is gained at the cost of losing the only power we really have that can change this insane society – our moral integrity, our ideals, and our principles. This may be a festive occasion for careerists who have used the ecology issue to advance their stardom and personal fortunes; it would be the obituary of a movement that has, latent within itself, the ideals of a new world in which masses become individuals and natural resources become nature, both to be respected for their uniqueness and spirituality.

Social Ecology

An ecologically oriented feminist movement is now emerging and the contours of the libertarian anti-nukes movement still exist. The fusing of the two together with new movements that are likely to emerge from the varied crises of our times may open one of the most exciting and liberating decades of our century. Neither sexism, ageism, ethnic oppression, the "energy crisis," corporate power, conventional medicine, bureaucratic manipulation, conscription, militarism, urban devastation, or political centralism can be separated from the ecological issue. All of these issues turn around hierarchy and domination, the root conceptions of a radical social ecology.

It is necessary, I believe, for everyone in the ecology movement to make a crucial decision: will the eighties retain a visionary concept of an ecological future based on a libertarian commitment to decentralization, alternative technology, and a libertarian practice based on affinity

groups, direct democracy, and direct action? Or will the decade be marked by a dismal retreat into ideological obscurantism and a "mainstream politics" that acquires "power" and "effectiveness" by following the very "stream" it should seek to divert? Will it pursue fictitious "mass constituencies" by imitating the very forms of mass manipulation, mass media, and mass culture it is committed to oppose? These two directions cannot be reconciled. Our use of "media," mobilizations, and actions must appeal to mind and to spirit, not to conditioned reflexes and shock tactics that leave no room for reason and humanity. In any case, the choice must be made now, before the ecology movement becomes institutionalized into a mere appendage of the very system whose structure and methods it professes to oppose. It must be made consciously and decisively – or the century itself, not only the decade, will be lost to us forever.

Essays which elaborate more freely on views only noted in this letter are available from Comment Publishing Project, PO Box 371, Hoboken, NJ 07030

Theological Ecology

An open letter to the ecology movement

Open Road, Summer 1980

Lessons of the 70s/80s Strategies for the

...has to begin its quest for ... the factory but also ... Bookchin.

Ecology maven Murray Bookchin

By Frank Stevens

And what brought an end to (the slaughter of witches)? That which brought an end to all magic, whether the holy rites of "our" religion or the blasphemous witchcraft of "their" religion. Science, making use of the natural laws of the Universe, and doing so in a demonstrably workable fashion, became the approved method of forcing man's desires upon the world.

—Dr. Isaac Asimov, 1975.

Well, not exactly. Dr. Asimov is a famous and very well-paid science writer. He could hardly be expected to notice that "science" does not exist apart from class society (like everything else). It has become painfully obvious in the last two decades that advanced capitalist "science" has proceeded in brazen ignorance and, in some cases, reckless disregard of "the natural laws of the Universe" and, consequently, has proven "demonstrably" unworkable if not hazardous.

Some of these failures, particularly the hazardous ones, have generated sizable opposition from many kinds of people, operating from many kinds of motives. As a kind of convenient shorthand, we lump all these people together as "the ecology movement."

But, in fact, most of these people don't really see themselves as part of a social movement. And they are probably right about that. Does "ecology" as an abstract conception mean anything more than any other abstract conception?

Does it really make sense to speak of "a movement" that includes: politicians on the make? companies out to make a profit cleaning up other companies' pollution? wealthy suburbanites trying to keep their neighborhoods small and exclusive? hunters and fishermen? working class victims of occupational and neighbourhood pollution?

This list could go on a long time. But what concerns me here is that seldom have I run across a serious attempt to examine ecological questions from an anarchist viewpoint. Still worse, it would appear that the most popular approach to these questions among anarchists is what I choose to call "theological ecology". Theological ecology is the view that regards the fundamental evil of capitalist society as "the forcing of man's desires on the world". All the forms of domination of human by human stem, in this outlook, from the domination of nature by humans. Anarchy, that is human freedom, cannot exist unless we give up attempting to control and dominate nature for our own ends.

In the ordinary course of things, I would be as inclined as not to dismiss theological ecology as just as nonsensical as any other theology. But when one picks up an issue of the **Open Road** (a widely-read anarchist newspaper published in Vancouver) and reads in Issue number 11 **An Open Letter to the Ecology Movement** by Murray Bookchin (a famous, widely-read anarchist) which simply reeks of theological ecology . . . well, it can't simply be dismissed. It is time, I believe, to take a critical look at just exactly what we are being asked to accept as "the anarchist view" of ecology.

(To be fair about it, Mr. Bookchin's article does not attempt to set forth the ideas of theological ecology in a systematic way. But the fragments that I have chosen to respond to are, I think, an accurate reflection of his views.)

Mr. Bookchin condemns the present order as "an inherently diseased anti-ecological society, a society riddled by an unbridled need for control, domination and exploitation of humanity and nature . . ."

At first glance, this is semantic noise. Since "unbridled" means without a bridle, Mr. Bookchin is just calling for us to control our desire to control or dominate our desire to dominate.

But at a more profound level, isn't Mr. Bookchin suggesting that the very existence of intelligence is suspect? All living organisms try to control their environment, but intelligent organisms are dramatically more successful at it.

For most people, it is the failure of advanced capitalist society to successfully control nature that provokes a critical view of that society. The capitalist that pollutes the air to make steel has not dominated nature; he has dominated certain elements at the cost of poisoning the air that we

> **Theological ecology is the view that regards the fundamental evil of capitalist society as "the forcing of man's desires on the world."**

have to breathe.

But for Mr. Bookchin, it would seem that the desire to make steel or to engage in any other purposeful activity is what is at fault. Insofar as a good working definition of intelligence is the act of imposing purpose on what otherwise has none, it would seem Mr. Bookchin is attacking the very existence of intelligence.

Further, in a social sense, is it not the desire to capture control over our own lives that lies at the root of anarchist politics? The passivity that Mr. Bookchin prescribes for our relations with the natural environment is precisely what characterizes far too much of our social existence. If a handful of people rule this planet, isn't it because the rest of us sit back and accept it because "that's the way things are"?

Mr. Bookchin looks forward to "a new ecological society" that "will yield not only a new harmony between human and human but between humanity and nature."

Really? Why is it, do you suppose, that whenever given the opportunity to choose, people flee from living in harmony with nature like they would the plague?

The plague is one good answer, for that is nature too. Mr. Bookchin talks about nature like a Walt Disney cartoon, but the reality is not so pleasant.

Suppose an accused man was brought before us to stand trial. This man is accused of killing or planning to kill every living creature and every creature that has ever lived, not just on our planet but throughout the universe. Those he has not killed outright, he has condemned to pain and suffering. If they survive his clever diseases and overwhelming disasters, his victims finally fall to progressive degeneration of their bodily organs and tissues. What punishment could we imagine for one guilty of such crimes?

But this is what nature is. Without malice or purpose, it is in harmony with nature that we are born in pain, suffer through brief lives, grow old and die.

It was not nature that built the campfire, chipped the ax, sowed the grain, built the town. It was not nature that eased the pain of childbirth, that rolled back the deadly germs, that delayed the collapse of old age. Nature has written no books and composed no symphonies.

Of course, there is much human misery that cannot be blamed on nature. (For example, nature fights no wars.) Still, given a choice, humanity's efforts to dominate nature seem to offer the chance of a more enjoyable and longer life. Living "in harmony with nature" means no life at all or, at best, a short and painful existence followed by a merciful extinction.

And this is as good a place as any to wonder just how it happened that "harmony" became part of the anarchist project. Anarchist society means that everyone gets the chance to take part in social decisions . . . not that there suddenly ceases to be any need to make decisions at all. That the forms of struggle and the content of the controversies will be different in a classless society than they are in a class society is not to be doubted. But that there will be no struggles and controversies at all??? Anarchism is for people, it seems to me, not angels.

"Ecology, in my view, has always meant social ecology: the conviction that the very concept of dominating nature stems from the domination of human by human."

I don't know if this is true or not, and neither does Mr. Bookchin in all probability. Certainly he produces no arguments to prove this assertion.

But the logic leads to a curious conclusion: if we stop dominating each other and set up an anarchist society, then we will give up trying to dominate nature at the same time. Somehow, I doubt it!

It's interesting to note, by the way, that Mr. Bookchin says that people got the idea of dominating nature from dominating each other . . . Whereas most theological ecologists (not being anarchists) say that the domination of nature came first. Since anarchism is "humanity-centered", Mr. Bookchin understandably gives precedence to humans dominating humans as the cause of humans dominating nature.

Mr. Bookchin says that the quest for freedom must begin " . . . not only in the material conditions of life but also the spiritual ones."

The only problem is that here as elsewhere, Mr. Bookchin is carefully vague about just what it is he's talking about. In this example, he goes on to talk about the nuclear family . . . which is a social relationship, not a "spiritual condition". What are the "spiritual conditions of life", anyway?

Mr. Bookchin says that as long as humanity is organized into a system of elites, "the project of dominating nature will continue to exist and inevitably lead our planet to ecological extinction."

What Mr. Bookchin overlooks in this pretty rhetoric is that extinction is just as much a part of his beloved "nature" as anything else. Even if the human race did not exist, this planet will become ecologically extinct in four or five billion years when our sun has exhausted its hydrogen and begins burning helium. At that far distant time, the sun will expand to many times its present size, and although its surface temperature will be cooler than

Ecology

it is now, the heat from its larger surface area will certainly char if not vaporize the earth.

But what worries Mr. Bookchin is not simply extinction, but rather the idea that we simply can't successfully dominate nature. He seems to feel that the only alternatives are (1) dominate nature by destroying the planet; or (2) submit to nature and whatever it offers. The third alternative, that it is possible to harness the forces of nature and make them serve our own desires without killing off everything in the process, is not even considered by Mr. Bookchin. He is like the capitalist who views all working people as hopeless fuckups, incapable by their very nature of social responsibility. The ruling class tells the working class that it is too stupid to run things; Mr. Bookchin tells the human race that it is too stupid to make nature serve us.

Mr. Bookchin criticizes what he calls "environmentalism", which he says "reflects an 'instrumentalist' or technical sensibility in which nature is viewed merely as a passive habitat, an agglomeration of external objects and forces, that must be made more 'serviceable' for human use, irrespective of what these uses may be."

But what else could one reasonably expect? Mr. Bookchin is not so spiritual that he does not eat, but when he gives in to this aspect of nature, does he not deprive another animal of food?

Humans disagree on how to use nature, but all of us do it constantly. Given the opportunity to shape nature nearer to our heart's desire, who turns their back and strives for ecological sainthood?

Oh yes, there are such people. There've always been people who preferred suffering in this life so as to curry favor with the gods and be rewarded in one or another form of afterlife. But that old con has lost its savor in recent decades. More and more, people are beginning to demand heaven on earth. Freedom *and* abundance, equality *and* luxury, autonomy *and* pleasure are what we want.

And ultimately, it may now be said, we will go after our oldest enemy, death itself. Those like Mr. Bookchin who prefer harmony with nature to technical sensibility will, of course, have the freedom to die. But I do not think it will be a freedom they will choose to exercise.

Mr. Bookchin speaks of "the underlying notions of the present society, notably that man must dominate nature."

Mr. Bookchin here accepts one of the more clever capitalist myths. To be precise about it, the real notion is that "some men must dominate nature", and we all know who they are.

The domination of nature that characterizes the present social era is domination for the purpose of enriching the lives of a small minority of the human race. If the rest of us benefit, that's just an accident; and if we don't, that's our tough luck.

In either event, we have little to say about it (except during revolutionary periods). Most of us don't dominate anything.

But, just supposing, if we did have a classless society with the opportunity to dominate nature for the purpose of enriching the lives of all of humanity, would we do it? The answer is obvious.

Mr. Bookchin speaks of "our grotesque imbalance with nature".

What is "balance"? The cockroach has been around for some 300,000,000 years and shows every sign of hanging around forever . . . and it doesn't threaten the ecosphere. But however much such an existence may commend it-

self to Mr. Bookchin, the life of a cockroach holds little appeal for me.

Yet, ugliness, like beauty, is in the eye of the beholder. Perhaps Mr. Bookchin's aesthetics are such as delight in the spread of cancer cells or the eruption of volcanos, while recoiling in horror from the sterile operating room and the polluting rescue plane.

Mr. Bookchin says "admittedly (solar power satellites, space colonies, giant windmills, etc.) are less dangerous to the physical health of human beings than power derived from nuclear and fossil fuels . . ."

But that isn't enough, according to Mr. Bookchin, because it isn't the revolution; it isn't the creation of an egalitarian society. If the ruling classes respond to popular pressures and their own self-interests by phasing out the more dangerous forms of energy production, that is to be deplored because it leaves social relationships unaltered.

However, I must disagree. You see, if the ruling classes have concluded that dead workers produce no profits, I can only applaud such a generous sentiment: dead workers also make no revolutions.

Further, Mr. Bookchin at least hints at the idea that unless people are severely harmed by ecological blunders, they won't perceive the need to destroy hierarchical social relationships. But millions of people have perceived that need during periods of history when no one had ever heard of ecology. I don't think that the possibility of people living in the reasonable expectation of not being suddenly wiped out by poisonous or radioactive substances will make people conclude that hierarchy is OK after all.

Mr. Bookchin recommends "the need to understand the meaning of the affinity group structure as a lasting, family-type form."

Well, wouldn't you know that just when people are finally breaking loose from one form of permanent, compulsory association (the family), some ass will suggest imposing another form. Isn't that

what the phrase "a lasting, family-type form" really means?

I can see it now. Joining an affinity group will be just like marriage. There will be a stupid ritual performed to mark these sacred ties, presided over by a nature priest. Someone will get up and make a pompous speech about how "the affinity group is the foundation of anarchist society". Everyone involved will make a lot of silly promises they can't possible hope to carry out. Afterwards, the neighbors may have to get up a committee to go over to their house and stop the fighting. There'll even be divorce — a ritual explusion of the nonconformist member.

I've said previously that I have no ready answers to the problems of forming new kinds of relations between people. But I will not settle for the same old shit in a shiny new container. To me, the principle of free association means exactly that: people joining together when they wish, staying as long as they like, and departing when they please. Ceremony is superfluous and pledges of permanence are just lies, well-meaning perhaps, but lies nonetheless.

Let me take this a step further. When people join together for a narrow purpose, that purpose itself will generate an appropriate structure. But the relationships of people who are involved with each other in deeper ways are so complex and so subject to constant changes that to impose any structure is probably not only beyond us now but may always be beyond us. Many people may choose a quasi-family-type structure, but many others will choose no structure at all. I think the latter choice is a more realistic one; but, at a minimum, it is contrary to anarchist politics to impose a structure on people's relationships. On the other hand, theologians are ever-ready to tell us how we have to live.

Mr. Bookchin says that anarchist politics are incomprehensible "to millions of people who live as soloists in discotheques and singles bars."

Is there anything as satisfying as a fully-developed contempt for people who choose to live differently from the way that you know is the only correct way? Think how you feel, looking down on those idiots from your commanding position at the heights of spiritual/political consciousness. Yes, it does feel fine . . . even if the air is a little thin and the wind a little chilly and those scum down there don't appreciate your concern for their spiritual backwardness. Guess it's time to go down and knock a few heads together . . .

Personally, all I can say to this is that it's too bad the prophetic tradition didn't die out with the Hebrew tribes. In some ways, the prophet-motive is even worse than the profit motive.

Mr. Bookchin lauds "the ideals of a new world in which masses become individuals and natural resources become nature, both to be respected for their uniqueness and spirituality."

Of course, masses are becoming individuals now . . . just not the kind of individuals Mr. Bookchin approves of ("soloists in discos and singles bars").

But that's a trivial objection. Let's go to the root of this "uniqueness and spirituality". Do we conduct a ceremony of prayer before we eat each unique plant and animal . . . or do we stop eating? Shall every solar satellite contain a built-in altar? Must the hypodermic needle containing the life-saving drug be blessed before it can be used? Must every launching of the space shuttle be accompanied by a reading of Genesis 1:1?

What is all this except just another attempt to mystify human existence? What is all this besides just another set of "anarcho-

spiritualist" chains to fetter the ambitions of humanity? It seems to me that as soon as one postulates anything to which people must submit, you have abandoned the anarchist project, the project of freedom unlimited.

Humanity cannot be half slave (to the purposeless forces of nature) and half free (of domination of human by human). We cannot be free in the material world while bowing to a ghostly world carried around in our heads. All of the spiritual roads lead to a common destination, and the name it bears is Jonestown.

We reject worship as we reject every other form of servility. We demand heaven on earth, in the solar system, in the galaxy, in the universe. Win or lose, we will no longer settle for theological horseshit as a substitute for what we really want. But, at least in my opinion, I think we will win.

It would be very easy to say: "To hell with such 'worker-ownership' schemes, and your jobs for that matter"; objectively we can not, since we are talking about fellow workers' livlihoods. But we can make known the fact that stock ownership is merely a ploy by the capitalist class, the State and the social democratic reformists to fool workers into believing they are really in control of their workplaces. By the same token it is imperative that our fellow workers begin to realize and discuss what actual self-managment and workers control is all about and how their self-activity and the reorganization of their workplaces on a massive scale will not only benefit themselves but society as a whole.

We invite all shop-floor militants to open a dialogue with us on this issue.

Humans disagree on how to use nature, but all of us do it constantly. Given the opportunity to shape nature nearer our heart's desire, who turns their back and strives for ecological sainthood?

The «Bufe-ooneries»* continue

A response to Chaz Bufe's «Primitive Thought», and to the Misery of Anarcho-syndicalism

Over the years, the anarcho-syndicalist Workers' Solidarity Alliance (WSA) organization has had little to say about the growing ecological crisis (in effect, only one article appeared). This changed abruptly, though, when in the Fall 1988 issue of their paper Ideas and Action, the WSA printed an article to "generate discussion" about "environmentalism".(1) But if Chaz Bufe's article entitled "Primitive Thought" is any indication, the WSA might be better off to simply forget it: Bufe's long piece doesn't even analyze the environmental crisis and is devoted almost entirely to attacking people who do take industrial capitalism's destruction of the earth seriously, such as the people in Detroit who put out the journal Fifth Estate. The present article will not go into Bufe's comments about Earth First!, most of which repeat critiques made by George Bradford and others; it's more than enough attempting to unravel his accusations about Fifth Estate and other anti-authoritarian "primitivists" (although there are a number of us in Earth First! too). Calling for "relatively rapid development in the 'underdeveloped' countries" (sic), Bufe blandly advocates that the industrial plague be spread to the remotest corners of the planet and portrays himself as a friend of the earth at the same time. Who does he think he's trying to kid?

A couple of years ago Ideas and Action secretary Tom Wetzel had the following to say about the content of their journal: "What we ask is that people conduct their political discourse in a civil and reasonable way, instead of the cheap shot, name-calling prejudiced misinterpretation of others views, rumour-mongering and campaigns to discredit and denounce, which is the sign of sectarian competitiveness."(2) But the WSA seems to have a certain amount of trouble playing by their own rules, because along with its lack of seriousness, another major feature of Bufe's piece is its sneering tone and the level of his attacks. We anti-authoritarian primitivists are "blind" (repeated 3 times), and our "blind" rejection of technology is "idiotic". We're "dogmatic" (repeated 5 times

*The title of this text was inspired by the title of Brian Kane and Lawrence Jarach's critique of Bufe's Listen, Anarchist!: "Hold Your Tongue, Demagogue; Turning a Deaf Ear to Pure Bufe-oonery".

-- Chaz tends to wax a bit dogmatic himself) and prone to "scummy behaviour." Our ideas would inevitably wipe out "millions, probably billions" of people, Chaz isn't sure which, but what's a few hundred million or a couple of billion either way? But we're too "hypocritical" to "dare to advocate what would really be required to achieve our vision: wholesale coercion and mass murder." What's ironic, or worse, is that in a recent special edition on deep ecology, George Bradford of Fifth Estate presents a detailed critique of authoritarian and even genocidal comments (being in favour of AIDS or its equivalent to reduce population) made by some Earth First! members in their paper and elsewhere; and John Zerzan ridicules Earth First! honcho Dave Forman in a recent article on technology in Anarchy and warns about the right-wing tendencies of some Earth First! members (see footnote #3 for a comment on the recent exchange between Zerzan and Bradford). But Bufe already knows what he wants to believe; he has no intention of letting evidence to the contrary get in his way.

If Tom Wetzel's statement about publication policy indicates a distance between WSA's ideas and their actions (à la Bufe), it also poses the question of relations between anti-authoritarian tendencies when outlooks are often polar opposites. Bufe's nasty, brutish and not-so-short piece (to paraphrase Hobbes) is not his first swipe at the Fifth Estate -- his pamphlet Listen, Anarchist! offered an overlapping set of accusations (for some responses to Listen, Anarchist!, see footnote #4). Bufe's bottom line is clear: our primitivist visions are absurd, impossible to put into practice, and we should fuck off and die (politically speaking), the sooner the better. Our dangerous heresy must be banished from his 19th century anarchist church (the word primitivist is used, by the way, with considerable reluctance in this essay, because among other reasons there is no agreement about what it means; on the other hand, I do not reject the term because it accurately describes my vision and desires).

But Bufe doesn't even set up a straw Fifth Estate to knock down. Nowhere is there a presentation or analysis of the Fifth Estate's ideas or are the sources of these ideas mentioned (Mumford, Ellul, Camatte, the Situationists, Perlman, anthropologists such as Clastre, Sahlins, Diamond, some

native authors, etc. -- these influences have never been hidden and Fifth Estate's movement to an anti-tech position was set out in rich and at times very personal detail in the many articles that appeared there in the late seventies and early eighties).

As the authors of a pamphlet critiquing Bufe's Listen, Anarchist! point out, "whatever the extent of Fifth Estate's rejection of technology it could hardly be said to be blind considering the lengths to which Fifth Estate editors have gone to describe the various forms of and the systematic (anti) nature of many forms of technology in their writings and the ways in which these degrade humanity."

To date the anarcho-syndicalists have yet to offer a real critique of Fifth Estate and the anti-authoritarian primitivists. Letters that have been published in Fifth Estate such as ones by Jon Bekken (5) and Lazarus Jones (6) have been little more than grumpy diatribes devoid of analysis, and in his completely uncritical homage to computer anarchism Modern Technology and Anarchism, Sam Dolgoff finds it prudent to simply ignore us (7).

In this sterile landscape, it's easy to find Bufe's (non)critique exasperating. "Chaz brings up serious matters, too bad he fails to discuss them seriously" comment the authors of the critique of Bufe's Listen Anarchist! cited above. But if Bufe's piece is insulting on a variety of levels, it is not my intention to play the victim: I'll have my share of negative comments about his political outlook as well. Perhaps our revolutionary goals are incompatible, despite our professed mutual desire to abolish the state, capitalism, hierarchy and bosses. It should be noted, though, that anarcho-syndicalism is not entirely monolithic. Some young Canadian anarchists who recently joined the IWW, for example, are saying things which at times strongly contrast with Bufe's approach. But they are located almost entirely in North America, and their assertions are often contradictory upon closer inspection.

Some of what follows will be speculative (unlike Bufe, I have no crystal ball). If the resistance to industrial domestication offered by the Luddites and Native peoples serves as an ongoing inspiration, there is no blueprint for an anti-authoritarian, anti-technological revolution. I would mention as well that the vision presented here is my own. Others may well be quite different. We are not an organization or a primitivist party, and hopefully a truly decentralized society will be the negation of the rigid orthodoxies inherent in massified industrial civilization.

But first to take a closer look at the anarcho-syndicalism from whence Bufe came:

Anarcho-syndicalism: A Historical Overview

Emerging in the 1870-80's anarcho-syndicalism quickly became one of the three major anarchist tendencies of the period (along with anarcho-communism and anarcho-individualism). Although similar to anarcho-communism in many respects, its primary emphasis, as the name suggests, was on the workplace, through the creation of specifically anarcho-syndicalist unions or by agitating in and attempting to radicalize unions that were already in place. The anarcho-syndicalists proposed that the state be eliminated, the bosses kicked out and the means of production taken over and managed by the people working in them (as opposed to the state socialists, who favoured nationalizations).

From Europe, Spanish, German, Jewish

18

and Russian immigrants spread anarcho-syndicalism to the Americas, where it played a role in the Industrial Workers of the World and was the initial imported revolutionary current in a number of Latin American countries. By the 1920's, except in Spain, anarcho-syndicalism (and anarchism generally) was in rapid decline, as authoritarian socialist formations such as Lenin's International became the barely-contested representatives of any possibility for radical social change. In France, in the previously anarcho-syndicalist CGT, for example, the anarchists were elbowed aside and the union was taken over by the French Communist Party (which dominates it to this day).

Spain represents a unique case, as it embodies both a high point and a considerable burden (because of the anarcho-syndicalist CNT's collaboration with the government). Although a detailed analysis of the Spanish Revolution is impossible here, it is important to note that although factory production and wage labour remained in the cities, money was abolished in some locations in the countryside.

By the end of World War II, anarcho-syndicalism had gone underground in Spain and was in eclipse elsewhere. That it did not disappear entirely in the English-speaking countries was due in large part to the efforts of individuals such as Sam Dolgoff and Albert Meltzer. With the end of the Franco dictatorship in the late seventies, unions were legalized and the anarcho-syndicalist CNT experienced a strong resurgence. However, splits and purges in the organization and a host of other problems resulted in an equally precipitous decline.

The 1970's also saw a certain renewal of interest in anarchist and anti-authoritarian ideas elsewhere in Europe. In North America, a new generation of anarcho-syndicalists joined with other class-struggle-oriented anarchists to constitute the Anarchist-Communist Tendency within the amorphous Social Revolutionary Anarchist Federation, and went on to form the short-lived Anarchist-Communist Federation (ACF). In 1982, former ACF members began to publish Ideas and Action, and as the Workers' Solidarity Alliance, soon became the American section of the anarcho-syndicalist International Workers' Association, which is active in 13, mainly European, countries.

Although the IWA remains the major pole of attraction for contemporary anarcho-syndicalism, some have found it preferable to organize outside it. For example, anarcho-syndicalists form a tendency within the 500-member French Anarchist Federation, which takes the position that all anarchists should work together within one federation. In the U.S., a small group of anarcho-syndicalists, some of them former ACF members, are publishing a journal called Libertarian Labour Review. And in Spain, a rival CNT organization has appeared.

Although it is not a specifically anarcho-syndicalist organization, it is within the IWW that some anarchists have been saying things which in ecological terms are qualitatively different (i.e. beyond throwing in a few anti-pollution devices almost as an afterthought). Their approach will be dealt with separately at the end of this text.

"The Everyday Activity of Slaves
Reproduces Slavery"
-- Fredy Perlman

With the period of the arrival of the anarcho-syndicalists in the late 19th century, the first phase of industrial domestication was already complete, and in the most pessimistic analysis, the battle already lost. Setting the stage for this initial phase was a period of capital accumulation stretching over several centuries. Trade expanded, markets developed, and cities grew. Separated from the land -- often ejected physically or having had their communal plots appropriated by ravenous capital (making subsistence farming impossible) -- people were pushed toward cities and large towns, and soon became wage slaves in the factories. Communities were shattered, and community itself, which had continued to survive evolving forms of capitalism, was put under constant siege.

This period also saw a parallel development of inventions and technique. Toward the end of the 18th century, the level of technological development, combined with the level of capital accumulation, produced a qualitative leap: the beginnings of the factory system, which immediately resulted in a qualitative leap in alienation as well. But the alienation of expanding industrialism had less to do with people's separation from their

control over the products of their labour, as theorized by Marx, than it did with their rapid dispossession from tools they could really control (not to mention, of course, the acute alienation of working in and living amongst the factories themselves, which was considered a necessary evil -- when it was considered at all -- by Marx and the other 19th century radical theoreticians).

As though a chemical process had taken place, neither capital nor technology were to be the same again. A kind of fusion began to occur; and it was to become increasingly difficult to tell them apart. Though to a lesser extent this had long been the case: when the projectile from a blunderbuss or

musket pierced a Native person, for example, it was already no easy matter to detect which "portion" of the projectile came from "technological advances" and which from the capital which placed the conqueror in the "New World" (not to forget the already strongly developed capitalization of the conquerors' way of thinking itself).

The beginnings of the factory process also coincided with an increasing autonomization of technology. Soon the machines and the ideology underlying them were to escape the control of the capitalists themselves, imposing their own rules and imperatives, to which people could only adapt. The mega-machine we know today was rapidly taking form. As well, capital became more diffuse (and insidious in its ability to penetrate our relationships at will). Class distinctions did not disappear of course, but a process was underway whereby even the poorest people were to internalize more and more aspects of the ideology of capital.

The Luddites

The syndicalists are rarely very verbose about the movement which directly preceded them and whose suppression set the stage for the rise of unionism. This is understandable -- in effect the Luddites posed a very direct threat to their attempts to recuperate people's multi-faceted struggle against the imposition of factory slavery. A couple of excellent accounts of this period can be found in John Zerzan's recent anthology Elements of Refusal. The following excerpts are taken from a translation of an article by a member of the French group Os Cangacieros:

"Luddism was the poor's response to this new order. During the initial decades of the 19th century, a movement dedicated to the destruction of machines developed in a climate of insurrectional fury. It was not only a nostalgia for the golden age of the craftsman. Certainly the reign of the quantitative, of mass-produced shoddy merchandise was a major source of anger. (...) But Luddism was above all an anti-capitalist war of independence, an "attempt to destroy the new society" (Mathius). (...) Luddism was heir to the millenarian movement of the preceding centuries, and although it no longer expressed itself as a universal and unifying theory, it remained radically foreign to all political outlooks and to every economic pseudo-rationalism. (...) In England, while the nascent trade union movement was weakly repressed, and even tolerated, destroying machines was punished by death. (...) Allegedly backwards, the

Luddites ... understood that the 'material instruments of production' are above all instruments of domestication whose form is not neutral because it guarantees hierarchy and dependance." (8)

Work, Syndicalism and the Self-Management of Alienation

With the suppression of the Luddites, a grotesque competition evolved between the Marxists, capitalists and anarchists to establish who was to succeed as the authentic vanguard of "progress". A feverish belief in science, reason and the liberatory potential of technology animated rival hallucinatory schemes which barely seemed to sense the increasing mechanization and impoverishment of daily life.

The Marxists proposed a "transitional" "dictatorship of the proletariat" in which the state ruled in the name of the people. But even more insidious than this farce were the "self-management" proposals of the anarcho-syndicalists, who, foregoing the buffer of the state, offered an even more intense internalization of developing industrialism.

First came the acceptance of the inevitability and desirability of work and of human beings as "workers". This in itself amounted to a severe blow delivered by the anarcho-syndicalists for capital, as people definitively began to see themselves in capitalist -- i.e. economic -- terms: as objects of the economy. This tradition is carried on unmodified to this day, for example in WSA's "Where Do We Stand?" statement, when they say that "in pursuing social change, we put our main emphasis on the role of people as workers ... because no sector of society can emancipate itself unless the power of capital is overthrown". But the power of capital is precisely its ability to define people as workers! And even if money is abolished, the tyranny of "fixed capital" (the factory system) remains.

Ironically, the anarcho-syndicalists will usually vigorously deny that they are worker-ist. But this claim might begin to merit consideration when they stop using the word to name their organizations (in the most recent issue of their paper, for instance, the WSA was organizing a conference with two other "Worker" organizations and a couple of obscure political parties -- and in effect one of the worker organizations in question also aspires to become a party). If this is partying, leave me out!

After attempting -- not always successfully! -- to hammer the nail of work into the coffin of possibilities for radical change, the coffin itself, as if by mystical transubstantiation, may well have become the unions themselves. But it is important to distinguish between several at times conflicting roles played by the unions. From the beginning, the major task of the union organizers was to integrate the wage slaves into developing industrialism: to assure that people actually came to work, to enforce labour discipline, to encourage self-policing and to convince people of the necessity of factory hell.

But at the same time the unions sought to better working conditions and raise salaries. An often very bitter conflict existed between capital and the people who were forced to work in the factories. But this conflict was defined by the various extollers of progress as a fight for a bigger slice of the same pie: the expanding urban mega-monster.

While some Marxists, such as Bernstein,

The Return of the Anarcho-Syndicalists

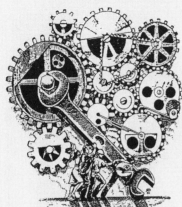

@ssures The ContinuAnce of WORK!

from Semiotexte USA

accepted the intrinsically reformist nature of the unions, other Marxists and the anarcho-syndicalists have persisted in seeing radical possibilities where none existed. "By organizing industrially the workers will be building a new society within the old" reads a pamphlet from the English section of the IWA (9). But "organizing industrially" should read industrially organized: organized by the logic of industrialism. This "shell" can only reproduce itself. As if evoking his worst nightmare, Tom Wetzel of the WSA informs us that "The old industrial structure cannot be scrapped all at once" before leading into an updated version of the same spiel: "Our aim is not to have the working class take over the existing capitalist industry in order to run it as it is at present, with the same methods of production." But this kind of verbiage comes into sharper focus in a statement to the April '88 congress of the IWA, where the WSA acknowledges the existence of an "ecological crisis", but goes on to offer no response/remedies/solutions of any type. Zilch. Not even the predictable anti-pollution devices. Everything is blamed on the "natural workings of capitalism" for the

thousandth time, as if anarcho-industrialism weren't an integral part of the problem.

When the anarcho-syndicalists grab (and slightly reform) the means of production, the story goes, we'll really be in control. There will be "real human mastery of production (rather than human enslavement to production as wage-worker cogs)" (Wetzel). But remove the word "wage" and no real difference between two parts of this formula exists. There is no self-managing industrialism; you can only be "self-managed" by it. Anarcho-syndicalism proposes to abolish our instinctive separation from industrialism; to make us fully participate in and take on its alienation as our own. This productivist, workplace-fetishist delirium attains its summit when Bufe refers to the factories as the wage slaves' "nests."

But little is said about the division of labour or the inherently centralizing, hierarchical nature of modern industry, or the techno-bureaucratic class necessary to run it. Sam Dolgoff of Libertarian Labor Review rapturously informs us that already "every year sixty million pages of scientific-technical information are freely (sic) circulated all over the world!" But he neglects to say how many pages people are expected to read to "self-manage" modern industrialism. And just how do you self-manage television? And how do billions of people really communicate through "their" desktop computers?

"The arrogance of the civilized mind is boundless"
— Bob Brubaker

In "Primitive Thought" Bufe never mentions the original inhabitants of this continent, or primitive peoples elsewhere on the planet; they simply disappear. In "Listen, Anarchist!", they disappear in a somewhat different way, when he complains of our "obsequious odes to 'primitive peoples'." By the quotation marks, Bufe clearly implies that they simply don't exist (which must come as a surprise to some! I can just see the anarcho-syndicalists clanking into the final enclaves. The assembled tribes are informed that progress has pronounced them guilty of "wholesale coercion and mass murder" and that furthermore it is highly likely they do not even exist. But if they obligingly proceed to self-manage a banana plantation and plug into global cybernetic planning, possibilities of atonement may well appear...).

As Dogbane Campion of the Fifth Estate notes, "It is imperative for those who share in this complex mythology of modern civilization to absolutely deny any legitimacy to the lifeways or visions of our primal ancestors." If this tie can be severed, and the unchallenged reign of industrial ideology established, we can be dismissed as a "fringe", as "screwballs", or in the unforgettable phrase of one regular Ideas and Action columnist, as "nuts and bolts". Even in humour, it seems, industrial terminology is inescapable, although he was referring to a wider range of undesirables as I remember the conversation; we're far from being the only anti-authoritarian

current that doesn't exactly fit into the WSA's picture.

When you realize you've been programmed by modern civilization, you begin to wonder who you really are. In the words of Feral Ranter:

Bufe puts down what he calls "obsequious odes to 'primitive people'". But it's obvious to anyone who cares to look carefully that primitive people had (and the few that still exist have) much fuller, freer lives than the average civilized person. Doesn't it make sense that those who desire fuller, freer lives would look to primitive folk to learn why they seem so much more alive than us? (One important factor seems to be that primitive people haven't developed the productivist mentality that so controls our lives and produces the technology to which Bufe is so attached)(10).

For most of those of us who have rejected civilization it is less a question of taking primitive peoples as a precise model (although we have many things to learn from them) than of (re)establishing a radically different, non-instrumentalist relationship with the earth and nature: what I see as a re-integration into nature, or as close to this goal as possible. As well, it's worth remembering that our own, often Celtic, ancestors also once lived a primitive lifestyle (as did everyone). You can't, of course, turn back the clock -- no one ever said you could -- though we could get rid of them. But that's no argument for not abolishing this society; the increasingly obvious bankruptcy of civilization only makes its negation more and more attractive...

Can't see the forest for the trees

The typical assertion of technology's neutrality is a trap that Bufe avoids. Instead, his modestly "more sophisticated approach than primitivism" leads to a more elaborate set of illusions. Warning that industrial technology is not a "monolith", Bufe would have us see it as "a great number of separate technologies" possessing positive and negative brownie points. "Even the worst technology might have some beneficial aspects", he notes, implying that we might have to put up with even that. Only, predictably, nuclear energy is singled out as being "inherently destructive", conveniently allowing the anarcho-syndicalists to rail against this highly visible monster without taking any risks, i.e. of finding themselves in a position where they can no longer promise "the workers" the same -- if not expanded -- commodity flow they presently "enjoy" (in the West that is) in exchange for industrial-urban slavery, and this for an unlimited period. But nuclearism cannot be wrenched out of context so easily: the techno-fix, cost/benefit productivist ideology underlying it makes it more a metaphor for modern tech than an anomaly.

Bufe's insistence on "a great number of separate technologies" is essential to the

factory nightmare

Demolition Derby I (1989)

20

WORK RESISTERS LEAGUE

Retinal Damage in Dead Time, Box 1425, NY NY 10009

anarcho-syndicalists: the last thing they need is for people to begin making connections and come to the conclusion that technology has established itself as an autonomous form of domination; we must remain mesmerized at all costs (as if by disconnected images passing on a screen). According to Tom Wetzel, it doesn't "make much sense" to talk about technology "in the abstract", while Bufe reduces Fifth Estate's rigorous analysis to "taking refuge in generalizations". Both put the word technology in quotation marks, as if this attempt to distance and neutralize the word somehow eliminates the problem (not to mention the one it causes their approach). Their flight from understanding, though, will not put the genie back in the bottle.

Even a glance at electricity, for example, is sufficient to demonstrate the interconnectedness (!) of modern technology (although this of course does not preclude rival bureau-

than a question of choice. Their nightmare is that people will refuse to "self-manage" the megamachine; that they will be repelled by industrialism's awesome amount of boring, stupid, unavoidable labour, the stacks of paperwork, the piles of computer disks, the endless meetings, the cars, the factories and perhaps even the cities themselves. "I like having a large variety of foods to eat the year long" says Bufe, whom I strongly doubt has recently grown or otherwise provided any himself. He simply assumes that agro-industry will continue on as before, and that people in the countryside will continue to work to feed the urban masses (as opposed to practicing subsistence farming or other methods of survival on the land), that the transportation and distribution network and everything needed to keep them functioning will continue as before, in short that all the soldiers of industrialism (and all its generals) will remain at their posts. Because if not, if even one essential sector says no thanks, the entire pyramid begins to crumble... To paraphrase John F. Kennedy, Bufe asks (and needs) what you can do for industrialism; what industrialism does to you is another matter.

And like capital, Bufe reduces people to producers, consumers and distributors; to mere "cogs".

Although accusing us of massive coercion, Bufe doesn't think twice about shoving his technology down our throats: that's industrialism as usual. But his us-and-them approach is highly distorted: we primitivists are not the only other fish in the anti-authoritarian sea; it's composed of diverse and frequently conflicting approaches. To go by the annual anarchist gatherings, anarcho-syndicalists comprise about 5-10% of the current milieu (compared to the Spanish Revolution, when they overshadowed everyone else and everyone was obliged to see themselves in relation to anarcho-syndicalism). What about, say, Freedom, Class War or Insurrection (to take a few examples from a non-North American context), groups or projects which aren't exactly bubbling over

in Canada.

Our differences with ultra-tech ideologues such as Bufe, though, are profound (and he's so sure of the future he doesn't hesitate to espouse a slightly-reformed image of industrialism whatever the ecological cost).

As the situation worsens though, approaches that would have appeared extremist not long ago are beginning to look more and more realistic. And de-industrialization can quite naturally be found near the top of the list of possible solutions to the eco-crisis. But as opposed to Bufe's implied vision of rampaging primitivist hordes, the onus for coercion would probably be on the anarcho-syndicalists. If the countryside can live without the cities, the reverse is hardly the case. Like capital, the cities see nature and the land as "natural resources" and "raw materials"; as something to be exploited. To feed the megamachine they need the country-side's food, minerals and transportation routes. But you don't have to blow up the factories -- all you have to do is desert them. Depending on the circumstances, people could try hunting and gathering, subsistence farming or a combination of both. But even communities based on subsistence farming (and Bufe doesn't claim the Earth isn't capable of feeding the present population) would directly threaten urbanism if they decided they were no longer repositories for pipelines, hydro-electric pylons, telephone wires, or sources of minerals and food for the cities and decided to shut off access. Even with a wall of China around us, we primitivists would still suffer technology's "democratic" pollution, acid rain, etc.

TECHNOFIX TIX

If Bufe avoids a rigorous examination of the effects of modern technology, it eventually becomes clear that it is not really considered important. Even the initial sentence of his text -- "The hottest topic in 'progressive' circles these days is the Earth First! controversy" -- succeeds in simultaneously emptying and turning any discussion of the eco-crisis into a spectacle. Bufe simply rolls out industrialism's big guns, as if the mere mention of their names should make us click our heels and salute. This technofix tic is the essence of industrialism's ability to become all that exists; its violent need to eliminate anything which does not speak with its codes or humbly adapt to its priorities, to its totalitarian project. With two generations of people who are unable to remember life without TV under its belt, techno-capital mops up the last native peoples and the show barely merits a thirty-second news clip; meanwhile, Bufe does his bit to make sure that no nasty neo-primitivisms rear their ugly heads to throw a monkey wrench into technology's harmonious advance. Any discussion of technology's gift to human-kind (since it sure hasn't done much for plants and animals!) is of little worth without

---

There is no self-managing industrialism; you can only be "self-managed" by it. Anarcho-syndicalism proposes to abolish our instinctive separation from industrialism; to make us fully participate in and take on its alienation as our own.

---

cracies within it). Everyone and everything is plugged in (directly or indirectly), and without electricity, or one of the many essential elements that compose it, everything collapses. And in effect guerilla groups like the FMLN have made attacking this highly-vulnerable hydro-electrical edifice a central feature of their campaigns.

Another example is the highly-publicized "virus" which affected the non-classified Arpanet computer system, shutting down hundreds of them across the U.S. by multiplying itself out-of-control, graphically demonstrating the potentially catastrophic effect of dependence on mass techniques.

Cities are constructed entirely around the circulation of automobiles, and everyone submits to their needs and whims (in a recent letter/article on transportation in Processed World, it's worth mentioning in passing, Tom Wetzel lets it be known that it's OK to criticize the automobile... as long as you don't propose to really do anything about them) (11). Real existing modern technology (as opposed to Bufe and Wetzel's elusive "technology") is a gridlock -- a complex of interlocking parts. Some are, in effect, expendable; but the core features need each other to survive, and tend to give birth to the more peripheral ones.

Technology's triumph, ultimately, has been psychological: our domestication and the process of reification (our reduction to the status of things) seem to have been accepted. Of the hypnotic power of modern technology there remains no doubt. But industrialism has also given rise to its negation. A friend relates, for example, that half the computer programmers where he works loathe "their" computers. The odds could be worse.

"Massive Coercion"

Massive coercion is the essence of modern technology (and as we have already seen, machines and their codes have repeatedly shown their ability to replace human beings as the slavemasters). Given their addiction to industrialism, the anarcho-syndicalists' workerism becomes a necessity rather

with enthusiasm about anarcho-syndicalism either. Are they guilty of "massive coercion" as well because at one point they might come into conflict with anarcho-syndicalism? And where do the Leninists and the other "revolutionary" statists fit in? If future revolutions turn out like recent ones (and even leftist revolutions are a rarity these days), the anarcho-syndicalists will simply be suppressed along with the primitivists.

MEANWHILE AT THE FACTORY 3 MILES AWAY

HOLY SHIT!! THERE'S A TOXIC GAS LEAK!!

THE YOUNG AND THE FRUSTRATED © 1988 BY VUNA TICKS

Luna Ticks, 424 S. 45th Street, Philadelphia, PA. 19104

So any revolution in which anti-authoritarians play a major role would be a qualitatively different one. And we primitivists expect to have our word to say along with everyone else (somehow you get the impression that Bufe expects us to just fade away because of the crushing weight of his arguments). If people are not interested in a primitivist approach, our influence will be minimal. And since we don't want to grab state power or the means of production, a typical putsch is out of the question.

But the concept of revolution is rapidly changing. The ecological crisis has aroused even the anarcho-syndicalists from their slumber (though there's little evidence that they're more than sleepwalking to date). And as the wounds inflicted by industrial capitalism have become harder and harder to conceal, ecological concerns have become the #1 issue

taking into account what has been lost (which is not to imply an idealization of previous forms of capitalism). The extreme difficulty -- if not impossibility -- of imagining life without movies, cars, and factories, etc. which people encounter is simply another example of the interiorization of industrial totalitarianism. Having almost entirely eliminated community, techno-culture has replaced it with its own mediated pseudo-community. Life has turned into a representation (and here the anarcho-syndicalists would have us believe that their flurry of mandated and revocable delegates are somehow not subordinate to the needs of industrialism).

Most modern technology is useless; in the end, it only serves the megamachine, without which its importance would disappear. The product of capitalism and the materialization of alienated labour, modern technology

21

is modern capital; the crystallization of its ideology. In a free society, most of it could simply be scrapped without hesitation. It is not surprising, then, that Bufe avoids unconvincing extrapolations about the joys of self-managing industrialism and emphasizes its showpiece: modern medicine. But here again, anti-authoritarians find themselves faced with unresolvable problems. As Feral Ranter points out, Bufe "chooses to ignore the way that modern medicine has stolen our health and our bodies from us and placed them in the hands of medical experts (hardly an anarchist ideal) who only know how to treat them like clockwork."

And not unexpectedly, as Ivan Illich points out in his book Medical Nemesis, the realm of medical experts, like that of sundry other experts, also turns out to be a techno-horror story: "The pain, dysfunction, disability and anguish resulting from technical intervention now rival the morbidity due to traffic and industrial accidents and even war-related activities, and make the impact of medicine one of the most rapidly expanding epidemics of our time." In fact, one easily gets the impression that doctors rarely know what they're doing at all: "In one instance," Illich reports, "autopsies showed that more than half the patients who died in a British university clinic with a diagnosis of specific heart failure had in fact died of something else. In another instance, the same series of chest X-rays shown to the same team of specialists on different occasions led them to change their mind on 20% of all cases. (...) Nor do machines seem to be any more infallible. In a competition between diagnostic machines and human diagnosticians in 83 cases recommended for pelvic surgery, pathology showed that both man and machine were correct in 22 instances; in 37 instances the computer correctly rejected the doctor's diagnosis; in 11 instances the doctors proved the computer wrong; and in 10 cases both were in error."(12)

But modern medicine's claims of omniscience, if patently false in practice, remain gospel in a legal sense and carry with them the entire weight of the state apparatus: "Medicine has the authority to label one man's complaint a legitimate illness, to declare a second man sick though he himself

does not complain, and to refuse a third social recognition of his pain, his disability, and even his death. It is medicine which stamps some pain as 'merely subjective', some impairment as malingering, and some deaths -- though not others -- as suicide." It is this autonomous power, which Illich rightly excoriates, that is perhaps the most sacred cow of science and reason worshippers like Bufe.

But even medicine's much-touted ability to control epidemics in a world in which "the new diseases of civilization kill as many as formerly succumbed to pneumonia and other infections" also appears suspect: "the study of the evolution of disease patterns provides evidence that during the last century doctors have affected epidemics no more profoundly than did priests during earlier times. Epidemics came and went, imprecated by both but touched by neither." Illich then goes on to discuss a variety of diseases such as scarlet fever, diphtheria, whooping cough, measles, rickets, pellagra, etc., which fit this pattern. After citing Illich's findings quoted above, George Bradford, in his recently published sequel on deep ecology, goes on to add that "the one in every two people that will suffer from cancer by the end of this century can generally assume that a major cause of disease is the industrial civilization that promised to conquer disease and death and which instead has made new diseases and poisoned the entire life-support system of the planet."(13)

But in no way do I wish to minimize the role of modern medicine: it may well be the link that inhibits people from achieving a qualitative leap beyond industrialism. But "urban-industrial dominance is the disease, not the medicine", as Theodore Roszak points out, and has poisoned our lands and bodies and turned us into neurotic hulks. From the ravages of this alienation, modern medicine offers at best temporary relief.

As I have previously stated, I have no crystal ball. Imagining a revolutionary movement is hard enough, much less a specifically anti-industrial one. As such, an anti-authoritarian primitivist approach has been around for about ten years. A full debate about medicine has yet to take place, and there is no consensus about this question (nor neces-

sarily should there be!) or many others, questions that in effect can only ultimately be resolved during the revolution itself (which, unfortunately, we are highly unlikely to witness).

Some aspects of modern medicine consist of information which can be used without reliance on modern technology. Others, such as widespread dependence on tranquilizers, bespeak the technofix pitfalls that industrialism avoids only with great difficulty. Most medical health care consists of basic information and simple techniques which could be easily learned, and whose generalization, as Illich points out, would attack the state of dispossession in which it is in the medical establishment's interest to keep us. People could also begin to learn about local plants and traditional remedies and start to self-manage their own health. Above all, getting rid of industrial capitalism would be the healthiest event imaginable, physically and mentally. People might decide they wish to keep most modern medical facilities but to get rid of the rest of the unrelated techno-superstructure, which would still result in massive de-industrialization. Or they may opt for "islands of industrialism" in a primitivist sea. These solutions, though, might create considerable strains or re-create the mega-machine. In that case, people might decide to forego industrial medicine entirely, which would signify a radical break with industrialism.

The poisoning of our earth, the daily slaughter and maiming caused by countless auto accidents, plane crashes, train wrecks, oil spills, industrial accidents, etc. and the washed-out neurotic horror of everyday urbanism -- this is industrial capitalism's logic and "morality". If Bufe and Wetzel occasionally indulge in ostentatious hand-wringing, they intend to do nothing about this nightmare beyond a little tinkering. More faithful upholders of industrialism-as-usual in the anti-authoritarian milieu than the anarcho-syndicalists there are none.

Bureaucratic Tangle

Not much has been said about organizations like the WSA as such up to this point, an aspect which should not go unmentioned. From the moment they are founded, organizational patriotism is the guiding light of these sects, distorting and emptying truth as armored reactions replace real communication based on affinity and trust, and people's profoundest desires and passions are squeezed into lowest-common-denominator platforms which are a caricature of freedom.

How "Primitive Thought" has been handled by Bufe, Wetzel and the WSA is a good illustration of this phenomenon. To review the facts:

1) Between 1982 and 1989, Ideas and Action prints one (out of 116) article on ecological issues, a fairly wretched piece on Bhopal, which argues for a "right-to-know" about what's poisoning us, but of course not for a right not to work as such, or not to work in the factories, or ultimately a right not to get poisoned and gassed in this or future anarcho-industrialisms in which "self-management" has kicked in and problems have magically disappeared -- Bufe, it's important to note, glibly accuses capitalists

Bufe simply rolls out industrialism's big guns, as if the mere mention of their names should make us click our heels and salute.

22

Demolition Derby I (1989)

of not "going to the expense of treating and properly disposing of" (...) "dangerous wastes", as if they -- or the anarcho-syndicalists -- could snap their fingers and resolve this and innumerable other problems which are caused by industrialism. But in the same paragraph, Bufe himself talks about scrubbers, which he says will "greatly reduce the amount of pollutants emitted by their plants." He doesn't claim, however, that they are going to eliminate pollution. We've seen what two hundred years of industrialism can do. How much more "greatly reduced" pollution can the planet take for, say, the next million years?

2) Bufe's article appears. Ostensibly published to "generate discussion" about "environmentalism", it's written by a guy who's hostile to it, who doesn't analyze the environmental crisis, and who only manages a sub-critique of Earth First! and a non-critique of the Fifth Estate. On top of that, its author has an axe to grind, if not an obsession about the Fifth Estate, considering that this is the third time he's publicly denounced them (if one includes his review of Perlman's "Against History, Against Leviathan"), and that after breaking off relations with them, he continued to correspond with them using a pseudonym.

3) Wetzel sends out disclaimers with the issue in question and afterwards, implying that Bufe's rant doesn't mean anything because it's "only his own viewpoint".

4) Things are expected to remain in suspended animation until the WSA tacks on a statement to their "Where Do We Stand" piece, offerings that are usually four short paragraphs long (and what of substance can be said about ecology -- or anything else -- in four paragraphs, as if we expected anything from these people anyway beyond a few platitudes and perhaps some rapid verbal smoke-and-mirrors if they ultimately find their ultra-industrialism unconvincing at this late date. They had nothing to offer in their April '88 statement to the IWA conference, but we're expected to hold our breaths until their next empty pronunciamento blaming it all on the "natural workings of capitalism").

Before beginning this essay, I wrote to Ideas and Action for a copy of Bufe's Listen, Anarchist!, the article on Bhopal, pamphlets outlining the WSA's positions and anything else they had printed on environmentalism. I received the material I requested, and the "only his own viewpoint" disclaimer. A week later, Wetzel sent me another package to clarify the WSA's positions, which contained the statement to the April '88 IWA conference, a letter/article by Wetzel (which has since appeared in Processed World) on transportation and a letter by Wetzel to Alien Nation (all of which have been quoted here -- if they're supposed to present a point of view which is different from Chaz's, the contrary is very much the case ...!). This package included a somewhat longer disclaimer about Chaz's Listen, Anarchist!. These nervous disclaimers are understandable because Chaz's article effectively blows the WSA's cover of "anti-sectarianism". At the risk of being boring, I'll repeat Wetzel's statement of a couple of years back, where he states that Ideas and Action does not publish "cheap-shot, name-calling prejudiced misinformation of others' views, rumour-mongering and campaigns to discredit and denounce, which is the sign of sectarian competitiveness" (anyone who's read Bufe's abusive article would understandably find this statement absurd). This myth of non-sectarianism still has to be trotted out, it seems, despite Wetzel's (and Bufe's) central

Demolition Derby I (1989)

ÉCOLE DE TECHNOLOGIE SUPÉRIEURE

Montréal tech school

role in purging Sally Fry, Brian Kane and Kevin Keating from No Middle Ground (see

Sally Fry's "On 'Antiauthoritarian' Purges, Or, A Purge By Any Other Name ..." in Rabies (14)), not to mention the activities of other IWA organizations, such as Albert Meltzer's diatribes against Freedom et al. in Black Flag or the gun-toting, iron-bar wielding reception given to "the other" CNT by the CNT-AIT at the former's founding conference.

Bufe and Wetzel, it should be noted, are not exactly strangers: they just happen to be in the same organization, live in the same city (San Francisco, where Ideas and Action is published) and Sally Fry, who worked on two projects with Wetzel, calls Bufe and Wetzel "sidekicks" in the above-mentioned text. As well, another person recently told me that they share an apartment, although this is not 100% certain. "We don't agree with his polemics (read diatribes) against Fifth Estate and Open Road -- at least some of us don't," says Wetzel (if these anti-sectarians really don't, then why do they publish and distribute them -- after all, that's what their "editorial advisory" group is for, isn't it?). It should be mentioned that apart from Fifth Estate and Open Road, Listen, Anarchist! also attacks Resistance, The Spark (now defunct), the Australian anarcha-feminist paper Everything, Fredy Perlman (who "babbles on" according to Bufe), "marginals", the Vancouver Five (Four), and the list goes on. Considering the WSA's "non-sectarianism" (and Bufe even manages to devote a chapter to denouncing it!), it's interesting to note Wetzel's contorted excuse for including Listen, Anarchist! in the WSA's publication list: "We distribute the pamphlet because the group here believes it is accurate about the Bob Black/Processed

SOLIDARIDAD OBRERA

Organo de la C.N.T. de Cataluña
III época - 65 ptas.

FUNDADA EN 1907

Portavoz de la Confederación Nacional del Trabajo de España
Diciembre de 1988 - núm. 197

CNT
AIT

PARA QUE TODOS TRABAJEN
the CNT wants full employment; we want full unemployment

World affair ..." Well, well. Nothing in the copy I received would have led me to discern this selective stamp of approval (and Brian Kane and Lawrence Jarach, who were "there for the whole show", report that "Chaz was not around to witness very much of anyone's activities" during the Processed World affair -- he was hardly even there!). And once again, one notes, Bob Black is hauled out in order to attempt to discredit all and sundry. But this "anti-sectarianism" also plays another important role: when the WSA gets chummy with rackets like the New Union Party, or the Socialist Party USA (two of four other groups they were organizing a conference with in their last issue), you're not supposed to complain about it, because that's sectarian.

Wetzel's statement that he dislikes Bufe's "polemics" is revealing from another viewpoint as well. My objection to Bufe's piece is not that it's a polemic -- which this essay obviously is -- but its lack of seriousness. Parts of the present essay could also be termed "rants", a term that also has a positive connotation from my perspective, one far removed from Bufe's sneering, withered, passionless pronunciamentos.

But Wetzel's objection, in effect, is that Listen, Anarchist! was not "endorsed" by the WSA, even though they distribute it through their very selective book service -- no ultra-left, situationist, anti-work, critique of technology/civilization, Native stuff, of course, nor much of anything that could really help people understand modern domination -- for the convoluted reasons given by Wetzel. Here Wetzel demonstrates a central feature of these organizations: the impoverished relations brought about as the mediation of the organization stunts desire and twists it according to its own alienated logic. What

Chaz says, therefore, really doesn't matter, which is why he can go on for page after page, while Wetzel -- with all the sincerity of any bureaucrat faithfully carrying out the anonymous dictates of his or her chosen organization -- cancels it out with a four-word disclaimer; only the organization's four-paragraph dictum really means anything. By negating the individual, the organization negates the possibility of true, unalienated community. Often these organizations only seem to erect mini-bureaucracies that don't even function: that simply thrash around in a self-inflicted tangle. For a more complete discussion of this question, Jacques Camatte's inexpensive On Organization (available from the Fifth Estate bookstore) (15) is highly recommended.

Chaz, one might say, individualizes this bureaucratic tangle, and is himself a mind-boggling "nest" of contradictions, which merit a partial separate listing. Here's a guy who complains about "malicious name-calling" and does it constantly, who smears revolutionary violence as "leftist" and "Marxist", despite the long history of militant anti-authoritarian resistance to the state and capital (although when, where and how much violence is appropriate of course remain fundamental questions), who denounces "personal attacks" and turns around and launches vicious attacks, but simply doesn't name the people he's attacking (that's what I call an impersonal attack!), re-writing events that actually happened to his own advantage (for example he launches an incredible attack on Sally Fry -- without naming her -- to explain why she was purged from No Middle Ground, hauling out the now-infamous "lone-nut" theory as an explanation, when in fact two

other people were also excluded from the project), who complains about "emotional manipulation" but does it constantly, who reviles "anarcho-sectarianism", when this phenomenon is nothing is not the essence of sects like the WSA and that "destructive sectarians pursuing personal vendettas" (Bufe's phrase) is, in effect, a precise definition of his ongoing preoccupation with the Fifth Estate (his "main whipping-boy", let there be no doubt), who lectures that "we should not cower behind pseudonyms" (and mentions George Bradford of Fifth Estate specifically in this context) and then pseudonomously corresponds with Fifth Estate, who inveighs against "ultra-correct political howling" and does it constantly, who complains about those who "call anarchists with whom they have disagreements 'Leninists' or 'Stalinists'," while on another page of the same issue of a journal he helps edit and produce, someone from the Bay Area compares the Fifth Estate to the Khmer Rouge and Sendero Luminoso, who "complains about the misuse of terms but does it frequently" (Feral Ranter), who castigates religion but reduces anarchy to the narrowest of orthodoxies, summarily issuing banishment proclamations against anyone who doesn't tread the true path of anarcho-salvation as defined by Bufe. All this while solemnly intoning that we must "attack irrationality ... wherever and whenever (it) arises", and that "If anarchism is ever to be a real force in society, it must be based on ethical behaviour" (excerpted and placed on the front cover of Listen, Anarchist!)!

☞

23

"One Shudders To Think Of The Impression They Leave With Anyone Who Comes In Casual Contact With Them"

Bufe -- Listen, Anarchist!

We primitivists must be purged (and by now it should be evident that we're not the only ones) in order to clear the way for an antiseptic image of anarchism which can be suitably packaged and presented to the working class. So what kind of a response to the present text can we expect from Bufe?

Well, it's instructive to look at the afterword of Listen, Anarchist!, where he responds to the critics of that masterpiece. Historians may still be searching for "the real Nixon", but this I think is where we get Essence of Bufe, the pure, distilled, high-octane variety. Here he goes on for two and half pages without naming any of his critics, much less giving their addresses so people can check out what they have to say for themselves (even his most ardent fans -- and he probably has a few -- must have been left scratching their heads wondering who the hell he's talking about). But considering that some of his critics know him and have worked on projects with him, and not only demolish most of his arguments but expose his lies and falsifications about local activities for what they are, this omission becomes all the more understandable.

Having provided himself with a clean slate, Bufe finds himself perfectly positioned to create the opponents he desires, and proceeds to roll them all up into one single hideous caricature (he had been criticizing a wide variety of heresies in his scatter-gun tract, and the responses were from a number of viewpoints).

"What is interesting about these denunciations is that none contradict any statements of fact I made," he informs us, as if people doing long denunciations could manage not to "contradict any statements" in what they're denouncing! This completely ludicrous assertion is also a complete falsification, because most of the denunciations refute his theses section by section. He then says that "all" of his opponents' critiques "consist of personal attacks primarily", which is proved false by someone who gave his tract a rave review, M. Valezcaviedes, who says in Guángara Libertaria that " ... it seemed to me that (Spider Rainbow -- the only person's response he read apparently) did a good critique from an ideological point of view" (me pareció que hizo una buena crítica desde el punto de vista ideológico) and two sentences later says that "No critique is of value if it becomes sectarian or personal" (ninguna crítica tiene valor cuando se hace sectario o personal)(16). It's true that Spider's critique is more straightforward, and that others are insulting at times. But what kind of response did Bufe expect to his contempt-filled tract? ... That people would turn the other cheek? All of these critiques, though, it should be mentioned, are substantive responses to his tract, and I'll gladly send copies to anyone who requests them (care of this journal). Although Bufe informs us that there are "a few outright lies" in these responses, he doesn't manage to name any, which doesn't make this claim any the more convincing.

The political patient (the caricature he's created) is then admitted to Dr. Bufe's consultation room, where a rapid diagnosis in the second paragraph detects "an extremely odd conception of Anarchism". By the seventh paragraph, this malady has taken on the proportions of a full-blown "screwball conception of Anarchism" and by the last paragraph, lo and behold, has evolved into an ultra-virulent "sick parody of Anarchism". Nothing left to do with these sickos, one gets the impression, than cart them off to the asylum ...

Most of Bufe's afterword consists of an attempt to contrast different interpretations of "the personal is political", with his being the "ethical" one, whereas the other folks are the sickos. He must have found his arguments pretty lame, apparently, because Bob Black (again!) is pulled out of a hat in order to attempt to discredit all and sundry, although by this time (April '87), Black was long gone from the Bay Area, had broken off contact with almost everyone, and was just beginning to tangle with the Subgenius/Small Publication Association milieu. No matter, though: gone, but not forgotten (I'm not attempting to imply, by the way, that Black is "sick", although I was threatened by him myself at the height of "the troubles"). Bufe's impoverished psychiatro-jargon doesn't help us to understand the Black phenomenon vis-a-vis anti-authoritarianism,

about which almost nothing worthwhile has been written to date).

According to Bufe, the responses to is tract are "entirely in line with their (authors') history of engaging in or condoning such practices as making anonymous death threats, vandalizing the offices of political opponents, using the state legal apparatus against political opponents, and violently physically assaulting political opponents" (all things Black did or is alleged to have done). But in fact, none of the people who responded to his tract "engaged in or condoned" any of these activities (with the exception of Black, who apparently wrote a response to Listen, Anarchist!, which I haven't been able to locate). In effect they specifically criticize Black's excesses and most of the very activities that Bufe mentions. Lawrence and Brian denounce "calling the police and using the courts" (although they're referring to both Black and Processed World -- Chaz doesn't seem to mind when the latter does it), and state that they "disagree" with activities such as "the alleged death-threat telephone call"; and Feral Ranter mentions that "Black can be violent and abusive". So ultimately his critics specifically mention three of the four things he accuses them of "engaging in or condoning". What an incredible liar and falsifier! No wonder he doesn't mention their names. I can only conclude that since this is a reprint, and presumably all the principals already have a copy, Bufe feels he can say absolutely anything because now that "the rush" is over, copies are only occasionally going out to Scotland or Australia or whatever, where people don't have a clue about what's going on (with the afterword, of course, simply confirming the text in spades).

Bufe's activities are one more proof, if more are needed, that just because someone calls him or herself an anarchist or anti-authoritarian it doesn't necessarily imply they're a comrade.

The IWW

(Note: Louis Prisco's letter referred to below was eventually printed in Industrial Worker).

If the WSA's reaction to ecology has been primarily one of indifference and hostility, at first glance the IWW's approach would seem quite the opposite. For example some IWW members have long been active in environmental and Native rights campaigns, and a local Wobbly informs me that 40% of the membership opted to reject the purchase of a computer in a recent vote. The IWW has come out strongly in support of Earth First! and 10,000 copies of the May 1988 Radical Environmentalism issue of their paper Industrial Worker had to be printed, compared to it's usual run of 3,000 six months earlier. To shed more light on their present approach, a long article on Earth First! in the September 1988 issue of Industrial Worker is worth quoting in some detail:

"Once the May issue hit the stands our wildest hopes regarding its impact were quickly exceeded. It became clear at once that young rebel workers are far more interested in radical environmentalism than even we had realized. Moreover, from all over the continent reports have been coming in showing that Wobblies and Earth First!'ers are eager not only to learn from one another but also to take action together to effect our common goals. And last but not least, more new memberships, new subscriptions, new bulk orders, renewals of lapsed subscriptions and contributions to the Industrial Worker sustaining fund have come into IWW headquarters since May than in any comparable period in anyone's memory.

"Yes, fellow workers, the IWW is grow-

ANARCHO-SYNDICALISM ATTEMPTS TO CHANGE ITS IMAGE

Circle the correct definition of **anarcho-syndicalism:**

1) A simplistic, economistic approach to complex social, economic and political issues.

2) A sexist, workerist 19th-century ideology with a fetish for blue overalls.

3) An animal species that became extinct in Spain in the 1930s.

4) A cult founded by Edward G. Robinson, George Raft, Humphrey Bogart and James Cagney in the 1940s.

5) None of the above.

If you chose 5 as the correct answer, then maybe you should check out the Workers Solidarity Alliance.

Popular misconception of an anarchosyndicalist.

Anarchosyndicalists in real life.

Alienation must be peddled with modernized and humanized images, as in this real-life ad from Ideas and Action #9 (reproduced here sans the predictable recruitment come-on). Accusations of workerism are denied (see #2) while it is at the same time cutsied up and marketed!
Images come and go, but the T-shirt remains the same . . .

24

Demolition Derby I (1989)

ing today as it has not grown in years, and there is no getting around the fact that one of the reasons it is growing is because of our fortuitous encounter now increasingly taking on the character of an active, ongoing combat alliance with the international Earth First! movement.

"One of our own tasks in the immediate future must be to spread the word of radical environmentalism throughout the broader labor movement and among working men and women everywhere" (17).

Quite a contrast to Bufe! Some initial remarks should be made, however, before further exploring the question of the IWW's approach to ecology. First, it seems that we immediately run into a bureaucratic tangle. Louis Prisco, a long-time San Francisco IWW activist, charges that the "pro-Earth First! slant" of the May paper was not "debated among the members at the Convention or in the pages of the GOB (General Organization Bulletin, the IWW's internal discussion organ)," and suggests that its adoption was "a unilateral and therefore undemocratic decision by the Industrial Worker staff." Along the same lines, the editors of Libertarian Labor Review state that although a "storm of protest" occurred after the May issue, "the editors refused to print letters from IWW members opposed to Earth First!" and that "in September, a few paragraphs of a highly-edited criticism were finally published, followed by a lengthy, two-and-a-half page response by a former member of the editorial collective." So it seems that although the Industrial Worker editors definitely articulate what appears to be an official position in the September issue, it's difficult to ascertain how representative it is of the membership (and of course the IWW's position towards Earth First! is not synonymous with a position towards ecology as such). An additional perspective on this question comes from a correspondent who has been active with the Washington Earth First! group, who writes that "mostly the wobs' attempted alliances with Earth First! have been instigated by a few wobs." This sound pretty far removed from a generalized embrace of Earth First! (Prisco, by the way, says that Fifth Estate and Earth First! "have helped the real culprit—Big Business—to divert attention from itself", serving up a helping of "objectively helping the bourgeoisie"-type rhetoric because, according to him, Earth First! and Fifth Estate have "insisted that the principal enemy is technology alone". Earth First!, of course, has never been specifically anti-capitalist, although in my opinion they have surely done more to shine a spotlight on the ravages of big business than to divert attention from them; as for the Fifth Estate, which has constantly emphasized the interaction between capital and technology and the multi-faceted impoverishment caused by the former, this is pure falsification).

Considering the purposes of this text, it should be reiterated that the IWW is not specifically anarcho-syndicalist; it has always contained Marxist and other radical tendencies as well. It should also be mentioned that it is not really a union in important respects. Since few shops have actually been organized, the essence of syndicalism -- bargaining over contracts -- is largely absent. In this sense, anything, however radical, can be said in the pages of Industrial Worker, but if the organization were mediating between capital and labour on a regular basis, hard choices would quickly have to be made...

As well, almost all of what has been said in previous sections of this essay about workerism, organizational patriotism and the "self-management" of industrialism goes for the IWW as well. The organization is nothing if not rooted in the past in the worst sense -- i.e. of dragging along most of the deadweight of what is useless in classical Marxism and anarchism. And the following quote from some former IWW members gives an impression of considerable confusion and incoherence as well: "However, the organization was even more thoroughly reformist than we thought, racked with crass factional manoeuvering, and lacking even rudimentary discussion. The only action consisted of either tailing leftist causes with a somewhat more radical line or organizing workers into capitalism further." (18) Yech!

Also disturbing is the continuing vitality of the "one big union" myth. Although I'm told that this archaism is not really taken

CIVILIZATION IS COLLAPSING ...

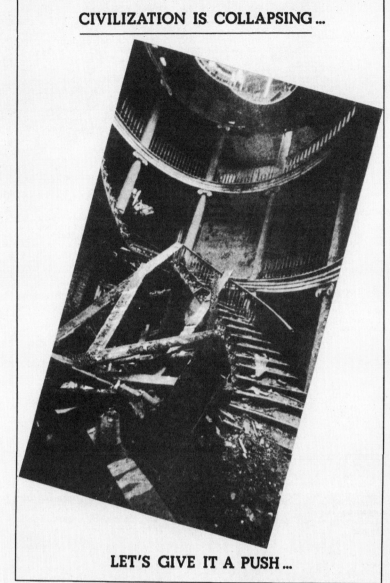

LET'S GIVE IT A PUSH ...

seriously, you still keep bumping into it everywhere in their literature. It has been chosen to name the newsletter of the recently founded Toronto IWW branch for example, and two of the pro-ecology responses in the September issue of Industrial Worker also mention it, one ending "Here's to one great union on a green and growing planet!" (19), and in the other an anarcho-syndicalist states that "The IWW is our only hope -- there is nothing else to look to for answers and action" (20) -- almost sounds like an evangelical revival!

The proposition that any organization, whatever its ideology, is going to grab the means of production on a global scale smacks

bined with the techno-bureaucracy necessary to run modern industrialism, would have a lethal effect on any possibility of people taking control of their lives in a truly decentralized manner.

Along with the one big union spiel goes the self-appointed role of organizer-of-the-working-class, an outlook which simply repeats the organizer/organized duality that is inherent in the modern spectacle (if you're not busy organizing, you're busy being organized). The IWW, ultimately, does not want people to self-organize: it wants to organize people into its organization and to mediate their relations.

This being said, there are obviously

Some Anarchists differ from Marxists only in being less informed. They would supplant the State with a network of computer centres, factories and mines coordinated "by the workers themselves" or by an Anarchist union. They would call this arrangement a State. The name-change would exorcise the beast.

-- Fredy Perlman

more of proposing a state than anything else, and one with distinct totalitarian inclinations at that (what happens if you don't want to join the "union": you starve?). As well, the impoverished communication implied by the computer networks necessary for such an arrangement (in effect the only way it could function on a worldwide basis), com-

people in the IWW who are sincerely concerned about the destruction of the earth and who are doing something about it. Unfortunately, the organization's reaction to Earth First!, as portrayed in Industrial Worker, if positive in the sense of being open to radical environmentalism, has also turned out to be another bureaucratic horror story. Replying

Orwellian World

In the Orwellian world of the IWW, words often mean the opposite, or are emptied of real meaning entirely. Thus workers' control really signifies that people will be controlled by modernized and streamlined industrialisms which will ultimately be physically little different from what capital and the state will soon be obliged to promote themselves <u>if they want to survive</u> (and are beginning to promote even now -- for example, recent capitalist/media hysteria about Brazilian rainforests, legislation to protect the ozone layer -- the so-called Montréal protocol -- or seemingly drastic three-step anti-smog legislation which has recently been introduced in Los Angeles).

Although <u>Industrial Worker</u> reads little differently from any other radical/leftist labour journal, to anti-authoritarians the anarcho-syndicalists in this catch-all outfit must of course present the most appealing image of the organization. In an article in the Spring '89 issue of <u>Kick It Over</u>, a green-anarchist-feminist journal from Toronto (24) for example, Ted Dyment, one of the founders of the Toronto IWW branch, says that "Initially, I was not too comfortable with the very term 'industrial', since it evoked in me images not in keeping with my pastoral vision of utopia ..." No problem, though. Dyment it seems has quickly adapted by simply convincing himself that his "pastoral vision" is identical to the IWW's refurbished industrialism: "I found that the IWW has a clearly stated desire to de-industrialize our world, through the seizure of all 'means of production' and the subsequent conversion to products and methods which <u>promote</u> human community according to the <u>will</u> of the community" (underlining in original). Whether this jumble of concepts signifies anything at all, or is simply total confusion is itself unclear. What "de-industrialization" means is nowhere explained, and in effect could not be other than specifically vague because the IWW's lowest common denominatorism precludes a radical movement towards clarification, which would threaten the don't-rock-the-boat consensus (the glue that keeps the organization together). It is simply floated as a politically correct buzzword. In fact I'd be very surprised if Dyment could come up with any kind of "clearly stated desire to de-industrialize this world" from the IWW -- i.e. something that would really threaten industrialism, or much of anything beyond a certain amount of grumbling about cars and perhaps television and a desire (but not an ability, with what they want to keep) to do away with industrialism's pollution and toxic wastes. Although there undoubtedly are people in the IWW who do desire radical de-industrialization, the organization's lowest common denominator approach will make an unequivocal anti-industrial stance highly unlikely.

What is more tangible in Dyment's statement is precisely what has always remained at the heart of the IWW project: "the seizure of all 'means of production'," in other words their factory fetishism. The "subsequent conversion" Dyment refers to will be less a question of adding anti-pollution devices and doing away with a few of the most noxious excesses of industrial capitalism than one of converting people from being the objects of the bosses' industrialism to being the "subjects" of "their industrialism" ... but either way, they only end up as objects of industrialism ...

In the "Typical Programs Discussed in the Toronto IWW" part of Dyment's article, the section "Ecology Actions" clearly reveals the poverty of this organization's approach: "The rather large roof area at the union hall could be converted to roof-top gardens that could involve the locals, particularly Chinese families who frequently dig up their front lawns for vegetable planting; sodding over ugly vacant lots and turning them into People's Parks; targeting a particular area for litter clean-up; wall murals and canvases to brighten up the brick and concrete." Far from feeling menaced by any of this, the capitalists I'm sure will be more than happy to watch the syndicalist boy scouts applying band-aid solutions to civilization's excesses ... all with unpaid labour on their own time. "That vacant lot eyesore is looking nice thanks to the syndicalist militants," I can just hear one yuppie saying to the next as they cut across Kensington Market toward a sushi bar. If we can't have a "caring capitalism", at least we can "brighten up the brick and concrete".

And IWW daydreaming, one can't help but notice, just happens to "involve the locals" in their union hall.

But an article in a recent issue of <u>Industrial Worker</u> entitled "Northwest Wobs Call for Support to Keep Louisiana-Pacific Mill Open"(25) reveals a realistic version of what can be expected from these alternative resource managers, who may turn out to be a revamped and "revolutionized" forest industry's best friend after all. "I'm asking environmentalists to fight to keep LP's Potter Valley mill open," blares IWW and <u>Earth First!</u> member Darryl Cherney, lamenting with respect to the companies in question that "they expect us to trust them with long-range forest management". But of course it's the One Big Union, Cherney doesn't have to remind us, to which this "forest management" should be entrusted. For now, though, some employees "are currently attempting to buy back the company", in other words to install a somewhat less hierarchical, self-managed capitalism, a process meriting hearty applause for the IWW eco-defenders.

But it is techno-capital, through wage slavery, which has gathered people around mines and "natural resources" and in industrial belts. Having internalized this constellation, the IWW can only conceive of people as resources, as "labour power" on a market, as cogs in a process of production, making it incapable of directly attacking capital and industry.

Is it "anti-labour" or "anti-worker", as the IWW would seem to give the impression, to wish to assault the incarnation of modern slavery and domestication itself -- the factory system? The IWW's work fetishism (and there's a big difference, one which it is in the IWW's interest to fudge, between being "anti-worker" and being anti-work!) and its unimaginative and defensive approach define the parameters of a project which in practice only amounts to preferring smaller companies to larger ones.

to a letter bringing up some of the outrageous comments made by some <u>Earth First!</u> members, the seven editors of <u>Industrial Worker</u> baldly state that "none" of these "crazy rumours" are true (!!), and refer the reader to a long defence of <u>Earth First!</u> written by Franklin Rosemont in the same issue (quoted at length at the beginning of this section). This article is an example of organizational patriotism in its most insidious form, as the truth is gutted (in a manner not at all dissimilar to the "solidarity" that is synonymous with hoisting "national liberation" rackets into power in the third world). Rosemont attempts to explain away a laundry list of outrageous statements by <u>Earth First!</u> leaders, doing a mind-boggling song and dance in the process.

He properly points out that statements made by some <u>Earth First!</u> members or leaders should not be taken as the official position of the organization (although their control of the organization's main paper certainly gives weight to this impression), as many of its critics have done often in order to simply write off radical environmentalism but obscures the fact, as Mikal Jakubal, who has been active in <u>Earth First!</u> notes, that "there are other <u>Earth First!</u>'ers—many in fact—who hold similar views as Forman, Abbey and the rest"(21). Instead of portraying <u>Earth First!</u> as it is and coming to obvious conclusions, Rosemont assails those who refuse to grace the unacceptable with the desired "solidarity," writing them off as "some obscure organs of the sectarian 'left'" (sounds like a pretty sectarian reaction itself). On another note, Rosemont says that <u>Earth First!</u> is "largely made up of working class folks", as if that were equivalent to advocating the abolition of the wage system.

This kind of plastic surgery, apart from distorting or trampling on the facts, suggests other bureaucratic implications as well. In this respect, Rosemont's use of the phrase "fortuitous encounter" (with regard to <u>Earth First!</u>) is revealing. Despite the previously mentioned support given to environmental and Native struggles by some Wobblies, the IWW has not exactly been a hive of ecological activity in the past. On the contrary, as its name implies, it has been a pillar of <u>industrialism</u>. To seriously question the IWW's "born again" radical environmentalism (especially considering the opposition it has engendered within the organization and how it's been handled) is only reasonable and necessary.

The magnitude of the eco-crisis, it should be mentioned, has shaken up the entire radical spectrum: organizations are scrambling to put forth positions and to hop on a perceived bandwagon (<u>Processed World's</u> "wannabe Green" (sic) (see <u>Processed World</u> #22) racket is classic in this sense). Rosemont's article makes it clear that <u>something</u> is happening in the IWW (although his distortions make it unreliable as to precisely what). Unfortunately, it is not people or the environment, but the <u>organization</u>, with its own needs and logic, which inevitably seems to come first. A prevailing "build the mass party" (oops, union) and professional organizer mentality (and you don't have to be a paid bureaucrat to be a professional organizer) quickly tend to reduce reality to, as Rosemont says, "new memberships, new subscriptions, new bulk orders and renewals of subs and contributions" (the trump card used to sell radical environmentalism to skeptical Wobblies). Since the IWW has been floundering for years, decades actually, one gets the strong impression that it would be willing to jump on almost any bandwagon that would spruce up its appeal. In this sense, radical environmentalism is seen primarily as a pool of potential recruits -- although according to Louis Prisco, the IWW's "new found alliance

goals unless they have already been educated at least a little. The Polarization Effect causes people to *turn away* from an "extreme" point of view, although they *turn towards* ideas closer to their own point of view. If we can start out just slightly to their left (or right, as the case may be) and keep moving closer and closer to the IWW's central beliefs, we're in business. We can also use cognitive dissonance to

DAVID ZATZ, MEMBER OF 1989 IWW GENERAL EXECUTIVE BOARD. FROM THE GENERAL ORGANISATION BULLETIN - NOV./DEC.89 ISSUE.

> **A slice of IWW manipulation**

Demolition Derby I (1989)

The above graphic appeared in the most recent issue of <u>Reality Now</u> and <u>Kick It Over</u> (caption suggested by Rip van Winkle)

is obviously a much bigger deal for us than it is for <u>Earth First!</u>. Once the shine is off, will the IWW drop radical environmentalism in favour of whatever other "greener pastures" turn up?

Reality Now

Those who haven't seen the most recent issue of <u>Reality Now</u> (<u>RN</u>) will be surprised to find their project included in this essay. In effect, three <u>RN</u> collective members, whose time and efforts account for a large portion of what goes into the project have joined the <u>IWW</u>, which formed a Toronto branch in January 1988. This has understandably led to changes in their journal. The following quote from a collectively-signed article entitled "The Environment is a Class Issue" gives an idea of their present approach: "But there has been a noticeable change in the character of anarcho-syndicalism in recent years ... (...) Anarcho-syndicalism needs these changes. It has had in the past a tendency towards needless bureaucracy and has been too focused on one area of struggle (the workplace) despite sharing the belief that struggles have to be expanded to the communities. (...) It may indeed have to change its entire nature of organization to be effective in the future. And it needs to adapt to an ecological consciousness which goes beyond merely believing in less pollution. Technology itself has to be challenged. We welcome anarcho-syndicalists who have been willing to challenge these things and ecology-minded anarchists who recognize that the urban struggles of workers, the poor and urban communities is where our strength to initiate change lies."(22)

It would be inaccurate not to recognize a qualitative difference between this statement and those of the Bufes, Bekkens, Wetzels and Dolgoffs. But what is new here would appear to be primarily what is being brought in from the outside; to the extent that the project has taken on the negative features of traditional anarcho-syndicalism, its ability to confront modern domination has clearly diminished.

Since <u>Reality Now</u> accuses the English journal <u>Green Anarchist</u> of being "profoundly ignorant on working people and union organizations", it is worth clarifying my own position. Unlike <u>Green Anarchist</u>, I supported the Wapping strike which took place in

London, England and which is the specific controversy referred to in the quote above, and spent time on the picket line when I visited London. However, my support was neither for union organizations nor for "workers", but for <u>people</u> who were attempting to defend themselves against one aspect of capital's assault (a <u>RN</u> collective member's phrase "supporting the spirit of the people fighting back" captures my approach well). The Wapping situation was precisely <u>defensive</u> and reformist, although positive aspects were strongly in evidence, primarily all-pervasive feelings of anger and revolt. But it is when this anger and revolt is directed against <u>industrial</u> capitalism itself, which was clearly not the case at Wapping, that it takes on a truly radical character (and one that will not be easily recuperated).

"Profound ignorance", or more precisely an inability to learn from the past, is a phrase that in my opinion could be appropriately directed at the <u>Workers' Solidarity Alliance</u>, when their organization speaks in glowing terms of the so-called "Workers' Charter" for example, a document which has been endorsed by a number of South African trade unions. Here is an excerpt from the "Workers' Charter", taken from an unsigned article in the most recent <u>Ideas and Action</u> (signed articles are not necessarily endorsed by <u>WSA</u> or the editorial group, so the one in question must be, according to their editorial policy): "Only the working masses, <u>under the leadership of organized industrial workers,</u> can truly liberate our country from the chains of capitalist exploitation; (...) Only under the leadership of organized workers over the mass democratic struggle of today and the <u>government of tomorrow</u>, will the demands of the Freedom Charter be fully and completely exercised in the lives of the working masses of our country" (my emphasis)(23). Unflinchingly endorsing statist, industrial fetishist, vanguardist, leftist garbage like this is the logical outcome of a certain reformism that is always looking for the "really radical" union to support -- usually an outfit that is under the thumb of a Communist party or some other embryonic state or "national liberation" racket.

Concerning the question of relations between anarcho-syndicalists and eco-anarchists, I can only speak for myself, and the anti-authoritarian primitivist tendency of which I'm a part is only one of several

within the broader eco-anti-authoritarian milieu. Before going further though I would like to call attention to the word used to describe "the change in the character of anarcho-syndicalism in recent years": "noticeable". The choice of the very weak adjective is in my opinion important and precise. If <u>Ideas and Action</u> and <u>Libertarian Labor Review</u>, the two specifically anarcho-syndicalist journals in North America, have finally begun to talk about ecology, after having almost completely ignored it for years, they have yet to "go beyond merely believing in less pollution", as <u>Reality Now</u> accurately puts it, nor has "technology itself been challenged".

As well, whatever other sectors of the anti-authoritarian milieu may think of us, the most virulent, and indeed near hysterical attacks on primitivists have come from the anarcho-syndicalists. Apart from Chaz Bufe's diatribe in the most recent <u>Ideas and Action</u>, the most recent <u>Libertarian Labor Review</u> has Jon Bekken shaking his magic wand again, trying to make us disappear, claiming that we've "repeatedly denounced" his "movement and ideals". But Bekken it seems will never understand that we're not on the outside; that because we also wish to abolish the state and capital, we're an integral part of the movement (more a milieu in my estimation) <u>whether he likes it or not</u> and that it was precisely his grumpy letter to <u>Fifth Estate</u> (and his hopelessly inadequate nineteenth-century anarchism) that was roundly responded to in their pages. This, then, is what "real existing" anarcho-syndicalism has had to say about us lately, and as you can easily imagine, as a rule we're not exactly in love with them either. As for the <u>IWW</u>, there is Louis Prisco's open letter about <u>Reality Now</u> in which he completely falsely claims that the <u>Fifth Estate</u> has "insisted that the principal enemy is technology alone" and thus has "helped the real culprit-Big Business-to divert attention from itself".

Much of the anarcho-syndicalists' hostility towards us derives from our attacks on work, productivism, and industrialism as such. In this respect, <u>Reality Now</u>'s reference to a "fundamental de-industrialization" further on in the "Environment is a Class Issue" article represents something of a milestone in anarcho-syndicalist literature -- the first such statement I'm aware of (see a critique of Ted Dyment's more recent use of this term in the Spring '89 <u>Kick It Over</u> in the "Orwellian World" section of this article). However, this approach seems to be contradicted in the following sentence of their editorial statement: "The setting up and running of collective 'industries' is generally a good short term solution in that it enables people to have direct control over that aspect of their lives, and provides the framework for an alternative society to replace the existing social structure". Why the word industries is put in quotation marks is unclear. But as with Bufe's elusive "technology", doing so does not remove its negative connotations in the least! Its use in effect underlines the problems inherent in <u>Reality Now</u>'s attempt to synthesize eco-anarchism and anarcho-syndicalism (their eco-anarchism disliking the term, one gets the impression, but their anarcho-syndicalism feeling obliged to employ it).

Without falling into the trap of decreeing which tools will be kept after the revolution in a void, by the same token we can only move toward de-industrialization by refusing technology's all-pervasive grip on our lives (although in this city this refusal is often primarily psychological/emotional/spiritual at this point). No one, certainly, wants to work for a boss. But from this perspective, self-managing industries is hardly a solution to wage slavery (see the section "Work, Syndicalism and the Self-Management of Alienation"), nor could these industries provide a "framework for an alternative society". There are surely collective projects which can be carried out which are not industries! But even self-managed projects such as anti-authoritarian bookshops and cafes I've worked in did not give those involved "direct control over that aspect of (our) lives". On the contrary, businesses within capitalism, self-managed or otherwise, seem to primarily foster a small business-persons' mentality... or you go out of business. Below the quote in question, <u>Reality Now</u> acknowledges that these projects can be problematic, but is vague about what these problems are, and in effect getting specific about them can certainly lead to a feeling of pessimism...

Also, there is no reason to assume that "In the long term, when speaking of worker control of industry, not only would a funda-

27

breaking the chains of work

mental de-industrialization occur due to decentralization, but the whole nature of industry would necessarily change due to control of projects and the destruction of multinational corporations". This is simply wishful thinking and contradicts the expansionist logic which is the essence of industrialism. On the contrary, by now industrialism is running on automatic; if de-industrialization is to occur, it will not be in a mechanistic, deterministic manner, but because people want it to happen (and act accordingly).

It is also important to point out that anarcho-syndicalists such as Sam Dolgoff are claiming even now that unions should be "fighting the de-industrialization of American industry" (!), when what is occurring is precisely a decentralization in the sense that now people are choking on industrialism and are being turned into factory slaves everywhere in the world (as opposed to primarily in Europe and North America). Only the delirium of a Dolgoff and cohorts could perceive a real de-industrialization taking place in the US, as if cars, TV's and the usual assorted techno-junk were somehow less in evidence. On the other hand, his comment is instructive about what can be expected from "real existing" anarcho-syndicalism.

I would also like to briefly touch on several other questions. In its editorial, Reality Now states that the IWW "is only

Another change worth noting is an invasion of "smoke-stack graphics", creating an almost eerie contrast with the frequent graphics showing views of pristine wilderness, such as the one on the front cover. And gone is most of the hesitation of a few years back. Although this is only natural, its replacement -- the special self-assurance of the organizers of the working class -- seems to have left little room for spontaneity and humour. The impression given is one of having taken on the burden of the entire world.

Up to now I have emphasized what appears questionable or contradictory in RN's approach. On a positive note, I would also mention that in a collective member's response to a letter from Fifth Estate, a distancing from the FMLN has taken place, cutting short the journal's free fall into political irrelevance (although in effect there is still a lack of clarity concerning the presentation of groups such as the Ohio 7, or the journal the Insurgent); and in spite of the impression that may have been given above, Reality Now's content remains essentially the same as before: Anarchist Black Cross and prison news, Native news and "tactical/practical" information. Apart from the two IWW articles (one an introduction to the IWW and the other on the IWW and prisons), there has been no invasion of "workerist" material or cheerleading for local union federations. On the other hand, there have been clear changes in its editorial

Along with the one big union spiel goes the self-appointed role of organizer-of-the-working-class, an outlook which simply repeats the organizer/organized duality that is inherent in the modern spectacle (if you're not busy organizing, you're busy being organized). The IWW, ultimately, does not want people to self-organize; it wants to organize people into its organization and to mediate their relations.

one of many ways we can organize ... " But without wishing to be overly repetitive, it's worth noting again that this is not what the IWW is saying. For example an article concerning the IWW Prisoners Organization Project reprinted from Industrial Worker states that "Our aim is to organize and unite all prisoners into one Big Union". My point is not to argue the merits or demerits or prisoners joining the IWW. But the primary reason given, "Active participation in a democratic union will also help us to become productive members of the working class" rings no different from what we are taught in school or learn in the media and from big business. What does this have to do with our real goals in life?! Ironically, an article on the same page entitled "Fuck School" talks about a "public burning of report cards" and entertains thoughts of "destroying the school system". The overall editorial feeling from the journal, though, is that this something kids do (or contemplate) ... until they grow up and become "productive" factory slaves.

A change toward a more anarcho-syndicalist approach is also evident in a recurring massification effect, whereby collectives become "unions" or "industries", and groups and individuals become "organizations", as in the following quote from their editorial statement: "The organizations we create may need to network successfully with other local organizations to work together towards common goals. These networks can hook up with organizations in other areas." This leaves out many of us who have no desire to form organizations and prefer an affinity group approach (and in effect just below this quote, the "organizations" in question are referred to as "such groups", in effect a more accurate representation of the present milieu).

outlook, so we'll have to see which way the journal evolves. My objection, by the way, is not to covering workplace struggles which have a radical edge, such as wildcats, which Fifth Estate and other anti-tech journals unfortunately ignore. The problem is how they are covered and the innumerable illusions which surround them.

* * *

If Reality Now openly calls itself "anti-technology" in an article entitled "Corporate Sabotage in the Computer Age", outside North America little has changed in the anarcho-syndicalist landscape, and continental projects such as Libertarian Review and the WSA are littered with clunkers as well. Anarcho-syndicalism is floundering, unable to analyze and confront modern domination, and if a book advancing its theory has been written since the Spanish Revolution, I'm unaware of it.

The leopard may yet change its spots, but I'm not holding my breath.

-- Michael William

AFTERWORD

The Summer '89 issue of Ideas and Action arrived just as this article was being typeset. The only response to Bufe's article which was printed, a brief, diplomatic letter from an "Earth First! organizer", focused mainly on reproaching Bufe for not taking into account the diversity of the Earth First! milieu.

As well, an article on CFC's and the destruction of the ozone layer by Al Chatfield was printed. Predictably, nothing in this seemingly obligatory piece goes beyond the parameters of what has been analyzed above (now that capital and governments are quickly facing the necessity of eliminating ozone-eating CFC's, the WSA can safely pipe up for their abolition!). Technology remains unanalyzed as usual, industrialism is let off the hook and "ultimately, the problem is the way that capitalism functions", we are reassured, and "as the crisis of the ozone layer demonstrates, the flaws of capitalism are a threat to all life." In Tom Wetzel's long obituary in the same issue concerning the death of Rik Winslow, a WSA militant who was killed in a recent car accident, there is of course no inkling that industrialism might have had something to do with his death either, and after the revolution, once the anarcho-syndicalists have removed the "flaws of capitalism", presumably fatal car crashes will disappear.

In a section of Chatfield's article entitled "direct action", direct action is in effect discouraged, since according to the author, "a more effective form of pressure than protests by irate individuals or small activist groups would be collective action by the workforces of companies that use or make CFC's." Chatfield's lack of examples of situations in which this "more effective form of pressure" has occurred, however, doesn't make his assertion very convincing.

For the anarcho-syndicalists, the community remains subordinate to those who control the factories or are forced to work in them, and remains at the mercy of what comes spewing out of them.

poster: Carel Moisewitsch

ART

Writing on the history of *Open Road*, Bob Sarti recalls that when the journal was first launched the editors were determined to make it different from standard text-heavy leftist publications. To that end each issue featured graphics, collages, drawings, and photographs, including centre-spread illustrations by artists dealing with issues such as feminism, prison liberation, the history of anarchism, and direct action. When I first encountered *Open Road* this was what struck me: it *looked* exciting. However art's contribution to anarchism in Canada has gone far beyond the printed page.

Anarchist artists are constantly striving to communicate their values in diverse media and spheres as varied as streets, protests, and art galleries. Artists such as Rocky Dobey have created stunningly beautiful posters. Poets and novelists like Norman Nawrocki and Jean Smith have given anarchism a lyric voice. Bands such as Black Kronstadt and Propagandi have toured across North America. And painters, video-makers, theatre groups, puppeteers, sculptors, photographers, architects, and graphic artists have all left their mark on the movement. Taking anarchist politics into the realm of culture, they have made creative work synonymous with activism, and anarchism has been the better for it.

This section does not encapsulate the entirety of anarchist artistic production. I would liken it to a snapshot that has been gleaned, for the most part, from the journals. What it does communicate is how art seeps into everything. Open any publication and chances are you'll find poems, drawings, and photographs. Go to an event and you may encounter a vibrant mix of dancing, music-making, banners, puppets and protest signs. Visit a space and perhaps discover home-made buttons and patches, graffiti and poetry scrawled in rebuilt nooks and crannies, art on the walls or music blaring through a sound system. Anarchists use art to express their ideals, and this is what makes their art so compelling: it brings to consciousness our own desire for a better world. And what could be more revolutionary than that?

– ALLAN ANTLIFF

many times i've sat here staring...

Many times I've sat here staring at the typewriter,
anxiously wondering if I had the writing ability to
express myself clearly. I so much want to communicate
feelings and thoughts to you. All those times sitting,
discussing, searching for the ideas that were to free us.
To think back on the creative ways in which I rebelled
against all the forces who tried to temper my spirit and
control the impulse to wonder. I think of where I once
was and to where I exist now. I live mostly within the
heart, my mind unable to tap into the soul weakening the
flow. I am a witch, healer, giver of life, the crone.
I see myself as no other sees me, careful to share
vulnerability. You must be able to recognize me, reflective
in my eyes is your pain. I've felt all the incredible depths
of emotion and I wait for you to spark them in me. When
my tears flow as milk of the mother, I'm offering you chanels
to live for a moment. When I'm rejected I retreat, hidden
in the rich dark soul of the ancient moon. There are times
when I lose my way, rhythms scattered. I'm frightened,
memories torment me. Rationale is weakened by strong forces
of anger, hurt and pain. I'm falling into a sea of doubt
and confusion, no points of reference to guide me. Only
one thing is familiar, lonliness. Here I am surrounded
by people and not one of them can save me. Panic shoots
through me and all I want is for someone to take the pain
away. It was clear to me that an injustice was done and
you were able to walk away with the power that indifference
holds. I tried to shut off all the mental pictures of
running you down. Too unkind were they and of course I'm
not really like that. Of course I wasn't to think those
thoughts. I'm not cruel, I'm angry. I've been pushed to
a place where I do not feel comfort and all the rotting
corpses of helplessness are dragging me down. With my
focus blurred and heart pounding I sensed the trap. This
has always been where recognition flashes before me. My
mother is here, her mother was here. I gather all the
strength of generations of feminine to guide me back, back
into the beginning of my time. The journey is of nothing
I've known although pain is so familiar. Are we ever
given everything we need to nurture us into full human
beings? Twisted and bent we grow, guilt flooding our
senses. Where was the original rejection and could I ever
get over it? Years later and I sometimes still feel that
I'm wandering, stumbling in isolation. I draw comfort in
acceptance of my aloneness. Wisdom is born of my pain and
this is how I now sense life. Intellect, good graces and
charm are the tools by which some live but I have little
understanding of how these work. I now know no other way
then to quietly feel and to scream when it all becomes
unbearable. Then the journey begins again...

                              Pauline

ART § 285

LITERATURE

Daily Life in Revolutionary Utopia:

Feminism, Anarchism & Science Fiction

By Lessa, Takver and Alyx

Whileaway, Amazonia, Canbe, Precipice, Gethen, Anarres, Matapoisett, Ecotopia—nice places to visit . . . you might even want to stay awhile!

SCIENCE FICTION HAS A PARTIC-ular appeal for those who are committed to radical social change. The construction of a parallel world embodying the worst of our fears and the finest of our hopes, delights, terrifies, stimulates and inspires us. Fantasy worlds are powerful tools. As ideas crystallize in the details of future societies, a psychological acceptance of certain possibilities is created. Attention to the unfolding of the fantasy worlds can be a practical political exercise for the readers as well as for the writers.

What it boils down to is that a vision for the future is an intrinsic part of our political position—how can we act to transform society without a conception of what we want to create?

Feminists have noticed that in most science fiction, the condition of women has not been a major focus for creative change. In fact, the "future" for women has been very gloomy: classic sex-role stereotypes abound, all the more appalling because of their persistance in the midst of technical marvels and incredible biological leaps.

It is suggested by Ursula K. Le Guin that the subjection of women in science fiction is "merely a symptom of a whole which is authoritarian, power-worshipping and intensely parochial." (in **Science Fiction Studies #7**, 1975). To demonstrate her analysis, LeGuin creates an anarchist society in **The Dispossessed** where the role of women corresponds to feminist ideals. A similar mutual reinforcement of feminist and anarchist principles is apparent in several other science fiction books.

Male-Female Roles

FEMALES AND MALES ARE virtually indistinguishable in Matapoisett, the future-anarchist village in **Woman On The Edge of Time** (by Marge Piercy). Connie, a chicana woman living in a mental hospital in present-day New York City, is guided to the future by Luciente who appears at first to be male:

Luciente spoke, she moved with that air of brisk unselfconscious authority Connie associated with men. Luciente sat down, taking up more space than women ever did. She squatted, she sprawled, she strolled, never thinking of how her body was displayed.

Not only do men and women in Matapoisett share all the possibilities and choices of life, but they are also referred to by a common pronoun, "per," for person.

Anarres, the anarchist world in **The Dispossessed**, is also androgynous. Shevek, an anarchist scientist, visits Urras, the parent world, and is constantly amazed and disgusted by the roles adopted by men and women there. He is asked, "Is there really no distinction between

men's and women's work [on Anarres]?" and replies, "Well, no, it seems a very mechanical basis for the division of labour, doesn't it? A person chooses work according to interest, talent, strength—what has the sex to do with that?"

As in Matapoisett, people's names give no clue to their sex. On Anarres, every person receives a unique name from the central computer. (Androgynous names always confuse and upset alien visitors who don't know how to act without information about gender.)

In **Ecotopia**, which is an environmentalist's dream come true, author Ernest Callenbach explores male and female differences rather than eliminating them. An American reporter describes the society as women-dominated:

While a majority of Survivalist Party [party in 'power'] members are women, many men are members also . . . The basic co-operation and biology-oriented policies . . . are usually considered to be derived mainly from female attitudes and interests; the chief Opposition party . . . continues to express what are alleged by Survivalists to be out-dated and destructive male attitudes towards individualism and productivity.

Le Guin's fascinating exploration of an ambisexual world in **The Left Hand of Darkness** is ably described by Pamela Sargent (in **Women of Wonder**):

The human narrator . . . is sent as an envoy to the Gethenians, inhabitants of the planet Winter.

> **In all of Whileaway there is no one who can keep you from going where you please, no one who will follow you and try to embarrass you by whispering obscenities in your ear, no one who will attempt to rape you, no one who will warn you of the dangers of the street.**
>
> — **The Female Man by Joanna Russ**

The Gethenians are neuter, but are subject to a monthly fertile season, called kemmer. Each Gethenian finds a partner; hormonal secretions make one Gethenian male or female. The other then becomes a member of the opposite sex and they mate. No Gethenian knows which sex "he" will become during kemmer.

Genly Ai, the Earthman, considers the implications of this physiological development: rape is not possible, since all sex must be by mutual consent. Since the Gethenians are neuter most of the time, sex plays no role in their daily lives except during kemmer when everything else is subordinated to it.

Genly Ai muses:

Consider: Anyone can turn his hand to anything. This sounds very simple, but its psychological effects are incalculable. The fact that every-one between seventeen and thirty-five or so is liable to be tied down to child-bearing implies that no one is quite so thoroughly "tied down" here as women elsewhere are likely to be—psychologically or phsyically; everybody has the same risk to run or choice to make. Therefore, nobody here is quite so free as a free male anywhere else.

Consider: There is no division of humanity into strong and weak halves, protective/protected, dominant/submissive, owner/chattel, active/passive. In fact the whole tendency to dualism that pervades human thinking may be found to be lessened or changed on Winter.   .

One is respected and judged only as a human being. It is an apalling experience.

Living Together

Some science fiction presents familiar feminist values in radically-changed family structures. There are surprises, too!

In **Woman On The Edge Of Time**, Connie is horrified to see a man breast-feeding an infant. Later she visits the "brooder" where several fetuses are "joggling slowly upside down each in a sac of its own, inside a larger fluid receptacle." Luciente explains:

It was part of women's long revolution. When we were breaking up the old hierarchies. Finally there was that one thing we had to give up too, the only power we ever had in return for no more power for any one. The original production. 'Cause as long as we were biologically enchained we'd never be equal. And males would never be humanized to be loving and tender, too. So we all became mothers. Every child has three. To break the nuclear bonding.

In **The Female Man**, Joanna Russ creates Whileaway, a world of women-only where advanced biology has made reproduction possible:

Whileawayans bear their children at thirty . . . These children have as one genotypic parent the biological mother (the "body mother") while the non-bearing parent (the "other mother") contributes the other ovum.

. . . A family of thirty persons may have as many as four mother-child pairs in the common nursery at one time. Food, cleanliness and shelter are not the mothers' business.

In **Ecotopia**, people live in groups of between five and twenty members where "women exert a power which in other societies is covert or non-existent: the right to select the fathers of their children . . . men participate extensively in the care and upbringing of the very young, but in cases of conflict, the mothers have the final say."

The Canbe Collective Builds a Be-Hive is a beautiful book for older children produced by Dandelion Press (see review in **Open Road #8**) about an anarchist community in the future. Employing the non-sexist pronoun, "se," throughout, the book describes life in one collective which is composed of three "affines" each including adults and children. As Pru and Able talk one evening about two of the children, Able wonders if they're getting possessive. Pru says:

. . . some of the collectives have tried to abandon the affine idea and have not liked it . . . I think it's not so much the possession idea, but the small group idea that matters . . . my base is my affine when it comes right down to it.

Sweet Friends

In these days of Anita Bryant and Judge Simonson, even *reading* about sexually liberated future worlds is heartening.

In Matapoisett, "all coupling, all be-friending goes on between biological males, biological females, or both." Persons have close friends ("sweet friends"), lovers ("pillow friends") or co-mothers ("coms") of either sex. No one shares a room, "only babies share space."

On Anarres, partnership is a "voluntarily constituted federation like any other. So long as it works, it works, and if it doesn't work it stops being." Both homosexual and bisexual couples move from the public dormitory to a single room as the only social limit on sexual activity is a mild pressure in favour of privacy. There is always the possibility that a partnership will be broken up if the people are needed for work in different areas. Many people choose not to partner but to be "promiscuous."

Amazon Planet by Mack Reynolds describes a world once dominated by women that has since chosen to become consciously non-sexist. A

—continued on p. 13

Open Road 7 (1978)

—continued from p. 8

visitor from Earth is told:

Here on Amazonia, for possibly the first time, we can contemplate a true love between the sexes. No longer does one economically dominate the other. No longer is one at the mercy of the other, because of unfair laws. Both are equal.

And on Whileaway,

Sexual relations—which have begun at puberty—continue both inside the family and outside it, but mostly outside it. Whileawayans have two explanations for this. "Jealousy", they say for the first explanation, and for the second, "Why not?"

Short People

IN THE ANARCHIST-FEMINIST future(s), children are the apples of their collective's eye, glowing with physical mental and spiritual health in a non-sexist, sexually-free atmosphere designed to enhance their fullest potential. Their "schools" have little resemblance to any present-day educational institutions. They are full members of their communities, respected by adults for their contributions as well as their needs.

Ecotopian children attend open-air schools, spending less than an hour a day in class. They participate each day in the work of the community, in factories and gardens, where "they need to use concepts in geometry and physics, do complex calculations and bring to bear their considerable skills in carpentry.

In **The Canbe Collective**, Patience and Dandelion dream up a unique idea for building a playdome which involves the entire collective in serious discussion and decision-making. As the two young people pursue their plan they have full access to the information and distribution network of their world.

Toys are not big items in Whileaway or Matapoissett, where children participate in the life of their community, soaking up its values. And from **The Dispossessed**:

A child free from the guilt of ownership and the burden of economic competition will grow up with the will to do what needs doing and the capacity for joy in doing it.

Appealing Work

EVEN IN THE FUTURE, PEOPLE have to work, although the distinctions between work and play have been significantly reduced. Much effort is put into making work appealing and integrating it into community life.

When work becomes pleasant and people can choose what they do, who does "the dirty work"? In Matapoissett, Jackrabbit tells Connie, "Fasure [this is all automated]. Who wants to stuff pillows?" On Anarres, where they don't have the technology to automate the disagreeable work, it's shared:

Nobody has to do it for very long, unless he likes the work ... The Community Management or Block Committee ... make rotating lists. The disagreeable work postings or dangerous ones like the mercury mines and mills are normally for one half year only.

When only the necessary work is done and shared equally, a more leisurely pace of life becomes possible. Jackrabbit explains:

After we dumped the jobs telling people what to do, counting money and moving it about, making people do what they don't want or bashing them for doing what they want we have lots of people to work.

On Amazonia, where work settings (although worker-controlled) remain more rigid and set apart, the visitor from Earth notes with surprise that "the enterprises tend to be just as concerned with conditions of work as they are with profits."

As well as being concerned for each other, the inhabitants of several of these future worlds exhibit a high degree of ecological consciousness. They try to grow food and to manufacture goods without destroying the soil or the sea or the air; they seem to have learned the folly of uncontrolled use of natural resources.

In **Ecotopia**, people who want to build a wood structure "must first arrange to go out to a forest camp and do forest service—a period of labor during which ... they are supposed to contribute enough to the growth of new trees to replace the wood they are about to consume." The example is especially exciting since Ecotopia has been established through revolution in Washington, Oregon and Northern California. (Saving all those redwoods and Douglas Firs!)

Technology is not synonomous with capitalism and destructive industrialism in many of these stories. Le Guinn's character in the **New Atlantis** knows his Bookchin:

We could completely decentralize industry and agriculture. Technology could serve life instead of serving capital. We could each run our own life ... The State is a machine. We could unplug the machine, now.

The major use of technology is to liberate people from the work no one wants to do. And computer technology is ingeniously used for information storage and access in almost every book described.

Anarchist Blueprint

The network was not to be run from the top down. There was to be no controlling center, no capital, no establishment for the self-perpetuating machinery of bureaucracy and the dominance drive of individuals seeking to become captains, bosses, chiefs of state.

The Dispossessed

All the systems of Anarres are worked out in detail for the eager student of anarchism, including a description of the transition from authoritarian centralized capitalism.

In the original plans for Anarres, decentralization was an essential element.

Odo, the major theoretician:

had no intention of trying to de-urbanize civilization. Though she suggested that the natural limit to the size of a community lay in its dependence on its own immediate region for essential

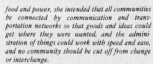

The women say they have learned to rely on their own strength. They say they are aware of the force of their unity. They say, let those who call for a new language first learn violence.

They say, where will you begin? They say, the prisons are open... They say that they have broken with the tradition of inside and outside, that the factories have each knocked down one of their walls, that offices have been installed in the open air, on the esplanades, in the rice-fields.

— The Guérillères by Monique Wittig

food and power, she intended that all communities be connected by communication and transportation networks so that goods and ideas could get where they were wanted, and the administration of things could work with speed and ease, and no community should be cut off from change or interchange.

A similar structure prevails in Matapoissett, where the informality and extent of people's participation astonishes Connie:

Twenty-five or thirty people sat around an oblong table arguing about cement, zinc, tin, copper, platinum, steel, gravel, limestone, and things she could not identify. Many of them seemed to be women ... they ranged from sixteen to extreme old age ... they spoke in ordinary voices and did not seem to be speechifying ...

'We have a five-minute limit on speeches ...'
'This is your government?'
'It's the planning council for our township.'
'Are they elected?'
'Chosen by lot. You do it for a year: three-month with the rep before you and three with the person replacing you and six alone.'

The resulting communities are not mainly rural, but not sprawling cities either. In **Shockwave Rider** by John Brunner, the anarchist city Precipice appears like a jewel in a sea of horror: "It's like a village—with the city implicit in it." In fact, the description of these cities of the future would seduce you into reading further, if the treatment of sex roles had not already captured your imagination.

Despite the complexity of matters to coordinate, attention to process and consensus decision-making are priorities **The Canbe Collective** describes meetings in vivid detail and here is the reporter in **Ecotopia**:

A meeting has no formal agenda; instead it opens with a voicing of "concerns" by many participants. As these are discussed general issues begin to take shape. But there are no Robert's Rules of Order, no motions, no votes—instead, a gradual ventilation of feelings, some personal antagonisms worked through and a gradual consensual focusing on what needs to be done.

Not so on Whileaway. A fiercely—female focussed society, its inhabitants are indoctrinated under a static coded system which naturally produces their "characteristic independence, dissatisfaction, suspicion and a tendency toward a rather irritable solipsism." The book's feminism is apparently not consistent with an anti-authoritarian structure.

Of course, all is not rosy in the future. Le Guin's Odo complains: "favoritism, elitism, leader-worship, they crept back and cropped out everywhere." And the first settlers on Anarres were aware that "unavoidable centralization was a lasting threat to be countered by lasting vigilance."

What of individuals who don't or won't fit into the society? All the authors take a creative crack at this issue. Here's **The Dispossessed**:

Well, he moves on. The others get tired of him, you know. They make fun of him, or they get rough with him, beat him up; in a small community, they might agree to take his name off the meals listing, so he has to cook and eat all by himself; that is humiliating.

Marge Piercy's handling of violent acts in **Woman on The Edge of Time** has some authoritarian elements.

First off, we ask if person wants to take responsibility for the act ... then we work on healing. We try to help so that never again will person do a thing person doesn't mean to do .... [If it was intentional] then you work out a sentence, maybe exile, remote labor ... you, your victim, and your judge work it out (or the family of your victim) ... the second time someone uses violence, we give up ... we don't want to watch each other or to imprison each other ... we aren't willing to live with people who use violence ... we execute them.

In **Ecotopia** there are small prisons rather than large ones. Prisoners participate in the general life of society, holding jobs with ordinary pay and rights. They are confined at other times, with husbands, wives or lovers if they choose. The underlying theory:

In the American system prisons were training grounds for crime. Humane policies give inmates time and opportunity to develop noncriminal modes of life.

The philosophy of anti-authoritarian individual responsibility is fully developed in **The Dispossessed**. A conversation between two characters:

'Listen, wasn't it Odo who said that where there's property, there's theft? ... and to make a thief, make an owner; to create a crime, create laws.'

'Nobody owns anything to rob. If you want things, you take them from the depository. As for violence ... would you murder me? And if you felt like it, would a law against it stop you? Coercion is the least efficient means of obtaining order.'

Keeping Watch

ALL THESE SOCIETIES MUST contend with hostility from other worlds or dangers even closer to home. Some have developed secret powerful weapons which are trained on their enemies; in **Woman On The Edge of Time** every individual must do a stint at the Front where war is waged interminably

Where on earth do all these stories leave us? We've checked out our ideas in "concrete" situations, followed our intuitions through to logical conclusions, imagined how we'd changed things if we were writing the future.

Science fiction doesn't give us a complete picture. There are some areas that leave us quite unsettled. Several books describe a need for coercion in work distribution; none of the authors successfully outlines a method for dealing with extreme anti-social behaviour. The militarism in most of the books is disturbing.

There isn't enough historical detail in science fiction to connect us from here to there. But, when all is read and done, it is our future we're working on. Imagination at the very least reminds us of our goals. Let's give the last word to Odo, talking about Amai, a young woman in her House:

Amai had grown up in Odonian Houses, born to the Revolution, a true daughter of anarchy. And so quiet and free and beautiful a child, enough to make you cry when you thought: this is what we worked for, this is what we want, this is it, here she is, alive, the kind, lovely future.

DRAWINGS BY CLIFF HARPER

Spring Cleaning.

Lawrence and Leslie. Two car-roads that meet here and continue through one of the richest neighbourhoods in the country. To the south-east lies a patch of bright new condominiums. The south-west corner opens to Edwards Gardens, an extremely large, meticulously maintained park abundant with vast freshly mowed lawn-fields surrounded by flowers and trees and winding trails, some of which travel over small bridges crossing the Don River, whose quiet curves intersect the entire park.

The north-east corner of the cross-roads is paved, allowing cars to drive lazily up to the rows of gasoline pumps for a drink. To the north-west lies a smaller park, followed by a maze of suburban homes, schools, a community centre, and more parks. The intersection is running smoothly. Green, red, green, red. The metal creatures crawl out of the Esso, wait at the red, and then upon the flashing green, spewing invisible fumes, they pull into Edwards Gardens so their drivers can experience some well-groomed 'nature'.

The sun is setting. Cars coming from the south, returning from work, turn and disappear into the rows of homes. Other cars, appearing from these same rows of brick baskets, turn south heading to the city's heart, for a nice dinner, or perhaps a movie, a musical, or maybe a leisure stroll through the mall. Teenagers glide by on their roller-blades laughing. Birds sing, as the orange sky reflects off the Don.

But wait, what is this? In the smaller park, in front of the homes and trees and grass and flowers, the landscape is interrupted by a woman. She shouldn't be here. She must be lost. Her head is resting on a wooden bench. The bench is holding up her weak, resting body. Her sleeping bag keeps her warm. Beside her, on the ground, a couple of shopping bags are filled with her belongings. No one will steal them here.

The woman, small and weak and surrounded by large trees and structures, is the most prominent figure for miles.

In the middle of Eden, she silently screams out that something is wrong.

Anarchives 4/2 (1997)

The neighbourhood children see her and don't understand. Why doesn't she sleep in her house, they wonder? Surely everyone has a house. Doesn't everyone have a house? Doesn't everyone have a family? They must! All of their friends have houses and cupboards of food from the Price Club. Why doesn't she sleep in her house, they wonder?

The woman is a hole in the fence. A glimpse through the facade, to another world. A world not too far away.

She's a little stream, leaking out of an underground cesspool, dribbling through a flower garden.

She's a cancerous tumour. A sudden sign of trouble that's been hiding underneath the skin.

I worried for the woman. They won't like her here. Here they plug the holes in fences, they fix all the leaks, and kill the tumours, hoping they don't come back. How will they plug this hole? Will they drag her away at night? Who would know? Who would care?

No. They won't do that. They don't break the law much around here. They don't have to. The laws are woven for them.

They know she has a right to claim the public bench and live on it. It's the only thing this city has provided for her. A bench. She accepts it, and it keeps her off the ground. All winter. Right on the corner, by the bus-stop, where everyone sees her. Every day.

But they're smart. I went past Lawrence and Leslie last week, and looked for the woman. I was right. They would never forcibly remove the woman. But they would make her leave, even if it meant taking away the one thing she had.

The sun set, the cars drank, the kids glided by.

But the bench, was gone.

LOOK AT US
LOOK AT US, WE ARE OF EARTH AND WATER
LOOK AT THEM, IT IS THE SAME
LOOK AT US, WE ARE SUFFERING ALL THESE YEARS
LOOK AT THEM, THEY ARE CONNECTED
LOOK AT US, WE ARE IN PAIN
LOOK AT THEM, SURPRISED AT OUR ANGER
LOOK AT US, WE ARE STRUGGLING TO SURVIVE
LOOK AT THEM, EXPECTING SORROW, BEING BENIGN
LOOK AT US, WE ARE THE ONES CALLED PAGAN
LOOK AT THEM, ON THEIR ARRIVAL
LOOK AT US, WE ARE CALLED SUBVERSIVES
LOOK AT THEM, DESCENDING FROM NAMECALLERS
LOOK AT US, WE WEPT SADLY IN THE LONG DARK
LOOK AT THEM, HIDING IN TECH NO LOGIC LIFE
LOOK AT US, WE BURY THE GENERATIONS
LOOK AT THEM, INVENTING THE BODY COUNT
LOOK AT US, WE ARE OLDER THAN AMERICA
LOOK AT THEM, CHASING A FOUNTAIN OF YOUTH
LOOK AT US, WE ARE EMBRACING EARTH
LOOK AT THEM, CLUTCHING TODAY
LOOK AT US, WE ARE LIVING IN THE GENERATIONS
LOOK AT THEM, EXISTING IN JOBS AND DEBT
LOOK AT US, WE HAVE ESCAPED MANY TIMES
LOOK AT THEM, THEY CANNOT REMEMBER
LOOK AT US, WE ARE HEALING
LOOK AT THEM, THEIR MEDECINE IS PATENTED
LOOK AT US, WE ARE TRYING
LOOK AT THEM, WHAT ARE THEY DOING?
LOOK AT US, WE ARE CHILDREN OF EARTH
LOOK AT THEM, WHO ARE THEY?

JOHN TRUDELL

No Picnic I (1988)

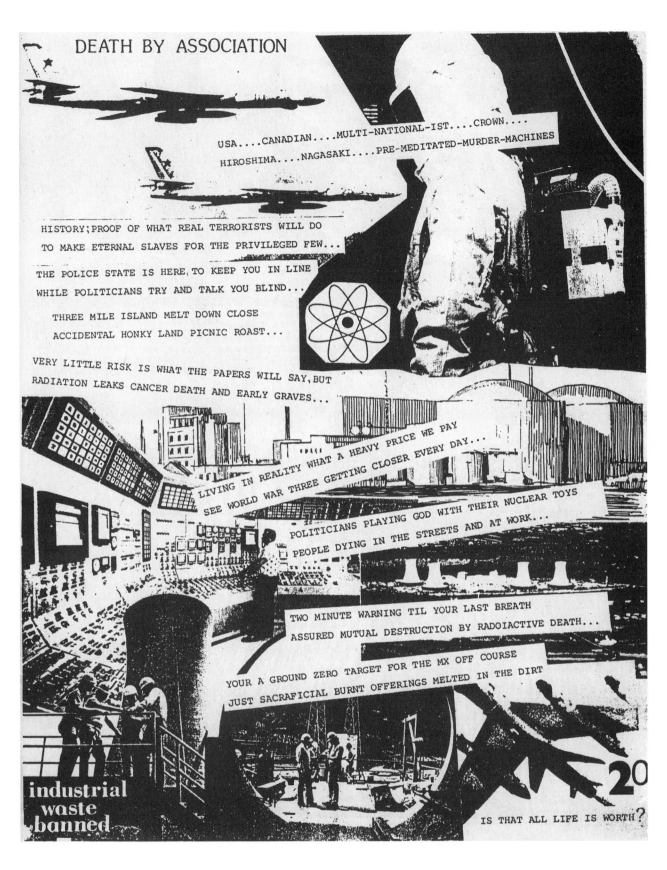

DEATH BY ASSOCIATION

USA....CANADIAN....MULTI-NATIONAL-IST....CROWN....
HIROSHIMA....NAGASAKI.....PRE-MEDITATED-MURDER-MACHINES

HISTORY; PROOF OF WHAT REAL TERRORISTS WILL DO
TO MAKE ETERNAL SLAVES FOR THE PRIVILEGED FEW...

THE POLICE STATE IS HERE, TO KEEP YOU IN LINE
WHILE POLITICIANS TRY AND TALK YOU BLIND...

THREE MILE ISLAND MELT DOWN CLOSE
ACCIDENTAL HONKY LAND PICNIC ROAST...

VERY LITTLE RISK IS WHAT THE PAPERS WILL SAY, BUT
RADIATION LEAKS CANCER DEATH AND EARLY GRAVES...

LIVING IN REALITY WHAT A HEAVY PRICE WE PAY
SEE WORLD WAR THREE GETTING CLOSER EVERY DAY...

POLITICIANS PLAYING GOD WITH THEIR NUCLEAR TOYS
PEOPLE DYING IN THE STREETS AND AT WORK...

TWO MINUTE WARNING TIL YOUR LAST BREATH
ASSURED MUTUAL DESTRUCTION BY RADIOACTIVE DEATH...

YOUR A GROUND ZERO TARGET FOR THE MX OFF COURSE
JUST SACRAFICIAL BURNT OFFERINGS MELTED IN THE DIRT

industrial
waste
banned

2⁰

IS THAT ALL LIFE IS WORTH?

Down By the River

"The path of progress in psychiatry is circular,
periodically returning to its starting point."
Thomas Szasz, M.D., *The Manufacture of Madness*

Here we are, ready
to plunge into this institution
by the river where everything
is the same and yet
so different. Another
state, an unknown set of rules,
and this new thing she's done,
this direct statement:
I do not want to live.

We are afraid and we do not
know what it is we can or
can't do, but we agree on this:
no shock treatments, never again,
and home as soon as possible,
maybe today, if we talk loud
and fast enough
and do not listen to the
roaring in our heads.

> (Professor Ugo Cerletti, inventor
> of electric shock therapy, recalling
> the first time he used the treatment
> on a human being, "When I saw the
> patient's reaction, I thought to myself,
> 'This ought to be abolished!' ")

A mockingbird sings
from a low branch; we open
our mouths and gulp a last
lungful of free air. We are
three humans, flesh
against stone.

When we push through the door
to the lobby, we are immersed
in a deep channel of water.
Lost creatures slide by us.
We are almost to the front desk
before someone calls out,
smelling fear and pity
pouring off us like sweat.
We feel something inside
ourselves turn on its back,
belly to the ceiling.

We sign our individual names
and relationships, but we know
we are family
and we do not agree
to this place.
We walk past offices, empty,
unlit treatment rooms, incomprehensible
machines. We wonder where
the torture takes place
and know it is deliberately
kept from us.

We surprise ourselves.
How is it each of us has decided
not to play Judas?
When we kiss her this time,
we will be shouting welcome:

Hello to the lost, the lonely,
these heretics and modern-day witches,
the oppressed: our mother, our wife.

> (1851. Illinois commitment statute
> enacted. Married women . . . may be
> entered or detained in the hospital
> at the request of the husband
> of the woman . . . without evidence
> of insanity required in other cases.')

We are certain
if we turn away from her,
we turn away from our *selves*.

We are on the ward;
there she is:
a skinny old woman,
locked away and muttering
to herself. When she sees us,
her eyes flame.
She comes to us drugged,
rigid, begging to go home.
We sit with her, a temporary island,
making conversation, trying
to ignore the swell and ripple
around us.

mythical dog painted in black on a large pear- shaped vase from Varvarovka, a Late Cucuteni site near Kishenev, Soviet Moldavia, fourth millenium BC.
(All material quoted in parentheses is excerpted from *The Manufacture of Madn*

A man visits his wife.
The woman is too loud,
she says damn
and FUCK and smokes
cigaret after cigaret.
He is gawky,
not enough chin
and too much Adam's apple.
Her jeans hang on her body.
He is dressed in chinos
and a thin, cotton shirt.
He hands her a package.
She rips the wrapping off:
a picture of Jesus in the
Garden of Olives. She waves
his offering and shouts:
JEy-ZU-uS KRi-I-sST from K-Mart,
for 67 cents. The figure in the print
is kneeling, robed in purple
and alone.

From the bricked-in garden
just off the ward,
a black man gestures to us.
He smiles. He is wearing
pajamas, a robe and slippers,
though it is well past noon
and lunch has been served.
He walks toward us,
a living piece of flotsam

cast up by the river.
He is polite and tells us
his name: Richard.
This is our first clue
we have entered another landscape
where nothing is accidental.
We introduce him to the Richard
in our family. The black Richard
grins at the white Richard,
leans over and asks my mother,
will she free him, too?
She clenches her fists
and hisses, "Yes!"

(1955. Egas Moniz is awarded
the Nobel Prize for Physiology
or Medicine for the treatment
of schizophrenia by prefrontal
lobotomy.)

I am caught by the drowned snags
of the river at last.
I walk to the nurses' station,
the territory marking the border
between the visitor's lobby and the ward.
I glance up
stare across a sudden expanse
of barbed wire,
into a woman's face.
She is walnut-skinned,
her eyes come at me
like deer.
Someone tells me
this is our Christina.
I nod. I know her.
My head hums. I ask her
where she lives
but I cannot understand
her dialect, her black rural
southern speech.
I wrap my arms
around her
with my eyes.

I want to throw my arms around
them all and shout:
we are locked in here

whether we are inside
these walls or not,
when can we be free?
I want to sing out:
let us go down
to the river
each and every one,
where we can walk
and run and move
our limbs in the ripe sun
and wait for the thunder, down
by the river flowing
out of the high green hills
to where the mockingbird sings.

We will listen
for the thunder
and pray the walls
crumble.

Christina V. Pacosz

Some Winded, Wild Beast

Black & Red   P.O. Box 02374   Detroit, Michigan 48202

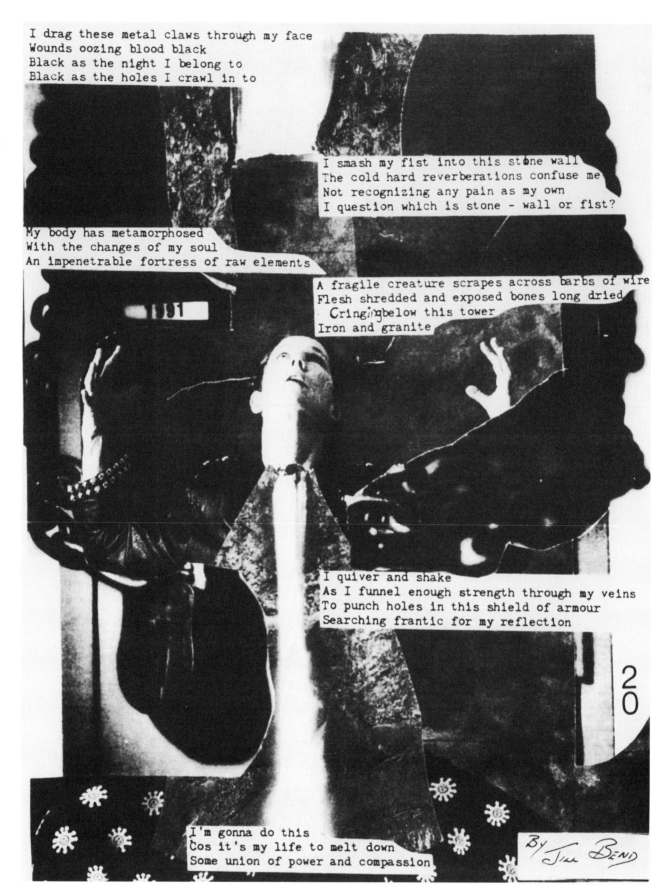

I drag these metal claws through my face
Wounds oozing blood black
Black as the night I belong to
Black as the holes I crawl in to

I smash my fist into this stone wall
The cold hard reverberations confuse me
Not recognizing any pain as my own
I question which is stone - wall or fist?

My body has metamorphosed
With the changes of my soul
An impenetrable fortress of raw elements

A fragile creature scrapes across barbs of wire
Flesh shredded and exposed bones long dried
Cringing below this tower
Iron and granite

I quiver and shake
As I funnel enough strength through my veins
To punch holes in this shield of armour
Searching frantic for my reflection

I'm gonna do this
Cos it's my life to melt down
Some union of power and compassion

By Jim Bend

BOA 4 (1992)

Blue collar poets boost production

By Tom Wayman

During the past fifteen years, something new in the history of English literature has appeared in North America.

For the first time ever, we now have a poetry about daily work and the working life that is written from *inside* the jobs that are described.

Previously, poets were largely from a social class which ensured that if poets considered work at all, they wrote of it from the outside: they did not participate themselves in what they were attempting to depict. Work, a central and governing aspect of human existence, was ignored in favor of the supposedly-sublimer themes of love and death.

Where writers were members of the working class they were most often moved to write by events or emotions connected with the struggle for unionism or socialism. Hence they saw no reason to describe the conditions of their own daily life except in the most general terms. They wrote with an eye on the future, not the present; they wanted to exhort others to action, to praise a victory or mourn a defeat, but always in terms of the millennium to come. Due largely to a lack of education, working poets wrote in an artistic style that was antiquated. They seemed unaware of, and certainly took no part in, the ordinary literary life of their age.

Radical Departure

The new work poets of the last fifteen years or so represent a radical departure from this. Their presence apparently parallels the spread of mass public education beyond secondary school, for many of the work poets have had some exposure to modern verse either in an enlightened high school class, or at a community college, university or technical institute. But their own writing, the new work poems, is something entirely unprecedented, in English language poetry.

Indeed, this poetry seems unique on the planet. Even the "proletarian" poets of the various Communist regimes write rather of the glories of the Party or the State than of the conditions of their own daily working lives. In other nations, the gap between those with much of an education and the rest of their countrymen is still too great. Left-wing writers, or those sympathetic to their working compatriots, mostly do not work themselves at ordinary jobs. So these poets can write of a worker's life only from *outside*, imagining themselves to be speaking *for* those whose labor keeps the whole society functioning.

The new work poems first began to appear in North America scattered in little magazines and anthologies, and in a few poet's own collections. In 1974 I gathered together a small anthology of such poems, and in 1976 edited a second, larger anthology called **A Government Job at Last** from which the poems here are taken. Most of the poets

"Speaking clearly about the conditions of daily life. . ."

are young, as might be expected, and many are somewhat familiar with, or take part in, the ordinary literary life of our time. But all contributors write their poems about jobs or the working life from inside their own experiences at these occupations, whether blue- or white-collar, paid or unpaid labor.

To me, the presence of these poets and these poems reflect developments in the work force in North America today.

About a third of the work force in most industrial enterprises can be considered "long-hairs." These young people have no particular commitment to staying in one job forever, and so work as a means to pay off debts and/or amass capital towards further enjoyment of life in the consumer world of long vacations, cars, stereos, drugs, further schooling, etc. About two-thirds of the work force might be considered "lifers." These are people of all ages who for various reasons *must* work for longer periods of time at one job, whether because they are supporting families, or are paying off vast mortgages, or to give their lives shape or meaning. Many, but not all, of the work poets are long-hairs: their senses are still finely tuned to the differences between wage slavery and the comparative (even if short-lived) freedom of not being employed, and to the effects of any particular job on human dignity, life off the job, interpersonal relationships, etc. Gwen Hauser's poem reproduced here about life in a glass factory is a good example of this. The usually-older lifer poets contribute a sharp sense of the absurdity of long-term industrial servitude. The work of Marty Glaberman, a 20-year veteran of the Detroit auto shops, will serve as an example of this. But all the work poets concentrate on presenting specific details of the writer's present life. As in the work force at large today, there is little sense in these poems of a better life just around the corner.

The work poems do, however, show once again that people are perfectly capable of speaking for themselves about the conditions of their lives. There is no need for any sort of professional "representative" to speak for us— whether a union bureaucrat, a politician of any stripe, or any form of writer, journalist or poet. And when we clearly articulate conditions at the core of our daily existence— our work—we demonstrate one more time our awareness that real social change must start here and must bring effective change *here*, not at city hall or the union hall or in some provincial or federal legislature.

There are also artistic lessons in the new work poetry.

For some time it has been assumed that the avant-garde in the art must be concerned with formal experimentation: developments out of Ezra Pound's dicta, or concrete poetry, or surrealism, or dada, or some other holdover from the artistic life at the beginning of this century. But I believe that the new is *always* new, and that what is new in poetry in our time is to be found in *content*—in these working poems, written from inside the job, the first time in the history of the language such material has been produced.

New Realism

These poems strive to speak clearly, precisely, luminously about the conditions of daily life of most of us. What is new is that it is *us* speaking of these realities in our own lives; this is what makes it a New Realism. In Canada, however, besides the endorsement of formal experimentation as the road to the future there has been much critical insistence on dragging poetry into the service of myth. I believe the new work poetry stands against this too. So much of humanity's history has been a slow, painful struggle to free ourselves from the spider-web of myth, superstition, and the whole range of elaborate metaphors, allegories, and verbal puzzles all of which obscure the realities of our condition. Not that the work poets eschew metaphors entirely; as has been shown, words themselves (our artistic medium) may be considered metaphors for the objects they describe. Also, as the Preamble of the Industrial Workers of the World reminds us, the new society begins within the shell of the old. But the contemporary work poets try to use words to make our lives *clearer* to us. They resist the urgings of academics to make our lives even more confusing.

After all, what could be more mysterious, hidden, than the myriad technologies and the hundreds of other human lives that in a complex industrial society such as ours are necessary to bring us the simplest of objects we use in our daily life? But there is nothing mythological in this. Just human work, and the lives, loves, deaths that work affects.

The more we understand all this complexity—and we are helped in this understanding by the careful depictions of the New Realist poets —the more we understand the great human solidarity that unites all our daily working lives. And this is the solidarity we must have as a weapon to defeat the masters of this life.

Tom Wayman is a Vancouver based poet whose most recent book is **Free Time**, *published by MacMillan of Canada, 1977.*

A GOVERNMENT JOB AT LAST is available from MacLeod Books, 350 West Pender St., Vancouver, B.C.

Drum

boom

    That's a helluva way
    to welcome a buddy

Boom

    who's just a few minutes
    late

BOOM

    trying to sneak by the foreman
    to avoid an argument

BOOM

    banging on a steel skid
    with a steal hammer lead hammer copper hammer

B O O M

    rythmically, louder and louder
    all work stopping to escort me to my machine

B-O-O-M

    and when I get there
    it just as suddenly

STOPS

    ALL EXCEPT THE MEMORY OF THE FOREMEN
    STANDING AROUND LOOKING STUPID
    AT SOMETHING THEY CAN'T CONTROL
      —Marty Glaberman

Thirty Below

Men on the pond
push logs through constant ice.
Faces stubble with frost.
No-one moves beyond the ritual
of work. Torment of metal
and the scream of saws.

Everything is hard. The sky
scrapes the earth at thirty below
and living things pull into pain
like grotesque children
thrown in the wrong season.

Someone curses.
Pulls his hand from the chain.
His skin has been left on steel,
blood frozen into hard balls.
He is replaced and the work goes on.

Everything is hard.
Cold lances the slow dance
on the pond. The new man trembles
out of control.
He can't hold his pole.
Someone laughs,
says it will be spring
before they shut this damn mill down.
      —Pat Lane

Ernie
(Poem for a Sweat-Shop Foreman)

Ernie, the foreman,
    never sweats.
he is cool and sweet-smelling
    in any weather.
standing beside Ernie
    is like standing beside
a flower-scented refrigerator
    with the door open.

why does Ernie
    never sweat?
no, it's not because
    he doesn't work.
he appears to work
    from time to time.
maybe it's because
    he has ice-water in his veins
instead of blood
    like ordinary humans;

why does Ernie
    never sweat
when we're all sweating to death
    & almost dying
because the company
    is too cheap to give us a fan?
it must be that Ernie
    is a God not a man.
      —Gwen Hauser

Some Jobs Are Not So Boring, O

when I was waitressing,
(running my ass off for $80 a week)

Jo, the cook, was a champion
of the working classes.

"Are they giving you a hard time,
honey?" he would ask, as I stood
in the kitchen in tears telling him
how rude Station Four was.

Then he would grandly run his hand
through their food,
      Backwards & Forwards,
      handsomely spreading germs,

before I took the dainty dishes back
to set before the king.

    —Nellie McClung

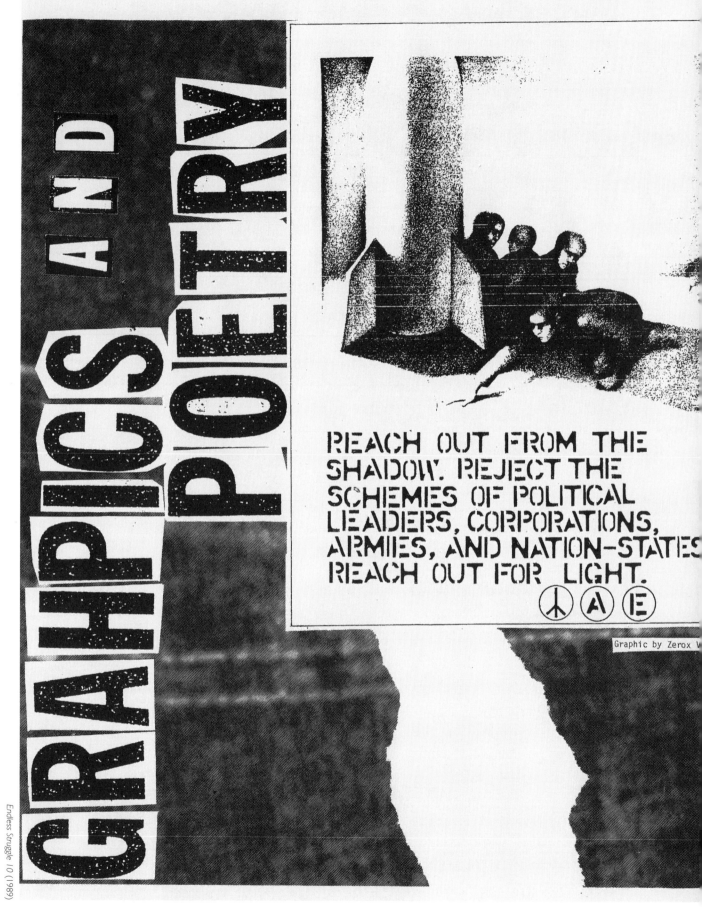

GRAPHICS AND POETRY

REACH OUT FROM THE
SHADOW. REJECT THE
SCHEMES OF POLITICAL
LEADERS, CORPORATIONS,
ARMIES, AND NATION-STATES
REACH OUT FOR LIGHT.

Graphic by Zerox W

automatons

they use words like alligators
snap go their jaws
to influence politically
outmanuever your enemy

in pressed and painted suit and tie
lawyers bankers landlords wankers
automatons like these deserve to die

don't you recognize the lies
their media feeds you every day?

citizens of the U.S.A.
what have you got to lose?

i say wooden shoes
i say erupting
i say erupting
i say erupting
interrupting the news
interrupting the words they use
to influence politically
outmanuever your enemy

citizens of the U.S.A.
what have you got to lose?

in pressed and painted suit and tie
lawyers bankers landlords wankers

don't you recognize the lies
their media feeds you every day?

-bob z
artists & writers underground
c/o sarris bookmarketing
125 e. 23rd st. #300
new York, NY 10010

▼ JOUNI WAARAKANGAS ▲

Revolution Time

"It's revolution time",
sounded the mime.
Imagine my surprise at this
news.
But alas, it was not to be,
you see The Revolutionaries
didn't ahve their shit together.
They spent too much time discussing Theories written by
the hands of empty men who
are long gone Dead, most of
them were too hung-over
anyway...
Oh well things wouldn't
have changed much anyway...
anyway.

                    Keith.

Aware

After years of repression
I got the impression
taht my oppression
was the slow succession
of a rulers procession
over my right to expression.

        Maggie 89.

In This World the Scum Rises To The Top

I've lain awake at nite with stabbing pains in my brain. Death in the crib. Death in the factories, fields & streets. The self-servers are constantly putting our health at risk. In the "happy" countries a steady rise in teen suicide deaths. Any one of us could be next. Well somewhere there is some one at fault. They're not gods or devils, they claim to be human(e), but surprise surprise they're just power grubbing scum! that love to dominate me & you. To them you're nothing & when you're nothing you've nothing to lose. when the suits can take away anything you cherish including your life...

Hateful scum! ...I hate scum! So when they push me into the corner gimme a board, brick, bottle or bomb, cause in-case you haven't heard cornered rats attack!
So you better look out you murderous fucks cause cornered rats attack!

k e v i n

Too Much Too Think

I think I've had a little bit too much to think
Don't seem to worry about Government anymore

Don't seem to think about the Third World War
Don't seem to care about much anymore
Perhaps, just maybe, somewhere along the line I had just a little too much to think....

Keith.

The Slaughterhouse

The bovine eyes hold
So much confusion,
certain only that they see no mercy.

Pain,oh, such pain.
But there cannot be.
It's been there since birth
It must be right.
Wait! Was that birth?
No miracles here.
It was only production.

A dim understanding.
Slowly lights wasted eyes.
In an unnoticed minute,
(as were all that came before)
The creatureslowly senses
This is not his life,
He only exists...

And now he doesn't anymore.

Maggie 89.

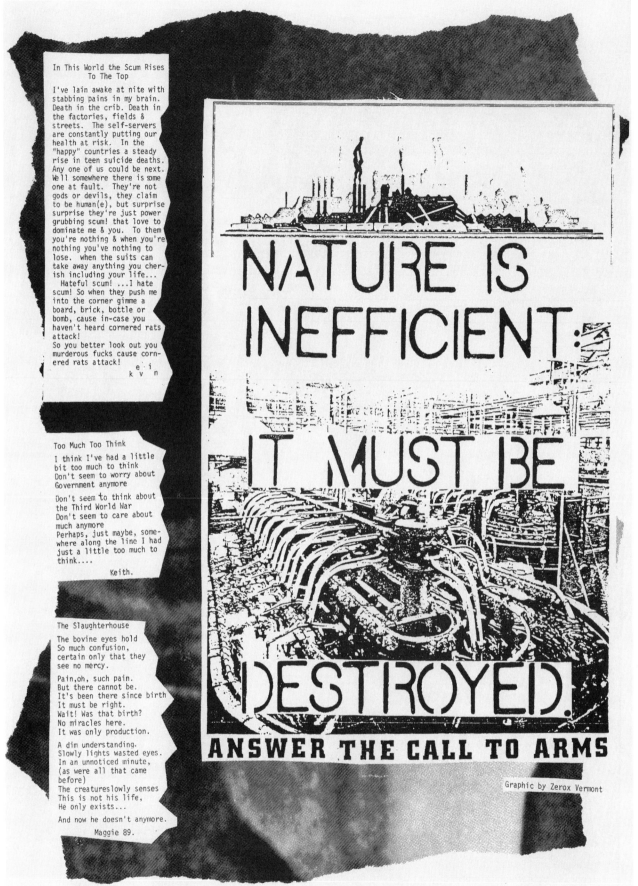

NATURE IS INEFFICIENT: IT MUST BE DESTROYED.

ANSWER THE CALL TO ARMS

Graphic by Zerox Vermont

Endless Struggle 10 (1989)

WiMMiN SURViViNG OPPRESSION

rae gabrielle
laura morrison
anne raven
pam solo
siobhan louise o'keefe
cerrolyn
pam cooley
deanna bowen
yvette jantzen
pj flaming
kim jackson
hella keese
persimmon blackbridge
carel moisewitch
pat chauncey
lone nielsen
sheila baxter
zöe lambert
dianne wood
margaret prevost
jancis m. andrews
katharine fischer
annie frazier
kelly white
michelle thrush
kenna fair
christine cumming
polly bak
julie o'rourke
sara orlowski
fatima jaffer
guttargie o'sullivan
patricia schneider
and more...

Women Surviving Oppression is a cultural event of some of the personal vitality, creativity, intelligence and spirituality on which wimmin draw to do battle in daily life.

Artwork by over 20 wimmin on display

March 11 to April 7
at the
Downtown Eastside Womens Center
44 E. Cordova
Wheelchair Accessible

Firehall Arts Centre
280 E. Cordova

Photos: pp. 32 - 36

Photos of some of the **many** amazing art works in BoA Show - March 1991

cabarets of poetry, music, dance, storytelling & surprises in a drug/ alcohol free space

Photos by Yvette Janzen

31

Laura Morrison

Ricochet

3
3

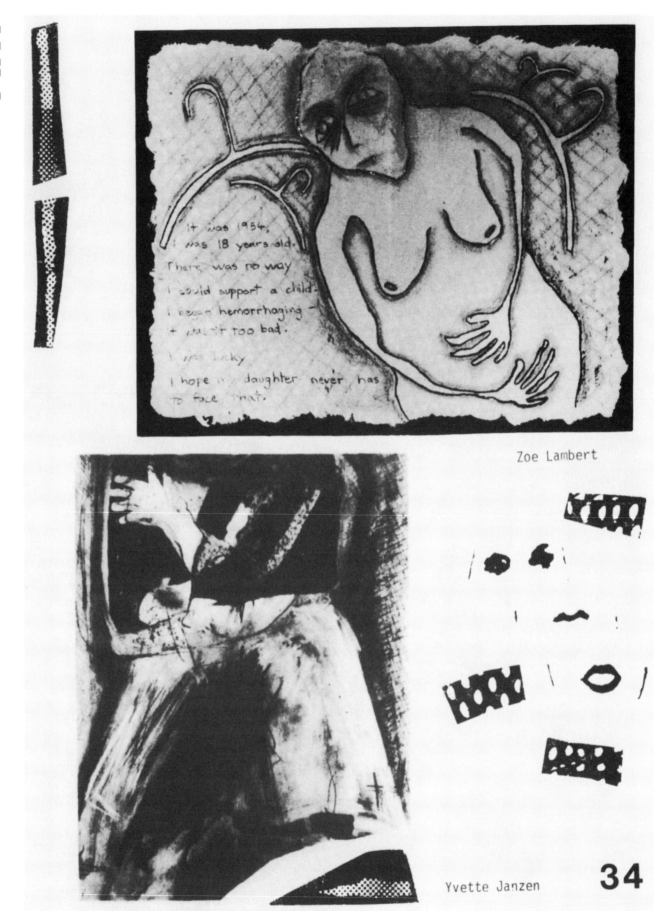

It was 1954.
I was 18 years old.
There was no way
I could support a child.
I began hemorrhaging —
+ wasn't too bad.

I was lucky.

I hope my daughter never has
to face that.

Zoe Lambert

Yvette Janzen

34

BOA 4 (1992)

...wimmin, in the forms of rape, battery, incest, assualt, is one
...ience under patriarchy. Besides overt physical violence,

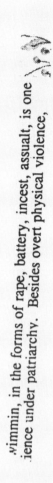

Patricia Shneider

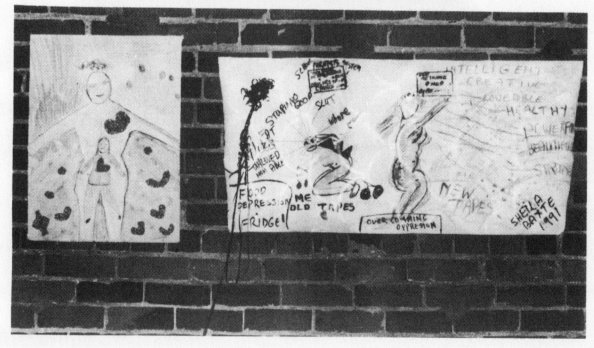

Sheila Baxter

ANARCHIST SANDWICH PARTY

Bloor/Danforth Subway, Toronto, May 1–5, 2004
ballpoint pen on paper, suite of five collaborative drawings
each drawing 111.8 x 127 centimetres (44 x 50 inches)

produced with the assistance of Nick Ackerley,
Christopher House, Peter Kingstone, Jeremy Laing,
Scott McEwan, Amish Morrell, Will Munro, Yvonne Ng,
Sandy Plotnikoff, Moh'd Shanti, Tina Shapiro, Fraser Smith,
Catherine Stinson, and Netami Stuart

Anarchist Sandwich Party consists of a suite of five large-scale ballpoint pen drawings. These collaboratively produced drawings themselves depict another collaborative project: an anarchist sandwich party held by the "Art and Collaborative Approaches" class of Toronto's Anarchist Free University.

The Anarchist Free University ("Anarchist U.," as it is affectionately called) operates as a volunteer-run collective that organizes a variety of weekly courses on social sciences and the humanities. The collective locates itself within the long tradition of community anarchist free-schools by its adherence to principles of openness, non-hierarchic organization, and the constant questioning of the roles of teacher and students.

Among the six weekly courses offered by the Anarchist U. during its first semester in the Fall of 2003 was the Art and Collaborative Approaches class facilitated by myself, which engaged some thirty participants. As the last class of the course, the group decided to produce a collaboration: an anarchist sandwich party held in the Toronto subway system.

On December 1, 2003, each course participant brought enough of one sandwich ingredient to make forty sandwiches.

The twenty people who attended this event assembled at Bathurst Station in downtown Toronto, boarded the subway train heading eastbound towards the suburb of Scarborough, and proceeded to form a sandwich-making assembly line. The first person brought out bread, then passed this bread to the next person, who added one ingredient to it. As it was passed from person to person in this way, a gradually growing sandwich was built until – filled with twenty different ingredients – it reached the end of the assembly line. In a mood of celebration, sandwiches were enjoyed by course participants and distributed to other passengers riding the subway train. This process resulted in the collaborative production of forty sandwiches produced en route as the train reached the eastern end of the subway line in Scarborough, traversed the city again to the western end of the line in Etobicoke, and arrived once again at Bathurst Station downtown.

Appearing somewhat like oversized ballpoint-pen sketches on high-school binders, the drawings comprising ANARCHIST SANDWICH PARTY; BLOOR/DANFORTH SUBWAY, TORONTO #1-5 document the project in a process that was itself collaborative. These drawings connect to the continuing evolution of self-initiated, collectively-operating, grassroots education.

They link the nutritional nourishment of our bodies to the educational nourishment of our minds and perspectives; and the making and sharing of food, to the creation and sharing of knowledge, experiences, and points of view. Produced with the assistance of people who do and who do not identify as artists, these drawings advocate for a culture of participation and creative engagement.

– LUIS JACOB

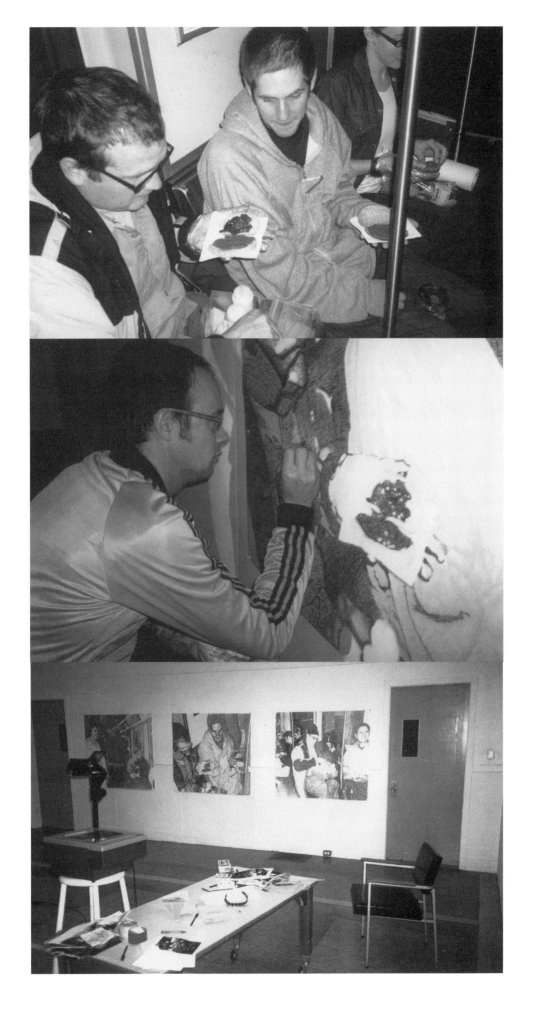

PUBLIC WATER CLOSET

modified portable toilet, 1998, Ottawa and Toronto

1. *Public water closet* (PWC) is an attempt to place art not simply in a public context, but also within a social and political dialogue. The project makes available one of the basic infrastructures of public space – a washroom. Its aesthetic and conceptual strategy acts in part as an alibi for the controversial proposition that public space should be open for use by any member of the public, regardless of their economic situation, and not merely as a publicly funded location for capitalist accumulation.

The form of the work overturns (or in Situationist terminology, detours) the basic function of the two-way mirror, which is to provide systems of power a safe venue from which to survey a population to be controlled. In PWC the hierarchy is reversed, so that people on the street who are currently being harassed and prosecuted for their expression of basic needs and functions, are allowed a location from which to watch the city without being seen. The project initiates an alternate relation between individuals and municipal infrastructure, which is currently being designed and constructed as one element in a paranoid fantasy of coercion.

Public water closet is a minimum architecture whose rationale and effects operate beyond mere functionalism. It specifically addresses desire and play in the city. Within the device, users appear barely protected by a thin sheet of glass from viewers on the street, creating a dialectic of voyeurism and exhibitionism.

The work is clearly influenced by the related practices of Robert Smithson who postulated sculpture as a mirroring of its site, Gordon Matta-Clark who literally cut buildings open, exposing their interiors to view, and Dan Graham whose use of reflective glass in the construction of fun houses and follies disarms one of contemporary architecture's most ubiquitous and problematic materials.

2. PWC is a prototype. It plays with the modernist ambition of universality. Theoretically it can go anywhere, but it works best in a city where washrooms are not available, and where their emergency provision would be useful.

It was conceived in the context of Premier Mike Harris's Ontario and Mayor Mel Lastman's Toronto. Both politicians prioritized tactics of police repression over economic redistribution or provision of basic public infrastructures. In the summer of 1998 the province shoved the Safe Streets Act down people's throats. This new law gave the police special powers to criminalize behaviours characteristic of homeless people, including aggressive panhandling and squeegeeing, the only means many individuals have to survive. Toronto city council voted to increase police funding to pay officers overtime to remove unwanted persons from the city's parks and other public spaces. These two tactics facilitate the urban design department's program of reurbanization. This agency is interested in increasing housing densities in downtown Toronto, ostensibly as a means of reducing sprawl at the periphery, but all new development in downtown consists of condominiums for individuals or couples, affordable primarily by affluent professionals. The city is more interested in raising property values than maintaining the current diversity of Toronto's downtown population. New policing policies are directly linked to strategies of gentrification through which the city itself acts as a commodity for global capital.

PWC is materialized as architecture to suggest an alternate approach to Toronto's urban design. In Toronto it was located at the corner of Queen and Spadina, the epicentre of the conflict surrounding squeegeeing, where local businesses, like Lettieri Café, demanded protection from these independent entrepreneurs. To install the water closet legally, I needed the permission of surrounding stores. Many were amenable to the project because it was an artwork, as long as the washroom was not placed directly in front of their store. However certain businesses were vehemently opposed, claiming they would take the issue to their councillor, and arguing that it would encourage people they considered undesirable to inhabit the city's streets. These responses transparently articulated an understanding, shared by the city and the province, as to who is considered a legitimate inhabitant of urban space.

3. *pwc* attacks what Samir Amin calls the "single thought" of contemporary capitalism – "globalized neo-liberalism" (Samir Amin, *Spectres of Capitalism* [New York: Monthly Review Press, 1998], 43). It proposes first of all that alternate frameworks for urbanism must be investigated. This is to say that at no moment can we accept the reduction of urbanism to its own capitalist single thought. Second, it specifically argues that the city cannot be segregated along class lines as the commodification of urban space currently insists; rather the city has to operate as an engine of difference and adjacency. Third, it attempts to invent an architecture of play. Public infrastructure could allow for sensuality and erotics, invented autonomously through participation and collaboration, rather than through the media's constantly increasing infiltration into our city's streets. Finally it creates an architecture that subverts the growing militarization of urban space, the corollary of current attempts to liberalize trade and investment under the stewardship of global capital.

Recent proposals such as Toronto's 2008 Olympic bid and those for waterfront redevelopment are only intensifications of existing ideologies and methodologies of contemporary urbanism. *pwc* participates in alternative strategies currently being developed by diverse groups around the world.

– Adrian Blackwell

MODEL FOR A PUBLIC SPACE

*plywood construction, Mercer Union, Toronto 2000,
Architecture Gallery, University of Manitoba, Winnipeg 1999*

In 1998 I made an unofficial entry to the design competition for a new public square at the corner of Yonge and Dundas streets in the heart of downtown Toronto. My proposal responded critically to the authoritarian and commodified conceptions of civic space imagined by Toronto's planners and politicians, experimenting instead with a conception of democratic space proposed by Richard Sennett in his lecture: *The Spaces of Democracy*. He argues that the focused Greek theatre and the open agora, or market, are two complementary and necessary discursive spaces in ancient Greek political life.

The proposed square is formed by taking a flat and open plane and cutting it in a single spiral line. This flexible surface is shaped so that continuous seating wraps the space forming a shallow dish. This square is open and varied: intimate, expansive, enclosed, and shaded. In response to the city's fantasies of a space that would innocuously serve the businesses surrounding it, while refusing to legitimate non-commercial functions, the proposal argued that a public square must be a space of dialogue in which conflicting visions and uses interact.

Model for a Public Space is derived formally from the project for Dundas Square, but it responds explicitly to my experience with non-hierarchical meeting forms at Toronto's Anarchist Free School (1998–2001). In its classes and meetings ideas were discussed and decisions reached by consensus, sitting face to face and talking together. Thinkers from Hannah Arendt to Guy Debord have argued for this basic method of political engagement, which is the form of both revolutionary and worker's councils.

The space is formed as a set of bleachers, constructed by cutting and unpeeling a plywood floor in a spiral and supporting it on spruce studs in an inverted cone. The single seat is tightly wound, so that people sitting across from one another are physically close, allowing intimacy in large groups. The structure both constructs, and undermines, hierarchies. If you sit towards the top, you are in a position of power surveying the space, but you remain on the periphery. In the centre you command attention, but people sit behind and high above you. The space is deliberately transparent, creating an openness to meetings, so that visitors can walk under the seats to stand and watch. *Model for a Public Space* appears contingent, it is not a permanent structure, fully realized, but a model used to create real, but circumscribed, discussion.

– ADRIAN BLACKWELL

BLACK KRONSTADT

"Its not my imagination, I've got a gun at my back!"

It was 1987 and I was fifteen years old. While the United States government was preparing to shoot down commercial airliners in the Persian Gulf and Israeli Defense Minister Yitzhak Rabin was slaughtering unarmed civilians in Palestine, I was listening to my first punk rock record, "Everything Went Black" by the L.A. based hardcore band Black Flag.

Being a working class kid living in a small logging town on the West Coast of Vancouver Island in British Columbia, Black Flag summed up my general outlook on life at the time. I hated school, hated work, the police pissed me off, and everyday existence with generally racist, ignorant red-necks drove me crazy. I needed an outlet.

I never thought of myself as a musician. I thought music was a highly specialized skill that only a "gifted" few could obtain. All that changed when I heard Black Flag. The crude sound of Greg Ginn bashing out three chords and strangling my eardrums with his non-conventional version of a "guitar solo" made me realize that, regardless of talent, anyone can pick up an instrument and express themselves. This sentiment was one of the great gifts punk gave to the working class youth of England, where the genre more or less originated. My confidence upped, I went out to find a guitar and amplifier.

After I'd equipped myself with some gear, I hitchhiked to Nanaimo in search of more punk rock records. There was a record store in a mall, I forget the name, where they stocked punk rock. The women at the counter said that she'd just received a record that I may be interested in, "but it's very noisy" she cautioned, and placed the disc on the turntable.

> "I am not he, nor master, nor lord, no crown to
> wear, no cross to bear in stations I am not he,
> nor shall be, warlord of nations …"

Eve Libertine's prophetic words, backed by sonic nuclear explosions, radiated anger and hatred towards religion, the status quo, and government. Crass sounded more serious and real than anything I'd ever heard before. They were angry and articulate. You could understand the reasons behind the anger and they offered solutions as well. When all was said and done, it was this band from the U.K. that changed my life forever. Black Flag may have encouraged me to pick up a guitar, but it was Crass that brought me to consciousness and introduced me to anarchism. I paid the five bucks and headed back home to put a band together.

I found three other misfits in town who wanted to play music and we started our first band, Contempt. Between smoking a lot of dope and drinking ourselves into oblivion, we managed to learn a few songs and started playing shows in the Ucluelet/Tofino area. We were the very first punk group from either of those towns and we paid the price by enduring regular beatings and general harassment from the local red-necks and police, but all of this simply justified our cause. We ordered classic anarchist literature through the local public library and, although it bored the shit out of us at times, began to arm ourselves with the history of anarchist struggles for a liberated world.

We watched closely what was happening in Oka, Quebec during the Oka crisis of 1990, when the Mohawk Nation took on the Canadian military. The impact was tremendous. Although we didn't really know the depth and complexity of the issues, we knew full well that the Mohawks were correct in their defense of their land. While local racists were driving around in their trucks looking for "chugs" to beat up, we stuck our necks out and supported the Mohawks. The City of Oka was illegally appropriating their land for a golf course? Give me a fucking break! The racists in Quebec really knew how to add insult to injury.

"Fuck the pigs. Fuck the pigs. Fuck the pigs."

I can still hear our wonderfully sophisticated attack on the local authorities blasting out across the gaping faces of a gathering of Ucluelet parents and elderly folks during the annual Christmas band concert at our local high school. How I had managed to convince Mr Stewart, the school's band teacher, to let us play I'll never know. Amidst a storm of thrown chairs and crude insults, the teachers yanked the plug on Contempt and banned us from their institution forever.

With our unbridled success we realized that Ucluelet was too small a place for an unruly punk rock band. In 1991, as George Bush was preparing to unleash Operation Desert Storm upon the unfortunate people of Iraq, we packed up our gear and headed to the nearest large urban centre, B.C.'s provincial capital, Victoria.

The "big city" proved too much for the small town boys of Contempt. In the small town our message and ideas had meaning, but in the city everything seemed more convoluted. Deep down we missed the simplicity and intimacy of our home town, where we knew what was what and who was who (or at least we thought we did). In Victoria, we were sucked into a punk scene saturated with drugs, alcohol, poverty, and depression.

Contempt split up in 1992 after playing about fifty shows and releasing two cassette tapes. It was our first experience with propagating dissident opinions as well as learning how to work collectively (which did not always go so well) while playing music together. Some members retreated to reclusive lives in various small towns on Vancouver Island, while others continued to play music in Victoria or Vancouver.

In 1993, I was homeless and squatting in a disused meat locker (Contempt's old practice space) that I shared with Dean, a new anarchist friend. Dean had recently moved to Victoria in order to escape the heroin-drenched depression of Vancouver's impoverished East End. From

liner notes from *Crimes of Capital / Crimes of the State*

the tiny speakers of a dumpstered portable radio, we listened intently to newscasts covering the FBI's all-out assault on a religious sect in Waco, Texas, known as the Branch Davidians. Twenty-three children and fifty-three adults were either shot to death or burned alive. It was the Salem witch trials all over again.

Dean was a different type of anarchist than I was used to. His politics were much more refined and rooted in the important political events of the second half of the twentieth century, such as the Soviet invasion of Afghanistan and Vietnam. While I had been reading anarchist texts from the nineteenth century, Dean was reading Noam Chomsky, Edward S. Herman, and Ward Churchill. He introduced me to the history of armed guerrilla groups such as Direct Action, the Red Army Fraction, Black Liberation Army, Weather Underground, etc. He was also much more up-to-date with what was happening in punk music. It was Dean who first played for me the driving crust sounds of Amebix, Nausea, Antisect, and Anti-Schism. Armed with his sharp wit, hatred of capitalism, and a bass guitar he proposed we start a new anarchist band. Since I was without a home, money, or any prospects for the future, I couldn't think of a better idea.

After a month or so of looking, vocalist Luke Puke and Dan Ware, the well-seasoned ex-drummer for Clusterfux, joined us. We vetoed the name Bludgeon, which I thought was "too metal" and finally decided, with the help of our friend Al, to call the band Black Kronstadt. The name memorialized the Kronstadt uprising that marked the end of anarchist insurgence during the Russian Revolution. In March, 1921 sailors on the Kronstadt Island naval fortress in the Gulf of Finland rose up against the Communist Party dictatorship. They declared Kronstadt a "free soviet" and appealed via radio for the people of Russia to join the revolt. The Communists responded by declaring marshal law in the major cities. They then bombarded Kronstadt with artillery rounds while thousands of soldiers were sent in waves to besiege the fortified city. After sixteen days the fortress fell and Lenin proudly proclaimed it "Red Kronstadt" as the blood of the rebels ran in the streets. Our band's name was a grim reminder of the treachery and deceit of Marxists during the Russian Revolution and throughout the twentieth century.

"The cycle of conquest perverts our daily lives,
there are those who don't want us to realize,
that alternatives exist if we can make the
change, the cages in our minds, to break down,
rearrange."
– Black Kronstadt, "Turning Point," 1992

People in Victoria either didn't know what to make of it or attacked us outright for having a "revolutionary" message. Vancouver, on the other hand, had a rich history of anarchist activity and welcomed us with open arms. We played with the great Vancouver anarchist bands of the day such as Peanut Gallery, Insult to Injury, The Dunderheads, Five Against One, and Submission Hold. In the summer of 1993 some Vancouver crust punks organized the last large scale anarchist gathering of the northwest coast for that decade. By juxtaposing workshops and lectures with punk shows by night, The Frenzy Anarchist Conference was a great success, attracting hundreds of people from all over Canada and the U.S. This event introduced us to the broader context of political punk. We met groups from various parts of North America including Destroy, Unamused, Naked Aggression, General Fools, and Shitfit, all of whom opened up windows to the international DIY anarchist underground, a network that Black Kronstadt eventually became a part of.

Black Kronstadt recorded their first record at Gary Brainless' studio the Rats Nest in the summer of 1993. It was a six-song seven-inch bearing the title *Crimes of Capital/ Crimes of the State*. We adorned the cover with a graphic from the Russian Revolution by the Latvian artist A. Apsit depicting the tyranny of the rich, the church, and the state. Without attaching too much importance to the record, this EP was the first out-and-out anarchist crust-punk release out of Victoria. It was 100 percent DIY, put out by our own label, Hierarkill Records. By participating in rent welfare scams and eating out of dumpsters, we were able to miraculously come up with enough money to press 1,000 records and produce a quite impressive "Crass-style" fold out sleeve. It was advertised in all of the anarchist journals and sold out within a few weeks. Although the record received great reviews from all of the outstanding anarcho-punk tabloids, Black Kronstadt was having serious internal problems; after the EP release, Luke and Dan decided to quit the band. Luke was more interested in the "old school" and "drunk-punk" scenes which were becoming very popular in the early '90s with bands like The Casualties. Dan was struggling with personal issues and wanted to move to the U.S.

After only a year and a half, Black Kronstadt was once again without a vocalist or drummer. At this point the Victoria scene was being swept up by a status quo, party-it-up ska scene. Needless to say it was difficult finding anyone who wanted to back anarchist politics and rant for social change. Six months later, when I had pretty much given up on Black Kronstadt, I was walking along a country road after a hard day's work at a local organic farm. A car stopped and I was offered a ride by young man named Dez who played drums and had heard that Black Kronstadt was looking for members.

Dez was a very relaxed person who provided the band line-up with some much needed stability. We were soon joined by Lorena on vocals. She wrote the lyrics to "Last Supper" and "News to You," two of Black Kronstadt's favourite class war songs. Lorena appears on two live tracks for an ALFSG tape released out of Victoria by Cory Pete, who also played bass guitar for Sub Genius and Sensory Crossover. Lorena left the band after six months and a young punk named Cliff, who'd been hanging around our neighbourhood, offered to replace her as our vocalist.

With the line up solidified we released our second seven-inch, *A World To Win* (taken from the title of an article in the B.C. anarchist journal, *Endless Struggle*), on Portland's Consensus Reality Records. This set the stage for our "Raze the System" marathon tour of the U.S. in the summer of 1995. We played approximately fifty dates and hit most of the country's major cities (as well as many not so major ones) in three months. This was the summer of the Gustafsen Lake standoff in British Columbia. Members of the Shuswap (Secwepemc) Nation set up a camp for a sun-dance ceremony at Gustafsen Lake, where they had been preforming the ceremony for centuries. However the land was now "owned" by a rancher who tried to force them to leave. The group refused and a stand-off began. This brought the issue of unceded territories (land that, by Canadian law, still belongs to Indigenous peoples) to the fore. The government sent in police and military personal to lay siege on the encampment. Things really heated up after a number of cops and military were killed by "friendly fire" during an ill-conceived assault on the camp. The stand-off finally ended with the Shuswaps' arrest and trial. Black Kronstadt spoke out consistently in support of the Shuswap during the tour and later wrote a song about Gustafsen Lake called "Paranoid Delusions."

Despite our car engine blowing up, encounters with U.S. neo-Nazis, and no money, the tour was a great success. We played with some of the best anarchist bands of the era, including Masskontrol, Assuck, Rice, Final Warning, 2.5 Children, Distraught, Aus Rotten, Defiance, Black Fork, Whorehouse of Representatives, Avail, State of Fear, Naked Aggression, Los Crudos, Propaghandi, I Spy, Swallowing Shit, Malefaction, Gojira, The Pist, Dystopia, and Detestation. We even played a few dates with the legendary U.K. anarchist band The Varukers.

The following winter Black Kronstadt added two new members, Danny playing second guitar and Nicki as accompanying vocalist. We also realized that if we were at all serious about promoting anarchist ideas and counter culture we had to expand our activities beyond the band. The result was Sabat!, the first anarchist-run books-and-records store in Victoria (at least to our knowledge). Sabat! filled in a gap left by a recently closed anarchist-run Activist Centre which had served as a resource centre and meeting space. Sabat! occupied a room in the back of John's Military Surplus in downtown Victoria (the owner, John Brown, was sympathetic to anarchism and provided us with the space free of charge). We formed a collective that soon outgrew the band, and filled the store with shelves of classic and contemporary anarchist literature, zines, journals, and music – all for sale at rock bottom prices. For the next three years Sabat! was an important cornerstone for the anarchist scene in the city. It was a positive project that built a sense of community.

When Black Kronstadt performed, we brought a good portion of the store with us. Our literature table created a different kind of atmosphere at local shows and one that people were not generally used to. As a result the anarcho-punk scene grew and our shows became larger-than-the-band events. Other great political bands formed in Victoria: War Without End, Jonas, Deadset, Patriotic Filth, Hiroshima 8/16, and Third World Planet. In the nearby city of Nanaimo the anarchist punk scene also thrived – Ninth Hour, Dementia, Ultra Vires, Sub Genius, Disaster Area, Plastic, and Offal Consumption – formed there. Bands were touring up and down Vancouver Island and better-known punk bands such as Defiance, Phobia, Assuck, Detestation, and His Hero is Gone started making Victoria a regular destination.

> "Fight the power, it's self defense!"
> – *Black Kronstadt*, "N.A.S.T.A.," 1995

Black Kronstadt toured the west coast of the U.S. in 1996 and recorded five new songs at Smegma Studios in Portland, Oregon. The songs were meant to be the first part of an LP scheduled for release by Mind Kontrol records out of Texas later that year. However, the group disbanded after the first round of recording, and the record was left unfinished. Our one and only LP, *The Free Spirit*, eventually came out about a year later using previously recorded tracks from 1995, as well as the Smegma tracks.

Although Black Kronstadt was only around for four years we did put Victoria on the anarcho-punk map. Our records got plenty of attention and respect – they're still in circulation worldwide. More importantly, we helped energize the anarchist scene in British Columbia and I am sure there are plenty of anarchists who would trace the beginnings of their radicalism to a Black Kronstadt performance.

— WOLF EDWARDS

G7 Welcoming Committee

G7 Welcoming Committee Records was begun in 1996 by members of the Winnipeg-based band Propagandhi and established itself on the second floor of Winnipeg's A-Zone building, where Mondragon Books is located. The founding of this collectively owned and organized rogue media outlet was inspired in equal parts by a constructive interest in anarchism (particularly ParEcon [participatory economics], a value-driven, as opposed to profit-driven, proposal for organizing human relations) and to counter the tendency of established, sustainable "punk" record labels to proclaim themselves "alternative" while embracing typically authoritarian, top-down workplace structures.

The aims were two-fold:

1. To provide an example of a functioning, sustainable, *visible* non-hierarchical, anarchist workplace.

2. To provide anarchist/anticapitalist/antiauthoritarian artists/activists/musicians with a supportive, dependable record label whose behaviour both internally and externally, would not contradict the radically progressive messages of their own words and actions. And vice versa.

With many successes and a handful of failures on both these counts, G7 Records has been home to an eclectic roster of domestic and international artists/ activists. Releases have ranged from hardcore punk to ambient spoken word, from fusion/urban grooves to bewilderingly extreme metal. Despite years working within the imposed framework of a profit-driven economy (where "indie" music is more often than not more about street-cred than radical vision) and a music industry whose mandate is to co-opt and water-down anything meaningful so as to make it commercially viable, G7 *still* believes in music's power to engage, compel, enrich, stir, effect, describe and undo. We carry on....

– G7 Welcoming Committee Collective

Transcription, Editing and Introduction by Glynis Sherwood

Lizzie Borden, a New York filmmaker, visited Toronto in September 1986 when her film, Working Girls, an empathetic portrayal of prostitution as an economic choice, premiered at the annual Festival of Festivals. Working Girls is Lizzie Borden's second full-length feature movie. Her first film, Born in Flames, depicts a futuristic scenario where a variety of feminist groups, from underground radio stations to anti-rape squads, to a Women's Army, attempt to revolutionize society along radical feminist lines. KIO collective members, Alexandra Devon and Catherine Tammaro, interviewed Lizzie Borden during her stay in Toronto.

Lizzie Borden has adopted a strong anti-censorship stance which is critical of the anti-pornography movement. Her position illustrates the divisions in the feminist movement in response to both the negative images of women conveyed by mainstream pornography and the overwhelming ability of the state to silence artistic expression. The KIO collective, while abhorring government interference in any area of life, including censorship, also acknowledges many of the arguments and analysis put forward by the anti-pornography movement. The goal should be not to enhance differences by siding with any particular "camp", but to find ways of dealing with and eradicating misogny, in any form, while rejecting censorship so that we may be free to create our own images as feminist filmmakers such as Lizzie Borden have begun to do.

Alexandra Devon: Tell us how you came to your current views on prostitution.

Lizzie Borden: My interest in prostitution and my coming to a totally different opinion about it [occurred when] I began to meet women who really "worked". I had mixed feelings about the anti-pornography movement from the beginning because it seemed too moralistic and a little too contemptuous of imagery without seeing how it worked. Also, there was a holy attitude that I objected to. But when I started to meet women who actually "worked" I began to see that it was wrong to see them as victimized or degraded. The more women I met, and the more houses I visited -- it was mostly brothels that I visited because those were the women I met -- the more I realized that they did not fit into the stereotype I had of working girls. They didn't wear short skirts or stiletto heels, they looked like any of us and they worked in houses and they chose to do it for many, many reasons.

There was a lot of controversy when **Not A Love Story** came out[1] in the States, and I actually was very critical of that film because I felt that what it did was make women who worked in the sex industry feel as if they were doing something wrong. There are a lot of women who are victimized by prostitution obviously: for example, an under-aged girl arriving at Grand Central Station caught up by a pimp and put out into the street is victimized. However that comprises only a small percentage of women who work as prostitutes.

When **Not A Love Story** came out with that back to nature mentality -- you know Tracy Lee cavorting along the beach at the end of the film and everything is back to normal -- the idea of an awakening to a choice was one thing, but a lot of women have chosen to work as prostitutes. For me it's an economic choice in this culture, where work is so abominable most of the time. To choose to work two to three shifts a week as a prostitute and make the same money or more as working a forty or fifty hour work week, where the work is demeaning, exhausting, not necessarily in somebody's field of passion so that it's morally dispiriting, is a real choice. Obviously in a future society where we would rethink the work ethic maybe there's a way that not only prostitution won't exist, but people can choose to work at the things they want to work at. Basically, my film **Working Girls** is about the idea of a woman choosing prostitution as an economic choice and not being pushed into it. She doesn't have a daddy problem, she doesn't have any psychological problems, she doesn't hate men, she doesn't have any axe to grind, in terms of doing it, except for the fact that she wants her own time. The other thing that I found too is that there are some prostitutes who love their work, there are others who tolerate it, but it's not that it's hurting them tremendously.

There aren't many women -- there are some but no more than the ordinary woman in the streets -- who get raped, attacked and hurt. Prostitutes are more visible in the streets so the percentage of rapes and attacks is relatively higher. But what practically every movie about prostitutes makes us think is that a hooker is a walking target, and there are so many prostitutes hurt by the end of these movies that you think it's the unsafest profession in the world. Women are smarter than that. There are a lot of safety mechanisms involved. What I found out about brothels is that there were safety mechanisms against violence in many forms from "Johns", but also from the police. There was a direct line to the police station in case somebody problematic came in. Say a customer had a gun or something, then they could buzz the police station. These women couldn't get arrested because they weren't calling the vice cops. There were also health protections. A lot of the women who "work" are healthier than most ordinary women, they're more educated about their bodies.

The major problem I saw was a bit of schizophrenia, if anything. You know just that sense of being touched/not being touched, having a sense where you have to do work and somehow cut your body off from feeling. There was an incredible labyrinth-like ability of these women to have another working name and then, when they leave work, become themselves again. Some of them had really decent relationships with lovers, male or female. Some of them had problems of course but who doesn't in this culture. Also I found that in a brothel a lot of the codes and rituals reproduce what we see in heterosexual social codes and rituals in places other than in a brothel, like singles bars. Any kind of a job that a woman has where she services mostly men has many, many parallels to prostitution. Waitressing, being a stewardess, being a PR person, working on many levels , like in the music industry, you have to service men. A lot of the exchanges I thought were really similar. For instance, "Would you like to sit down, make yourself comfortable, can I get you something to drink," etc. That was shocking to me in a way when I first saw the parallel.

When I finished this film, a feminist came up to me and said, "How can you do this, this is very anti-feminist, your stance is anti-feminist." People saying you are making an apology for prostitution, refusing to see it as an equivalent exchange. What I tried to do in **Working Girls** was to show that Molly, the lead character, or the other women, but especially Molly because we follow her throughout the whole day, is not exploited by the men. It's an even exchange, and there's a lot of humour and even some compassion back and forth. She knows what she's getting, she wants money, she'll be able, during that hour or half-hour, to do her job as well or not as well as she can. She has a commodity so she can choose the conditions, the framework, who she sees, who she doesn't see, the amount of involvement -- all of that. Because she has that to rent, not to sell, it's an even exchange.

Who I did find was the enemy was the Madam, just as a pimp would be the enemy because of the profiting off the bodies of the workers. So it ends up being like a regular employment situation. I didn't see it as that much different, always trying to get the most work for the least return. Of course, the girls in the house try to redress that imbalance by ripping off the Madam -- not counting their sessions, not writing down the right number of hours, etc.

AD: How did you become a feminist?

LB: Around 1972, I got really interested in what could be said to be the beginnings of radical feminism. It just brought everything together for me. Somehow the whole Vietnam thing was so male oriented, and a lot of the issues were about men. The women's movement brought things together in such a vital way that I was able to start to see parallels in almost every other political situation, from anti-war movements to libertarian struggles in other countries, all of that, but through the viewpoint of feminism.

At that point I was a painter and an art critic, when I first came to New York, and then realized that I didn't like the visual and the verbal so separated. I was really jealous of people making films. I would see people making films, like Goddard, and think, "I'm really jealous of this." So then I thought, "OK, I should be making films if I'm responding this way." So I taught myself everything. I just decided that I'd had too much of school -- school had destroyed art for me, really. I knew too much about it. I didn't want to learn anything about film other than what I needed to know -- to shoot, do sound and edit. I loved editing, it's so much like writing, and I became good at it so that I was able to support myself as a film editor -- usually small films and documentaries.

Making a film was a way to get involved politically. I never was involved in consciousness-raising groups. Somehow making a film itself was a political process for me. **Born In Flames** came out of a lot of the inequalities I saw when I came to New York. Also, the alternative movements -- the gay movement, the women's' movement -- were very divided and reproduced the divisions of the dominant culture. For example, Black women were still very isolated from white women, who were very isolated from Latin and Asian women, who were invisible. So that was one of the things I was interested in doing **Born In Flames** about. I began to be involved with Black women for the purpose of making the film. I wanted to construct a paradigm that I didn't see happening in the culture. For me, film is a political exploration. I'm totally not involved politically except in so far as I make films. I mean I don't go to meetings, I don't go to anything! But the films are a way to have a reason to be involved. The film about prostitution is the same thing. That, as opposed to being overtly political, it is, in fact, still a very political film because it is asserting a position. Every time you assert a position it has to be somehow standing against some dominant position you see or somehow trying to present another way in. I don't know why, I think I felt that I could be more influential or helpful or make a stronger statement by making a film. I'm really bad at meetings, I'm bad at panels, my brain stops working. Although I sign petitions, I may have gone to maybe one march in my life. Sometimes I feel guilty, I go "maybe I'm not politically involved enough". But making films is all about exploring an issue that I find absolutely fascinating and difficult. That's my way to motivate myself, to start to do research and explore it, and I put myself totally within it. In **Born In Flames** I was totally within the framework of what it's about. The women involved in it were who they really were. By doing the film I learned a lot. I always want to do a film about something I know nothing about and use that process to educate myself. So that to me is my main reason.

Catherine Tammaro: I wanted to ask you a couple of questions about your visual concerns in the film **Born In Flames**.

photo by Bill Banning

Anarcha-Filmmaker:

An interview with Lizzie Borden

Kick It Over 18 (1987)

2

FILM & VIDEO

I'm a painter myself, and you mentioned that you started out as a painter and then gave it up to make film. What were your visual concerns in that film, and do you feel that they were well carried through or well represented? Were you perhaps making a political statement by the visual sparseness of the film?

LB: Born In Flames was a response to having very little money. The film was done for no more than $40,000 and no less than $30,000 over a period of four or five years. I couldn't pay people very much, and I had to do it over a long period of time, so my aesthetic had to be about grabbing images, and getting them without worrying about a well-defined aesthetic which would combine everything. Starting from an aesthetic of "cheapness" I then had to develop a kind of visual aesthetic which I decided was going to be montage[2]. I decided that I would not worry about what each individual looked like, but really try to create an energy about the juxtaposition of images. I couldn't worry that people gained and lost twenty pounds from one six month period to another, or that they shaved their heads or did strange things. I had to somehow manage to bind together a lot of images without having people worry too much about that. The structure of it also reproduced a lot of political ideas that were at the bottom of **Born In Flames**. I couldn't have an aesthetic unity based on consistent lighting, continuity and all of that because that wasn't what the film was about.

by Robyn Turney

It was so much about discontinuity and dysfunction. It was about different groups somehow coming together and the explosion of when that happened. I thought much more about diagonals, as opposed to horizontals or verticals or anything that would lead to continuity of visual experience.

You try to make virtues out of your problems, and with **Born In Flames** I really tried to do that. It would have been impossible otherwise, because so much of the film was constructed in the editing. I would get a piece of something where there was no script to start with. So much of it was trying to be open to what the ideas of these women I was working with.

In **Working Girls** I had to have a completely different visual aesthetic. I had $100,000 for production, and that in itself is not very much. But when I decided I was going to make the film all take place in one day I knew that I had to have a very good looking image that was very controlled, otherwise people would get tired of looking at it. I couldn't use any kind of wild editing really. It actually surprises me sometimes because people say, "Oh

my god, **Working Girls** doesn't look anything like **Born In Flames**, like shock." But each idea has its own needs. Wild shooting would have been too subjective. **Born In Flames** is all about subjectivity, really. With **Born In Flames**, what seemed to me interesting was to try to get something very raw whether or not people really believed in it as actors or not. They were never intended to be actors. But they were almost playing out their fantasies of the characters, somewhere between who they were and who they fantasized themselves as being. In **Working Girls** it was strictly actors. I was really lucky to get Louise Smith who played the lead role of Molly because she had to do a lot of very hard work. In fact we did a week and a half of bedroom scenes and she really felt like a hooker. By the end she did everything. She is a nice Catholic girl who'd never been in a film and had never taken her clothes off before. But she was so willing to stretch herself to the experience. What was interesting to me in dealing with actors was overcoming their prejudices of what "working" girls were. They came to rehearsals in stilettos and I made them all go to the real place that the film was based

on and apply for a job so they could see what the girls who really worked there looked like, what the Madam was like, and they changed their opinion.

The reason I didn't want to do a documentary was that I felt that I would deal with a lot of restrictions, and I also wanted to go into the bedroom and demystify the sex that happens in that prostitute/"John" relationship -- I couldn't have done that in a documentary. I did a lot of research and forged ahead. A friend of mine worked in a particular brothel on 24th Street and I went in there with a tape recorder and took notes, and met women and even clients. They weren't defensive since I wasn't going to use them -- their images. I was going to base characters on them and then spend a lot of time writing the script.

AD: I've heard in number of articles you described as an anarcha-feminist. Are you in fact an anarcha-feminist? Is this a label people have put on you? Are you comfortable with it?

LB: I'm comfortable with it by process of elimination because I never quite figured out what it is, but I feel closer to it than any other political identification. I'm so critical of any kind of organized left wing just because of bureaucracy really becoming another class, and the relationship of women to whatever organized left there is. So the idea of anarchism has always

appealed to me simply because it's always calling into question that which is. I somehow see anarchism as that. I see it as not necessarily excluding different political identifications. For example, on one issue it might be possible to side with a socialist stance, on another issue a very Western stance. But the thing about anarchism is that it allows you not to have to be over-programmed. The other thing is about feminists. What gets me now is people saying that they're not feminist anymore. Feminism is such a mild word for how I consider myself, that I'm absolutely a feminist. Anarcha-feminism to me has always been about stirring things up. You try to constantly ask those questions which will prevent stasis from setting in. Even at the expense of sometimes being seen as contradictory or saying things that go against what you said a year before or a minute before. For me it's a process. We all know what's wrong with Western capitalism and we all know what's wrong

with the extreme left, so anarcha-feminism -- it just seems to be the only viable identification, if one is to identify at all.

AD: Would you tell us some of the problems you've had with your films getting censored.

LB: When **Born In Flames** came out I went through this big thing with the [Ontario] Censor Board. The same thing occurred with my "dick shots" in **Working Girls**. This year it's been pretty outrageous because the film was appealed, then they decided I had to make one cut. Since I had to make that cut for American distribution, I said alright. As it turns out, I just put tape over that scene. But in a way the controversy about the censorship of my film made it possible for the Andy Warhol film, which has twenty-eight minutes of a blow job, to just breeze right through. That I resent tremendously.

But the irony is that censorship by the economic market is just as strong. No distributor is going to take my film unless I cut that scene out. They say, "Fine, you can have that shot in your film but we're just not going to distribute it." And if it doesn't get distributed it doesn't get seen. So, in fact, that's a form of censorship as well. I feel that a lot of feminist issues get cut down in the market place. It's fine to deal with certain issues and people say, "Sure, go right ahead." But it's harder to get grants, it's harder to get the film seen and you get torn apart totally. It's something which I feel is highly contradictory and does end up being a form of censorship. Here in Canada at least it's overt, you know what your fighting against, which is the only advantage. Still it's hard because it means nobody can see things.

In the US, there is at least a chance, you know what the situation is. You can always put something up and have some people come to see it.

AD: What were you trying to say about feminism in **Born in Flames**?

LB: One of the points of **Born In Flames** was about "feminisms" -- the plural rather than the singular. That's been the problem of some political movements and feminism too -- the idea that you have to codify a platform. There are a million feminisms, there are a million types of different women who consider themselves feminists but don't have the same agenda. The idea of plurality as opposed to democracy is something that is really, really difficult. Especially where there's this

myth in America, and probably in Canada too, of the melting pot. To melt together, to become uniform, to agree on a platform. It will never exist and there's no reason to have it exist. In fact, one of the issues, in terms of race, is how do you allow, encourage, appreciate racial autonomy with all of its distinctions, and at the same time not discriminate because of all those things? How do you allow people to not feel that they have to conform to a white feminist program? One of the things about **Born In Flames** was that each of the different sub groups, the Black underground radio station, the white underground radio station worked together without losing their autonomy. For me it seems really important to make those links. That was also a response to a lot of NOW[3] platforms. **NOW** was afraid to have lesbians work with them. They were afraid to have this group and that group because of one national image that they were promoting, which I thought was highly damaging and still is.

Now all of a sudden everything has wound up in the women against pornography movement, at least until a few years ago. It ends up being an issue that people have to feel one way on. Then there's a lot of hatred against the women who try to have another viewpoint. So that the Andrea Dworkin[4] types are totally against the women who are saying, "Hey look we don't want to be censored." Then there's the women who are much more exploratory in terms of sexual practice. It ends up tearing everything apart -- which is great -- the media loves it! It allows potent movements to be so diffused that nothing can happen. That's scary!

CT: I wanted to ask you a question about the white radio station in **Born In Flames**. It's a different topic but appropriate in terms of a wider vision of anarcha-feminism. Adele (the disk jockey) makes a statement about the return of a female prophet, about a spirit. What are your feelings on spirituality and how they fit in with a unified vision of anarcha-feminism?

LB: I don't think there is any fitting into a unified vision of anarcha-feminism. That character, the female prophet, she's very much like that in any case, as a representative of a kind of artist/poet type. What generates a lot of poetry is some kind of a connection to notions of spirit. It's not a political notion so much as an artistic one. She's somebody who very consciously within the film kept saying something different. She was identified first with Arabs and she had a headdress on. Then she had corn rows, and then it was reggae stuff, and then it was rock. So it was all about that kind of shifting identification which is very suspect. I wanted her to not be this person you could totally identify with, but somebody who was hopping all over the spectrum of what was possible. To deal with some of the ideas, because that's in fact how people learn and how people grow within any sort of artistic imagination. Her sources would have been very different from the Black underground woman whose source would be much more a sort of local oppression, a certain kind of way of seeing. Her speeches came a lot from Malcolm X[5] but transposed to feminism, whereas Adele, the artist/poet, was all over the place. It was all about music too, and what music generated and the kind of poetry that spontaneously comes out of life's events. So, in fact, Adele was very anarchist because her response to everything was totally spontaneous. It was, "I feel like saying this, and I feel like saying it right now.".

I personally have been such an atheist all my life that I have no views on spiritual stuff, except in so far as passion is spiritual, or the need to make something is spiritual, and the need to come together is spiritual. Spiritual in that there is a collective body of feeling that ends up being bigger than the sum of its parts. Not that there's an external goal -- I don't believe in "The Goddess", I don't believe in any of those things, because I never have. I've never had a God that I had to shift to Goddess. But I think spirit is about a sense of something greater, and that greater can be what gives you the courage to keep fighting in the face of a lot of cynicism. So, for me, that's the only spiritual knowledge or feeling of passion I have, which is transcendence of a current situation and hope. It's the hope that sends a spark when you do come together with other people. There is a sense of power. So spirituality is that kind of power, not power over but power to transform. That's a magical feeling in a way. But you also

know it as an artist. When you're writing, you have an idea and every little bit of your being tingles. That feeling can also be expanded to larger things. Even seeing those anti-rape marches with everyone with candles -- there's something so extraordinary.

For me spirituality is also about aesthetics. There is something of beauty that has to transcend the ugliness and sense of despair that you see. That's why at the end of **Born In Flames**, Adele says this thing about turning shit into gold, which is her own formulation. She's a wacky person, she's so much playing herself in that film and she wrote her own stuff. One of the things I liked to do with people was to have them, well some of them, say what they wanted to. So Adele would come one day dressed one way and speaking one thing. That's the way that kind of person is. She reminded me of a lot of artists that I knew. There is a "devil-may-care" and even what one may call political irresponsibility on the part of the artist. I'm attracted to that, on the one hand, because a more considered, responsible position can sometimes be more solid but it can also be a drag. I saw that element in the women's movement. One can become a prisoner of logic.

One of the reasons I decided to concentrate on work was that, as I said before, so much of the work in this culture is spiritually draining. It flattens you out, there is no spirit. You give time for so little return that it's horrifying. That diminishment of spirit is something which I was concerned about. That's a point that I wanted to make in **Working Girls**. There were a lot of things I know that I wanted to have read through without necessarily having one statement. One of my ideas in terms of making the film was that of choice. Sometimes, time to develop yourself is more important than whatever the culture may think of you renting your body for sex, if you can make so much more money that way. I really think that it's a choice in this culture. It's something that people just can't have a ready moral judgment about. What happens is that the moral judgments are handed down. What is extremely dangerous is for any woman to have the scarlet "A" on her who has happened to work as a prostitute for any length of time -- for six months, for six years, for her life. To be seen as a fallen or degraded person or woman is a horror. That has to be revised, simply because for others to decide who is degraded and who isn't is really hard.

When people ask me why **Working Girls** is feminist, my feeling is that

women have to control our images and prostitution, too. If prostitution exists in this culture -- and it has existed and probably will exist for a very long time -- we can't just say it's bad, that it's feeding into the male trip of power over women. If it exists, we as women cannot only control the images of prostitution, but all of the works about it -- for example, movies. If women in prostitution can be seen as not necessarily victims, or if, in fact, some of them can be allowed in this culture to achieve a position of strength, it can only help. It's a feminist position, women being powerful in any area is feminist. Even within prostitution, if one can say 3,000 years from now hopefully there will be no prostitution that's great, we all hope that. As long as it's here we need to deal with those images a little bit differently. I'm just so tired of some of these movies -- high class call girls or street hookers who are addicts. There's a million kinds of prostitution just like there a million kinds of feminism. But what happens is that the media makes it look like there's one kind, one judgment upon it, and that's simply not true. We don't deal with one kind of businessman or one kind of secretary.

LB: Anyone who knows women who "work" would have a different opinion than mainstream portrayals of prostitution. Men who have gone to prostitutes have a different opinion. It's the people who have never had any experience that buy into pictures of prostitutes in the media, which is a little much.

AD: What is next for you?

LB: I have a lot of ideas but it's hard to talk about it right now because I just finished **Working Girls** for the Cannes Festival[6] in May and haven't had a lot of time to evolve other ideas. I've been writing -- I'm a slow writer. I always like to go into areas of the forbidden, so it will be something -- I'm not sure.

At this point too I think that what happens is the more films I make, and the more expensive they become, the more I start to see what a financially restricting position I am in. You can't get grants that will allow you to make films. You have to deal with ideas that can be a little bit commercial, but I don't want to deal with things only on the basis of commercialism. You start to wonder how practical it can be to make films.

I would also not be adverse to working on someone else's script if I got a script that was interesting, just because with the last two films I've either written them in the editing room or, as with **Working Girls**, written the scripts myself. I do have

some ideas. One is about a reform school, the other is about a Black jazz musician who discovers a cure for drug addiction. There's these different ideas. The drug addiction/jazz musician one is about a two million dollar movie -- God knows where I could get that money.

The reform school one, actually written by Adele who plays the punk in **Born In Flames**, is based on her experiences in reform school. It might be a reform school musical. That's another example of stereotyping too -- reform school movies are usually horrible, they're real snake pits. Even the Miles Edderling film **Scrubbers** that everybody loves, I really didn't like. Adele was moaning on the floor saying, "It's not like that." So these things are being written, and in some cases I'm helping with an overall plot and somebody else is writing it, or I'm co-writing it.

The other idea I have is the exploration of the sexual relationship of two people over the age of fifty-five because nobody ever sees sex between older people. I'm interested in all these things, but which happens first is so much a question of financing at this point. I'll never not make movies; if I have to I'll go back to the **Born In Flames** way which is to shoot once a month. You begin to learn that there are ways of getting movies made and it's based a lot on scripts and who you go to. **Working Girls** should make it easier. So one of these will be next. Hopefully not too many years in the future. □

NOTES

1.   Not A Love Story, a Canadian-made film, circa 1982, is both an expose and condemnation of pornography and the sex industry as a form of degradation and violence against women.

2.   A "montage" is the combination of elements of different photographic pictures.

3.   NOW (the National Organization for Women) is a powerful US womens' lobby group with a membership comprised of millions.

4.   Andrea Dworkin is the author of many radical feminist works, including the well-known Minneapolis anti-pornography legislation which was adopted then repealed recently in that American city.

5.   Malcolm X was a Black nationalist orator who was something of a competitor in the early 60's with Dr. Martin Luther King (unlike King, he advocated liberation "by any means necessary"). His assassination in 1965 is believed to have been carried out by agents of the police or by former Black Muslim associates.

6.   The Cannes Film Festival is an annual mega-event held in France, which premieres, and grants awards to, big budget mainstream films, and occasionally alternative films, primarily from Europe and North America.

WORK

Work *(1999) 11 minutes, video, colour*

director: Kika Thorne
soundtrack: Peaches
starring: Shary Boyle
also featuring: Nancy van Keerbergen, Shelton Ramsey
Deveral, Ronda Bean, Louise Liliefeldt, Simeron Heath
art director: Adrian Blackwell
camera: Daniel Borins
sound: Chris Johannsen
editors: Julie Robinson, Andrew Bee

*distributor: V-Tape (*vtape.org*)*

Work, with its circuitous demands, leaves us little room for anything else, and so the work of love, the work of play, art and invention, the manufacture of intensities, is often pushed for time.

When X gets fired from her day job, the work begins. An unsettling form of emancipation, the firing is what delivers X back to the world, to us, to trade stories, sing and ride bicycles, to make out and make art.

The video *Work*, starring realtime artist Shary Boyle, with a soundtrack by Peaches, is a digital split-screen with ten scenes, each a minute long. The ten minutes describe an allegorical day-in-the-life and as a generic cycle, points to the work one does, to make the work one loves to do.

That she gets fired early in the day means she has more time to herself for the rest of the movie. After the initial blast of despondency: red couch, red pajamas, the heavy minimalist metal of Feedom, (a side project by Peaches, Chilly Gonzales, and Taylor Saavy), the effect is a story of freedom, of finding freedom in unlikely modalities.

Current working conditions for youth, for most of us, in a neo-liberal, union busted, temporary flexible economy, confounds worker solidarity, and has all but eliminated the concept of job security. But in the traversal of this labourscape, one finds a wrinkle in time. And as we siphon hours away from the non-sequitur of drudgework to bring ourselves back into the picture – make meaning, deepen friendships, construct community, flirt with cashiers, – we produce multiple nodes of resistance, we become revolutionaries of the instant, no! instant revolutions.

– KIKA THORNE

Immediatism

by Hakim Bey

All experience is mediated--by the mechanisms of sense perception, mentation, language, etc.--& certainly all art consists of some further mediation of experience.

However, mediation takes place by degrees. Some experiences (smell, taste, sexual pleasure, etc.) are less mediated than others (reading a book, looking through a telescope, listening to a record). Some media, especially ``live'' arts such as dance, theater, musical or bardic performance, are less mediated than others such as TV, CDs, Virtual Reality. Even among the media usually called ``media,'' some are more & others are less mediated, according to the intensity of imaginative participation they demand. Print & radio demand more of the imagination, film less, TV even less, VR the least of all--so far.

For art, the intervention of Capital always signals a further degree of mediation. To say that art is commodified is to say that a mediation, or standing-in-between, has occurred, & that this betweenness amounts to a split, & that this split amounts to ``alienation.'' Improv music played by friends at home is less ``alienated'' than music played ``live'' at the Met, or music played through media (whether PBS or MTV or Walkman). In fact, an argument could be made that music distributed free or at cost on cassette via mail is LESS alienated than live music played at some huge We Are The World spectacle or Las Vegas niteclub, even though the latter is live music played to a live audience (or at least so it appears), while the former is recorded music consumed by distant & even anonymous listeners.

The tendency of Hi Tech, & the tendency of Late Capitalism, both impel the arts farther & farther into extreme forms of mediation. Both widen the gulf between the production & consumption of art , with a corresponding increase in ``alienation.''

With the disappearance of a ``mainstream'' & therefore of an ``avant-garde'' in the arts, it has been noticed that all the more advanced & intense art-experiences have been recuperable almost instantly by the media, & thus are rendered into trash like all other trash in the ghostly world of commodities. ``Trash, '' as the term was redefined in, let's say, Baltimore in the 1970s, can be good fun--as an ironic take on a sort of inadvertent folkultur that surrounds & pervades the more unconscious regions of ``popular'' sensibility--which in turn is produced in part by the Spectacle. ``Trash'' was once a fresh concept, with radical potential.

By now, however, amidst the ruins of Post-Modernism, it has finally begun to stink. Ironic frivolity finally becomes disgusting. Is it possible now to BE SERIOUS BUT NOT SOBER? (Note: The New Sobriety is or course simply the flipside of the New Frivolity. Chic neo-puritanism carries the taint of Reaction, in just the same way that postm odernist philosophical irony & despair lead to Reaction. The Purge Society is the same as the Binge Society. After the ``12 steps'' of trendy renunciation in the ' 90s, all that remains is the 13th step of the gallows. Irony may have become boring, but self-mutilation was never more than an abyss. Down with frivolity--Down with sobriety.)

Everything delicate & beautiful, from Surrealism to Break-dancing, ends up as fodder for McDeath's ads; 15 minutes later all the magic has been sucked out, & the art itself d ead as a dried locust. The media-wizards, who are nothing if not postmodernists, have even begun to feed on the vitality of ``Trash,'' like vultures regurgitating & re-consuming the same carrion, in an obscene ecstasy of self-referentiality. Which way to the Egress?

Real art is play, & play is one of the most immediate of all experiences. Those who have cultivated the pleasure of play cannot be expected to give it up simply to make a political point (as in an ``Art Strike, '' or ``the suppression without the realization'' of art, etc.). Art will go on, in somewhat the same sense that breathing, eating, or fucking will go on.

Nevertheless, we are repelled by the extreme alienation of the arts, especially in ``the media,'' in commercial publishing & galleries, in the recording ``industry,'' etc. And we sometimes worry even about the extent to which our very involvement in such arts as writing, painting, or music implicates us in a nasty abstraction, a removal from immediate experience. We miss the directness of p lay (our original kick in doing art in the first place); we miss smell, taste, touch, the feel of bodies in motion.

Computers, video, radio, printing presses, synthesizers, fax machines, tape recorders, photocopiers--these things make good toys, but terrible addictions. Finally we realize we cannot `` reach out and touch someone'' who is not present in the flesh. These media may be useful to our art--but they must not possess us, nor must they stand between, mediate, or separate us from our animal/animate selves. We want to control our media, not be Controlled by them. And we should like to remember a certain psychic martial art which stresses the realization that the body itself is the least mediated of all media.

Therefore, as artists & ``cultural workers'' who have no intention of giving up activity in our chosen media, we nevertheless demand of ourselves an extreme awareness of immediacy , as well as the mastery of some direct means of implementing this awareness as play, immediately (at once) & immediately (without mediation).

Fully realizing that any art ``manifesto'' written today can only stink of the same bitter irony it seeks to oppose, we nevertheless declare without hesitation (without too much thought) the founding of a ``movement,'' IMMEDIATISM. We feel free to do so becaus e we intend to practice Immediatism in secret, in order to avoid any contamination of mediation. Publicly we'll continue our work in publishing, radio, printing, music, etc., but privately we will create something else, someth ing to be shared freely but never consumed passively, something which can be discussed openly but never understood by the agents of alienation, something with no commercial potential yet valuable beyond price, something occult yet woven completely into the fabric of our everyday lives.

Immediatism is not a movement in the sense of an aesthetic program. It depends on situation, not style or content, message or School. It may take the form of any kind of creative play which can be performed by two or more people, by & for themselves, face-to-

5

Anarchives 3/I (1996)

face & together. In this sense it is like a game, & therefore certain ``rules '' may apply.

All spectators must also be performers. All expenses are to be shared, & all products which may result from the play are also to be shared by the participants only (who may keep them or bestow them as gifts, but should not sell them). The best games will m ake little or no use of obvious forms of mediation such as photography, recording, printing, etc., but will tend toward immediate techniques involving physical presence, direct communication, & the senses.

An obvious matrix for Immediatism is the party. Thus a good meal could be an Immediatist art project, especially if everyone present cooked as well as ate. Ancient Chinese & Japanese on misty autumn days would hold odor parties, where each guest would bring a homemade incense or perfume. At linked-verse parties a faulty couplet would entail the penalty of a glass of wine. Quilting bees, tableaux vivants, exquisite corpses, rituals of conviviality like Fourier's ``Museum Orgy'' (erotic costumes, poses, & skits), live music & dance--the past can be ransacked for appropriate forms, & imagination will supply more.

The difference between a 19th century quilting bee, for example, & an Immediatist quilting bee would lie in our awareness of the practice of Immediatism as a response to the sorrows of alienation & the `` death of art.''

The mail art of the '70s & the zine scene of the '80s were attempts to go beyond the mediatio n of art-as-commodity, & may be considered ancestors of Immediatism. However, they preserved the mediated structures of postal communication & xerography, & thus failed to overcome the isolation of the players, who remained quite literally out of touch. We wish to take the motives & discoveries of these earlier movements to their logical conclusion in an art which banishes all mediation & alienation, at least to the extent that the human condition allows.

Moreover, Immediatism is not condemned to powerlessness in the world, simply because it avoids the publicity of the marketplace. ``Poetic Terrorism'' and ``Art Sabotage'' are quite logical manifestations of Immediatism.

Finally, we expect that the practice of Immediatism will release within us vast storehouses of forgotten power, which will not only transform our lives through the secret realization of unmediated play, but will also inescapably well up & burst out & perme ate the other art we create, the more public & mediated art.

And we hope that the two will grow closer & closer, & eventually perhaps become one.

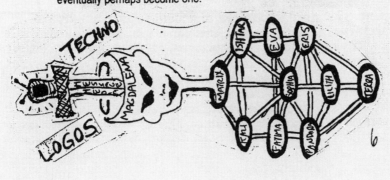

LIVING THEATRE

An interview conducted this winter [1979] in Dublin, Ireland, with three anarchist players – Julian Beck, Judith Malina and Ilian – who have helped bring revolutionary drama to the theatres and streets of North America and Europe since the early 1950s . . .

OR: *You left North America three years ago, and have only recently begun performing again on stage. What have you been doing in the interim?*

JULIAN: Now we're in a much more active street theatre phase, performing not only in the streets but in elementary schools and high schools, not only at the factory gates but inside the factories, in gymnasiums, skating rinks, sports palaces, mental hospitals and again and again and again in the big piazzas. But the significant change that took place in the organization of our work here was that we began to work more and more with activist groups and this had particular significance in, for instance, Spain, where we spent several months in 1977, and in Italy, where we have done the greater part of our work since we've been back in Europe. With anarchist groups and sometimes also with anarchist pacifist groups and sometimes simply with pacifist groups. In Germany too, I should add, because we did several weeks in Frankfurt, organized by the Spontis, and people working in Frankfurt, including Danny Cohn-Bendit, who helped arrange the whole possibility of our going there and working there.

Organized Events

This is a significant development, because the anarchists in these places have been able to organize theatrical events, get the permits, get the places, do the public relations work necessary, find us other groups to work with, and have themselves been the participant actors in the preparation of many of the plays. For instance, when we were in Spain, the CNT [Spain's anarchist-syndicalist union] organized a tour for our play *Seven Meditations on Sado-Masochism*, all over Catalonia, and even arranged for a single performance as part of a street fair of a street theatre play we did on sexual liberation in Barcelona.

OR: *Do you see the work of your group as part of the conscious anarchist tradition?*

ILIAN: Rather than in the tradition, we are within the meaning of anarchism, not only theoretically, but practically, in the way we live. We try to live in an alternative way, as a collective. Living Theatre has been calling itself a collective already for ten years, and so our living is an experiment on an anarchist basis. Our work is directed toward the

agitation of the word anarchism, propaganda by the word and propaganda by the deed in the sense that we look for workers, students, anti-militarists, feminists, people that are anarchists, people that are active politically, and we work with them and try to further as much as we can an anarchist reality in the existing politics.

JUDITH: We were in Spain in the period when the CNT was on the verge of turning from a clandestine and illegal workers' organization into a very strong representative of working people – no longer clandestine, but now openly organized. This was a very important time, and in bringing anarchist theatre with a clear and undisguised anarchist thesis, to that scene was very important for us, it was very important for them, and it was very important in developing our concept of what is possible, what is historical and what is historically obsolete in anarchism and what is historically futuristic.

Hopefulness

Certainly, I think anarchism is a basic human desire; that is, people want to be free on a most fundamental level. Everyone has a desire for freedom; how much they've been taught, "it's impossible to have what you want," determines how anarchistic they actually are. If they've despaired totally, they tend to be strongly conservative, cautious, even fascistic, if you become too frightened of what is really possible. If people are very optimistic, if the political situation seems to be opening out, as for instance today in Italy, then generally the Left becomes more libertarian because there's a hopefulness you can organize things in a reasonable and humane manner with less and less authoritarian structures.

OR: *How do you adapt to language differences? Do you have to keep changing languages from one country to another?*

ILIAN: Yes, we are an international group. This is important. We have performed in six different languages.

JULIAN: We do the plays in Italy essentially in Italian, in France in French, in Germany in German, in Ireland or England in English. We've performed in Spanish, and in Portugal we did street theatre in Portuguese. We decided to concentrate on Italy because, already ten years ago, we had decided we wanted to use the work we do in the theatre in support of the libertarian movement where we felt we could be useful. It seemed to us that in Italy there is a very distinct movement to the Left. I think it's happening everywhere....

ILIAN: The left is very wide and varied in Italy.

Open Road 9 (1979)

Libertarian Solutions

JULIAN: This left in Italy is looking for libertarian solutions; it is not looking, really, for bureaucratic or leadership solutions. Even our friends in the Communist Party are looking for some form of communism that has a libertarian colouring, and if you can make the communist colour sufficiently libertarian, it begins to spell out anarchism. At first, the Communists were mistrustful of us; we provoked them considerably. Our newest play, *Prometheus*, with its portrait of Leninism, has again provoked them. They were just getting to settle down with the Living Theatre and feel there was a working relationship and the portrait of Leninism has disturbed them again.

OR: *How would you characterize your portrayal of Leninism in* Prometheus?

JULIAN: I think it's a re-examination of the nature of the party leadership, and it is our attempt to show it as a double and a reproduction of that authoritarian model which has plagued humankind for many thousands of years. We're talking now of a revolution against this authoritarian model which reasserts itself again and again and again in terms of being beneficent, in terms of being efficient or efficacious and which is really basically part of a psychological power drive perhaps more than anything else. What we wanted to show was Lenin's, and the Leninists' oversight of the need not only to change society economically and politically, but also socially and therefore also psychologically. The failure to understand that need allowed the authoritarian principle to assert itself, to the point at which it became in fact uncontrollable, and has created another authoritarian form, which we anarchists know has to be transformed.

OR: *Another political element that seems to run through most of your work is pacifism. How does pacifism fit into the overall picture?*

JUDITH: If we examine the basic principle of anarchism, which is not to impose force upon anyone else, it seems that the fundamental definition of anarchist behaviour, and the fundamental definition of pacifist behaviour, can't really at bottom be any different. That is, if we want liberty, we can't remove other human beings' liberty by shooting them through the head any more than we can remove it by exploiting them to work twelve hours a day. If we are going to develop into a whole ambience, a whole form of human behaviour based on mutual aid and loving each other in a brotherly/sisterly manner, then to exclude those who oppose us from this love and this altruism because they are violent, because they are exploitative, seems to contradict the entire basis of anarchism.

Self-Defense

OR: *Do you see a role for violent self-defense, either individually, or as a group, a community, a class or a people?*

JULIAN: I think all violence and all punition are based ultimately on the illogic of the theory of self-defense. I think even the glaring examples of our own times, of, let us say, fascist Germany or fascist Spain, are based on the defense of certain principles: honour, land, hegemony, of certain classes in the defense of their rights and their freedoms against other classes and other groups and other lands whom they felt were invading and encroaching on those rights. I think that the human mind has its structure of logic, and I think the human mind works essentially logically, even in its most surreal associative manners – everything that it does is based on various kinds of structures of logic. Now sometimes these structures of logic have flaws in them, and these flaws, these little holes, are the places where all the truth runs out, and the process of creating an anarchist society is the process of creating a society in which the truth doesn't run out and doesn't evaporate and doesn't escape. Nobody, or on most rare occasions, arbitrarily says now is the opportunity to express myself and to assert my freedom by punishing that person over there or shooting that man or that woman or that child. It simply doesn't happen. We begin the logic of self-defense when we feel violently that we must "Defend the poor!" We must defend the poor against the insufferable exploitation of the rich. We must defend a country against the colonial master. We must defend the land that belongs to the peasants against the latifundists who own it all. "We must defend the right of children to eat." We build up progressively a tremendous logic of force and coercion and violence out of that concept of our right to defend. If we're going to change the society and build an anarchist society, we have to create a new terrain for the logic.

OR: *You referred to the CNT. They are working in a peaceful way now, but they reserve the right, at the end, to have an armed confrontation with the State, and most other anarchist movements have that attitude, too.*

ILIAN: I'm not so sure about that. I think in Spain the anarchists are probably closer to pacifism than, for instance, in Italy. They have had terrible bloodshed in the so-called Civil War [1936–39], and there is much more of a questioning of the uses of violence right now in Spain than there was ever before. I think that anarcho-syndicalism is basically, on principle, non-violent in the sense that the general strike – taking the means of production and starting *autogestion* (workers' self-management) – is a non-violent way of changing society. Of course, in the moment that *autogestion* threatens the ordinary authoritarian hierarchical order of society the bosses will call the police, and I think it is the work of the most importance now to start to open up a dialogue with the direct servants of the rich – those who have the legal use of arms – the soldiers and the police who do not belong to the upper class, but have their origins in the lower strata of society. This is a work of utmost importance to us right now as revolutionists – to open up a dialogue to overcome the isolation of these brothers and sisters of ours who defend the power structure against their own people. This is a contradiction of this system that we must dig up and make clear. When we end the play that we do now (*Prometheus*) in front of the prison, usually we originate a dialogue with the police who come to ask who we are and what are we doing. It creates a confrontation which should never lead to violence. It is a provocation that we do, but not a provocation to violence; we would not offer resistance if they attacked us, for instance. We would rather retreat and make it possible for it to happen again.

Pacifism

OR: *What sort of response do you get from the groups that are active in the streets of Europe when you talk about pacifism and non-violence?*

JUDITH: Very often with such groups, we do plays about the subject of violence and non-violence, in which we and they can develop on a theatrical level this debate. We do a play called *Where Does The Violence Come From?* which we do in the streets with all kinds of groups, sometimes activist groups, sometimes groups that are quite neutral on this subject and perhaps interested in another kind of work. We have worked, say, with groups of mental patients and people from the Wilhelm Reich Centre in Naples, who are interested in therapeutic changes and who are specifically political in the way that Reichians are political and are making important community experiments. We did with them in a very, very violently-oriented neighbourhood – *Where Does the Violence Come From?* – in fact, we were attacked by a fascist group during the production of the play on the street. This leads to a deepening of the understanding of the problem. To confront the question of non-violent tactics against violent tactics, to enter into debate, to be part of an educational process, and in the course of that to be educated ourselves, to change ourselves, is thrilling for us – to encounter people who consider themselves revolutionaries, but using very different tactics than ours.

OR: *Do you see any prospects of bringing this message back to North America fairly soon?*

JULIAN: There is no immediate prospect. We would like to, but there is no immediate prospect. It would depend on finding a considerable financial solution to the question, how do you bring over a group of twenty people and all

that theatrical gear, and find some way of getting financial support for that?

OR: *How do you actually finance yourselves now?*

JULIAN: In Europe, we have much less of a problem than in the United States, because we've found we were able to work with anarchist comrades who were able to get gigs for us in city after city in Italy, sometimes even getting money, contradictorily but interestingly enough, from the city, who have paid us to do weeks and weeks in some locations, even in Sicily and the south of Italy, to do what they call animation, street theatre work – cities like Bologna and Genoa, which are large and well-known, but also cities that are small, such as Massa or Cosenza, which is located in the toe of Italy's boot.

Year After Year

OR: *How do you sustain this tremendous out-pouring of energy year after year when so many other groups, not only theatre groups but other types of political action groups, fold up, or go through such radical transformations that they no longer really exist in the same way anymore? It seems that the Living Theatre has reached the stage of being an institution.*

JUDITH: We have had certain advantages. We have the advantage of having each other, as it were; in some way, we inspire each other, because we're a group of people who have come together as an affinity group and a working collective. Now, there have been other affinity groups that have been working collectives and have not been able to sustain and endure through the terrific difficulties of trying to be a free collective in an un-free and un-collectivized world. But in a certain sense sharing a certain viewpoint, which would represent a kind of optimalist position, kind of an extreme position as to be totally anarchist in our hopes and endeavors, and totally pacifist in our hopes and endeavors, with every member of the group being really concerned with being a part of a collective, which hopefully can become more and more collective and more and more libertarian ... so that when anyone of us falters there's all the others, when there are divisions among us we make a conscious effort to resolve those differences on a good pacifist and a good anarchist level. And we have work that inspires us, that always keeps us moving to the next step, the next production, the next play, the next action, so that we can't, as it were, drop out of our cycle of energy, and we can keep that going and keep energizing each other in that way.

OR: *Were you in West Germany during the Schleyer episode?*

JULIAN: Yes, we were at that time in Munich performing the *Seven Meditations*, and in that play there is a meditation on

Open Road 9 (1979)

violence, in which we discuss police violence and we read a fact-sheet, essentially, in which we demonstrate electric shock torture, and we talk of the use of torture in various countries, giving ten specific incidents. We choose ten specific out of a possibility of 500 things we could cite; it varies from place-to-place and time-to time – we usually try to speak of something that goes on in the country in which we are performing, among other facts, and we did mention the fact that in Germany there is use of what is known as the "white torture" – isolation and sensory deprivation – in which people are confined in areas that are constantly illuminated by electric light bulbs, in which there are no sounds and no human contacts. I was arrested and charged with – and this pleased me very much as an anarchist – defamation of the State. We left behind about $1,000 in bail and got out. The most courageous and impressive thing that happened, to my knowledge at that time, immediately was a silent march of about 200 people in Munich through the centre of town – young people, who then came to the jail where I was held for a brief time, about nine hours.

JUDITH: It was courageous because this was a period during which all street demonstrations were banned because the country was thrown into total panic in the crisis of the killings.

North America

OR: *Looking at it from Europe, what does the situation look like to you in North America? Do you see anything hopeful?*

JULIAN: You know, the national barriers are very strong, and it's very hard to get through and to get information. We get so busy with our own activities that we don't get to see publications or get to know precisely what is happening. I assume, however, that the world is so united now that what is happening in one country is happening in another. We find that what we think is unique in Italy is in fact also happening in France, is also happening in Germany, also happening, as we see it here, in Ireland. When we did this play (*Prometheus*), we thought we would have difficulty, for instance, finding volunteers to play the anarchists when we came to Ireland. In the second act of this play, you know, we ask the people to play Bolsheviks and terrorists and anarchists and pacifists and a theatrical group, and we find we get the most volunteers, everywhere, to play the anarchists. In Italy, but also here in Ireland. So that my measure of what's going on in North America is measured by what we see happening in the places that we work.

Anarchists in Italy

There's a very big anarchist movement in Germany, Italy and France. There must be 500 groups at least in Italy that

identity themselves as anarchist groups, that have their anarchist headquarters, that do their propaganda work in the cities spreading a certain open-minded consciousness, and I expect this must be the case in the United States. The anarchist movement, which has been declared dead repeatedly again and again and again by its opponents on the Right and on the Left, is again reasserting itself; it's going to keep reasserting itself as long as we're deprived of freedom. We find that when we work in Sardegna, when we perform plays like *Seven Meditations* in town after town in Sardegna, the people there – fishermen, mountain people, people of so-called non-sophistication – are able to talk with us until three o'clock in the morning about various applications of anarchist principles. And when we perform in occupied factories around Torino or Milano, as we have done, there is no problem in talking to people who are standing next to machines eight or ten hours a day about what it means not only to organize in the shop but what the principles of anarchism would mean in relation to their own families, in relation to the sexual revolution, in relation to organizing food distribution, in relation to leisure hours, what we would do with people who don't want to work, what you would do without money, all of these things that we once thought were guarded secrets of the anarchist movement, everywhere there's a knowledge explosion going on, certainly in Europe.

OR: *What are your plans for the immediate future?*

JULIAN: The immediate future is always to keep living from week to week and our plan now is to go to France and tour for six weeks and to try to collect enough money from the tour we're doing now in France, Belgium and Luxembourg to return to Italy and, after another Italian tour, we hope to have amassed enough money to make a concentrated campaign of activity in the streets and plazas of the city of Rome and the area around Rome, where we have not had a real opportunity as yet to work as in-depth as we want to.

OR: *So if somebody wants to get in touch with you, how do they do it?*

JULIAN: The best thing is to contact as in Rome. The address there is Living Theatre, Via Gaeta 79, 00185 Rome. And if anybody felt they could get together work in the United States or Canada for us that would be terrific. Somebody did speak to as about the possibility of going to the Montreal festival in the summer of 1979. That might be a possible way of paying our way over to North America and back again to Europe – at the same time it might then be possible to arrange several months of work in Canada and several months of work in the United States.

[Editor's Note: In 2003, the Living Theatre returned to New York City, where they are now building their own theatre.]

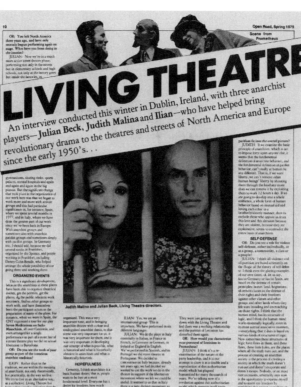

Scene from
Prometheus

LIVING THEATRE

An interview conducted this winter in Dublin, Ireland, with three anarchist players—**Julian Beck, Judith Malina and Ilian**—who have helped bring revolutionary drama to the theatres and streets of North America and Europe since the early 1950's . . .

Judith Malina and Julian Beck, Living Theatre directors.

The Living Theatre takes to the stage in Italy.

poster: Susan Simensky-Bietla

AUTONOMOUS ZONES

Perhaps the best known Western example of an autonomous zone in the modern era is the Paris Commune. On March 18, 1871, armed Parisians who had long chafed under Napoleon the 3rd's dictatorial Second Empire rose up and took over their city. The resulting commune was not only an exercise in self-governance, economic justice, and gender egalitarianism on a mammoth scale; it was a reclamation of space. Parisians transformed their city into zones of liberation where, for two months, social experimentation, creativity, and idealism flourished before the French army invaded to restore "order" at the end of the bayonet. Thousands were killed and the commune was no more, yet the dream of the autonomous zone continued. And it does so to this day in anarchism's collectivist projects – its bookstores, protests, and centres for radical organizing, education, and culture. The autonomous zone – a term coined by Hakim Bey in his publication *T.A.Z.* – is a weapon against capitalism and hierarchy and a radical sphere where social cohesion and tactical diversity can prosper. Theoretically, the anarchist web site is the ideal instance of Bey's TAZ: it combines both the transitional (a floating byte of information in the ether of the information network) and the fixed (a reliable site or address which can be repeatedly accessed). But whether an autonomous zone is, in Bey's definition, "temporary" (a Reclaim the Streets party, the WTO protests) or "fixed" in space and time (a bookstore or free-space), it is always a circumnavigation of authority.

The anarchist autonomous zone is the most practical way to overcome the artificial separation of the "personal" and "political." It is an act of stepping outside borders, of taking control of *space* for anti-authoritarian activities, where one can recognize and realize desires outside the boundaries of commodification. As Rebecca Solnit asks in her book *Wanderlust*, how many people get involved in large anti-globalization movements just to be in the street,

a constructed and rigidly-ruled space they would normally have trouble walking across due to traffic? The personal and political meet at this juncture: a protest against cars, for example, is both a quality of life issue and a political issue. It addresses everything from the destruction of nature to curtailed civil liberties for non-drivers. The subversive character of the autonomous zone is asserted precisely through the zone's presence: it reconstructs public space as a zone of anarchy in the act of refusing it's privatization and dismantlement. Anarchist gatherings, Quebec City's 2001 Carnival Against Capitalism, Reclaim the Streets, and Critical Mass – they are as much a part of the fluctuating autonomous zone as Toronto's Anarchist Free School or Winnipeg's Mondragón Bookstore and Coffeehouse.

Space, the autonomous zone reminds us, is the most serious matter facing any anarchist. Land, geography, borders – they all mean the same thing for those without capital, those who, in pre-modern terms, remain "landless." The dialogue that controls issues of space and land, after all, stems from authoritarian rule. The nation state begins and ends with "space." To the State, space is something to be conquered, colonized, and owned. Land means empires and empires mean protection of the sanctimonious institution called "property" by way of prisons, reservations, militarism, and war. It is an abstraction made real by the creation of artificial distinctions and obstacles to impede free movement. For this reason, autonomous zones have the potential to be the most radical form of reclamation yet. As Bey writes, "The question of land refuses to go away. How can we separate the concept of space from the mechanism of control?" Autonomous zones are a point of access to freedom for all, because the autonomous zone is a non-place that transgresses the geography of control.

– KERRY MOGG

Bookstores are a mainstay in anarchist culture, and for good reason. They serve as centres for organizing and are the first place activists go to discover what is going on in a community. Most importantly, these centres are where you find books, journals, stickers, buttons, and posters you won't find anywhere else. They connect you with the wider movement.

Montreal's Alternative Bookshop began in 1973 in a shared storefront located on Crescent Street (below Saint Catherine's Street). In 1980, a collective interested in establishing a local hub for anarchist activity bought the building where the bookstore is currently located. The bookstore moved into the ground floor of the new building and then relocated to the more spacious second floor in 1984. In 2003, it moved back down to a newly refurbished ground floor. The Alternative Bookshop is run by a collective on the basis of consensus and everything sold is first vetted for content. Over the many years of its existence the store has served as an info centre for thousands – I, for example, made regular trips to Montreal to pick up books and journals in the early 1980s. Collective members have been involved in some of the most notable events in Montreal, such as the May Day celebrations held in 1986 and, more recently, the Montreal Anarchist Book and Freedom Fair. The store has served the community well, and its endurance is an inspiration.

— ALLAN ANTLIFF

Poster (1986)

LIBRAIRIE ALTERNATIVE

844~3207

2033, boul. St~Laurent   MTL

Livres et périodiques
EN FRANÇAIS, ANGLAIS ET AUTRES LANGUES
pour la révolution sociale

ANARCHISME

Communisme Anti-autoritaire

ANARCHO-

SYNDICALISME   Internationale Situationniste   HISTOIRE SOCIALE   Ecologie

PACIFISME / Antimilitarisme RÉVOLUTIONNAIRE

Vie quotidienne

FEMINISME

Etc.

AUTOGÉRÉE / ANTI-PROFIT

Poster (1985)

On April 25, 2004, a fire destroyed a heritage building on Hastings Street in downtown Vancouver, and one of North America's oldest radical institutions was lost. Spartacus Books had just celebrated its thirtieth anniversary at that location in 2003, and was thriving in its many roles when the tragedy occurred.

Spartacus Books, named after the slave who led a revolt against the Roman Empire, originated at Simon Fraser University in 1972. Roger Perkins (who worked in the SFU bookstore) and a group of students saw the need to make radical political literature available. Initially a buying co-op, books and pamphlets were stored in lockers and sold from book tables. This initiative met with so much enthusiasm that radicals from the community were approached and a larger collective was formed to found a store. The first Spartacus Books opened in the spring of 1973 above a pool hall in Vancouver's downtown Eastside. This warehouse space was large – there was an area for public meetings behind the store and Spartacus was able to share the space with the American Exiles Association – deserters from the U.S. military.

Within a year, we moved to a more visible location on Hastings Street, where the store remained until the recent fire. It was a good building, housing organizations like *Open Road* magazine. At the new location the stock grew and became more comprehensive, carrying an especially broad range of anarchist theory, history, and current newspapers, magazines, and zines. From the beginning, a space was set aside with couches and comfortable chairs, providing a reading area for those who couldn't afford to pay for what they wanted to read. In recent years, this area also had public access computers that were heavily used for organizing.

More than a non-profit bookstore, Spartacus was a meeting hub and organizing space. The store educated and informed activists, providing tools to those who challenged the state and capitalism's monopoly on information and opinion. The walls displayed over thirty years worth of posters documenting on-going struggles. This agitator's art gallery covered everything from the American invasion of Vietnam to recent Indigenous resistance and anti-WTO protests. Posters celebrating Emma Goldman and other anarchists were on display too.

What was most unique about Spartacus at its founding was its collective, volunteer structure and non-sectarian approach. We ran with a volunteer base of twenty to fifty members using consensus decision-making. There never was a "boss" and all problems were resolved in meetings. Admittedly, they were often long and tedious for some, but an anarchist approach to management proved its value over the decades. With a constant turnover of people leaving for jobs or school, well over a thousand activists participated in what everyone saw as a vital project.

Starting in very sectarian times (the early 1970s), our non-sectarian principle was crucial to our survival – it avoided the disruption of divisive disputes. Anarchists co-operated with self-identified pacifists, syndicalists, greens, feminists, social democrats, (and even Leninists in the early days), and the broad range of anti-authoritarian activists without labels. Through decades of struggles, Spartacus provided pertinent up-to-date information and a meeting and organizing space for learning about and working against war, racism, misogyny, state authority and oppression, and for global justice and liberation.

The fire and loss of everything – books, computers, furnishings, posters and the space itself – isn't the end of our story. The Spartacus collective has started fund-raising with the goal of rising from the ashes and reestablishing the store: because the need for Spartacus is no less now than it was in 1972.

– ALEXANDER DAUGHTRY

EXPLOSIVE TITLES

ANARCHISM • FEMINISM
SOCIALISM • THIRD WORLD
PRISONS • LABOUR HISTORY
ART • LITERATURE

Spartacus Books
311 West Hastings Street
Vancouver, B.C.
688-6138

photos: Kerry Mogg (2000)

Winnipeg's Old Market Autonomous Zone was founded in 1995 with the purchase of a local historic building by a small collective. Housed in a turn of the century building – once a textile factory and later home to the Jewish Y – the Emma Goldman Grassroots Centre was the first project to take shape in the new A-Zone. Located on the second floor, it is inhabited by radical activist collectives and projects of all stripes, providing accessible office space well below market value. Here direct action groups work side by side with magazine collectives, record companies, publishers, radical librarians, and international organizations such as Food Not Bombs and Anarchist Black Cross. A common room hosts discussions on topics ranging from the practical to the theoretical. Grassroots Centre participants regularly hammer out the nuts and bolts of how the space should be shared and kept up. Issues such as sexism in the community and the maintenance of a critical practice in daily life are also grappled with. Since the common room was opened, a number of fledgling and established groups in the larger community have gathered there to forge consensus decision-making and collective practices worthy of and consistent with the Centre's historic coinage.

In the summer of 1996, the A-Zone expanded with the opening of the Mondragon Bookstore and Coffeehouse on its ground floor. This has given the location a thriving street-level presence. Winnipegers walk in off the street and experience anarchist principles "materialized" in the form of a bookstore and vegetarian restaurant/coffee shop. The storefront is peopled with radical artists, workers, and neighbourhood folks in search of radical literature and cafiennation. Run by a collective of ten, Mondragon brings in speakers, holds lectures and film screenings, and serves as a meeting place for informal organizing. Six years and many collective members later, Mondragon is still going about its business of making ideas accessible in print and in person, promoting a sustainable food politics, and providing a healthy example of workplace anarchy.

– RIA JULIAN

WHO'S EMMA

Who's Emma was a volunteer-run storefront operation in Kensington Market in Toronto. Named after Emma Goldman, it started in 1996 and ran for over four years. The project developed from discussions within the punk scene dating back to the early 1990s, from the Toronto Hardcore Hotline and several punk collective houses in the city. It was also an attempt to revive an anarchist scene in the city. The tension between punk subculture and anarchist politics marked the entire history of Who's Emma. This was played out in the daily life of the storefront and in large monthly collective meetings. The storefront opened at 69½ Nassau Street. Its organization was explicitly modelled on the Epicentre in San Francisco, a volunteer-run punk record store, zine library, and community centre. From the beginning, the store was open seven days a week and staffed by volunteers who worked one four-hour shift a week. On Mondays, the volunteers were all women. There were working groups to order records, books, zines, to take care of finances, and to organize workshops. The workshops were on topics from silk-screening, to setting up a pirate radio, to the history of political movements such as MOVE. Working groups were free to take decisions on their own, but reported to the monthly general meeting.

From the beginning Who's Emma was committed to anarchist principles of non-hierarchical organizing and decision-making by consensus. A whole new generation of facilitators emerged and the skills of listening and participating in meetings were central to the project. During the initial period of the project a black bloc of punks spontaneously emerged in Toronto. Its most spectacular action was an attempt to close down the stock exchange during a citywide Day of Action to protest the neoliberal policies of Mike Harris's conservative government. Who's Emma also had several memorable punk shows in the street outside the space, including two annual all-day music festivals. We frequently had tables at punk shows in the suburbs.

The first major debate at Who's Emma concerned whether we should stock records on major labels. Some punks argued that important music was on these labels. They resisted arguments that punk subculture is necessarily in opposition to large corporations. This heated debate lasted several months and took place informally, in small discussion groups and in crowded monthly collective meetings. It was essentially a debate between relatively non-political punks and anarchists. Eventually consensus was reached to exclude records on labels run by major corporations. The second major debate involved issues raised by the women's group about anti-abortion lyrics of some straightedge punk bands and objectionable artwork on some record covers. Who's Emma was aware that punk subculture is dominated by boys and some women felt uncomfortable in the space. From the beginning we stocked women's music and feminist books. Monday was always for women volunteers and we had feminist posters on the walls. Every second monthly meeting was facilitated by a woman. Continually educating boys about these issues was central to the project. However, after months of meetings it proved impossible to reach consensus about anti-abortion lyrics and sexist record covers. Women within the collective took different positions on these issues. Who's Emma was not officially involved in the organization of the Active Resistance (AR) anarchist gathering held in Toronto in 1998. However, our space was used for meetings and several members of the collective were heavily involved. Unresolved personal conflicts and two serious break-ins involving the loss of large amounts of CDs ultimately led to the closure of Who's Emma.

— ALAN O'CONNOR

If I can't dance, I don't want to be part of your revolution

For the last year of Who's Emma's existence I was a staff person and collective member. My picture is, of course, only a partial snapshot of Who's Emma as I experienced it. By most accounts, the first two years of Who's Emma? were the most invigorated and invigorating. Volunteer energies were up, the project was still novel and full of hope, and there was a certain clarity of purpose. This energy continued until just after the Active Resistance anarchist gathering. Planning for AR 98 and the work of pulling it off created some tensions among Toronto anarchists and this had an impact on Who's Emma? After AR it became more and more difficult to fill volunteer shifts. From two people per shift, it became difficult to find one person for many shifts. Towards the end the space was only open reliably for about four shifts per week (out of fourteen).... If not for the tireless efforts of the Oakville punk crews who held regular benefit shows Emma would have died months before it did. There was always an aspect of the carnivalesque in Who's Emma: whether it was the crass hardcore music, the quirky zines, humorous buttons, joyful camaraderie, or the clarion of agit-prop, the space signalled its difference from its surroundings, its "otherness." It was a place of transformation from the present to the future, a glimpse of the "new world in the shell of the old."

Autonomous zones are hubs of DIY culture and politics. In scenes where transience and the ephemeral often predominate, such spaces offer some permanence, some rootedness. There the "underground" can move above ground and engage in everyday discussions with non-activists, with people who want to find out what this anarchy stuff is all about. Perhaps the real legacy of Who's Emma can be found in the new projects which were born of the space. Current efforts which would likely not have gotten started without the existence of Who's Emma include the zine *Sabcat*, Books to Prisoners, and Hunger Artist Press. The space brought many new people into anarchist activism before it finally closed on September 2, 2000, after over four mostly good years.

— JEFF SHANTZ

photos: Allan Antliff (1999)

ANARCHIST FREE SPACE

The Anarchist Free Space was begun in April 1999 by artists and activists who were then running the Toronto Anarchist Free School (AFS). Backed by funding from one of their members, the Anarchist Free School set up shop in a roomy storefront location in Toronto's Kensington Market, a stone's throw from it's sister organization, Who's Emma.

The Free Space was intended as a venue for committed anarchists, novices and non-anarchists alike to come together and share ideas about the prospects, difficulties and strategies for creating new, anti-authoritarian social relations. The primary vehicle for this was an ambitious schedule of AFS classes on diverse issues. Courses reflected the desire for openness – they weren't all about anarchists talking to anarchists about anarchy (though a few of them were just that). Some of the courses included "Love Songs of the 20s and 30s," "Street Art," "Understanding Violence Against Women," and "Alternative Economics." Not just the mind but the body was taken care of in a yoga class and in shiatsu workshops. For most of the year at least one class was running every weekday evening. Far and away the most successful and long-running were "Introduction to Anarchism" and "Class Struggle Anarchism: Syndicalism and Libertarian Socialism."

In addition to classes the AFS tried to revive the anarchist salon tradition. As the 1999 course booklet noted: "Salons have a colourful history throughout the world and in particular within Anarchist Communities. Salons are intentional conversational forums where people engage in passionate discourse about what they think is important." At the AFS the third Friday of every month was reserved for lively discussions on various topics decided upon by participants. Often the salons included a potluck dinner and performance. By all accounts the salons were enjoyable and engaging affairs.

In activist terms the AFS was at its liveliest during the spring and summer of 2000. Taking the view that the Free Space could (and should) be a worthwhile organizing centre members reached out to other activists in the city. The Ontario Coalition Against Poverty (OCAP) was invited to hold their movie nights at the space every Saturday and held several successful large "screenings." Several members of the space participated in the OCAP-initiated protest at Queen's Park on June 15, which ended in a full-scale police riot. The class struggle anarchist zine *Sabcat* was also produced out of the Free Space and met with tremendous enthusiasm locally and abroad. This was in addition to the AFS *Anarchist Notebook*, which provided a forum for anarchist organizational principles and artistic creativity. A Books to Prisoners program was also started and became quite successful. Poetry readings and hardcore shows brought in hundreds of book donations along with the help of some independent publishers and distributors. Before long the first shipments went out from the Free Space to prison inmates.

Almost everything I've ever read about autonomous zones or infoshops raises the nasty business of gentrification in North American cities. This story is no exception. Members of the Free Space took a leading role in the battle against gentrification in the Kensington Market area. In May, 2000 a petition had begun circulation against plans for a soup kitchen and hostel for homeless people to be opened on Augusta Avenue just north of the Free Space. The viciously worded petition openly attacked poor people, saying they were unwelcome in the Market. The Free Space collective and members of nearby Who's Emma met and decided without delay to interview every store-owner or manager in the Market to see who was carrying the petition. Teams of two spent the next few days talking to people throughout the Market. Where petitions were found, and thankfully very few places had accepted them, it was made clear that such anti-poor propaganda was unacceptable and that those businesses which persisted in circulating it would be targeted.

Later in the summer another battle developed over harassment by the City of Toronto of a few homeless men living in the Market. The situation came to a head when one of the men asked a couple of us at the Free Space for help in keeping city workers from taking his stuff to the dump. We confronted the workers and, after several discussions, worked out a deal where the city workers promised not to touch any belongings in the area fronting the Free Space. We also asked OCAP to get involved and they put pressure on the union to do a little education with their members. With street-space secured, homeless guys started hanging out and selling their wonderful array of used goods in front of and alongside the Free Space. For a couple of months it was like a real street bazaar. Shoppers loved the piles of stuff and there was always serious bargaining going on.

The Free Space offered an alternative way of living in Toronto before it closed in 2001. Participants maintained it in a spirit of openness and inclusion. Anarchy is not some fanciful idea, something for philosophers and mystics to ponder. Anarchy only has meaning when it is lived.

Anarchist Free Space: April 1999–April 2001. "Don't mourn – organize!"

— JEFF SHANTZ

photos: Jeff Shantz / Rachel Rosen (2000)

AUTONOMOUS ZONES § 339

During the Toronto Active Resistance gathering in 1998 a discussion group on "Community Organizing" came up with a proposal to found a free school in Toronto. I and others were approached to participate in the effort, and before too long a core group of about eight people were meeting twice a week to hammer out the logistics. From the start we envisaged the school serving as a centre for anarchist organizing and activism. To that end we resolved to call our organization the Anarchist Free School (AFS) and to operate along anarchist lines, with a stated commitment to explicitly anarchist educational projects. The school got up and running in fall, 1998 and lasted until the winter of 2001. From the beginning it attracted lots of people and radicalized many. The project was publicized in newspapers and on the radio; the AFS, a storefront locale for classes in downtown Toronto's Kensington Market, was established; and anarchists from the United States and Canada visited to speak on various issues in the winter of 1999 at an Anarchist Free School Lecture Series. Over 2000 a publication was produced (*Anarchist Notebook*) and classes continued until the winter of 2001, when the Anarchist Free Space project began to wind down. By this time the Free School's most dynamic participants were heavily involved in other projects – Reclaim the Streets, communal housing, etc. It seemed as good a time as any to move on.

How did we operate? At monthly meetings courses, workshops, and related projects were proposed and discussed. Once someone committed to preparing and facilitating a course or workshop they set a time for meetings and wrote up a description to be added to the school's schedule of courses. We published a new calender every four months, but courses could be added at any time. Each event was free and open to anyone to participate. Some of the courses included "Alternative Health Practices," "Art, Anarchism, and Culture," "Spanish Conversation,"

"Anarchism and Cities," "Wild Plants of Toronto," and "The Conflict in Chiapas." The goal was to share our respective skills and knowledge without discriminating between the practical and the theoretical in the belief that any sphere that a Free School participant wanted to explore merited exploration. This fostered a type of education that was profoundly anarchistic, since hierarchy was anathema to the learning process and no one assessed, instructed, or profited from it – each and every individual charted his or her own program as he or she saw fit.

One key to the school's success was its ability to break down patterns of generational division which so often undermine the viability of anarchist communities. Where there is community, as there was in the Free School, the benefits are certainly tangible. For example, the oldest in our group – Garry Moffit – generously provided us with the rent-free space in Kensington Market from which to operate. Others chipped in with a myriad of skills in graphic design, communications, poster-making, painting, and publicity. The school was a great solidarity-builder, quite apart from its educational purpose.

This brings me to the question of theory. At a symposium on anarchism and education held by England's *Green Anarchist* journal in 1998, there was general agreement that education is crucial for any long-term strategy bent on creating an anarchist society. "Most anarchist movements are drifting from day to day," the participants observed, and therefore neglect the role education can play in this regard. What sort of education could further anarchism was also a topic of debate, with at least one person denouncing the very idea of schools for their built-in role as a "cultural" force in which "something abstract" is "imposed to homogenise and control people ideologically." This critic identified schooling with status quo "domestication" that suppresses "instinctive resistance to dehumanization" – the

the reading list | first meeting taking place on dec.02/2001/7pm @ mondragon bookstore & coffeehouse

a n a r c h i s t
b o o k
r e a d i n g
c l u b

Winnipeg 2001

"primitive" force dwelling in every pre-educated child. Here we have echoes of the 19th-century Russian anarchist Leo Tolstoy, who similarity condemned the school system of his day in favour of more "authentic" (and therefore liberated) forms of knowledge. However, unlike his *Green Anarchist* counterpart, Tolstoy clung to the category of "culture," arguing that it resided in the creative knowledge of the Russian peasantry, unsullied by imposed learning and deadening indoctrination. What unites Tolstoy and the *Green Anarchist* critic is their shared conviction that "schooling" itself is at the root of the problem. *Green Anarchist*'s anti-educator put it this way: "Fundamentally schools are about getting people to accept boredom and discipline and the content of what's taught is pretty incidental to this. We're indebted to Foucault's *Discipline and Punish* for pointing out that modern schooling came from the same organizational principles as modern prisons, factories, and military organization."

Fair enough, but we also know that Tolstoy's unschooled "learning-by-doing" peasantry perpetuated oppressive social relations. In fact, *Green Anarchist*'s critic was careful to note that "non-schooling" is no guarantee of escaping anti-libertarian influences. The resolution of this issue, as I see it, is to initiate a learning process that fuses anarchist content with anarchist practice. An anarchist education, after all, should strive to reach beyond educational parameters because it's ultimate goal is the liberation of society. Toronto's Anarchist Free School was a step in that direction.

After the Free School folded, many AFS participants continued to meet under the auspices of the Random Anarchist Group. Others poured their energy into the Ontario Coalition Against Poverty (OCAP) and the anarchist-communist journal, *Ye Drunken Sailor*. And in 2003 former Free Schoolers renewed the tradition by founding an Anarchist University with a website and a range of courses that has attracted hundreds of participants. Though the AFS is no more, its legacy lives on.

— ALLAN ANTLIFF

Toronto 1998

Edmonton 2002

Anarchist Notebook

no.1

A publication of the Anarchist Free School

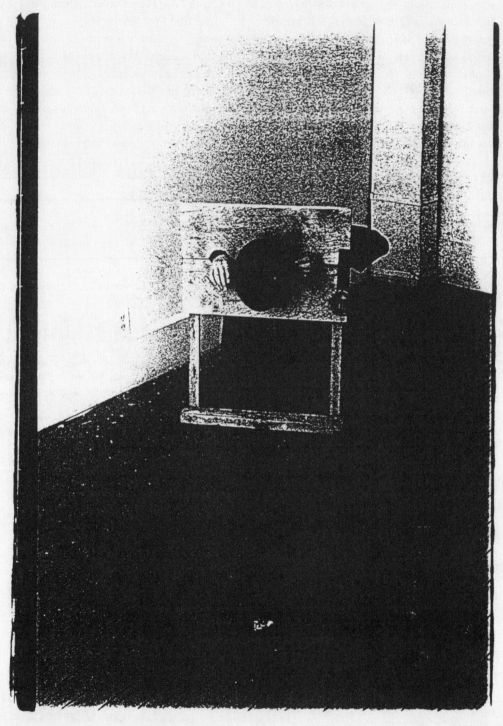

The Anarchist Free School is a counter community dedicated to effecting social change through the application of anarchist principles in every sphere of life. The location on Augusta provides a place for people to explore these alternatives. It includes a bookstore, a library, and an open space for classes and events. The Anarchist free Space welcomes all applications for use, proposals for new courses, and submissions to the Anarchist Notebook.

Anarchist Free Space 254 Augusta Ave. Toronto M5T 2L7 (416) 203-0191 in Kensington Market, S of College, W of Spadina.

Anarchist Notebook I (2000)

Consensus is the way to eliminate power

Consensus reduces alienation. If there is not consensus, it means that some people are being forced to live with situations they do not want.

The most important thing about making consensus work is that each person wants all the other people, not just themself, to be happy with the decision.

Either a group making decisions against the opposition of some of its members *or* some members making decisions independently of the rest of the group, can cause people to be alienated from the result, and these are cases of power being applied.

There is no way that either decentralization or centralization can end alienation. People should use consensus to decide how much decentralization there will be.

The main point about consensus is the elimination of the group as a power distinct from the members of the group. There are not people making rulings about other people. Everyone's view of what is the correct decision is equally important, and no one can say that one person is incompatible with the group, since the group does not exist except as the consensus of *all* the members of the group. Consensus, by definition, means that individuals can disagree with each other, but the group can not disagree with an individual, since the group does not have a position against the opposition of any of the individual members.

There should be consensus on how committees will work; one of the best methods is that committees can make decisions that are a) within their own areas, b) consistent with decisions made by the whole group, c) do not introduce new policies that would normally have to be discussed by the whole group and do not have results known to be controversial with members of the whole group, and d) if there is any lack of consensus of the whole group on a decision made by a committee after the decision was made by the committee, the decision should be changed by the whole group to a decision that there is consennsus on. This will actually help to increase the amount of decentralization since people will know that it will not be used against them.

How to make consensus work in divergent or large groups

Be clear about decisions that have been made and about the committee process.

If controversies arise, the whole group should want to reach a conclusion that is a consensus.

If an individual or some members of the whole group want to take an action which other members of the whole group do not consent to, the group of people who want to take the action should take the action in the name of themselves as a group, not in the name of the whole group.

Anarchist Notebook I (2000)

ANARCHIST FREE SCHOOL
FALL SEASON LAUNCH
THURSDAY OCTOBER 7 8PM

CHECK OUT THE SPACE, REGISTER FOR CLASS, SUGGEST COURSES
IF YOU WANT AND PICK UP THE FIRST ISSUE OF THE NOTEBOOK.

FRIDAY NIGHT FILMS
Beginning Friday, October 1, the Anarchist Free School will play videos of films that
document anarchism, resistance and the integrity of the human spirit. 7pm, couches.
October 1: Kanehsetake: 270 years of Resistance. A documentary about the tense
standoff between Mohawk Warriors and the Canadian Armed Forces.
October 8: Soy Cuba (I am Cuba). A Russian take on American imperialism in
pre-communist Cuba.
October 22: No Blade of Grass. A feature film projecting the results of a planet
suddenly unable to feed its urban population.
October 29: The New Babylon. Russian silent film about the 1871 Paris Commune.
November 5: The Horse's Mouth. A British feature comedy about a dissolute artist.

Friday Night Films will continue with further input. Film and video artists and curators
are welcome use this time and space to show. With our couches and casual atmosphere this is an excellent forum to invite an intimate discussion about the work.
We can also seat up to 50.

SAVAC South Asian Visual Arts Community BOOK LAUNCH PARTY
Saturday, October 16th, after 10pm is the night to celebrate the publication of the
Street Art Postering Project: a series of 3 posters curated by Kevin D'Souza,
with essays by Ashok Mathur, in affiliation with Desh Pardesh. DJ Vashti will spin.

SALONS
Third Friday of every Month at 7pm Oct 15, Nov 19, and Dec 17 after 7pm.
Salons have a colourful history throughout the world and in particular within Anarchist
Communities. Salons are intentional conversational forums where people engage in
passionate discourse about what they think is important. I am proposing that we continue this tradition here in Toronto with monthly "Salons" at the Free School this Autumn.
Look for our first Salon on the third friday of October. There will be food (potluck), conversation, and performance. The theme will be music. Be prepared to join in an
improvation of drums and other hand instruments. Just show up to participate. At the
end of each Salon we can pick a topic or activity for the following month.

anarchist free space

254 Augusta Ave in Kensington Market, Toronto.
(416) 203-0191. S of College, W of Spadina.

LOVE SONGS OF THE 20'S + 30'S
Ah, don't we all yearn for fireside comfort with song, not for trained singers as such;
the material will focus on American folksongs based on 20's and 30's recordings just
for the sake of singing with friends. Songsheets provided. Facilitated by Dave Szigeti.
Starts October 18, 1999.
Mondays 6:30-8pm

STREET ART
The urban landscape is a monotonous concrete canvas for corporate billboards and
elite city planners. It's time to infuse the city with impromptu political art and creative
concoctions from the community. This course tries to look at various movements in
street art from graffiti to subvertising, while focusing heavily on group work to produce
art that will be installed in the middle of the night. Come with an ambitious, creative,
agitative spirit. Faciltated by karen
okamoto. Starts October 11, 1999.
Mondays @ 8:30 pm

ARTS AGAINST THE MACHINE
This arts group is part of the Coalition
Against Technological Unemployment.
CATU is working to publicize the fact
that advancing technology is the cause
of the increase in poverty and accelerat-
ing environmental damage. Technology
is destroying the economy and making
us poorer. The arts group will have supplies and assistance of artists to produce
things like: sculptures, giant puppets,
paintings, patches, stickers, etc. Starts
October 12, 1999.
Tuesdays 1-4pm

CRITICISM OF TECHNOLOGY
We will look at technology as a force in society; development as rejection of one's self;
and historical and political battles over technology. Starts October 12, 1999.
Tuesdays 4-5pm

UNDERSTANDING VIOLENCE AGAINST WOMEN
Come and join a feminist discussion group organized to explore issues surrounding
violence against women. We will be covering various types of violence: sexual assault/
harassment, date/acquaintance rape, emotional/physical abuse in intimate relationships, and the impact of abuse on women and children. Ultimately, all violent acts committed against women are attempts to exert power and control by instilling fear. In
addition to dispelling existing myths and stereotypes, we will also examine the patriarchal roots of male violence. By understanding the social climate which sanctions and
perpetuates domination over women, it becomes possible to advocate for change.
Therefore factors such as the privacy of the home, traditional gender roles, and the
media backlash against the battered women's movement, will all be integral topics for
discussion. Starts October 12, 1999.
Tuesdays 6-9pm 6 - 7pm (women only) and continues 7 - 9pm (all are welcome!)

ANARCHIST
FREE SCHOOL

Education is a political act. By deepening our knowledge of ourselves and the world
around us, sharing skills and exchanging experiences in an egalitarian, non-hierarchical
setting free of prejudice, we challenge disempowering habits and broaden our
awareness of alternatives to the inequalities of a capitalist society.
The Anarchist Free School is a counter-community dedicated to effecting social change
through the application of anarchist principles in every sphere of life. This Space represents an opportunity for the community at large to come together and explore these
alternatives. The Anarchist Free School welcomes all applications for use of the Space.

INTERNATIONAL BUREAU OF RECORDIST INVESTIGATION
A weekly meeting, open to those with an interest in Recordism, Surrealism, and
other currents of the Fantastic and the Absurd in contemporary art and culture (and
spirituality, and politics, etc., etc.), for the exploration of those topics via discussion,
presentations, game-playing and other collective activities, and general nonsense
and tom-foolery. Never ended but begins again October 12th, 1999.
Tuesdays @ 9:23 pm

super8anarchy
Taking up were we left off, we will gather in small groups on a weekly basis until
the film is done. Then we can screen it, perhaps at the Safepark itself. Starts up
again October 13th, 1999.
Wednesdays @7pm

YOGA
Wear loose comfortable
clothing and bring a yoga
mat or blanket. No experience necessary. Instructed
by Christie. Starts October
14th, 1999.
Thursdays 6-7:15pm

INTRODUCTION TO ANARCHISM
This course will be a broad
introduction to anarchist
theory and practice, as
well as a look at the history
of, anarchism and anar-
chist struggles. There will
be readings taken from
some of the major anarchist thinkers such as: Bakunin, Kropotkin, Goldman and
others. Also, the class will be structured in such a way that the participants may
suggest the focus and direction of the readings and discussion topics. Facilitated
by Dan and Allan - contact allan.graham@utoronto.ca Starts October 14th, 1999.
Thursdays 7:30-9:30pm

WILD PLANTS OF TORONTO
A hands on course introducing people to plants that grow in ravines and parks and
waste spaces of Toronto. As well as identifying the plants, there will be lessons on
their uses as food and medicine. The class will meet outdoors, weather permitting.
Facilitated by Stu. On October 16th meet at the main gate of Riverdale Farm
(Carlton and River Streets). Call for future meeting locations (416) 462-1072 .
Saturdays @ 1pm

**THE FREE SCHOOL OPENS OCTOBER 7TH @8PM, 254 AUGUSTA AVE
IN KENSINGTON MARKET, SOUTH OF COLLEGE, WEST OF SPADINA
COME CHECK OUT THE COURSES, MEET PARTICIPANTS, PARTY...**

Anarchist Free School (1999)

poster: Rocky Dobey (1988)

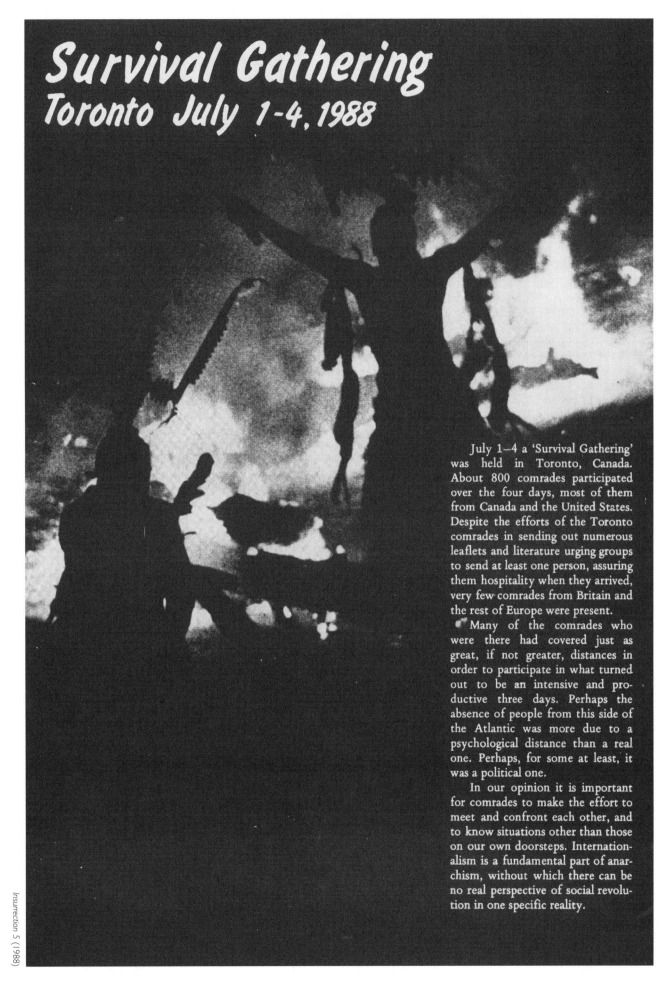

Survival Gathering
Toronto July 1-4, 1988

July 1–4 a 'Survival Gathering' was held in Toronto, Canada. About 800 comrades participated over the four days, most of them from Canada and the United States. Despite the efforts of the Toronto comrades in sending out numerous leaflets and literature urging groups to send at least one person, assuring them hospitality when they arrived, very few comrades from Britain and the rest of Europe were present.

Many of the comrades who were there had covered just as great, if not greater, distances in order to participate in what turned out to be an intensive and productive three days. Perhaps the absence of people from this side of the Atlantic was more due to a psychological distance than a real one. Perhaps, for some at least, it was a political one.

In our opinion it is important for comrades to make the effort to meet and confront each other, and to know situations other than those on our own doorsteps. Internationalism is a fundamental part of anarchism, without which there can be no real perspective of social revolution in one specific reality.

Insurrection 5 (1988)

Certainly, the comrades who hosted the Gathering had worked for months to make it possible for this to happen in Toronto. All comrades who arrived had somewhere to sleep. All had good food to eat for the whole duration of the Gathering, regardless of whether they could contribute to the cost or not. This Gargantuan undertaking by the organisers had a considerable effect on the conditions of the meeting itself. It was possible to dedicate the whole time to discussion and all the other exchanges of such a unique occasion to meet comrades from so many different realities. It was also a chance to meet in person many comrades whom one had known only through correspondence until then.

The self-sufficiency of the Gathering also meant that media attempts to scare the good people of Toronto with horror stories before the event remained a ridiculous farce. Nor were faint hearts subjected to scenes of long-haired anarchists and punks crowding into the city's cafes in the fruitless attempt to find vegetable patties in the place of hamburgers.

This brings to mind another anarchist 'gathering' which took place a few years ago in Venice, and which, through the photograph album that was produced following it, was apparently a source of inspiration to some of the Toronto comrades. That was a different situation indeed. In fact, in Venice there were two gatherings: the official one that was organised by the comrades of *Rivista A* in Milan, with its conference hall and worthy speakers with their brief cases and hotel room keys (and their passive audience in a more or less similar position). Then there was the unofficial meeting, which consisted of the many punks and other young comrades who had come from all over Europe. Many had hitch-hiked to get there and did not have the money to frequent cafes and bars to benefit from their toilet facilities. Some ended up peeing in the canals of Venice, to the consternation of the local people, council and press. Young comrades roaming the streets after 'curfew' were threatened by the organisers. The following day there was almost a rebellion amongst comrades.

ORGANISATION

Compared to this situation where two distinct and separate entities passed each other by (when they were not in conflict) in Venice, the Toronto Gathering maintained a homogenity throughout the whole four days. There was obviously contrast within that homogenity, but never a situation where one part of the comrades was excluded from what the other was doing. This can be explained by the presence of two factors: one, that the 'official' North American (and European) movement had abstained from participation; two, the structure of the Gathering itself. This was such that comrades coming from outside found themselves in a condition to participate in not only the discussions of their choice, but also in the management of the Gathering itself: defence, bookstalls, decisions concerning the media (it was unanimously decided to keep them out), food distribution, etc. Instead of conference tables and microphones there was an informal structure of workshops which enabled comrades, even in such a great number, to find a dimension in which they could participate directly. There were 63 workshops in two days, and ample space in which to hold them. The comrades had the use of a university building and a community centre for the weekend. They had also printed 1,500 pamphlets, laying out the whole programme of workshops, orientation in the city, evening gigs, etc. Workshop subjects ranged from technology to feminism to the middle east, to national liberation, to the anarchist movement in Greece and much more. It is impossible, for reasons of space, to go into any of these here. Discussions were often disjointed due to the numbers of people participating in them, sometimes speaking in rotation rather than discoursively. In any case, few could had been under the illusion that something specific could come from the workshops themselves. They were more a filtering process which made it possible to get to know the comrades in whom one recognised most affinity. It was then possible to meet and talk in smaller groups. This, in my opinion, is what the

Insurrection 5 (1988)

Gathering succeeded in doing: it created an informal structure within which it was possible to gain an understanding of some of the positions and ideas of the comrades present. From there onwards it was up to us.

A FEW WORDS ON THE MOVEMENT

It would be presumptious to think one could give an account of the anarchist movement in North America after such a short stay. A few considerations can be made, however. Beyond the various publications that we are all familiar with, there is a feeling of a young movement that is still in embryo. It is a movement that is basically informal, apart from some syndicalist or industrially orientated groups. This movement breathes a desire for freedom, despises the social reality of the American Dream. It feels close to the native people of the north American continent, and some comrades are involved in the struggles of the latter against cultural and physical annihilation.

Other comrades project a strong sense of guilt towards the people of the continents from which the western world extracts its trashy wealth. Many address themselves towards the ecological question, sometimes through 'alternative' projects in isolated attempts to redress the ecological holocaust of

the multinationals. Many are isolated by vast distances which it is hard for we Europeans even to imagine. The predominant form of organisation is that of groups that could loosely be called affinity groups. But one element seemed to be lacking: a revolutionary projectuality, an analysis and methodology leading towards a clear class perspective in the struggle against capitalism as a whole. This is understandable from a country where capital is unevenly distributed between extremes of advanced levels of post-industrialism and backward areas. There seemed to be a lack of projectuality and political awareness, perhaps due to the tendency of the movement to look for an alternative life-style approach to the refusal of capital.

One proposal did come forth, however, like a brick. It was the third day of the Gathering, which had now moved away from the university and community centre to a leafy park. Comrades were assembled to discuss future meetings and to exchange contact addresses. Out of the blue, a two or three page long document was produced proposing that a highly structured national organisation be formed. The document contained detailed indications as to how meetings should be held, decisions be made, members be expelled, etc, similar to the kind of papers that circulate among the anarchist communist comrades. It was not a pro-

posal for struggle, but rather, it seemed, an attempt to capture a captive audience. Strangely archaic and out of context in such a situation that had had been prepared and had functioned informally, one might say almost to perfection. No one was disposed to being shackled in this way and after some time a group of comrades proposed to publish the document for debate within the movement.

Certainly one left feeling a sense of a great potential within a part of the North American movement, a potential that lacks some of the instruments necessary for it to come to the fore concretely in the struggle. And the same movement is looking towards Europe for some of its indications.

To sum up, the Survival Gathering was an intensely worthwhile experience which, in our case at least, will lead to a far closer contact with the comrades and struggle in North America. In future events of the kind (one is being planned for San Francisco next year), it would be useful and productive to have more analysis, perhaps comrades could write something brief on the subjects that interest them. This will only be possible if the 'post-gathering' period is one which addresses itself towards the reality of the struggle. Events such as conferences and the Gathering in question are important instruments in the movement, but that is all they are.

Jean Weir

Anarchist
Survival
Gathering

An Anarchist Unconvention

July
1·4

Toronto Anarchist Gathering, July 1-4.

"The Gathering has meant growth for us as a community. It acted as a focus to draw us together & make us stronger. But it has also revealed to us where we need to strengthen the bonds & explore our differences. So for us the Gathering has already been very worthwhile." (From the intro. of the Gathering booklet)

COUNTER-CULTURE?

Although I myself was only in Toronto for about 2 weeks, it did seem like the Toronto anarchist/anti-authoritarian community had been connected & made stronger as a result of the Gathering, but time will tell if the bonds can remain.

The diversity of the N. American anarchist movement (& I suppose as a whole), to me, is both it's strength & its major weakness. The diversity exists in both forms of anarchism &, to a certain extent, lifestyles of anarchists themselves. The forms of anarchism, such as anarcho-syndicalism, ecological anarchists, anti-technology, anarcho-communists etc. have proved to be a major division. For example, generally speaking, anarcho-syndicalists see a society based much more on an industrial worker-controlled situation while ecologists & anti-technologists see this as moreof a danger to earth & individual freedom. This is very general & simplistic but I think it point out some major difference in anarchist theory & approach.

So at the Gathering it was indeed interesting to see 800 anarchists co-operating & inter-acting. Segments of the counter-culture were well represented, with many hippies, punks, gay anarchists, feminists (excuse all the labels), & this brings us back to lifestyles. These cultural groups are very oppressed & spat upon by mainstream society, which is conditioned to despise all non-comformity, yet in this anarchist community these groups are accepted, respected, & welcomed. (One thing is importantly missing; more racial groups. Why was almost the whole Gathering young & white? The peoples of colour are much more the targets of the racist government system...). As I said before, this diversity & respect for different cultural groups, minority's etc. is one of Anarchisms strongest points. I say this because I myself saw this, felt this, & Ibelieve it was the strongest arguement _for_ anarchism... that of individual freedom yet a sense of responsibility to the community.

ORGANISATION

The amount of work put into the Gathering was staggering, considering lunch & dinners (supplied free), accomodation, the 63 workshops in 2 days, banquet on the first day, 2 gigs on Saturday night, Networking day in Alexandra park, films, Anarchist poster show, all organised in a non-hierarchal way- demonstrating how something on this large of a scale _can_ be managed by anarchists, & done very well!

FRI. JULY 1st

Friday morning was a general meeting at the 519 Church st. Community centre. Some Trotskyists attempting to sell literature were dealt with fairly quickly after a bit of discussion, as well as a few media-types. The Toronto Anarchists had purposely kept a distance from the media as we all know their "odd" habit of distorting everything they report! This distrust of the media wasn't helped with articles like "15,000... white supremists... neo-nazis... " to be attending. Reactionary articles designed to stimulate fear & hatred of the Anarchist community.

After the meeting people went off to workshops or just meet people. Over 63 workshops went on during the first 2 days,on subjects like; Anarchy in Greece, squatting, ecology, National liberation struggles, anarcha-feminism technology, racism, dumpster diving, CSIS etc. Few of the workshops were actual lectures, most were discussions sharing opinions or experiences.

In the evening was the banquet, and the first police hassles. 2 Americans were arrested for "Entering the country under False Pretenses", meaning they didn't tell the border guards they were heading for the Gathering, & whether or not they did was unimportant as the people were held all weekend & missed the Gathering. Countermeasures were quickly taken & no more bogus arrests were made.

SAT. JULY 2nd

More workshops & I missed the ones I really wanted to see as I slept in. In the evening was the gigs- MDC, Scream, Fail-safe, PLO, Mr. T Experience, & another band I can't remember. This was such an excellent gig, _all_ the bands were great, & MDC played all their great stuff like "John Wayne was a Nazi", "Business on Parade", "No More Cops", fucking great! The whole gig was fun & had a really cool atmosphere. At another venue the Lay-Abouts reportedly played an excellent gig

Endless Strugle 8 (1988)

Endless Strugle 8 (1988)

KOPS IN KONTROL?

(Fun-fact #1- some kops at 52 division are ex-members of the Royal Ulster Constabulary, the bloody kops in N. Ireland. Fun-fact #2- 52 division has been investigated by Amnesty International for beatings & torture.)

During the actual protest it may have seemed like the police were in control, but on closer examination it's obvious how fucked up they were. This is clear for 2 reasons 1) we had no pre-planned route, so the kops couldn't predict where we'd go or what we'd do, it was totally spontaneous, & 2) the kops were constantly reacting to what we did. This was obviously a situation which these kops were unfamiliar with. One thing the kops did do was prevent us from attacking our real targets-corporations, capitalism, consumer society etc. If anything the police instigated more of the violence in their attempts to protect property. Despite this a few thousand dollars worth of property damage was inflicted.

In one newspaper account a kop said "Usually they go limp, we pick them up & take them away. This is definately new- running in the streets", & another said "We can't pen them in, this is like Europe". Not quite like Europe, but you get the point. When I was at the 52 Division Hqs, I listened in on many radio conversations & kops discussing the days actions, & through the radio one officer reported "They're heading up such-and-such a street", to which one kop replied "Why don't we just let them have the whole damn city?", & the other kop said "We already have."

The kops use of "snatch-squads" was also quite interesting. About 4-5 kops would rush in on a pre-selected protester & tackle him/her. This was often done at intersections where the crowd would be effectively thinned out, making it easier to grab someone. Perhaps an article on police tactics in situations like this will be done in future issues?

CONCLUSION

How much positive affect the DOA had is hard to say. In a sense it's much like any anarchist paper, leaflet, book etc. as it is in itself a critiscism of the state, an attack against its institutions, a loud voice raised in protest. Perhaps it will stimulate some people to think more by themselves & also critically of the state, but how

as well & everyone had gobs of fun, so that's cool, right?

SUN. JULY 3rd

This was a day of Networking in Alexandra park, where groups involved in Anarchist Black Cross or ALF work etc. could get together. Bands & musicians & poets played/performed through-out the day, with lots of Kops patrolling through the park.

MON. JULY 4th DAY OF ACTION

Originally the DOA was intended as a general protest against <u>many</u> state institutions, corporations & other scum who attempt & make our lives nothing more than numbers & dollars, but on Sunday the US shot down an Iranian airliner killing 290 people, & this obviously made people very angry! We gathered outside the US consulate at 12 noon & as I arrived I noticed the heavy police presence. After demonstrating outside the Consulate we began moving down the street & were corralled into a tight barricade that kept us on the side-walk. Graffiti was left everywhere as we moved on & crossed the road. The media began posing a problem as they began blatantly filming peoples faces & getting in the way. We stopped at a S. African war memorial where a nazi flag, a US flag, & then the black flag of Anarchy were torched. The militancy & anger of the

protest grew & we quickly took to the streets, laughing & yelling "No War, No KKK, No Fascist USA". Soon the Kops made their first charge, lunging in with horses & night-sticks, & from here on it became like a running street-fight through the down town core of Toronto. When the Kops moved in to arrest people, other people would fight bakc &"unarrest" the person. At one intersection we started hauling out some of the kops own barricades & moving them up to block the horses, but the kops quickly charged us.

We wandered out of the down-town area & some wimmin took off their tops in defiance of the ridiculously sexist Public indecency" laws which forbids wimmin from exposing their chests but allows men to. Some more people were arrested & we moved on, making our way to Queens Park. At this point the fun ended for me as I was arrested for allegedly "Assault" on a reporter, haha! Everyone stopped in Queens park. The kops were growing in numbers, Ontario Provincial police & the cities "Public Order Unit" were called in, so at this point the crowd dispersed. About 31 people were arrested, most on "Assault Police" or "Assault". The brutality of the police was no surprise, just as it was no surprise that 6 of the bastardd were injured & 3 sent to the Hospital!

many? Will more of society just think Anarchists are violent & stupid (now that this reminds them we're still here)? I don't really know, but there's only so much reading & writing one can do, & besides it was a lot of fun! The Toronto Anarchist Gathering was very succesful in my mind... can't wait for next years Gathering in San Francisco!

Threat 'serious'

TORONTO — Immigration officials say they're taking seriously a threat by U.S. anarchists to kill an immigration officer at the Fort Erie Peace Bridge. A guard said he overheard the threat as nine anarchists were trying to enter Canada Thursday for a court appearance Friday. *prov. July 11*

Endless Strugle 8 (1988)

In 1997, a number of younger Toronto anarchists involved in the *Anarchives* journal decided to mark the 1988 Survival Gathering with their own week-long gathering, called Active Resistance (AR). Held during August 17 to 23, 1998, AR attracted over 700 people, culminating in a 1,000 plus "Hands Off Street Youth" demonstration on Saturday, August 22. Participants also staged an impromptu demonstration in front of the U.S. consulate in response to U.S. bombings of non-military targets in Sudan and Afghanistan (the bombings were a retaliations for attacks on military bases overseas) and protested outside a reactionary business establishment that had called for the city police to "crack down" on homeless people.

But AR was about much more than demonstrating. Apart from meeting old friends and making new ones at the AR convergence centre, there were a number of evening events at various venues, including a rowdy night of films and talks on subjects such as "Indigenous Struggle in Chiapis," "Native Struggles and Spirituality," and "Political Prisoners/Prisoners of War." An agit-prop crew also convened every night to put out a zine called *In the Streets*. This kept everyone abreast of any changes in scheduling, etc. that arose and provided a forum for people's concerns and ideas. AR also featured a very effective email/internet media infrastructure and pirate radio.

The gathering featured a host of daily workshops held by AR participants and four "Core" meetings that ran each afternoon – "Building Revolutionary Movements," "Alternative Economics," "Community Organizing," and "Art and Revolution." Art and Revolution is where I hung my hat. Over thirty people made giant puppets, banners, theatre, and drums for AR's culminating demonstration which we decided would protest police brutality against the homeless, particularly street kids. The Art and Revolution group who ran AR's protest workshop had been founded during a second anarchist gathering held two years before in Chicago to protest that year's Democratic Party Convention. A group of artists and performers from San Francisco invited local activists to join a week-long street theatre workshop for the gathering's preplanned march on the convention. This gave the Chicago demonstration unprecedented energy, and afterwards the San Francisco group resolved to form the Art and Revolution Convergence Collective, "dedicated to infusing radical social movements with art, theatre, and creativity." They took their show on the road and out of this a loose-knit federation grew up. At Toronto, Art and Revolution people from San Francisco, Olympia, and Boston were all on hand to help out with preparations for the Saturday "Hands Off Street Youth!" protest.

Art and Revolution's impact was dramatic. The demonstration began in a park, where an opening theatre piece spelled out the reasons for the protest. Then the demonstrators took to the streets. Toronto police were confronted with a 1,000-plus crowd marching behind a giant puppet whose out-stretched arms unveiled a banner declaring, "Hands Off Street Youth!" Radical cheerleaders waved police-line pom-poms and chanted, demonstrators parodying cops on horseback strutted around on stilts, banners and flags were raised, and a masked theatre contingent snaked through the procession while a drum crew pounded out rhythms. Babies waved from street cars and bystanders were drawn in by the atmosphere, which was joyful and boisterous.

Art and Revolution not only reached out to spectators who might have perceived the AR demonstration as a threat: it coalesced the demonstrators around a celebration of their freedom, rather than a confrontation with their oppressors. Demonstrations often end up focussing on the inevitable phalanx of heavily-armed riot police poised to attack, whose ugly presence dominates the proceedings. The cops are there to take control by representing a demonstration as a sphere rife with danger. Their presence can be chilling or it can fill people with hate and anger. Either way, the police police the minds of demonstrators and spectators alike with their ritualized surveillance-and-attack behaviour, while the media end up reporting the event from the cop's perspective, thus marginalizing both the marchers and whatever issue they attempt to bring to the public's attention. This time around the demonstrators set the agenda, creating a free space for protest that was not only serious, but also fun and inclusive, rather than exclusionary and threatening. Parents with children, people in wheelchairs, and older folk could join the march in safety, but that didn't stop the "illegalities." Demonstrators squatted in the streets, stopped the traffic for chants, fired-up anti-cop/anti-poverty speeches at major intersections, and occupied the front of a downtown precinct station, where they presented a second demonstrative theatre protest against police attacks on street people.

Over all, Active Resistance was a great success. Both the Anarchist Free School and Anarchist Free Space were direct out-growths of AR, and the Ontario Coalition Against Poverty (OCAP) gained an infusion of young activists who have since transformed the politics of that organization. These achievements are real and meaningful. And they never would have happened without AR.

– ALLAN ANTLIFF

awww yeah we're fuckin'

in the streets

a daily publication bringing you all the news from yer friends at @gitprop. aye?

august 22, 1998
toronto, canada

DEMO TODAY!!!

hands off street youth!

today 3pm alexandria park @ bathurst n. of queen

Active Resistance '98 Schedule

Monday 17	Tuesday 18	Wednesday 19	Thursday 20	Friday 21	Saturday 22	Sunday 23
9am Anti-Press Conference @ Symptom Hall	9am - BREAKFAST & PLENARY @ The Bakunin Bop	9am - BREAKFAST & PLENARY @ The Bakunin Bop	9am - BREAKFAST & PLENARY @ The Bakunin Bop	9am - BREAKFAST & PLENARY @ The Bakunin Bop	10am BREAKFAST & PLENARY @ Symptom Hall	10am BREAKFAST & CLOSING PLENARY @ Symptom Hall
10am - all day long Registration! @ Symptom Hall	10am - 12pm freeskool (workshops, caucusing, forums)	10am - 12pm freeskool (workshops, caucusing, forums)	10am - 12pm freeskool (workshops, caucusing, forums)	10am - 12pm freeskool (workshops, caucusing, forums)	11am - 1pm freeskool (workshops, caucusing, forums)	2pm picnic/wrap-up gathering @ Trinity-Bellwoods Park Dundas between Bathurst & Ossington
3pm Food Coordination Meeting @ Symptom Hall	12pm - 1pm LUNCH @ Symptom Hall	12pm - 1pm LUNCH @ Symptom Hall	12pm - 1pm LUNCH @ Symptom Hall	12pm - 1pm LUNCH @ Symptom Hall	2pm STREET THEATRE/ DEMO PREP Meet @ Alexandra Park (below Scadding Court Community Center)	SAY GOODBYE, HEAD HOME TO AGITATE & ORGANIZE!
3pm Art & Revolution Introduction Meeting @ Symptom Hall	1pm - 4pm CORES Building Revolutionary Movements: @The Bakunin Bop Community Organizing: @ The Bakunin Bop Alternative Economics: @ The 360 Art & Revolution: @ K.Y.T.E.S.	1pm - 4pm CORES Building Revolutionary Movements: @The Bakunin Bop Community Organizing: @ The Bakunin Bop Alternative Economics: @ The 360 Art & Revolution: @ K.Y.T.E.S.	1pm - 4pm CORES Building Revolutionary Movements: @The Bakunin Bop Community Organizing: @ The Bakunin Bop Alternative Economics: @ The 360 Art & Revolution: @ K.Y.T.E.S.	1pm - 4pm CORES Building Revolutionary Movements: @The Bakunin Bop Community Organizing: @ The Bakunin Bop Alternative Economics: @ The 360 Art & Revolution: @ K.Y.T.E.S.	3pm ACTION/DEMO! ARA, OCAP, AR98 Anti-cop brutality demonstration. (see zine 'Events' section for details) Meet @ Alexandra Park (below Scadding Court Community Center)	
4pm Agit-prop orientation (print/radio/photo/video/postering/stenciling/daily reports) @ Telegraph Office in Symptom Hall	4pm - 6pm freeskool (workshops, caucusing, forums)	4pm - 6pm freeskool (workshops, caucusing, forums)	4pm - 6pm freeskool (workshops, caucusing, forums)	4pm - 6pm freeskool (workshops, caucusing, forums)	6pm DINNER @ Symptom Hall	
6pm DINNER @ Symptom Hall	6pm DINNER @ Symptom Hall	6pm DINNER @ Symptom Hall	6pm DINNER @ Symptom Hall	6pm DINNER @ Symptom Hall	9pm Performance Night Party @ The 360	
8pm AR'98 OPENING PLENARY! @ Innis pre-Revolutionary Town Hall	8pm Forum Indian Struggle & Spirituality! @ Hart House Anarchist Debates Room	8pm Forum Indigenous Struggle In Chiapas! @ Koffler is a capitalist pig Institute	8pm Forum Political Prisoners and Prisoners of War! @ Hart House Anarchist Debates Room	7pm Art & Revolution rehearsal for Saturday's demostration location tba.		
	10pm AGIT-PROP Nightly Meeting @ Telegraph Office in Symptom Hall	10pm AGIT-PROP Nightly Meeting @ Telegraph Office in Symptom Hall	9pm AR98 Film Night @ 66 Portland Street, unit 202 (south of King, east of Bathurst St)	7pm The Ontario Coalition Against Poverty - Camp-Out (see zine 'Events' section for details)		
			10pm AGIT-PROP Nightly Meeting @ Telegraph Office in Symptom Hall			

**Schedule is subject to change during the week.
Updates & freeskools will be posted @ Symptom Hall.**

photos: Susan Simensky-Bietila (1998)

The Montreal Anarchist Book and Freedom Fair was founded in 2000 and is modelled on the example of similar annual bookfairs in London and San Francisco. Based in a large elementary school converted to a community centre, the Book and Freedom Fair is more than simple bookselling. Several floors are given over to venders of posters, buttons, stickers, journals, zines, and info-tables run by anarchist collectives of every stripe. A vegetarian cafeteria service makes sure no one goes hungry and workshops are held on everything from biotechnology to the history of anarchism and art. Benefits connected with the yearly event add to the excitement. For example, the first Fair, held in 2000, featured "Paroles Rebelles" – a spoken-word show that raised funds for the Book and Freedom Fair, Montreal's Books to Prisoners chapter (this anarchist organization distributes books to prisoners for free), and Mexico City's anarchist library, the Biblioteca Social Reconstruir. In 2001, the Book and Freedom Fair included an evening of inspired, off-beat musical performance held in a spacious community hall which succeeded in attracting a large and diverse crowd. Proceeds raised that year were split between the Fair and a land occupation action by Uruguayan activists. The Montreal Anarchist Book and Freedom Fair is a compelling model of co-operative diversity that attracts thousands under the canopy of a friendly and accessible environment, firmly rooted in the local community.

– KERRY MOGG

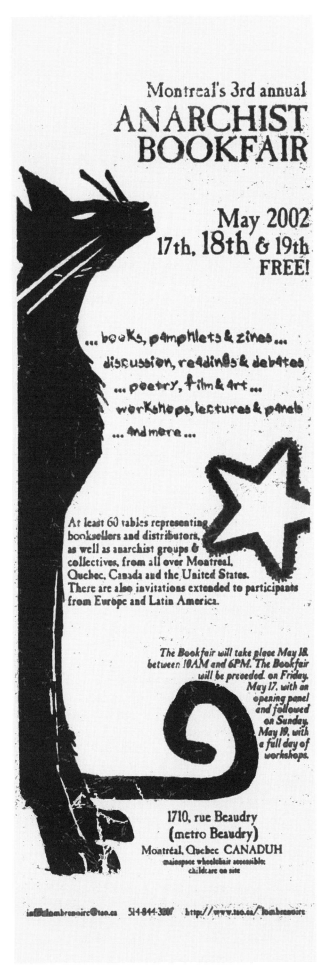

"I repeat, this is not a protest: it's something creative."
– Police Officer on the radio at
Reclaim the Streets, Toronto 1998

Reclaim the Streets (RTS) is a response to capitalist and state restraints on public space and city life. It usually looks like a big party/festival and takes place in the most domineering space in the city – the roads. RTS began in Britain when rave, squatter, and anti-road activists combined forces in the autumn of 1991. Protesters camping on a highway construction site appealed for help from rave scene organizers who had thrown "underground" parties in abandoned urban spaces to support squatting. When the ravers and squatters showed up, they turned the anti-highway protest into a giant street party. In late 1994, in reaction to this new threat, the British government passed the Criminal Justice and Public Order Act, a draconian law that made public assembly, civil protest, outdoor partying, and any broadcasting of repetitive beats a criminal act. This galvanized activists to form the Reclaim the Streets movement.

In 1995, RTS organizers staged an illegal party on a major thoroughfare in downtown London. Soon RTS events spread around the world to cities such as Helsinki, San Francisco, Sydney, Tel Aviv, and Tokyo. The internet played a major role in co-ordinating RTS events and in 1998 a series of world-wide RTS actions were called for May 16, the date of that year's G7 summit. Activists in Toronto were already planning a RTS, so they were ready. The first Toronto RTS action began at the intersection of Bloor Street and Parliament Street, with 250 people parading west down Bloor. The parade had a carnivalesque feel: it included stilt walkers, jugglers, fire-breathers, a huge drum kit on wheels, and anti-car placards. When the marchers reached the corner of Bloor and Brunswick streets – a hub of cafes and bars – they stopped and declared an impromptu street party. RTS strung up strips of cloth and banners, creating a huge web that enmeshed the entire intersection. They also set up a music system with DJs while people chalked the street with slogans promoting anarchism and the anti-car movement. After forty-five minutes the police arrived. They used horses to clear the area and there were some arrests.

The Toronto action was a classic RTS event: a street was taken over by ravers who partied it up with militant activists to the beat of music and celebration. The 1999 RTS took place in the same location, but the street-occupation was shorter and the party moved on to a nearby park with no hassles. RTS 2000 was more ambitious. People gathered at the base of Toronto's landmark CN tower and then paraded up York Street in the downtown core to the corner of King Street and York Street There they had the usual RTS festivities: people jumped rope, chalked slogans, and danced to a DJ's sound system. The cops were getting anxious to clear the area, but RTS organizers had a trick up their sleeve – a dump-truck full of grass sod was delivered to the site via a side street. Some organizers in the know asked people for help just before the truck arrived. The surprise hit full force when people in the back of the dump truck began throwing sod down to busy RTSers. In a flash, the street became a lawn. It was quite a sight – skyscrapers, fifty cops, and a street covered in grass and protesters.

RTS 2001 started on Friday August 17 at seven PM in Grange Park, a small inner-city public space. Four hundred people marched to a major shopping street – Queen Street West – and stopped. Traffic halted and the street party began. Local artists had brought an "Urban Disco Trailer"; a hardtop camper with a DJ booth and a stereo system on the roof. They also had a large white tarp that people played with in the street and later used to cover a police cruiser. The event featured a barbecue corn roast, 16 mm films, music, and carnival activities. The police eventually intervened, but not before everyone had thoroughly enjoyed themselves.

So, what makes RTS different from say, an arts festival or a normal street party? First, it is done illegally, with no permits and no payoffs. Secondly, it creates a new space outside the discipline of everyday capitalism and fills it with dancing, celebration, rebelliousness, and creativity. RTS is where artists and activists liberate their cities.

– DAN YOUNG

poster: Jason Hallows

"If you want to change the city - you have to control the streets"

STREET PARTY!

FRIDAY AUGUST 25, 2000

Meet at 6:30 pm at the east field of Old Scona
High School -10523 84 ave
ROAD RAVE NOT ROAD RAGE!
www.reclaimthestreets.net

WHY RECLAIM THE STREETS?

WHAT DO YOU WANT:
PARKS OR PARKING LOTS?
GREY OR GREEN?
CARS OR COMMUNITY?
FUMES OR FLOWERS?
ROAD RAGE OR ROAD RAVE?

THE ROAD IS MECHANICAL, LINEAR MOVEMENT EPITOMIZED BY THE CAR. THE STREET, AT BEST, IS A LIVING PLACE OF HUMAN MOVEMENT AND SOCIAL INTERCOURSE, OF FREEDOM AND SPONTANEITY. THE CAR SYSTEM STEALS THE STREET FROM UNDER US AND SELLS IT BACK FOR THE PRICE OF GASOLINE. IN EDMONTON OUR COMMUNITIES AND ITS CITIZENS HAVE BEEN SPLINTERED BY FREEWAYS, SUBURBAN SPRAWL, AND MEGAMALLS.

A STREET PARTY IS TO DEMONSTRATE THAT WE CAN MAKE OUR OWN FUN WITHOUT ASKING THE STATE'S PERMISSION OR RELYING ON ANY CORPORATION'S LARGESSE. FOR A FEW HOURS, THE LONGING OF FREE SPACE IS NOT ABOUT ESCAPE BUT THE TRANSFORMATION OF THE HERE AND NOW.

BRING YOUR GOOD TIME: DRUMS, COSTUMES, WHISTLES, BELLS, JUGGLING BALLS, BEACH BALLS, SKIPPING ROPES, DANCING SHOES, POETRY, BUBBLES, AND HUGS...BUT NO DRUGS OR THUGS.

photo: Kerry Mogg (2000)

Black Bloc At the Mexican Border

photo by Peter Maiden

12:53 PM, Sunday, April 22, 2001

The Black Bloc marches along the Mexican border
to raise border issues and help resist the FTAA.

Quebec Teddybear Catapult

photo by Devin Asch

11:41 AM, Saturday, April 28, 2001

Flags & Gas

photo by Devin Asch

11:54 AM, Saturday, April 28, 2001

Gas Lobbing

photo by Devin Asch

11:46 AM, Saturday, April 28, 2001

METAPHOR CITY: QUEBEC

By Jonathan

Québec City was where the wall came down. I'm not talking about that goddamn fence - though that was something to behold, all those befuddled insurrectionaries looking upon their works and gasping a collective 'what the hell do we do now?' in the calm before the storm. There was actually a guy tramping around and pleading with protesters to come through the hole in the fence, to 'fill the space!' That was something. But the wall I'm talking about was of my own making, because I'm a video guy, and at every demo my camera is my security. You know how watching a protest on television just isn't the same as being there? Well, video activists are watching TV while it's happening! In high school theatre, they called this the 'fourth wall' - the invisible shield separating actors from audience. I'm sure the video role amounts to an evasion for some poor souls, a conscious deferral of commitment, but for me it started as a way in and has evolved into a real sacrifice - I give up the immediacy of experience to fulfill my duty. Yelling at the cops messes up your soundtrack, after all, and Haskell Wexler himself couldn't keep his framing while throwing rocks with his free hand. But, somewhere in this gaseous torrent, I just stopped caring. I broke at around 11 p.m. on Friday. Nothing much was going on - the locals were having a good drunk up by the felled fence on Rene Levesque; the protest component had been reduced to a small circle of hippies singing happy-happy folkie shit. There was just one guy who kept breaking away from his circle and stepping up to the line, screaming unknowable French curses at the jackbooters in plain, uncalculated human despair. Even he was kept well in line by his friends, who were better able to contain their agonies. But it is the screamer I will remember. Soon, the media trucks turned their well-vandalized tails. Apparently the TV folks were a bit dumbfounded at the attacks on their poor objective selves, but the surest sign that the streets are free is the slaying of the sacred cows. And when they put their cameras out to pasture, the police seized the moment in time-honoured fashion, played some spirited Gas the Onlooker, and rustled themselves up some hippies. Ah, tear gas. The armchair fascists loved that stuff - they were patting their boys on the back all weekend over the minimal 'physical engagement' between cops and protesters. Better optics, for sure - it's easier to photograph a tackle than a cloud of noxious gas, which fits the armchair geezers fine. But, damn it to hell, oppression is still oppression from a block away. In fact, long-distance brutality is what the FTAA and its idiot ancestors are all about - faceless, monolithic, and so seemingly unstoppable that you may be tempted not to try. Another fine metaphor. But I digress. Those members of the crowd who felt compelled to breathe did what had to be done. I was doing the same, lagging behind a bit to photograph the arrests, when a canister hissed to the ground not far away. And here I was. Alone - just me and this sputtering, hateful hunk of chemical artillery, one of thousands, each one an indiscriminate hate machine. I had been breathing their bullshit all day, I had seen the agonies that this tool of 'crowd control' had inflicted on people, and to be selfish, blindness had screwed up some of my best shots. So without thinking much of it, I walked up to the thing and kicked it. It was a bad kick - it didn't move at all. So I kicked it again. It wobbled a pathetic foot or two toward the distant riot line. And then I heard, and felt, this: BANG. No time to think, but I knew what that meant. I had been shot. I don't know what it was - maybe a rubber bullet, maybe another tear gas can, maybe one of the other precious tinker toys that we bought them for Christmas. But it took the skin right off a chunk of my left thigh - two inches above my knee, thank heavens - and it hurt like I have not hurt before. Maybe I should have expected this, but I didn't. Shot? Me? But, I'm Canadian. We're nice fellows, right? Old civics lessons die hard, I guess, but for me they died in a hurry, limping my retreat, yelling "You fucking shot me in the leg!" into the night to announce the reality of what I was feeling. Here I was, thirty years old, never even managed to pick a fist-fight in grade school, but now I'm a bad boy, and BANG I have just got The Strap. It's kind of an honour, but it sure is confusing. I don't want to suggest that this paltry bit of torture stacks up against anything that our boys are inflicting on your friendly neighborhood maquiladora, but once again, I smell a microcosm: the pigs decide they want our turf; we offer whatever feeble fight-back we can offer; BANG. This is what it's all about, folks. The mask is off, the wall is down.   Get used to it.

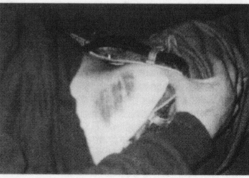

Kick It Over 39 (2001)

TAO Services

TAO has been known to offer the following services, either on a pay-what-you-can basis, or under contract. TAO workers are unionized with the IWW.

Network:

linux shell
email addresses and lists
web sites
databases
irc meetings
general server admin
training
general consultation
custom

Computer:

linux (installation and maintenance)
training
general consultation
destruction

Research:

(anti)corporate
network
media
activism

Organizing:

meetings (facilitation/planning)
conferences/fora
workshops
direct action
vegan feasts
therapy

Media:

tactical
production
publishing
writing and editing
general relations
infiltration

Theatre:

improv
street
script
workshops

Child Care:

single or group
camp or activity based
from computers to
theatre

Urban Renewal:

public art
gardening
agriculture
landscaping

Contact TAO:

TAO Toronto
P.O. Box 108, Station P
Toronto, ON, Canada
M5S 2S8
416.812.6765

TAO Northern Ontario
920 O'Brien Street
North Bay, ON
P1B 5X1 Canada
705.497.1057

TAO Ottawa
200 Cooper St. Suite 3
Ottawa, ON
K2P 0G1 Canada
info: 613.236.9052
human: 613.236.4103

TAO Vancouver
Phone: 604-255-6967
Fax: 604-251-6747

TAO USA
PO Box 7037
Syracuse, NY
13210 USA

Contact Geography:

Maritimes - maritimes@tao.ca
Quebec City - onze@tao.ca
Montreal - montreal@tao.ca
Ottawa - ottawa@tao.ca
Toronto - toronto@tao.ca
Guelph - guelph@tao.ca
Niagara - niagara@tao.ca
Northern Ontario - north@tao.ca
Winnipeg - winnipeg@tao.ca
Edmonton -edmonton@tao.ca
Vancouver - vancouver@tao.ca
Saskatoon - saskatoon@tao.ca
Syracuse NY - mag@tao.ca

NYC - nyfma@tao.ca
Washington D.C. - dc@tao.ca
Memphis - memphis@tao.ca
Southern US - south@tao.ca
Ireland - ainrial@tao.ca
UK - freedom@tao.ca
Germany - i-afd@tao.ca
Finland - anarko@tao.ca
Israel - israel@tao.ca
Sweden - frihet@tao.ca
Denmark - quique@tao.ca
Australia - arts@tao.ca
Asia - a-asia@tao.ca

For More Infomation:

About TAO - www.tao.ca/sky
Join TAO - new.tao.ca
TAO Help - help.tao.ca
TAO Email - mail.tao.ca
TAO Email Lists - major.tao.ca
TAO Event Listings - events.tao.ca
or email tao-org@tao.ca

TAO Communications is a co-operative identity that changes with time and develops with space. We are a diverse group of individuals with talents and interests that range across the multi-disciplinary fields of media, communications, art, activism, organizing, peace, and love. We live and work in open communities, and encourage others to participate in our efforts. Please contact us (as humans) if the information in this pamphlet appeals to you.

TAO Communications

www.tao.ca

Tao Communications is a regional federation comprised of local autonomous collectives and individuals. We organize networks as a means of defending and expanding public space, exercising the right to self-determination. We create knowledge through independent public interest research, and distribute it freely through participatory education.

We actively promote the establishment of worker-owned and operated autonomous zones. Under the belief that information should be free, we operate against capital or market-regulated forms of political, economic and cultural organization, and towards socially just, ecologically sound, international liberation. We advocate democratic exercise of the means of production to help achieve these beliefs. We also create tactical arts intended for such practical and inspirational application, as to encourage other autonomous groups and individuals to join us in our struggle for democracy and equal rights.

---

1) We want freedom. We want the power to resist tyranny and inevitability.

We believe in community based participatory democracy arising from direct action and public accountability. In this we belive that people will not be free until we are all able to effectively engage our society as equals in a process of voluntary co-operation. This process includes the freedom for everyone to become, belong, and just plain be, in a manner that does not violate the rights of others.

2) We want full employment and support for all people, engendering political, economic, and social egalitarianism.

We believe that every person is inherently entitled to either full employment or a guaranteed income. We believe that the means of production should be placed in the hands of the people, so that communities are able to organize full employment, providing a responsible standard of living which sustainably tries to meet the needs of all people now and in the future.

3) We want an end to the robbery of our communities by capitalists.

We believe that that the global ruling class and it's corporate economic entities have been built on plunder, pillage, conquest, and tyranny. We demand an end to economic slavery and dependence, with the cancellation of all debt, and restitution to be paid to all aboriginal and formerly colonized peoples.

4) We want free and decent housing, fit for the shelter of human beings.

We believe that if the landowners and landlords will not freely give decent housing, then the land should be made into co-operatives, so that local communities, if necessary with aid, can build and make decent housing fit for their people.

5) We want free participatory education for all people that allows us to explore the diverse histories found in our cultures, and the diverse roles we all play in the present-day society.

We believe in an education system that enables people to develop a knowledge of self within a participatory and democratic learning process that also allows and encourages the transcendence of self.

6) We want an end to all forms of war. We want all people exempt from military service.

We believe that people should not be forced into military service, while also recognizing that people will protect themselves from violence and attack, by whatever means necessary. In this we support communities' efforts to organize self-defence groups to defend and protect their safety from the violence of the state.

7) We want an immediate end to the oppression and victimization of peoples at the hands of the state.

We support and are involved in feminist, as well as aboriginal, black, queer, youth, human, and animal liberation struggles, including the valuation of elders. We are anti-fascist, anti-sexist, anti-racist, anti-ageist, anti-homophobic, anti-speciest, anti-ableist, anti-authoritarian, and against neo-liberalism and neo-conservatism. We support the liberation of identity, and the right to self-determination.

8) We want freedom for all political prisoners, and a gradual abolition of all prisons, jails, and authoritarian mental-health institutions.

We belive that the legal system is neither just, nor representative of the needs and demands of the people. We envision a society that employs community engagement rather than social ostracization in dealing with those most disaffected.

9) We want a justice system that resides in the communities it affects, responds to the needs of all within those communities, protects the inalienable human rights of all, and seeks resolution rather than revenge, equality rather than the protection of elite interests.

We believe when all parties are represented, equally and fairly, as part of a due democratic process, that conflict resolution, aiming towards consensus, tends to sufficiently resolve crises, and leave all parties content. In this we admire and take as a model a number of aboriginal justice systems.

10) We want clean air, clean water, free universal access to all forms of media, health care, and public transportation, as well as the ability to produce and consume foods, herbs, and drinks, free of industrial toxins, pesticides, genetic engineering and manipulation.

We believe that our environment and our interaction with and within it, determines not only our health and well-being, but our ability to participate as active members of our society.

Tao Communicatoins Website (2001)

resist.ca (2001)

Endless Struggle (1989)

ZINES & SMALL PRESS

The production of zines and other small press items is a mainstay of the anarchist community. They combine an individualistic Do It Yourself ethos with a desire for the un-mediated communication that never occurs in capitalism's censored, for-profit news-making. Zines and the small press are personal and anarchically unrestrained. They embody the sustained efforts of those who create them in order to realize freedom on a micro level, often using the most accessible tool available: the common office photocopier. These publications are, in short, an amazing demonstration of how self-publishing and self-expression can flourish in radically political terms.

Whether the intent of the authors is to generate discussion around daily local/national/international events (*BC Blackout, Ecomedia*); the active rebellion of a marginalized group against the forces that repress it (*Queer Terrorist*); or the laying bare of personal viewpoints (*Smarten Up!*), zines and small press publications are a vocal and necessary anarchist presence. The authors are creative in a way that only those forced by necessity can be: the resulting graphic art forms are unique and important historical documents. These publications express an indomitable articulation of the unruly sensibilities of activists so often misrepresented in history, if not excised from it altogether. They also serve as guides to the issues and debates emanating from those in the underground, highlighting the diverse voices that have contributed in myriad ways to the anarchist movement.

Ecomedia is a case in point. The project was begun in Toronto by David Barbarash and was inspired by the example of Vancouver's *BC Blackout*, Canada's first anarchist info-bulletin. The Toronto counterpart began in April 1984 as the *Anti-Authoritarian News Network* bulletin and started carrying news from the international anarchist Ekomedia Network that October. Offices of the Ekomedia Network published news bulletins in London, Berlin, Madrid, Athens, Copenhagen, Trondheim, Stockholm, San Francisco, Paris, and Geneva. Ekomedia Toronto served as an alternative/anarchist wire service before founding its own *Ekomedia* bulletin in April 26, 1985. By 1986, the Toronto branch had evolved from Barbarash's one-person operation into a collective and the "k" in *Ekomedia* was changed to *Ecomedia*. The bulletin increased in frequency and circulation, and in September 1986, *Ecomedia* also began airing ten to fifteen minute long news reports on Toronto's community-run CKLN Radio. During its seven year existence (the last issue came out in 1992), Ecomedia Toronto was loosely affiliated with *Reality Now*, The Animal Liberation Front, Anarchist Black Cross (Canada), Toronto's Community Switchboard Anarchist Phone Network, and the *Anti-Authoritarian News Network* bulletin (which folded in January 1986). In this way it helped knit together the community, giving anarchist projects in Toronto a public presence they otherwise might never have achieved.

Though overshadowed by that concurrent late 20th-century phenomenon, the internet, operations such as *Ecomedia* and the many zines and small press productions suffusing the anarchist movement are worthy of notice because their low-tech output is so individualistic and hence, radically democratic. Even in the case of publications with impressive production values, small press anarchists still work against domination in their refusal and/or appropriation of elitist and expensive computer equipment. They thereby resist – as "incorrect users" – the subordination and regulation of creative production by corporate monoliths flogging mass-produced desk-top publishing programs. And, as this selection shows, they leave behind a more rich and lasting legacy than any web site ever could.

– KERRY MOGG

Bad British Columbia BLACKOUT

AUTONOMY NEWS SERVICE
#112 JULY 27 - AUG. 17, 1984

FREE!
(election goody)

Nobody keeps campaign promises.
Nobody deserves to live off your taxes.
Nobody can legislate your freedom.

NOBODY IS THE PERFECT CANDIDATE!

If *you* think that Nobody represents your interests,

VOTE FOR NOBODY

If *you* think Nobody should run your life,

VOTE FOR NOBODY

If you *think*,

VOTE FOR NOBODY

British Columbia BLACKOUT

AUTONOMY NEWS SERVICE
#86 JULY 15-29, 1983

OUR PRICE
FREE!
CHEAP

TURNING OFF THE TAP

A WORKSHOP ON ELECTRONIC SURVEILLANCE & THOSE WHO USE IT

CHILDCARE AVAILABLE

THURSDAY JULY 21 7:30 PM
1ST UNITED CHURCH, 320 E. HASTINGS
--- NO CAMERAS, PLEASE ---

(Snoop around to page 3.)

AUTONOMY NEWS SERVICE
#122 JAN. 18-31, 1985

FREE!
(the Five!)

Bad British Columbia BLACKOUT

HIDING AWAY UPPITY WOMEN

When he sentenced the Vancouver Five last summer, judge Sam Toy said they were "common criminals"-- and then handed them uncommonly severe prison terms.

But the special treatment didn't stop there. It took a life-threatening hunger strike and persistent public support to win Doug Stewart's return to B.C. after a suprise transfer to the toughest hole in the country, Quebec's Archambault prison.

And for Ann Hansen and Julie Belmas the distinction of being "dangerous women" who challenged both the state and the patriarchy has compounded their isolation from the outside community of friends and supporters. Stashed away thousands of miles from home in Canada's only federal women's prison, they were immediately classed high security risks--a first for the women's prison. Even in men's prisons, it's a measure reserved for inmates accused of the gravest internal offences, like attempting escape or assaulting guards.

Prison authorities use the women's security status to justify a virtual ban on visitors for Ann and Julie. Applications to visit are mostly rejected or ignored. Approval takes three months. People with any hint of a media connection are strictly prohibited.

Even when a suitable visitor is approved (4 to date for Ann), the customary open visit is denied. Visiting times are restricted to 60 minutes (including strip

searches), with a guard never more than 10 feet away to monitor the conversation.

Ann and Julie have already launched grievances against the security classification, and a court battle is also being considered.

"I'm going to fight this," says Ann, "because I realize how important the hands of friendship are to maintain strength and a sense of identity." For these women, it's a crucial battle; not only will their isolation continue for years if unchallenged, but prison authorities are planning even harsher measures.

Thick glass walls will separate Ann and Julie from even the few visitors they are permitted, after a special screened visiting area is built this year. Also slated for this year is a "special handling unit" to house high security prisoners apart from the general prison population.

Funding for the prison grievances, Julie's upcoming sentence appeal and Brent's Litton defense will come from the Free the Five Defense Fund. But what with last year's trials, the fund is close to depletion. A campaign to raise more money is just beginning, so if you can help, or have ideas for fundraising events, write the fund at: PO Box 48296, Bentall Station, Van., V7X 1A1. Also check out the latest update on the Five from the Defense Fund.

Letters to the Five can be sent directly to them at these addresses:

Julie Belmas & Ann Hansen: Box 515, Kingston, Ontario. Brent Taylor: Box 280, Bath, Ontario. Gerry Hannah: Box 4000, Abbotsford, BC. Doug Stewart: Box 2000, Agassiz BC.

OPEN ROAD BENEFIT DANCE: JAN. 18 AT UBC GRAD CENTRE

SPECIAL
ANTI-WAR
ISSUE

ISSUE #93
JANUARY 29 TO FEBRUARY 11
FREE

Toronto's Anarchist Bi-Weekly

Ecomedia
BULLETIN

Ecomedia, P.O. Box 915, Stn F, Toronto Ont. M4Y 2N9
All Material Is Anti-Copy right!

GULF WAR
CRISIS
HOTLINE
535-8673

Disobey
THE NEW WORLD ORDER

This is a special issue of Ecomedia on the current war in the Middle East. Inside we've got material on tons of anti-war resistance that's been blacked out by the media, some different perspectives on the issues behind the war and the anti-war movement, a calendar of local anti-war activities, and more.

But first let's get a couple of things clear. The war is not about morality or the United Nations. Canada sent troops in before the UN made any resolution, and in fact, the UN resolutions were created by the very countries which have pushed for war. And besides, if Canada was so concerned about the integrity of the UN, why did they flagrantly disregard it when, in 1989, they condemned Canada's treatment of the Lubicon Lake Indian Nation and demanded that no further irreparable harm be done to the Nation? Canada can't talk of upholding the UN—moreover, it's the UN that's upholding our government's push for war. Besides, has anyone really asked just what is so holy about the United Nations in the first place? Is it a democratic, peaceful organization? If we're expected to kill and die for this organization, shouldn't we at least be sure this is the kind of world organization we want?

Secondly, just because the troops are killing people now doesn't mean we have to turn coat and support them. This war is still wrong. And if we really want to support 'our women and men' then we should bring them back while they're still in one piece.

Let's make it clear that the war is really about consolidating economic interests. Our government, with the USA, wants to control the region and especially the oil buried there. Some of the more blunt warmakers are clear on this fact. They say our economy depends on it. If that's true, then opposing the war should not merely about bringing home the troops, but about changing any economic system that requires such sacrifices. It's about changing any political system that allows a handful of men to send us to war without any consultation with the people of this country. It's about fighting the inherent racism that tells us we have any right whatsoever to determine the future and control the resources of Arab lands. *(Continued on page 4)*

WE'RE NOT ALONE
Chronology of Anti-War Resistance

We have attempted to give a glimpse of the anti-war movement in North America and other parts of the world. The deliberate lack of coverage by the media has made it difficult to gauge the size and diversity of the anti-war movement. The crowd estimates given here may be inaccurate, since the mainstream media generally uses police figures which are much lower than the actual numbers.

One of the best sources for information we have received is the New Liberation News Service (NLNS) — a news service comprised of mostly university and college papers. They put together packages of news items from the various papers and journals in the NLNS network. With the outbreak of war, they are now producing "war update" packages of news and information on the anti-war movement. A great deal of this chronology has come from these "war updates". We encourage people to send information on ongoing protest and resistance in their areas to us and to the NLNS. Their address is: NLNS, P.O. Box 41, MIT Branch, Cambridge, MA, 02139 USA (Phone: 617 253 0399)

January 14

● CHICAGO - 5000 people show up at what was supposed to be a civil disobedience at the Federal Building. Organizers only expected 200-400 people. The action began with a picket, and later people blocked the building's entrances and an intersection. A total of 130 people were arrested during the course of the CD. Three more arrests were made after protestors surrounded police paddy wagons.

● TORONTO - over 2000 people march

(continued on page 2)

ECOMEDIA TORONTO BULLETIN ISSUE #93 JANUARY 29 TO FEBRUARY 11, 1991

A Chronology of Anti-War Resistance

—Continued from page 1—

through downtown core, blocking traffic and intersections, and ended up at the U.S. consulate. This took place at midnight when the so-called U.N. deadline expired.
● SAN DIEGO - a city-wide demo with at least 10,000 people.
● WASHINGTON, D.C. - 6000 people march from the National Cathedral to the White House where they meet up with 1000 more demonstrators (500 of which were from the Military Family Support Network).
● SEATTLE - the largest anti-war demonstration ever with over 60,000 people taking part. They marched to the Federal Building, blocking streets and highways.
● NOUAKCHOTT, Mauritania - police fire teargas to disperse thousands of university students protesting against U.S. intervention in the Gulf.

January 15

● AMHERST, MA - 6000 protest at Westover Air Base in Chicopee (a major staging area for U.S. troops).
● CINCINATTI - over 4,000 attend an anti-war rally at the University of Cincinatti.
● SAN FRANCISCO - 4000-5000 people block the doors of the Federal Building during the morning and early afternoon, preventing over 8,000 Federal employees from going to work. 400 people are arrested during the blockade. Afterwards, the Bay Bridge is occupied by over 1000 people.
    Another demonstration, organized by Roots Against War, starts from the Mission District in Latino and Chicano communities and proceeds towards the Financial District. Police claim 30,000 participated, but the number was much higher. People riot and built huge bonfires in the streets. They smashed windows, spraypainted and broke into a Citicorp bank. Later, 1000 people attempt to occupy the Bay Bridge again but are attacked by police.
    By 11:15 pm it is believed that every police official in the city is on duty. The day ended with over 600 arrests.
● BOSTON - protestors take to the streets all day, they block the Federal Building, stop traffic, etc. At least 70 people are arrested for participating in various c.d. actions.
● MADRID, Spain - over 40,000 people march against the war, another 35,000 march in Barcelona.
● FRANKFURT, Germany - 8000 march against U.S. intervention in the Gulf.

January 16

● TORONTO - about 500 people show up at the U.S. consulate after news breaks out that the U.S. has started bombing Iraq. Protestors march through downtown streets. Traffic is stopped in both directions in front of the consulate. Old City Hall doors are covered in anti-war graffiti.
● MADISON, WI - a solitary man, upon hearing the U.S. attacked Iraq, sits down in the middle of a busy street in protest. He was arrested, but goes back every day.
● WASHINGTON, D.C. - over 3000 people protest during the night and 15 arrests are made by the police.
● NEW YORK CITY - when U.S. attack is announced, hundreds of people converge on Times Square and block traffic for an hour. People then march to the United Nations where they meet a wall of police. From there they head back to Times Square and through the West Village.

January 17

● VANCOUVER - over 3000 high school students walk out of their schools and march through the downtown core. Protestors shut down the Skytrain (subway) and attempt to occupy the offices of federal M.P. Kim Campbell.
● TORONTO - protestors attempt to occupy an Army recruiting centre.
● BOSTON - gathering at the Government Centre blocks JFK Building's entrances. Police in riot gear arrest 40 but the blockade continues to grow, culminating in 2500 people. They later march past the State House and surprise the police by heading to the highway and block traffic.
● MINNEAPOLIS - 3000 people march through downtown area.
● HAMILTON, ON - 500 high school students march through downtown streets and later attempt to occupy the mayor's office. SANTA CRUZ, CA - thousands of demonstrators congregate downtown and march to a highway where two students were hit by a car. The University of Santa Cruz is reported to have been shut down by students.
● AUSTIN - a youth group blocks downtown traffic for four hours, 26 are arrested. Protestors spend the night at the capital building.
● NEW YORK CITY - At 2 am, 300 demonstrators try to close down the Brooklyn Bridge. A car drove into protestors and injured eight. One woman fell 90 feet onto an entrance ramp and died the next day from her injuries. Police delayed calling emergency services and began to hit demonstrators with their clubs. The car was going 60 mph when it hit the crowd who proceeded to destroy it.
● MADISON, WI - protestors blackout media coverage of college b-ball game for full five minutes, 50 people arrested as a result.
● CHICAGO - every campus in the city holds an anti-war rally, followed by a march to the Federal Building. Over 4,000 people take to the streets.
● SAN FRANCISCO - actions take place all over the city. In the largest, thousands block the entrances to the Federal Building. Police start arresting people in the early afternoon and many are detained inside the building. According to reports, a recruiting centre is trashed and two police cars are set on fire. That evening, a march through the Financial District is attacked by police with teargas or mace (we're not sure which). Late at night protestors attack banks and other targets in the Financial District.
● MILAN, Italy - molotovs are thrown at a British school and an American library in protest of the U.S. attack.
● PESHAWAR, Pakistan - police charge

Youth in Madrid, Spain protest the deployment of Spanish armed forces in the Persian Gulf.

into 800 students marching on the U.S. cultural centre.
● AMMAN, Jordan - the Egyptian ambassador's residence is stoned by protestors because of Egypt's role in the coalition forces.
● KHARTOUM, Sudan - at least 10,000 students protested against the U.S. attack.
● GERMANY - hundreds of thousands protest against the U.S. attack. Demonstrators and police clash in Hamburg, Frankfurt and Berlin.

January 18

● SEATTLE - 1000 people close down the Federal Building where there has been ongoing demonstrations.
● MISSOULA, MO - Young activists stage die-in at college basketball game, receiving national media attention.
● GERMANY - over 250,000 people took the streets throughout the country. Eight campuses went on strike: Gottingen, Marburg, Bremen, Siegen, Mannheim, Freiburg, Bielefeld and Chemnitz (Karl Marx-Stadt).

January 19

● SAN FRANCISCO - over 30,000 people march in conjunction with a national demonstration in Washington, D.C.
● TORONTO - 3000 peolpe march down main streets. Flags are burnt, spraypainting.

January 21

● DHAKA, Bangladesh - over half a million people march against the U.S. attack in the Gulf.

January 25

● ATHENS, Greece - November 17 (a Greek revolutionary organization) takes responsibility for the following bombings in Athens: Citibank (U.S. bank), Barclays (British bank) and the residence of the French Military Attache.

January 26

● PARIS, France - a large anti-war demo later turns into a riot. A bomb goes off at the offices of the leftist newspaper Liberation. The paper supports the U.S. attack in the Gulf.
● LIMA, Peru - the U.S. consulate is machine-gunned and a car bomb goes off at the airport. A running gun battle is reported to have taken place between security forces and unknown individuals.
● BONN - 200,000 at an anti-war demo; over 500,000 across Germany.
● TORONTO - 2000 people in an anti-war march.
● VANCOUVER - 10,000 people march; others go to a reserve armoury and to spraypaint, remove the flag, etc. They later attempt to occupy a recruiting office and are met by riot police.

● MONTREAL - 10,000 people march against the war.
● WASHINGTON - anti-war demo: police claim 75,000 people attended, organizers claim 250,000. During the march, some people throw paint bombs, smash windows and spraypaint various targets including the FBI, Justice and Treasury buildings. A number of bank windows are smashed and, in particular, the World Bank gets spraypainted and some smashed windows.
● ADANA, Turkey - the U.S. consulate and a Turkish-American organization are attacked (no one has claimed responsibility at this time). Earlier in the week, the Turkish revolutionary group, Dev Sol, attacked a NATO facility and two organizations with U.S. links.
● BEIRUT, Lebanon - banks affiliated with France and Saudi Arabia are attacked. Apparently, seven foreign interests have been attacked to date in Lebanon.

January 27

● ATHENS, Greece - the Greek revolutionary group, November 17 is believed to be responsible for the bombing of the Inter-American insurance company and for firing a rocket grenade at the American Express offices. No one is injured, but lots of property is damaged.

January 28

● ATHENS, Greece - an explosion near the British Petroleum offices is again believed to be the work of November 17. Again, no one is injured. All actions in the last few days are against the U.S./U.N. attack in the Gulf.

January 29

● CANADA – High school students in 23 cities across the country stage walkouts to protest the war. In Toronto approximately 250 attend a teach-in on anti-war organizing, civil disobedience, and are addressed by a Kuwaiti dissident.

It should be clear from even these incomplete reports that opposition to the war is much wider and diverse than the mainstream media is letting on. Hopefully we can all take this as inspiration to continue organizing and to try out some of the many different approaches and actions documented here.

A Climate of Fear

Prior to and since the war began, the establishment media has been saturated with reports of what authorities are doing to protect their countries from a "terrorist threat". This has created a near hysteria allowing the intimidation and harassment of Arab communities by security and intelligence groups to be met with no resistance in the western world. Both the RCMP and Canadian Security Intelligence Service (CSIS) in Canada and the Federal Bureau of Investigation (FBI) in the USA have admitted to "interviewing" a majority of the Arab, specifically Iraqi and Palestinian, community. Britain has already detained or deported 172 Arabs. Canada has detained 2 Arabs. Detroit, the city with the largest Arab population in the US, declared a state of emergency and requested that the National Guard be called in. This request was denied.

Adeeb Abed, a Palestinian living in New York, believes that such a level of harassment is being implemented in preparation for when the atrocities committed against Iraq by the western Coalition come to light. For when this occurs, a groundswell of resistance and protest will come from the Arab communities most affected by news of the carnage. However, this can be curtailed if the repression begins before the community comes together around the issue.

Another aspect to this hysteria from which the state can benefit is a climate making the invoking of emergency powers plausible. Although the War Measures Act no longer exists in Canada, it has been replaced by the Emergency Powers Act. The Act sets out four levels of emergency of which one is war. During a war, the Act allows Cabinet to make and enforce any law, order or regulation, except conscription. This ranges from prohibiting public assembly to imposing martial law. Given the Canadian state's declaration of the War Measures Act in 1970 to crush the growing Québecois independence movement and its invocation of the Defence Act over the summer to use the Canadian Army against the Mohawks at Kanesetake and Kahnawake, the existence of the EPA is far from reassuring.

Even less reassuring is the state admitting that CSIS and RCMP agents are working overtime and using every available resource and personnel and that more funds have been allocated to surveillance and security since the war began. In Toronto, a young Palestinian student was arrested on January 23 by police and RCMP agents, alledgedly carrying hand grenades. These police forces are also alledging that weapons and explosives were in this man's apartment. CSIS and the RCMP were 'investigating' him prior to his arrest. He was to appear in court again on January 31. This arrest is, to our knowledge, the first in Canada resulting from CSIS and RCMP investigations into "possible terrorism". It's not likely to be the last, and it's for this reason that as an anti-war movement we must be prepared for increased surveillance and harassment.

To better understand the role CSIS and the RCMP could play in thwarting our movements, let's look at their role in a historical context. During the 60's and early 70's, the RCMP did their damnedest to destroy the mass Québecois independence movement. It was not only the FLQ (the armed expression of the movement) that was targeted, but also legal parties such as the RIN and unions like the CSN, in the form of surveillance (both visual and electronic) and intimidation. Indeed, while many Québecois lived in poverty, and Montreal was chosen as the site for Expo '67, countless separatists were "interviewed" by the RCMP to prevent them from effectively organizing against Expo. François Bachand, who organized two massive demonstrations in Québec which turned into riots, was murdered while living in exile in France in 1971. Since no investigation was launched into his death, many of his compatriots believe that Canadian security officials killed him.

The peace movement has also suffered from RCMP infiltrators. Many people might remember that in 1983, during opposition to cruise missile testing in Canada, Andy Moxley publicly came out as an police informant in Ottawa. Just weeks previously the Solicitor General had claimed there was no police infiltration in the peace movement. Moxley had been offered a deal—be let off on a drug charge if he'd inform on the peace movement. He was living at the Peace Camp on Parliament Hill at the time, and had worked in the Alliance for Non-Violent Action, the Young Communist League, and was a founding member of Students for Non-Violent Action at Carleton University.

History shows us that counter insurgency forces in Canada will use militant expressions of a movement to justify targetting it in the hopes of destabilizing it. Our response to this must not be to shy away from militant and what the state defines as illegal tactics, but to build a movement using a variety of approaches while offering mutual support to its diverging elements. If not, history will repeat itself and we will be left picking up the pieces of an anti-war movement instead of stopping the war.

We must keep the reality of domestic counterinsurgency in mind while organizing. This should not have the effect of paralyzing our movements but instead strengthening them.

DISOBEY...

Continued from page 1

And most of all, let's make it clear that we don't propose peace at the expense of justice. We don't oppose this war because we feel only peaceful means are okay. In fact sometimes force is necessary to fight tyrants. It's just that we differ on who our enemies really are. We'll go to war if it'll end poverty, racism, sexism, and other social and institutional problems. We'll go to war if it'll eliminate economic classes. We'll go to war if it'll create a society that can finally live in harmony with the environment and with each other. But that war is one we'll have to fight against those who hoard power the world over, not against Iraqi civilians.

Our strategy in this anti-war struggle will reflect a few common understandings. For one, popularity has never concerned this government. The letters and petitions sent in are of no concern to them. That's not to put down the people that are creating and signing them, as every positive effort is nice to see, it's just that as a strategy no amount of lobbying is going to do the trick. It's only when the cost of this war—politically, economically, socially—becomes too high, when they can no longer maintain business as usual, that we can force changes. In this issue many different actions are reported and many are based on this perspective.

The war cannot become a single-issue 'give peace a chance' campaign, because the issue is not merely the use of violence but the question of power—who has it, who doesn't. The war is a crucial juncture in the division of world power, although if the world rulers have their way power will still remain firmly in the hands of industrial nations, whether it's the USA or Europe or Japan. It's only by developing a movement including all the powerless and excluded, a movement that addresses those power divisions on every level, that we can begin to take

power back into our own hands. War may be necessary to change the current division of power, but only a war that gives 'power to the people' is worth our lives. By making the movement broad enough to encompass the 'power' issues of racism, sexism, heterosexism, ageism, and all the manifestations of power, we can get to the heart of why there is a war at all.

Demonstrations, and mass action, are crucial in showing that those who oppose the war are not a small minority or a collection of 'Iraqi agents'. Those who put in the tremendous effort to organize these rallies should be thanked for those efforts. Those who want to do other things (and there's so much more still to do) should take the initiative themselves to organize themselves and others who are interested and make these things happen! In fact, those who oppose the war need to do our best to strengthen the resistance that is growing, by adding our perspectives, our energy, and our presence to the movement. There are many different perspectives and methods within the movement, but many of these differences are not our primary concern. We can build solidarity by naming our common ground first and finding the means of working together on those points.

Finally, it's in our interests to organize ourselves in ways that will carry us beyond this war. After the Vietnam war the anti-war movement fell apart, for many reasons. Yet the problems and the issues that caused that war are obviously still there. In fact this current battle isn't really an isolated war; the same war (over who has economic and political power worldwide) is being fought out in El Salvador, in Ireland, in South Korea, and here in Canada. So look at things with a long term perspective. Look at continuing this resistance 'til the whole thing is turned around.

We can make changes through collective action. But that means that each individual has to throw their lot in with the rest of us and organize as best we can. Anishnabe elder Art Solomon says each person has power. If we hold this to be true, then now is the time to use it.

Ecomedia Toronto

Ecomedia is an international "wire service" that acts as an alternative to regular news services. We focus on news and often censored information on autonomous and anarchist resistance and analysis of current events.

Ecomedia Toronto is a local office involved in three main projects: a radio show every Wednesday on CKLN 88.1 FM between 7 and 8 pm on the "Word of Mouth" program; also another radio spot at 12:15 pm Fridays on CIUT 89.5 FM; and the bulletin in your hands, published bi-weekly and free at locations around the city. Subscriptions are $18/yr (26 issues) mailed monthly to cut costs. Order from the address on the front. Make cheques or M.O.'s payable to Ecomedia.

ANTI-WAR AGENDA

To date the majority of demonstrations opposing a war in the Gulf have been peaceful and relatively free of arrests or confrontations, as they remain within parameters set by police. There is no indication that this will change, though organizations are encouraging people to take on more diverse actions in smaller groups

The following is a list of upcoming events:

Feb. 2, Saturday - Rally at City Hall, begining at 1 p.m.

Feb.3, Sunday - Troops Out Now are having a meeting to plan future events at the Christian Resource Centre, 40 Oak st., at 1p.m.

Feb.8, Friday - Civil Disobedience and demonstration, meet at City Hall, 4 p.m.

Feb. 9 - 27 - YOU FILL IN THE GAP !

Feb.28, Thursday - T.D.N. and Greenpeace are holding an anti- war event at the Bloor Cinema.

March 3rd., Sun. Teach in Convocation Hall, U of T.

Peace groups are admitedly planning on a short-term basis, therefore more events are sure to occur. A 24hr Gulf Crisis Hotline has been set up, and can be contacted for up-to-date event listings. The Hotline number is 535-8673. Good luck.

OTHER ACTIVITIES:

February 6, 7:15 10th anniversary of resistance to the Bath House Raids of 1981. Cawthra Sq. Park (Church North of Wellesley). Cool speakers. Stop Police Violence, fight homophobia, fight racism.

February 2 - Let Them Live, a benefit for the Lubicon Lake Indian Nation, featuring Syren and the Eagleheart Singers, celebrating the release of their benefit cassette. 7pm, 58 Cecil St., $5-8 sliding scale.

Ecomedia 93 (1991)

ECOMEDIA

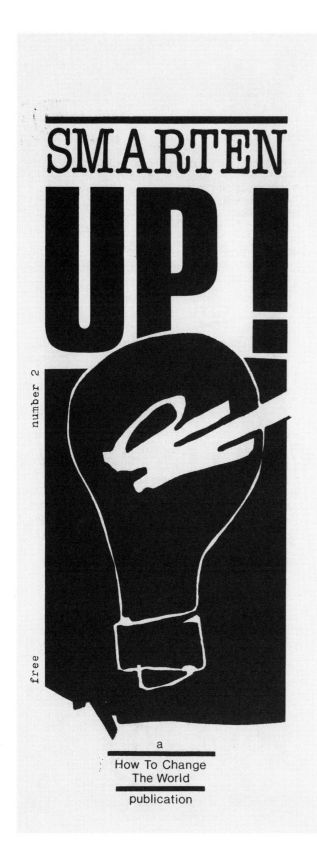

BETTER YET!
GET TO THE POINT
#4-1320 Salsbury Drive, Vancouver
Canada V5L 4B?

Click-Break

Thought-head must learn more how-why.
I am sitting on a beach, without words
watching you picture-take
click-break
the reason you are here.
Apply a narrower-specifier to
to your brain
and slice-dice the what gets too near.
Close to an edge,
this,
maybe you don't know,
could take you, take you some place
you don't want to go.
You might realize a sweet contempt
for things shoved-caught in your throat.

Close to the edge.
Hard waves smash and suck away the earth.
At home your sprinklers are screaming
in pain, continuing their unaffected rhythm.

Go!

This publication was concieved,
written and printed within 7 hours.
Printed at Budget Printing,
200 copies - $26 plus tax.

Now you do something. K?

black ● dot

I'm An ANARCHIST

I'm an anarchist. More and more I'm becoming less and less intimidated about saying this. Just like, I'm a feminist. It took me a while before I wanted to say that too. Now? Of course I'm a feminist and of course I'm an anarchist.

A really good book — ANARCHISM by Daniel Guerin. The sections in it are - The Basic Idea of Anarchism
       In Search of a New Society
       Anarchism in Revolutionary
       Practice

Why do you think anarchism is misunderstood by people? It is a way of organizing society without government. Governments and their supporters (usually people who have some something to gain by maintaining a system that uses people for the benefit of a few, or people who, in my opinion, have not considered ways to improve human existence) want you to believe that anarchism is equal to violence and disorder. It is simply self-protection for them to make this the accepted definition.

The other major question about anarchism is - How will it work? Contrary to popular belief anarchy is an organized society. This book outlines different people's ideas for setting up a society without authority. It also describes the situations where anarchists have been successful, if only for a short time.

Read this book. It fills in a lot of gaps in the question of anarchism and politics in general.

"The state has always one purpose: to limit, control, subordinate the individual and subject him to the general purpose."   Stirner

372 § ONLY A BEGINNING

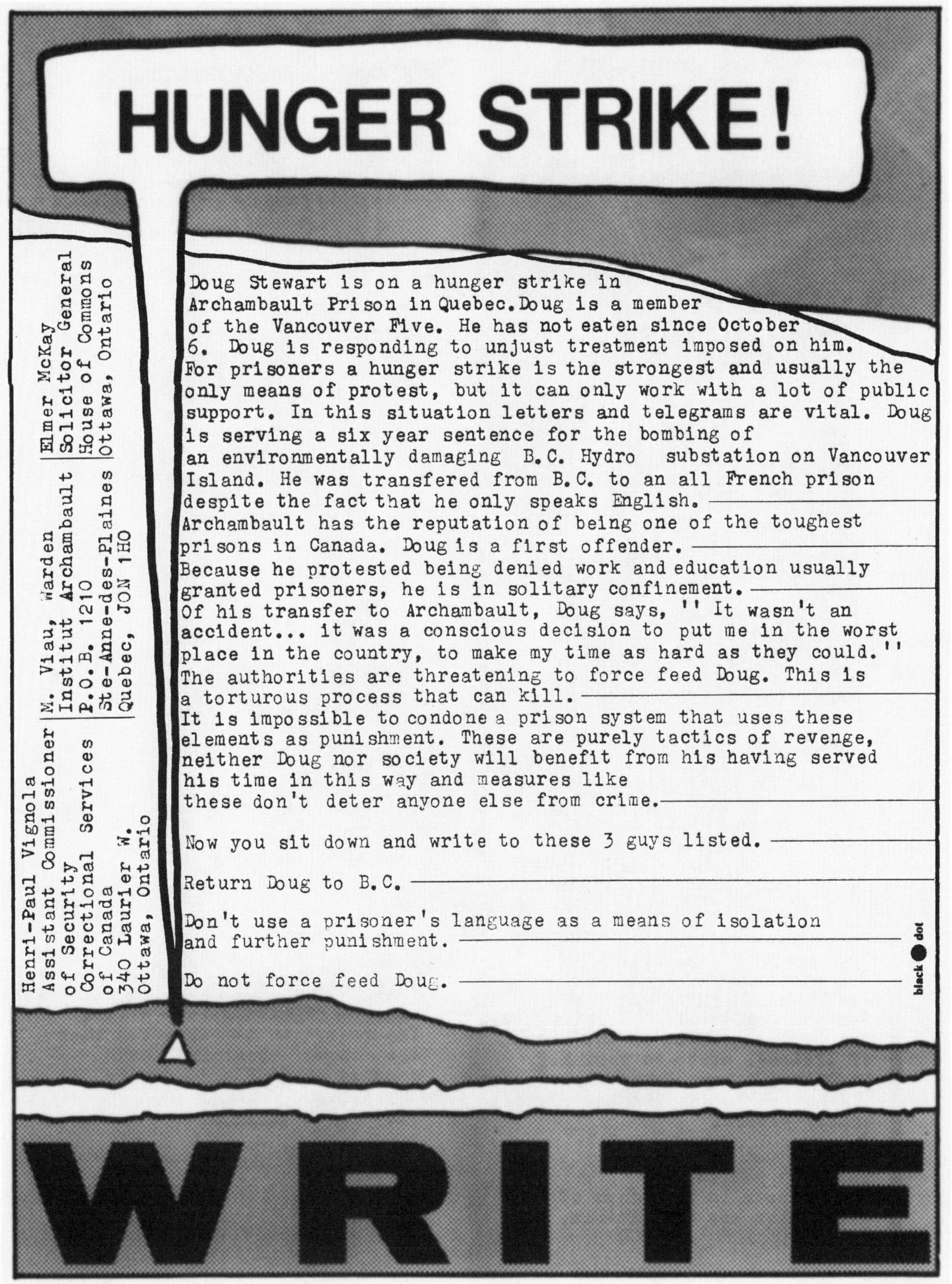

HUNGER STRIKE!

Henri-Paul Vignola
Assistant Commissioner
of Security
Correctional Services
of Canada
340 Laurier W.
Ottawa, Ontario

M. Viau, Warden
Institut Archambault
P.O.B. 1210
Ste-Anne-des-Plaines
Quebec, JON 1HO

Elmer McKay
Solicitor General
House of Commons
Ottawa, Ontario

Doug Stewart is on a hunger strike in
Archambault Prison in Quebec. Doug is a member
of the Vancouver Five. He has not eaten since October
6. Doug is responding to unjust treatment imposed on him.
For prisoners a hunger strike is the strongest and usually the
only means of protest, but it can only work with a lot of public
support. In this situation letters and telegrams are vital. Doug
is serving a six year sentence for the bombing of
an environmentally damaging B.C. Hydro substation on Vancouver
Island. He was transfered from B.C. to an all French prison
despite the fact that he only speaks English.
Archambault has the reputation of being one of the toughest
prisons in Canada. Doug is a first offender.
Because he protested being denied work and education usually
granted prisoners, he is in solitary confinement.
Of his transfer to Archambault, Doug says, '' It wasn't an
accident... it was a conscious decision to put me in the worst
place in the country, to make my time as hard as they could.''
The authorities are threatening to force feed Doug. This is
a torturous process that can kill.
It is impossible to condone a prison system that uses these
elements as punishment. These are purely tactics of revenge,
neither Doug nor society will benefit from his having served
his time in this way and measures like
these don't deter anyone else from crime.

Now you sit down and write to these 3 guys listed.

Return Doug to B.C.

Don't use a prisoner's language as a means of isolation
and further punishment.

Do not force feed Doug.

black ● dot

WRITE

Riot Grrrl Montreal 2 (2001)

EDUCATE YRSELF! (ej)

YESTERDAY THIS GUY CAME UP TO ME IN CLASS AND LAUN-CHED A VERBAL ATTACK. HE PUFFED UP HIS CHEST AND SAID LOUDLY:

Why are you Against Free Trade?

I HAD NEVER TALKED TO HIM ABOUT THIS SUBJECT BEFORE. HE JUST ASSUMED MY POLITICAL STANCE BECAUSE I WAS READING FLYERS ABOUT THE FTAA SUMMIT. [IF I WAS READING A BOOK ABOUT WORLD WAR II WOULD HE HAVE ASSUMED I WAS A NEO-NAZI?] I GAVE HIM ALL THE REASONS I COULD THINK OF. LATER I REALISED THAT HE NEVER GAVE ME EVEN ONE REASON THAT HE DIDN'T OPPOSE FREE TRADE.

Why DiD HE Make me responsi-Ble FOR HIS EDUCATION? WHY DID HE DEMAND REASONS FROM me BUT NOT FROM HIMSELF?

HE JUST DEFAULTED TO THE PRO FREE-TRADE SIDE BECAUSE IT'S EASIER, RESERVING HIS RIGOROUS QUESTIONS FOR ME. I DIDN'T DESERVE THAT ATTACK YESTERDAY AND NEXT TIME I DON'T KNOW IF I'LL OFFER MY REASONS BECAUSE PEOPLE LIKE HIM SHOULD BE LOOKING UP BOOKS IN THE LIBRARY & NOT PINNING THAT RESPONSIBILITY ON ME. EDUCATE YRSELF asshole ☆ ☆ ☆ ☆

watch me
make up
my MIND

instead of
my FACE

Riot Grrrl Montreal 2 (2001)

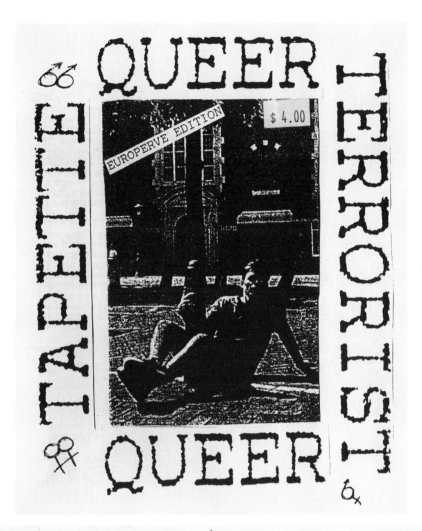

RANT, RANT, RANT!!!

THIS IS FOR ALL THOSE CLONE FAGS WHO THINK THEY CAN EXERCISE
THEIR QUEER COLLECTIVE VOICE BY SNATCHING UP ALL THE CLINIQUE OFF
THE SHELVES... FOR ALL THOSE WHO BELIEVE THAT RENTING THEIR
VIDEOS FROM GAY PORN STORES ACTUALLY LIBERATES DESIRE... FOR ALL
THOSE MINDLESS FAGS (AND DYKES) WHO GLEEFULLY DROP BUNDLES OF
MONEY ON ALCOHOL IN "GAY-OWNED" ESTABLISHMENTS BECAUSE THEY
SOMEHOW CARE ABOUT "US" MORE THAN OTHER BUSINESSES... TO ALL
THOSE WHO RUN OUT TO BUY THE LATEST BRONSKI BEAT REMIX BELIEVING
THAT SOMEHOW THIS HELPS CONTRIBUTE TO THE BUILDING OF "GAY
CULTURE"... TO THOSE WHO DON THEIR LEATHER JACKETS PLASTERED WITH
"QUEER" STICKERS IN THE INTERESTS OF MAKING A "POLITICAL"
STATEMENT... TO THOSE WHO THINK THAT "PUNK" MEANS HAVING WEIRD
HAIR AND LOTS OF BODY PIERCINGS... TO THOSE WHO THINK THAT
WEARING DOC MARTENS MEANS THAT YOU'RE A RADICAL... AND TO ALL
THOSE EVERYWHERE WHO WOULD RATHER SIT BACK AND BE TOLD WHAT TO
WEAR, WHAT TO LISTEN TO, AND WHO TO BE, RATHER THAN FIGURING OUT
WHAT "CULTURAL RESISTANCE" COULD POSSIBLY MEAN FOR THEMSELVES...

YOU ARE PART OF THE PROBLEM!!!

YOUR COMPLACENCY, YOUR REFUSAL
TO ACKNOWLEDGE HOW THIS SYSTEM
OF CORRUPTION HAS CO-OPTED YOU,
AND YOUR BELIEF THAT BY SPENDING
MONEY ON THESE CULTURAL
REPRESENTATIONS, YOU OFFER ANY
TYPE OF MEANINGFUL RESISTANCE,
INDICATE THAT YOU ARE AS

HOPELESSLY IDIOTIC AS THIS
SYSTEM TREATS YOU AND WANTS YOU
TO BE. YOU THINK THAT "BUYING
GAY" HELPS TO CARVE OUT A SPACE
OF RIGHTS AND EQUALITY FOR "GAY
PEOPLE", WHEN IN REALITY IT
SERVES TO REINFORCE THE VERY
SAME SYSTEM OF OPPRESSION
RESPONSIBLE FOR CREATING
DIVISIONS OF RICH/POOR,
BLACK/WHITE, GAY/STRAIGHT...

YOU FAIL TO REALIZE THAT YOUR
IDENTITY AS "GAY" FITS IN
PERFECTLY WITH THEIR CONCEPTION
OF WHO YOU SHOULD BE, HOW YOU
SHOULD ACT, AND EVEN HOW YOU CAN
RESIST...

DON'T "BUY GAY"; YOU'LL JUST
ENCOURAGE THEM

DON'T CONSUME CULTURE; CREATE IT!

RADICAL FAERIES

Queer Tapette/Queer Terrorist 2 (1990)

WHO ARE WE?
WHERE HAVE WE BEEN?
WHERE ARE WE GOING?

The gay movement has left these central questions unaddressed. In fact, some gay people would have us believe we're just the same as the straights, except for what we do between the sheets. But others of us hold to the gut feeling that we *are* different—that we gay people are *a people*. As a people we have ways that are peculiar to us and a language that characterizes us. We have our own past and, even more importantly, our own future.

We have searched through our childhoods for roots and clues to our special identity, and we have come up with the word FAERIE. As gay children we delighted in stories of faeries—those playful, magical, pansy-faced beings who assumed human shape. We have even been known as faeries throughout our lives to those around us.

So we are faeries. We spell it variously—as faerie, fairy, faery. No matter how we spell it, our aim is to explore and celebrate our nature. We want to build *real* community on the fullest possible understanding of who we are. Therefore we feel it necessary to address the question of our identity.

FAERY GATHERINGS

Since 1979, many gatherings of radical faeries have been called to explore this question: Who are we? The gatherings take place in rural, isolated, safe settings. Radical faeries are invited to bring their fantasies, arts, memories, dreams and reflections. The gatherings are a provisional sanctuary in which we take off the masks we wear for the hetero world, suspend judgment and open ourselves to each other.

So, who are we? Answers so far are over-simple and tentative. But here are some clues:

THE GREAT MOTHER

We feel a special love of nature. Growing up as faerie boys, we talked with trees and stones—as do all children. But unlike the mortal children, we still share our thoughts and feelings with trees and stones—and vice versa. As faeries, we recognize ourselves as part of the balance of nature. Our part in nature is exhilarating, awesome and humbling. We know that when we lose a part of nature's sacred theater to the ravages of Men, we have lost a part of ourselves. Faeries therefore are cautious, caring stewards of country space. We are one with nature, with her variety and timeliness.

MAGIC

We faeries have also explored our magical power. Our ability to communicate, to organize, to heal, and to create exceeds the limitations of mortal reality. We use meditation and group ritual to celebrate ourselves. Magical awareness is the connection to our own immanent power. In mundane society, magic has been mystified, confused and heterosexualized. We faeries are reclaiming the value of magic.

SEX

It comes as no surprise that faeries love sex. In sex, as in all things, we enjoy variety. Our sexual relations are characterized by an enjoyment of each other's enjoyment. In this regard, every sharing of energy between faeries is sexual, whether or not it involves genitalia.

GENDER

As faerie babes we were each born with a penis and (because of this penis) a burden of social expectation. As faeries we are sharply aware of the inappropriateness of society's gender expectations when applied to us.

We faerie boys had queer ways of trying to throw a baseball. The boys (those who would grow up to be Men) told us we threw like the girls. But the girls, when we asked them, said we didn't throw like boys *or* girls—we threw like a *sissy*. There's the clue to our real gender. We are not-Men. We are other. We are sissies. We are faeries. As adult males we still fail gloriously at being Men. Even in 501s and sport shirts there's no mistaking a faerie for a real Man.

POLITICS

Whenever faeries vote, they can usually count on numbering among the smallest minority. The democratic system tends to bypass us.

Politically, faeries incline toward cooperation. We protest against abuse of power. When we come together, faeries do so as a *circle*. We link all around, with neither a head nor a foot, neither a leader nor a follower. We prefer to make decisions based on loving, caring, sharing consensus. We find that consensus excellently serves circles of 50 or fewer faeries. But circles of even many hundreds of faeries have not found it necessary to fall back to hierarchical, subject-OBJECT politics.

FEMINISM

As faeries we are very interested in what our sisters have to say. The feminist movement is a beautiful expansion of consciousness. As faeries we enjoy participating in its growth.

THEATER/COSTUME

The play of life and its myriad possible permutations bring ceaseless delight to faeries. As faerie boys we loved pirate and Robin Hood stories as much for the costumes as for anything else. We have all aspired to become actors and actresses. Colorful and fantastic costuming is one of our gifts to the world, if the world will but accept it.

SUBJECT-SUBJECT CONSCIOUSNESS

Mortal society is a dog-eat-dog world—a survival of the fittest, full of give and take, where push comes to shove and the early bird gets all the worms. It pains a faerie's heart that human creatures could feel at home in this economy of rape. The world could just as easily be a dog-love-dog place. We prefer to respect the sanctity of life. Faeries see the universe as wholly alive and sacred. We are subject-SUBJECT with our environment, with all its inhabitants and manifestations. We relate to others as we relate to ourselves—as subjects.

This is queer behavior in the dog-eat-dog world. Subject-SUBJECT consciousness is the essence of faerie vision. It underlies our respect for nature, our magical practice, our sexuality, and our relationship with women. Sadly, today's world is in short supply of this consciousness. The world needs our gifts, and our time as faeries has come. Together we can sprout and nurture our visions. That is why we will continue to gather as faeries and share.

SHADOWS

Oh, yes. Faeries aren't all light and clarity. We have anger and rage within us too. We have all internalized aspects of the dog-eat-dog world. Faeries come together to examine their projections and their sense of wrong and evil. We work to integrate the ''dark side'' of ourselves into our awareness.

No Masters! No Gods!

Dare to dream

Norman **Nawrocki**

TEARS ARE TRUE

I saw a grown man crying
sittin' on the stairs
I said
'Whatcha doin' cryin'
sittin' on the stairs?'

He said
'The Truth's gone & left me
sittin' on the stairs
I'm all alone now
sittin' on the stairs

I said
'If the Truth's gone and left you
sittin' on these stairs
Get up and we'll go find it
somewhere else'

'It's probably round the corner
I said, 'Come walk with me
It's probably round the corner
Come on, you'll see
Let's go find it,
Come on, walk with me'

No Masters! No Gods! Dare to Dream (1999)

ZINES & SMALL PRESS § 379

I Talk So Fast … (2001)

BY
BERNIE

UNCOPYRIGHT
2001

Under shimmering diversions of the spectacle, *banalization* dominates society the world over and at every point where the developed consumption of commodities has seemingly multiplied the roles and objects to choose from.

The world already possesses the dream of a time whose consciousness it must now possess in order to actually live it.

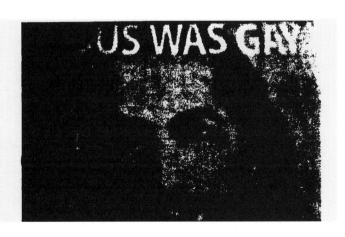

Vivez *sans* temps mort.

live without dead time.

This society which eliminates geographical distance reproduces distance internally as spectacular separation.

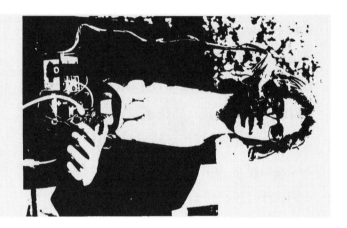

All branches of knowledge, which continue to develop as the *thought of the spectacle*, have to justify a society without justification, and constitute a general science of false consciousness. This thought is completely conditioned by the fact that it cannot and will not investigate its own material basis in the spectacular system.

FOLLOW THE MONEY

Where Authority Exists (2001)

minus tides!

for
those
on
the
other
side
of
life

fiction   essays   poetry   art   life

Summer 2000   vol.12 #1 $3.00

VOTiNG WiLL KiLL YOU

In the present political context of the Canadian State, the rulers of this small but well-oiled machine sense that their subjects are losing interest in the self gratifying games of their politicians.

Having no major war at hand they have decided to use old nationalist theatrics, tested and approved at other times and other places: The Nation is threatened by economic collapse and neighbors with bad intentions! Everybody at their posts! Save the Nation!

Everyday, even in the remotest places, the citizenry of this nation is being bombarded with patriotic rhetoric like the meaning of being Canadian, the uniqueness of this country, the paradise we'll all live in if only we vote and give money to one of the political rackets on the stage.

Meanwhile the meaning of being human, the uniqueness of each individual , of each community, of each bioregion, the fulfilled lives we shall have when humans stop grovelling in front of talismanic State-Stamped Bank Notes, all that is forgotten, brushed aside as the concerns of dreamers, heretics, tramps, " dysfunctional persons', in short, as the stuff of losers. Only Real Politiks counts. Winners want Power!

To balance the budget, reduce the deficit, to have " honest politicians" (sic), to expand the realm of wagedom, to have a united country all marching in unison to the rhythms of the punch clock and the rulers speeches! A country united by the belief in its greatness! Jobs for all, responsible government, Law and Order! These should be your dreams, these should be your concern!

Grow up and get a job you say! Yes, for you to grow up means to learn how to build your own chains, to fasten other peoples chains onto yourself and your own chains onto other people. Which is why your reply to a debate or a rant which concerns freedom is always: Get a job. Who can blame you? It took half of your life to learn to keep a job and the other half to love it.

But for me growing up means a lot. It means undoing the chains put on me by previous generations. It means getting to know my limits and learning from those previous generations, their wisdom , their mistakes, their false assumptions. For me growing means getting out of one's parents place, getting out of the jail house of the State, breaking the long leash of Capital , so that I can grow with out being stunted by coercion and false promises.

Doesn't the idea of government imply the immaturity of the governed? How can you mature if some thing keeps you in a state of perpetual immaturity? How can you try your hands at things when somebody else does it for you?
But these ideas are not entertained by those who preach the gospel of authority. Do as you are told, it's as simple as that. But if I have any brain, any spirit, any shred of integrity left, it is not simple to do as I am told.

When I am told to deny and forget the majority of my authentic desires, when I am told and forced to participate in empire-building, fortune accumulation and biological meltdown, when I am told to accept that abstractions like the Economy , the Leader, the Well-Being of the Nation, Humanity, History, etc,. Etc., ad nauseam, that those are ideas that have more importance and more meaning than my own fucking life, then something is wrong! It's not that simple.

Minus Tides! I (2001)

THE OPPORTUNITIES OF LIVING
ARE DIMINISHED IN PROPORTION
AS WHAT ARE CALLED
THE "MEANS"
ARE INCREASED.

THOREAU

TODAY IS TOMORROW

CLASS WAR MOUNTAIN BIKE CLUB
P.O. BOX 4051, STATION E, OTTAWA, ONTARIO, K1S 5B1 (613) 231-4392

Today is Tomorrow (1989)

AUTOCRACY

Macho Hunters?

Automobiles are a product of a specific type of hierarchical culture. They are one result of the values of western civilization of which an obvious characteristic is its patriarchal dictatorship. The parallels between men's treatment of their cars and their female lovers and the interchangeability of the vocabulary men use in relation to both 'possessions' is well known. Men ride cars and 'ride' women. They even call their cars 'she'. This is because men view women and cars not only as 'beautiful objects', but as objects which have a certain power that they enjoy controlling. Men have traditionally justified their domination of women by defining them as wild, chaotic, mysterious, etc. Thus, by virtue of their supposed lack of rationality, women need domestication, taming, control. This view is one of the central ideological tenets on which the patriarchy is based and seeks to justify itself. It is graphically expressed in the Christian religion, with its evil women myths and hatred and fear of the 'wilderness'. Ever since males began to organize and consolidate their domination of females, perhaps succeeding generations of males have lapped this oppressive shit up because they had so much to gain in terms of material possessions and because they were seduced by power. I believe this perception of women extends to everything outside the male ego/self and that it originates in our separation from nature, possibly through agriculture and religion. But that is not the issue here. What is interesting to me is that the automobile seems to have become a contrived representation of a similar type of 'wild power' that has been tamed, a kind of fake potential that is kept under control. It's as if the collective male psyche created a toy for itself that fit its model of the cosmos. A dangerous, wild machine that has been harnessed, a sort of permanent hunters' trophy to exhibit as proof of the superiority of the male, an artificial creature that is kept on display as a warning that we (men) are the most cunning and strong of all. We are at the helm of a metal beast posessing hundreds of 'horse'power, as if to reassure ourselves (white, western,males), and to convince others, that we are indeed awesome. The car is, in many ways, a pretend monster, one that reflects a patricentric cultures' obsession with subduing and dominating the world around it.

Home

For the past six months I've lived on a small island in the gulf between Vancouver Island and the mainland of British Columbia. There are about 850 people who live here during the winter and almost four times that many during the summer. Many people here find their home unique. They like to think of it as a community, and there are several projects that testify to this description. More specifically, however, they like to describe it as an alternative community. There is a well organized recycling depot and a 'free store' where everyone brings stuff that they no longer need or want so that someone else will get a chance to use it. Really quite remarkable. There are also other initiatives that are aimed at promoting skill sharing and mutual aid, as well as a fairly developped 'informal economy'. All in all though, the combined influences of New Ageism and Christianity have neutralized a lot of the effort that might have posed a real threat to the status quo.(These ideologies are both blind to socio-economic causes of our misery.) There is, however, still a basic aspiration of achieving community control over their lives and environment among many islanders. It is this basic desire, and the extent to which it will avoid being recuperated

or negated by religion and liberal, authoritarian leftist or even conservative ideologies, that I am interested in encouraging.

One of the most promising devellopments in terms of subversive potential has been the recent suggestion of reducing our car dependency. The idea seems to have originated partly as a strategy to help the island maintain its uniqueness in face of increasing numbers of tourists and visitors who converge on it during the summer. Many bring their urban consummerist lifestyle with them and are willing to pay for 'conveniences' and goodies. The island ends up with ice cream stands with Coke ads plastered all over them and even police.(There had never been police here until two summers ago when they were apparently invited to deal with increased traffic problems as a result of the extra summer residents. What it will mean is the increased criminalization of island traditions like a healthy tolerance of nudity on the beaches, etc.) More cars also means more dead deer, accidents, danger for children, speeding(urban folks tend to have internalized rigid schedules more than rural

folk), more noise and pollution and of course the need for parking lots where there were once trees or a peaceful meadow. One way visitors could respect local lifestyles more, it was suggested, would be to expect them to walk, cycle or use an alternative transportation system that we could set up. Someone circulated a 'poll' asking whether we would like to implement some type of system that would help us to reduce our dependency on cars, possibly by abolishing them from the island! The respondents' hostility was as dissapointing as their apparent conformity. "This is the twentieth century, dough brain." was a typical response and it about sums up the majority view. There were, however, only about 56 people who answered, and 6 of them were in favor. There were also a few of us who didn't receive a copy of the poll who would like to see cars abolished not only from our neighborhoods but from the face of the planet. As someone commented: " The first response was negative, but the seed's been planted."

Metal Armor

And yet the auto is more than a toy that the collective male ego has created in a subconscious desire to flatter itself, or an example of an urge to dominate and control. In a society in which suspicion and competition have replaced trust, allowing ourselves to be vulnerable is considered strategically stupid. And so we build walls, shields and armor to protect our selves, behind which nobody can reach us, nobody can hurt us. In this sense the automobile has become a metaphor for the emotional armor that that the patriarchy wraps around men. Driving my car, shielded by fifteen hundred pounds of steel, I appear and feel confident, impregnable, secure, safe. Yet I go nowhere: around and around in circles, a cog in a hyper-rationalized, mechanistic, tedious world. Furthermore, reflecting the almost complete disintegration of authentic community (which is most obvious in the extreme atomization of our existences) nowadays we almost always ride in our cars alone. An obnoxious radio announcer we don't even know and the unsatisfactory sounds of recorded music are our only company. Not only in the cities, but everywhere, travelling by automobile has become a solo activity. It is not only a question of the decadent waste and inefficiency this represents, but how well it illustrates the stark loneliness of living in contemporary western civilization.

Freedom and sensuality of movement negated

Our ancestors once lived, played and dreamed together. I believe that one of the reasons they consciously refused to keep large surplusses of food either through agriculture or the domestication of animals was because the trade-off simply wasn't worthwhile. The work (alienating, dreadful activity) this would require was weighed against the pleasure of living together in communities of leisure, celebration, ritual, sensuality, humor, etc., and pleasure always took precedence. Also their relationship to nature was such that they had no desire to conquer it. They simply viewed themselves as an actual part of it. The planet was not a threatening wilderness that, if tamed, would give them abundance, it was abundant as is, and they were part of that abundance and celebrated it.

Thus, the chosen lifestyle was that of gatherer-hunters who were essentially semi-nomadic. They usually travelled and wandered together, moving on with the seasons within a particular geographical area that was familiar to them, but never fully 'known' in the modern sense, because they never dissected their environment into meaninglessness the way science does. And, although they may have travelled through the same valley before, for instance, each voyage was probably appreciated as a new experience. Perhaps a different path was chosen each time, one with different smells, sights, sounds, different herbs and roots and fungi to taste and experiment with, different bark and stones and leaves and moss to touch. Perhaps sometimes they even thought it was worth the risk of being hungry or tired for an extra day in order to explore and wander through another valley. In these respects their travels were meaningful, as were their simpler wanderings away from the temporary campsites, as individuals or smaller groups.

I have wished to share this description of travelling/wandering in order to contrast it with the so called 'leisure travelling' of today, which has been described as 'purely formal'. Sitting inside metal boxes, often alone, we experience the 'scenery' only with

Today is Tomorrow (1989)

THE TYRANNY OF CARS

our eyes, at a speed which blurs even this experience. Pseudo-travellers, we follow all
the instructions: speed, direction, rest-
stoos,"scenic viewpoints", wonderlands...
Everything is organized and chosen for us:
the freedom to choose this paved highway
or that one, Pepsi or Coke. It's all part
of the sensory deprivation project of
modern power. The ultimate aim is complete
dehumanization: a society of robots and
spectators so plugged into the Machine that
we become reduced to mere components of it.

" a system that does not
manufacture objects which
we need but manufactures
the need for objects "

Clearly the auto is more than a 1950's
cultural icon (evoking memories of the first
time at the wheel, wholesome drive-in movies
with the family, the first sexual encounter,
etc.). Nor is it a simple form of transportation, not the best, but the only one we have
at the moment in a world in which such things
are necessary, a sort of unrefined necessity.
These perceptions are the result of an incredible public relations and advertising campaign propagated by a system that does not
manufacture objects which we need but manufactures the need for objects. The continuation of this system relies not only on our
submission to it, but on our internalization
of it. The present necessity of automobiles is
the result of a deliberate strategy propagated
by the monopolistic power of the automobile
and petroleum industries, which cunningly influenced the organization of our cities (and
consequently our daily lives) so that we would
be forced to purchase this commodity. In fact
the auto has become the cornerstone of the industrial economy. There are mines for the raw
materials, factories to assemble them, roads,
expressways, highways and bridges to drive
them on, ferries to carry them and parking lots
to leave them in. All this means that millions
of people give their lives away to work just
to produce or accomodate a machine that is destroying the planet and making a few men rich.
It also means that some of us will spend an
incredible amount of time working only to make
enough money to buy a machine the primary
function of which is to drive us to work!

A Traffic in Slaughter

Cars are more alive and are deadlier than
had been anticipated. Each and every year
millions of hectares of land around the planet
are cleared, destroying or disrupting ecosystems, to accomodate this industrial plague,
and millions of animals will be killed or injured on the worlds highways. Every year the
lives of hundreds of thousands of humans are
snuffed out in traffic accidents, millions
more are maimed, amongst us those who
work at producing them. All in all pretty grim
carnage. And we are expected to accept
this slaughter.

Automatons

To merely reform cars into safer, more
efficient, more environmentally sane versions
of the same thing would miss the point. This
includes self-management schemes that would
have us all shuttled about in worker-controled
mass transit systems. As though the project
for a libertarian community and mass society
were not irreconcilably opposed. Cars are
useful for transportation only within a capitalist, hierarchical social system. They
rely on a specific organization of our lives
in which 'work', 'leisure' and 'home' occupy
three distinct geographical areas, because
capital does not allow them to be unified.
To confront the rule of capital is to confront
the ideology of work and our atomized existences. Cars are deadly and they belong in
a world of death. To imagine them as part of

free, communitarian societies is to imagine
those societies as mere replicas of the world
we now live in.
The auto is just another prop in a hideous
existential nightmare made real by thousands
of years of law and order. Trapped inside
these machines I feel not only like an extension of them, but also of the society
that they in turn help to define. Which
brings me back to that quiet island where
some folks are discussing whether they should
or shouldn't abolish cars. It seems that to
the extent to which cars epitomize alienated,
industrial, atomized, mass society, the question isn't whether we should or shouldn't,
but when and how. My suggestion is that because
cars are dependent on a society founded on
power and domination, a sure way of ridding
ourselves of them would be to rid ourselves of
that society. In the meantime I'm optimistic
about our capacity to come up with sane,
creative alternatives, but have no illusions
that even if we did, the real source of our
problems would be solved. For a world without
domination, including cars,
                                        Amigo

(I can see it now. Grass and weeds and herbs
reclaiming deserted streets. Trees and
berry bushes gathering together to overcome
the crumbling highways. The cities are more
quiet...there are other sounds...birds,
insects,wind...)

Today is Tomorrow (1989)

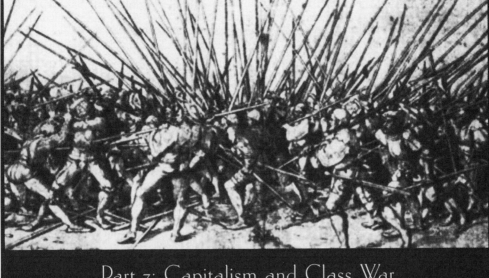

Part 3: Capitalism and Class War

Behind what is called "globalization" behind "free trade" behind Structural Adjustment Programs and debt payments, at the root of the problem with the economy, is capitalism. Capitalism is the economic system based on accumulation of money (capital), private property, commodity production and markets.

In a capitalist society, things are produced to make a profit. These things are called commodities. In order to make a profit, there must be a "demand" for the commodities--there must be someone who wants the commodity and has enough money to pay for it. The price of the commodity must always be higher than the cost of producing it, so that the producer makes a profit. The problem is that there are many things that people need that they may not be able to pay for. If people have no money, for example, they still need food. Unfortunately, it is simply not profitable to produce food for people who do not have enough money to buy it. So it is not done. Today about 1.1 billion people in the world are undernourished. This happens not only with food, but with almost everything. In almost every area, the economy could produce much more than it does. To produce more, however, would be "inefficient"--it would not be as profitable.

It is not the actual producers who make the profit, however. Under capitalism there is a small class of people who have accumulated money (capital) and who can buy and own fields, factories and workshops.

14

These capitalists then hire people to work for them and produce for them. They pay their workers a small amount of money to work for them and make all the profits off their work. People who work for capitalists do not do so because they want to, they are forced to. If you don't have capital to live off of, you have no other choice but to sell your labour and your time. If you don't, you will have no money to pay for the things you need. You will have no place to sleep and nothing to eat and eventually you will die. Capitalism forces most people to sell their labour and their time to the rich. This is both a form of slavery and a form of theft. Most people spend their whole lives working and get very little for it, at the same time as the owners of the corporations they are working for get richer and richer.

There is no democracy here. At your job, you have no say as to what will be produced or what will be done with the product. You are paid to do what you are told, and if you don't, you are fired. You could quit, but then you would have to get a job in some other place where you have just as little say in what goes on. Decisions are made by the elite in government and business for the purpose of making profit and ensuring the climate necessary to make profit--the climate in which there is a ruling class and a working class. This means ensuring that there is enough inequality and poverty so that there is a class of people who are forced to work for others. This

15

wage slavery and class oppression are built into the very logic of capitalism.

The main argument given to defend capitalism and "free trade" is that profits for the rich will make everyone better off, by trickling down to the rest of the population. This is utterly ludicrous. If an entire interlocking political and economic system is designed to make

profit for a small rich ruling class, by exploiting the rest of the population, it should be of no surprise to anyone that this is what happens. It would be truly miraculous if taking from the poor and giving to the rich somehow made poor people better off. This Reaganite propaganda is reserved for public speeches, however. When talking internally, the ruling classes are somewhat more honest about how the logic of capitalism plays itself out.

In an internal memo in 1991, the World Bank's Chief economist at the time, Lawrence Summers, argued that more polluting industries should be encouraged to relocate to poorer countries. A polluting industry tends to increase the chances that people in the surrounding area will have health problems. If pollution kills someone or makes them unable to work, the cost to the economy (or to the industry in the case of a lawsuit) would be roughly equal to the projected wages that that person would have earned in the rest of their life. In a country with low life expectancy and low wages, this cost will be lessened. Summers writes, "I think the economic logic behind dumping a load of toxic waste in the lowest wage country is impeccable and we should face up to that." Summers was later appointed United States Treasury Secretary, under the Clinton Administration and is now president of Harvard University.

16

An Anarchist Critique of the Global Economy (2001)

Capitalism does not help the poor. It creates poverty and inequality. Since 1950, the total dollar value of the world economy has increased 5-fold, while the number of people in absolute poverty has doubled. The 3 wealthiest people on the planet are now wealthier than the 48 poorest countries. In the past few decades, almost every country in the world has seen a decrease in real wages and an increase in income inequality. From 1994 to 1998 the total wealth of the 200 richest people in the world more than doubled to about $1 trillion ($1000 billion). Today about 1.3 billion people survive on less than a dollar a day, and about the same number do not have access to clean drinking water. Approximately 3 billion people (half the population of the world) live on less than 2 dollars a day; and 2 billion people (a third of the world) are suffering from anaemia.

The state of the world today is not the result of some abstract natural laws. It is the result of a specific set of interlocking institutions. These institutions are designed to generate massive wealth for the few and poverty for the rest. Capitalism is and has always been in league with the state, not opposed to it. The same people who make the decisions make the profit. The same small class of wealthy capitalists and bureaucrats run the governments and the corporations. They create a tight concentration of power. The current trend that is called "globalization" is really just a further concentration of that power. The IMF, through Structural Adjustment Programs, now directly runs the economies of over 70 countries. That means that about 1000 capitalist economists control the economic policies for 1.4 billion people in these countries. This tight cooperation between bureaucrats and capitalists is nothing new. Not that long ago, the state was killing off the native population of North America from east coast to west coast and maintaining millions of Africans in slavery in the United States and Canada--all to fuel profits.

Then as now, the oppression caused by capitalism and the state overlapped and reinforced other

Ratio of the wealth of the richest country compared to the poorest country.

1830	3 to 1
1913	11 to 1
1950	35 to 1
1973	44 to 1
1992	72 to 1

Ratio of the wealth of the richest country in 1820 (Britain) to the poorest country today (Ethiopia) is 6 to 1.

Ratio of the income of the richest 20% of the world's population to the income of the poorest 20%.

1960	30 to 1
1997	74 to 1

17

An Anarchist Critique of the Global Economy (2001)

oppressive structures in society, such as racism and sexism. Of the millions put in jail today in the United States, a hugely disproportionate amount are African Americans. Black people make up less

patterns. The people that profit most from the global economy are white people. The people who are most oppressed by the global economy are people of colour.

Similarly, the people who profit

from capitalism are overwhelmingly men, while women are the most oppressed by capitalism. In 1997, Zimbabwe had a Structural Adjustment Program imposed on it. As school fees doubled, female children were the first to drop out. As health spending by the government was cut by a third, the number of maternal deaths during childbirth doubled.

than 15% of the United States population, and yet about half of the United States prison population is Black. 1 in 14 Black men in the United States are currently in jail, and about 1 in 3 Black men in the US will go to jail at some point during his life. There is a racist dynamic to the increase in economic inequalities. They follow old colonial

In many cases, as men become unemployed, women have to get a paying job, in addition to doing the unpaid labour to maintain the household. In the world today, women do 2/3 of the work hours and yet receive only 5% of the wages and own less than 1% of the property. Of the 1.3 billion people living on less than a dollar a day, 70% are women.

18

An Anarchist Critique of the Global Economy (2001)

The entire planet is in a state of low intensity civil war. The ruling elite profit off of the exploitation of the rest of the world. When hundreds of Mexicans die every year, trying to get across the US-Mexico border--many dying of thirst in the desert--that is an act of aggression. When 30,000 people a day die easily preventable deaths, that is an act of aggression. When people's housing is taken away and they are forced into the street, that is an act of aggression. When people are forced to work under totalitarian conditions, that is an act of aggression. When toxic chemicals are dumped where people are living, that is an act of aggression. When people are denied basic necessities, that is an act of aggression. When protesters in Quebec, Gothenburg, Genoa or Washington D.C. are beaten, tear-gassed or shot, that is an act of aggression. In 1989, there was a huge protest in Caracas, Venezuela, against the IMF, after the price of bread rose 200%. The police and military were called in and opened fire on the crowds. More than 200 people were killed before the Caracas morgue was filled up and stopped keeping track. Unofficially probably more than a thousand people were killed. That is war, class war.

20

An Anarchist Critique of the Global Economy (2001)

It is not something new. It has been going on so long as there have been rich people and poor people, so long as there has been a class of people who make the decisions, and a class who have no control over their lives. And it will continue and intensify with the expansion of "free trade". When US Space Command issued a document called Vision 2020, calling for orbital gun platforms with laser weapons that can fire on the earth below, the report said that the weapons would be necessary as "the globalization of the world economy will continue, with a widening between 'haves' and 'have-nots.'" US Senator Bob Smith summed it up when he said, "It is our manifest destiny... You know we went from the East Coast to the West Coast of the United States of America settling the continent and they call that manifest destiny and the next continent if you will, the next frontier, is space and it goes on forever."

21

An Anarchist Critique of the Global Economy (2001)

Call to Action

Piqueteros

In spite of all the rhetoric, global governance does not provide a framework for overcoming the vast inequalities that stratify the globe along lines of race and class and gender. And the G8 Summits are not forums in which poverty reduction can be coordinated. When the heads of state of the wealthiest and most powerful countries meet together, they work out how to further their own agenda and that of the capitalists who keep them in power. When the give loans and when they give debt relief, when they send troops and when they send aid, when they talk about development and when they talk about poverty reduction, it is all guided by the control and profit logic of class war. Their policies and PR all reflect the basic and underlying strategies of capitalism and government: control people, and divide them, so that you can profit off them. Alongside the plainly stated economic and military ideology of capitalism, an ideology of so-called alternatives develops.

Some people argue for a kinder, gentler capitalism. They say that we should strengthen government, national and international, in order to counterbalance capitalism's most oppressive manifestations and predatory tendencies. This line of thinking still falls well within the logic of capitalism that drives global governance and poses no fundamental threat to either. The rulers of government and business appropriate the language of reform and continue the plunder. They talk about poverty reduction while imposing poverty. They appeal to human rights to justify mass murder. They talk about partnerships while perpetuating global apartheid. The rhetoric of global governance becomes the fuzzy mittens on the hidden hand of the market and the iron fist of the military.

Global governance should not be negotiated, it should be attacked.

The attack is already underway. The worldwide struggle against capitalism is led by movements in the global South where the poverty and the repression are more concentrated. In Argentina, for example, a country that has been in the grip of neo-liberal economic policies for decades, a strong movement of unemployed workers, called the *Piqueteros*, has developed. Organized in neighborhood assemblies, they block major highways in order to paralyze commerce and press demands on a corrupt and complicit government. They form the backbone of the protest movement that forced the president out of office in December 2001. [1][2] In Brazil, members of the MST, which comprises hundreds of thousands of landless peasants, occupy land and grow crops to survive, while setting up alternative health and education centers. [3]

Inspired by these and other struggles, anarchists are organizing as part of the grassroots resistance within the global capitalist empire.

We reject the logic of profit, and instead we are organizing toward an economy that produces to fulfill everyone's needs. We are trying to create a classless society, without private property, in which economic decisions are made democratically by communities. We are imperfectly enacting decentralized forms of direct democracy in which collective decisions are directly in the hands of the people and communities who are affected by them. We are pushing the imaginary boundaries that divide people and arguing for a true internationalism that refuses borders that impede the free movement and full dignity of human beings. We hope to create a society without government, based on liberty, equality and international solidarity.

But we realize that those who profit off of misery and exploitation will do everything in their power to maintain the world as it is, and only through a prolonged struggle on many different fronts will we move toward such a society. Instead of easy answers, we offer a call to action, solidarity and struggle.

Anarchy?

The word "anarchy" comes from Greek and means "no rulers." As a political philosophy, anarchism is based on the belief that organization does not require hierarchy. Society can and should be organized based on mutual aid and free association, without police, politicians and bosses; domination and exploitation should be attacked wherever they exist. Only for those who mistakenly believe that organization is necessarily tied to hierarchy, does "anarchy" mean "chaos".

graffiti at protest against joint meeting of G20/World Bank/IMF in Ottawa

HEART
-THE CENTRAL ORGAN-
of the Anarchist Party of Canada (Groucho Marxist)

NUMBER THREE

Heart 3 (1982)

OH ANARCHY   (tune: Oh Canada)

Oh Anarchy
our rabid raging cause
We'll smash the state
because because because

with old black flags
flying free and high
as we shall someday be
we shall rid ourselves
of the patriarchs
and end wage slavery

through Anarchy
not through lotteries
we'll fight to win
the whole damn bakery

Oh Anarchy
Our rabid raging cause
we are correct
because we have no flaws

by the guiding light
of a burning bank
we will be quite nicely free
and through bloodshot eyes
in the coming time
We'll drink to Victory.

(Winner of the 1982 slander your
country's national anthemn contest)

ACKNOWLEDGMENTS

No book of this scope could ever have been produced without the generous support of many people. I am especially indebted to Jim Campbell: he first suggested the project and provided invaluable assistance in tracking down contributors, copies of journals, posters, and photographs. Wolf Edwards, Bob Sarti, Jill Bend, Don Alexander, and David Lester generously loaned materials from their private archives. Bob Melcolme, Michael William, Norman Nawrocki, Moishe Dolman, Karl Leveque and Dale, Alexandre Popovic, and Jaggi Singh all pulled through with hard-to-find materials and much appreciated advice. Thanks for the same goes to the *BOA* collective – Zoe Lambert, Kim Jackson, and P.J. Flaming. While gathering material in Winnipeg I enjoyed the hospitality of Ria Julian, Eton, and Tomek Jasiakiewicz. Rocky Dobey shared his art and first-hand accounts of Toronto anarchism, circa 1988, and David Barbarash helped with matters related to *Ecomedia*. Thanks go to Adrian Blackwell, Jeff Shantz, Alan O'Connor, Rachel Rosen, Dan Young, Daniel Allen, and Bernie Munich for documentation related to the TAO, Anarchist Free School, and Anarchist Free Space. All those who contributed essays on various journals, actions, and organizations have my heartfelt thanks. So too does Mark Antliff for his commentaries on French-language articles and Susan Simensky-Bietila for her photos of the Active Resistance Gathering. I am indebted to Kerry Mogg, who kept the accumulated chaos of photos, pamphlets, posters, journals, zines, etc. in workable order as the project progressed. A final bow goes to Clara Chung for her wonderful book design and Blaine Kyllo, Brian Lam, and Trish Kelly of Arsenal Pulp Press for seeing the anthology to completion.

Allan Antliff (foreground), Canada Research Chair, University of Victoria, is the author of *Anarchist Modernism: Art, Politics and the First American Avant-Garde*. He has written extensively for the anarchist press and is currently a contributing editor to the *Alternative Press Review* and art editor of *Anarchist Studies*.

photo: Susan Simensky-Bietila